Aboriginal History

Aboriginal History
A Reader

Edited by **Kristin Burnett & Geoff Read** | Second Edition

OXFORD
UNIVERSITY PRESS

OXFORD
UNIVERSITY PRESS

Oxford University Press is a department of the University of Oxford.
It furthers the University's objective of excellence in research, scholarship,
and education by publishing worldwide. Oxford is a registered trade mark of
Oxford University Press in the UK and in certain other countries.

Published in Canada by
Oxford University Press
8 Sampson Mews, Suite 204,
Don Mills, Ontario M3C 0H5 Canada

www.oupcanada.com

Library and Archives Canada Cataloguing in Publication
Aboriginal history : a reader / edited by Kristin Burnett and Geoff Read.
— Second edition.

Includes bibliographical references.
ISBN 978-0-19-901533-7 (paperback)

1. Native peoples—Canada—Historiography. 2. Native peoples—Canada—
History. I. Burnett, Kristin, 1974–, editor II. Read, Geoff, 1975–, editor

E78.C2A1457 2016   971.004'97   C2015-907719-2

Cover image: friends-united.ca.

Oxford University Press is committed to our environment.
This book is printed on Forest Stewardship Council® certified paper
and comes from responsible sources.

Printed and bound in the United States of America

2 3 4 — 19 18

Contents

13   Health, the Environment, and Government Policy

14   Treaties, Self-Governance, and Grassroots Activism

Contributors

Betty Bastien
University of Calgary

Sarah Carter
University of Alberta

Lori Chambers
Lakehead University

Jaime Cidro
University of Winnipeg

Laurie Meijer Drees
Vancouver Island University

Dorothy Harley Eber

Lorena Sekwan Fontaine
University of Winnipeg

Adam Gaudry
University of Saskatchewan

Brian Gettler
McGill University

Celia Haig-Brown
York University

Travis Hay
York University

Jonathan Lainey
Library and Archives Canada

Bonita Lawrence
York University

Lianne C. Leddy
Wilfrid Laurier University

John Lutz
University of Victoria

Dennis H. McPherson
Lakehead University

J.R. Miller
University of Saskatchewan

Jarich Oosten
Leiden University

Shiri Pasternak
Columbia University

Thomas Peace
Huron University College

Sherry Pictou
Bear River First Nation, Dalhousie
University

Liza Piper
University of Alberta

J. Douglas Rabb
Lakehead University

Cornelius H.W. Remie
University of Nijmegen

Daniel K. Richter
University of Pennsylvania

Robert Robson
Lakehead University

Brett Rushforth
College of William & Mary

Paul Rynard

Joan Sangster
Trent University

Hugh Shewell
Carleton University

Kelly Skinner
University of Waterloo

Martha Stiegman
Concordia University

Elizabeth Vibert
University of Victoria

Cora Voyageur
University of Calgary

Todd Webb
Laurentian University

William C. Wicken
York University

Acknowledgements

We would like to acknowledge and thank the following people who contributed to the publication of this volume:

Olive Patricia Dickason, whose groundbreaking book, *Canada's First Nations: A History of Founding Peoples from Earliest Times*, redefined the teaching of Aboriginal history in Canada and remains a powerful text and pedagogical tool. Sadly, she passed away in March 2011; we dedicate this volume to her memory.

Lawrence Barkwell, Lynn Berthelette, Shannon Stettner, Sarah Carter, Chris Dooley, Mary Jane McCallum, Carolyn Podruchny, Colin Read, and Robert Robson, for their advice and guidance.

Lori Chambers, Jaime Cidro, Lorena Sekwan Fontaine, Adam Gaudry, Brian Gettler, Travis Hay, Jonathon Lainey, Bonita Lawrence, Lianne Leddy, Dennis McPherson, J.R. Miller, Shiri Pasternak, Tom Peace, Sherry Pictou, Doug Rabb, Hugh Shewell, Kelly Skinner, Martha Stiegman, Elizabeth Vibert, Cora Voyageur, and William Wicken for contributing original essays to the second volume, working hard to meet deadlines and make revisions, and, in some cases, helping to identify and secure primary documents.

Julie Bennett, Robin Jarvis Brownlie, Lauren Kolodziejczak, Roger Lewis, Leah Otak, and Christina M. Thompson, who helped us acquire the primary documents.

Chris Blow and Steve Gamester, who helped us locate relevant films.

Travis Hay whose invaluable work saved us many hours.

The staff at Oxford University Press, particularly Alan Mulder, who suggested we undertake this project in the first place, and our editors: Tamara Capar, Caroline Starr, and Gillian Scobie whose patience and hard work was and continues to be much appreciated.

Our children, Adrian Burnett and Zachary, Zoe, and Parker Read, who felt the impact of the demands this project placed on our time. Kristin's furry children—Frankie, George, Mary, Sam, and Stevie—who love when Kristin spends so much time at her computer and provides a nice warm lap to sleep in. Geoff's partner, Sarah Read, who shouldered more than her fair share of the housework and childcare at times so that work could be done on this volume and yet remained supportive throughout the process, despite working full time.

The final product is very much our own; any errors have been made in the editing process are our responsibility. Nevertheless, the book could not have come to fruition without the contributions—both great and small—of all the people listed above, and for that we are deeply grateful.

Kristin Burnett and Geoff Read
Thunder Bay, ON and London, ON
23 January 2015

Introduction

Indigenous Histories

Kristin Burnett with Geoff Read

Here We Are Again

We were pleasantly surprised when Oxford University Press asked us to undertake a second edition of *Aboriginal History: A Reader*. We agreed to do so on the condition that there be substantive revisions to the text. Drawing on the excellent recommendations we received from reviewers, we updated terminology and replaced or revised over half the articles, focusing on exchanging the previously published works with new pieces written specifically for the reader and updating the original articles. We also included new primary documents, revised the introductory chapter and chapter introductions, and updated the additional resource sections. Significantly, the collection tries to situate current politics, events, and crises—such as the call for a national inquiry on missing and murdered Indigenous women—within the context of past, present, and ongoing federal policies and settler structures of white supremacy and colonialism. While it sounds very clichéd and pedestrian to say that we need to know in greater intimacy and richer detail the histories of Turtle Island, this is especially true if we want to critically understand what is taking place on these stolen territories.

In her work *Dancing on Our Turtle's Back: Stories of Nishnaabeg Re-Creation, Resurgence and a New Emergence*, Leanne Simpson questions whether or not reconciliation between Indigenous peoples and non-Indigenous peoples is possible when currently "the majority of Canadians do not understand the historic or contemporary injustice of dispossession and occupation"; Simpson suggests that when one fails to know these histories and acknowledge them, it is impossible to "make any adjustments to the unjust relationship."[1] Idle No More, the anti-fracking movement in New Brunswick led by the Elsipogtog First Nation, the more than 17 First Nations (Beaver Lake Cree First Nation, Athabasca Chipewyan, Fort McKay First Nation, Mikisew Cree First Nation, and Frog Lake First Nation, to name a few) that are fighting oil sands development in Northern Alberta, and the community protests from across the Far North on social media forums, like the Feeding My Family Facebook group page that focuses the high cost of food in the North, are all current instances of the consequences of these histories playing themselves out in people's lives and communities. These stories signal the need for us to know our histories better.

The last introduction we wrote for this text began with a lament over the paucity of material covering the history of Turtle Island since the arrival of Europeans and could serve as a complement to Olive Patricia Dickason's influential work, *Canada's First Nations: A History of Founding Peoples from Earliest Times*. The popularity of our reader suggests that, despite the growing number of outstanding works that focus on the specific experiential, theoretical, and disciplinary aspects of Indigenous histories and politics, there remains a shortage of collections in the field that are geographically and temporally broad enough for a survey course. As one of the first works of its kind in Canada, Dickason's text was significant. *Canada's First Nations* provided a synthesis of Indigenous history in the geographical area that came to be known as Canada. When Dickason wrote her textbook in 1992, she did so as a challenge to non-Indigenous Canadians who believed "that Canada [was] a country of much geography and little history"[2] and to force non-Indigenous Canadians to rethink what constituted Canadian history.

In his recent book, *The Inconvenient Indian: A Curious Account of Native People in North America*, Thomas King points out that "[m]ost" of us think that history is the past. It's not. History is the stories we tell about the past … the stories are not just any stories. They're not chosen by chance."[3] King's words remind us that how history is written and by whom it is written matter. Much of the history we learn in university classrooms and in secondary schools fails to connect the establishment of Canada as a nation-state with the stealing of Indigenous lands, for example. These events are taught in isolation from each other—as if one could have been achieved without the other. For instance, the "triumph" of responsible government and the Confederation debates, while identified as key components of Canada's nation-building narrative, are not taught alongside the fact that these events occurred without the consent of the traditional landholders of Turtle Island. The passage of the British North American Act in 1867 is taught without reference to Indigenous peoples. Still further, Indigenous peoples largely disappear as political and economic actors after the war of 1812 in the orthodox and normative Canadian historical record. Deeply connected to the erasure of Indigenous peoples' past and the misrepresentation of Canadian history is the failure of history teachers to teach students about colonialism, a failing that was most recently and infamously exemplified by Prime Minister Stephen Harper when he boldly but erroneously asserted that Canada has "no history of colonialism" at a meeting of the G20 in 2009.[4] The history of newcomers coming to Turtle Island is not taught in relation to colonialism but rather as a story of heroic exploration. Instead, colonialism is either not addressed in the Canadian context (as if it is something solely carried out by Europeans on continents like Africa) or talked about only as it pertains to Indigenous peoples, and this implies that it is somehow only the problem and concern of the colonized.

Although the last several decades have witnessed efforts on the part of the dominant society to be more inclusive of colonized and racialized groups within the historical discipline, and in Canadian history textbooks specifically, Indigenous peoples remain largely peripheral to Canada's political, cultural, intellectual, economic, and religious history, often appearing only in brief ghettoized chapters. Indeed, the very narrative structures of how we write "Canadian" history perpetuate this problem.[5] Historian Mary Jane McCallum observes that Canadian survey texts begin with an introduction that relegates thousands of years of Indigenous histories to a brief chapter which "represents Aboriginal lives as if they were conducted 'in a sort of anteroom,' giv[ing] First Nations history a sense of timelessness distinct from what becomes the central narrative—European colonization and settlement."[6] The identification of trading networks, large-scale agriculture, animal husbandry, urban settlement, and resource development on Turtle Island, with minor exceptions, is possible only because the arrival of Europeans is a form of violence, which renders static and uniform the complexity and diversity of Indigenous histories, societies, and cultures before the arrival of Europeans, and serves to make understanding the past, present, and the future extremely difficult.

We are definitely not claiming that this text reveals the "true" history of Turtle Island or that we, as settler historians, are in a position to write that history; rather, the collection seeks to offer alternative perspectives that complicate the narratives that we are taught in high schools and fed by the media that characterize colonialism in Canada as a "dark chapter" or a minor glitch in what is otherwise a just and laudable national history.[7] We need to think very critically about the messages we are fed by the popular press and consider how they perpetuate misunderstandings and colonial violence towards Indigenous peoples. For instance, a recent survey of editorials in Canadian newspapers over the past 100 years by Mark Cronlund Anderson and Carmen Robertson found that representations of Indigenous peoples have changed very little in that they remain deeply disparaging and racist. When discussions of Indigenous peoples by non-Indigenous people appeared in newspapers, Indigenous peoples were always framed in one of three ways: as "adhering to a retrograde past, childish, or incapable of full social evolution."[8] Recent and infamous examples of this dehumanization and denigration can be seen through discussions of the housing crisis in Attawapiskat during the state of emergency that was declared in 2011. Teenagers and children attending school in the community were shocked and frightened over the venomous and hateful comments that many non-Indigenous Canadians made about the situation.[9] We need to consider why these stereotypes are so pervasive: they do nothing but malign and degrade Indigenous peoples and, what is more, they justify a fantastic lack of curiosity and critical thinking about the present social, political, and economic landscape of Turtle Island.

Terminology

It is often difficult to know which terminology is appropriate to use and in what contexts. We need to be cognizant that words have power and come with histories that are embedded in the social, legal, and political relationships between Indigenous peoples and the Canadian state. What follows is an overview of the terms used to refer to Indigenous peoples in Canada with regard to their historical and legal contexts.

There is no universal term for Indigenous peoples on Turtle Island. The terminology has evolved to reflect a growing awareness and understanding of Indigenous peoples and cultures both in Canada and around the world. In Canada, the term *Aboriginal* has become commonplace. It is used by the federal government to refer to all the "Aboriginal people in Canada collectively, without regard to their separate origins and identities,"[10] and came into common usage following its inclusion in section

35 of the 1982 Constitution Act. Section 35 of the Constitution recognizes and affirms the existence of Aboriginal rights and treaty rights. The federal government defines Aboriginal rights as "rights that some Aboriginal peoples of Canada hold as a result of their ancestors' long-standing use and occupancy of the land."[11] However, not everyone uses the term *Aboriginal*, and some Indigenous scholars and activists have chosen to reject it because they regard the term as a colonial imposition and the embodiment of state violence wrought on Indigenous bodies. More specifically using "Aboriginal" forces Indigenous peoples to construct their identity solely through their "political–legal relationship to the state" thus undermining and erasing the centrality of cultural practices, histories, geographies, and community to Indigenous identities.[12]

While the term *Indian* is considered outdated and historically inaccurate in contemporary academic circles, it reflects legal categories that have very real meanings and implications for Indigenous peoples in Canadian society. The three legal categories of Indians as defined under the Indian Act are Status Indians (individuals who are registered with the federal government according to specific criteria), Non-Status Indians (individuals who are members of a First Nation but whom the federal government does not recognize as Indians), and Treaty Indians (individuals who are Status Indians and recognized as members of a First Nation that signed a treaty with the Crown). *First Nation* is also used to refer to individual bands, for example, the Pelican Lake First Nation. Chapter 8 in this collection is particularly concerned with the history and politics of language, and looks at the complicated and problematic ways in which the state has tried to legislate Indigenous identities.

Métis is another frequently misunderstood term. People often interpret it literally and reduce Métis to simply meaning people who are of mixed Indigenous and European ancestry.[13] However, this is not the case. Its meaning is more complex and applies to distinct cultural groups whose multiple identities, cultures, communities, geographies, and histories have diverse origins that include unions between Indigenous peoples as well as between Indigenous peoples and Europeans.[14] Recent constitutional and judicial developments have both enhanced and complicated Métis identities as defined by the state. For instance, in the 2003 Powley decision, the Supreme Court of Canada ruled that Métis peoples possess Aboriginal hunting and fishing rights in a particular area only if they can prove that they have ancestors who lived there before Confederation. The 1982 Constitution Act also recognizes Métis peoples as one of Canada's founding Aboriginal peoples, but they are considered part of that founding nation only if they self-identify as Métis and can trace their ancestry back to a historical Métis community. Adam Gaudry's piece in Chapter 6 defines Métis identity as referring only to those descended from the historic Métis nation that developed on the northern Plains. These definitions are further complicated by the individual membership criteria of different Métis organizations across Canada. Such processes have constructed narrowly defined categories of identity that often bear little relationship to the realities of people's lives and how identity and group cohesion become historically constituted.

Language is complicated and we acknowledge that none of the aforementioned definitions captures all of the personal, political, cultural, legal, geographic, or historical complexities adequately. We have chosen to use the term *Indigenous peoples* in the pieces that we have written ourselves for this collection. We think scholars Taiaiake

Alfred and Jeff Corntassel offer the most comprehensive explanation for our decision to use Indigenous:

> [Indigenous peoples are] Indigenous to the lands they inhabit, in contrast to and in contention with the colonial societies and states that have spread out from Europe and other centres of empire. It is this oppositional, place-based existence, along with the consciousness of being in struggle against the disposing and demeaning fact of colonization by foreign peoples, that fundamentally distinguishes Indigenous peoples from other peoples of the world.[15]

The authors of the original articles in this collection use the terminology that they believe to be most appropriate, often in direct reference to the legal language or in regard to how they personally identify as Indigenous peoples. Some of the reprinted articles use terminology that is considered outdated today. Readers will also note our decision to refer to North America as Turtle Island. We do so to acknowledge and highlight the fact that when Europeans arrived they renamed everything they laid claim to (this included lands, places, and peoples). By doing so, newcomers ignored and undermined the "original place, community, and family names" that were used by the many and diverse Indigenous nations that had called Turtle Island their home since time immemorial.[16]

We also use terms such as *colonialism, settler colonialism, and newcomer/settler* throughout the reader. Conventional definitions of colonialism describe it as the "implanting of settlements on a distant territory."[17] However, as this reader clearly shows, colonialism is messy and, at times, nebulous. At its root, colonialism can be understood as a relationship of domination by one group over another that is simultaneously a social experience, a political and economic arrangement, and an intellectual or knowledge-making process. Put simply, colonialism is a system whereby people (colonizers) from one nation or nations expand into the territories/lands of another group and appropriate resources (broadly defined to include people, natural resources, knowledge, etc.) and exploit them for their own benefit.[18] Settler colonialism differs from colonialism in that it acknowledges the significance of permanent occupation and settlement and the erasure or at least containment (read assimilation) of Indigenous peoples and identities.[19] In other words, "settler colonialism destroys to replace" so that settlers can claim stolen territories for their own and thus distinguish themselves from their countries of origin. Patrick Wolfe refers to this process as the logic of elimination.[20]

Finally, in defining the terms *settler* and *newcomer*, we borrow from Adam Barker, who rejects the notion that defining settlers/newcomers as merely non-Indigenous is too simplistic. Settlers/newcomers is not a racial category and "includes most peoples who occupy lands previously stolen or in the process of being taken from their Indigenous inhabitants or who are otherwise members of the 'Settler society,' which is founded on co-opted lands and resources."[21]

In short, the terminology in the field of Indigenous history is sometimes complex and often contentious. To help guide readers we have included a glossary at the end of the book.

The Volume

The collection contains a variety of primary sources that reflect the breadth and diversity of available materials. Many were created by Indigenous people, contradicting the common perception that their histories are at risk of being "lost" because "Indians," as supposed primitives, did not leave their own records behind. We include photographs, oral history accounts, maps, newspaper articles, government documents, letters, diary excerpts, baptismal records, and more. In this diverse set of documents, Indigenous peoples' voices come through loud and clear, ensuring that their stories are told and remembered, demonstrating, in many cases, their past and present struggle to counter the Eurocentric narratives of the colonizing newcomers. We need to decentre how we understand these histories. Given that, as Gayatri Chakravorty Spivak suggests, silencing Indigenous voices and erasing Indigenous histories is an integral part of the colonial project,[22] such documents are invaluable for historians who wish to deconstruct the Eurocentrism of traditional Canadian history.

In specific instances, we chose to draw on records created by the Canadian government and non-Indigenous people. We did so with great caution because many records penned by non-Indigenous people and representatives of the state contain misrepresentations and derogatory and racist descriptions of Indigenous peoples. Emma LaRocque refers to the uncritical use of such materials as "textual dehumanization."[23] Thus, we include these documents, not because we believe that they accurately reflect the experiences or realities of Indigenous peoples but because they trace the constraints Indigenous peoples were subjected to, as well as the contexts within which they were forced to operate. The Indian Act, for instance, remains "an aggressive colonizing project of assimilation"[24] and continues to govern the day-to-day lives of Indigenous peoples. To cite only three of its invasive provisions, the Act determines who is legally considered a Status Indian, controls where Indigenous peoples can live, and requires that Indigenous peoples obtain permission from their Indian agent to sell agricultural produce. Because the Act clearly (though unfortunately) continues to exercise a powerful influence over the lives of Indigenous peoples, it is important for students to consider and critique it. In examining the Act, students can learn about the restrictions placed upon Indigenous peoples as well as the racist and discriminatory means by which Canada, as a settler colonial state, has sought to control, subjugate, assimilate, and (at times) eradicate Indigenous peoples and cultures. Looking at primary sources of diverse types and authors also forces people to think about the different media historians use to learn about the past, how individuals can look at and interpret the same text in different ways, and how Eurocentric biases and western historicities dominate the documentary record relied upon by the large majority of historians.

This volume is divided into 15 chapters. With the exception of Chapters 12, 13, and 14, each chapter includes two articles, and with the exception of Chapter 1 all chapters are supplemented by primary documents and/or photos. Although the geographic coverage provided by the articles is by no means comprehensive, it does encompass the histories of Indigenous peoples in regions we now know as the West, the provincial norths and Far North, Central Canada, Quebec, and the Maritimes. To a degree, the content is shaped chronologically, which is also how history survey courses are generally taught. Ideally, this reader would follow Indigenous societies from their births to the present and include the origin stories of each Indigenous group, stories that identify Turtle Island as the place of origin for Indigenous peoples. Recent archaeological evidence illustrates that human beings were present in the Americas as early as 70,000 years ago.[25] To cover 70,000 years of history of the diverse nations and cultures present within the (artificial) boundaries of present-day Canada in one reader is a vast and impossible undertaking. Instead, we have chosen to draw on the historical knowledge and perspective of Indigenous peoples and scholars regarding particular periods within Indigenous histories so that we can try and shift conventional interpretations and focuses of Canadian history.

This volume seeks to decentre those historical events and processes of Canadian history that have been highlighted as part of our national narrative—such as the establishment of Quebec City, the Conquest, the War of 1812, Confederation, the building of the intercontinental railway, Vimy Ridge, peacekeeping, and the patriation of the Constitution—while excluding alternative histories, particularly those that account for Indigenous histories and ways of knowing. As Germaine Warkentin and Carolyn Podruchny suggest, in undertaking an examination of Indigenous histories we must subject what we "know" of history to scrutiny and recognize that it "is only recently that we have attempted to do so from the point of view of the Indigenous peoples who were living here when the Europeans arrived, inhabiting the same historical epoch but with very different ideas of its history."[26]

In Chapter 1, Dennis H. McPherson, J. Douglas Rabb, and Betty Bastien inform readers that Indigenous peoples have their own histories and historical traditions (which should be an obvious statement but, sadly, is necessary). Writing from an Ojibwa perspective, McPherson and Rabb state that "Native spirituality and identity have, despite all odds, survived colonialism." Together with Bastien, they show how western knowledge and perspectives often run contrary to Indigenous peoples' ways of knowing and understanding the past and the world around them. Indeed, McPherson and Rabb's article is a rallying cry to Indigenous peoples to reclaim their histories and traditions, to resist the erasure or re-telling of the past, and to suggest that settlers have a great deal to learn from Indigenous values of diversity and principles of non-interference.

Bastien argues that "learning is premised on a "knowing" that is generated through a participatory and experiential process." To illustrate, Chapter 2 offers Indigenous perspectives of contact with Europeans and suggests a range of possibilities in imagining the first encounters that took place along the eastern coast of North America. When different peoples first came into contact with each other, they did not "discover the unexpected" but "went into new territories full of expectations, ideas, and stereotypes: what they found was—in large measure—what they expected to find."[27] In other words, Indigenous peoples and Europeans alike used pre-existing cultural meanings and categories to interpret what they witnessed, heard, and experienced when they met new people. Both Daniel K. Richter and Dorothy Harley Eber point out that Indigenous peoples and Europeans understood and experienced their first encounters with each other in radically different ways. Therefore, contact with the European world, while drastically affecting the Indigenous nations that lived on Turtle Island, needs to be re-imagined and re-examined from different points of historical reference and "knowing," and incorporate Indigenous world views and perspectives. "First contact" can no longer be understood as a single event with a clear beginning and end. Instead, we should perceive contact as both a "spatial and temporal movement" that sweeps through what Mary Louise Pratt has called the "contact zone."[28] Within this contact zone, cultures met, grappled with each other, and arrived at some sort of accommodation, however unequal. Contact initiated a series of "dialogue[s] which, once commenced, could not be easily broken off" and, indeed, continue to this day.[29]

Chapter 3 looks at the history of treaties in the geographical area that is now called Canada. Treaty-making has a long history on Turtle Island. Before Europeans arrived, Indigenous nations and communities came to agreements and formed relationships with one another which continued long after the arrival of Europeans. Today, Indigenous peoples question the validity of litigating treaties in courts because it forces Indigenous peoples to "conform to European-Canadian perspectives and modes of evidence in proving their rights." Instead, we need to pay attention to the "language, culture, relationships, and Anishinaabe normative values" in order to understand the original meaning and intent of the treaties.[30] In his article, J.R. Miller charts the histories of treaties, how they reflected the different kinds of relationships that formed between Indigenous peoples and newcomers on Turtle Island, and how those connections changed across time from kin-based relationships based on reciprocity to their current iteration. Miller argues that the passage of the Indian Act in 1876, in the midst of negotiating the numbered treaties, created an atmosphere of suspicion and duplicity which permeates present-day negotiations and anticipated the demise of respectful and reciprocal relations between Indigenous peoples and newcomers.

William Wicken's article uses a series of treaties signed by the Mi'kmaw and Wustukwiuk with British colonial authorities between 1726 and 1779 to examine the role that professional historians have played in "helping" the courts interpret the original intent and meanings of the treaties. Wicken astutely observes that because "Indigenous people are not one homogenous group not every community made a treaty and not every community encountered European settlers at the same time." Wicken thinks it is impossible to deduce, with virtually no evidence, what people thought and intended when they signed the treaties—something that the courts demand of historians and Indigenous peoples. That courts persist in making such demands suggests that the acceptance of Indigenous world views and knowledges in the courtroom is merely window-dressing. We know that the federal government has failed to live up to its treaty promises, but simply focusing on that element misses the mark: Indigenous legal scholars call for a deeper consideration of Indigenous world views, laws, and relationships and their meaningful integration into the current western-dominated justice system.

Chapter 4 seeks to explore a more complex picture of geopolitics in the seventeenth and eighteenth centuries. Conventional histories of North America have focused on those events that fuelled economic and geographic expansion of European empires and led to the building of modern nation-states, concentrating in particular on the wars of empire and conquest. Until recently, Indigenous peoples and nations were seen as peripheral to, or at best casualties of, this enterprise. We argue that not only were Indigenous peoples and nations not peripheral but that they also had very different understandings of, perspectives on, and agendas during these events. Because Indigenous peoples did not conform to contemporary definitions of nations and states, their histories of territorial expansion and political maneuverings during the seventeenth and eighteenth centuries have been overlooked, especially in conjunction with the jostling of European empires that was occurring in North America. However, Indigenous peoples were not marginal figures: they negotiated political, economic, and social agreements with other Indigenous nations and Europeans. Sometimes the interests of Indigenous peoples and Europeans were compatible, and at other times they were not. Brett Rushforth examines the nature of French–Indigenous alliances during the eighteenth century and how they were profoundly shaped by the France's Indigenous partners. These allies reshaped the geopolitical map to their advantage by establishing and perpetuating New France's reliance on slaves, especially those from the Fox Nation. In doing so, they ensured a state of perpetual war with the Fox.

Jonathan Lainey and Thomas Peace's article uses biography to investigate the multifaceted relationships that formed between Indigenous peoples, colonial governments, and settlers in the eighteenth and nineteenth centuries. Examining the life of Louis Vincent Sawatanen, chief of the Wendat Nation's council, Lainey and Peace look at the "events that shaped the colonial boundaries between British North America and the United States, the Wendat—as well as their other Indigenous neighbours." Using the life of Sawatanen as a lens, the authors show how convoluted the social, political, and economic terrain of colonial/Indigenous relations were on Turtle Island. Further, Lainey and Peace show that cultural adaptation and pluralism is far more complicated than currently acknowledged. Looking at Sawatanen, the authors found that while the Wendat may have adopted certain cosmetic French practices like housing and western-style agriculture, they remained culturally and linguistically distinct and fundamentally Wendat.

Chapter 5 revisits the history of the fur trade which, until the 1970s and 80s, was largely characterized by non-Indigenous historians as an enterprise established by Europeans with the help of their Indigenous "sidekicks" and undertaken principally by men. After being granted access to the Hudson's Bay Company Archives in 1975, historians started to write histories about the fur trade that placed Indigenous peoples and societies at the centre rather than the margins and incorporated a more intersectional analysis of gender and race. It has also been recognized that the fur trade produced its own socio-cultural complex that drew on Indigenous and European traditions. Such works clearly showed that without Indigenous peoples, their knowledge, and extant trading networks, a large-scale intercontinental fur trade would have been impossible. Even more recently, historians have begun to question the degree to which we have allowed the fur trade to dominate histories of Turtle Island and Indigenous peoples. The historiographical and explanatory power of the staples thesis[31] and our dependence on a non-Indigenous record base has blinded many historians to the fact that not all Indigenous peoples participated in the fur trade or, if they did, they did so intermittently and for specific reasons that fur traders did not comprehend or record.

Elizabeth Vibert's article considers how fur trade records have produced particular ideas and knowledge that has continued to shape present-day perceptions of Indigenous peoples and their pasts. Vibert encourages people to read against the grain and appreciate how fur traders wrote reflections of themselves and their own cultures into the records. Concentrating on descriptions about food and hunger in fur traders' accounts, Viberts argues that "notations like "gatherer-hunter," "gatherer-fisher-hunter," or even "eclectic subsister" would more closely reflect the relative contributions of various methods of food production" than descriptors like hunters or fishers. These latter terms were ones first employed by fur traders and then adopted and normalized by historians to characterize Indigenous foodways. In Brian Gettler's work, we read about the participation of the Innu, who lived along Lac Saint-Jean, the Saguenay River, and the north shore of the St Lawrence, in the fur trade. Gettler's piece traces how the rapid social and economic changes that took place in Quebec society during the late-nineteenth and the first half of the twentieth centuries affected the Innu living in Saguenay-Lac-Saint-Jean region of Quebec. From the 1880s, when the arrival of the railroad brought increasing numbers of European Canadians into the region as agricultural settlers, the Innu adopted a range of activities and strategies to remain competitive in the fur trade well into the 1930s.

Chapter 6 examines the Métis in Canada, looking at how identity is formed, articulated, and recognized. Over the past decade, the diversity and depth of scholarship on the Métis has exploded. This research has moved beyond just looking at the struggles between Métis free-traders and the Hudson's Bay Company and those between Louis Riel and the Canadian state as the only significant moments and places of Métis identity formation. Debates have arisen about what constituted the Métis identity and when they were recognized as a nation. In the first article, Geoff Read and Todd Webb show how the identity of the Métis took on national and international importance as journalists, politicians, and social commentators from Australia to France discussed the Métis Nation. Indeed, the Métis were not an unknown people confined to the periphery of empire, but "the degree to which the broader international community acknowledged Métis claims and nationhood shaped the socio-political terrain upon which the Métis had to operate." The second article by Adam Gaudry focuses on the historic Métis community of the North West in order to illustrate that the making of the Métis as a cohesive community is a historical process that is embedded in the cultural, political, familial, and economic. Gaudry critiques how the focus on the "mixedness" of the term *Métis* has diminished a "coherent Indigenous people to a state of mere biological mixedness." Gaudry observes that mixed-race marriages are normal in all societies but still do not constitute the creation of a "unique Indigenous peoples." Indeed, Gaudry persuasively argues that "[j]ust because the government labeled families as Half-breed or Métis for administrative purposes" (read the delivery of social services) does not make them a distinct people or "reflect how they understood their own identities." By creating legal identities, the federal government is trying to control how groups define themselves and undermine what constitutes unique and distinct peoples, cultures, and nations. Increasingly, Indigenous scholars are critiquing what they refer to as the politics of recognition wherein some groups are recognized as "Métis," with the attendant rights and privileges associated with that recognition, and others are not. Glen Sean Coulthard argues that the "politics of recognition" are implemented by states who do not always rely on the exercise of state violence alone and instead "rest on the [state's] ability to entice Indigenous peoples to identify, either implicitly or explicitly, with profoundly asymmetrical and nonreciprocal forms of recognition either imposed on or granted to them by the settler state and society."[32]

Chapters 7 to 10 explore the state's assimilationist efforts and the resistance of Indigenous peoples. Two years after Confederation, the federal government passed its first Indian Act in accordance with section 91(24) of the British North American Act, which gave Canada exclusive jurisdiction over "Indians and lands reserved for Indians."[33] This 1869 Act mapped out Canada's vision of its relationship with Indigenous peoples. In 1876, the government consolidated all legislation pertaining to Indigenous peoples, reflecting the government's preoccupation with land management, First Nations or band membership, and local governance. These years witnessed tremendous shifts in federal Indian policy and signalled the hardening of boundaries between Indigenous and non-Indigenous peoples in Canada. During the 1870s, the numbered treaties were negotiated, Indigenous peoples were increasingly confined to reserves, alien systems of governance were imposed, and the pass system was instituted. In 1880, the government created the Department of Indian Affairs (DIA). These events made it extremely difficult for Indigenous peoples to resist the growing intrusion of the colonial Canadian state. Dwindling food resources led to starvation and an increasing incidence of diseases associated with poverty and poor living conditions. The late nineteenth and early twentieth centuries and the operations of the DIA laid the foundations of Canada's Indian policy, which remained remarkably constant over the next century.

In 1920, Duncan Campbell Scott, one of the major architects of Canadian Indian policy, stated the following before a special parliamentary committee:

> I want to get rid of the Indian problem. I do not think as a matter of Fact, that this country ought to continuously protect a class of people who are able to stand alone. That is my whole point. Our objective is to continue until there is not a single Indian in Canada that has not been absorbed into the body politic, and there is no Indian question, and no Indian Department and that is the whole object of this Bill.[34]

Such opinions shaped government policies that sought to transform Indigenous peoples into European-Canadians through education in residential schools, the transformation of families, and the imposition of individualist capitalist wage labour.

Chapter 7 examines the development and implementation of Indian policy within both federal and provincial jurisdictions. Beginning with the repressive administration of Scott and ending with the Conservative government of Stephen Harper, Hugh Shewell looks at the rise and entrenchment of the bureaucratic administration and management of Indigenous nations in Canada at the federal level from 1913–2013. Shewell astutely observes that very little has changed in the form and function of Indian policy despite the current espousal of so-called liberal and multicultural values. He concludes that state policy towards Indigenous peoples remains "assimilationist, seeking to dissolve First Nations into white, liberal Canadian society."

The second article, by Lori Chambers, considers state policy towards Indigenous peoples, especially children, through an examination of child welfare policy and what is infamously known as the "Sixties Scoop." Chamber's analysis includes provincial programs and policy—a frequently overlooked and largely neglected component of Indigenous experiences in Canada. Under Section 91 subsection 24 of the British North American Act of 1867 all "Indians and lands reserved for Indians" are under federal jurisdiction.[35] However, responsibility for infrastructure and key social and health and welfare services are under provincial jurisdiction (these include roads, bridges, airports, drinking water facilities, sewage, health care, and schools). Given that the 1950s witnessed the beginnings of federal efforts to download responsibility for Indigenous child welfare (and other social and health care services) onto the provinces without adequate funding, it is extremely important to look at the provinces' roles in determining Indian policy. Echoing Shewell, Chambers regards Indigenous child welfare policy as an assimilatory undertaking by the state that is ongoing.

Chapters 8 and 9 outline the personal consequences of Indian policy on Indigenous peoples and communities. In Chapter 8, both Bonita Lawrence and Jaime Cidro unveil the intimate violence that the Indian Act has perpetrated on the lives of Status and Non-Status Indians. This race-based legislation has not only created inequities between Indigenous and non-Indigenous peoples but has also led to intergenerational violence in Indigenous communities. Lawrence discusses how federal policies towards Indigenous peoples have "caused profound chaos within communities, including the fracture of family ties; the loss of knowledge of language, ceremonies, songs, and rituals; and the demise of a daily living relationship to the land." Cidro looks at Bill C-31, an amendment to the Indian Act passed by Parliament in 1985, and how the Indian Act and its attendant legislation have had extreme and often destabilizing effects on Indigenous families. The federal government continues to legislate membership and identity. For instance, the Gender Equity in Indian Registration Act (or Bill C-3) came into effect on 31 January 2011. This legislation was passed in response to the legal challenges brought forward by Sharon McIvor, a member of the Lower Nicola First Nation located in British Columbia. Bill C-3 is intended to address the consequences of women who lost their status as a result of marrying non-Status individuals; the consequences of this legislation are pending.

Chapter 9 focuses on the ongoing impact of residential schools on Indigenous peoples and their communities. Drawing on the voices of residential school survivors, Celia Haig-Brown and Lorena Sekwan Fontaine reveal the ways in which the trauma of residential schools are present realities of colonialism, not merely a "dark chapter" of Canada's history. From our own experiences as teachers, we are constantly surprised at how little students know about the history and objectives of Canada's residential school system or how long this system lasted. Similarly, Fontaine describes how, after she taught a history course on residential schools, many students told her that they had not considered the continuing effect that the residential schools have on Indigenous communities or the ongoing pain that survivors experience. In particular, Fontaine looks at the ongoing legacies of the residential school system and the possibilities of reconciliation. Fontaine asserts that reconciliation is not a "one size fits all" solution and that many people chose not to participate for a variety of very understandable reasons. Nor, notes Fontaine, is reconciliation guaranteed at this juncture, especially when the federal government remains less than committed to the process and continues to refuse to release all residential school records. In order to understand the bureaucratic roadblocks involved in this ongoing history, we need only consider how residential school survivors had to sue the federal government to release the records of the RCMP investigation (which the federal government is required to do under the terms of the Truth and Reconciliation Commission) into the treatment of children at St Anne's Residential School in Fort Albany. The school had its own electric chair that school employees used to "discipline" students.

Chapter 10 looks at society and culture in the Far North. The first article, by Cornelius H.W. Remie and Jarich Oosten, surveys a number of phenomena in the northern Inuit community of Pelly Bay (Kugaaruk) in present-day Nunavut. The efforts of Roman Catholic missionaries to convert the Inuit at Pelly Bay had important consequences, but the authors also reveal how the Oblates transcended their religious roles and took on important functions within the community, providing social welfare, food, and other necessities during periods of crisis. Mission organizations and their workers often stepped in when the federal government failed to act or refused to do so. Moreover, Remie and Oosten argue that our understanding of conversion needs to be more complicated because the Inuit's Catholicism was of a decidedly syncretic bent. In their words, the Inuit "integrated [their own cultural beliefs and traditions] into Catholicism, thus developing a form of religiosity that was reshaped to suit their own existential and cultural needs." Conversion was no top-down affair: the Inuit did not receive the benefits of Christianity passively from their European "betters," but selectively adopted the teachings of the missionaries to suit their own purposes and circumstances.

While media coverage in 2011 of the housing crisis in Attawapiskat First Nation, a community located in Northern Ontario on James Bay, brought international and national attention to the housing conditions experienced by many Indigenous peoples living in rural and northern communities, these conditions are nothing new. The housing crisis in the North has a long history, and a better understanding of federal Indian housing policies and the forced settlement and relocations of Indigenous populations are necessary to appreciate current circumstances. In the second article, Robert Robson traces the development and delivery of housing programs in the Northwest Territories after the Second World War. Robson identifies these programs as an integral part of the federal government's "wide-ranging program of northern expansion" and a central feature of the state's efforts to assert its authority and sovereignty in the region. The housing programs implemented by the federal government in the post–WWII period served to "redefined northern communities as well as the system of community hierarchy that had existed in the north for generations." Indeed, such programs transformed the landscape of the Inuit communities according to what the federal government "perceived the needs of community to be as opposed to the actual or real needs of the local population." Thus, northern housing programs have had long-ranging and in many respects negative impacts on the social and cultural practices and the health and well-being of the communities they were supposed to benefit.

The works in this reader also seek to make Indigenous peoples visible in those areas of political, economic, and social history in which they have been traditionally written out of the narrative. In Chapter 11, John Lutz's article highlights the important roles that Indigenous peoples played in the development of British Columbia's economy, making them visible in the wage economy of the post–fur-trade era. Similarly, Joan Sangster seeks to rescue Indigenous women workers from obscurity and looks at labour placement programs aimed at Indigenous women in the post–Second World War period. Conventional histories of labour in Canada do not include Indigenous peoples, let alone Indigenous women. Indeed, in a traditional survey of Canadian history, the role of Indigenous peoples in the development of the Canadian economy tends to disappear with the decline of the fur and robe trades of the mid-nineteenth century. Indian policy and residential schools wanted to produce a particular type of Indigenous worker: Indigenous men would fill positions as the most menial of labourers and Indigenous women would be domestic servants. The perpetuation of this fallacy and the exclusion of Indigenous peoples from Canadian economic history are part of the process of making them appear as outsiders, remnants of the past, and objects of tradition. Lutz and Sangster both take important steps towards correcting this misrepresentation.

Chapter 12 turns to Indigenous women and their growing marginalization under the Canadian state and women's responses to these processes. In this context, Indigenous women faced a double bind, disadvantaged both as women and as Indians. Under the 1876 Indian Act, Indigenous women lost many of their social, political, and economic rights. The Acts of 1868 and 1869 gave Indian women fewer rights under the law than Indian men. For example, women could not vote in band elections or inherit property from their husbands. Accordingly, their maintenance upon the death of their spouses became the responsibility of their children. Women also lost their Indian status if they married non-Indigenous men. These policies tried to recreate European-style patriarchy in Indigenous communities by making Indigenous women dependent on both men and the colonial state. The chapter begins with Sarah Carter's article and shows how the process of erasing Indigenous women from the landscape of Western Canada was central to the colonial project and facilitated the efforts of newcomers to make the newly formed white society appear natural and neutral and Indigenous women out of place, particularly in urban areas, through the use of passes and public humiliation.

Lianne C. Leddy's article picks up on many of the themes raised in Carter's article, but she suggests that the picture is more complicated. The federal government intended the establishment of Indian Homemakers' Clubs to help instill a particular vision of white Canadian domesticity in Indigenous communities, especially in response to the official view that Indigenous motherhood was simultaneously inadequate and threatening. However, Leddy argues "that Anishinaabe kwewak[36] took leadership roles in Indian Homemakers' Clubs and made them their own, focusing their efforts on issues that they deemed to be important," including when those endeavours were contrary to the paternalistic desires and goals of Indian Affairs. Leddy contends that the clubs worked as means through which Indigenous women could continue to operate within their "traditional realm of practice and expectations." In some instances, women used the Clubs to assert their independence, voice dissent, and "provide a 'check' for elected band council representatives" when they could not formally do so before the 1951 amendments to the Indian Act. Where Leddy concentrates on little-known Indigenous women at the grassroots level, Cora Voyageur's work offers an examination of Elsie Knott, the first Indigenous woman to be elected chief of her band under the Indian Act. Knott's election was possible only after the Act was revised in 1951 to allow women to participate in band politics and to hold office. Like Leddy, Voyageur demonstrates that Indigenous women rejected the passive roles ascribed to them by Canadian authorities and worked to help their communities in multiple ways.

The next two chapters explore the interconnectedness of land, culture, well-being, and sovereignty and the impact that western world views embodied in government policy and capitalism have had upon the health of Indigenous peoples and their communities. In Chapter 13 Liza Piper, Laurie Meijer Drees, Kristin Burnett, Travis Hay, and Kelly Skinner discuss the health and well-being of Indigenous peoples from a variety of perspectives. Piper illustrates how the aquatic environment was degraded as a result of the desire of non-Indigenous people to obtain access to the rich fisheries in the region. Indeed, the avarice of non-Indigenous people in collusion with provincial and federal governments led to extensive environmental damage and growing incidents of ill-health in the region, particularly among Indigenous peoples.

Exploring similar themes, Meijer Drees investigates the Nanaimo Indian Hospital, one of the major centres of tuberculosis treatment and containment, as well as a site of cultural resistance and persistence. Drawing on oral histories, Meijer Drees shows how Indigenous peoples resisted the DIA and understood their experiences at the hospital both as patients and visitors. The last article, by Burnett, Hay, and Skinner, illuminates how federal government policy and corporate practices have produced food insecurity in northern Indigenous communities. The high cost of food and the corresponding chronic food shortages and malnutrition have had real and long-lasting consequences on the health and well-being of communities.

The final chapter, which uses Chapter 3 as its starting point, looks at the efforts of the state to abrogate treaties and agreements negotiated in good faith with Indigenous nations. These articles show that the illegal and corrupt actions of the state are not a function of the distant past but a very real part of the present. Looking at the Algonquins of Barriere Lake, Shiri Pasternak outlines how the Comprehensive Land Claims Policy (CLCP) transforms the "nation-to-nation relationship [Indigenous nations have] with the federal government into a set of circumscribed practices and regulations that fall under provincial and municipal jurisdictions." Thus, while the CLCP offers the appearance of reconciliation, it also undermines the "social, political, and ecological relations of each nation to their lands" by transforming them into a form of "individualized land ownership." Yet the Algonquins of Barriere Lake have resisted this process at great cost and proposed a tripartite agreement that allows for co-management between federal, provincial, and Algonquin governments. Next, Paul Rynard considers the negotiations that took place around the James Bay Agreement and the role of the federal and provincial governments. He argues that "public policy needs to be analyzed in light of the Canadian state's chronic subservience to the needs of powerful social interests and the exigencies of the market economy."

Pasternak is echoed by Martha Stiegman and Sherry Pictou, who discuss how recent court challenges, while seeming to address immediate problems, do not change the fundamental nature of the system—a liberal capitalist economy and a colonial state—that underpins it. The authors look to the dynamics of accumulation by dispossession, a concept coined by David Harvey, who argues that the neoliberal capitalist practices of western countries after the 1970s centralized wealth and power in the hands of a privileged few, to understand the appropriation of Indigenous lands. The authors connect accumulation by dispossession with the current framework used to "resolve" land claims through the elimination of Indigenous sovereignty. Accordingly,

Stiegman and Pictou suggest that present-day Indigenous activists would be well-served to build alliances with non-Indigenous producers, as many have begun to do.

These articles provide an appropriate conclusion to the volume by tying together many of the themes emphasized by the other essays, including the interconnectedness of Indigenous peoples with their environments, the acquisitive nature of the Canadian state, the resistance of Indigenous peoples to European and Canadian colonialism, and most important, the need to draw on alternative world views for solutions.

It is obvious that it is necessary for non-Indigenous Canadians to develop a better understanding of Indigenous histories on Turtle Island; yet, as mentioned earlier in this introduction, the lack of knowledge of Indigenous histories among the settler population remains a real problem, which prevents the actualization of honest dialogue between Indigenous peoples and settlers. Furthermore, the constant disparagement of Indigenous peoples and the retelling of history by public figures, the popular media, and many non-Indigenous Canadians continues to distort the past, perpetuate pernicious stereotypes of Indigenous peoples, and sustain the distance between Indigenous peoples and settlers. There are several relatively recent examples. The first occurred in an interview conducted by the Montreal newspaper *La Presse* with Richard Pound, former vice-president of the International Olympic Committee, in August of 2008. When asked to compare China and Canada, Pound stated that "400 years ago, Canada was a land of savages, with scarcely 10,000 inhabitants of European origin, while in China, we're talking about a 5000-year-old civilization."[37] In a demonstration of just how widespread Pound's fallacious view was and is, many social commentators rushed to defend it, including *The Globe and Mail*'s Margaret Wente, whose piece surpassed Pound's original comments in terms of its racism.[38]

Less than a year later, as mentioned above, the prime minister of Canada, Stephen Harper, denied Indigenous peoples' experiences of colonization. Before the international community, Harper described how wonderful Canada was because we had "no history of colonialism. So we have all of the things that many people admire about the great powers but none of the things that threaten or bother them."[39] In other words, Harper does not see the current circumstances and challenges that confront Indigenous peoples as having anything to do with the arrival of Europeans over 400 years ago, the theft of Indigenous lands, or assimilationist and violent state policies; accordingly, he believes bullheadedly that the "issue of missing and murdered indigenous women was not part of a 'sociological phenomenon,' but, rather, a crime, and should be treated as such."[40] Echoing Harper's 2009 sentiments was the 2013 Speech from the Throne, which characterized the "founding" of the Canadian state as follows:

> [W]e draw inspiration from our founders, leaders of courage and audacity. Nearly 150 years ago, they looked beyond narrow self-interest. They faced down incredible challenges—geographic, military, and economic. They were undaunted. They dared to seize the moment that history offered. Pioneers, then few in number, reached across a vast continent. They forged an independent country where none would have otherwise existed.[41]

Such statements are always made in isolation from the history of colonialism and dispossession that has formed the very basis of the Canadian state. The persistence of such comments is evidence of the power that such beliefs continue to have. Moreover, this erasure of Canadian colonialism, especially when articulated in public forums by influential political leaders, legitimizes the commonly held perception that Indigenous peoples are the architects of their own impoverished circumstances; likewise, ignoring the colonial context facilitates a belief that Indigenous peoples' struggle for justice is antithetical to the well-being of the Canadian state. In turn, such perceptions produce the conditions in which the racist and often criminal treatment of Indigenous peoples is seen as acceptable.

In choosing the articles for this reader, we sought to accomplish several objectives, but chief among them was to counter Eurocentric views of Canadian history, such as Harper's, by showcasing the diverse and dynamic histories of Indigenous peoples on Turtle Island. The topics of the reader seek, then, not to "reduce [Indigenous peoples] to our own categories"[42] but rather to show that the histories of Indigenous peoples and non-Indigenous peoples are deeply interconnected and at times separated by a gulf of misunderstanding. Different moments held greater significance and meaning for Indigenous peoples than for European-Canadians. Their perceptions were frequently vastly different than those of settler Canadians but in no way inferior or subservient to them. We want to expose students to the diversity of primary sources that are available to learn about the past, particularly those created by Indigenous peoples. In doing so, we show that Indigenous histories are not at risk of being lost and that Indigenous peoples are not relics of a, to use Pound's term, "savage" past. Finally, the reader serves as a challenge to those individuals who would erase the past of Indigenous peoples by denying their histories and experiences. Indeed, such denials are part of a larger project to "rid Canada of its Indian problem." Clearly, this eradication of the "Indian problem" has not taken place—Indigenous peoples have resisted and flourished in spite of the best efforts of the state. We end with the words of Kiera L. Ladner and Leanne Simpson about the importance of knowing Indigenous histories: "Honouring and revealing Indigenous resistance is of critical importance to our communities, because the struggles are not well documented in mainstream Canadian history. They are manipulated by mainstream Canadian media and are hidden from Canadians and often Indigenous Peoples alike."[43]

Notes

1. Leanne Simpson, *Dancing On Our Turtle's Back: Stories of Nishnaabeg Re-Creation, Resurgence and a New Emergence* (Winnipeg: Arbeiter Ring Publishing, 2011), 21.

2. William Lyon Mackenzie King, 18 June 1936. As cited in *Colombo's Canadian Quotations*, John Robert Colombo, ed. (Edmonton: Hurtig, 1974), 306.

3. Thomas King, *The Inconvenient Indian: A Curious Account of Native People in North America* (Toronto: Anchor Canada, 2012), 3.

4. As quoted in Aaron Wherry, "What He was Talking About when He Talked About Colonialism," *Maclean's*, 1 October 2009, accessed 19 February 2015, www.macleans. ca/politics/ottawa/what-he-was-talking-about-when-he-talked-about-colonialism/.

5. Recent and exciting exceptions are Mary Jane Logan McCallum, *Indigenous Women, Work and History, 1940–1980* (Winnipeg: University of Manitoba Press, 2014) and *Indigenous Women and Work*, ed. Carol Williams (Champaign: University of Illinois Press, 2012).

6. Mary Jane McCallum, "Condemned to Repeat? Settler Colonialism, Racism, and Canadian History Textbooks," in *"Too Asian?" Racism, Privilege, and Post-Secondary Education*, ed. R.J. Gilmour, Davina Bhandar, Jeet Heer, and Michael C.K. Ma (Toronto: Between the Lines, 2012), 75.

7. "Dark Chapter" is a reference to Stephen Harper's Indian Residential School apology delivered on 11 June 2008 in which he refers to the "treatment of children in Indian Residential Schools as a sad chapter in our history." For a copy of the full speech see www.aadnc-aandc.gc.ca/eng/1100100015644/1100100015649, accessed 26 December 2014.

8. Mark Cronlund Anderson and Carmen Robertson, *Seeing Red: A History of Natives in Canadian Newspapers* (Winnipeg: University of Manitoba Press, 2011), 176.

9. *The People of the Kattawapiskak River*, Directed by Alanis Obomsawin, DVD. 2012.

10. Indian and Northern Affairs Canada, Communications Branch, "Words First: An Evolving Terminology Relating to Aboriginal Peoples in Canada" (Oct. 2002), accessed 15 Dec. 2010), www.collectionscanada.gc.ca/webarchives/20071124233110/http://www.ainc-inac.gc.ca/pr/pub/wf/wofi_e.pdf.

11. Aboriginal Affairs and Northern Development Canada, "Terminology," accessed 3 February 2015, www.aadnc-aandc.gc.ca/eng/1100100014642/1100100014643.

12. Taiaiake Alfred, Wasase, *Indigenous Pathways of Action and Freedom* (Toronto: University of Toronto Press, 2005), 23–5.

13. Métis Community Services, "Definition of Métis," accessed 16 Jan. 2011, www.metis.ca/index.php/metis-people/The%20definition%20of%20Metis%20Peoples.

14. Indigenous Foundations. Arts, ubc.ca. re terminology UBC "Métis," http://indigenousfoundations.arts.ubc.ca

15. Taiaiake Alfred and Jeff Corntassel, "Being Indigenous: Resurgences against Contemporary Colonialism," 597.

16. Indigenous Nationhood Movement, "Rename Campaign," posted 22 October 2013, accessed 26 February 2015, http://nationsrising.org/campaigns/rename/.

17. Edward Said, *Culture and Imperialism* (New York: Vintage Books, 1994), 9.

18. Lorenzo Veracini, "Settler Colonialism: Career of a Concept," *The Journal of Imperial and Commonwealth History* 41, 2 (2013): 317.

19. Lorenzo Veracini, "Understanding Colonialism and Settler Colonialism as Distinct Formations," *interventions*, 16, 5 (2014): 615–33; Adam Barker, "The Contemporary Reality of Canadian Imperialism: Settler Colonialism and the Hybrid Colonial State," *The American Indian Quarterly*, 33, 3 (2009): 325–51.

20. Patrick Wolfe, "Settler Colonialism and the Elimination of the Native," *Journal of Genocide Research*, 8, 4 (2006): 387–409.

21. Adam Barker, "The Contemporary Reality of Canadian Imperialism: Settler Colonialism and the Hybrid Colonial State," *American Indian Quarterly* 33, 3 (Summer 2009): 328.

22. Spivak argues that the colonized subject—the "subaltern" in her words—cannot speak in a colonial context. Gayatri Chakravorty Spivak, "Can the Subaltern Speak?" in C. Nelson and L. Grossberg, eds, *Marxism and the Interpretation of Culture* (Basingstoke: MacMillan Education, 1988), 271–313. While other scholars agree with Spivak that the suppression of Indigenous voices is a key part of the colonial project, they insist on the ability of colonized peoples to make themselves heard. See, for example, Julie F. Codell, "The Empire Writes Back: Native Informant Discourse in the Victorian Press," in Codell, ed., *Imperial Co-Histories: National Identities and the British and Colonial Press* (Madison: Fairleigh Dickinson University Press, 2003), 188–218; Alan Lester, *Imperial Networks: Creating identities in nineteenth-century South Africa and Britain* (London: Routledge, 2001), 5–8, 189–92, Edward Said, *Orientalism* (New York: Vintage Books, 1979). In *The Location of Culture* (New York: Routledge, 1994), Homi Bhabha argues that as inhabitants of "liminal" or "interstitial" space, colonized peoples are uniquely placed to transcend colonial narratives.

23. Emma LaRoque, *When the Other is Me: Native Resistance Discourse, 1850–1990* (Winnipeg: University of Manitoba Press, 2010), 62.

24. John S. Milloy, "Indian Act: A Century of Dishonour, 1869–1967." Research Paper for the National Centre for First Nations Governance, May 2008. Available at http://fngovernance.org/search/results/c216c72eca0d2b6839ae9aeb9c22f521/.

25. To put the duration of Indigenous people's presence on Turtle Island into perspective, imagine if a home video covering the last 70,000 years ran for one year, 24 hours a day. In this video, Jacques Cartier, who came to North America in 1534, would not appear in the video until 11 a.m. on 28 December. Or if the video was to run for just one full day, Europeans would not arrive until after 11:49 p.m. In this light, recent comments made by academics such as Tom Flanagan, which characterize all Canadians (Indigenous peoples included) as "recent

immigrants," are ludicrous. Such comments need to be viewed as part of a broader project to try to make Indigenous peoples appear out of place in the North American landscape. Erasing the history of Indigenous peoples on this continent allows non-Indigenous people to escape the discomfort of confronting Canada's own Eurocentric creation mythology and colonialist underpinnings. See Tom Flanagan, *First Nations, Second Thoughts?* 2nd edn (Montreal: McGill-Queen's University Press, 2008).

26. Germaine Warkentin and Carolyn Podruchny, "Introduction: Other Land Existing," in *Decentring the Renaissance: Canada and Europe in Multidisciplinary Perspective, 1500–1700* (Toronto: University of Toronto Press, 2001), 10.

27. John Sutton Lutz, "Introduction: Myth Understandings; or First Contact, Over and Over Again," in Lutz, ed., *Myth and Memory: Stories of Indigenous-European Contact* (Vancouver: UBC Press, 2007), 2.

28. Lutz, "Introduction: Myth Understandings, or First Contact," 4. Mary Louise Pratt defines contact zone as "shift[ing] the centre view. It invokes the space and time where subjects previously separated by geography and history are co-present, the point at which their trajectories now intersect. The term *contact* foregrounds the interactive, improvisational dimensions of imperial encounters so easily ignored or suppressed in accounts of conquest and domination told from the invader's perspective. A contact perspective emphasizes how subjects get constituted in and by their relations to each other. It treats the relations among colonizers and colonized, not in terms of separateness, but in terms of co-presence, interaction, interlocking understandings, and practices, and often within radically asymmetrical relations of power." See Mary Louise Pratt, *Imperial Eyes: Travel Writing and Transculturation*, 2nd ed. (New York: Routledge, 2008), 8.

29. Pratt, *Imperial Eyes*, 31.

30. Aimee Craft, "Living Treaties, Breathing Research," *Canadian Journal of Women and the Law*, 26, 1 (2014): 1–22.

31. An economic theory of development that posits the establishment of Canada as a function of East–West trade driven by the exploitation of natural resources. For an example of this, see *Harold Innis, The Fur Trade in Canada: An Introduction to Canadian Economic History* (Toronto: University of Toronto Press, 1999 (originally published in 1930).

32. Glen Sean Coulthard, *Red Skin White Masks: Rejecting the Colonial Politics of Recognition* (Minneapolis: University of Minnesota Press, 2014), 16.

33. Cora Voyageur and Brian Calliou, "Various Shades of Red: Diversity Within Canada's Indigenous Community," *London Journal of Canadian Studies* 16 (2000/2001): 112.

34. As quoted in E. Brian Titley, *A Narrow Vision: Duncan Campbell Scott and the Administration of Indian Policy in Canada* (Vancouver: University of British Columbia Press, 1986), 50.

35. Constitution Act, 1867 (U.K.), 30 & 31 Vict., c. 3, reprinted in R.S.C. 1985, App. II, No. 5.

36. Anishinaabek refers to the Council of Three Fires, which comprises Ojibway, Pottawatomi, and Odawa peoples and their allies. Anishinaabe is the singular adjective, whereas Anishinaabek refers to the people as a whole. Kwewak is the Anishinabemowin (Anishinaabe language) word for women.

37. Cited in Margaret Wente, "What Dick Pound Said Was Really Dumb—And Also True," *The Globe and Mail* (25 Oct. 2008).

38. Wente, "What Dick Pound Said."

39. David Ljunggren, "Every G20 Nation Wants to be Canada, insists PM," Reuters, 25 September 2009, www.reuters.com/article/2009/09/26/columns-us-g20-canada-advantages-idUSTRE58P05Z20090926.

40. Staff Writer, "Murdered and Missing Aboriginal Women Deserve Inquiry, Rights Group Says," CBC News, 12 January 2015, www.cbc.ca/news/politics/murdered-and-missing-aboriginal-women-deserve-inquiry-rights-group-says-1.2897707.

41. Staff, "Full Text: Throne Speech 2013," Global News, 16 October 2013, http://globalnews.ca/news/906578/full-text-throne-speech-2013/.

42. Jacques Derrida, "Structure, Sign, and Play in the Discourse of the Human Sciences," in Richard Macksey and Eugenio Donato, eds, *The Structuralist Controversy: The Languages of Criticism and the Sciences of Man* (Baltimore: Johns Hopkins University Press, 1972), 251.

43. Kiera L. Ladner and Leanne Simpson, "This is an Honour Song," in Leanne Simpson and Kiera L. Ladner eds, *This Is an Honour Song: Twenty Years Since the Blockades* (Winnipeg: Arbeiter Ring Publishing, 2010), 4.

World Views

Introduction

This chapter is an exploration of Indigenous world views. One of the most damaging aspects of the colonial project lies in its attempt to erase the traditions and bodies of knowledge of Indigenous peoples and societies. This epistemological violence has several consequences. It makes the attempts of Europeans and then European-Canadians to assimilate Indigenous peoples appear benevolent and makes Indigenous peoples seem in need of "salvation and civilization." By creating the fiction that Indigenous peoples are without knowledge, history, or culture, colonial discourses simultaneously cast them as naive children and as newcomers. Doing so reaffirms the European explorers' descriptions of North America as a *terra nullius*, Latin for "land belonging to no one." And, so the logic goes, if no one owned this land, it was available for the taking.

The two articles in this chapter encourage us to think about how people from different cultures and traditions understand the world around them and their histories. Dennis H. McPherson and J. Douglas Rabb believe that, in spite of the state's best efforts, concepts of Indigeneity have survived and that, in order to learn about the past, Indigenous peoples and students of Indigenous histories must use the beliefs of contemporary Elders and Indigenous scholars in conjunction "with early contact accounts in the historical record." To do so, we would have to "dig beneath the foreign matter" to repatriate the histories of Indigenous peoples. McPherson and Rabb also suggest that non-Indigenous peoples have a great deal to learn from Indigenous peoples in regards to respect for diversity and values like non-interference.

The second article, by Betty Bastien, outlines the world view of the *Siksikaitsitapi* (Blackfoot-speaking people), offering an alternative to the western lens through which most North Americans see the world. Bastien, a member of the Siksika Nation, urges us to move away from Eurocentric individualism, the typically western desire to dominate and control the natural world, and the characterization of everything outside the western tradition as primitive and outmoded. Instead, she encourages people to see themselves as part of a complex system of kinship relations that require respect and reciprocity. In her discussion, Bastien uses several Blackfoot terms, which are defined in an accompanying glossary.

Using these articles as a starting point, we challenge you to examine history from Indigenous perspectives, to examine what is a documentary record penned largely by non-Indigenous people with a healthy skepticism, and to question the Eurocentrism of traditional western historical narratives. European explorers and empires that described Turtle Island as a *terra nullius* did so deliberately in order to justify their conquest and possession of it. Indeed, Europeans invoked elaborate ceremonies to legitimize their assertions of sovereignty over the continent.[1] More insidious still was the characterization of Indigenous peoples as "primitive" and without "civilization." Such depictions initiated an ongoing tradition of undervaluing Indigenous perspectives and ways of knowing.

Chapter Objectives

At the end of this chapter, you should be able to

- identify elements of Indigenous epistemologies and their influence on Indigenous world views;
- identify some of the major differences between Indigenous and western world views;
- identify and discuss Indigenous polycentrism and its implications for both Indigenous peoples and non-Indigenous Canadians;
- consider how Eurocentric world views of Indigenous peoples contributed to elements of the colonial project in Canada; and
- examine critically the development of Indigenous studies programs in western institutions, such as in universities.

Note

1. Patricia Seed, *Ceremonies of Possession in Europe's Conquest of the New World, 1492–1640* (Cambridge: Cambridge University Press, 1995).

Secondary Source

Aboriginal History and Native Philosophy

Dennis H. McPherson and J. Douglas Rabb

Is it possible to discuss Aboriginal history without discussing Native philosophy? Joseph Boyden, in his award-winning historical novel, *The Orenda*, perpetuates the stereotype of the vicious American Indian through his detailed description of war between the Huron and the Iroquois, and through his depiction of the Iroquois torturing Jesuit missionaries and other outsiders. Some of his descriptions are particularly gruesome. For example, Boyden writes in the person of a Huron warrior talking about how he and his companion, Fox, torture to death some captured Iroquois:

> Fox and I walk over to the younger of the two who continued to sing his death chant, the skin of his back stinking from the heat of the ashes upon which he lies. His chant has allowed him . . . to enter his trance, and it becomes my mission now to break him from it so that he begs. After untying the prisoner's hands Fox takes one in his while I take the other, and we proceed to break each of his fingers and then, using a rock, the bones in his hands. When still he makes no sign of crying out, I take a burning stick again and insert it in his ear. . . .[1]

Contemporary Native philosopher Lee Hester, and others, drawing on traditional knowledge and evidence from first and early accounts of contact, reject this stereotypical version of the savage, warlike redskin, arguing that "hundreds of indigenous cultures have existed side by side on this continent 'forever' without the 'violent ethnic conflict now plaguing the world.'"[2] A few mainstream historians like Calvin Luther Martin agree, arguing that "the romantic myth of the 'Noble Savage' . . . might not be so mythic and romantic after all."[3]

Not everyone is willing to let go of negative stereotypes, however. Environmental philosopher J. Baird Callicott, for example, has reacted strongly against Hester et al.'s claim that "[i]t was, in fact, the acceptance (and even *celebration*) of a rich cultural and ethical diversity . . . that made it possible for hundreds of cultures to flourish side by side. . . ."[4] As Callicott puts it, "No historical evidence whatever for this claim is offered; and the evidence that does exist supports an opposite conclusion."[5] Callicott dismisses contemporary Native voices like Hester's as simply irrelevant:

> [Lee] Hester et al. write with complete certainty about indigenous thought. But search their footnotes for the cultural artifacts—or any evidence at all—upon which their pontifications are based. . . . Why then, when weighed against the cultural artifacts that I have amassed, meticulously studied, synthesized, and summarized . . . should we trust Hester et al.'s account of the beliefs, attitude and values of indigenous peoples and accept their criticism of mine? Apparently, because two of the authors identify themselves as indigenous.[6]

Callicott seems to believe that most contemporary Indigenous people have been assimilated into mainstream culture. He argues that "[t]o buy guns, motors, and mackinaw jackets is to buy, however unintentionally, a world view to boot."[7] He also suggests that the adoption of "nonnative technologies (such as the automobile and the television) and the replacement of native languages by European languages (such as Spanish and English) as mother tongues, . . . have further attenuated the process of cultural transmission and reproduction."[8]

In fact, however, there is considerable documentation that "describe[s] natives who are caring, loving, and sharing among themselves and with others."[9] Christopher

Columbus, for example, describing the Natives he first encountered, wrote in his journal that

> [t]hey are so . . . free with all they have, that no one would believe it who has not seen it; of anything that they possess, if it be asked of them, they never say no; on the contrary, they invite you to share it and show as much love as if their hearts went with it. . . .[10]

Similar acts of hospitality from the American West of the late 1600s are well documented in Frank Waters's *Book of the Hopi*. There we find a revealing description of the arrival of the Navaho, often regarded as particularly violent, and the traditional enemy of the Hopi:

> . . . [L]ittle **bands** of men, women and children came, all dressed the same way, all hungry and homeless. The Hopi were good to these barbarians. They fed and sheltered them. They taught them to work in the fields, to weave baskets, and to spin cotton.[11]

The Navaho eventually outstayed their welcome, as did, incidentally, the Spanish, and hostilities finally did break out. But, as Waters also reports, even after the Hopi were victorious over the Spanish, in the **Pueblo Revolt of 1680**, and shortly thereafter over the Navaho,

> [t]he Hopi were left with a great sadness. They were a people of Peace who did not believe in war, yet they had been forced into killing both [the Navaho] and the Castillas [Spanish] in order to protect their homes and their religion.[12]

It is important to note that the Hopi are reported to have gone to war to *preserve* their religion and their way of life, not to *impose* their religion or their way of life on anyone else.

In *The Jesuit Relations*, Christian missionaries working among the Huron, in what would become Canada, recorded similar acts of hospitality:

> We see shining among them some rather noble moral virtues. . . . Their hospitality towards all sorts of strangers is remarkable; they present to them in their feasts, the best of what they have prepared, and as I have already said, I do not know if anything similar, in this regard, is to be found anywhere. They never close the door upon a Stranger, and once having received him into their houses, they share with him the best they have; they never send him away, and when he goes away of his own accord, he repays them with a simple "thank you."[13]

Of course *The Jesuit Relations* also contain some Boyden-like descriptions of horrific torture. The death of Father Jean de Brébeuf is probably the most famous example. It is described in the document as "a vivid and sympathetic account of the martyrdom of Brébeuf and Gabriel Lalemant, written by Christophe Regnaut." Regnaut did not witness the torture himself; he was told about it by Christianized Hurons who had escaped from their enemy, the Iroquois. Regnaut thus based his report on highly partisan hearsay evidence. He tried to make up for this by giving a detailed description of his own "eyewitness" examination of the bodies of these tortured missionaries.

> Father de Brebeuf had his legs, thighs, and arms stripped of flesh to the very bone; I saw and touched a large number of great blisters, which he had on several places on his body, from the boiling water which these barbarians had poured over him in mockery of Holy Baptism. I saw and touched the wound from a belt of bark, full of pitch and resin, which roasted his whole body. I saw and touched the marks of burns from the Collar of hatchets placed on his shoulders and stomach. I saw and touched his two lips, which they had cut off because he constantly spoke of God while they made him suffer.
>
> I saw and touched all parts of his body, which had received more than two hundred blows from a stick. I saw and touched the top of his scalped head; I saw and touched the opening which these barbarians had made to tear out his heart.
>
> In fine, I saw and touched all the wounds of his body, as the savages had told and declared to us.[14]

Two things jump out from this "eyewitness" account. The first is that the wounds Regnaut says he "saw and touched" are described in terms of the account given him by the Huron Christian converts. For example, he says he saw blisters on the body. He does not really know how they got there for he has not seen them being inflicted. He has been told that they were caused by boiling water used in a mock baptism. But that detail is hearsay; he has not seen it himself. And so it is for his description of all of the wounds he says he saw and touched. Further, Regnaut's frequent repetition of the words "I saw and touched" is suspicious. He is using a highly piteous and evocative rhetorical strategy, repeating the formula, "I saw and touched this wound, I saw and touched that wound" over and over again. This suggests that he wrote his account not as an objective retelling of the facts of the case, so to speak, but as a Jesuit missionary seeking to elicit sympathy and support for missionizing among the Huron and other Indigenous peoples of the Canadas. Readers and researchers will have to decide for themselves just what weight to give Regnaut's account, compared, for example, to the documents cited above praising noble virtues and hospitality. There may be some truth in both.

However, we are reminded of a story told by the late Mohawk historian, Deborah Doxtator, as part of her keynote concluding address to the First Biennial Aboriginal Peoples Conference at Lakehead University, October 1994:

> When I was twelve I had a very important confrontation with history that I don't think I will ever forget. My history teacher in a largely non-Native school was my aunt, actually my father's cousin but because she was the age of my aunts that was what I called her. I remember she had someone from the class read aloud from the history text the school board said we were supposed to use for the class. The book was talking about the "bloodthirsty Iroquois" and went into great descriptive detail concerning the tortures endured by the Jesuit martyrs at the hands of the "savage" Mohawk. The book had pictures of men in breechcloths, their heads half-shaved of hair, looking mad and brandishing what looked like small axes, ready and willing to

"Anishnawbe World View" by Ahmoo Angeconeb

incomprehensibly murder someone. Anyone. I looked up from that book at my aunt.
She told the class that would be all for history that day and when the bell rang and
we were to go to the next class she motioned for me to stay behind to speak to her.
She told me not to believe everything that's written in books. She told me that story
about the Iroquois, well, it just wasn't true. I was somewhat confused by what happened, but it was a different time in a very conservative white-dominated community.
Publically as the teacher she couldn't tell me that, but privately as my aunt she did.

It was an important lesson about what writing Native history was really about then. I guess it was also part of what lured me into trying to write it myself.[15]

If, as Doxtator's history teacher told her, the story in the history text about the "blood-thirsty Iroquois" in fact "just wasn't true," then we have to ask if the Roman Catholic Church in 1930 was misguided in sanctifying Jesuit missionaries such as "Jean de Brébeauf, Isaac Jogues, Gabriel Lalemant, Charles Garnier, Noel Chabanel, René Goupil and Jean de la Lande."[16] There is no question that these and other missionaries did indeed "suffer hardships for the Christian faith."[17] However, they were also interfering intruders in a foreign land, and unwitting instigators in a clash of cultures. They learned Native languages not to converse with the Natives, but to convert them.

Native Values

Conversion of the Natives over time became a relatively easy endeavour for the missionaries. This may be due in part to the fact that "Indigenous communities accept more diversity than most linguistic communities," as **Mi'kmaq** scholar Marie Battiste and her Chichasaw husband, Sa'ke'j Henderson, argue in their classic study, *Protecting Indigenous Knowledge and Heritage: A Global Challenge*.[18] In our study, *Indian from the Inside: Native American Philosophy and Cultural Renewal*, we recognize diversity as a Native value within what we have called the polycentric perspective. This polycentrism is nicely illustrated in the following account of a traditional "sharing circle" by Cree scholar Michael Hart:

> Symbolically, the topic is placed at the centre of the circle and everyone has a chance to share their views about the topic. Since everyone is in a circle they will each have a different perspective of the topic or part of the picture. Everyone expresses their views so that a full picture of the topic is developed. Individual views are blended until consensus on the topic is reached.[19]

Drawing on our work, Cherokee philosopher/historian Jace Weaver recounts a story told by Osage scholar George Tinker. Weaver explains the significance of polycentrism in Native cultures:

> Imagine two Indian communities who live in close proximity to each other, separated by a mountain. A non-Native visitor arrives at the first community. In the course of the stay, she is informed that the tribe's council fire is the center of the universe and creation myths are told to demonstrate this concept. The following day, the outlander and representatives of the first tribe travel to the other community. The elders of the new tribe declare that their council fire is the center of the universe, and the members of the first tribe nod their assent. Confused, the visitor asks her host, "I thought you said that your fire was the center." The Indian replies, "When we're there, that is the center of the universe. When we are here, this is the center." Tinker concludes, "sometimes a single truth is not enough to explain the balance of the world around us. . . ." [As Weaver makes clear] We need to examine as many different cultural codes as we can to re-create the structure of human life—self, community, spirit, and the world as we perceive it.[20]

This polycentrism leads not only to respect for diversity but also to other values such as non-interference that are manifest in Native cultures. As can be seen in many of the first contact documents that we cited above, respect for diversity and non-interference were, at least at first contact, widespread among Native people from different regions of the Americas.

The value of non-interference served as the governing principle in treaties and other agreements between Indigenous nations. This is apparent in the famous **Iroquois Confederacy**. In the traditional story of the founding of the Confederacy, Deganawidah (Dekanaweda) creates a symbol of the union by taking an arrow from each of the Five Nations "which," he says "we shall tie up together in a bundle which, when it is made and completely tied together, no one can bend or break." Immediately after declaring, "We shall tie this bundle of arrows together with deer sinew which is strong, durable and lasting and then also this institution shall be strong and unchangeable," Deganawidah introduces a further symbol—the autonomous members of the Confederacy united as a single person. "This bundle of arrows signifies that all the lords and all the warriors and all the women of the Confederacy have become united as one person."[21] This ideal person is a unity, not a uniformity. The individual members of the Iroquois Confederacy are all one person yet maintain their individual identities: "Before the real people united their nations, each nation had its council fires. . . . The five Council Fires shall continue to burn as before and they are not quenched."[22]

To say that the "five Council Fires shall continue to burn as before" is to say that the Confederacy recognizes and accommodates the diversity and autonomy of the five member nations. Deganawidah's narrative states explicitly that "[w]henever a foreign nation is conquered or has by their own free will accepted the Great Peace, their own system of internal government may continue . . . but they must cease all strife with other nations."[23] This Indigenous ideal of diversity in unity is recommended for the present day by Lumbee tribal member Robert A. Williams Jr. in his 1997 study *Linking Arms Together*. He argues: "Deganawidah's message envisioned a multicultural community of all peoples on earth, linked together in solidarity under the sheltering branches of the Tree of the Great Peace."[24]

Historian Olive Dickason describes the Confederacy as "the Great Peace," which "was not an overriding authority, but a 'jural community' charged with maintaining the peace through ceremonial words of condolence and ritual gifts of exchange."[25] It is important to note that Dickason here talks about the Confederacy "maintaining the peace," not "creating the peace." The tendency among non-Native scholars is to interpret the "Great Peace" as a peace treaty or type of instrument designed to end conflict between two or more warring parties. A typical example of this tendency to view the Iroquois as warlike appears in the historical novel *The Master of Life* by Canadian philosopher William Douw Lighthall (1857–1954). In this fictionalized account of the founding of the Iroquois Confederacy we hear Hiawatha responding to the claim by his adopted Onondaga father that the war with the Mohawk is evil: "'All war is evil,' returned Hiawatha bitterly; and as he said it he realized that the gods were speaking by his lips, for he had not thought so wide a thing . . . This thought was—to abolish war . . . By alliance forever might come the death of war forever . . . War against war!"[26] But, as we said, the Great Peace was to maintain harmonious relationships, not to restore them.

In *The Master of Life*, Lighthall also suggests that British success in North America occurred in large part because the British linked themselves to the "Silver Covenant Chain of the Iroquois League," meaning the Confederacy. As he puts it,

> [w]hen . . . the white men came, they came in two directions. The Frenchman, Champlain, came up the St. Lawrence; the Netherlander, Hudson, up the Hudson. The former rashly took up the unjust quarrel of the Huron and the Algonkian against the Mohawk; the League replied by crippling the colony of France until its doom was written before all eyes and its dominion passed away. The Netherlander linked his future with the Silver Chain; he held to it for himself and the Britons; and the League was the bulwark which protected them during years of weakness and prepared the way for the spread of British principles in North America.[27]

Douglas Rabb argues "that if current members of the Iroquois Confederacy really thought that they had 'prepared the way for the spread of British principles in North America,' they might well say, with deep regret, that they had much to answer for."[28] Whoever is to blame, British principles have certainly spread throughout the North American continent, influencing everything from English translations and interpretations of the "Iroquois Confederacy Great Law of Peace" to twenty-first-century Supreme Court judgments on Aboriginal rights and Aboriginal title.

Section 35 of The Constitution Act, 1982, of Canada recognizes and affirms Aboriginal rights already in existence. The first case of the Supreme Court adjudicating Aboriginal rights was the Sparrow decision, in which the Supreme Court recognized fishing in a traditional fashion as such a right.[29] Subsequent cases established a method for the recognition of Aboriginal rights: "[A] practice, custom or tradition which is integral to the aboriginal community must be shown to have continuity with the practices, customs or traditions which existed prior to contact"[30] with Europeans. A derivative of Aboriginal rights, Aboriginal title, was first delineated by US Chief Justice John Marshall in such cases as *Cherokee Nation v. Georgia and Worchester & Georgia*,[31] and has recently been upheld in the Canadian context in the Tsilhqot'in Supreme Court decision. The Supreme Court asserts, "Aboriginal title is . . . the unique product of the historic relationship between the Crown and the Aboriginal group."[32] As we argue,

> [i]t is important to realize that this concept of Aboriginal Title was equally alien to the Indians and to the [European] estate system [stemming from the Holy Roman Empire], which was attempting to accommodate the reality of the New World. . . . Though aboriginal and treaty rights are "recognized and affirmed" in *The Constitution Act, 1982*, . . . "aboriginal title" is still, to this day, not clearly defined.[33]

In *Indian from the Inside* we argue at some length that the "British regarded 'aboriginal title' as a right that must be extinguished. . . . And, of course, the easiest method of extinguishing such title is [was] for the Indians to cede it, to give it all away."[34] But what were they really giving away? In The Royal Proclamation of 1763, King George III recognized the use and possession of the land by the Nations or Tribes of Indians under his protection. This is the document from which Aboriginal rights emerge.

Aboriginal title does not appear in The Royal Proclamation. It was first described by US Judge Marshall and is really a British/European invention for dealing with the cloud hanging over sovereign rights to land, because Aboriginal peoples did not see land as something to be owned.

Native World Views

Even the most cursory understanding of Native philosophy raises serious questions about what Indigenous people thought they were selling or ceding in giving up Aboriginal title. Indeed, one might well ask whether "selling" and "ceding" are even the right concepts here.

In looking at Native philosophy, it is important to get at traditional world views that are as close as possible to authentic pre-contact views. Though difficult, this is not impossible. Some considerable work has already been done in this field using philosophical and literary analyses of traditional narratives, early contact descriptions such as the Jesuit Relations, and accounts by contemporary Elders as well as ethnologists and anthropologists. By cross-referencing this diversity of sources, a reliable picture does emerge.[34] As professors of Native philosophy we have always seen our role as acquainting Native students with these kinds of philosophical and research methods so that they can return to their home communities to do effective community-based research, because this is where Native philosophy is to be found: in Native communities. Though this research is still in its infancy, some important philosophical questions have emerged.

Using some of the checks and balances mentioned above, Overholt and Callicott argue that the Ojibwa concept of *person* differs significantly from the Euro-American one. Though it still carries the ethical significance of a being deserving of moral respect, it has a much broader application that extends to what they call other-than-human persons:

> While in the Western world view only human beings are fully persons, the Ojibwa acknowledge other-than-human persons, among them "plants and animals" and even "soils and waters." . . . Animals, plants, and minerals are not . . . rightless resources, as is the case in Western economic assumptions. . . . Human beings must assume appropriate attitudes toward the non-human members of their polymorphous community. For one thing human beings must not be arrogant. . . . Above all non-human beings must be *respected*.[35]

If this is, indeed, the traditional Ojibwa world view it follows that whatever else they were doing in the treaty-making process, they could not have been putting a price on land. They may have been willing to share their traditional territory with others and accept something in return, but that is quite different from treating land as an object to be sold or ceded. Given their world view, the Ojibwa could not have seen their treaty as interfering in any way with the way they had been living with the land since time immemorial. It is important to note that the expression is "living with the land," not "living on the land," as if the land were an object to live upon or a resource to be exploited. Michael Pomedli, one of the few western-trained philosophers to take

Native philosophy seriously, gives an extensive analysis of the concept of "living with" in his appropriately entitled book *Living with Animals: Ojibwe Spirit Powers*:

> "Living with" has many meanings ranging from a mere juxtaposition or geo-positioning of one being with another, to a co-mingling and near identification of one being with another. On the psychological and dispositional level "living with" can range in meaning from despising or hating the other, to varying ways of being-with, of showing affection, love and care. "Living with" can be viewed on the level of social and political structures ranging from the sometimes extreme differences between leaders and followers, to much smaller differences among those who assume leadership roles while retaining more or less equal status to others.[36]

For the Ojibwa and other Native people, "co-mingling and near identification" with the land and other animals is emphasized as well as "equality" and "showing affection, love and care"; in short, showing "respect." This comes out in Pomedli's discussion of the role of specific animals in Ojibwa ceremony and philosophy, including otters, owls, and bears, as well as water creatures and thunderbirds. This discussion gives Pomedli an Indigenous lens through which to view the nineteenth-century Ojibwa historians Peter Jones, Andrew Blackbird, George Copway, and William Warren. It is beyond the scope of this paper to examine Pomedli's discussion of these Native historians but his methodology is of interest here. As far as we are aware, this is the first time these four Ojibwa historians have been approached as Aboriginal voices in the context of Native philosophy. Pomedli sharpens the focus of his Indigenous lens by including line drawings derived from Ojibwa rock art and birch-bark scrolls throughout his book. He explains:

> Petroglyphs are images carved on rock surfaces. Pictographs are images drawn or painted on rocks. Petroforms are patterns or shapes arranged with small or large rocks on the ground or on rather flat rocky surfaces. These three types of representation are often called rock art. Other forms of communication are the line drawings and images on birch bark scrolls or other materials indicating ideas, speech, and songs.[37]

Using the "editorial we," Pomedli writes, "We have included these illustrations to give meaning to our written text, and also as another and sometimes parallel articulation of Ojibwe culture."[38] He also observes that

> [t]hese voices in line drawings, stone formations, and incised stone speak of performances that were vital to the Ojibwe peoples. . . . These performances and visions are continued in many cultural representations—for example, on clothing and utensils, as images carried or tattooed on the person, and in contemporary art.[39]

As an example from contemporary art we include, as a primary source document, a drawing by Ojibwa artist Ahmoo Angeconeb titled *Anishnawbe World View*. This artwork should be studied carefully. It says a great deal about Native values and world views. At the top it features a sky world represented by a traditional image of a thunderbird. Directly below that is a middle world consisting of three humans, a mother and a father with a toddler standing between them. On either side of this family are a wolf and a bear both standing upright on two legs like the humans, thus representing "other-than-human persons," suggesting the kinship among them all. There are also water creatures in this middle world, a fish and a turtle depicted in stylized form, suggesting that they are more-than-human spirit beings. Below the middle world there is an underworld represented by a horned serpent. Though these worlds are depicted one above the other, we should be careful not to draw the conclusion that they represent a hierarchy of any sort. They are all equal, as is more obvious in Angeconeb's earlier piece, *Abneesheenabpay Sky World, Middle World & Underworld*, in which the three worlds are presented side by side in a triptych.[40] The late art historian Patricia Vervoort, who spent much of her distinguished career working with and writing about Native artists, discusses how ancient petroglyphs and pictographs have inspired a number of contemporary Native artists, who can be seen as "reclaiming this imagery as part of their history."[41] Vervoort's discussion of Angeconeb's triptych is revealing:

> *Abneesheenabpay Sky World, Middle World & Under World* (1989) . . . is a three-part, triptych-like, lino-block print, which employs traditional legendary figures such as the Horned Serpent of the Under World. In the Middle World are human beings with trees, fish, and land animals such as loons and bears, while the Thunderbeings on the left represent the Sky World. All of these images have strong silhouettes and, other than the human figures, have strong internal patterns of linear detailing. On the right, the notion of the Under World is conveyed by two large snake-like creatures whose shape again relates to snake-like forms painted on the rocks at Agawa and other sites. The strong shapes echo the curving contours of traditional rock paintings and indicate Ahmoo's source of inspiration. Each of his print blocks is precisely balanced in composition.[42]

Vervoort's discussion confirms that the Native world view depicted here is anything but hierarchical. Sky World is to the left of Middle World, and Under World, despite its name, is to the right. They are all equal, they are each sacred. The original triptych art form is found in medieval churches and was devoted to sacred Christian art. This is probably why Vervoort uses the term *triptych-like* in her article. But Angeconeb's use of the triptych is intended to convey his belief that the ancestral art forms he employs, ancient pictographs and other forms of rock art, are just as sacred as anything found in medieval Christian churches.

There is much more Native philosophy contained in these works of art than we have discussed here. Vervoort goes a little further than we have, in drawing attention to the turtle supporting the land in *Anishnawbe World View* (1991), for instance.[43] Many Native peoples refer to North America as "Turtle Island." The images here each tell a story. But those unfamiliar with Native traditions may not recognize these stories and their significance. Euro-American and Native world views are incommensurable.[44] This incommensurability is even expressed in the languages themselves. Authentic Native languages are process oriented, describing relationships and events in the present.[45] Pomedli tries to capture this in noting that for the Ojibwa, "stones, trees, clouds, and animals are not merely physical and passive; they are active agents in the world."[46] But to understand the philosophical import of concepts like "other-than-human persons" and how this relates to, for example, the animal–hunter relationship, requires what we have called a transformative philosophy.[47] Pomedli agrees. Drawing on some of our work he argues, "Those of us who are attempting to understand these cultures must engage in some form of transformation from our present-day technical and post-European formulations. We need to acquire a sense of wonder whereby the old becomes new, the past is understood in the present, the strange and unfamiliar are accepted on their own terms."[48]

Conclusion

As we gain a deeper understanding of Native philosophy with community-based research, it becomes more and more obvious that first-contact histories will have to be rewritten. In rewriting these histories a number of important philosophical questions arise. Do we need to reinterpret or renegotiate the present recognition and affirmation of constitutionally protected Aboriginal rights? Are such rights and Aboriginal title itself based on legal fictions designed simply to separate Aboriginal people from the land, and make room for the settler populations? Should Aboriginal rights be ignored altogether, and other ways sought to make amends for the oppression of Aboriginal peoples, ways more compatible, more in harmony, with Native philosophy?

Notes

1. Joseph Boyden, *The Orenda* (Toronto: Penguin Books, 2013), 273.
2. Lee Hester, Dennis McPherson, Annie Booth, and Jim Cheney, "Indigenous Worlds and Callicott's Land Ethic," *Environmental Ethics* 22, 3 (2000): 278.
3. Calvin Luther Martin, *In the Spirit of the Earth: Rethinking History and Time* (Baltimore: The Johns Hopkins University Press, 1992), 16.
4. Hester et al., "Indigenous Worlds," 278.
5. J. Baird Callicott, "Many Indigenous Worlds or the Indigenous World? A Reply to My "Indigenous" Critics," *Environmental Ethics* 22, 3 (2000): 302.
6. Ibid., 294.
7. J. Baird Callicott, *In Defense of the Land Ethic: Essays in Environmental Philosophy* (Albany: State University of New York Press, 1989), 212.
8. Callicott, "Many Indigenous Worlds," 293.
9. Dennis McPherson, "A Definition of Culture: Canada and First Nations," in *Native American Religious Identity: Unforgotten Gods*, Jace Weaver, ed., (Maryknoll, NY: Orbis Books, 1998), 81. See also Dennis H. McPherson and J. Douglas Rabb, *Indian from the Inside: Native American Philosophy and Cultural Renewal*, 2nd edn (Jefferson, NC: McFarland, 2011), 125–39; Dennis H. McPherson and J. Douglas Rabb, "Indigeneity in Canada: Spirituality, the Sacred and Survival," *International Journal of Canadian Studies* 23, (Spring 2001): 60–3.
10. Samuel Eliot Morison, *Admiral of the Sea: A Life of Christopher Columbus* (Boston: Little Brown and Company, 1942), 231.
11. Frank Waters, *Book of the Hopi* (New York: Ballantine Books, 1963), 312.
12. Ibid., 314.
13. S.R. Mealing, ed., *The Jesuit Relations and Allied Documents: A Selection* (Ottawa: Carleton University Press, 1990), 45.
14. Reuben Gold Thwaites, ed., *The Jesuit Relations and Allied Documents: Travels and Explorations of the Jesuit Missionaries in New France 1610–1791*, vol. 34 (New York: Pageant Books, 1959), 9–35.
15. Deborah Doxtator, "Issues in Writing Native History," in *Indigenous Learning: Proceedings from the First Biennial Aboriginal Peoples Conference*, Sylvia O'Meara et al., eds, (Thunder Bay, ON: Lakehead University Aboriginal Resource and Research Centre, 1996), 115.
16. Michael Pomedli, *William Kurelek's Huronia Mission Paintings* (Lewiston: Edwin Mellon Press, 1991), 108.
17. Ibid., 108.
18. Marie Battiste and James (Sa'ke'j) Youngblood Henderson, *Protecting Indigenous Knowledge and*

Heritage: A Global Challenge (Saskatoon: Purich Publishing, 2000), 105.

19. Michael Anthony Hart, "Sharing Circles: Utilizing Traditional Practice Methods for Teaching, Helping, and Supporting," in *From Our Eyes: Learning from Indigenous Peoples*, Sylvia O'Meara et al., eds (Toronto: Garamond, 1996), 65.

20. Jace Weaver, *That the People Might Live: Native American Literature and Native Community* (New York: Oxford University Press, 1997), 32–3.

21. Arthur C. Parker, "The Constitution of the Five Nations," in William N. Fenton, ed., *Parker on the Iroquois* (Syracuse: Syracuse University Press, 1968), 101.

22. Ibid., 55–6.

23. Ibid., 10.

24. Robert A. Williams Jr., *Linking Arms Together: American Indian Treaty Visions of Law and Peace, 1600–1800* (New York: Oxford University Press, 1997), 60.

25. Olive Patricia Dickason, *Canada's First Nations: A History of Founding Peoples from Earliest Times*, 3rd ed. (Don Mills: Oxford University Press, 2002), 53–4.

26. William Douw Lighthall, *The Master of Life: A Romance of the Five Nations and of Prehistoric Montreal*. (Toronto: The Musson Book Co. 1908), 143.

27. Ibid., 260–1.

28. J. Douglas Rabb, "The Master of Life and the Person of Evolution: Indigenous Influence on Canadian Philosophy" in *Hidden In Plain Sight: Contributions of Aboriginal Peoples to Canadian Identity and Culture*, Cora J. Voyageur, David R. Newhouse, and Dan Beavon, eds, (Toronto: University of Toronto Press, 2011), 211.

29. *R. v. Sparrow*, [1990] 1 S.C.R. 1075.

30. *R. v. Gladstone*, [1996] 2 S.C.R. 723.

31. *Worcester v. Georgia*, 31 U.S. (6 Pet.) 515 (1832).

32. *Tsilhqot'in Nation v. British Columbia*, 2014 SCC 44.

33. Dennis H. McPherson and J. Douglas Rabb, *Indian from the Inside: Native American Philosophy and Cultural Renewal*, 2nd ed. (Jefferson, NC: McFarland, 2011), 37.

34. Ibid.

35. See J. Baird Callicott, *Earth's Insights: A Multicultural Survey of Ecological Ethics from the Mediterranean Basin to the Australian Outback* (Berkeley: California UP, 1994); "American Indian Land Wisdom? Sorting Out the Issues" in *In Defense of the Land Ethic: Essays in Environmental Philosophy*, (Albany: State University of New York Press, 1989); Michael M. Pomedli, *Ethnophilosophical and Ethnolinguistic Perspectives on the Huron Indian Soul* (Lewiston: Edwin Mellen Press, 1991); Thomas W. Overholt and J. Baird Callicott, *Clothed-In-Fur and Other Tales: An Introduction to an Ojibwa World View* (Lanham MD: University Press of America, 1982); J. Douglas Rabb, "Prologues to Native Philosophy," *European Review of Native American Studies*, 9, 1, (1995): 23–5; Dennis H. McPherson and J. Douglas Rabb, "Some Thoughts on Articulating a Native Philosophy," *Ayaangwaamizin: The International Journal of Indigenous Philosophy* 1, 1 (1997): 11–21; Dennis H. McPherson and J. Douglas Rabb. "Transformative Philosophy and Indigenous Thought: A Comparison of Lakota and Ojibwa World Views," *Proceedings of the 29th Algonquian Conference* (Winnipeg: University of Manitoba Press, 1999), 202–10; Dennis H. McPherson, and J. Douglas Rabb, *Indian from the Inside*.

36. Overholt and Callicott, *Clothed-In-Fur and Other Tales*, 154–5.

37. Michael Pomedli, *Living with Animals: Ojibwe Spirit Powers*, (Toronto: University of Toronto Press, 2014), xxv.

38. Ibid., 243.

39. Ibid., xxv.

40. Ibid.

41. Ahmoo Angeconeb's *Abneesheenabpay Sky World, Middle World & Underworld* can be seen in *Thunder Bay Art Gallery Newsletter* (Spring 2013), 3, accessed 12 August 2014. http://theag.ca/events/mitakuye-oyasin-all-my-relations/, accessed 14 May 2015.

42. Patricia Vervoort, "Re-present-ing Rock Art," *American Review of Canadian Studies* 31, 1–2, (2001): 209.

43. Ibid., 216.

44. McPherson and Rabb, "Transformative Philosophy," 202–10.

45. Dennis H. McPherson, "Living with Bees, W.A.S.P.s, and Other Stinging Critters: A Reply to Ryan Heavy Head and Elizabeth Wilson," *APA Newsletter On American Indians in Philosophy* 5, 2, (2006): 17.

46. Pomedli, *Living with Animals*, xxvi.

47. McPherson and Rabb, "Transformative Philosophy," 202–10.

48. Pomedli, *Living with Animals*, xxv.

Secondary Source

Indigenous Pedagogy: A Way Out of Dependence

Betty Bastien

This article explores the pedagogical practices of *Siksikaitsitapi*. Traditional learning is premised on a "knowing" that is generated through a participatory and experiential process involving kinship relationship networks known as alliances. In the Indigenous paradigm, an understanding of the dynamic and intricate relationships among *Mokaksin*, *Pommaksinni*, and *Aistommatop* knowledge originates and is experienced from the living, fluid, and transforming world of the Blackfoot people. The organic nature of the universe is understood and emulated through the powers of life, which *Siksikaitapi* call *Ihtsipaitapiiyo'pa*. Referring to *Ihtsipaitapiiyo'pa* reminds us of the sacred spirit. In this context, the word *spirit* is understood as universal consciousness.

This sacred power structures all relationships among and between humans, nature, and the universe. The *Siksikaitapi* perspective thus emulates natural patterns of the universe. The universe's patterns constitute a web of interconnectivity, a system that maintains balance and harmony that preserves and strengthens *Ihtsipaitapiiyo'pa*. By echoing these natural relationship and life processes, *Siksikaitapi* harmonize with nature. Harmony is achieved through their relationships, as revealed through their relationship with *Natosi*, the manifestation of the source of life that is at the core of human and planetary survival. Subsequently, *Natosi* is an integral partner in our renewal of responsibilities in maintaining balance and thus is central to the Blackfoot world. The inclusive nature of relationships with the natural and cosmic world and with the sacred is at the heart of the Blackfoot ontological perspective. Self/identity is premised on the integrative spirit of *Ihtsipaitapiiyo'pa*.[1]

Ontological Perspective

Siksikaitapi ontological theory is premised on experience with the sacred *Ihtsipaitapiiyo'pa*. The individual's experience of the sacred guides *Niitsitapi* (real people, as in the Blackfoot-speaking people) in understanding what it means to be human. Therefore, human development is based on experiences, which connect the individual to the transformational powers of the universe. This includes a complex system of kinship relationships through which *Niitsitapi* teach their children the meaning and purpose of life. Children discover the meaning of life through experiences grounded in the sacred relationships of alliances. The understanding of what it means to be a human being is premised on the connections with the sacred and on transformational experiences. In essence, the identity of the people and the theory of human development are based on a framework of moral and ethical relationships.

These spiritual relationships have been referred to generically as the spirituality of Indigenous people. They are the basis of becoming and being *Niitsitapi*. The tribal identity of *Siksikaitsitapi* begins with having good relations. Prayer is not only the path for good relations among one's alliances, but it is also the process of making alliances and acknowledging them. This has been expressed as follows by one *Kaaahsinnooniksi*: "In order to regain our identity and maintain our way of life we need to have good relations. We don't leave out prayer in anything that we do. This is our way."[2]

The Indigenous and Eurocentred conceptions are diametrically opposite in their approach to relationships and to defining the purposes of human activity. The most striking cultural difference is that in the Eurocentred concept an objectified self represents the universal nature of humanness. This denies the cosmic essence of humanity originating with *Ihtsipaitapiiyo'pi* as the source of the relationships of *Siksikaitsitapi*. The nature of humanity in the *Siksikaitsitapi* world view orginates from spiritual relationships. Human development and governance are shaped through these relationships, and human beings strive to be in balance with all relationships. In summary, the ontological experience of the sacred arises within a complex system of kinship relations.

Niitsitapi's conception of self is intricately linked with an organic universe; alliances with the natural world are the relationships from which life is lived. *Niitsitapi* cosmic self is understood as part of the natural order and is ethically and morally located in all of time. Subsequently, knowing is the knowing of all time. On the other hand, in the Eurocentred view, the objectified self stands alone and powerless. The ideas of self are totally reversed between these two paradigms. Understanding these differences means recognizing and distinguishing the construction and the dynamics of dependency.

Using the European self-image and concept of power automatically victimizes tribal people, since these conceptions continually reconstruct powerlessness, victimization, deficiency, or inferiority as characteristics of Indigenous peoples. A post-colonial paradigm must not only deconstruct the assumption of the Eurocentred ideological process but also begin by reaffirming and reconstructing tribal concepts, the fundamentals of Indigenous theories and ontological assumptions. The validation and use of tribal ontologies begins the process of the reconstruction of self and the identification of one's place in a cosmic universe allowing for Indigenous ways of knowing. For *Siksikaitsitapi*, the beginning point is the awareness of their alliances that are at the heart of the culture. Alliances shape tribal and personal identities. Through these relationships, *Niitsitapi* identity can manifest and express itself outside the colonial paradigm, wholly and self-sufficiently engaged in its own discourse.

By advancing a universal definition of self, the Eurocentred perspective denies other forms of knowledge, other forms of knowing, and thus other forms of humanity. This denial of other views has been central to genocide and colonialism. As a result, for many Indigenous persons, the self has become disassociated from the natural world. In this experience, knowing is understood as a cerebral activity located in the intelligence of humankind, and science is seen as an isolated and objective exercise dependent upon the ability to separate the self from the world. In fact, in the context of the Eurocentred mind, to understand the self as a cosmic being is to be powerless and without much agency. It is politically unwise and undesirable; furthermore, it is considered morally reprehensible, primitive, and outmoded.[3]

The general framework that constructs *Niitsitapi* dependency is the objectified self and subsequent analysis of deficiency and pathology that support the paradigm. "The North American indigenous self has been seen as deficient. Further, the indigenous self has become contaminated or damaged through the effects of genocide. 'Damaged,' in this context, refers to the individual's inability to achieve his/her purpose in life as framed within the value system of the dominant society."[4]

The concept of an objectified self is consistent with and part of the Eurocentred concept of culture. "Self" is seen as composed of characteristics that are distinguished by intelligence and by the ability to separate and isolate phenomena. Notions of reality are intricately linked with this concept of self (as with any other), a self premised on an absolute autonomy. A clear distinction is made between what is and what is not self. This autonomous conception of self has been forced upon tribal peoples. Subsequently, pathological characteristics have also been imposed and projected on the now isolated Indigenous self. As a result, the objectification of self is one of the fundamental bases for the denial of the existence of other forms and expressions of humanity. This objectification has been imposed via Eurocentred theories of human development and education, which are used to interpret the behaviour of tribal peoples. The abstracting definition of self is a premise fundamental to Eurocentred science and knowledge and determines how reality is perceived and how a society comes to knowledge.[5] Culture and self thus have become abstractions that can be controlled and manipulated in accordance with the values of Eurocentred societies.

Siksikaitsitapi Ways of Knowing: Epistemology

Epistemology concerns itself with theories of knowing and provides frameworks for discussing validity issues. It provides cultures with a philosophical and theoretical structure for seeking knowledge as well as for processes that define truth. Epistemology affects the informal and formal educational process that is dependent upon theoretical interpretations and understandings of the nature of the universe, reality, and truth. The educational foundation of a culture originates from its epistemological assumptions, its pivot of reality interpretation and maintenance.[6]

Most Eurocentred epistemologies are premised on rationality and the objectification of knowing. As a result, nature is understood to be made of identifiable qualities that are potentially knowable. Scientific inquiry is the pursuit of discerning the knowable qualities of an objectified universe. The rational goal of objectified observation is to identify the discrete parts that are assumed to exist and from which understanding and knowledge are derived. By identifying the component parts of the universe, or understanding how these parts are interconnected, the knower garners the power to control, manipulate, and predict the movements of people and objects.[7] Scientific rationality and objectivity are considered possible because of the assumption that humans are fundamentally rational beings. The Eurocentred paradigm distinguishes human beings not only as separate from each other but also as separate from the natural world by virtue of their intellect or ability to reason.

In this model, we must control an object in order to gain knowledge of it. We can do this only if we are emotionally detached from it. And we gain emotional distance from the "object" by first and foremost gaining control over ourselves, by placing our intellect in control of our emotions. Marimba Ani describes Eurocentred epistemologies as invoking certain ontological foundations that have a cognitive bias.[8] These assumptions are embedded in the structure of the English language. Language in general is the medium through which structures of power are perpetuated, and concepts of "truth," "order," and "reality" established.[9] "Truth" is what counts as true within a system of rules for a particular discourse; "power" is that which annexes, determines, and verifies truth.

Truth is never outside or deprived of power, and the production of truth is a function of power; we cannot exercise power except with the production of truth.[10] Power lies in the understanding that truth is contextual to the science and methods of a culture.

For *Niitsitapi*, intelligence means participating within the world from which one has acquired the wisdom of nature and the knowledge of experience. The objectification of knowledge through the manipulation and control of observation has negated alternative epistemologies, modes of cognition, and world views, thereby limiting the ability for people to experience the universe as cosmic.[11] *Niitsitapi* epistemologies are premised on a set of assumptions through which knowledge and validity are constituted. Within these assumptions, all knowledge rests within a cosmic union of human beings who are interconnected with the natural order through the spiritual forces coming from *Ihtsipaitapiiyo'pa*. They constitute the collective consciousness of *Niitsitapi*, which is based on the spirituality of a cosmic order. A *Kaaahsinnoon* shares his experience with *Siksikaitsitapi* epistemologies:

> I had moved to the Sundance with my parents. X (an older person who was a member of *Omahkohkanakaaatsiisinni*) approached me to assist him with his dancing [ceremony]. He said, "Would you assist me when I dance out from *Tatsikiiyakokiiysinni*, the centre tipi?" I did not want to do it. I did not feel good about doing it." Y (another man, who overheard X asking for my assistance) interjected and said, "He is asking for your assistance, why don't you want to assist him?" I then agreed to help X with his dancing. X said, "You watch me, when I come out of *A'mii, Tatsikiiyakokiiysinni*. I will wave to you." X did as he said and I entered the center and danced with *Omahkohkanakaaatsiisinni*.
>
> In the morning, I was sleeping and was awakened by the sound that people make when they want to enter a lodge. The sound is a way of announcing their arrival. My mother called to them to enter. Three *Omahkohkanakaaatsiisinni* members had come to visit my father.[12]

One of the *Omahkohkanakaaatsiisinni* began with,

> "Your son created a grave imbalance yesterday [by dancing with the *Mopisstaan* without proper preparation], it is not good. He went to the center and danced with the bundle." X continued, "When it is midday, he will go to the center lodge. The person who is going to paint his face will be sitting waiting for him." X did not say whether I would dance with the Bundle again. After they left, my mother told me, "Do as you are told, go to the center lodge." She gave me offerings (gifts) for *Kaaahsinnoon* who was going to paint my face.
>
> At midday I went to the center lodge. X was there. He pointed to *Kaaahsinnoon* who was going to paint my face. Later, I danced with the bundle. This was an imbalance I made. It bothered me.[13]

In the above narrative, *Kaaahsinnoon* addresses how he was guided by the ancestors and the alliances among *Omahkohkanakaaatsiisinni* in becoming a grandfather.

His participation began with an imbalance that could have had severe consequences for him and his family. However, he was protected by the members' advice.

Through this experience, *Kaaahsinnoon* began to live in balance and harmony. In particular, he shared the proper movements within the lodge, which maintain an agreeable equilibrium among the occupants.

Pommaksinni, a process of transferring spiritual knowledge through kinship relations, is central to *Siksikaitsitapi* epistemology. "Kinship" in this context has a wider meaning than a biological/genealogical relationship. *Siksikaitsitapi* ontology and epistemology are inextricably intertwined. The following epistemological assumptions illustrate these relationships:

- The nature of the universe is interconnectedness;
- The universe is interconnected through *Ihtsipaitapiiyo'pa*;
- It is the nature of the universe to work for balance;
- The universe has sacred power and influence; it works in reciprocal ways among its interdependent parts.

Siksikaitsitapi epistemology creates a way of being, a way of relating to the world that embodies the kinship–relationship system. Relationships entail responsibilities that connect to an experiential "body" of knowledge. In this way, knowing becomes a part of the knower. *Mokaksin*, meaning knowledge itself, has spirit that is "transferred" in the relationships between the knower and known. Through these methods and rules of knowing, knowledge and self become one.

Additionally, transformation is achieved by changing the relationship between knower and known. In describing an experience of *Siksikaitsitapi* epistemology in action, a *Kaaahsinnoon* said,

> There are certain things in our way of life that I understand are given to us. You have to do certain things. That is your life. These are the real personal things that *Siksikaitsitapi* must do. These things cannot be handed down. I think that in some cases those of you, who are attempting to learn our ways, you are trying to understand this aspect of our way of life.
>
> It comes directly from *Ihtsipaitapiiyo'pa* to you. It will be shown to you in one way, shape, or form. It will be taught to you.
>
> It is given to you, for you to use in a good way.[14]

In this example, *Kaaahsinnoon* refers to one of the most powerful assumptions of Indigenous epistemologies: it is in the nature of the universe to give gifts, blessings, and lessons, which are meant to be used in a positive way.

Our theory of knowledge is found in the sacred stories, which are the living knowledge of the people. These stories, accumulated over millennia, explain the nature of reality, and the science, and economic and social organization of *Siksikaitsitapi*. The knowledge contained in the stories remains alive because it is applicable across generations. Each generation of *Kaaahsinnooniksi* is responsible for retelling the stories to the next, which must adapt the lessons and apply them to the present. The ways of knowing, of acquiring knowledge and truth, are dependent upon observational skills, or *Kakyosin*. Knowledge lives in the process of observing, in reflecting on connections among observations, and in applying the experiences of *Akaitapiwa*, our ancestors.

Knowledge also derives from applying one's personal observations and experiences to the interrelationships of alliances.

Niitsitapi epistemologies represent knowledge as being experienced in an infinite and all-encompassing moment. Following *Niitsitapi* logic means experiencing the whole, the interconnectedness of an indivisible universe. Rationality, on the other hand, denies the spiritual nature of knowledge and sacrifices the wholeness of human beings.[15] One example of the denial and sacrifice that results from Eurocentred logic comes from my friend, colleague, and ceremonialist Duane Mistaken Chief. He shared the following with me regarding the use of plants and herbs: "Eurocentred scientists dissect the herb and extract the elements of the herb that they have found to have medicinal properties. However, what they don't understand is that the plant functions as a whole—other properties of the plant may be important because of their cleansing functions."[16]

The nature of the universe to function as an interdependent whole has profound implications for education and the process of learning. The following principles encompass the epistemologies of *Niitsitapi*:

- Knowledge, truth, and meaning are revealed to *Niitsitapi* through their relationship with *Ihtsipaitapiiyo'pa* and through a network of interdependent kinship relations. Knowledge is holistic and every aspect of nature contains knowledge that can be revealed;
- Knowing, learning, and teaching are reciprocal in nature. *Niitsitapi* learn the nature of existence through the guidance of kinship alliances;
- The reciprocal nature of knowing is understood and appreciated through *Pommaksinni*. The reciprocal nature of knowing is premised on creating and generating the knowledge necessary for maintaining balance.

These principles of coming-to-knowing correlate with the manner in which education and human development processes and practices are traditionally organized among *Niitsitapi*. The primary medium for seeking to understand *Niipaitapiiysin* and, for *Mokaksin*, *Ihtsipaitapiiyo'pa* is kinship relations. Knowledge is transferred through these relationships and exists in a process of renewing and generating alliances for knowing.

A common sense of transformation and transcendence is experienced through ceremonies. The meanings associated with *Pommaksinni* are shared by the people.[17] As long as the people retain their transfers, they will retain their connection to the transformational ways of being. The people will continue to renew their responsibilities as instructed in the original *Pommaksinni* described in the old stories. Song, prayer, dance, and other mimetic movements were given that embody the vibrational patterns by which the power of the alliances can be transferred to *Siksikaitsitapi*. For example, in *Pommaksinni* of sacred power and knowledge of *Niinaimsskahkoyinnimaan*, *Ksisstsi'ko'm* said,

> Here is my pipe. It is medicine. Take it and keep it. Now, when I come in the Spring, you shall fill and light my pipe, and you shall pray to me. . . . For I bring the rain which makes the berries large and ripe. I bring the rain which makes all things grow, and for this you shall pray to me, you and all the people.[18]

Furthermore,

> Whenever you transfer the Pipe to anyone, steal quietly upon them just before day-
> break, the time I am on the move, and take him by surprise, just as I do, chanting
> my song, and making the sound of a bear charging. When you catch a man and offer
> him the Pipe, he will not dare refuse, but must accept it and smoke it. It is sure death
> to refuse, because no one dares to turn away from the grizzly bear. The owl is also a
> prominent figure in the Pipe because he is a bird of the night. When the society is after
> a new member, they chant Owl songs and pray to Owl for sacred power to enable them
> to catch him in a deep sleep. In this way, a spell is cast over him and he cannot escape.[19]

The *Niinaimsskahkoyinnimaan* story lives in the ceremonies and through the lives of *Aawaatowapsiiks* and *Kaaahsinnooniksi*, who renew these alliances to bring peace and prosperity to the people. Each year after *Ksisstsi'ko'm* is first heard, *Niinaimsskaiks* know it is their responsibility to hold the annual Thunder Pipe dance. The narrative illustrates the reciprocal responsibilities of prosperity and balance between *Ksisstsi'ko'm* (including all the alliances represented in the bundle) and the people. The protocol requires people to show respect, seek good relations, and maintain alliances with *Ksisstsi'ko'm* each year when *Niinaimsskahkoyinnimaan* are opened, the ceremonial dances are performed, and songs are sung to honour and renew the *Siksikaitsitapi–Ksisstsi'ko'm* alliances for another season.

Thunder Pipes are used for curative purposes. In contemporary Indigenous societies, many individuals abuse drugs and alcohol; one-third of Aboriginal people die violent deaths; and incarceration and unemployment are at unprecedented levels that continue to rise. These conditions indicate the need to reconnect with the healing knowledge generated through sacred alliances, such as with the Medicine Pipes (a form of Thunder Pipe). Healing in this sense means reclaiming and regaining the tribal ways of generating knowledge and restoring the responsibilities to life itself. Learning the responsibilities of traditional alliances is the path of coming to know one's purpose in life and of learning the sacred knowledge that can address adversity experienced by contemporary *Niitsitapi*.[20]

The sacred power of the universe is pervasive and reveals itself through all of creation, including thoughts, objects, speech, and actions. It speaks through rocks and animals and may take the form of an animal that transforms into a person or begin with a person who transforms into an animal.[21] As part of the transformational power of the universe, people migrate regularly into "dream worlds." These migrations provide the meaning and knowledge sought and acquired by *Siksikaitsitapi*. In fact, all human beings, according to the Plains cultures, transcend the limits of their embodiment through these dream-world migrations. They are considered unexceptional experiences.[22]

Knowledge is Coming-to-Know *Ihtsipaitapiiyo'pa*

In the traditional context, knowledge comes from *Ihtsipaitapiiyo'pa* and knowing means connecting with *Ihtsipaitapiiyo'pa*. Knowledge not only has spirit but also *is* spirit. Knowledge grows through the ability to hear the whispers of the wind, the teachings of the rock, the seasonal changes of the weather. By connecting with the knowing of the animals and plants, we strengthen our knowledge. As in all relationships, consent must be given and obligations and responsibilities observed.[23] Ceremonies embody the delicate balance of the cosmic order and thus provide connections to knowing. These relationships are also evident in creation stories and cosmology.

The social organization of *Niitsitapi* reflects the influence and teaching role of *Akaitapiwa*. As Ronald Goodman illustrates in his discussion of Lakota star knowledge, the star world and the microcosmic world of the Plains are intricately interconnected.[24] The same connections are considered important among *Siksikaitsitapi*. In partial fulfillment of this relationship, we have four annual major ceremonies that correspond to the seasons: *Niinaimsskahkoyinnimaan*, the Medicine Pipes, which are opened after the first *Ksisstsi'ko'm* in spring; *Aako'ka'tssin*, the Sundance, which is held in July or when the Saskatoon berries ripen; *Ksisskstakyomopisstaan*, the Beaver Bundle, held after the ice breaks in the spring; and *Kano'tsisissin*, the All Smoke, held in the winter when the nights are long. These ceremonies are the collective consciousness of *Siksikaitsitapi*, which places them at the centre of their universe. During these ceremonies, we acknowledge and give thanks to our alliances for another cycle. We ask for continued protection, prosperity, long life, growth, and strength.

This knowledge is a living knowing. It is illustrated through the heart of *Siksikaitsitapi* epistemologies and pedagogy: *Pommaksinni* is the central approach to teaching the traditional knowledge of the tribe. In this way, the initiated take care of the bundles and pipes that are the connections of alliances, the partners of *Siksikaitsitapi* in maintaining the delicate balance of life. This includes an all-encompassing responsibility to teach and pass on the knowledge to the next generation of initiates and to ensure the survival of all. *Pommaksiistsi* are the ceremonies that transfer knowledge and maintain the tribal integrity of *Siksikaitsitapi* ontology and epistemology.

The basic ontological responsibility, *Kiitomohpiipotokoi*, of giving and sharing is embedded in the fundamental philosophical premises of *Siksikaitsitapi* education. Sharing and giving connect to and perpetuate *Ihtsipaitapiiyo'pa*. They are consistent with the natural order of the universe and help to maintain it in balance. According to *Siksikaitsitapi*, a fundamental aspect of the cosmic universe is reciprocity, which is experienced in *Aipommotsspists*, the practice of ceremonial transfers. As a *Siksikaitsitapi* word, *Aipommotsp* means "We are transferred; it was given, or passed on." The word depicts reciprocal responsibilities or an exchange of responsibilities among participants. The natural law of reciprocity is not limited to ceremony but is extended by *Siksikaitsitapi* to their daily customs and activities.

The ethical and moral behaviour identified through customs, language, values, and roles is often referred to as protocol or ritual. Protocols and rituals encapsulate the *Kiitomohpiipotokoi* that are the means for returning to a state of balance or ensuring good relations. This was mentioned earlier in regard to joining sacred societies for ceremony and living arrangements of the tipi. A few daily examples are the strictures to give food and drink to visitors, to not walk in front of ceremonial people or *Kaaahsinnooniksi*, to greet and acknowledge everyone with some gesture, and to always move in a sun-wise direction if you are moving in a circle. Tribal protocol acknowledges the sacred state or the good relations of food, the energy of individuals, and the movement of life. One *Kaaahsinnooniksi* shared the following comment on the seeming inexplicability of the rationale behind these protocols:

These are the things for which we cannot give you an answer. I ask why is it that you cannot enter the lodge (home) of a *Niinaimsskaiks* with a cigarette. Why is it, if I have given you something to eat when you come to visit me, that you have to tell four stories, if you want to take the food out of the home? This is our way of life. These are the things that are taught to us.[25]

Through generations of *Aipommotsspists*, *Kaaahisinnooniksi* have been taught the rigorous and sacred science of participating in ceremonies. The knowledge inherent in their ceremonial protocols transcends the classical Eurocentred conceptions of reality and nature. However, experiments in quantum mechanics have revealed that reality is the manifestation of a "set of relationships," which, upon interacting with an observing system, change knowledge and physical reality discontinuously.[26] This particular scientific view is consistent with *Siksikaitsitapi* understanding. *Ahkoyinnimaan* can be said to be a web of kinship relationships that, through active participation of *Siksikaitsitapi*, alters and transforms reality. Included in this web of interconnectivity are *Siksikaitsitapi* relationships with animals, who also have roles and responsibilities in the transformation of life. Through participation, *Siksikaitsitapi* become a conscious part of an interactive system and are transformed in the process. Once the transfer has occurred and become part of the living body, the initiated becomes *Aipommotsp*. The alliances collectively strengthen life for the sake of life, for the survival of humankind, and for the universe.

In the sacred story of *Ksisstsi'ko'm*, this knowledge is given to the people as *Aipommotsp*, the transfer of *Ahkoyinnimaan*. The relevant alliances that are active here are illustrated in the following excerpt:

A long time ago, Thunder struck down a man. While he lay on the ground, the Thunder Chief appeared to him in a vision, showing him a pipe and saying, "I have chosen you that I might give you this Pipe. Make another just like it. Gather together also a medicine bundle, containing the skins of the animals and birds which go with it. Whenever your people are sick, or dying, a vow must be made and a ceremony given with a feast. The sick will be restored to health.' The Grizzly Bear afterwards appeared to the man and said to him, "I give you my skin to wrap around the sacred bundle, because it is larger than the skins of other animals." The owl possesses knowledge of the night. The Medicine Pipe is wrapped with raw hide and decorated with feathers and the winter skins of the weasels Many animal and bird skins are gathered for the sacred bundle, wrapped in a large grizzly bear skin. In the spring, when the first Thunder is heard, the Pipe is brought out and held up.[27]

Niitsitapi education is distinct from the Eurocentred educational system in that it is governed by the natural law of balance and harmony. *Aipommotsspists* are the means of maintaining the reciprocity and generosity required to preserve balance among *Siksikaitsitapi*. Transfers also sustain the natural order that makes possible the gifts of life; reciprocity is essential for the survival of all life. *Aipommotsspists* are the embodiment of this way of life, forming the fabric of *Siksikaitsitapi* culture and the social organization of a people.

Aipommotsspists: Transfer of Knowledge and Ontological Responsibilities

Aipommotsspists exemplifies the concept that traditional learning is experiential. Transfers bring *Siksikaitsitapi* ontology, epistemology, and pedagogy together by transmitting sacred responsibilities and knowledge from generation to generation. They are the initiations into sacred knowledge and responsibilities that are passed down through each generation to ensure the renewal of cosmic alliances. These medicine bundles have been transferred to *Siksikaitsitapi* with the original instructions for coming-to-knowing, *Akaotsistapi'takyo'p*, so that "we have come to understand (not merely know) it."[28]

During the original *Aipommotsp* of the medicine bundles, the initiates were instructed on how to conduct the ceremonies. In essence, the transfer ceremony is working with *Ihtsipaitapiiyo'pa*, from which knowledge is revealed or transferred. As such, the transfers are the processes of renewing the original responsibilities as taught to the *Siksikaitsitapi* in the original transfer.

Kaaahsinnooniksi said,

> Tribal identity is learned through experience. Conversely, students and non-Native people who want to learn of our ways often will use the literature; they do not realize that the literature is fraught with inaccuracies and false information. The language and the experience of our relationships has been our way of teaching and learning.

Aipommotsspists are a medium for becoming one with the universe. They are the connections to all time, as well as the ancestors and ancients, and ensure the continuance of *Siksikaitsitapi*. As one ceremonialist said,

It is our responsibility, in the *Siksikaitsitapi* way, to give back what we have been transferred. . . . For example, those who have received an education return and give it back to the people. The *Siksikaitsitapi* way, our way, the *Niitsitapi's* way, is to help, to assist, and then *Ihtsipaitapiiyo'pa* will help us.[29]

The ontological theory is a complex kinship system of relationships from which knowing originates. Coming-to-knowing involves a lifetime process of learning, understanding, and knowing. Knowledge is a way of living and being, a way of being in the world, and also a way of learning. Humans' participation in this process creates partnerships in the co-creation of balance in our physical reality. Knowledge is thus relational, acquired through experience and relationships. However, it is also spirit and independent of human beings and a relationship that human beings engage in. Through coming to understand the process of renewal, one understands balance and the process of living that strengthens the balance.

Science currently describes the nature of reality thus: "Everything is intimately present to everything else in the universe." In other words, material objects are no longer perceived as independent entities but as concentrations of energy of the quantum field. The universe is portrayed as a quantum field that is present everywhere in space, while its particles have a discontinuous, granular structure.[30] Indigenous people have long understood the universe to be, as physicists now suggest, an indivisible whole.

The ways of knowing and understanding manifest in the interactive exchanges within the context of relationships. These relationships are based on the responsibilities as understood through the reciprocal nature of the universe. *Niisitapi* come-to-know through connection with family, environment, geography, the animal world, the universe, and so on. In their relationships, they experience the knowledge and achieve an understanding of their responsibility for maintaining the balance of their world.

In conclusion, protocols and ethics of Indigenous knowledge are embedded in our responsibilities and place in the universe. The academy must begin to respect the reality that, in the generation of knowledge and in respecting Indigenous epistemologies and pedagogy, Indigenous people will regain their independence. From the inner strength of an Indigenous/tribal identity, *Siksikaitsitapi* will remember how to apply the traditional knowledge in the following aspects:

- knowing one's tribal and cosmic responsibilities;
- experiencing the knowing of tribal alliances;
- incorporating knowledge and skills acquired for the well-being of a cosmic universe; and
- passing on one's knowledge and skills to the next generation.

Indigenous ways of knowing live in the experience of being in tune with the source of life; our responsibility is to pass it on, do the transfers, so that others too will live. Indigenous pedagogy teaches *Niisitapi* and others the ways of knowing and being within the Blackfoot world so that all will thrive and survive. The Elders quoted here have lived the *Siksikaitsitapi* ways of knowing, making possible the doctoral research that produced my book *Blackfoot Ways of Knowing*. It is their lived experiences with sacred knowledge that ensure another generation's survival.

Notes

1. For an expanded discussion of Blackfoot beliefs, practices, and pedagogy, see Betty Bastien, *Blackfoot Ways of Knowing* (Calgary: University of Calgary Press, 2004). Much of this essay is based on the research for my book. Hereafter, information taken from this book is not referenced, with the exception of quotations.
2. Ibid., 84–5.
3. Marimba Ani, *Yurugu: An African-Centered Critique of European Cultural Thought and Behaviour* (Trenton: Africa World Press, 1994), 10.
4. Bastien, *Blackfoot Ways of Knowing*, 159–60.
5. Ani, *Yuruguru*, 45–7.
6. Ibid., 98.
7. Ibid.
8. Ibid., 37.
9. Bill Ashcroft, Gareth Griffiths, and Helen Tiffins, *The Empire Writes Back: Theory and Practice in Post-Colonial Literatures* (London and New York: Routledge, 1989), 7.
10. Ibid., 167.
11. Ani, *Yuruguru*, 37–9.
12. Bastien, *Blackfoot Ways of Knowing*, 100.
13. Ibid., 100–01.
14. Ibid., 102–03.
15. Ani, *Yuruguru*, 32.
16. Duane Mistaken Chief, Personal Communication to Betty Bastien, Dec. 1998. See also Bastien, *Blackfoot Ways of Knowing*, 105.
17. Howard L. Harrod, *Renewing the World* (Tucson: University of Arizona Press, 1992), 67.
18. Ibid., 70.
19. Walter McClintock, *The Old North Trail: Life, Legend and Religion of the Blackfeet Indians* (University of Nebraska Press, 1992), 253–4.
20. Bastien, *Blackfoot Ways of Knowing*, 109.
21. Harrod, *Renewing the World*, 23.
22. Ibid., 25.
23. David Peat, *Lighting the Seventh Fire* (Secaucus, NJ: Carol Publishing Company, 1994), 65.
24. Ronald Goodman, *Lakota Star Knowledge, Studies in Lakota Theology* (Rosebud, SD: Sinte Gleska University, 1992).
25. Bastien, *Blackfoot Ways of Knowing*, 143.
26. Gary Zukav, *The Dancing Wu Li Masters: An Overview of the New Physics* (New York: Bantam Books, 1979), 54–79.
27. McClintock, *The Old North Trail*, 253–4.
28. Bastien, *Blackfoot Ways of Knowing*, 141.
29. Ibid., 140–1.
30. Zukav, *Dancing Wu Li Masters*, 257.

Glossary

A'mii, Tatsikiiyakokiiysinni The centre tepee; over the centre tepee.

Aako'ka'tssin Sundance; literally, circle encampment.

Aawaatowapsiiks Ceremonialist; those who have the right to take part in sacred activities and ceremonies; in certain ceremonial contexts, an individual.

Ahkoyinnimaan Pipe.

Aipommotsp (Aipommotsspists) We are transferred; it was given or passed on.

Aistommatop Transformed; literally, embodying the knowledge.

Akaitapiwa (Akaitapiiks) Ancestor; literally, the old [days] people or people of the past.

Akaotsistapi'takyo'p "We have come to understand (not merely know) it"; to be cognizant of and discern tribal connections; sacred science; knowing as experiential knowing.

Ihtsipaitapiiyo'pa Sacred power, spirit, or force that links concepts; life force; term used when addressing the sacred power and the cosmic universe; source of life; sun as manifestation of the source of life; great mystery; together with *Niitpaitapiiyssin*, identifies the meaning and purpose of life; that which causes or allows us to live. It is through *Ihtsipaitapiiyo'pa* that all "natural laws" are governed.

Ihtsipaitapiiyo'pi The reason we are caused to live through the source of life.

Kaaahsinnoon Grandfather.

Kaaahsinnooniksi "Our grandparents"; used by *Niitsipoyi* to refer to familial grandparents and by members of the various societies or bundle and pipe holders to refer to previous society members, bunder holders, pipe holders, etc.

Kakyosin Observational skills; "to align" or "to balance," referring to the *Siksikaitsitapi* understanding that there is an order of things or pattern that we can discern if we are observant. Through *Kakyosin*, we align ourselves with these patterns and can achieve the same things the observed beings can. For example, one time a man was starving and he came upon a decomposed carcass of a *Makoiyi* (wolf). When he slept, the spirit of the *Makoiyi* spoke to him in song and gave him its pelt as a gift. The spirit told him how to conduct a ceremony around these gifts and instructed him to conduct it every time before using them. With this knowledge, the man was able to transform into a *Makoiyi* and hunt sucessfully.

Kano'tsisissin All Smoke ceremony; a night ceremony attended by past and present members of the various societies, bundle holders, medicine pipe holders, and others, all of whom have had sacred transfers, or *Iipommowai*, at one time or another.

Kiitomohpiipotokoi Role and responsibilities; "what you have been put here with."

Ksisskstakyomopisstaan (Ksisskstakyomopisstaani stsi) Beaver Bundle.

Ksisstsi'ko'm Thunder.

Mokaksin Knowledge; intelligence; wisdom; coming-to-know.

Mopisstaan Bundle (object).

Natosi "Sacred power"; the sun.

Niinaimsskaan (Niinaimsskaiks) "The Medicine Pipe holders"; the Thunder Pipe holders.

Niinaimsskahkoyinnimaan Thunder/Medicine Pipe; reference is to the ceremonial bundle of the Thunder Pipe, which would include the alliances of the pipe.

Niipaitapiiysin Way of life; constant motion of breath; together with *Ihtsipaitapiiyo'pa* identifies the meaning and purpose of life; to teach the way of life.

Niitsitapi Generic term for real people or all Indian, Aboriginal, or Indigenous peoples.

Omahkohkanakaaatsiisinni Big All Comrades Society; the ultimate sacred society, which has the central role in the annual Sundance ceremonies.

Pommaksinni (Pommaksiistsi) The practice of transferring; the method of teaching.

Siksikaitsitapi All Blackfoot-speaking tribes; "Blackfoot-speaking real people."

Tatsikiiyakokiiysinni The centre tepee.

Questions for Consideration

1. How do McPherson and Rabb define Indigeneity?
2. How might Indigenous polycentrism and respect for "non-interference" inform Canadians' understanding of both the past and the present? What potential benefits to this do McPherson and Rabb see? Do you agree with their perspective?
3. What does Bastien say lies at the heart of the "Eurocentred concept of culture"? How is that different from its *Siksikaitsitapi* counterpart?
4. In Bastien's understanding, how do the *Siksikaitsitapi* view and understand their natural environment? How might that understanding conflict with a Eurocentred conception of the environment?
5. Has a Eurocentric perspective led non-Indigenous Canadians to misunderstand Indigenous world views? If so, how?

Further Resources

Books and Articles

Bastien, Betty. *Blackfoot Ways of Knowing*. Calgary: University of Calgary Press, 2004.

King, Thomas. *The Truth about Stories: A Native Narrative*. Toronto, ON: House of Anansi Press, 2003.

LaRocque, Emma. "Introduction: Representation and Resistance," in *When the Other is Me: Native Resistance Discourse, 1850–1990* Winnipeg: University of Manitoba Press, 2010, 3–17.

McPherson, Dennis H., and J. Douglas Rabb. *Indian from the Inside: A Study in Ethno-Metaphysics*. Thunder Bay, ON: Lakehead University Centre for Northern Studies, 1993.

Weaver, Jace. *That the People Might Live: Native American Literature and Native Community*. New York: Oxford University Press, 1997.

Printed Documents and Reports

British Columbia Ministry of Advanced Education. *Native Literacy and Life Skills Curriculum Guidelines*. Victoria: Ministry of Advanced Education and Job Training and Ministry Responsible for Science and Technology, 1989.

Mealing, S.R., ed. *The Jesuit Relations and Allied Documents: A Selection*. Ottawa: Carleton University Press, 1990.

Morris, Alexander. *The Treaties of Canada with the Indians of Manitoba and the North-West Territories: Including the negotiations on which they were based, and other information relating thereto*. Toronto: Prospero Books, originally published in [1880]—2000.

Films

First Nations: The Circle Unbroken. DVD. Directed by Geraldine Bob, Gary Marcuse, Deanna Nyce, and Lorna Williams. NFB, 1993.

The Medicine People: First Nations' Ceremonies. DVD. First Nations Films, 2000.

Totem: The Return of the G'psgolox Pole. DVD. Directed by Gil Cardinal. NFB, 2003.

BabaKiueria (Barbeque Area), dir. Don Featherstone, 1986. Available online at www.youtube.com/watch?v=oUMpPgMGCe8.

Calloway, Colin. *First Peoples: A Documentary Survey of American Indian History.* Boston: Bedford/St. Martin's, 2004.

Waban-aki: People from Where the Sun Rises. DVD. Directed by Alanis Obomsawin. NFB, 2006.

Websites

Canadian Museum of Civilization: Storytelling: The Art of Knowledge
www.civilization.ca/cmc/exhibitions/aborig/storytel/introeng.shtml

First Nations Pedagogy Online
http://firstnationspedagogy.ca/index.html

2

Encountering Europeans

Introduction

In mid-October 1492, Christopher Columbus and the Tainos people of the Caribbean first encountered each other in present-day Bahamas. Conventional histories of "first contact" have located this momentous meeting as the "starting point" from which all other contacts flowed. However, this myopic view lacks complexity. Contact was not a singular moment but occurred for various groups at many different times over the last thousand years. In 1000 CE, Indigenous peoples encountered the Vikings at present-day L'Anse aux Meadows, NL, more than 500 years before Jacques Cartier made landfall on the northeastern shores of Turtle Island. On the west coast of present-day Canada, Indigenous people first met the Spanish aboard their vessel, the *Santiago*, in 1774. This contact was soon followed by the penetration of fur traders into the interior of present-day British Columbia from the East.[1]

Indigenous peoples who occupied the interior of Turtle Island and the far North also encountered Europeans at wildly different times and in varied ways. Given the extensive Indigenous trading networks that penetrated the entire continent, the acquisition of European goods and technology often took place long before Indigenous peoples met Europeans face to face. Both Daniel K. Richter and Dorothy Harley Eber's articles capture this point beautifully. Information about Europeans trickled through these networks and "rumours and objects, not men and arms, were the means of discovery." Imaginations must have run wild with the "skimpy evidence that reached them."[2]

The meanings and understandings that have been applied to contact have fascinated historians and have sparked what historian Bruce Trigger refers to as "a large body of speculative literature."[3] As both articles reveal, culture was a deciding force in the shaping of contact; the ways in which people understood themselves and their place in the world shaped the contours of these meetings. Until recently, most of this speculation has come from the European perspective. However, drawing on the stories and memories of Inuit Elders, as Eber does, offers extremely different and interesting versions of and perspectives on contact. Indigenous peoples saw Europeans through their own cultural lens. Initially, many Indigenous groups were willing to co-operate to some degree with Europeans. However, this readiness could and usually did change over time. For instance, while initially welcoming, the Stadaconans quickly tired of Jacques Cartier and his crew. Similarly, the arrival and departure of the *Fury* and the *Hecla* at Igloolik under William Edward Parry in 1822–23 was marked by conflict. According to Igloolik Elder Rosie Iqallijuq, the misbehaviour of Parry's men resulted in the prolonged isolation of the region until the curse laid by a local shaman was lifted. Most notably in these encounters, contrary to the narratives constructed by European accounts of contact, Indigenous peoples did not perceive themselves as inferior to Europeans.[4] Indeed, from an Indigenous rather than European perspective, some of the Europeans' behaviours and misadventures, such as the unpreparedness of Cartier and his followers for the North American winter of 1535–36 and the corporal punishment that Parry carried out over a minor theft, were likely taken as evidence of European inferiority, cruelty, and ignorance.

Chapter Objectives

At the end of this chapter, you should be able to

- identify some of the core myths and beliefs about Indigenous peoples that resulted from the story of first contact and how they continue to inform people's perceptions;
- identify ways in which Indigenous peoples first reacted to European travellers;
- understand better the different Indigenous and European perceptions of contact; and
- query the chronology and geography of contact.

Notes

1. Jean Barman, *The West Beyond the West: A History of British Columbia*, 3rd edn (Toronto: University of Toronto Press, 2007), 22, 34–6.
2. John Lutz, "Introduction," in Lutz, ed., *Myth and Memory: Stories of Indigenous-European Contact* (Vancouver: UBC Press, 2007), 2.
3. Bruce Trigger, *Natives and Newcomers: Canada's "Heroic Age" Reconsidered* (Montreal & Kingston: McGill-Queen's University Press, 1986), 121.
4. Ibid., 89.

Secondary Source

Imagining a Distant New World

Daniel K. Richter

"History," said Carl Becker, is "an imaginative creation."[1] Perhaps no historical subject requires more imagination than the effort to reconstruct the period when Indian country first became aware of a new world across the ocean. All we have to go on are oral traditions of Indians who lived generations after the events described, written accounts by European explorers who misunderstood much of what happened in brief face-to-face meetings with Native people, and mute archaeological artifacts that raise more questions than they answer. Yet this very lack of information places us in much the same situation as most eastern North American Indians during the era of discovery. They probably heard mangled tales of strange newcomers long before they ever laid eyes on one in the flesh, and when rare and novel items reached their villages through long-standing channels of trade and communication, they discovered European *things* long before they confronted European *people*. Rumours and objects, not men and arms, were the means of discovery, and we can only imagine how Native imaginations made sense of the skimpy evidence that reached them.

On the coast of what will one day be called either Newfoundland or Labrador, Native hunters find that several of the traps they had set are missing, along with a needle they need to mend their fishing nets. In the place where of these items had been is a smoothly polished upright timber crossed near the top by a second piece of wood, from which hangs the carved effigy of a bleeding man. Flanking this remarkable construction are two other poles from which pieces of some woven substance flap in the breeze: one is white with two strips of red, mimicking the shape of the crossed timbers; the other bears an image of a four-footed, two-winged beast holding something in its paw.

Somewhere near the mid-Atlantic coast, an old woman hides in the woods with her daughter and several grandchildren. Both women scream as some 20 pale, bearded men, sweating in heavy armour and helmets, stumble upon them. The Elder's suspicions abate a little when the men courteously offer her something to eat, but the younger disdainfully flings the food to the ground. As the women try to fathom the strange sounds issuing from what they consider to be incredibly ugly hairy faces, the men suddenly snatch one of the male children away from the grandmother and lunge for the young woman, who flees screaming into the forest, never to see her nephew again.

In an Indian dwelling, a woman tells her granddaughter about the first meeting between Native people and Europeans. One day, she says, a floating island appeared on the horizon. The beings who inhabited it offered the Indians blocks of wood to eat and cups of human blood to drink. The first gift the people found tasteless and useless; the second appallingly vile. Unable to figure out who the visitors were, the Native people called them *ouemichtigouchiou*, or woodworkers.

These three scenes are imagined, but they are rooted in verifiable historical events. The hunters' missing traps were purloined in 1497 by explorer John Cabot and his crew; the mid-Atlantic child was snatched from his kinswomen in 1524 by a detachment of Giovanni de Verrazano's mariners; and the tale of sailors who ate sea biscuits and drank wine was told to a French missionary in 1633 by a Montagnais who in turn had heard it from his grandmother years earlier.[2] This much we know from surviving documents, which also explain the nature of what the Europeans left behind and took with them. Cabot's crucifix and flags were sacred symbols that laid legal claim to the land for, respectively, his God (whose Son was portrayed dying on the wooden cross), his English sponsors (whose patron, Saint George, was evoked on the kingdom's white banner by a red cruciform), and his home republic of Venice (whose patron, Saint

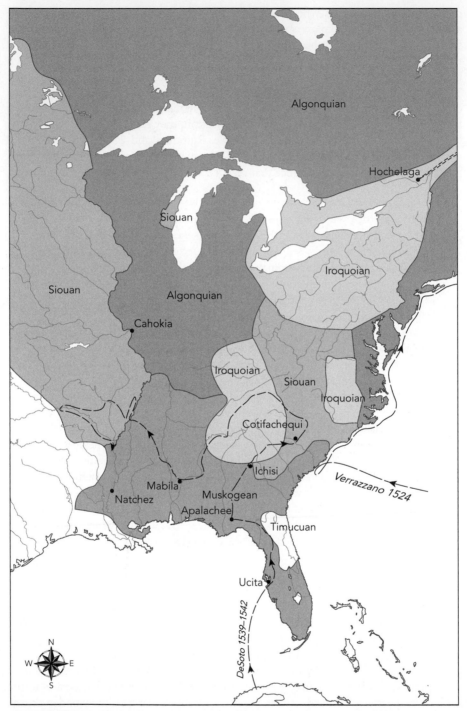

Map 2.1 Eastern North America and the sixteenth-century discovery of Europe: Approximate distribution of major Native American linguistic families and routes of principal European incursions. (Source: *Facing East from Indian Country: A Native History of Early America*, by Daniel K. Richter, Copyright © 2001 by the President and Fellows of Harvard College.)

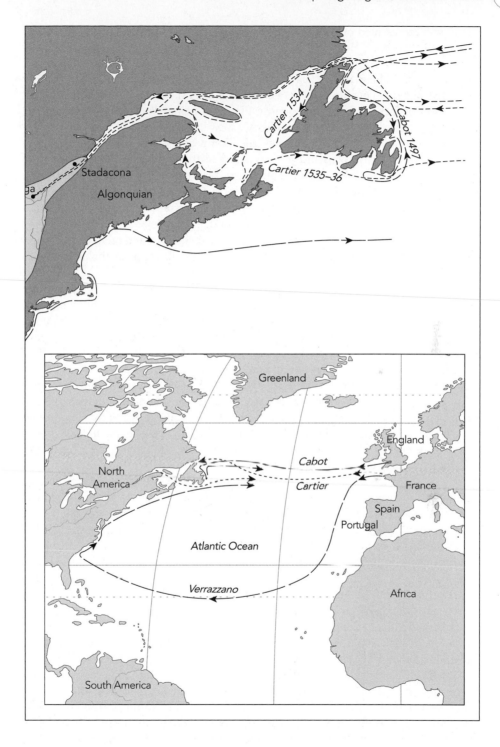

Mark, was represented on its flag by a winged lion bearing a book of the Gospel). To convince his sponsor, Henry VII of England, that a land in which "he did not see any person" was indeed populated, Cabot collected "certain snares which had been set to catch game," along with a large, red-painted wooden "needle for making nets."[3] Similarly, Verrazano justified taking "a child from the old woman to bring into France" in terms of his need to bring his sponsor, Francis I, living proof of his exploits and a potential interpreter to aid future travellers.[4]

Documentary evidence illuminates the European cast of characters, yet only imagination can put Indians in the foreground of these scenes. There is no record of what happened to Cabot's crucifix and flags. Yet we know that if the Indians who owned the missing snares and needle had come upon them, they would not have found the idea of symbolic memorials to important events unfamiliar: northeastern Native people sketched elaborate pictographs in their houses or on the bark of living trees to record the success of war parties, hunting expeditions, and other exploits, and they carved images that they either raised on poles or affixed near the entrances to their houses.[5]

For eastern Indians, the world was a morally neutral universe of potentially hostile or potentially friendly spiritual forces—some human, most other-than-human—with whom one had to deal. All of these relationships depended on reciprocal exchanges of goods and obligations, material or ceremonial. Especially when dealing with beings whose power was greater than one's own, it was important to fulfill ceremonial obligations that demonstrated not only reciprocity but respect.[6]

In light of this emphasis the exchange of goods—gift giving—becomes a dominant motif in each of our three scenes. Yet the gifts are always unanticipated, if not disrespectful. To our conjectured hunters, the unseen Cabot apparently reciprocated for a red needle an incomprehensibly abstract red-and-white symbol, and for an animal trap an image of a strange beast. The crucifix he also left behind was carved with a degree of detail inconceivable to people unfamiliar with iron tools, but it clearly represented a man enduring torture. What kind of gift was this? And what kind of gift givers were Verrazano's men, whose unexpected behaviour lay not in the matter-of-fact arrogance with which they seized a child (Indian war parties routinely took captives of all ages), but in their offering of food, which deceived the grandmother into believing they were allies rather than enemies? And gifts of food also define the unanticipated in the story of the floating island: the wood was worthless, the blood inhumane.

The gifts defined the givers. Montagnais people, the grandmother said, called Europeans "woodworkers"; elsewhere in eastern North America, Indians commonly described them as "clothmakers," "metalworkers," or "axemakers."[7] Whoever the bestowers of such things were, they seemed—initially at least—to come from a world quite unlike that in which ordinary human persons lived.

In the early decades of the sixteenth century, European ships regularly converged on the Atlantic coast. Sometimes they stopped to trade with the Natives; when Verrazano in 1524 reached the shore of what later would be known as New England, he found Indian people ready and waiting with the furs they already knew that the newcomers coveted.[8] At other times, particularly on the vast coastline of the territory the Spanish called *la Florida*, which stretched from the peninsula northward to Chesapeake Bay, raiders such as Ponce de Leon in 1521, Lucas Vázquez de Ayllón in 1526, and Pánfilo de Narvàez in 1528 came ashore to seek gold or slaves to work in the mines of Cuba and elsewhere. An occasional castaway or newcomer taken in battle learned a Native language and provided the first firm clues about the customs and intentions of the invaders. Welcome or unwelcome, the travellers left behind weapons, tools, jewellery, and clothing that fell into the hands of Indian people.

On two extended occasions during the 1530s, flesh and blood replaced rumours and things in the North American discovery of a new European world. Because the Europeans involved in these contacts wrote about their experiences, we have slender platforms from which to observe the events and—reading against the authors' grain—to imagine how the arrival of Europeans might have looked from a perspective in Indian country.[9] Transporting ourselves to the shores of Tampa Bay on the Gulf coast of Florida on Sunday, 25 May 1539, we barely see the sails of nine Spanish ships anchored three miles or so off the coast to avoid the treacherous shoals closer in. A party of 10 Timucuan-speaking Natives watching with us are familiar enough with Spanish sails to know that these are no floating islands and that although their inhabitants may wield considerable spiritual power, their disembarkation is unlikely to be beneficial. As the first small boats set out for shore, they send word for those women and children not already dispersed to spring fishing or hunting camps to abandon their villages, and they set signal fires to warn others at a greater distance. The wisdom of those preparations becomes clear when the scouts encounter a Spanish advance party and find themselves in a skirmish. The Timucuas kill a pair of Spanish horses before being forced to retreat, but they leave two of their own people dying on the ground.

We are not sure if this is the first time these particular Florida Natives have encountered horses, but we are certain they have never seen so many of the great beasts: more than 200 land in the first boats. During the next week some 600 men follow with a contingent of dogs trained for war and with at least 13 pregnant sows. In command of this assemblage—which far outnumbers the force any village in the area can mount—is Hernando de Soto, the recently appointed governor of Cuba and *adelantado* of *la Florida* [who] bears royal authority to invest his considerable personal fortune in an effort to conquer the people and presumed riches of southeastern North America. Within a week his army takes over an abandoned village named Ucita or Ozita and rechristens it *Spiritu Sancto*, "Holy Spirit." As the *adelantado* ensconces himself in the chief's residence, his men dismantle the remaining houses and destroy a temple topped by a carved wooden bird, salvaging the materials to build barracks for themselves. Meanwhile they brutally seize replacements for four previously captured Timucuan men brought with them to serve as interpreters and guides. When three of these in turn escape, a Native woman who supposedly helped them is thrown to the dogs. The same fate meets the remaining interpreter when he proves a less than co-operative guide.[10]

In a village a couple of days' journey inland are two people who regard the Spaniards' arrival more positively than do the kin of the Ucita victims. One used to call himself Juan Ortiz, although now he uses a Timucuan name and has nearly forgotten the language of his native Seville. A dozen years earlier he was captured on the coast by the people of Ucita. Subsequently he escaped to the rival town of a headman named Mocoço. There he abandoned any real hope of seeing Spaniards again, despite his host's repeated assurances "that, if at any time, Christians should come to that land, he would release him freely and give him permission to go to them."[11] The promises were neither empty nor disinterested. Mocoço apparently hopes his guest will broker an alliance with the Spanish that will help him defeat his coastal enemies of Ucita and three other towns and, presumably, open a channel of trade with the newcomers previously blocked by his inland location.

When word of de Soto's landing reaches Mocoço, therefore, he sends Ortiz along with a reception committee that, taking no chances in enemy territory, travels well-armed. The Timucuans show themselves to the mounted Spanish, but before any pleasantries can be exchanged, the invaders' horses charge and send the Native people fleeing into the woods. Ortiz barely escapes death by making the sign of the cross and shouting the name of the Virgin and a few other remembered Castilian words.

To the *adelantado*, Ortiz, with his mastery of two Timucuan dialects and his knowledge of Indian culture and diplomacy, is a welcome discovery, yet little else seems promising. The small coastal villages of Tampa Bay hoard no gold or silver and, particularly in the spring well before harvest time, do not even contain enough stored maize to feed his troops. In what seems like a deliberate attempt to protect their immediate neighbourhood, both Ortiz and Mocoço deny any knowledge of the wealth the Spanish desire, but they speak vaguely of a much larger town a hundred miles or so to the north, where a chief extracts tribute from all the villages in the region and where the land is "more fertile and abounding in maize."[12] So, taking Ortiz along as interpreter, the army vacates Tampa Bay, and a pattern is established: No, one set of Native leaders after another tells the invaders, there is no gold and little food here, but if you travel farther (into what just happens to be the country of my enemies), you might find what you seek. Thus, when de Soto is disappointed at the town of the Paracoxi, his destination becomes Anhaica Apalachee (modern-day Tallahassee). To that southernmost of the surviving Mississippian cities, his army fights its way by late October. There de Soto finds sufficient food to support his men and settles in for the winter, apparently only slightly inconvenienced by Native raiding parties that attack work details or set fires in the town.

By March de Soto is ready to resume his quest. His entourage plods northeastward through present-day Georgia, perfecting tactics first used in the previous year's march through the Florida peninsula. Occasionally the Spaniards capture a hunting party and, if the Indians fail to provide satisfactory information on what lies ahead in words Juan Ortiz can fathom, throw a victim to the dogs or burn him alive to encourage others to talk. More often, de Soto goes through the motions of Mississippian diplomatic ritual; the *adelantado* even carries a chair in which to seat himself during ceremonies with chiefs carried on their retainers' shoulders. Invariably the formalities end when leaders agree to provide several hundred men, who are shackled together to haul the army's equipment. Also likely to be requisitioned are several dozen women, who, after a hasty baptism by one of de Soto's four priests, will satisfy what one Spaniard describes as the soldiers' "lewdness and lust."[13] To preclude trouble, the chief and his retinue are held hostage until the army—pillaging corn supplies, burning the occasional refractory village, and planting crosses on temple mounds—reaches the territory of the next chiefdom, when the cycle begins again.

Native leaders repeatedly claim that the riches the Spanish seek lie farther on, in the chiefdom of Cofitachequi. In May 1540, near present-day Camden, SC, de Soto's army finally reaches a spot directly across the Wateree River from its capital. The town's inhabitants are already familiar with Spanish goods, if not with Spanish people; they not only have carefully preserved glass beads and metal items but have also fashioned leather helmets, armour, and footwear in styles that seem strikingly familiar to the Castilians. We watch as a young female leader—the Spanish call her "The Lady of Cofitachequi"—is carried to the riverbank in a white-cloth-draped litter, from which she enters a canoe graced by a canopy of a similar material. When she reaches de Soto's side of the stream, she removes a string of freshwater pearls from her neck and places it over the *adelantado*'s head. Gifts of blankets and skins, turkeys and other foods, follow.

De Soto rends the ceremonial drama with a blunt inquiry about where more of the pearls might be found. The Lady directs him to one of several nearby towns abandoned two years earlier when "a plague in that land" forced the inhabitants to seek new homes.[14] There, he and his officers loot a mortuary temple of more than 200 pounds of pearls preserved in the body cavities of the deceased.[15] The corpses also yield European glass beads, rosaries and crucifixes, and "Biscayan axes of iron."[16] The pearls are loaded with other booty on the backs of the inevitable requisition of Cofitachequi porters, and the army sets off again holding the Lady hostage.

And so we follow de Soto's trek: across the Appalachian Mountains into the modern states of North Carolina, Tennessee, Georgia again, and Alabama, always chasing reports of wealth in the town over the next hill or down the next river. Armed resistance builds steadily until, in October, the Spaniards' luck runs out in the Tascaloosa city of Mabila, in what will later be called western Alabama. Several thousand warriors hide inside Mabila's houses as a ceremonial welcome for de Soto and his advance party provides cover for Indians waiting in ambush. When the attack comes, several Spaniards die before the remainder flee the town and regroup for a daylong battle that culminates in ruthless slaughter. When it is over, Mabila lies in smoking ruins. Inside are the bodies of perhaps 2000 Tascaloosas, along with the ruins of all the pearls and other treasure de Soto has collected. Twenty or so Spaniards, including de Soto's nephew, are dead. The wounds of some of the nearly 200 invaders who are seriously injured are treated with the fat of their slaughtered enemies.

For nearly a month de Soto's now ragged army, reduced by cumulative losses to closer to 400 than 600 men, tries to recover its strength. It sets off again and huddles for a brutally cold winter in a small abandoned village in what will be known as northeastern Mississippi. In March 1541 the town's former inhabitants burn the Spanish camp, and with it most of the invaders' remaining saddles and padded armour. Still the Spanish plod on, in a journey as increasingly nightmarish for them as for the Indians whose countries they continue to pillage and whose people they continue to enslave when they can. They move across the Mississippi River and into the country of the Caddos in modern-day Arkansas, another winter comes and goes, and in March 1542 Juan Ortiz dies after a brief illness. In May, in the Natchez country, when disease also claims the *adelantado*, his men sink the corpse in the Mississippi River to protect it from the indignities they are sure Indians will perpetrate on it. At last, after the survivors wander through much of what will later be Arkansas and east Texas, they improvise a forge on the banks of the Mississippi and pound the chains of their slaves into nails and hardware for boats. In June 1542 they board the seven vessels they have been building and float out of sight, down the river to the Gulf and the Spanish settlements on the Mexican coast. As they fade from view, a few of the pigs they leave behind—later residents of the area will call their descendants "razorbacks"—remain with us on the shore, but surviving documents reveal nothing about how, if at all, Native people recovered from the devastation the conquistadors left behind or what stories they told themselves to make sense of invaders from another world.

As de Soto lay dying in the spring of 1542, far to the north, in what is now called St John's Harbor, NL, Frenchman Jacques Cartier prepared to head home, convinced that he had found not only the gold the *adelantado* had been looking for, but diamonds too. This was Cartier's third voyage to a country he called Canada. [W]hen Cartier returned to France, experts confirmed that his ship contained nothing but iron pyrite ("fool's gold") and commonplace quartz crystals.[17]

In search of how Cartier and his entourage may have looked to the people of Canada, we might travel back in time to July 1534, when the Frenchman arrived on the first of his three voyages.[18] Standing on the southern coast of what is now called the Gaspé Peninsula, we see 40 to 50 canoes full of Micmacs abandoning their fishing as two ships come into view. Hoisting the skins of fur-bearing animals aloft on pieces of wood, they try to lure the newcomers ashore to trade. Inexplicably to the Indians, Cartier's ships turn about and sail for the opposite shore. Micmac canoeists give chase and surround the ships, waving and shouting "We wish to have your friendship!"[19] but two panicky musket shots drive them off. Shortly, however, they return and get close enough to be struck by a pair of lances wielded from the decks before they have to retreat again. The next day, when the Europeans' nerves have calmed and they have found safe anchor for their ships, they send two men ashore with a load of knives, hatchets, and beads. Soon some 300 Micmac men and women are wading through the shallows dancing and singing and rubbing the arms of Cartier's crew as a sign of welcome. Trading proceeds until the Indians have "nothing but their naked bodies" left to exchange![20]

That the Natives have clearly come to trade demonstrates that European ships are already familiar sights to the Micmacs. Fifty miles or so to the northeast, on the Bay of Gaspé, however, a group of **St. Lawrence Iroquoians** from the interior is far less acquainted with floating islands, although they almost certainly have heard of their existence. Later in the month, as the Iroquoians, fishing for mackerel, look up to see Cartier's vessels approach, they therefore hesitate before surrounding the ships with their canoes. The now more experienced Europeans almost immediately toss them iron knives, glass beads, and other small items, but the Iroquoians are not prepared with anything to exchange for these gifts.

As the French get ready to sail on, they erect a 30-foot wooden cross, in the centre of which they place a shield decorated with fleur-de-lis and letters spelling out *Vive le roi de France*. The Iroquoians' leader boards a canoe with his brother and three sons and follows the Europeans to their ships.[21] Luring the canoe closer with a gesture that promises an iron axe in exchange for the bearskin the headman wears, the Europeans drag the whole party on board. By gestures, Cartier assures the Indians that he means them no harm and offers them food and drink. The cross, he dissimulatingly explains, stakes no claim to their territory; it is merely a marker to allow the French to find the spot again when they return along with two of the headman's sons, who will be taken home to be trained as interpreters.[22] How much of the message gets through clearly is uncertain, but, after an additional bestowal of iron gifts and brass necklaces, the headman, his brother, and one of the young men return to shore reasonably amicably. The others, named Taignoagny and Domagaia, remain on deck wearing ill-fitting French shirts, coats, and caps.

Cartier and—perhaps more astonishingly to their kin—Taignoagny and Domagaia return to Canada within the year, this time with three ships and plans to stay the winter. We know almost nothing about the intervening experiences of the two Iroquoians in [Europe]. During those months, however, they apparently learned enough French, and their hosts enough St Lawrence Iroquoian, to communicate some important pieces of information about their native land. Their home village (or at least the principal of the five communities that spoke their language) lies far inland along a broad river (the St Lawrence), whose entrance Cartier had missed in his survey of the gulf. From that village of **Stadacona** (the word means "here is our big village"), on the site of present-day Quebec City, the river continues much farther to a large town called **Hochelaga** ("place at the mountain") at modern Montreal, and thence far onward, perhaps toward a passage to Asia.[23] Taignoagny and Domagaia also speak vaguely about what the French understood to be a fabulously wealthy "Kingdom of Saguenay," located far to the north and west along a river flowing into the St Lawrence. In part, the tale includes wishful thinking on the part of Cartier, a desire to please (or dupe) their hosts on the parts of Taignoagny and Domagaia, and the same kind of rumour of riches over the next hill that de Soto chased through the southeast.

As the fleet casts anchor near what the French would christen the Île d'Orléans, a few miles down the St Lawrence from Stadacona, Taignoagny and Domagaia struggle to make themselves recognized in their strange clothing and the long hair that has replaced the partially shaved heads with which they left home. When the confusion is cleared up, a group of women dances, sings, and brings all the visitors fish, maize, and melons. The next day Donnaconna, the principal headman of Stadacona, leads a fleet of canoes to conduct a welcoming oration; Cartier reciprocates with the ubiquitous sea biscuits and wine, carried to Donnaconna's canoe. According to the region's diplomatic customs, the visitors should debark from their vessels for additional ceremonies outside the village gates and then enter the town to take up lodging in the houses of its leaders. Days of feasting, speeches in council, and exchanges of gifts should follow to seal the alliance.

None of this happens. Instead, Cartier finds a harbour for his two larger ships at the Île d'Orléans, and, before even visiting the village itself or distributing more than a few token metal items, he demands that Taignoagny and Domagaia guide his third craft on to Hochelaga. Not surprisingly, after an evening of consultations with Donnaconna and other village leaders, the two weary Native travellers lose their enthusiasm for the voyage and offer excuses, warnings, and ruses designed to prevent the French and their precious cargo from going to a rival town. Donnaconna ceremoniously gives three children to the French for adoption; one is his own niece, another Taignoagny's brother. Cartier reciprocates with a gift of swords and brass bowls, but, despite a visit the next day from three shamans bringing warnings from the spirit world of dangers upriver (and a similar call from Taignoagny and Domagaia, who deliver messages allegedly from Jesus and Mary), he persists in his design. Without Native guides, Cartier and some of his men set off for a visit to Hochelaga and several villages and fishing camps along the way.

Donnaconna is less than enthusiastic in welcoming Cartier back [in mid-October]. While their leader was gone, the French had constructed a trench, palisade, and artillery emplacements to protect the ships on which they continued to sleep and eat. Spurning their hosts' hospitality, the Europeans settle in for the winter behind their trench and palisade on the Île d'Orléans. While to all appearances most of the Stadaconans nonetheless interact with the French "with great familiarity and love," a minority, led by Taignoagny, expresses considerably less pleasure with their ill-mannered guests.[24]

In December Cartier forbids all contact with Stadaconans of both factions, when he learns that disease has killed some 50 villagers. Despite the precautionary quarantine, the French are soon falling desperately ill as well. By March 1536, 25 of the 110-member crew have died, and only a handful can walk. We do not know what is killing the Stadaconans, but the French ailment is an uncontagious nutritional disorder, **scurvy**. Were Cartier not so intent on concealing from his Native hosts the extent of his men's weakness (on one occasion he has them throw stones at Stadaconans who get too near, and on another he orders the few who are able to lift tools to make a furious racket to suggest that the entire crew is busily preparing the ships for departure), he might learn far sooner from Domagaia that a concoction brewed from the vitamin C–rich bark and leaves of the white cedar would restore his men to health.[25]

During the winter the French, shivering in their sickbeds, remain incommunicado for weeks on end, encouraging their hosts to suspect the worst of them. In April Donnacona and Taignoagny bring several hundred newcomers to Stadacona. Perhaps this is a normal seasonal migration of the sort typical among many of the Iroquoians' Algonquian-speaking neighbours, whose small winter communities commonly join much larger agglomerations for the spring and summer. Or the newcomers may be allies whom Taignoagny has convinced Donnacona to recruit for an assault on guests who have long overstayed their welcome. We will never be sure, because, under cover of a friendly council, Cartier takes Donnacona, Taignoagny, Domagaia, and two other leaders prisoner. In a replay of events in 1534, Cartier then assures his prisoners, and the women who bring strings of shell beads to redeem them, that he will restore them safely the next year. Donnacona publicly pledges to return in a few months, and the ships set off downriver.

Five years pass before we see Cartier's ships at Stadacona again. With him in 1541 are several hundred prospective French colonists but none of the Iroquoians who left Canada in 1536. When Donnaconna's successor inquires after their fate, Cartier admits that the chief has long since died in France, but then claims that the others "stayed there as great lords, and were married, and would not return back into their country."[26] In fact all but Donnaconna's niece have perished, and she has been prevented from returning to keep the distressing news secret. The Stadaconans, who remember Taignoagny's less-than-enthusiastic tales of Brittany, no doubt suspect as much, but their new headman welcomes Cartier nonetheless, by placing his head-dress on the Frenchman's brow and wrapping shell beads around his arms. Cartier reciprocates with "certain small presents," promises more to come, and partakes of a feast![27] At a place he calls Charlesbourg-Royal, some nine miles above Stadacona, at the mouth of the Cap Rouge River, the French build a fort, plant a crop of turnips, and find their worthless fool's gold and quartz crystals. As the colonists settle into Charlesbourg-Royal for the winter, our ability to imagine the scene suddenly ends. The published narrative left by a participant ends abruptly with the words "The rest is wanting."[28]

Yet other sources reveal that Cartier's people—or most of them—survived until spring, as increasingly unwelcome guests. Not only had they settled in the Stadaconans' territory without permission, but they had also done so at an upstream location likely to cut the town off from any trade benefits the Hochelagans and other inland peoples might enjoy. Come spring, Cartier, having lost perhaps 35 men in skirmishes with his hosts, packed up his colonists and sailed for home. In the Newfoundland waters where we first imagined meeting him, he encountered a fleet bearing more colonists under the command of Jean François de la Roque, sei-gneur de Roberval, who replaced Cartier at Cap Rouge. We know few details of the reception this party encountered except that, after a punishing winter during which untreated scurvy killed at least 50 of their number, in 1543 they too abandoned Canada. As far as we know, no Europeans travelled up the St Lawrence River for another 40 years.[29]

If anything emerges from the shadows of the sixteenth-century Indian discoveries of Europe, it is a persistent theme of conflict and distrust. But the nature of that conflict bears close attention, for its most remarkable aspect is not the violence that erupted between Natives and newcomers. Cartier clearly wore out his welcome, and nothing can be said in defence of the vicious de Soto. Nonetheless, almost everywhere they went, these Europeans found people trying to make some kind of alliance with them, trying to gain access to the goods and power they might possess, trying to make sense of their flags, their crucifixes, and their sea biscuits. These efforts to reach out to people of alien and dangerous ways are more striking than the fact that, in the end, enmity won out over friendship. But most striking of all is the way in which the arrival of the new-comers exacerbated conflicts of one Native group with another: Mococo versus Ucita, Micmacs versus Stadaconans, Stadaconans versus Hochelagans; everyone discouraging advantageous Europeans from travelling to the next town, but encouraging dangerous ones to pay their neighbours a visit. Both within and among Native communities, con-tact with the new world across the seas inspired bitter conflicts over access to what the aliens had to offer—conflicts that would spiral to unimaginably deadly levels in the decades ahead.

Notes

1. Carl Becker, "Every Man His Own Historian," *American Historical Review* 37 (1932): 228, 231.

2. Julius E. Olson and Edward Galord Bourne, eds, *The Northmen, Columbus and Cabot, 985–1503* (New York: C. Scribner's Sons, 1906), 423–4; Samuel Eliot Morison, *The European Discovery of America: The Northern Voyages, A.D. 500–1600* (New York: Oxford University Press, 1871), 206–09; Peter E. Pope, *The Many Landfalls of John Cabot* (Toronto: University of Toronto Press, 1997), 11–42; [Richard Hakluyt the Younger], *Divers Voyages Touching the Discoverie of America, and the Ilands Adjacent until the Same, Made first of All our Englishmen, and Afterward by the Frenchmen and Britons* (London: Thomas Woodcooke, 1582), fols. A1–B4 (2nd pagination); Reuben Gold Thwaites, ed., *The Jesuit Relations and Allied Documents: Travels and Explorations of the Jesuit Missionaries in New France, 1610–1791*, 73 vols. (Cleveland: Burrows Brothers, 1896–1901), 5, 119–21.

3. Olson and Bourne, *Northmen, Columbus and Cabot*, 423.

4. Hakluyt, *Divers Voyages*, fol. A3v.

5. E.B. O'Callaghan and B. Fernow, eds, *Documents Relative to the Colonial History of New York*, 15 vols. (Albany: Weed, Parsons, 1853–87), 47–51.

6. See, for example, Ruth M. Underhill, *Red Man's Religion: Beliefs and Practices of the Indians North of Mexico* (Chicago: University of Chicago Press, 1965), 20–9.

7. Charles T. Gehring and Willliam A. Starna, trans and eds, *A Journey into Mohawk and Oneida Country, 1634–1635* (Syracuse: Syracuse University Press, 1988), 62; Johannes Megapolensis Jr, "A Short Account of the Mohawk Indians" (1644), in Dean R. Snow, Charles T. Gehring, and William A. Starna, eds, *In Mohawk Country: Early Narratives about a Native People* (Syracuse: Syracuse University Press, 1996), 45.

8. Hakluyt, *Divers Voyages*, fol. A5v.

9. The following is based on documents published in Lawrence A. Clayton, Vernon James Knight Jr, and Edward C. Moore. eds, *The De Soto Chronicles: The Expeditions of Hernando De Soto to North America in 1539–1543*, 2 vols. (Tuscaloosa: University of Alabama Press, 1993), particularly the accounts attributed to "A Gentleman of Elvas" (I: 19–219) and Rogrigo Rangel as compiled by Gonzalo Fernandez de Oviedo y Vakdes (I: 247–305).

10. Ibid., I: 257.

11. Ibid., I: 62.

12. Ibid.

13. Ibid., I: 288–9.

14. Ibid., I: 83.

15. Carol Ortwin Sauer, *Sixteenth-Century North America: The Land and the People as seen by the Europeans* (Berkeley, University of California Press, 1971), 158.

16. Clayton, Knight, and Moore, *De Soto Chronicles*, I: 279.

17. Bruce G. Trigger, *Natives and Newcomers: Canada's "Heroic Age" Reconsidered* (Montreal & Kingston: McGill-Queen's University Press, 1985), 129–35.

18. The published first-hand accounts of Cartier's three voyages to North America, on which the following section is based, are reprinted in Henry S. Burrage, *Early English Voyages Chiefly from Hakluyt, 1534–1604* (New York: C. Scribner's Sons, 1906), 1–102.

19. Ibid., 19.

20. Ibid., 21.

21. Ibid., 25.

22. Ibid.

23. Percy J. Robinson, "The Origin of the Name Hochelega," *Canadian Historical Review* 23 (1942): 295–6; and Robinson, "Some of Cartier's Place-Names," *Canadian Historical Review* 26 (1945): 401–05.

24. Ibid., 71.

25. Trigger, *Natives and Newcomers*, 131–2.

26. Burrage, *Early English and French Voyages*, 96.

27. Ibid.

28. Ibid., 102.

29. W.J. Eccles, *The Canadian Frontier, 1534–1760*, rev. ed. (Albuquerque: University of New Mexico Press, 1983), 12–18.

Primary Document

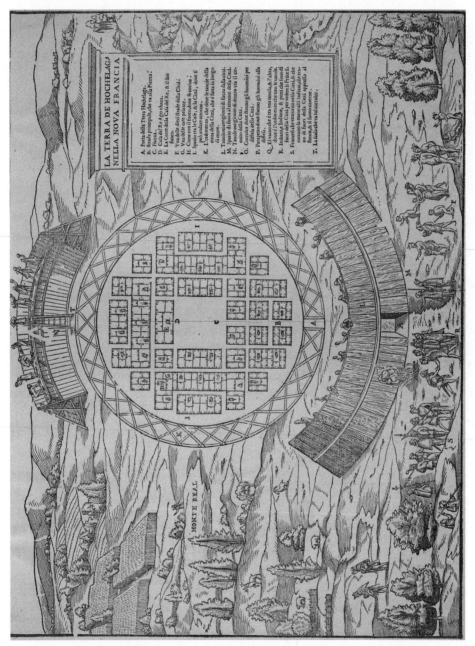

Plan of Hochelaga picturing contact, Cartier, 1556, by Ramusio (Italian chronicler of voyages). (Library and Archives Canada/Peter Winkworth Collection of Canadiana/e002140137.)

Primary Document

Jacques Cartier and his first interview with Indians at Hochelaga, 1850, by Andrew Morris. (Andrew Morris. Library and Archives Canada Acc. No. R9266-3339.)

Secondary Source

Into the Arctic Archipelago: Edward Parry in Igloolik and the Shaman's Curse[1]

Dorothy Harley Eber

The colours of the Arctic today are blue and dove grey, like a Toni Onley watercolour, and on this brilliant clean morning John MacDonald, director of the Igloolik Research Centre, is driving us over the road that leads to the point off which William Edward Parry of the Royal Navy—whom **Inuit** call Paarii—anchored his expedition in the winter of 1822–3.

Vehicles pass us on their way to a summer tent colony at Igloolik Point, where hunters and their families are camped for the walrus hunting, a resource as sustaining today as it was during Parry's visit. Large herds, he wrote on the day he drew within sight of Igloolik, "were lying with their young on almost every loose piece of ice we saw."[2] "We're going to visit Mr Elder," says MacDonald. In fact, five of us are going to picnic at Mr Elder's grave.

After a while, we stop at a circle of tumbled stones just off the road. They and a tombstone, which juts out of the centre, are encrusted with golden and crimson lichen. The words on the tombstone read:

Mr. Alexander Elder
Greenland Mate

HBM
Ship Hecla
Obit April 15, 1823
Aged 36 years

[Elder] was buried here, near where Parry's observatory stood, having died, wrote Parry, from "confirmed dropsy which having attacked the region of the heart, rapidly terminated his existence."[3] But the late Igloolik Elder Mark Ijjangiaq left another version of his end:

That man's death was caused by a **shaman**. It had something to do with a thing that someone wanted from him. One of the higher officials refused the request. Of course,

Parry's Farthest, attained on his first voyage into the Arctic archipelago during 1819–20. The sketch shows HMS *Griper* off the west end of Melville Island. (HMS *Hecla* is round the point, a few miles to the west). Watercolour over pencil on wove paper. By Midshipman Andrew Motz Skene (1796–1849), 1820. (C-132217. Library and Archives Canada.)

they were low on their supplies and had to turn the request down. But that man wanted the thing so badly that with the help of his shaman's powers he killed that white man. That is what I have heard.[4]

The *Fury* and the *Hecla* were the first ships ever to reach Igloolik. No more would come for a hundred years, and this isolation too was the shaman's revenge. I learn the reason why from Rosie Iqallijuq, Igloolik's most senior citizen:

> When the two ships were leaving, they were cursed by a shaman never to return. Naturally the crew of the ships had been getting girlfriends—no wonder, they were men! Perhaps the Inuit men were jealous types. One of the wives who got involved with a crew member was the wife of the shaman Qimmungat and he—the shaman— *suvijavininga*—he blew the ship away! From that day on, no ship arrived. The curse of the shaman persisted for a long long time and so no ships were able to make it to this area.[5]

The Start of Nineteenth-Century Arctic Exploration

When Parry anchored off Igloolik, he was 32 and already well on the way to his position as Britain's towering figure in nineteenth-century Arctic exploration. Deeply religious, diligent but daring, his rapid rise to prominence began after he captained the *Alexander* on the British Navy's first attempt to reach the Pacific from the Atlantic via a Northwest Passage.

The British Admiralty had decided to energetically pursue a program of Arctic exploration. In the aftermath of the Napoleonic wars, a window of opportunity had opened up: vessels and men were freed up with the peace and needed employment, and climate conditions were propitious. Whalers reported open water in high latitudes and a remarkable melting of icefields.

It was known that above continental North America a polar sea existed. But the geography of the Arctic Sea and its fractured land masses was unknown. The Northwest Passage was still to be discovered.

Parry's Farthest

[The task to discover the passage went first to John Ross, but] after [his] failure to discover that Lancaster Sound was a Strait, the Admiralty readied a new expedition. They gave the command to William Edward Parry, and, still a lieutenant but in command of his own expedition, Parry made his most revolutionary voyage: he sailed through Lancaster Strait, across the Arctic archipelago, and wintered triumphantly with the *Hecla* and the *Griper* far to the west in Winter Harbour at Melville Island. Ice blocked his further progress—no one would sail farther west for 30 years—but Parry knew he had discovered that a sea route existed from Baffin Bay to the Pacific.[6]

He had, in fact, explored one of the several routes by which a Northwest Passage can be accomplished. But the heavy pack ice he encountered had made him believe there was likely to be a more southerly, superior passage.

It was the search for this passage, which he rightly thought would lie close to the coast of continental America, that brought Parry in the years 1821–3 through

Hudson Strait and the Bay on a voyage during which he would winter twice in the ice, the second time off Igloolik Island. Igloolik lies at the eastern end of what is now the Fury and Hecla Strait. This ice-choked strait separates the north shore of Melville Peninsula from Baffin Island. It would not provide the route he sought. In fact, the records he and second-in-command, 25-year-old George F. Lyon, kept and published of their close contact with Native people would supply for many years to come the best accounts of Inuit life. These accounts, with their geographic and ethnographic data, endure as classic texts of exploration.

But Igloolik Inuit now have their own well-filed, well-shelved historical record. Since 1986, when the first interviews were recorded, many of the contributors have died, but their stories are alive and readily accessible through the archives of the Inullariit Elders' Society in the Igloolik Research Centre. They grow more valuable year by year.

Portrait of Edward Parry, drawn during Parry's 1821–3 expedition. The word *Captain* at the left was added by the collector, George F. Lyon, who brought the drawing back to England. (Reprinted with permission from the University of Cambridge.)

Paarii in Igloolik, as Inuit Tell It

As soon as possible after I arrive in Igloolik, I go with interpreter Leah Otak to visit Rosie Iqallijuq, the community's foremost authority on Paarii and his times (sadly, Rosie died in 2000). We find her sitting on her bed. "I know of explorers from what I have heard," she says. "It is a long time ago that Igloolik first saw a ship."

I am anxious to pursue the story of the shaman's curse, its origins and outcome—but, to begin with, from the Inuit point of view, why did Parry come to Igloolik in the first place? From her own Elders, the famous Ataguttaaluk and her husband, Ituksarjuat, whom southerners called the King and Queen of Igloolik, Rosie learned a version of the ancient Inuit creation myth that links Parry's arrival with the coming into existence of the Inuit, white people, and Indians (who traditionally were enemies):

> There once was a girl called Uinigumasuittuq who was married to her dog. Because she was married to her dog, her father got bothered in his sleep. So he took his daughter to the island of Qikiqtaarjuk, so she could have her husband with her there. She gave birth to six babies—two were Inuit, two were intimidating half-Indian half-dogs, and two were half-white half-dogs. The father brought the half-Indian half-dogs over to the mainland, and it is said that is why there are unapproachable people there—because of the dogs the father took to the mainland.

The two half-white half-dog babies were put into the sole of a *kamik* [a boot made of caribou hide or sealskin] with two stems of grass and let go into the ocean. Then all of a sudden there was fog; there were bells ringing in the air, and the father could see a mast from the grasses, and sails of a boat like the sails of the boat in which Paarii came. You could see this boot sole, with the two babies in it, leaving the shore. There were only the two babies in the boot sole—a girl and a boy—but that's how the white people multiplied; they had children from one another. Uinigumasuittuq created the white people—these two children who had so many babies. Paarii and his people came around here for the skull of their mother and took it from Qikiqtaarjuk—but we didn't see that![7]

John MacDonald makes the case that to the Inuit of Parry's day this creation story made good sense. "White men had never appeared around Igloolik before. People must have wondered why they were there; the nature of their mission was difficult to comprehend. Given Parry's interest in the island and obsession with the bones he found lying around, what better interpretation could there be?" For Parry and his crews did take away skulls.

We learn about this in Parry's journal entry for 23 July, when shortly after his arrival in Igloolik he goes to visit an abandoned Inuit winter camp:

In every direction around the huts were lying innumerable bones of walruses and seals, together with the skulls of dogs, bears, and foxes. . . . We were not a little surprised to find also a number of human skulls lying about among the rest, within a few yards of the huts; and were somewhat inclined to be out of humour on this account with our new friends, who not only treated the matter with the utmost indifference, but on observing that we were inclined to add some of them to our collections, went eagerly about to look for them, and tumbled, perhaps, the craniums of some of their own relations, into our bag.[8]

Inuit today will tell you that before the missionaries came they did not put their dead in boxes—indeed, they had no wood. "We put rocks around the body and eventually the animals scattered the bones." And for a long time there were Elders who asked to be buried in the old Inuit way. "Some people feared the priests' burial—they feared their spirits would be caught by the weight of the rocks on top of them."[9]

Rosie heard many of her stories from Ulluriaq, a potent personality of the past with whom she once shared the igloo. Ulluriaq lived to a great age and, according to local tradition, was a child herself when Paarii came to Igloolik. Rosie met Ulluriaq when she was about 13, after she had travelled by dog team from Chesterfield Inlet to begin her arranged marriage to an older man:

I first saw Ulluriaq when I got to this area. She was already very old—handicapped by old age—and was sharing the abode with us. I was married to Amaroalik, an old man, very much older than me. Ulluriaq used to tell me stories of the shamans, stories of the explorers. It was basically to put a smile on your face . . .

Ulluriaq told of the time when the ship first arrived—Paarii and his group. Ulluriaq's family were living in Pinngiqalik—Pinger Point—and the ship was travelling towards

Igloolik. The hunters got on their kayaks, taking some women with them, and followed the ship, and when it anchored the kayaks went down to the anchored ship.

Describing this same event, on 16 July 1822, Parry wrote:

> At thirty minutes past nine A.M. we observed several tents on the low shore immediately abreast of us, and presently afterwards five canoes made their appearance at the edge of the land-ice intervening between us and the beach. As soon therefore as we had satisfactorily made out the position and state of the ice, I left the *Fury* in a boat, accompanied by some of the officers, and being joined by Captain Lyon went to meet the Esquimaux.[10]

Says Rosie, "It was then that the community of Igloolik was first established. They wintered at Ungaluujat, past Igloolik Point. You can see the camp grounds today, and you can see that it was a very well established camp."

There were always Inuit camps—and there still are seasonal Inuit camps—at Igloolik Point, but Parry anchored five miles away in what he called Turton Bay (Inuit call the bay Ikpiarjuq—"raised beaches") off Ungaluujat. On this point near Parry's anchorage, the expedition set up tents. Quite soon Inuit began to visit and camp out, building their own sod houses, and sometimes using old Thule houses.

Qallunaat [people who are not Inuit] Gifts

When the Inuit first met the white men, Rosie says, their goods initially seemed useless:

> Apparently Inuit received some tobacco from the ship and at that time the tobacco came in the form of squares which had to be cut into small pieces—and apparently Ulluriaq started using these tobaccos as her toys—they were perfectly square. In those days, they were still living in sealskin tents, and one day it started to rain. As a result, the square chunks of tobacco got wet, and when her parents . . . came into the tent, they started to smell something foul. They wondered what it was. So they went over to where Ulluriaq kept her toys and realized it was those square things. The tobacco had gotten wet and was stinking up the tent. Ulluriaq told her parents, "The smell is coming from my pretend blocks." Her father collected all the square tobaccos and threw them away. . . .

Foodstuffs were similar puzzles:

> When the ice broke up and the ships were leaving, Ulluriaq's parents received sacks of flour, and at that time flour came in large bags. They also received tea, sugar, and biscuits from the ship. . . . And not realizing that biscuits were made for eating, Ulluriaq and other children started tossing them back and forth. And the sacks of flour were also discarded. When the children realized when you hit the sack it would appear to smoke, they had themselves a time hitting the flour sacks. They hadn't a clue about flour or biscuits—they dare not cook them or eat them, because they didn't know they were food in the first place.

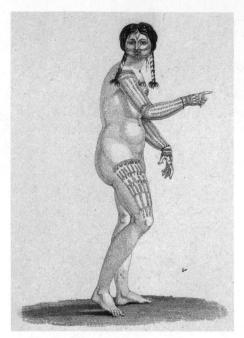

The Manner in Which the Esquimaux Women Are Tattooed. Drawn by George Lyon, 1822–3. (Library and Archives Canada/Canadian Historical Prints and Watercolours collection/C-099264.)

In Parry's account, flour was carried in barrels; but was flour perhaps sometimes distributed in bags? Or is this an instance of blended oral history, a later story now contributing to Rosie's account of Parry's largesse, but which perhaps originally related to supplies received from other sources, possibly the whalers, and heard by Rosie during her childhood?

Certain things were rapidly integrated into the culture. "At that time," says Rosie, "they started drinking tea and using sugar." And suddenly all the women were resplendent with beads. "They liked the beads so much they started beading and used them for bracelets. . . . I've heard that those who received beads for the first time—when the first white man wintered here—made bracelets from the beads."

In fact, at the time of Parry's visit, beads were not unknown. Parry wrote that he found beads already in use among Igloolik women. Like other goods, beads spread through inter-Inuit trade. Trade beads came to Canada with the first explorers. Merchants and explorers took beads with them as objects of trade, and when the first Europeans entered the Gulf of St Lawrence, Venetian beads arrived in their vessels. The **Hudson's Bay Company (HBC)** established its first post at Churchill on the west coast of the Bay in 1685 and intermittently sent sloops up the coast to trade for oil, whalebone, and ivory. In all probability, on board were glass seed trade beads. Igloolik Inuit may also have begun to receive beads from the whalers, who in 1817 had begun operating high off the east Baffin coast. But the expedition's presence made beads abundant. "Many of the [women], in the course of the second winter, covered the whole front of their jackets with the beads they received from us."[11]

The Inuit women also made themselves beautiful with tattoos. [Lyon] had himself tattooed:

> She took a piece of caribou sinew, which she blackened with soot. She began the work by sewing a rather deep but short stitch in my skin. When the thread was drawn beneath the skin, she pressed her thumb on the spot so as to press in the pigment . . . The work went slowly . . . When she had sewed forty stitches and the strip was about two inches long, I felt it was enough.[12]

Lyon's skin was then rubbed with whale oil.

Why the Curse Was Laid

Despite some squeamishness about Inuit burial practices, relations between the visitors and the Inuit during their winter of residence were harmonious. By the time the expedition left, it had altered the Inuit material culture. The expedition had been peacefully received—its presence useful to the Inuit, and the Inuit helpful to the expedition. The Inuit wanted to trade and were eager to barter, though the white men often gave freely without expecting return. The Inuit had drawn maps, repaired and sewn clothes, and on occasion hospitably hosted officers and crews in their sod houses and tents. Parry had tended the Inuit sick, had set up a makeshift hospital, and shortly before the *Fury* and the *Hecla* began their journey home, he left sledges, wood for bows and arrows, and many useful items for Inuit use, spreading them out around Igloolik so that as

Beaded Amautik. The artist, Germaine Arnaktauyok, is the niece of Igloolik storyteller Rosie Iqallijuq. Private collection of the artist. (Arnaktauyok, 2005.)

many as possible would benefit. Before departure, as per Admiralty instructions, he set up a flagstaff at a site on the Melville Peninsula, which almost certainly did not stand long. "The wealth of materials invested in the site—wood, metal, canvas, and rope—must have been too valuable an asset for reasonable Inuit to leave intact," says MacDonald. "They may well have considered the mast a final, though curious, parting gift from Parry."[13]

But unfortunately, towards the end of the expedition's stay, harmonious relations were disrupted—a missing shovel brought forth the *qallunaat*'s wrath. Parry wrote:

> On the 3d of March [1823], the Esquimaux were excluded from the *Fury* for some hours, on account of a shovel having been stolen from alongside the preceding day. Soon after this, Oo-oo-took, a middle-aged man, who had seldom visited the ships, was in Mr. Skeoch's cabin, when that gentleman explained to him the reason of his countrymen being refused admittance; upon this he became much agitated, trembled exceedingly, and complained of being cold. There could be no doubt he thought Mr. Skeoch had dived into his thoughts; for hastening upon deck, he was a minute or two afterwards detected in bringing back the lost shovel from the place where he had buried it behind our wall. A day or two before this occurrence, Captain Lyon had in a manner somewhat similar recovered a knife that had been stolen from him, for which, by way of punishment, the offender was consigned to solitary confinement for some hours in the *Hecla*'s coal-hole.

As, however, the Esquimaux only laughed at this as a very good joke, and as the time was shortly coming when numerous loose stores must be exposed upon the ice near the ships, I determined to make use of the present well-authenticated instance of theft, in trying the effect of some more serious penalty.

Parry administered naval discipline:

The delinquent was therefore put down into the Fury's store-room passage, and closely confined there for several hours; when having collected several of the natives on board the *Fury*, I ordered him to be stripped and seized up in their presence, and to receive a dozen lashes on the back with a cat-o'-nine tails. The instant this was over, his country-men called out very earnestly, "*Timun, timunna*," (That's right, that's right) and seemed much relieved from the fright they had before been in while the fate of the thief seemed doubtful. . . . This example proved just what we desired; in less than eight-and-forty hours, men, women, and children came to the ships with the same confidence as before, always abusing Oo-oo-took, pronouncing themselves and us uncommonly good people, but evidently more cautious than before of really incurring our displeasure.[14]

But according to the stories told today, the Inuit were not as pleased about this retribution as Parry appears to have thought. "*Taima, taima*" can be interpreted as "the end, the end," or "enough, enough." When the story was told more than 40 years later, the thief had become a heroic victim.

[Charles Francis] Hall heard his version from a woman called Erktua, who had visited Parry and Lyon's ships:

Oo-oo-took, a superior *an-nat-ko* [shaman] was charged by Parry when at Ig-loo-lik with the crime of theft for taking a shovel . . . Then Parry caused him to be whipped with something that was made of ropes with knots in them—cat-o'-nine-tails. The Innuits [sic] standing around and witnessing all this wanted to help Oo-oo-took defend himself, but he said: "Let the *Kob-lu-nas* to kill me; they cannot, for I am an *an-nat-ko*." Then Oo-oo-took's hands were untied, after which the *kob-lu-nas* tried to cut his head and hands off with long knives—probably swords. Every time a blow was struck, the extreme end of the knife came close to Oo-oo-took's throat; occasionally the blade came just above the crown of his head, and when the attempt was made to cut off his hands the long knife came down very near his wrists; but, after all he was uninjured because he was a very good *An-nat-ko*.

After the flogging, the shaman was confined below decks:

After Oo-oo-took had been one day and one night in the dark hole, he thought he would use his power as an *an-nat-ko*, and destroy the vessel by splitting it through the middle from stem to stern. So he commenced calling to his aid the Good Spirit, when a great cracking noise was made, now and then, under the ship, and at the end of the two days and two nights' confinement, the *kob-lu-nas*, fearing from such great and terrific noises that the ship would be destroyed, let Oo-oo-took go.[15]

For generations this story has circulated not only in Igloolik but all along the Arctic Ocean coast, sometimes melded with stories of other expeditions, and certainly with additional colourful elements. In the versions people tell today, sometimes the theft of the shovel is mentioned; sometimes it is not.

Lena Kingmiatook of Taloyoak tells a particularly full and dramatic version:

These white people took an **Inuk** prisoner whose name was Eqilaglu. This little man was also a shaman and the reason he became a prisoner was because he didn't want his wife to be abused by these white people. He was probably trying to protect his wife. These authorities took him and tied him upside down to a mast so he would agree that these white people could do whatever they wanted to do to his wife. That's why they captured him and treated him very roughly. They had a big axe and they tried to kill him, but since he was such a powerful shaman the axe would go right through him and just cut the wooden pole. No marks on him!

The little man had a tent made of sealskin probably—not cotton as we have today, for sure. Every time they tried to kill him, every time they swung the axe, other Inuit watching could see him walking into his tent, his spirit going to his tent. . . . At that time we didn't have the rifles or guns or weapons that the white people had. All we had were harpoons, spears, and knives made of bones. So although there were some Inuit there watching, they were not helping him. The white men tortured him, tried to kill him with an axe, and hung him upside down so the blood would go up to his head and he would go crazy and be unable to use his power.

The little shaman was very helpless. He didn't want to give up his wife and also his steel snow knife, but he didn't have enough power. The other Inuit people know he is asking for help. All the shamans get together and they mumble and mumble in a low, low voice and it sounds like thunder roaring in the tent. It was a prayer to bring help to the little man. He began getting more power from the other shamans; that way he got harder and harder to kill.

Even though he was tied up, as soon as people looked away from him, he'd completely disappear and walk right into his tent. Each time, someone would bring him back, and tie him up, and try to kill him again. The ice was breaking up and they tried to get him to agree they should take his wife along. But he wouldn't agree and the ship stayed there even though they could travel now. Then the captain told them: "Now it's up to me. We leave this man alone now and give him back his wife. We cannot do anything more because we do not have his power."

They brought Eqilaglu back to his tent and gave him back his wife. And they began to rush, rush, getting ready to leave at a certain time of day. But the little man said to himself, "That ship, those white people, have treated me so badly." Then the little man said a certain word, "*Pamiuluq!*" That's old language. *Pamiuluq* is a spirit with a bad tail. The little man said, "*Pamiuluq* will chew up their ship." That's what he said, looking at the ship. "The white people treated me so badly so *Pamiuluq* will chew up their ship."

Hervé Paniaq of Igloolik gives a horrific account of the shaman's sufferings and subsequent action:

> He had stolen a shovel so he was taken. He was made to lie on his back on deck with his hands tied. The white people wanted to axe off his arms . . . He was made to lie on his back, but his arm could not be axed. When they tried to axe his arm, it looked as if his arm was severed, so much so that the blade would stick fast to the deck, but each time his arm was untouched. After numerous attempts had been made, they gave it up. When they were done with him, he blew them away and told them never to return again. As the ship had spent a good deal of time in the region, they kept wanting to return but it was no longer possible.[16]

Pauli Kunnuk also recorded his version of how the shaman took revenge:

> . . . An Inuk had stolen a shovel. It is said that the white person really got mad over the incident, which is understandable because of the theft. Because of the way the man got mad over it the Inuk made it not possible for ships ever to return on account of the ice. That's what I heard; whether there is any truth in it or not I cannot say. But it is said that through shamanism it was no longer possible for ships to make it here. Certainly without a doubt, shamanism was practiced in those times.[17]

After Paarii wintered, for more than a hundred years, no vessel came to Igloolik. This was the shaman's curse.

The Lifting of the Curse

As a small boy in the early 1900s, Mark Ijjangiaq believed white men were rare. "I thought there were only a few worldwide. . . . I thought Inuit were numerous in comparison—because I knew there were a lot of them."[18]

In fact, by the early 1900s, Inuit in certain areas of the Canadian Arctic had had contact—often close—with *qallunaat* for three-quarters of a century. The whalers *Elizabeth* and *Larkins*, which appeared high off Baffin Island's northeast coast five years before Parry wintered at Igloolik, were harbingers of many more. In pursuit of the bowhead, Scottish and English vessels whaled in numbers down the east Baffin coast and eventually into the whale-rich waters of Cumberland Sound. Here, Americans joined the chase; they introduced wintering and set up shore stations, and then in the 1860s their vessels sailed into Hudson Bay and Roes Welcome Sound. The Inuit soon became necessary partners in the North's first industry. When the whalers took their leave, for the most part before the First World War, the traders, in pursuit of white fox furs, were there to take their place. They set up permanent trading posts, and the missions and sometimes the Royal Canadian Mounted Police (originally the Royal North West Mounted Police) set up shop next door.

But because of ice conditions—and the shaman's curse—Igloolik Inuit remained profoundly isolated.

Igloolik has a vigorous tradition about how the curse of the shaman was vanquished.

Aya, I think I have heard—
(He has heard from the wind)
I think I have heard—
(He thinks he has heard)
The sound of wood out in the wild
Aya, Aya, Aya.

[The late] Noah Piugaattuk recalls that around the turn of the twentieth century (some consider the song is of earlier origin, even predating Parry), an Igloolik Inuk made up this song for use in a drum dance. The composer, whose name was Imaruittuq, danced with the drum, while his wife and another woman sang his song. In many verses, the song tells that after years without contact the white man will soon come again to Igloolik. But will he come by water or by land? The verses of Imaruittuq's song allow for either possibility.

I think I have heard
He thinks he has heard from the sea
I believe that I hear
He believes that he hears
The sound of wood from the sea.

The song that asked the question was sung in the giant igloo when Piugaattuk was a child. "The song was made long ago, knowing the inevitability of white settlement."[19]

Igloolik people say the first white man came by land—in 1913, by dog team. They say he was the French-Canadian explorer Alfred Tremblay—whom Inuit call "Tamali." (In fact, Charles Francis Hall had visited Igloolik just 44 years after Parry. Inuit received him hospitably and told him their stories. They called him "Mistahoh," and Rosie made a brief reference to him after Leah and I asked if she had ever heard of him: "He was here for a while; then he went on towards Hall Beach and on from there." Rosie expressed the opinion that he was related to a member of the lost Franklin crews. "That's why he was anxious to find them. . . .")

According to Igloolik Elders, it was Tremblay who broke the shaman's spell. He had shipped in 1912 with Captain Joseph Bernier on the *Minnie Maud*, an old fishing schooner hastily fitted out to pursue a rumour of "a new Eldorado" in North Baffin Island. Gold nuggets were said to have been found in the bed of the Salmon River flowing into Eclipse Sound. Tremblay set off overland with Inuit guides to look for minerals, game, and anything else of interest.

He reached Igloolik on 20 March 1913. "When morning broke I saw the low lying land of Igloolik Island ahead of me . . . we struggled into the native village, at the south-eastern extremity of the island, about noon, and standing on the shore I saw four Eskimos. . . ." Tremblay had no knowledge that Hall had preceded him. "These natives were very astonished when they saw me as I was the first white man to visit Igloolik since Sir W.E. Parry . . . Some of these natives had never seen a white man before and held them in fear. They had heard of Parry and his men only through tradition." Tremblay and his guides were too exhausted to explain their presence. They slept for 24 hours in their host Eetootajoo's igloo. But on 23 March, Tremblay set out to explore Igloolik Island.[20]

Noah Piugaattuk was a little boy when Tremblay arrived. ". . . He walked to Igloolik Point and looked at [remains of] the old sod houses there. On his return from his walking journey, he said his exploration had been like capturing an animal—which then becomes available for food. Now people would easily come here and do whatever they needed to do."[21]

Rosie says Tamali shot up the island. "It is said that he had a pistol and with it he shot up the island of Igloolik as he walked around the shoreline. Afterwards, he said Igloolik was dead—ships would now be able to get to the island."

Though Tamali had lifted the curse, it would still be two decades before Igloolik saw a ship. The pace of change quickened after the HBC and the Catholic **Oblate** Mission arrived at Chesterfield Inlet in 1913. But, say Igloolik people, "Igloolik was the last to have white people." Only in 1931 did the first ship since the *Fury* and the *Hecla* appear offshore.[22]

Rosie, who had spent her childhood around Chesterfield Inlet when there were already white people, was there to watch when the ship bringing the wood to Igloolik for the first mission came into view:

> I recognized that boat when it was arriving. It was the *Tiriisikuluk* [the *Theresa*], only a small one. The women who were living in the same camp as me began yelling out "*Umiaq juaraaluuk*!!—A huge big ship!" They seemed to have lost their minds. I became scared of these ladies who went crazy over the ship . . . but they were only happy because the boat was arriving. I said it was really not such a very big ship. They were amazed!
>
> Ever since that time, ships have come regularly again. It seems in the past they had been blown away by the shaman."[23]

Notes

1. This article draws chiefly on the author's interviews conducted in Igloolik in 1998 with Rosie Iqallijuq and interpreted by Leah Otak. These are augmented by interviews recorded both with Rosie Iqallijuq and other Elders for the Inullariit Elders' Society and held at the Igloolik Research Centre. All quotations from the Inullariit Elders' Society archives are identified in the notes by the archive file numbers in parentheses.

2. W.E. Parry, *Journal of a Second Voyage for the Discovery of a North-West Passage . . . in the Years 1821–22–23* (London: John Murray, 1824), 269.

3. Ibid., 15 and 17 Apr., 425.

4. Mark Ijjangiaq, Inullariit Elders' Society archives (253).

5. In this article, the author has quoted on a number of occasions from interviews with Rosie Iqallijuq in the Inullariit Elders' Society archives held in the Igloolik Research Centre, notably file numbers 26, 204, and 395.

6. W.E. Parry, *Journal of a Voyage for the Discovery of a North-West Passage . . . in the Years 1819–20* (London: John Murray, 1821), 296.

7. Rosie Iqallijuq, Inullariit Elders' Society archives (445).

8. Parry, *Journal of a Second Voyage*, 230.

9. From personal interviews with the author: Pitseolak Ashoona, Cape Dorset, 1970; Louis Kamookak, Gjoa Haven, 1999.

10. Parry, *Journal of a Second Voyage*, 270.

11. Dorothy Harley Eber, "Eva Talooki: Her Tribute to Seed Beads, Long-Time Jewels of the Arctic," *Inuit Art Quarterly* (Spring 2004): 12–17; Parry, *Journal of a Second Voyage*, 270–2.

12. From "Tattooing, a Discussion of the Practice across Arctic Regions," in Jens Pederhart Hansen, Jorgen Meldgaard, and Jorgen Nordqvist, eds, *The Greenland Mummies* (Montreal & Kingston: McGill-Queen's University Press, 1991), 102–15.

13. John MacDonald, "Parry's Flagstaff near Igloolik, Northwest Territories," *Arctic* 48 (Sept. 1992): 308–12.

14. Parry, *Journal of a Second Voyage*, 410–12.

15. J.E. Nourse, ed., *Narrative of the Second Arctic Expedition Made by Charles F. Hall: His Voyage to Repulse Bay, Sledge Journeys to the Straits of Fury and Hecla and to King William's Land, and Residence Among the Eskimos during the Years 1864–69* (Washington: US Naval Observatory, 1879), 112–14.

16. Hervé Paniaq, Inullariit Elders' Society archives (141).

17. Pauli Kunnuk, Inullariit Elders' Society archives (87).

18. Mark Ijjangiaq, Inullariit Elders' Society archives (86).

19. Noah Piugaattuk, Inullariit Elders' Society archives (303).

20. Alfred Tremblay, *Cruise of the Minnie Maud: Arctic Seas and Hudson Bay, 1910–11 and 1912–13,*

trans. and ed. A.B. Reader (Quebec: Arctic Exchange, 1921), 153.

21. Noah Piugaattuk, Inullariit Elders' Society archives (303).

22. Captain Robert Abram Bartlett, with his famous vessel *Effie M. Morrissey*, visited western Baffin in 1927, but he sailed through Hudson Strait and across Foxe Basin to the Strait of Fury and Hecla only in 1933.

23. Rosie Iqallijuq, Inullariit Elders' Society archives (395).

Primary Document

Excerpt from an Interview with Rosie Iqallijuq

Interview and translation by Louis Tapardjuk
Edited by Leah Otak

Q: Have you ever heard of Ulluriaq?

A: Ulluriaq was from originally a Kivammiut [people of Kivalliq] but she got married to someone that lived in this area so she was taken here where she made it her home from that time on, this also happened to me.

She lived at Uqquat (pn) until her husband died who was known as Pittiulaaq, not the Pittiulaaq that we know but his namesake. She was brought over by her half son who actually was the son of [her] former husband. She remarried but I cannot remember the name of the person whom she got married to.

She had spent her formative years in this area, it was in her childhood that she remembered the time when white people arrived by boat. She remembered the time when white people came, as a matter of fact she was the first Inuk to have seen white people before anyone else as the rest of the people that saw those white people died but she lived on so she was the only one that ever saw white people for a long time in this area. She said that the ship wintered in this place.

According to her recollection of that particular time they were given things that were really good to play with. One item that made a good toy was black hard cubes which turned out to be tobacco plug. They would use them in their play house as utility boxes; they smelled but nevertheless they were good toys. Another was the biscuits used as *sakkattangit*. They were not considered to be food as a matter of fact they would play with them. They would be given some food from the ship but they did not know what they were so they would just play with them for they did not know what they were.

That is all I have heard about her, she did not bear too many children. I knew one of her children but I have forgotten what she was called. Her grandchild is still alive and that is the wife of Kunuruluk.

Q: Have you ever heard of anything more about the white people that wintered here, I believe they were referred to as Paarii?

A: Yes, that is right they were Paarii and the rest. I believe they wintered here for two winters where their ships were frozen in just in front of us where they sometimes made camp at the point Ungaluujat. The reason why it is called Ungaluujat is connected to the tent rings where there would be a tent and a wall of stones for wind break. They used to have stones surrounding the tent for wind break because it would be a long time before they got enough snow in the autumn for them to make snow dwellings. There are a few of them around so these were used for the winter camp. Some were staying at Igloolik in *qarmaq* [sod house] using whale bones for rafters and the walls made with stones and sod at the time when Paarii wintered here. At Ungaluujat (pn) there is a grave of a white man who is said to have died at the time when Paarii wintered.

I heard at the time when Paarii wintered there was a shaman who was jealous over his wife when she started to go around with some white people. When the ships departed it is said that with the help of his helping spirit he blew the ship away so that no other ship can ever make it back to Igloolik.

From that time on no ship ever came this far. Then there were some others that went to Igluligaarjuk (pn) [Chesterfield Inlet] and Aivilik (pn) [Repulse Bay area]. When they met with some people at Mittuq they made it known to them that they wanted to go to Igloolik. But most of the people refused to go with them except for one individual who was not very smart. When he was asked to go with them he readily agreed to go as he barely ever refused anyone as he was the type of a yes man. It was at that time he came to Igloolik, this was after Paarii voyage. I have not heard if they ever wintered here or not.

After this a white man by the name of Taamali was brought over by dog team from Mittimatalik (pn) [Pond Inlet]. It was said that he was clerk of the trading post. This story is what I have heard from Ittuksaarjuat. They had arrived here from Mittimatalik by dog team which happened before Ittuksaarjuat was born.

It is said that he had a pistol so with it he shot the island of Igloolik as he walked around the shoreline. After he had shot the island he said that Igloolik was dead and that a ship will now be able to get to the island.

It was not until very recently when I had started to live in this area that we were able to get a ship into Igloolik. This was a small ship called *Tiriisikuluk*; they brought over the materials for the mission to be built. From that time on we finally started to get ships once in a while.

Before I came to this area I used to see ships so when the people in this area saw this small ship they said that it was big ship, but it was a small one slightly larger than a scow.

. . .

Q: Do you recall the time when they started to get converted to Christianity?

A: Yes, as a matter of fact I had arrived to this place when they were just getting converted to Christianity. Before that time I witnessed an experience where people started to get converted to Christianity. This was the parents of Ujarak, which are Ava and Urulu along with Qaunnaq and his wife. I saw them at the time when they were just getting converted to Christianity. This day walruses and seals were caught. Liver was cut into small pieces and placed to the edge of a small plate; in addition there was the heart, piece of the intestine and part of the head. These were all cut into small pieces;

they were too small for one to get a good bite of. They were about the same size as a pill placed on top of the plate.

At this gathering there was a general confession to all the people that were gathered in the central location. As they confess their wrong doings they would be filled with remorse and would cry in their confession. This process of *siqqitiqtut* [converting to Christianity] was called siqqitiqtut. After everything that needed to be said had concluded a prayer followed. All the adults in the gathering were offered a piece of meat from the plate where they swallowed the meat which was a voluntary breach of taboo. From this time on they no longer would have taboos to follow. This all happened while we were at Pituqqiq (pn).

I just realize that I never did go through the process of *siqqitiqtut*. I knew about Christianity at that time but I still had not been baptized.

That spring I was taken to this area by Amarualik where we first went to Iqaluit (pn), on our return trip we had to walk home as the ice almost left before we got back. When we arrived I went over to our tent just to discover that there was no one in it. Then I went to Uuliniq's tent but it too was vacant. At that moment I could hear some voices from the dwelling of my in-laws that is Iqipiriaq since they had the largest tent. I told Amarualik that all the people might be in there, he replied that was true. He added that they might be *aaniaqtut* [sick], that his confessing their wrong doings to the gathering. I immediately told him that we should go there, but he found no point in going as it was pointless to go. So I went there alone leaving him behind as he had things to do.

I went in and discovered that there were two plates with meat in them, I immediately got a flash back to the time when I saw people going through the process of *siqqitiqtut*. As it turned out with each of the animals caught this process would continue with each different animals. It was comparable to that of receiving a Communion. When I resided at Igluligaarjuk (pn) before this I use to go to church when the priest were saying Mass and saw when they were giving Communion, so this process of *siqqitiqtut* reminded me of that particular time. This was the time when they started to convert to Christianity and the time when they started to let go [of] the taboos that they were restricted.

Certainly there were those that did not know what to do and how to go about being a Christian. My real mother-in-law Ukkanngut thought it was useless to go through the process of *siqqitiqtut*.

Q: Who was instrumental in getting the people to convert to Christianity?

A: It was Umik, who is said to have been started off by a minister called Uqammak. He had shown the people how to go about converting the people to Christianity, so since Umik was from this region the minister sent him over to convert the people to Christianity.

He was the grandfather of Louis Alianakuluk, Piujukuluk and the rest of the kinship from their mother's side.

Umik soon experienced mental imbalance for he was trying hard to convert the people to Christianity, at the same time his son committed a murder who was taken away to a penitentiary. It was so pitiful to see him in his state. He would hurt himself and he just kept on talking and talking, he was trying to keep his physical abuse to himself and very careful that he did not hurt other people.

He talked so much when he was in that state. I remembered the time he shook my in-law's hand, which is Ukkanngut and Itturiligaq, when he arrived at Ugliarjuk (pn) [Chesterfield Inlet] when we were the only people in that place at that time. They had passed through on the way back from their journey to Mittimatalik (pn) [Pond Inlet], it was at that time his son was arrested and taken away. He said as he shook hands with my father-in-law: "*Gutip irninga qallunaat nunaannut angirraujaungmat, paliisillu kanaitallu piungittumik piqujijunniiqtualuungmata.*" ["The son of God had been taken home to the land of the white people, the police and the Canadians have discouraged anyone from doing wrongful acts"].

This was the first time I ever heard of Canadians mentioned, as I was young at that time I would not forget what I just heard.

Qattuuraannuk and Ittuksaarjuat were living at Akunniq that year; my brother-in-law had gone to Akunniq so that Qattuuraannuk could be advised. So I found that their dwelling did not have anyone so I made up the sleeping platform for them. I was tired but all along Umik just talked and talked, so I went to sleep. After I woke I discovered that he was still talking. The following day they took him to Akunniq where he did the same thing, just talked and talked so that no one could get to sleep on account of it.

The following spring he passed way from exhaustion.

. . .

Questions for Consideration

1. What did Indigenous peoples and Europeans think of each other when establishing contact and why? What did they want from each other?

2. Do you find Richter's "imaginings" to be an effective method of capturing Indigenous perspectives on contact with Europeans? Why or why not?

3. Discuss whether Ramusio's plan of Hochelaga (see the photo on page 43) should be understood as his "imagining" of the Huron settlement and whether it is comparable to Richter's imaginings of contact.

4. What evidence of cultural misunderstanding between Parry's expedition and the people of Igloolik exists in both the Inuit Elders' testimonies and the writings of Parry and George Lyon?

5. How do you assess oral histories such as those of the Igloolik Elders? Do you see them as more, less, or equally as valid as written historical documents such as Parry and Lyon's observations? Why or why not? How might considering this question from an Inuit perspective produce a different answer than considering it from a western or Eurocentric one?

6. Based on the interview with Rosie Iqallijuq, how would you say the Inuit perceived Parry and his men? According to her testimony, what effect did "contact" with Europeans and Canadians have on her community?

7. Considering the evidence provided in this chapter, would you say that contact should be understood as a single momentary event or as an ongoing process? Give reasons to support your answer.

Further Resources

Books and Articles

Calloway, Colin G. *One Vast Winter Count: The Native American West before Lewis and Clark*. Lincoln: University of Nebraska Press, 2006.

Eber, Dorothy. *Encounters on the Passage: Inuit Meet Explorers*. Toronto: University of Toronto Press, 2008.

Richter, Daniel K. *The Ordeal of the Longhouse: The Peoples of the Iroquois League in the Era of European Colonization*. Chapel Hill: University of North Carolina Press, 1992.

Trigger, Bruce. *Natives and Newcomers: Canada's "Heroic Age" Reconsidered*. Montreal: McGill-Queen's University Press, 1986.

Printed Documents and Reports

Burrage, Henry S. *Early English and French Voyages, Chiefly from Hakluyt, 1534–1604*. New York: C. Scribner's Sons, 1906.

Clayton, Lawrence A., Vernon James Knight Jr., and Edward C. Moore, eds. *The De Soto Chronicles: The Expeditions of Hernando De Soto to North America in 1539–1543*, 2 vols. Tuscaloosa: University of Alabama Press, 1993.

Parry, W.E. *Journal of a Second Voyage for the Discovery of a North-West Passage . . . in the Years 1821–22–23*. London: John Murray, 1824.

Snow, Dean R., Charles T. Gehring, and William A. Starna, eds. *In Mohawk Country: Early Narratives about a Native People*. Syracuse: Syracuse University Press, 1996.

Films

Canada: A People's History, Episode 1. DVD. Executive produced by Mark Starowicz. CBC, 2000.

Websites

Nunavut Research Institute
www.nri.nu.ca/about-us

Library and Archives Canada, Aboriginal Peoples Collection
www.collectionscanada.gc.ca/aboriginal-peoples/index-e.html

3

Treaties and Self-Governance

Introduction

Treaties between Indigenous nations and newcomers have played an enormous role in shaping the social, political, and economic terrain of Turtle Island. In order to settle the geographic area that came to be known as Canada, and obliged to do so by the Royal Proclamation of 1763, the British Crown and after 1867, the federal government of Canada, negotiated a series of treaties with Indigenous nations, initiating a process of treaty making that continues to this day. The "modern" treaty making process began in the 1850s with the Robinson treaties (Robinson-Superior Treaty and Robinson-Huron Treaty located in present-day Ontario).[1] William Robinson negotiated the Robinson Treaties primarily with the Ojibwa of the northern Great Lakes region. These early treaties established the template upon which the federal government would negotiate what became known as the "numbered treaties." All possessed similar characteristics (with minor variations): the cession of land and creation of reserves, the guarantee of annuities, the description of the government's obligations and responsibilities, and the Indians' continued right to hunt and fish on Crown lands.[2] The treaty process then moved further west and then north to cover most of Canada except for British Columbia and the Arctic.[3] Only two treaties were ever signed in British Columbia—the Douglas Treaties. These two treaties were negotiated in the early 1850s on present-day Vancouver Island. No treaties were negotiated in the Far North with the Inuit.

These treaties have widely different interpretations. In 1952, historians such as George Stanley described the treaties as agreements in which terms were set by the state and accepted by uncomprehending Indigenous peoples, whom he tended to describe as one homogenous population.[4] Such an interpretation tends to characterize Indigenous peoples as naive children who possessed no concept of land ownership and misunderstood what they were "giving up." This analysis, with slight variations, has remained shockingly resilient in the popular imagination. In part, its persistence rests upon the assumption that the British Crown and later the Canadian government would not bargain in bad faith—that they would, in other words, follow through on their treaty obligations—and therefore the disastrous outcomes of the treaties must lie with the misunderstandings of Indigenous peoples, not the failure of governments to hold up their end of the deals.

Court challenges from the 1970s to the present have sought to correct this misinterpretation and show that what was negotiated at the time was often not reflected in the written documents or in the verbal promises made by government officials. More important, the Indigenous peoples who negotiated the treaties were fully cognizant of what they were doing and, in order to address the changing social, political, and economic landscape that faced them, sought to arrive at the best possible terms with the state under difficult circumstances. Indigenous peoples consistently called for clothing, housing, farm equipment, animals, agricultural training, education for their children, and medical services as well as for aid during periods of scarcity and famine.[5] Moreover, they perceived the treaties differently than the colonial and Canadian authorities.

The articles in this section outline the history of the treaties in the geographical area that came to be known as Canada. J.R. Miller focuses on tracing how treaties were

Map 3.1 Historical Treaties of Canada. (Source: Indian and Northern Affairs Canada.)

and remain a reflection of the changing relationships between Indigenous peoples and settlers over the last four hundred years. Initially treaties were premised on kinship relations and informed by Indigenous world views. However, these relationships have changed dramatically over time. William Wicken looks at the treaties of Atlantic Canada and the role that the courts have played in mediating the original intent and

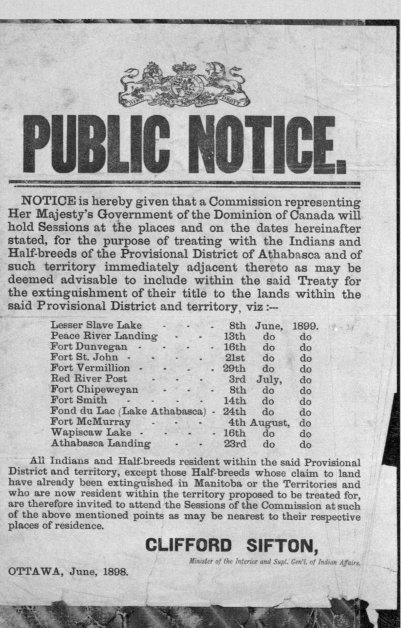

PUBLIC NOTICE.

NOTICE is hereby given that a Commission representing Her Majesty's Government of the Dominion of Canada will hold Sessions at the places and on the dates hereinafter stated, for the purpose of treating with the Indians and Half-breeds of the Provisional District of Athabasca and of such territory immediately adjacent thereto as may be deemed advisable to include within the said Treaty for the extinguishment of their title to the lands within the said Provisional District and territory, viz :—

Lesser Slave Lake - - -	8th June,	1899.
Peace River Landing - -	13th do	do
Fort Dunvegan - - -	16th do	do
Fort St. John - - -	21st do	do
Fort Vermillion - - -	29th do	do
Red River Post - - -	3rd July,	do
Fort Chipeweyan - - -	8th do	do
Fort Smith - - -	14th do	do
Fond du Lac (Lake Athabasca) -	24th do	do
Fort McMurray - - -	4th August,	do
Wapiscaw Lake - - -	16th do	do
Athabasca Landing - -	23rd do	do

All Indians and Half-breeds resident within the said Provisional District and territory, except those Half-breeds whose claim to land have already been extinguished in Manitoba or the Territories and who are now resident within the territory proposed to be treated for, are therefore invited to attend the Sessions of the Commission at such of the above mentioned points as may be nearest to their respective places of residence.

CLIFFORD SIFTON,

Minister of the Interior and Supt. Gen'l. of Indian Affairs.

OTTAWA, June, 1898.

Notice for treaty making, 1898. (Library and Archives Canada/Department of the Interior fonds/c140890.)

meaning of the signatories. Wicken cautions against the homogenization of historical treaties and questions the ability of the courts and so-called experts to determine what people intended.

Chapter Objectives

At the end of this chapter, you should be able to

- understand and explain the motivations of both Indigenous peoples and the Canadian government in the process of treaty-making;
- understand and trace the changing relationships between Indigenous peoples and newcomers;
- understand why the idea that Indigenous communities did not understand or negotiate the terms of their treaties remains so pervasive;
- identify the different types of treaties that were signed between Indigenous nations and colonial authorities and Canada;
- understand the role that courts and historians have played in defining treaties.

Notes

1. Robert Surtees, "Treaty Research Report: The Robinson Treaties (1850)" (Ottawa: Treaties and Historical Research Centre, Indian and Northern Affairs Canada, 1986.
2. Treat 7 Elders and Tribal Council et al., *The True Spirit and Original Intent of Treaty 7* (Montreal: McGill-Queen's University Press, 1996), 297–326.
3. For more information on treaties, see John Long, *Treaty No. 9: Making the Agreement to Share the Land in Far Northern Ontario in 1905* (Montreal: McGill-Queen's University Press, 2010); Ottawa [Indian and Northern Affairs], *A History of Treaty-Making in Canada*, (Ottawa: Government

of Canada Depository Services Program, 2010); Maurice Switzer, *We Are All Treaty People* (North Bay: Union of Ontario Indians, 2011); and J.R. Miller, *Compact, Contract, Covenant: Aboriginal Treaty-Making in Canada* (Toronto: University of Toronto Press, 2009).

4. George F.G. Stanley, "The Indian Background of Canadian History," *Report of the Annual Meeting of the Canadian Historical Association* 31, 1 (1952): 14–21.
5. Jean Friesen, "Magnificent Gifts: The Treaties of Canada with the Indians of the Northwest, 1869–76," *Transactions of the Royal Society of Canada* 1, 5 (1986): 41–51.

Secondary Source

Canada's Treaty-Making Tradition

J.R. Miller, University of Saskatchewan

Although Canada's post-Confederation treaty-making was fuelled by the immediate needs of nation-building politicians, the process of negotiating treaties was shaped by precedents that reached far back into Canadian history. The seven numbered treaties that the Dominion of Canada concluded with First Nations in the Northwest in the 1870s were a necessary prelude to populating the plains in particular with farmers who would grow crops for export via a transcontinental railway. The imperative to acquire Rupert's Land, as the Hudson's Bay Company's (HBC) territory was known, arose from the Confederation bargain that the architects of the new state had hammered out. Acquiring the Northwest was essential to expanding Ontario, whose leaders viewed it as a potential hinterland for Ontario agriculturalists, capital, and finished goods. Also, the commitment in 1871 to build a railway to the Pacific to induce British Columbia to join Confederation made securing control of the western interior all the more pressing. Without good relations with the First Nations there it would be impossible to settle immigrants on western lands and build a railway through the region. In short, immediate needs to complete and solidify a transcontinental state lay behind treaty-making in the 1870s.

But if the reason for making treaties was a recent one, the process of concluding the agreements with western First Nations was largely dictated by century-old precedents. Behind the short-term thinking of Canadian politicians lay the influence of the Royal Proclamation of 1763. In turn, underlying and shaping that cardinal document of imperial policy was one hundred and fifty years of First Nations–European relations in the fur trade and in diplomatic and military relations between First Nations and the Crowns of France and Britain. In other words, the roots of the treaties of the 1870s and later can be found in Native–newcomer relations of the seventeenth and eighteenth centuries.

All the motives that pushed Europeans to make contact with the northern half of the North American continent meant that the newcomers would be dependent on the Natives they encountered. In the early seventeenth century French and other ships came in search of fish, furs, routes to Asia, and people to evangelize for the Christian god. To pursue fish, fur, exploration, and evangelization necessarily meant that the French had to find ways to get along with the Indigenous inhabitants who vastly outnumbered them. At a minimum, they required Native toleration of the newcomers' presence on their lands and waters. If First Nations opposed the small ships that came each year in search of cod, whales, and other marine life, the puny Europeans would not have been able to maintain their fishery. Certainly, the presence of those who, like the English, practised a fishery that entailed drying their catch on shore before packing it for shipment home, had to be acceptable to local people. So, too, local guides had to advise mariners on exploring the waterways, especially the St. Lawrence, in pursuit of the elusive route to Asia. And, of course, if First Nations did not co-operate, the missionaries who wanted to tell them about the Christian god would fail. Native acquiescence in Europeans' activities was thus essential.

More than toleration of newcomers by First Nations was needed by those who came in search of furs or, later, for alliances against other Europeans. Indigenous people were critically important in the fur trade because of their knowledge, skills, familiarity with the North American environment, and labour. The First Nations who were France's principal partners in the commerce knew how to survive in the northern climes and where the best fur pelts were to be found. They had vital transportation skills, making birchbark canoes that could manoeuvre through the turbulent waters of rivers in the Precambrian Shield and using snowshoes in the winter drifts. They also knew how to harvest the resources of their environment—game, fish, vegetables, herbs, and berries—that were essential for living off the land as furs were collected or transported to sites where they were exchanged for European goods. They were experienced at harvesting fur-bearing animals, and they were accustomed to sojourning in the woodlands in the cold season, when the best furs were to be obtained but when most Europeans wanted to be in warmer quarters.

The specific case of the beaver, the animal whose pelt was in greatest demand in the seventeenth century, best illustrates the newcomers' dependence on Native skills and labour. In the 1600s the beaver was in demand in Europe because its pelt could be made into a smooth, shiny felt from which men's hats were manufactured. Since the broad-brimmed beaver headgear was all the rage, and since European sources of beaver were largely exhausted, the North American beaver was the principal target of the fur traders. But not just any beaver pelt would do; one particular version of the fur was desired above all others. The French were particularly anxious to acquire what they called *castor gras d'hiver*—literally, greasy, winter beaver fur—because it lent itself best to hat-making. The prime pelt was a beaver skin from which the long, coarse guard hairs had been removed, leaving the soft, downy fur underneath so well-suited to making beaver fur felt. And how was *castor gras d'hiver* produced? First Nations people wore cloaks fashioned from several raw beaver pelts with the fur on the inside. Over a season or several winters, the combination of heat, abrasion, smoke, and oils from the body caused the guard hairs to fall away leaving only short, downy filaments attached to a supple hide. Voila! *Castor gras d'hiver*. No doubt First Nations peoples thought it amazing that newcomers were keen to take their worn furs for a good price. More to the point, the case of *castor gras d'hiver* illustrated European dependence on First Nations. Although the furs of other species did not involve the "processing" by Natives that the beaver did, it was true that in all aspects of the fur trade Europeans relied on Indigenous producers.

For mostly similar reasons newcomers were also dependent on First Nations when it came to making alliances for diplomatic and military purposes, a motive that gained in prominence from the late seventeenth through to the mid-eighteenth century. For their part, First Nations did not distinguish between commercial and diplomatic relations. As a Haudenosaunee diplomat put it in a council in 1735, "Trade & Peace we take to be one thing."[1] What the Iroquois speaker meant was that in First Nations society one did business only with those with whom one had a guaranteed, stable relationship. Both French and British governments sought such alliances with First Nations because from the end of the 1600s until the Peace of Paris in 1763, the two European powers were vying for control of eastern North America, a struggle in which the British eventually prevailed. Naturally, given the large numbers of skilled, experienced First Nations in the territories over which the two European states contended, each government was keen to secure the friendship and support of First Nations as they manoeuvred against their rival. For their part, First Nations entered into alliances with Europeans only if they regarded such co-operation as being in their best interests, and always alongside a thriving commercial relationship.

A key challenge for newcomers was finding a way to establish the relationships that were vital to their success in either trade or alliance. What they quickly discovered from the earliest days of trade with First Nations was that Indigenous peoples had their own ways of creating such relationships. In Native societies, one had to assume that a stranger was a potential foe who meant harm unless that foreigner could be converted to a reliable associate. First Nations accomplished this transformation by ascribed or fictive kinship: they made a stranger into a benign relative by a process that converted the potential danger into reliable kin. This change was accomplished by participating in a series of ceremonies with the unknown person, rituals whose solemn and sacred nature ensured that they would not be taken lightly. The ceremonies included formal speeches of welcome, feasting, gift exchanges, and smoking the pipe. The participation of two groups that had previously been strangers in these ceremonies converted them into kinfolk and friends. Henceforth they would address each other using the rhetoric of family: "brother," "cousin," and even "father." Moreover, whenever the two parties were reunited after an absence, the ceremonies would be enacted anew, thereby maintaining the kin tie that ensured good relations. Europeans found themselves drawn into First Nations' circles of kinship via ceremony from the earliest days of contact. Champlain, for example, became an ally and trade partner of the Montagnais (Innu) as early as 1603, when the chief, Anadabijou, and his party smoked the pipe, feasted, and exchanged expressions of mutual friendship and support.[2] The practice of making and renewing kinship by means of First Nations' ceremonies remained a prominent part of Native–newcomer relations from contact to the nineteenth century.

Europeans' employment of Indigenous ceremony to create kinship that facilitated trade reveals several important features of early Canadian history. First, that newcomers adopted Native rituals, often very skilfully and successfully, is a further illustration of Europeans' dependence on First Nations. Like reliance on Indigenous knowledge, skills, and experience in trade and war, regular use of ceremonies to strengthen kin-like ties shows which party had the upper hand in the relationship in these early decades of interaction. Second, these practices—ceremony and kinship—created both commercial and diplomatic treaties between First Nations and Europeans. Commerce and alliance were merely two sides of a single coin, and that coin was kinship created by ceremonies. Thus, in early trade and diplomatic rivalries are found the first two forms of treaty, the commercial and the diplomatic. These treaties were usually not formalized in the European fashion with treaty texts, but diplomatic relationships were often solemnized in wampum, belts of white and dark-coloured shells strung on deer gut, that First Nations of the northeastern woodlands fashioned and exchanged with their partners from across the sea. In the eighteenth century, the British in the Maritime region of Canada often made formal, written treaties with the Mi'kmaq in a vain effort to secure the friendship of an ally of the French, but commercial compacts still were recorded only in the ceremonies that created and sustained them. Finally, the use of ceremonies and kinship became a barometer of the Native–newcomer relationship. When healthy, stable relations prevailed, Indigenous ceremonies and familial rhetoric were evident; when relations cooled, the Europeans often stopped participating in ceremonies.

The third stage of treaty-making emerged at the end of a period of intense alliance-building and warfare in the 1760s. By the early eighteenth century, treaty-making was dominated by agreements that dealt with alliance rather than trade as Britain and France contended for control of territory. This was the period when Britain vainly tried to secure the neutrality of France's allies, the Mi'kmaq of the Maritimes, through formal written treaties in 1726, 1749, 1752, and 1760–61. In the end, Britain was victorious by 1760, although between 1763 and 1766 a coalition of former French allies led by the great Shawnee leader Pontiac controlled the interior, killing 2000 civilians and capturing key British forts. It was revealing that the false step that triggered this war was the decision by a British general to stop giving presents to First Nations. Groups that had hitherto had associated with the French interpreted General Jeffrey Amherst's foolish action as severing the link between themselves and the newly victorious British. If Britain's representatives did not participate in ceremonies by continuing to give presents, did that refusal not signal enmity that justified armed action? Pontiac's War was the culmination of a period of uneasy relations between Great Britain and First Nations that led the Crown to articulate a new policy.

Although Britain's principal reason for creating the Royal Proclamation of 1763 had nothing to do with First Nations, it is the document's clauses related to First Nations that have had the greatest historical significance. Most of the Proclamation dealt with the boundaries and institutions of governance that the United Kingdom had to develop for the new colonies it had obtained from France by the Peace of Paris. The last five paragraphs of the Proclamation, however, focused on First Nations in the eastern half of North America. First, Britain sought to ensure peace and tranquillity in the interior of the continent where France's erstwhile allies were so restive by closing the region to settlement. In the past, Anglo-American farmers's penetration of First Nations' lands had frequently led to bloodshed as the Indigenous populations sought to protect their territory from agricultural settlers who would disrupt their hunting and gathering. Britain thus forbade settlement west of the height of land along the Appalachian mountain chain. It also regulated entry into the territory, for trade was regulated: would-be traders had to obtain a license from the governor of the nearest colony before going into the interior. The Proclamation defined all lands beyond the "Proclamation line" as lands "reserved to them . . . as their Hunting Grounds" and also said that "the several Nations or Tribes of Indians, with whom We are connected and who live under Our Protection, should not be molested or disturbed in the Possession" of their lands.[3]

The Proclamation's provisions to promote peace gave the document its lasting historical and legal significance. Having established that the Natives' lands were "reserved to them," Britain outlined the means by which those lands could be surrendered. The limitations were necessary, said the Proclamation (speaking in the royal plural), because of the "great Frauds and Abuses [that] have been committed in the Purchasing Lands of the Indians, to the great Prejudice of Our Interests, and the great Dissatisfaction of the said Indians." Henceforth, "no private Person" was allowed to acquire First Nations' lands. Should First Nations wish to divest themselves of some of their lands, continued the Proclamation, they "shall be purchased only for Us, in Our Name, at some public Meeting or Assembly of the said Indians to be held for that Purpose by the Governor or Commander in Chief of Our Colonies respectively within which they shall lie." These provisions laid out the requirements for making treaties concerning First Nations' lands. A surrender could be made only to the Crown, and only after a public meeting to discuss surrender had been convened by the Crown's representative. George III and his advisors thus unwittingly established the ground rules for making territorial treaties, which have prevailed since 1763.

The Royal Proclamation's clauses dealing with Indian lands were carried out over the century following 1763. Before then, there had been two forms of treaty between

Indigenous peoples and Europeans in what is now Canada—commercial compacts and treaties of alliance. In fact, Britain's Indian Department leader, William Johnson, created a new peace and friendship treaty on the spot from the Royal Proclamation. During the winter of 1763–64 he distributed copies of the Proclamation throughout Indian communities, and he invited the leaders to a conference at Niagara in the summer of 1764. There, he explained the provisions of the Royal Proclamation to the First Nations chiefs and got their agreement. These actions converted the Royal Proclamation from a unilateral Crown document into a binding treaty between First Nations and the Crown.[4] After 1764, territorial treaties, a third type of agreement based on the Royal Proclamation, would emerge as the dominant type of treaty between the Crown and First Nations.

The Proclamation's land provisions were implemented as Indian Department practice in the future province of Ontario in the century between 1763 and Confederation. In three phases, Crown representatives made treaties to gain access to territory held by the Mississauga, an Anishinabe First Nation, and other groups in response to non-Native desires to obtain lands and resources. The first stage was a series of treaties made with the Mississauga principally along the north shore of the St. Lawrence and Lake Ontario from 1784 on to prepare the way for the peaceful immigration of thousands of United Empire Loyalists, former Americans who had supported Britain in the revolutionary war.[5] Given the small number of British officials in the region, it made sense to negotiate with the local landholders before attempting to settle immigrants on First Nations lands. In this early era of territorial treaty-making, making treaties in advance of settlement was only prudent, especially with the horrors of Pontiac's War still a fresh memory. These early pacts were notable for the way in which both Crown negotiators and Mississauga leaders employed the traditional ceremonies and rhetoric for making kin. For example, after he concluded a treaty with some Mississauga on the St. Lawrence in 1783, Captain Crawford reported to his superiors that following negotiations "a large one [wampum belt] was Delivered to the other Chiefs concerned in the Sale, with the usual ceremonys [sic] to be kept in the nation [as] a memorial to their Children that they may know what their Fathers had done at this Time."[6]

After treaties had been concluded to accommodate Loyalists, some negotiations continued in other parts of Upper Canada as a steady trickle of immigrants made its way to the colony. Crown negotiators did not always adhere to the terms of the Proclamation, resulting in the governor general in 1794 issuing instructions that basically repeated the requirements of the Proclamation. On the whole, however, the spirit, if not always the letter of the Proclamation was adhered to in the period prior to the War of 1812. For example, at an 1811 conference at Port Hope, east of York (the future Toronto), the Crown representative, James Givins, addressed the assembled First Nations: "Children—I am happy to see you, and I return thanks to the Great Spirit, that has been pleased to enable us to meet at this place in good health. Children—I am sent by Your Father the Governor to make an agreement with you for the purchase of a small piece of land, the plan of which I now lay before you . . . Children—As your women and children must be hungry, I have brought some of your Great Father's Bread and milk, and some ammunition for your young men, which I will give you before we hear this."[7]

After the War of 1812, the nature of Upper Canadian treaty-making changed. Perhaps the most significant difference was the form that remuneration to First Nations now took. In the first phase of treaty-making, the Crown made one-time payments to its Mississauga partners in the interests of reducing expenditures. Crown payments would take the form of annuities, smaller amounts paid annually, which could be recouped from the revenues generated by a growing population. And the population of Upper Canada was growing, especially from 1820 onward when large numbers of immigrants arrived from the United Kingdom to start farms or work in towns in what had formerly been forests. The other change in treaty-making was that Crown officials now referred to the agreements they made for territory as "indentures," signifying that they thought of them more as contracts than as kin-based pacts that had typified the first set of Upper Canadian treaties. Ceremony was still generally used, and the language of family relationships was usually heard, but the tone of mutual respect that had been evident before now seemed muted as the original inhabitants found themselves greatly outnumbered. The passing of the Indian Department officials who had learned their diplomatic craft in the days of ceremonies and familial language also hastened a shift away from the earlier treaty relationships.[8]

The final phase of Upper Canadian treaty-making, from the 1840s to the early 1860s, confirmed that non-Native respect for the requirements of the Royal Proclamation had declined. The focus of Crown officials shifted northward, first to the mineral-rich lands around Lakes Huron and Superior, and then to the fishery near Manitoulin Island. In the mid-1840s, the colonial government rashly issued exploration licences to mining companies in the Sault Ste Marie area, despite messages from First Nations leaders there that they expected to be dealt with before mining began. It took resistance from First Nations leaders who shut down a mining operation at one site to get the government in Toronto to pay attention. Ultimately, two treaties— Robinson Huron and Robinson Superior—were negotiated in 1850, but the way they had come about showed little awareness of the Royal Proclamation. The government even ordered its negotiator not to provide a feast, presumably in the interest of saving money, although Commissioner Robinson did in fact feed the local First Nations. A similar lack of awareness of or respect for the Proclamation was evident in the background to the Manitoulin Island treaty of 1862. Again it took protests, this time against non-Native fishers, to get the government to send a treaty commissioner who secured agreement with most, though not all, of the groups on Manitoulin Island. Clearly, a century after William Johnson convened the 1764 Niagara Conference, Crown representatives were a long way from operating in the spirit of the Royal Proclamation.[9]

The Robinson Treaties of 1850 were revealing in another way. As Alexander Morris, negotiator of four of the seven numbered treaties in the 1870s, observed, the Robinson Treaties "were the forerunners of the future treaties, and shaped their course." He pointed to the fact that the 1850 treaties provided for large reserves, annuities, and recognition of First Nations' continuing right to hunt and fish on their lands—all features of the numbered treaties.[10] In a broader sense, the entire succession of Upper Canadian treaties foreshadowed the western agreements. They implanted the Royal Proclamation procedures in public policy and influenced many of the political leaders who would oversee later treaty-making on the plains.

The achievement of Confederation necessitated the negotiation of treaties in the West in the 1870s. An essential part of the Confederation bargain was a commitment to Ontario that the Dominion would acquire the Hudson's Bay Company lands known as Rupert's Land. Ontario's leaders wanted the West as a field for settling young agriculturalists, as a place where Toronto-based transportation and manufacturing interests could find markets, and as a region where financial institutions could operate. In addition, when Canada negotiated the admission of British Columbia to the Dominion in 1871, one of the terms was the construction of a railway to the Pacific within ten years. Clearly, if the young country was going to acquire Rupert's Land, promote immigration there, and build a railway across the West, Canada would have to get the agreement of the tens of thousands of First Nations who controlled the region. Without their agreement, the Canadian northwest would replicate the angry Indian frontier that the Americans would soon experience when they tried to conquer their West with troops. For the Dominion of Canada, the obvious approach was to negotiate treaties instead.

If Canada pursued treaty-making largely for economic reasons, what of western First Nations? Left to themselves, they faced little pressure to forge links with strangers from far away. Plains First Nations were still numerous and strong in 1870, with a reputation for warlike tendencies and martial skills. But they knew they would not be left to their own devices for very long, and they had reason to fear that several forces were eroding their strength. Many of their concerns were expressed succinctly by Plains Cree leaders, such as Sweet Grass, who sent a message to Canada's governor in Winnipeg in 1871:

> Great Father,—I shake hands with you, and bid you welcome. We heard our lands were sold and we did not like it; we don't want to sell our lands; it is our property, and no one has a right to sell them.
>
> Our country is getting ruined of fur-bearing animals, hitherto our sole support, and now we are poor and want help—we want you to pity us. We want cattle, tools, agricultural implements, and assistance in everything when we come to settle—our country is no longer able to support us.
>
> Make provision for us against years of starvation. We have had great starvation the past winter, and the small-pox took away many of our people, the old, young, and children.
>
> We want you to stop the Americans from coming to trade on our lands, and giving firewater, ammunition and arms to our enemies the Blackfeet.
>
> We made a peace this winter with the Blackfeet. Our young men are foolish, it might not last long.
>
> We invite you to come and see us and to speak with us. If you can't come yourself, send some one in your place.[11]

As Sweet Grass indicated, the chiefs' reasons for concern were many.

Though the chiefs were firm in saying they owned their lands, they also suggested that they were willing to discuss an accommodation with the Dominion. "I shake hands with you, and bid you welcome," said Sweet Grass. "We invite you to come and speak with us." Why? They were concerned about the noticeable decline in animal resources, especially the bison, the foundation of the Plains economy. Moreover, they had recently suffered losses to smallpox, and intertribal warfare had been another blow. As their resources declined, they reached out to Canada for help: they knew they needed cattle, tools, and advice if they were to respond to the reduction of the bison by shifting to agriculture. Unstated in Sweet Grass's message was the fact that they knew that settler immigration was imminent because Hudson's Bay officers and Christian missionaries had told them so. Pro-treaty chiefs like Sweet Grass saw many reasons to speak with a representative of the "Great Father."

Some First Nations chiefs opposed treaty-making, but they lost the debate with those who favoured negotiations. Leaders like Poundmaker spoke forcefully against the government's approach once treaty-making began, and his fellow Plains Cree chief, Big Bear, initially refused to accept the treaty favoured by Sweet Grass and others. As was made clear in a private caucus of chiefs prior to the negotiation of Treaty 6 in 1876, the pro-treaty chiefs had the more convincing case. Chief Mistawasis supported treaty-making by conjuring a picture of looming crisis and challenging anti-treaty chiefs for an alternative to an agreement. He reminded his listeners of "the destruction of the buffalo as the chief source of our living, the loss of the ancient glory of our fore-fathers." And then he challenged those opposed to making treaty. "I speak directly to Poundmaker and The Badger and those others who object to signing this treaty. Have you anything better to offer our people? I ask, again, can you suggest anything that will bring these things back for tomorrow and all the tomorrows that face our people?" He thought not. "I for one think that the Great White Queen Mother has offered us a way of life when the buffalo are no more . . . I for one will take the hand that is offered. For my band I have spoken."[12]

Mistawasis and his colleague Chief Ahtahkakoop carried the day in 1876 and ensured acceptance of Treaty 6 by Plains Cree leaders. Not all First Nations throughout Rupert's Land confronted the same problems as the Plains peoples, but they all faced uncertainty. Forest dwellers to the north of the Prairies, for example, were adversely affected by changes that the Hudson's Bay Company was introducing to its transportation system, alterations that eliminated a lot of the seasonal wage work on which they depended.[13]

Although these factors made many western leaders amenable to considering treaties, they did not guarantee success in negotiations. Talks leading to the seven numbered treaties between 1871 and 1877 were characterized by protracted discussions. Bargaining for Treaty 1 (1871), the Stone Fort Treaty, in southern Manitoba was one example, as were the negotiations of Treaty 3 (1873) in northwestern Ontario, Treaty 4 (1874) in southern Saskatchewan, and Treaty 6 (1876) in central Saskatchewan and Alberta. Nonetheless, at the end of the day Canada managed to conclude agreements that permitted immigration and settlement in a vast territory that stretched from the Lake of the Woods to the foothills of the Rockies, and from the international boundary on the south to a point midway up the present-day Prairie provinces. In return, First Nations received cash remuneration, both a lump sum at signing and smaller annuities thereafter, reserves of 32 or 160 acres (12 or 45 ha) per person depending on the treaty, promises of schooling, and assistance with a transition to sedentary farming. Canada did not expect First Nations to switch immediately to agriculture, shown by guarantees in Treaties 3 through 7 of continuing rights to gather and promises of ammunition and twine to make nets for fishing. Treaty 6 was unique in containing both "medicine chest" and "famine" clauses that promised government medical aid and assistance in the event of a major famine.[14] These clauses, for which Cree negotiators argued strenuously, reflected the concerns that Sweet Grass had expressed in 1871 about disease and the decline of the bison.

The numbered treaties continued the tradition of using First Nations protocols, although events elsewhere showed that Canada did not plan to maintain the kin-like relations created by these ceremonies. In the West, where fur-trading with the Hudson's Bay Company over 200 years had instilled the use of ceremonies, First Nations spontaneously came to the discussions with their ritual practices. With the exception of Treaty 4, where many First Nations leaders were angry about not receiving a share of the money that Canada paid for Rupert's Land, pipe ceremonies, formal speech-making, and other rituals were observed. Among the Plains peoples these ceremonies included elaborate equestrian demonstrations that impressed treaty commissioners. As well, the rhetoric of family—references to Great Father, Great White Queen Mother, my brother, the Queen's children, etc.—was prominent. Indeed, one of the striking features of the negotiations was the way in which government representatives became more comfortable with and adept at using such language each year. Events soon would soon show that such rhetoric was hollow.

In April 1876, more than a year before treaty-making was concluded with Treaty 7, the Canadian Parliament passed the Indian Act. This statute was a consolidation of existing legislation affecting First Nations, but it also made it explicit that Canada intended to treat First Nations as people needing control and instruction as they moved towards adopting Euro-Canadian ways. The Act established the relationship as one between a trustee and its wards, a bond that meant that the Crown would treat First Nations peoples as legal children. For example, no Indian's will was valid unless it was approved by the Minister of Indian Affairs. The imposition of a legal parent–child link contradicted the ceremonially based relationship that had typified earlier interactions. First Nations who assumed they had made kinfolk of the queen's Canadian children through their ceremonies and treaty soon found themselves treated not as kin with whom the Crown would share but as children who were to do as they were told by federal officials. This "bait and switch" treatment of First Nations in the 1870s has permanently poisoned the Crown–First Nations relationship and accounts for much of the friction, distrust, and bitterness that have prevailed until today.

Given the double-cross that Canada perpetrated in the 1870s, it is not surprising that the history of treaty-making since has been problematic. The Dominion made four more numbered treaties with First Nations in the provincial norths and parts of the North West Territories between 1899 and 1921, but neither the negotiation of nor the experience with the northern treaties has been harmonious. Because Canada has always insisted that the Indian Act trumps treaty relationships, and since it also regards only its own written versions of all the treaties as authoritative, treaty-making and treaty implementation have been difficult. Indeed, after making two minor treaties in Ontario in 1923, Canada refused to negotiate any more treaties for half a century. Only when First Nations forced Canada back to the negotiating table through a land claims process that was set up in the 1970s, were new treaties—now viewed by government as comprehensive claims settlements—negotiated. Canada's paternalistic approach to interpreting existing treaties and negotiating new agreements has made contemporary treaty-making prolonged and contentious. For example, in British Columbia, negotiations under the British Columbia Treaty Commission, set up in 1993, have gone on for more than two decades and yielded only three agreements to 2014. An approach to treaty-making that does not honour historic kin-based practices has proven a demonstrable failure.

Canadian treaty-making has gone through several phases over the past four centuries with varying results. In the first two centuries after contact in the east, commercial compacts and treaties of peace and friendship that were founded on Aboriginal ceremonies flourished. Beginning with the Royal Proclamation of 1763, a third form of treaty, territorial agreements, emerged, though initially they were still negotiated within a regime of Aboriginal protocols and kinship. A sign of things to come was the fact that whenever settlement overwhelmed hunting-gathering, governments that depended on the votes of settlers began to disregard the old style of relations. Ceremony and kinship were revived at the insistence of First Nations in the negotiations of the 1870s, but Canada's adoption of the Indian Act in 1876 foreshadowed the demise of the kin-like relations that had once prevailed. In the twenty-first century Canadians find themselves having to deal with a legacy of distrust that their federal governments' deviation from the paths first blazed in the woodlands of the northeast in the 1600s has left the country.

Notes

1. Peter Wraxall, *An Abridgment of the Indian Affairs Contained in Four Folio Volumes, Transacted in the Colony of New York, from the Year 1678 to the Year 1751*, Charles Howard McIlwain, ed. (1915; New York: Benjamin Blom, 1968), 195.

2. H.P. Biggar, ed., *The Works of Samuel de Champlain*, 6 vols. (Toronto: Champlain Society, 1922–26), 1:98–101, 104

3. Royal Proclamation of 1763, in British Royal Proclamations Relating to America, 1603–1783, Clarence S. Brigham, ed., Vol. 12 of *Transactions and Collections of the American Antiquarian Society* (Worcester, MA: American Antiquarian Society, 1911), 215–18. For brief articles on how the Proclamation is interpreted today, go to www.activehistory.ca, accessed 16 Sept. 2014, and search under "Royal Proclamation" and "Magna Carta."

4. John Borrows, "Wampum at Niagara: The Royal Proclamation, Canadian Legal History, and Self-Government," in *Aboriginal and Treaty Rights in Canada: Essays on Law, Equality, and Respect for Difference*, Michael Asch, ed. (Vancouver: University of British Columbia Press, 1997), 155–72.

5. J.R. Miller, *Compact, Contract, Covenant: Aboriginal Treaty-Making in Canada* (Toronto: University of Toronto Press, 2009), Ch 3.

6. Library and Archives Canada [LAC], MG21, b 158, Sir Frederick Haldimand Papers, 366, reel 746, Capt. W.R. Crawford to F. Haldimand, 9 Oct. 1783.

7. LAC, CO 42, 351, Colonial Office Correspondence, Upper Canada, 1811 Despatches, reel B295, 138–9, Minutes of a meeting with the Mississauga Indians of the River Moira, Smith's Creek, 24 July 1811. At this time, "milk" was often used metaphorically as a euphemism for alcohol.

8. See Miller, *Compact, Contract, Covenant*, Chapter 4.

9. Ibid.

10. Alexander Morris, *The Treaties of Canada with the Indians of Manitoba and the North-West Territories* reprint (Saskatoon: Fifth House 1991; Belfords, Clarke, 1880), 16.

11. Message of Sweet Grass, Kihewin, Little Hunter, and Kiskion to Governor Adams Archibald, Red River, 13 April 1871, in Morris, *Treaties*, 170–1. The portion quoted here is the message of Sweet Grass, the most senior of these chiefs.

12. Peter Erasmus, *Buffalo Days and Nights*, Irene Spry, ed. (Calgary: Glenbow Alberta Institute, 1976), 247–9.
13. Miller, *Compact, Contract, Covenant*, 132–3.
14. Lists of the terms of the seven treaties can be found in Arthur J. Ray, Jim Miller, and Frank Tough, *Bounty and Benevolence* (Montreal and Kingston: McGill-Queen's University Press, 2000), 217–44; and less conveniently in Morris, *Treaties*, 313–75.

Primary Document

Excerpt from *The Treaties of Canada with the Indians of Manitoba and the North-West Territories, including the Negotiations on which they were based, and other information relating thereto*

Alexander Morris

Hudson's Bay Company Messages from the Cree Chiefs of the Plains Saskatchewan to His Excellency Governor Archibald, our Great Mother's representative at Fort Garry, Red River Settlement.

1. The Chief Sweet Grass, The Chief of the country.

    GREAT FATHER,—I shake hands with you, and bid you welcome. We heard our lands were sold and we did not like it; we don't want to sell our lands; it is our property, and no one has a right to sell them.

    Our country is getting ruined of fur-bearing animals, hitherto our sole support, and now we are poor and want help—we want you to pity us. We want cattle, tools, agricultural implements, and assistance in everything when we come to settle—our country is no longer able to support us.

    Make provision for us against years of starvation. We have had great starvation the past winter, and the small-pox took away many of our people, the old, young, and children.

    We want you to stop the Americans from coming to trade on our lands, and giving firewater, ammunition and arms to our enemies the Blackfeet.

    We made a peace this winter with the Blackfeet. Our young men are foolish, it may not last long.

    We invite you to come and see us and to speak with us. If you can't come yourself, send some one in your place.

    We send these words by our Master, Mr. Christie, in whom we have every confidence.—That is all.

2. Ki-he-win, The Eagle.

    GREAT FATHER,— Let us be friendly. We never shed any white man's blood, and have always been friendly with the whites, and want workmen, carpenters and farmers to assist us when we settle. I want all my brother, Sweet Grass asks. That is all.

3. The Little Hunter.

    You, my brother, the Great Chief in Red River, treat me as a brother, that is, as a Great Chief.

4. Kis-ki-on, or Short Tail.

    My brother, that is coming close, I look upon you, as if I saw you; I want you to pity me, and I want help to cultivate the ground for myself and descendants. Come and see us.

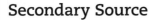

Secondary Source

The Treaties of Atlantic Canada

William C. Wicken, York University

From the 1950s, the Mi'kmaw and Wustukwiuk communities of Atlantic Canada launched several court challenges arguing that current governments were not honouring promises made to them in the eighteenth century. These promises, they said, were made in a series of treaties that the Mi'kmaw and Wustukwiuk had signed with British colonial authorities between 1726 and 1779. Since 1982 and the repatriation of the Canadian Constitution, these challenges have assumed more importance in altering the Crown's responsibilities. At least five cases have made their way to the Supreme Court of Canada (SCC). In this chapter, I provide an overview of the treaties and of the cases that they have spawned. Since I have also testified as an expert witness in many cases, including some that have reached the SCC, I inject a more personal and perhaps less objective view than someone who has not been so involved. It could be argued that my professional expertise as an historian has been compromised by my role as a witness. Is it possible to be both a professional historian and to provide unbiased expert testimony? In this chapter, I explore this issue and argue that the relationship between the professional historian and the courts is as ambiguous as the historical documents discussed in the courtroom.

The Aboriginal Population

Before 1784, there were two main Indigenous communities inhabiting the Atlantic region who would afterwards live within the Canadian state: the Mi'kmaq and the Wustukwiuk. The Mi'kmaq were the more populous and lived in what is now mainland Nova Scotia, Cape Breton Island, Prince Edward Island, the eastern coast of New Brunswick, as well as the Gaspé Peninsula. They also lived in southern Newfoundland, though dating their presence there is difficult. Despite this, we can say that the Mi'kmaq frequented Newfoundland from at least the late 1600s and probably had travelled back and forth from the mainland before then. The second major community was the Wustukwiuk, who lived along the St. John River Valley. Not much is known about these people before 1700 but it is probable that they were ethnically similar to communities further west.

    Another community, the Passamaquoddy, also lived in the area but their present-day legal status is unclear. Before 1784, they lived near the present-day border of Maine and New Brunswick and were closely related to the Wustukwiuk. After the creation of the American republic, their identity and legal status changed as many people chose to live on the Maine side of the border. Therefore, while the Passamaquoddy were parties to the same treaties as the Mi'kmaq and Wustukwiuk, their present legal status in Canada and to the treaties is ambiguous.[1]

The precise population of these communities in the 1700s is unknown. At contact, the French estimated that there were probably about 3000 Mi'kmaq and about 1000 Wustukwiuk. These totals, however, are estimates and the actual number may have been higher, as the introduction of European-borne diseases would have devastated the population.[2]

The Historiography

Historians did not pay much attention to the treaties until the late 1980s,[3] when the Union of Nova Scotia Indians and the Union of New Brunswick Indians began challenging provincial and federal laws, which restricted when their people could fish and hunt. Such challenges had been initiated before 1982 but the repatriation of the Constitution in that year forced the courts to revisit the treaties' legal status. This was mainly due to section 35 of the 1982 Constitution, which recognized Indigenous peoples' "aboriginal and treaty rights." Though the federal and provincial governments had planned to define those rights in more detail, they never did so and as a result, the courts were left with the task. After 1982, Indigenous communities and organizations began using section 35 to defend their members against prosecutions, which, they argued, impinged on rights, which came from their status as the indigenous inhabitants of Canada or the promises that British colonial or federal Canadian officials had recognized in treaties made with them. Because section 35 gave these rights constitutional protection, governments had less success after 1982 in arguing that statutory laws overrode them, which had been the governments' position before then. The courts were asked to determine what rights the Constitution provided Aboriginal people, whether these rights were inconsistent with legislative statutes, and therefore how the two might be reconciled.

However, since Indigenous peoples are not one homogenous group, not every community made a treaty and not every community encountered European settlers at the same time. For these reasons, the historical evidence that Indigenous communities have used to make section 35 arguments has varied. Because Aboriginal rights are more difficult to prove in court, litigants in the Atlantic region have usually focused on the eighteenth-century treaties when arguing that their constitutional rights have been violated.

Though the first test cases in Atlantic Canada referred to various historical documents, no historians were called to testify. This was true for instance in *R. v. Simon*, a case the Supreme Court of Canada decided in 1985. In that case the defendant, Jimmy Simon, had been charged with having a firearm and ammunition in his possession. Since Simon was carrying the rifle in the off-season, the legal issue was whether the Nova Scotia provincial game laws violated his treaty right to hunt. The SCC determined that a treaty the Shubenacadie Mi'kmaq had signed in 1752 was valid and that provincial legislation contravened Section 88 of the Indian Act. According to the Supreme Court, this section made the treaty paramount when it conflicted with provincial statutes.[4] After the Simon decision, Indigenous communities in Atlantic Canada made additional section 35 defences. Most of these cases came to trial because the Crown charged individuals with violating either federal or provincial statutes. In some cases, these individuals were successful in securing the political support of provincially based organizations, like the Union of Nova Scotia Indians, who had the financial resources to mount a Constitutional defense.

After the Mi'kmaq and Wustukwiuk began invoking section 35, governments began relying on expert witness testimony to discredit their claims. From the late 1980s, their principal witness was Stephen Patterson, a history professor at the University of New Brunswick.[5] Patterson's evidence forced Indigenous organizations to rely on experts too. The problem was that there were few individuals with the requisite knowledge. This was the reason I was enlisted in 1993 despite not having a university position at the time. John Reid of St. Mary's University was also recruited. Afterwards, other scholars entered the fray, including Stephen Augustine, Janet Chute, Robert Cuff, Olaf Janzen, Andrea Bear Nicholas, Gerald Penney, Harald Prins, Gary Semple, Laurier Turgeon, Alexander Von Gernet, and others.[6] Most of the subsequent litigation focused on the eighteenth-century treaties, though at times, Aboriginal title and the geographical scope of Mi'kmaw occupancy also figured in the courts' proceedings.[7]

In terms of the eighteenth-century treaties, court testimony and published work has divided into two camps. On one side is Professor Patterson, who has tended to interpret the treaties literally. For Patterson, the most important aspect of the treaties is the relative power that European nations exercised over Indigenous people. This, he argues, affected the terms concluded. According to Patterson, the Mi'kmaq and Wustukwiuk agreed to live within the British Empire and to become subjects of his Majesty King George, which meant that they agreed to abide by his laws. Though at one time, they might not have fully understood what it meant to obey British law, by the eighteenth century they had lived with French colonials for more than a century and so would have understood what the British wanted.

The other major aspect of Patterson's court testimony is his view of the relationship of the earlier treaties to the later ones. The British made six separate treaties in all. Patterson, however, has discounted the earlier treaties of 1725/26, 1749, and 1752, arguing that they were abrogated by conflict between the British and the Mi'kmaq and Wustukwiuk. The earlier treaties therefore have no legal force. The only treaty that matters, says Patterson, is the 1760–61 treaty.

Not everyone agrees with Patterson's views. I, John Reid, and others have tended to view British power at the time the treaties were signed as unstable. Great Britain's tenuous position in the Atlantic region affected how each party understood the treaties.[8] This, we said, was especially true when the first treaty was negotiated in 1725, a time when the British presence in Nova Scotia was limited to a 300-man garrison at Annapolis Royal. The inability of the British to control the Atlantic region meant that they lacked the power to force their will upon the Mi'kmaq and their allies. As well, unlike Patterson, we believed that each treaty built on the earlier ones and continued to have legal force despite the periodic resumption of war. This was clear, we said, from the ways in which later treaties modified earlier articles or introduced new ones.

Despite our disagreements, everyone who has testified in court probably agrees that the treaties' interpretation is not easily deciphered. This occurs for three reasons. First, unlike the numbered treaties, which the federal Canadian government made with various western and northern Indigenous peoples between 1871 and 1929, there are few conference minutes. As a result, we do not know what the delegates discussed, how the British interpreted each article, and how these phrases were translated from English into French and then into each community's language. Second, European documentation about Mi'kmaw and Wustukwiuk society is limited. European officials rarely, if ever, visited their villages or talked to their leaders. For this reason, we lack a solid basis for evaluating their society's evolution from the early 1600s to the 1780s. Without a clear understanding of their societies, interpreting how they understood the treaties is difficult. Finally, deciphering a treaty's meanings in court is difficult because the questions asked are derived from the law. These questions emerge from a contemporary context, which could not have been envisioned at the time a treaty was made. In *R. v. Donald Marshall Jr.,* for instance, the legal question was whether the federal government's commercial licensing system was an unreasonable burden on Mi'kmaw constitutional rights. Patterson, Reid and I were asked to examine the 1760 treaty, which the defense said showed that the British had engaged in a commercial fish trade with the Mi'kmaq. Specifically, we were asked if the British and the Mi'kmaq had intended that eels should be traded at the truckhouses, which the British agreed to establish and where trade with the Mi'kmaq and Wustukwiuk would take place.

There are two reasons this was not a question an historian would ask. First, the British were interested in furs, not eels. Thus, in discussing what items the Mi'kmaq might bring to trade at the truckhouse, neither party would have mentioned eels. Second, there was little documentation which showed that the Mi'kmaq did barter eels. For these reasons, historians would normally not have considered whether eels would have been traded. Whether they did, however, was only a question because the defense had to make a connection between the right claimed and the 1760 treaty. In sum the historians were being asked to decide an issue that had no historical significance and for which there was no evidence.

The Treaties

The Mi'kmaw, Maliseet, and Passamaquoddy negotiated and signed treaties with the British in 1725/6, 1749, 1752, 1760–61, 1778, and 1779. Not every community signed each treaty. Nonetheless, the federal government today accepts that every community at least signed a treaty once. The only possible exception, says the government, is Conne River, a Mi'kmaw community on the south shore of Newfoundland.

These treaties are generally called treaties of peace and friendship. This is because each agreement ended conflict between the British and the Mi'kmaq and Wustukwiuk. This distinguishes them from treaties that the colonial and Canadian governments later signed with various communities in Ontario and western and northern Canada. These later treaties resulted in Indigenous people surrendering land and also led to creating reserves. The peace and friendship treaties did neither; they did not result in land surrenders and they did not lead to creating reserves.

What then did the treaties do? They established guidelines to govern British–Indigenous relations. They were, as Peter Hoffer has suggested, "law at the edge of Empire." The British made treaties where they could not maintain political and military control and where traders were active and few settlers lived.[9]

For most of the eighteenth century, Great Britain exercised an unsteady dominion in the Atlantic region. French settlers, later called Acadians, had first settled there in the early 1600s. By 1755, their population was more than 15,000. Though Great Britain had obtained sovereignty over Acadia from France at the conclusion of the War of Spanish Succession (1702–13), until the founding of Halifax in 1749, the number of British settlers, soldiers, and administrators in the region remained small. Counterpoised to them was a growing French presence on Cape Breton Island and Ile St. Jean (Prince Edward Island), epitomized by the Fortress of Louisbourg on the northeast coast of Cape Breton. The fortress was both commercially and politically significant, serving as an entrepot between Canada and the French Antilles as well as guarding the entrance to the St. Lawrence River. Louisbourg also maintained a semblance of unity with the region's Indigenous population. It was here, for instance, that the French governor entertained Indigenous leaders as well as where missionaries gained succor and guidance for their work among the Mi'kmaq and Wustukwiuk. For the British, the French presence undermined their ability to create relationships with either the Mi'kmaq or the Wustukwiuk. The treaties, though imperfect, provided one method of doing so.

The 1725–26 Treaty[10]

The first treaty was negotiated in December 1725 and was ratified during the summer and fall of 1726. The treaty ended three years of war between the New England colonies (mainly, Massachusetts and New Hampshire) and eastern Indigenous peoples, a group that included the Mi'kmaq, the Wustukwuik, the Passamaquoddy, the Penobscot, and the Abenaki. The Penobscot and Abenaki lived within the present-day state of Maine. These communities were all members of the Wabanaki Confederacy, a constellation of peoples who were allied with the French and who opposed New England's expansion into their territories.

The war began in 1722, precipitated by a dispute between the Abenaki and New Englanders who had settled on the Kennebec River. The settlers claimed to have purchased land but the Abenaki said they had not. The Wustukwiuk and Mi'kmaq were not directly affected, but were upset with New England's exploitation of the Atlantic fishery. This in addition to disagreements about the limits of Great Britain's sovereignty precipitated their entry into the conflict.

The treaty was negotiated in November and December of 1725 in Boston. Two separate treaties were made. One was done with the Abenaki. Another was made with the Mi'kmaq, the Passamaquoddy, and the Wustukwiuk. After both treaties were finalized, the four Penobscot negotiators sent runners, bearing belts of wampum, to their allies, informing them of the agreement. Beginning in the summer of 1726, both treaties were ratified. The Abenaki ratified their treaty at Casco Bay, the others at Annapolis Royal, the British garrison on the Annapolis Basin in mainland Nova Scotia. Seventy-seven individuals signed the latter, attaching their mark to the treaty. A copy is reproduced in below.

The 1725–26 Treaty was composed of two parts, the Articles of Submission and Agreement, which the Aboriginal delegates signed and which outlined what they had promised to the British, and the reciprocal promises, the articles that outlined British promises.

The Articles of Submission and Agreement contained five articles and the reciprocal promises contained three. Each article established guidelines that the parties would abide by to maintain peace. Some of these articles are easily interpreted across time and culture. For instance, the third clause of the Articles of Submission and Agreement reads that *the Indians shall not help to convey away any Soldiers belonging to His Majesty's forts, but on the contrary shall bring back any soldier they shall find endeavouring to run away.* This article appears to brook little misinterpretation as it suggests that the Mi'kmaq would return any soldiers who deserted the fort. Other articles are less easily understood.

For example, the first article reads that "the Indians shall not molest any of His Majesty's Subjects or their Dependents in their Settlements already made or *Lawfully to be made* or in their carrying on their Trade or other affairs within the said Province." What is unclear here is *"Lawfully to be made."* What law? British law? Indigenous law? Or does *"Lawfully to be made"* mean lawful within the context of the treaty? Unfortunately, there are no auxiliary documents to clarify this clause, though we might argue that because the treaty was written in English, "lawfully" means according to "British law." Language, however, is never neutral. It cannot always be read across time but must be understood within a specific historical context. In other words, language is historically contingent. For this reason, I think it is reasonable to conclude that "lawfully" must be understood within the context in which the words were spoken.

The most contentious article of the 1726 treaty, which would be a focus of the courts after 1982, is in the preamble to the Articles of Submission and Agreement and which is later repeated in 1749, 1752, and in a modified form in 1760–61. In this clause, the Mi'kmaq and Wustukwiuk acknowledged King George as their sovereign. In doing so, they submitted to the king. However, the phrasing of the article is ambiguous. It reads: *"and make our submission to His said Majesty (King George) in as Ample a Manner as wee have formerly done to the Most Christian King."* In other words, the delegates made their submission to King George in the same manner as they had to the French king. This might be relatively unproblematic to decipher if the Mi'kmaq and Wustukwiuk had signed treaties with the French. However, they had not. Thus, to know how the Indigenous representatives would have thought about this article, we would have to understand their relationship with the French. Did French authorities treat them in the same manner as the Acadians? Were they also subject to French law? The lack of documentation about French–Mi'kmaw relations before 1713 leaves an interpretative vacuum. Though there are reasons to suppose that the French treated the Mi'kmaq and Wustukwiuk as inferiors, the historiography emphasizes the flexibility of French policy and the French need to maintain good relations with their Indigenous allies.[11] This would suggest that the Mi'kmaq were re-affirming with the British what had been true of their relationship with the French: the Mi'kmaq would not disturb the British and the British would not disturb the Mi'kmaq.

In *R. v. Marshall*, this clause was particularly contentious. In the 1760/61 treaty, the reference to the French monarch was dropped and instead the Mi'kmaw and

Wustukwiuk delegates pledged that *"we do make Submission to His Majesty (King George III) in the most perfect, ample & Solemn Manner."* For Patterson, this phrase demonstrated the submission of the Mi'kmaq and Wustukwiuk to British law. Reid and I argued that this literal interpretation was misguided and that this phrase should be read in the context of earlier treaties. And even if this was not true, how the Mi'kmaq and Wustukwiuk understood the word "submission" is unclear. If they were agreeing to abide by all of His Majesty's law, why then did the 1760/61 treaty outline the details of Mi'kmaw and Wustukwiuk obligations? Would it not have been enough for the delegates to swear to uphold British law? This contradiction between the *act of treaty making* and *the language of treaty making* "underlines the paradox of British–Mi'kmaq relations."[12]

The Later Treaties

After 1726, a long period of peace followed, for three main reasons. First, the 1725–26 treaty dealt with the major difficulties that had characterized British relations with eastern Indigenous peoples. Second, until 1749 and the founding of Halifax, the British did not expand their presence in the region. Thus, Indigenous communities continued to live much as they had done before, and had the added benefit of being able to trade with French merchants at Louisbourg and with Acadian traders on the mainland. Third, peace between Great Britain and France prevailed in Europe and so also in North America. As historic allies of the French, the Mi'kmaq and Wustukwiuk, had previously been drawn into the French–British conflict. Stability in French–British relations therefore translated into peace between the British and the Mi'kmaq and Wustukwiuk.

This changed in 1744, with the French entry into the War of the Austrian Succession. Soon afterwards the Mi'kmaq and Wustukwiuk were drawn into the conflict on the French side. With the signing of the Treaty of Aix-la-Chapelle in 1748, peace again prevailed. However, with the arrival of more than 2000 British settlers and soldiers in June 1749 to build a settlement at Halifax, an uneasy relationship began with the neighbouring Mi'kmaq. The new British governor, Edward Cornwallis, renewed the 1725–26 treaty, though only the Wustukwiuk and one Mi'kmaw community signed. Other communities were upset with the British decision to settle Halifax. Sporadic tensions continued over the next three years. This conflict ended with the signing of a new treaty in 1752.

Interpreting the 1752 treaty illustrates some of the tensions between contemporary Indigenous communities and university-based historians. Some Mi'kmaq have argued that the Grand Chief of the Grand Council signed the treaty and did so on behalf of all Mi'kmaq in Atlantic Canada. The Grand Council, these proponents argue, was an organization, predating contact, which acted as the political arm of the Mi'kmaw nation and was composed of seven Captains, who represented the seven different Mi'kmaw districts. At the head of the Council was the Grand Chief. In 1752, the Grand Chief was Jean Baptiste Cope of Shubenacadie, a community about 45 to 50 kilometres inland from Halifax.[13]

University-based historians, including me, have tended to be skeptical of this conclusion. I as well as Patterson have argued that there is no European-produced evidence that the Grand Council existed at this early date and therefore conclude that only the Shubenacadie community of mainland Nova Scotia signed the 1752 treaty.[14]

However, should the lack of such documentation render contemporary Mi'kmaw arguments spurious? Is it always necessary to confirm issues of Indigenous history in European documentation? Are there not other methods of determining such questions besides referring to British or French records? After all, we might ask, how could the British have possibly known or understood the subtleties of Mi'kmaw political organization? And that lack of knowledge would account for the British not mentioning the Grand Council in their correspondence. This contradiction between Eurocentric ideas and Indigenous oral histories is a source of disagreement among those who study Indigenous history. It is also an issue that is not easily resolved in the courtroom.

The 1752 treaty was quickly overtaken by events in Europe and in the Ohio Valley, where land speculators and settlers were encroaching on Indigenous lands and upsetting French claims to the region. This set off seven to nine years of war in North America and globally between Great Britain and France, which only ended with the Treaty of Paris in 1763. That treaty forced France to surrender most of its remaining territory in North America, including Ile Royale (Cape Breton) and Ile St. Jean (Prince Edward Island), to Great Britain. It was during these years that the 1760–61 treaty was signed.

There are many similarities between this treaty and the earlier ones. For instance, some articles modified the earlier 1725–26 treaty, whereas others introduced new laws to govern interactions between the Mi'kmaq/Wustukwiuk and British settlers. There was one significant difference. The 1725–26 treaty had included two parts, the articles of submission and the reciprocal promises. The treaty, which the British signed with the Wustukwiuk in February 1760, renewed the articles of submission word for word. However, the reciprocal promises were not mentioned. In the case of the Mi'kmaq, no mention of the earlier treaties was made.

Patterson has argued that the absence of the earlier treaties in the text of the 1760–61 treaty indicates a British intent to establish a new basis, which would govern relations with the Mi'kmaq and Wustukwiuk. Because previous attempts to create a lasting peace had failed, the British, he maintains, rejected the earlier agreements and wrote a new treaty. Thus, the reciprocal promises the British made in 1725–26 that the Mi'kmaq and Wustukwiuk "shall not be molested in their Persons, Hunting Fishing & planting on their Planting Grounds nor in any other their Lawfull (sic) occasions" were superseded by the 1760 treaty. The legal consequences of this supersession were that since the Wustukwiuk delegates had made "their Submission to His Majesty in the most perfect, ample & Solemn Manner," the contemporary Indigenous population had no claim to fish or hunt outside the regulatory systems created by the federal and provincial governments.

Patterson makes a number of good points that cannot be ignored. It is true that the Mi'kmaq and Wustukwiuk sued for peace. It is also true that in 1760, they were in a weaker bargaining position than they had been in 1725. However, neither should we over-emphasize the omnipotence of the British Empire at this time. As Linda Colley points out, in the eighteenth century the British were still in the process of building their global empire, and depended on maintaining a variety of relationships with various colonial peoples, a group that would have included the Mi'kmaq but also included Acadians and blacks.[15] While the British therefore did assume a harder line than before in interpreting their relationship with the Mi'kmaq than before, they nonetheless wanted to maintain peaceful relations with them. Indeed, the British could not do otherwise, because when the treaties were signed the fate of New France was still unclear. Though the British had successfully taken Quebec in September 1759, its final fate would not be decided until May of the following year when the British fleet arrived.

The Litigation

Several high-profile court cases since the early 1990s have focused on these eighteenth-century treaties. The most significant case, from a legal standpoint, was *R. v Marshall*. In October 1993, the federal government charged Donald Marshall and two companions with fishing without a license and selling fish without a license. Since they had been fishing in Pomquet Harbour, a small community on the north shore of Nova Scotia, Marshall was charged with violating federal statutes. At the time, there had been mounting pressure from non-Indigenous fishers in the region for the federal government to crack down on Mi'kmaq who were fishing lobster without licenses and out of season. Previously, Department of Fisheries and Oceans (DFO) officers had been unsuccessful in collecting the evidence needed to secure a conviction. One DFO officer, however, had seen Marshall sell eels to a commercial vendor. As a result, there was no question that Marshall had sold fish without the requisite commercial license.

The problem for the federal government, however, was twofold. First, Marshall was selling eels, not lobster. Nonetheless, the government chose to proceed, knowing that the case would be used as a test case to determine if the Mi'kmaq had a constitutional right to engage in the commercial fishery, regardless of federal legislation that forced fishers to purchase licenses from the federal government. The second problem for the government, which probably did not figure into the final Supreme Court decision, was the identity of the defendant. Marshall was no ordinary Mi'kmaw man. He had been wrongfully imprisoned for 11 years, and had the added distinction of being the first person released from jail in Canada as a result of a wrongful conviction. After his exoneration, Marshall tried to pick up the pieces of his life. One of the things he did was fish.

In Marshall, the defence lawyers, Bruce Wildsmith and Eric Zscheile, argued that in 1760 the British had promised that the Mi'kmaq could bring any items to trade with the British. The common intention of the parties, they argued, was that this could include fish. This suggested that the British intended that the Mi'kmaq would be involved in a commercial trading relationship, which would have included the Mi'kmaq trading fish for whatever they needed or wanted. This promise was constitutionally protected and therefore the licensing system, which forced the Mi'kmaq to buy a commercial license from the federal government, was an unreasonable burden on the contemporary Mi'kmaw community. In 5–2 decision released in September of 1999, the Court agreed. However, the Mi'kmaw rights to fish and to sell fish were not open-ended, said the Court, and governments retained the ability to restrict when, where, and how the Mi'kmaq might fish and sell fish. Conserving a species, for instance, was a justifiable restriction. The court also ruled that the Mi'kmaq could engage in the commercial fishery only to earn a moderate livelihood. Just what the court meant by "moderate livelihood," however, was unclear, and no doubt future litigation or negotiations will attempt to define that phrase.

The Court's decision was not popular among non-Native fishers. The decision also sparked a number of Mi'kmaw fishers to engage in a more extensive commercial fishery. This led to a second ruling on Marshall in November of 1999. This ruling, in which the Court clarified its earlier decision, and which is often called "Marshall II," outlined additional ways in which the Mi'kmaw commercial fishery might be restricted. The court's ruling was unprecedented, as the Court has never before issued a second ruling clarifying what it originally meant.

Marshall was only one of several section 35 cases that have come before the courts in Atlantic Canada over the past 30 years. Three other cases have also resulted in Supreme Court decisions. Though it is possible that future litigation will also find its way to Canada's highest court, that possibility is becoming less likely. This is because past Supreme Court rulings have forced the federal and provincial governments to adopt more conciliatory policies towards Indigenous peoples including fishers and hunters. In Nova Scotia, at the present time, for instance, all interested parties are holding ongoing negotiations to resolve their disagreements rather than using the courts to do so. The same process is occurring in New Brunswick and Quebec.

Conclusion

Historical documents are, by their very nature, ambiguous. This is as true of words written ten years ago as it is of words written 300 years ago. There is a difference, however. The more recent the events, the more extensive the documentation. Sometimes, this additional information allows us to better situate the historical context in which the words were written. For the eighteenth century, however, there are few documents and so often we do not know much about what transpired when treaties were made. We would like to know more about what was said during the discussions that preceded the treaties' signing. We would like to know what each party said to the other and how the interpreters translated the English text into Mi'kmaq and Wustukwiuk. Did the Indigenous delegates really understand what the English text said? We might also wonder whether our interpretation of the text and of the intentions of the British officials who drafted it, are accurate. Today we assume that terms like "submission" and "lawfully" mean certain things but in eighteenth-century Nova Scotia, it is also reasonable to think that British governors conceived of these words differently.

This reminds us that historians, despite their best efforts, can never know exactly what people thought. But that is precisely what the courts have demanded. The Courts have insisted that a common intention emerged when the delegates signed a treaty. This wrongly assumes that we can understand what was in the minds of those who were there. To know precisely what each delegate who signed the 1725–26 or 1760–61 treaty thought as they put pen to parchment, is, I believe, impossible. This ambiguity therefore makes us wonder to what degree historians who testify in court are impartial. I do not think there is a good answer except to say that a good historian will make reasonable conclusions and allow the courts to make reasonable judgments based on what we can and cannot know.

Notes

1. William C. Wicken, "Passamaquoddy Identity and the Marshall Decision," in *New England and the Maritime Provinces*, Stephen J. Hornsby and John G. Reid, eds (Montreal & Kingston: McGill-Queen's University Press, 2004), 50–8.

2. Historical and modern overviews of these communities are in Bruce G. Trigger, *Handbook of North American Indians. Vol 15: The Northeast* (Washington: 1978). See Philip K. Bock, "Micmac," 109–22; and Vincent O. Erickson, "Maliseet-Passamaquoddy," 123–36.

3. For example, see L.F.S. Upton, *Micmacs and Colonists: Indian–White Relations in the Maritimes, 1713–1867* (Vancouver: University of British Columbia Press 1979).

4. Thomas Isaac, *Aboriginal Law: Commentary, Cases and Materials* (Saskatoon: 2004), 110–14.

5. Stephen E. Patterson, "Indian–White Relations in Nova Scotia 1749–61: A Study in Political Interaction," *Acadiensis* 23, 1 (Autumn 1993): 33–59; "1744–1763: Colonial Wars and Aboriginal Peoples," in *The Atlantic Region to Confederation: A History*, Phillip A. Buckner and John G. Reid, eds (Toronto: University of Toronto Press 1994), 125–55.

6. This is likely an incomplete list and only includes individuals of whom I have a personal knowledge. Andrea Bear Nicholas was involved in litigation at an early date and before I and John Reid testified in Marshall.

7. In *R. v Drew*, for instance, the question before the court was the date at which the Mi'kmaq had occupied the south shore of Newfoundland and therefore what constitutional rights, if any, the present-day community of Conne River enjoyed, either from a treaty or aboriginal right. See The Queen v. Drew, NLSCTD at http://caselaw.canada.globe24h.com/0/0/newfoundland-and-labrador/supreme-court-of-newfoundland-and-labrador-trial-division/2003/07/17/queen-v-drew-et-al-2003-nlsctd-105.shtml. Wustukwiuk people who had used and occupied land on the south shore of the St. Lawrence River and who are associated with the Viger band posed similar types of questions. As well, since 2001 the three Mi'kmaw Gaspésie communities, Listuguj, Cascapedia, and Gaspeg have undertaken, research that is different than that done in either New Brunswick or Nova Scotia. Finally, the Prince Edward Island Mi'kmaq face a different set of problems, centred on the question of whether or not they are signatories to any of the treaties.

8. John Reid and I later published our own views of the treaties, though separately. John G. Reid, "Pax Britannica or Pax Indigena? Planter Nova Scotia (1760–1782) and Competing Strategies of Pacification," *Canadian Historical Review* 85,4 (2004): 669–92; William C. Wicken, *Mi'kmaq Treaties on Trial: History, Land, and Donald Marshall Junior* (Toronto: University of Toronto Press 2002).

9. Peter Charles Hoffer, *Law and People in Colonial America*, revised edition (Baltimore and London: 1998), 50–75.

10. Much of the following discussion follows the argument made in Wicken, *Mi'kmaq Treaties on Trial*.

11. There is a great deal of literature on this subject. However, the best-known and most widely cited analysis is Richard White, *The Middle Ground: Indians, Empires, and Republics in the Great Lakes Region, 1650–1815* (New York: Cambridge University Press 1991).

12. Wicken, *Mi'kmaq Treaties on Trial*, 218.

13. For instance, James (Sakej) Youngblood Henderson, "First Nations Legal Inheritances in Canada: the Mi'kmaq Model," *Manitoba Law Journal* 23, 1 (1996): 12–13.

14. Wicken, *Mi'kmaq Treaties on Trial*, 52–5.

15. Linda Colley, *Captives: Britain, Empire, and the World, 1600–1850* (New York: Random Books, 2002).

Primary Document

Articles of Peace and Agreement: Annapolis Royal 1726

London, England, Public Record Office, Colonial Office Series 217/5: 3r–5r

Whereas by the Articles of Peace and agreement Made & concluded upon att Boston in New England the Fifteenth Day of Decr: One Thousand Seven Hundred & twenty five by our Delegates & Representatives Sanguarum (alias Loron) Alexis Francois Xavier &

Meganumbe as appears by the Instrument then Sign'd Seal'd & Exchanged in the Presence of the Great & Generall Court or Assembly of Ye Massachusetts Bay by our Said Delegates in behalf of us the Said Indians of Penobscott, Norrdigewalk, St. Johns, Cape Sable, and the other Indian Tribes belonging to & inhabiting within these His Majesty of Great Britain's Territories of Nova Scotia & New England & by Majr Paul Mascarene Comissioner from this said Province in behalf of His Majesty by which Agreement it being requir'd tht the Said Articles Shoul'd be ratified with Full Power & Authority by an Unanimous Consent & desire of the Said Indian Tribes who are Come in Complyance with ye Articles Stipulated by our Delegates as aforesaid and do in Obedience thereunto Solemnly Confirm & ratifie ye Same & in Testimony thereof with Hearts full of Sincerity. Wee have Sign'd & Seal'd the Following Articles being Conform to what was requir'd by the Said Majr Paul Mascarene & Promise to be perform'd by our Said Delegates.

Whereas His Majesty King George by the Concession of the Most Christian King made att the Treaty of Utrecht is become ye Rightfull Possessor of the Province of Nova Scotia or Acadia According to its ancient Boundaries, wee the Said Chiefs & Representatives of ye Penobscott, Norridgewalk, St. Johns, Cape Sables & of the Other Indian Tribes Belonging to & Inhabiting within This His Majesties Province of Nova Scotia or Acadie & New England do for our Selves & the said Tribes Wee represent acknowledge His Said Majesty King George's Jurisdiction & Dominion Over the Territories of the said Province of Nova Scotia or Acadia & make our Submission to His said Majesty in as Ample a Manner as wee have formerly done to the Most Christian King.

That the Indians shall not molest any of His Majesty's Subjects or their Dependants in their Settlements already made or Lawfully to be made or in their carrying on their Trade or other affairs within the said Province.

That if there Happens any Robbery or outrage Comitted by any of our Indians the Tribe or Tribes they belong to shall Cause satisfaction to be made to ye partys Injured.

That the Indians shall not help to convey away any Soldiers belonging to His Majesty's forts, but on the contrary shall bring back any soldier they shall find endeavouring to run away.

That in case of any misunderstanding, Quarrel or Injury between the English and the Indians no private revenge shall be taken, but Application shall be made for redress according to His Majesty's Laws.

That if there are any English Prisoners amongst any of our aforesaid Tribes, wee faithfully promise that the said Prisoners shall be releasd & Carefully Conducted & delivered up to this Government or that of New England.

That in testimony of our Sincerity wee have for ourselves and in behalf of our Selves & in behalf of Our Said Indian Tribes Conforme to what was Stipulated by our Delegates at Boston as aforesaid, this day Solemnly Confirmd & ratified each & every one of the aforegoing Articles which shall be punctually observed and duly performed by Each & all of us the Said Indians. In Witness Whereof wee have before the Honourable John Doucett & Councill for this His Majesty and the Deputies of the French Inhabitants of Sd Province hereunto Sett our Hands & Seals att Annapolis Royall this 4th day of June 1726 in the twelvth year of His Majesty's Reign.

* * *

Reciprocal Promises Made by Captain John Doucett: 1726

London, England, Public Record Office, Colonial Office Series 217/4: doc. 321

This is a shortened version, which does not include a two-paragraph preamble.

Whereas the Chiefs of the Penobscott, Norrigwock, St. Johns, Cape Sable Indians and of the other Indian Tribes & their Representatives Belonging to and Inhabiting within this his Majesty's Province of Nova Scotia Confrome to the Articles Stipulated by their Delegates, Sangarumn (alias) Laurens, Alexis, Francis Xaver, & Meganumbe, at Boston in New England The Fifteenth day of December one thousand Seven hundred & twenty five have come to this His Majesty's Fort of Annapolis Royal and Ratifyed said Articles and made their Submission to his Majesty George by the grace of god of great Britain France & Ireland King Defender of the Faith &c and Acknowledged his said Majesty's Just Title this his said Province of Nova Scotia or Acadia & promised to Live peaceable with all his Majesty's Subjects & their Dependants & to performe what Further is Contained in the Severall articles of their Instruments. I do therefore in His Majesty's name for and in Behalf of this his said Government of Nova Scotia or Acadia Promise the Said Chiefs & their Respective Tribes all marks of Favour, Protection & Friendship.

And I do Further promise & in the absence of the honble the Lt. Govr of the Province in behalf of the this said Government, That the Said Indians shall not be Molested in their Persons, Hunting Fishing and Shooting & planting on their planting Ground nor in any other their lawfull occasions, By his Majesty's Subjects or their Dependants in the Exercise of their Religion Provided the Missionarys Residing amongst them have Leave from the Governor for So Doing

That if any Indians are injured by any of his Majesty's Subjects or their Dependants They shall have Satisfaction and Reparation made to them According to his Majesty's Laws whereof the Indians shall have the Benefit Equall with his Majesty's other Subjects

That upon the Indians Bringing back any Soldier Endeavouring to run away from any of His Majesty's Forts or Garrisons, the Said Indians for this Office Shall be handsomely rewarded

That as a Mark and token of a true Observation & Faithfull Performance of all and Every Article promised on his Majesty's part by the Government I have by and with the Advice of the Council for said Government Releas'd and Sett att Liberty the Indian Prisoners

Given under my hand and Seal at his Majesty's Fort of Annapolis Royall this 4th day of June in the Twelvth year of his Majesty's Reign.

John Doucett
Lieu Govr of Annapolis Royal

Questions for Consideration

1. Why did the British Crown and later the Canadian government pursue treaties with Indigenous nations? Conversely, why did the Indigenous nations pursue treaties with the British Crown and, later, the Canadian government? Did both sides achieve their intended goals? Why or why not?

2. How much bargaining power did Indigenous nations have in negotiating treaties with the British Crown and Canadian governments? How and why did this change over time?

3. What do the letters from the chiefs of the Cree Chiefs of the Plains Saskatchewan to Governor Archibald at Fort Garry reveal about 1) their motives for treating with the Canadian government? 2) the conditions then pervasive on the plains for Indigenous peoples?

4. What are some of the difficulties of historical interpretation that William Wicken identifies, when historians examine treaties between Indigenous nations and European governments? How do these difficulties affect the testimony offered by historians as "experts" in the courtroom? Given these difficulties, do you think courts are able to render good judgments on the meaning of treaties as understood by those who signed them?

5. In what ways does Wicken argue that understanding the historical context in which treaties were framed and signed is essential to interpreting them properly? Do you agree?

6. What is being agreed to in the "Articles of Peace and Agreement: Annapolis Royal 1726"? How would you explain your interpretation of this document if asked to do so in a court of law?

7. Should treaties be viewed as binding agreements between sovereign nations, or as promises extended to subject peoples on behalf of the British Crown and later the Canadian government? Whose interests have been served by treaties and why?

Further Resources

Books and Articles

Boldt, Menno, and J. Anthony Long, eds. *The Quest for Justice: Aboriginal Peoples and Aboriginal Rights*. Toronto: University of Toronto Press, 1985.

Cottam, Barry. "Compact, Contract, Covenant: Aboriginal Treaty-Making in Canada." *The Canadian Journal of Native Studies* 30, 1 (2010): 183–4

Issac, Thomas. *Aboriginal and Treaty Rights in the Maritimes: The Marshall Decision and Beyond*. Saskatoon: Purich Publishers, 2001.

Long, John. *Treaty No. 9: Making the Agreement to Share the Land in Northern Ontario in 1905*. Montreal & Kingston: McGill-Queens University Press, 2010.

Luby, Brittany. 'The Department is Going Back on These Promises': An Examination of Anishnaabe and Crown Understandings of Treaty" in *The Canadian Journal of Native Studies* 30, 2 [2010]: 203–28.

Quantick, Robin. "Natives and Settlers Now and then: Historical Issues and Current Perspectives on Treaties and Land Claims in Canada." *The Canadian Journal of Native Studies* 28, 2 (2008): 432–3.

Peters, Evelyn J. "Native People and the Environmental Regime in the James Bay and Northern Quebec Agreement," *Arctic* 52, 4 (Dec. 1999): 395–410.

Treaty 7 Elders and Tribal Council with Sarah Carter, Dorothy First Rider, and Walter Hildebrandt, eds. *The True Spirit and Original Intent of Treaty Seven.* Montreal: McGill-Queen's University Press, 1996.

Wicken, William C. *Treaties on Trial: History, Land, and Donald Marshall Junior.* Toronto: University of Toronto Press, 2002.

Printed Documents and Reports

Alfred, Taiaiake. *Peace Power Righteousness: An Indigenous Manifesto.* Toronto: Oxford University Press, 1999.

Grand Council of Micmacs, Union of Nova Scotia Indians, and Native Council of Nova Scotia. *The Mi'kmaq Treaty Handbook.* Sydney & Truro: Native Communications Society of Nova Scotia, 1987.

Grand Council of the Crees. *Never Without Consent: James Bay Crees' Stand Against Forcible Inclusion Into An Independent Quebec.* Toronto: ECW Press, 1998.

Films

Dancing Around the Table. DVD. Directed by Maurice Bulbulian. NFB, 1987.

Encounter with Saul Ralinsky, Part II: Rama Indian Reserve. DVD. Directed by Peter Pearson. NFB, 1967.

Is the Crown at War with Us? DVD. Directed by Alanis Obomsawin. NFB, 2002.

Websites

Treaties No. 1 and 2
www.aadnc aandc.gc.ca/eng/1100100028664/1100100028665

Treaty No. 3
www.aadnc-aandc.gc.ca/eng/1100100028675/1100100028679

Treaty No. 4
www.aadnc-aandc.gc.ca/eng/1100100028689/1100100028690

Treaty No. 5
www.aadnc-aandc.gc.ca/eng/1100100028699/1100100028700

Treaty No. 6

www.aadnc-aandc.gc.ca/eng/1100100028710/1100100028783

Treaty No. 7 (copy)

www.aadnc-aandc.gc.ca/eng/1100100028793/1100100028803

Treaty No. 8

www.aadnc-aandc.gc.ca/eng/1100100028813/1100100028853

Treaty No. 9 (original text)

www.archives.gov.on.ca/en/explore/online/james_bay_treaty/treaty.aspx

The Robinson-Superior Treaty (copy)

www.anishinabek.ca/download/Robinson%20Superior%20Treaty.pdf

4

War, Conflict, and Society

Introduction

The relationship between history, Indigenous peoples, war, and conflict is complicated. Until recently, stories of white women being held captive, scalping, and "blood thirsty savages" held a great deal of currency in colonial narratives of Indigenous warfare and settlement. While inaccurate, the salacious stories of white captivity and the potential for Indigenous violence have fascinated European-Canadian audiences and driven the formulation of British and Canadian colonial Indian policy.[1]

Recently, historians seeking to reclaim and make respectable the military traditions of Indigenous peoples have cast them as "long-standing allies of the Crown from the colonial era through to the twentieth century."[2] Historian J.R. Miller argues that, during the eighteenth century, relations between Indigenous and European peoples were defined by military alliances—a function of the protracted conflicts in which Europeans found themselves embroiled in North America and beyond.[3] While Indigenous peoples were undeniably involved in what are perceived as "European conflicts," they entered these struggles for their own geopolitical reasons, switching alliances between European powers and various Indigenous nations in order to secure and pursue their own interests. Brett Rushforth's piece outlines how Indigenous nations allied with the French used the Europeans' conflict with the Fox Nation to ensure that they controlled access to European goods and weapons. In doing so, Indigenous nations retained their dominant position as middlemen in the lucrative trade between Indigenous nations farther west and the French to the east. Jonathan Lainey and Tom Peace's article seeks to complicate what constituted "society" in the eighteenth century and illuminate the intricate web of relations that existed between Indigenous peoples and newcomers by looking at the life of Louis Vincent Sawatanen. These authors show that in spite of the drastic social, political, and economic changes that were taking place on Turtle Island during this period, the Wendat had a tremendous capacity for economic, cultural, and social adaptation alongside a firm determination to preserve a uniquely Wendat identity, community, and way of life. This remarkable combination of dexterity and continuity was achieved in part through the strength of Wyandot communities and extended families.

Chapter Objectives

At the end of this chapter, you should be able to

- explain why New France and its Indigenous allies went to war with the Fox;
- appreciate and articulate the subtleties of the diplomatic relationship between the French and their Indigenous allies;
- explain how and why historians' former views of the Wendat were erroneous;
- explain how individuals like Louis Vincent Sawatanen and the Wendat communities from whence he came were able to thrive in difficult circumstances;
- identify how Indigenous people shaped events as well as their own lives as the French, British, and Americans expanded their territories and influence.

Notes

1. Sarah Carter, *Capturing Women: The Manipulation of Cultural Imagery in Canada's Prairie West* (Montreal: McGill-Queen's University Press, 1997).
2. P. Whitney Lackenbauer, "Introduction," in Lackenbauer and Craig Leslie Mantle, eds, *Aboriginal Peoples and the Canadian Military:*

Historical Perspectives (Kingston: Canadian Defence Academy Press, 2007), xi.

3. J.R. Miller, *Skyscrapers Hide the Heavens: A History of Indian–White Relations in Canada*, 3rd edn (Toronto: University of Toronto Press, 2000), 123.

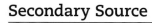

Secondary Source

Slavery, the Fox Wars, and the Limits of Alliance

Brett Rushforth

On the bitterly cold evening of 13 December 1723, Jean Becquet, master of the house at the governor's residence, called for Father Étienne Boullard. When Boullard arrived, he found an ailing Indian woman called Marguerite-Geneviève, whom he promptly baptized. Returning to his small residence at the seminary, the priest recorded what he had learned about the woman during his visit. She was 35 years old. She had a 14-year-old daughter called Marie Louise, whom he also baptized. She was a Fox Indian. And she was a slave, "captured in Fox territory by the Marquis de Vaudreuil," the governor of **New France**, "with whom she presently resides."[1]

Only two months earlier, Vaudreuil had written a letter to France congratulating himself on successful peace negotiations with Marguerite-Geneviève's people in an ongoing conflict historians call the Fox Wars. Pitting New France's Indian allies against a coalition of Fox, Sauk, Kickapoo, and Winnebago, this series of clashes claimed thousands of lives and destabilized the Upper Country for the better part of 30 years. Charged with maintaining the region's Indian alliances, Vaudreuil proudly announced that he had thwarted recent plans by his Native allies to attack Fox villages by sending a well-respected French officer to the region "to Persuade them to be Reconciled and to Live in peace."[2] As he had done many times before, Vaudreuil pressured Upper Country Indians to embrace the Fox as allies rather than enemies, seeking greater regional stability to facilitate French commercial and territorial expansion.

Governor Vaudreuil never mentioned to his French superiors that his household, like scores of others in New France, was served by Fox slaves who had been captured in the very attacks he claimed to oppose. For the previous 10 years, these slaves had trickled into Canada as allied Indians attacked Fox villages, making Fox men, women, and children the primary source of enslaved labour in the St Lawrence River Valley during the 1710s and 1720s. Because these slaves do not appear in the official reports that have informed earlier studies, their lives have been noted, if acknowledged at all, as interesting but insignificant side notes to the story of French–Indian diplomacy.[3] Yet the records discussing these slaves, produced by parish priests, notaries, and court reporters, offer a valuable new perspective on the Fox Wars.

This reassessment of the Fox Wars suggests that it was neither inherent Fox aggression nor domineering French leadership that fuelled the violence. Instead the Fox Wars grew out of a much more mundane disagreement over the limits of the emerging French–Indian alliance. Whereas French imperial officials sought to enlarge their influence in the west, connecting with an ever-growing number of commercial and military partners, those Natives already attached to the French wished to limit this expansion, blocking their enemies' access to French goods and support. As the French embraced the Fox, allied Indians violently asserted their prerogative to define the parameters of alliance, demanding that the French honour their friendship by shunning their historical enemies.

By raiding Fox villages for captives, and then giving or selling these captives to the French as slaves, [New France's Native allies] drove a deep and eventually fatal wedge between the French and their erstwhile Fox allies. French colonists' demand for Fox slaves supported this strategy, ultimately ensuring its success by alienating the Fox from French interest and finally compelling them to war. In addition to illuminating the role of Indian slavery in structuring the western alliance system, the wars also powerfully illustrate the ways in which Indians shaped the contours of the alliance to their advantage against French wishes.

Throughout the latter part of the seventeenth century, the French and the Fox shared a mutual desire for friendship. With the Iroquois threat looming, each side profited from the other's assurances of protection, and both could benefit from the trade that accompanied such relationships. But it was clear from the beginning that the French had a problem. New France's allies, including the Illinois, Ottawas, Ojibwa, Miami, and Hurons, detested the Fox. Even as these peoples needed Fox co-operation during the Iroquois Wars, they expressed deep enmity toward their Fox neighbours, seeking their exclusion from French protection and trade.

During the 1670s and 1680s, Fox villages came under attack from all these groups, sparking rounds of reprisals. These conflicts ebbed and flowed with the currents of the Iroquois threat, but animosity remained the norm. The cramped proximity forced by Iroquois attacks often sparked new violence among these historical enemies, creating a tense atmosphere in western refugee villages. Illinois, Ottawa, Ojibwa, and Huron war parties clashed with the Fox throughout the 1680s and 1690s, even as they faced a common Iroquois enemy.[4]

By the time of the general peace conference in Montreal in 1701, the Fox delegate to the peace negotiations expressed his desire to have a French presence in their territory. If the Fox "had a black robe, a blacksmith, and several Frenchmen among us," he pleaded with the French governor, "the Chippewa [Ojibwa] would not be bold enough to attack us." Although each of these peoples agreed to French alliance, the Ojibwa were not the only ones who wanted to drive the Fox out. The Illinois described the Fox as "devils on earth, they have nothing human but the shape. . . ." Still the French wanted the Fox within the alliance, so they invited the Fox to the 1701 peace as full partners.[5]

The French decision to establish a new settlement at Detroit the same year only deepened these divisions. Although never exclusive middlemen in the Great Lakes fur trade, the Ottawas, Ojibwa, and Illinois lived much closer to the French and thus could command a larger proportion of their commerce. As the French moved westward, these peoples were faced with the dual threat of having the Fox become better armed and of losing their position of strength within the region's fur trade networks.[6]

Meanwhile the absence of the Iroquois threat removed what little incentive Ottawas, Ojibwa, and Illinois felt to remain at peace with the Fox. In 1703 and 1708, Fox warriors attacked the Ojibwa near the southeastern corner of Lake Superior, killing several warriors and seizing a large number of Ojibwa captives. Counter-raids began later that year. Despite these conflicts French officers persisted in their efforts to join these peoples "together in feelings of peace and union," hoping to avoid taking sides in a dispute among peoples they considered allies.[7]

In this tense environment, the French naively invited the Fox to live among the allied peoples whose villages surrounded Detroit. Articulating his vision of an expansive western alliance, Governor Vaudreuil ordered Jacques-Charles Renaud Dubuisson, Detroit's new post commander, to "give all his attention to preventing the Indian allies from making war on one another."[8]

Instead violence erupted almost immediately. During one attack the Fox struck two Huron and Ottawa villages, capturing the wife of a powerful Ottawa chief who vowed revenge. Needing little encouragement a group of Ottawas, Hurons, Ojibwa, Illinois, Potawatomi, and some Miami surrounded the fortified Fox town near Detroit, threatening to kill all of them unless they released their prisoners and returned to their lands west of Green Bay.[9] Rather than embracing the Fox as kin like Vaudreuil had hoped, the Native alliance violently articulated their intention to define the Fox as enemies.

Besieged and badly outnumbered, the Fox desperately appealed for French mediation. At a hastily arranged meeting in late 1712, Fox War Chief Pemoussa begged French military officers for mercy. Following protocol for cementing alliances, Pemoussa offered several slaves to signify his friendly intentions, defining himself as a kinsman to the French and their allies. "Remember that we are your brothers," he said to the assembly of Native leaders.[10] In this dangerous world of symbolic diplomacy, no gift carried greater weight than a human body, and Pemoussa wisely offered slaves as his best hope to save his people.

Still, speaking for the French-allied nations, an Illinois warrior rejected Pemoussa's claim to kinship. Defined as enemies, the best [the Fox] could hope for was to be kept alive as slaves. Making one final appeal to kinship, this time depicting the Fox as the most beloved Elder in a young man's life, Pemoussa begged again: "Remember . . .

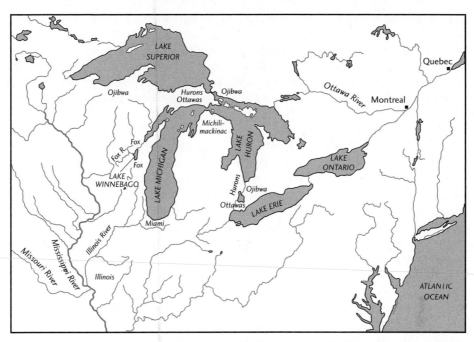

Map 4.1 Location of major participants in the Fox Wars, c. 1701. Adapted from Helen Hornbeck Tanner, ed., *Atlas of Great Lakes Indian History* (Norman, OK: University of Oklahoma Press, 1987), 32–3, 40–1; R. David Edmunds and Joseph L. Peyser, *The Fox Wars: The Mesquakie Challenge to New France* (Norman, OK: University of Oklahoma Press, 1993), 12–13; and Gilles Havard, *Empire et métissages: Indiens et Français dans le Pays d'en Haut, 1660–1715* (Paris: Les Éditions du Septentrion, 2003), 227. Drawn by Rebecca L. Wrenn. (Helen Hornbeck Tanner, ed., 2003.)

that you are our grand-nephews; it is your own blood you seem so eagerly to thirst for; would it not be more honorable to spare it, and more profitable to hold us as slaves[?]"[11]

Rejecting Pemoussa's offer of peace, the Fox's enemies surrounded and attacked them. One French observer reported that, after allowing Pemoussa a safe retreat, "all the [Fox] were cut in pieces before they could regain their weapons. The women and children were made slaves, and most of them were sold to the French."[12]

These events fit rather uneasily into the prevailing model of French–Indian relations, first developed in [Richard White's] *The Middle Ground*, which presumes a fundamental "tension between the Algonquian ideal of alliance and mediation and the French dream of force and obedience."[13] At Detroit in 1712, this formulation was turned on its head. French officials pursued a policy of mediation with the Fox, while their Algonquian-speaking allies manoeuvred for dominion over them. Rather than a cultural compromise initiated by Native diplomats, orders to mediate came from the highest levels of French imperial authority.

Indeed, Dubuisson's most notable concession to Native demands came when he agreed to participate in the bloodshed. This represented French acknowledgement of their allies' expectations. From the perspective of many allied nations, the French did not breach the terms of alliance through violence but rather when they sought mediation and peace with enemy nations.

But as violence around Detroit dragged on, French officials wearied of the fighting. From 1713 to 1716, French policy wavered between grudging support for the war against the Fox and efforts to secure a peaceful resolution. After three years of intermittent warfare, in 1716 French and Native forces defeated a large group of Fox, grinding the violence to a bloody halt.[14]

That fall, under heavy pressure from the French, the Fox and their enemies gathered in the St Lawrence River Valley to negotiate peace. Once again led by Pemoussa, the Fox arrived at Quebec hoping to restore their standing as French allies. Pemoussa performed several public displays of friendship. He gave gifts to French officers, returned prisoners to allied nations, and allowed himself to be baptized. The Fox would return prisoners and give symbolic gifts, including slaves captured in distant regions, to their fictive kin, both Native and French. Through this process they would replace the dead who had fallen, restoring the bonds of kinship severed by the war.[15]

Obviously pleased by this turn of events, Governor Vaudreuil praised the agreement.[16] To the Ottawas and other Indian peoples, however, it must have seemed the height of arrogance for the French governor to dictate how they should feel about their enemies. After all, the military commander who first proposed the armistice claimed to have the support of New France's Native allies, yet one Frenchman admitted that "he deceived himself, if he really thought so."[17] Asserting their prerogative to define the limits of the French–Indian alliance, these groups rejected French efforts to force mediation. During the following decade, they would slowly draw the French into renewed, and far more destructive, war with the Fox, limiting the expansive reach of French imperialism through strategic violence.

The 1716 treaty acknowledged the symbolic power of slaves to end French–Fox bloodshed. But if slaves offered the greatest hope for peace, they could also spark renewed warfare. The French had received scores of Fox slaves during the previous four years. By accepting these slaves, French colonists had symbolically acknowledged their enmity against the Fox, implicitly committing military support to their allies in future disputes.

Visiting Montreal two years later, a Fox delegation begged the French to "dissipate the fear which still Possessed them, by restoring to them some of their Children—that is, some of their people who were Slaves among the French."[18] Beginning in 1718 every recorded complaint made by the Fox against the French and their Native allies centred on the return of Fox captives, the most significant issue perpetuating the Fox Wars into subsequent decades.

Despite clear instructions to the contrary—issued repeatedly from Versailles and Quebec—French colonists retained and continued to acquire new Fox slaves following the 1716 peace accords. Emanating from every level of Canadian society, the French demand for slaves offered ample opportunity for Ottawa, Ojibwa, and Illinois warriors to capture Fox villagers and offer them to the French, thereby driving a wedge between these erstwhile allies. Over time the French enslavement of Fox would erode whatever hope for peace existed in 1716, sparking the second, and far more destructive, phase of the Fox Wars.

New France's appetite for Fox slaves originated in the bloody battles of 1712, when the French and their allies captured large numbers of Fox women and children. Many French officers and merchants returned from the Fox campaigns with young captives. From 1713 to 1716, about 80 Fox slaves appear in the colony's parish and court records, belonging to as many as 60 different French families. The actual number of slaves and slaveholders was certainly much higher, given the improbability that every slave and every master appear in surviving records.[19]

These Fox slaves served families in Montreal and Quebec, as well as in smaller seigneurial villages. In 1714, for example, a Sulpician priest baptized a young Fox slave, named François-Michel, who belonged to Jean Baptiste Bissot de Vincennes. Vincennes had been second-in-command in Detroit during the 1712 siege of the Fox. During the final stages of the standoff, a Fox emissary addressed him: "I will surrender myself; answer me at once, my Father, and tell me if there is quarter for our families. . . ." Vincennes responded with a promise that he knew he could not keep. According to the French report, "Sieur de Vincennes called out to them that he granted their lives and safety." When the Fox surrendered, and slaughter ensued, Vincennes gave his own sort of quarter to this young boy, who became his slave in Montreal.[20]

In another example Pierre Legardeur de Repentigny baptized his Fox slave, Mathurine, in 1713. Repentigny, a captain in the colonial troops, participated actively in several western campaigns. The potential to return home with slaves gave French military officers a personal stake in supporting violence against the Fox, but lower-ranking soldiers also benefited by obtaining Fox slaves. In Batiscan, for example, Marie Catherine Rivard-Loranger appears either as owner or godmother to several slaves from 1713 to 1716. Her son, a **voyageur** among the Illinois who fought in the early battles of the Fox Wars, returned with the Fox slaves in 1714.[21]

Occasionally, voyageurs and merchants connected to the war also obtained Fox slaves. Michel Bisaillon exemplifies this type of trader. He used his long-standing trade relationships with Illinois Indians to mobilize their support for French attacks during the first phase of the war. As a result he acquired several Fox captives that he subsequently sold as slaves to Montreal merchants. In 1717, for example, he sold a young female slave to René Bourassa, dit La Ronde for 400 livres.[22]

Many other merchants active in Detroit also acquired slaves during the early Fox campaigns, including the well-positioned Pierre Lestage, who garnered at least two young Fox slaves, Ignace and Marie-Madeleine. The children's godfather, Ignace Gamelin, also traded Indian slaves in Montreal and Detroit, acquiring one for his own household by early 1714. Pierre Biron, who supplied goods to the military during the Fox Wars, obtained a young Fox girl as his slave the same year. Called Marie-Joachim, she would serve as a house slave for nearly 20 years until her death in 1733.[23]

Many well-placed French officials also received their share of Fox slaves during the first four years of the conflict. François-Marie Bouat, a powerful Montreal judge, baptized his Fox slave, Marguerite, in 1713. In 1713 François, a Fox boy, was baptized as the slave of Augustin Lemoyne, with highly visible and powerful godparents: Charles Lemoyne de Longueuil and Catherine de Ramezay, daughter of Montreal's governor and future interim governor of the colony. Even more visible was Guillaume Gaillard, a member of New France's Superior Council and Governor Vaudreuil's close associate, who had purchased at least three Fox slaves by 1716 to serve in his home as domestics.[24]

[The] growing rift between the French and the Fox weakened French claims of the Fox as allies, subtly but steadily edging them out of the alliance just as the other Native allies had hoped. To deepen the divide, allied Indians continued to attack Fox villages in violation of the 1716 peace agreement, trading or giving slaves to French officers as tokens of alliance. The Illinois, especially, raided the Fox for captives and sold them as slaves to their French allies.[25]

Fox men, women, and children captured in these raids continued to stream into Montreal even after the French-brokered peace. Many colonists buying these slaves either hid their purchases or identified their slaves as *panis*, rather than Fox, Indians. For instance, when Joseph-Laurent Lefebvre bought a Fox slave in 1722, the notary initially recorded that she was a Fox Indian. In an apparent attempt to conceal the slave's origins, the notary then boldly struck out *Renard* and replaced it with *panise* (feminine of *panis*). With diplomats clamouring for the return of Fox prisoners, a notarized acknowledgment of a Fox slave's origins could undermine the slave owner's claim to legal possession. Despite obvious French efforts to obscure the identity of Fox slaves, nearly 100 more appear in New France's colonial records following the 1716 treaty. The distribution of these slaves, like those captured before the peace negotiations, suggests a pervasive acceptance of and demand for the enslavement of Fox Indians.[26]

These slaves performed many tasks, including domestic service, urban skilled labour, and even fieldwork. During the 1710s, for example, the tiny village of Batiscan acquired a disproportionate number of Fox slaves, who were employed in a hemp-growing scheme supported by the colony's intendant, Michel Bégon. Other Fox slaves worked on Montreal's riverfront, loading and unloading canoes for western trade. Most were house servants, many of them selling for as much as 400 livres—a third of a French officer's annual salary.[27]

During the early 1720s, the Fox four times requested French intervention to prevent the Illinois and other allied Indians from attacking their villages for captives. Finally, their patience grew thin and they retaliated with great force. Vaudreuil conceded that "the [Fox] were less in the wrong than the Ilinois for the war they have had together . . . ." The Fox, he explained to the commandant of Illinois country, "claim to have Grievances against the Illinois, because the latter detain their prisoners. I am convinced that, if they were to give satisfaction to the [Fox] on this point, it would not be difficult to induce The latter to make peace." Although Vaudreuil owned at least two Fox slaves from these very attacks, and saw many others serving his neighbours, he blamed the Illinois rather than the French colonists who made slave raiding so advantageous.[28]

By 1724 the Fox made it clear to the French that they would resume intense warfare with the Illinois and their French defenders unless Fox captives were returned. "They Are indignant," wrote Constant Le Marchand de Lignery, "because, when peace was made in 1716, they sent the illinois back Their prisoners while The illinois did not return Theirs, As had been Agreed upon in The treaty."[29]

To placate the Fox and their allies, Vaudreuil proposed an inspection of Illinois villages to determine if they held any Fox prisoners. Reporting the results of the inspection conducted in 1725, a French officer flatly declared, "Our Illinois have no Slaves belonging to the Foxes." An Illinois chief, Anakipita, offered a similarly calculated denial: "[The Fox chief] says that his Slaves have not been given back to him. Where are they? Is there a single one in our villages?" Anakipita and his French counterpart spoke a literal truth to conceal Illinois guilt in the Fox attacks. As Vaudreuil knew the disputed Fox slaves were already in French hands, far from the Illinois communities that had initially seized them.[30]

Even at this late date, the Fox still seemed willing to return to the French alliance if they could secure the return of their captives. In 1726 the Fox again approached the French, this time at Green Bay, begging for the governor to mediate these disputes. French authorities, wishing to expand trade in the area, were only too happy to oblige.[31]

Yet by this time hundreds of French colonists had given a decade of support to anti-Fox slave raids, rewarding their allies' violence with valuable goods and often with military support for the expeditions themselves. Many French post commanders had private interests in the slave trade, placing them in a poor position to negotiate a peace. And both of New France's governors who dealt with the Fox problem—Philippe de Rigaud de Vaudreuil and Charles de Beauharnois—owned a host of Indian slaves, including several Fox. Despite their need to avoid warfare among potential allies, French officials supported the Illinois, Ottawas, Ojibwa, and Hurons against the Fox.

Faced with continuing raids in violation of French assurances, and never receiving the promised return of their captives, Fox warriors finally abandoned their efforts to secure a French alliance, declaring open war on New France and all its Indian allies. In the spring of 1727 they murdered a party of seven French soldiers, launching a series of attacks. These new raids bred deep and mutual resentment among the French, their allies, and the Fox, finally putting an end to French–Fox efforts to expand the Upper Country alliance.[32]

The warfare that followed brutalized the Fox. Convinced by western post commanders to pursue the war wholeheartedly, French authorities invested soldiers and money to crush a people they had once called children. From 1728 to 1731, French–Indian war parties scored a series of victories over Fox warriors, but each triumph proved ephemeral, followed shortly by a Fox resurgence. Frustrated and facing pressure from his superiors, Beauharnois issued an order for his soldiers and his allies to "kill [the Fox] without thinking of making a single Prisoner, so as not to leave one of the race alive in the upper Country." In the process, Beauharnois hoped to maintain the supply of slaves that had been one of the Fox Wars' greatest benefits to his colony (and to his own household: he owned at least eight Fox slaves). "If [the Sieur de Villiers] is obliged to exterminate the Men," he added, "the women and Children who remain will be brought here, Especially the Children."[33]

This bloody contest exacted a costly toll from the Fox, who dwindled from a population of several thousand in the 1710s to only a few hundred by the mid-1730s. Yet, this victory came at a high price for the French. Not only did thousands of men, women, and children die in the conflict, but the Fox's retaliation limited French commercial and imperial expansion, blocking New France's westward reach just as its allies had hoped to do.[34]

During the height of the fighting, New France's intendant, Gilles Hocquart, sent a letter and a gift to his friend, a Monsieur de Belamy, in La Rochelle, France. The

Slave of Fox Indians or Népissingué slave, ca. 1732, anonymous. (Estampes et photographie, OF-4(A)-FOL, Bibliothèque nationale de France.)

letter contained "news of the defeat of the Foxes" by the French and their Native allies, detailing the heroics of the French officer who had led the charge. Sent on the same ship, Hocquart's gift supplied tangible evidence of the news. He instructed the captain of the ship to "remit to M. de Belamy a Fox slave" who was on board.[35]

In a similar move, Beauharnois, the colony's governor, apparently sent a Fox slave to his brother, François, who served as the intendant of Rochefort, France. As he had done with at least one African slave from Saint Domingue, Beauharnois likely registered his slave with French authorities, claiming that he brought the slave to France "to have him instructed in the Catholic religion and to have him learn a trade." Rather than returning to the Americas with improved skills, however, Beauharnois's Fox slave remained in France until his death, eventually encountering an artist who rendered his dubious likeness.[36]

Like these unfortunate survivors of the Fox Wars, hundreds of slaves entered New France as tokens of alliance between that colony and its Native allies. These slaves permeated, and powerfully influenced, the history of the Fox Wars. When the Fox wanted to forge an alliance with their attackers in 1712 [and when they made peace in 1716], they offered slaves. When Fox diplomats pressured the French for greater support, it was invariably to recover those of their nation captured by enemies. Perhaps most significantly, when Indian allies perceived that the French wanted them to embrace the hated Fox, they used slave raids to register their dissatisfaction with the French, defining the limits of alliance through strategic violence.

This violence allowed New France's Indian allies to exert their control over the alliance system, blocking French expansion whenever it threatened to strengthen their enemies. When French officials sought to bring the Fox into the alliance, their allies fought what they perceived to be a betrayal of their friendship. By raiding the Fox for slaves, and then placing these slaves into French hands, Illinois, Ottawa, Ojibwa, and Huron warriors alienated their Fox enemies from their French allies, drawing the two sides into war.

By shifting the angle of vision from French imperial aims to the local objectives of their Indian allies, it becomes difficult to view intercultural relations in binary terms, with Euro-Americans on one side, Indians on the other, and a world of mutual invention in between on a middle ground. This was a much more complicated world where fault lines formed between peoples with competing interests but not necessarily between those with incomprehensible cultures. Through a process of negotiation that White describes so elegantly, Vaudreuil and Pemoussa found a common ground on which to work out their differences. Yet the relatively similar cultures of the Fox and the Ottawas could not.

The Fox Wars also highlight important divisions within the French and Algonquian societies that generally constitute the units of analysis in the history of the Upper Country. Personal interest, overlapping spheres of authority, and local demands combined to make French imperial policy highly complex and difficult to predict. In the 1710s and 1720s, for example, the closer one got to Versailles the more likely one would be to support generous mediation with the Fox. Driven by their own set of interests, post commanders in the Upper Country clamoured for war, whereas governors and crown officials ordered peace.

"Algonquian" offers an even more problematic western bracket for the middle ground. The very fact of war between the Fox and their neighbours calls into question the presumed unity of the region's Algonquian-speaking peoples. Despite French insistence that Algonquian peoples shared the bonds of kinship as children of a French father, the Natives themselves had other ideas. When Pemoussa expressed his concurrence with the French vision of inclusive Algonquian kinship, his would-be brothers denied his claims and violently enforced the divisions they wished to maintain.

By doing so these Indians ensured that they, rather than the French, would determine the limits of the Upper Country alliance. They also defined its character. But if this alliance was "largely Algonquian in form and spirit," that is not because it reflected an Algonquian culture of mediation rather than a French culture of "force and obedience."[37] Such false dichotomies obscure the intimate connections between warfare and alliance that placed the slave trade at the heart of the Fox Wars. Like Marguerite-Geneviève—a Fox slave serving a French governor who wanted peace with her people—all Fox captives embodied the tensions between mediation and violence that riddled both Algonquian and French societies. During the Fox Wars and beyond, Upper Country Indians used these tensions to their advantage, compelling their French father to accept their enemies as his own.

Notes

1. Baptism, 13 Dec. 1723, in Gaetan Morin, ed., *Répertoire des actes de baptême, mariage et sépulture du Québec ancien, 1621–1799*, CD-ROM, record no. 65055. Registres Notre-Dame-de-Québec, 13 Dec.1723, Family History Library, Salt Lake City, Utah; Marcel Trudel, *Dictionnaire des esclaves et de leurs propriétaires au Canada français*, nouvelle édition revue et corrigée (Ville LaSalle, QC: Hurtubise, 1990), 141. Marguerite-Geneviève's 1725 burial record indicates that she was still Vaudreuil's slave two years later (burial, 2 Oct. 1725, in Morin, *Repertoire*, no. 73772).

2. Vaudreuil au ministre, 2 Oct. 1723, in Correspondence générale, Canada, série C11A, Vol. 45, fol. 136–41v, Le Centre des archives d'outre-mer, Aix-en-Provence, France; Vaudreuil to French minister, 2 Oct. 1723, in Reuben Gold Thwaites, ed., *Collections of the State Historical Society of Wisconsin* (Madison: State Historical Society of Wisconsin, 1902), 16: 431 (quotation).

3. Only one historian of the Fox Wars has even acknowledged the slave trade: Joseph L. Peyser, "The Fate of the Fox Survivors: A Dark Chapter in the History of the French in the Upper Country, 1726–1737," *Wisconsin Magazine of History* 73, 2 (Winter 1989–90): 83–110.

4. R. David Edmunds and Joseph L. Peyser, *The Fox Wars: The Mesquakie Challenge to New France* (Norman, OK: Oklahoma University Press, 1993), 14–17; Louis Hennepin, *A New Discovery of a Vast Country in America* (1698,

repr., Chicago: A.C. McClurg, 1903), 1: 134; Claude Charles LeRoy, Sieur de Bacqueville de la Potherie, in Emma Helen Blair, ed. and trans., *The Indian Tribes of the Upper Mississippi Valley and Region of the Great Lakes . . .* (Cleveland: A.H. Clark Co., 1911), 1: 356–72.

5. Gilles Havard, *The Great Peace of Montreal of 1701: French-Native Diplomacy in the Seventeenth Century*, trans. Phyllis Aronoff and Howard Scott (Montreal & Kingston: McGill-Queen's University Press, 2001), esp. Ch. 5; appendix to W. Vernon Kinietz, *The Indians of the Western Great Lakes: 1615–1760* (Ann Arbor: University of Michigan Press, 1965), 383 ("devils on earth").

6. Lettre de Lamothe Cadillac au Ministre à propos de l'établissement du Detroit, 18 Oct. 1700, in série C11A, 14: 56–9, Le Centre des archives d'outre-mer.

7. Edmunds and Peyser, *Fox Wars*, 59–61 (quotation, 59). For 1703 and 1708 raids, see Réponse de Vaudreuil aux Indiens, 29 July 1709, in série C11A, 30: 85–92v (quotation, 89), Le Centre des archives d'outre-mer.

8. Vaudreuil à Dubuisson, 13 Sept. 1710, in série C11A, 31: 79v, Le Centre des archives d'outre-mer. Vaudreuil au ministre, 1710, in série C11A, 31: 81–8v, Le Centre des archives d'outre-mer.

9. Edmunds and Peyser, *Fox Wars*, 64–71.

10. Pierre François Xavier de Charlevoix, *History and General Description of New France*, ed. and trans. John Gilmary Shea (New York: F.P. Harper, 1900), 5: 260.

11. Charlevoix, *History*, 5: 261, 263.

12. Dubuisson to governor, [1712], "Official Report . . . to the Governor General of Canada . . . 1712 . . . ," in Thwaites, ed., *Wis. Hist. Coll.*, 16, 282.

13. Richard White, *The Middle Ground: Indians, Empires, and Republics in the Great Lakes Region, 1650–1815* (Cambridge: Cambridge University Press, 1991), 145.

14. See documents in Thwaites, *Wis. Hist. Coll.*, 16: 345.

15. Vaudreuil au Conseil de Marine, in série C11A, 36: 59–60v, Le Centre des archives d'outre-mer; baptism, 1 Dec. 1716, Sainte-Famille de Boucherville, Archives nationales du Québec, Centre régional de Montréal. For treaty, see Délibération du Conseil de Marine sur des lettres de Vaudreuil et Louvigny, 28 Dec. 1716, in série C11A, 36: 280v, Le Centre des archives d'outre-mer; Vaudreuil to the Council of the Marine, 14 Oct. 1716, ibid., 36: 71–4v; Thwaites, *Wis. Hist. Coll.*, 16: 341–4, 343 (quotation).

16. Vaudreuil au Conseil de Marine, 30 Oct. 1716, in série C11A, 36: 59–9v, Le Centre des archives d'outre-mer.

17. Perrot, in Blair, *Indian Tribes of the Upper Mississippi*, 1:268; Charlevoix, *History*, 5: 306.

18. Vaudreuil to Council, 30 Oct. 1718, in Thwaites, *Wis. Hist. Coll.*, 16: 377–8.

19. Morin, *Répertoire*, records for "renard," "renarde," "renards," "outagami," and "outagamis"; supplemented by Trudel, *Dictionnaire*, 7–263.

20. Baptism, 2 Feb. 1714, in Morin, *Repertoire*, no. 44212. For Vincenne at the Fox siege, see [Gaspard-Joseph Chaussegros de Léry], "1712: Another Account of the Siege of Detroit," in Thwaites, *Wis. Hist. Coll.*, 16: 294 (quotations).

21. Baptism, 21 Sept. 1713, in Morin, *Répertoire*, no. 44145; Registres Notre-Dame-de-Montréal, film 111, Archives nationales du Québec, Centre régional de Montréal. For Repentigny's activities, see Paul-André Dubé, "Legardeur de Repentigny, Pierre," in *Dictionary of Canadian Biography*, Vol. 2, s.v. "Legardeur." For Rivard-Loranger, see baptism, 17 Feb. 1714, in Morin, *Répertoire*, no. 7941; baptism, 13 Jan. 1715, ibid., no. 7962; Trudel, *Dictionnaire*, 7.

22. Francis Jennings, "Bisaillon (Bezellon, Bizaillon), Peter," *Dictionary of Canadian Biography*, Vol. 3, s.v. "Bisaillon"; sale dated 28 Nov. 1717, Greffe Barrette (Montreal), Archives nationales du Québec, Centre régional de Montréal.

23. For Gamelin, see baptisms, 21 Sept. 1713, in Registres Notre-Dame-de-Montréal, film 111, Archives nationales du Quebéc, Centre régional de Montréal. For Gamelin's slave trading, see Brett Rushforth, "Savage Bonds: Indian Slavery and Alliance in New France" (PhD dissertation, University of California, Davis, 2003), 141–2. For Gamelin's own slave, see baptism, 11 Feb. 1714, in Morin, *Répertoire*, no. 44219. For Biron, see baptism, 19 May 1714, Notre-Dame-de-Montréal, Family History Library film no. 375842; burial, 14 Feb. 1733, ibid.; trial beginning 17 July 1725, in Les dossiers de la Juridiction royale de Montréal, Cote TL4, S1, file no. 053-3159, Archives nationales du Québec, Centre regional de Montréal.

24. Baptism, 21 Sept. 1713, in Morin, *Répertoire*, no. 44146; baptism, 3 June 1713, ibid., no. 44087; baptism, 26 Nov. 1713, ibid., no. 63501; baptism, 9 July 1719, ibid., no. 64333; Trudel, *Dictionnaire*, 331.

25. See Vaudreuil to French Minister, 2 Oct. 1723, in Thwaites, *Wis. Hist. Coll.*, 16: 428.

26. For Lefebvre, see sale of 7 Oct. 1722, Greffe Barrette (Montreal), Archives nationales du Québec, Centre régional de Montréal.

27. For hemp, see Rushforth, "Savage Bonds," 71–3. For riverfront, see trial beginning 13 June 1728, in file no. 059-3432, Les dossiers de la Juridiction royale de Montréal. For prices, see, for example, sale of 7 Oct. 1722, Greffe Barrette (Montreal), Archives nationales du Québec, Centre régional de Montréal; "Vente d'une Sauvagesse nommee Angélique, de la nation des Renards," 5 Oct. 1733, in Greffe Dubreuil, Family History Library; "Vente d'une Renarde de nation nommee Therese," 14 Sept. 1737, in Greffe Boisseau, ibid.; "Vente d'une femme âgée de 36 ans, Sauvagesse de nation renarde, esclave," 31 Oct. 1740, in Greffe Pinguet de Vaucour, ibid.

28. Vaudreuil to French Minister, 2 Oct. 1723, in Thwaites, *Wis. Hist. Coll.*, 16: 430. Vaudreuil to Boisbriant, 17 Aug. 1724, in Thwaites, *Wis. Hist. Coll.*, 16: 442–3 (quotation). Baptism, 13 Dec. 1723, Notre-Dame-de-Québec, Family History Library; Trudel, *Dictionnaire*, 407.

29. De Lignery to Boisbriant, 23 Aug. 1724, in Thwaites, *Wis. Hist. Coll.*, 16: 445.

30. Du Tisné to Vaudreuil, 14 Jan. 1725, in Thwaites, *Wis. Hist. Coll.*, 16: 451.

31. For the 1726 meeting, see Lignery à Deliette, 15 June 1726, in série C11A, 48: 415-18v, Le Centre des archives d'outre-mer.

32. Conseil de marine à Perriers, 22 July 1737, in série B, 50: 543, Le Centre des archives d'outre-mer; Beauharnois et Depuy au ministre, 25 Oct. 1727, in série C11A, 49: 48-49v, ibid.; Beauharnois à Liette, 20 Aug. 1737, ibid., 49: 120–1.

33. Beauharnois to French Minister, 1 July 1733, in Thwaites, *Wis. Hist. Coll.*, 17: 182–3. For Beauharnois's Fox slaves, see Trudel, *Dictionnaire*, 276–7.

34. Charlevoix, *History and General Description of New France*, 5: 256–7. For Fox population, see Résumés de lettres concernant les Renards, n.d., 1733, in série C11A, 60: 448–63, Le Centre des archives d'outre-mer.

35. Hocquart au ministre, 14 Nov. 1730, in série C11A, 53: 207-8v, Le Centre des archives d'outre-mer. Belamy never received his gift, however, since the ship wrecked on its first day of sailing from Quebec (see Beauharnois et Hocquart au ministre, 15 Jan. 1731, in série C11A, 54: 3–9v, Le Centre des archives d'outre-mer).

36. Archives départementales de la Charente-Maritime, La Rochelle, série B, Vol. 225, fol. 2–3 (quotation, 3). Transcript, film C-9182, National Archives of Canada.

37. White, *Middle Ground*, 143, 145.

Primary Document

Baptisms, 21 September 1713[7]

B Marg Marguerite Guichard	On the twentieth of September of the year seventeen hundred and thirteen was baptized marie marguerite nee [. . .] daughter of jean guichard, master surgeon, and marguerite gerbau, his wife. the godfather was mr. françois poulain and the godmother miss marguerite la morille daughter of [. . .] la morille [. . .].
	[signatures] Guichard [. . .] Poulin marguerite la morille Belmont priest
B Ignace Lamage	On the twenty-first of september of the year seventeen hundred and thirteen was baptized ignace lamage, roughly seven years old, from the fox nation living in the service of mr. Lestage a town merchant. The godfather was ignace gamelin, the godmother miss françoise le maître wife of mr. guillemin.
	[signatures] gamelin [. . .] guillimin Belmont pr.

B Marie Medelene Lamagelle	On the twenty-first of september of the year seventeen hundred and thirteen was baptized marie madelene lamagelle, roughly seven years old, of the fox nation also living in the service of the aforementioned mr. Lestage. The godfather was mr. Ignace gamelan. The godmother Marie Trudeau, wife of mr. Arnault.
	[signatures] Guillimin Marie [. . .] Belmont pr.
B Mathurine Lamagelle	On the twenty-first of september of the year seventeen was baptized Mathurine Lamagelle, roughly seven years old of the fox nation, living in the service of mr. Serapentigny. The godfather was mr. charles guillimin town merchant. The godmother mrs. agathe de [. . .] Wife of mr. serapentigny.
	[signatures] Agathe [. . .] Guillimin Belmont pr.
B Marg Lamagelle	On the twenty-first of september of the year seventeen hundred and thirteen was baptized Marguerite Lamagelle, roughly seven years old, of the fox nation, living in the service of mr. Charles de [. . .] The godfather was mr. charles guillimin, the godmother mrs. Agathe de [. . .].
	[signatures] Agathe de [. . .] Guillimin Belmont pr.
B Marg Lamagelle	On the twenty-first of september of the year seventeen hundred and thirteen was baptized Marguerite Lamagelle, roughly six years old, of the fox nation, living in the service of mr. Boriat. The godfather was françois le pallieur, son of Mr. Michel Le pallieur. The godmother Catherine Le pallieur also daughter of the aforementioned Mr. Le pallieur.
	[signatures] Lepallieur [. . .] le pallieur Belmont priest

Note

1. This baptismal register was transcribed and translated by Geoff Read. Illegible words are indicated by [. . .] and names as signatures by [signature].

Secondary Source

Louis Vincent Sawatanen: A Life Forged by Warfare and Migration[1]

Jonathan Lainey and Thomas Peace

At Indian Lorette, Louis Vincent, one of the Chiefs of the Hurons or Wyandots of that village, and father of the Grand Chief now in England. He was educated at Dartmouth College, and in the latter part of his life employed himself as a schoolmaster.[2]

This obituary appeared in Salem, Massachusetts's local newspaper, *The Salem Gazette*, on 17 May 1825. It recounts the life of an extraordinary man. Louis Vincent Sawatanen was a chief of the Wendat nation's council and a relative of the Grand Chief, as well as a college graduate and schoolteacher. Over his nearly 80 years, he witnessed the fall of France's North American empire, the rise of the United States, and the evolution of a new political culture within a space increasingly called British North America. Despite the significant geopolitical reorientation that these events brought to northeastern North America, Sawatanen's obituary reveals that they were not as transformative as we might assume. This short biographical sketch, published in coastal Massachusetts, nearly 300 kilometers from his home in Jeune-Lorette and 250 kilometres from his alma mater at Dartmouth College, suggests that Sawatanen's death resonated beyond his local community to other jurisdictions in the northeast, transcending the colonial boundaries that defined British North America. In permeating colonial borders, defined through imperial and colonial warfare, his obituary presents another way of seeing this period of the region's history. Though Sawatanen and a number of his Wendat kin and neighbours participated in, and helped define, the events that shaped the colonial boundaries between British North America and the United States from the 1770s to the 1820s, the Wendat—as well as their other Indigenous neighbours—continued to live in a world beyond either of these imposed colonial realities. While the northeast was being carved up by imperial and settler colonial interests, Sawatanen, and his kin and community, continued to live in a unified space defined broadly as northeastern North America.

The Wendat and Jeune-Lorette in the Eighteenth Century

Born at Lorette around 1745 to Vincent Aronchiouann (c. 1725–1762), a Wendat man, and Marguerite Bergevin, a Canadien woman, Sawatanen was the product of the community in which he grew up.[3] Lorette was a Wendat village allied with a Jesuit mission, 13 kilometres from the colonial centre of New France at Quebec. The community was small, measuring only one kilometre wide by three-and-a-half kilometres long, with between 150 and 200 people. Its growth was constrained by the expanding presence of French farms and poor soil quality. As a result of its size and location, the Wendat needed to draw on land and resources beyond the village's boundaries. In doing so, they expanded their influence both around Quebec and also more regionally across the northeast.

The size and location of the village were a result of the Wendat's longer history. Though the Wendat had important ties to this place before the French arrived in North America, Sawatanen's ancestors permanently moved into the St Lawrence Valley during the 1650s and 1660s. Their eastward migration from the shores of Georgian Bay followed decades of devastating European-introduced disease and warfare with the Haudenosaunee Confederacy (People of the Long House/Five Nations Iroquois). Although French Catholic influence was important in shaping their decision to move nearer to Quebec, we should be careful not to assign it too much weight.[4] Of at least equal significance were the Algonquin and other Indigenous peoples living north of the river. They accommodated the new permanent Wendat presence, building on alliance structures that predated the French arrival.[5]

Many Wendat were reluctant to interact with the French missionaries. Those who did not want to live near the French—the majority—chose one of two options. The first group moved west, strengthening their relationship with Anishinaabe trading partners on the northern shore of Lake Huron. The second group, who appear less frequently in the historical record, were either taken captive or chose to join

Haudenosaunee communities south of Lake Ontario. Though enemies, as another Iroquoian-speaking people the Haudenosaunee shared many linguistic and cultural similarities that would have helped this transition. Importantly, as Kathryn Labelle has shown, with the exception of those taken captive, Wendat decisions about migration were intentional and were often reached based on deeply held and long-lasting relationships.[6]

In truth then, there was no one decision about where and when to relocate; nor did the choices made break down clearly along tribal lines. Before 1650, the Wendat comprised a confederacy of four tribes: the Attignaouantan (bear), Attingneenongnahac (cord), Arendaronnon (rock), and Tahontaenrat (deer).[7] Initially, many members of the Attignaouantan, Attingneenongnahac, and Arendaronnon tribes moved to Quebec with the Jesuits. Warfare throughout the 1660s and 1670s led many people to leave while, conversely, a considerable number of Haudenosaunee moved into the community.[8] By 1680, the community had a half-dozen times, and considerable in- and out-migration left Attingneenongnahac people as the village's primary Wendat residents.[9]

As the Wendat migrated east, the French migrated west across the Atlantic. It is important to remember that the French population at Quebec was less than 1000 people when the approximately 600 Wendat arrived. Indeed, it would be another 13 years before the French Crown assumed direct administration of the struggling colony. In comparison with their Indigenous neighbours, therefore, it is incorrect to see the French as having more power or control—let alone sovereignty—over the region. Nonetheless, in addition to conflict with the Haudenosaunee, the relatively rapid expansion of French farms was influential. Each time the village moved it was located further and further from the St Lawrence and Quebec, while at the same time the Wendat became more integrated into the rural life of the colony. As both communities established themselves, the two peoples strengthened ties with each other. Not only were the Wendat allied with the Jesuits, they also frequently participated in French military endeavours and, by the time Sawatanen was born, their village was surrounded by Canadien farms.

Living so close to the French required adaptation. When they lived on the shores of Georgian Bay the Wendat were primarily an agricultural people. They lived in relatively large fortified villages built of longhouses and extensive fields of maize, beans, squash, and sunflowers growing beyond their village walls. By Sawatanen's lifetime, however, the Wendat had adopted a more moditional economy.[10] Although the community near Quebec initially lived in longhouses, by mid-century no fortifications divided Wendat and French spaces and the Wendat lived in French-style houses.[11] The Wendat continued to farm, though with significant modifications. The Wendat raised livestock and, in addition to the plants listed above, harvested European crops such as wheat and rye. Hunting and fishing also took on greater importance, becoming central to the village's economy by the end of the century. Additionally, the Wendat produced or harvested goods for Quebec's market economy and supported French military endeavours, serving as guides and producing essential equipment (snowshoes, canoes, paddles, etc . . .).[12] With such a small land base, the community capitalized on its position near a large colonial centre and market to ensure it had the resources to sustain itself.

In spite of living so close to the French, the Wendat remained culturally and linguistically distinct. In the middle of the American Revolution, the German chaplain Friedrich Valentin Melsheimer stated that the Wendat were continuing to use their language to communicate among themselves, and they could be easily distinguished—being much larger and stronger—from their French neighbours.[13] That same year, another German named August du Roi met the Wendat during a public audience with the colony's governor general. Like Melsheimer, he was struck by their poor French language skills, large size, and muscular and swarthy bodies. He specifically noted their long hair and carefully shaved heads, their painted faces and bodies, and their pierced and decorated ears and noses. Even their stare left an impression: "Their eyes have a remarkable brilliancy and fire."[14]

Wendat naming practices also remained distinct. Known to most of the colonial world by his French name (Louis Vincent), to the Wendat he was known as Sawatanen. Though we cannot be certain of its meaning, which likely changed over time, some believe it means "man of memory" and was passed along to subsequent generations through family lines.[15] Prosper Vincent, the great grandson of Louis Vincent's uncle and the first Wendat to be ordained a Catholic priest, carried the name at the end of the nineteenth century.[16] Much like his earlier namesake, Prosper Vincent served as an important liaison between Wendat and French worlds, suggesting that anyone bearing this name may have played a role in maintaining the community's memory and history.[17]

For well over a century and a half, then, the Wendat lived beside the French, allied with the Jesuits, while maintaining a tribal system of governance. Much like Sawatanen's ancestors, the clan remained the central social institution. The Wendat continued to belong to exogamous clans, determined through their mother's family line. This grouping formed their extended family and their principal allegiance. Over time their names and composition have changed. In the mid-eighteenth century, there were at least three clans at Lorette: Turtle, Vulture, and Wolf.[18] Though we know little about how this system worked, the clan structure likely shaped the relationships that Sawatanen, and others, developed as they moved throughout the northeast and Great Lakes.

The Vincents: A Well-Connected Family

By the early eighteenth century, Sawatanen's family had risen to prominence in the colonial world. Family members appear frequently in the historical record, both in reference to local events and as key actors in regional political and military campaigns. Many of the actions in which the name Vincent appears resonate strongly with the suggested meaning of Sawatanen's name—"man of memory"—involving the transfer of wampum or the preservation of diplomatic messages. As the century progressed and the nineteenth century developed, members of this family increasingly occupied important cultural and political positions within village life.

Early in the century, the historical record refers only to men named "Vincent." Most likely, these references were to Sawatanen's grandfather, Vincent Onehatetaionk (c. 1700–1764), who would have been an elder member of the community at the time, rather than his father, Vincent Aronchiouan (c. 1725–1762), who died in his late thirties. One of the earliest references to a "Vincent" comes from the 1740s when, upon learning that some of the community's wampum belts had gone missing at Kanesatake, Onehatetaionk declared their council fire extinguished and took the remaining belts back to Lorette. This was a significant decision. Leaders from Kanesatake complained that "since their fire had been removed, they no longer had any credit with their youth" and "that there was nothing they could do to respond."[19] On another occasion, five years later, when Sawatanen was just an infant, warriors from the community joined the French and Mi'kmaq in a vain attempt to retake Acadia. Capturing a merchant vessel, Onehatetaionk took its captain—William Pote—captive and brought him back to Quebec. According to Pote's journal, Onehatetaionk boasted that he was "In Subjection to no king nor prince In ye Universe."[20] Taken together, these early references suggest that the Vincent family played a prominent role in maintaining and developing regional relationships between their community and neighbouring Indigenous societies.

This continued throughout the eighteenth century. During Pontiac's War, an Indigenous uprising that nearly removed the British from the Great Lakes and Ohio Valley, a Wendat man named Vincent was part of a delegation from the St Lawrence Valley that carried four wampum belts to "open the path in Upper Canada that Pontiac, king of the Natives, had blocked." Put another way: the valley's Indigenous peoples asked those of the Great Lakes to respect the peace they had recently made with the British.[21] Laurentian Indigenous peoples had a clear interest in ensuring that the treaties of neutrality and alliance, agreed to in 1760 following the British conquest of New France, were maintained. Without them, these communities were vulnerable to British reprisals for violence further west.

The presence of a Wendat man in this delegation was not by chance. Although they left the shores of Lake Huron in the mid-seventeenth century, the Wendat maintained an extensive diplomatic network throughout the northeast and Great Lakes. These relationships were likely enhanced by connections to Wendat who had moved west rather than east during the 1640s and 1650s. The noted eighteenth-century historian Pierre-François-Xavier de Charlevoix observed in the 1720s that "the Wendat, who hardly comprise a Nation, and reduced to two small mediocre villages many miles apart, no less remain the soul of all the councils, whenever they encompass more general affairs."[22] Note Charlevoix's choice of words: the opinion of the Wendat was solicited beyond purely local affairs. It was this role in northeastern and Great Lakes affairs that the Wendat, often helped by the Vincent family, continued to play throughout the eighteenth and nineteenth centuries.

Regional Relationships during 40 Years of Warfare[23]

Born into a world contested by empire, during the War of the Austrian Succession (1740–48), Sawatanen's life was shaped by warfare. Living in close proximity to France's administrative capital, no one at Lorette could escape the violence that erupted between European empires in the latter half of the eighteenth century. Though the War of the Austrian Succession began as a conflict over continental concerns, it quickly extended to North America. The Wendat participated alongside the French by building necessary equipment and fighting in campaigns as far away as Nova Scotia.

The war ended in a stalemate and shortly thereafter France and Britain renewed their conflict. This time, though, it was sparked in the Ohio Valley as the two empires' westward expansion collided.

This war, the Seven Years' War (1755–63), was transformative. Though France had some initial success in the war's early years, by the late 1750s Britain had the upper hand. Beginning with the fall of the fortified French town at Louisbourg (1758), the conflict ended in North America with Britain's successful capture of Quebec (1759) and Montreal (1760). Though Sawatanen was only a young boy when the community was forced to abandon their homes during the winter of 1759, these conflicts shaped his experiences over the coming decades. The British conquest of New France brought Anglophone and Francophone colonial worlds together, providing Sawatanen with opportunities that would have been unavailable in earlier decades.

Wendat warriors were heavily invested in protecting Quebec. They joined over 1000 Indigenous warriors who had come to the Plains of Abraham to defend French interests. In the aftermath of the conflict, though, the Wendat quickly made peace with the British. From the war's start, the British sought to sever France's Indigenous alliances. Central to this goal was the newly created Indian Department. Coinciding with the outbreak of war, this imperial department centralized the Crown's relationships with northeastern Indigenous peoples, moving Britain away from policies shaped by individual colonies towards a more overarching imperial approach. The department's superintendent, Sir William Johnson, actively sought Indigenous neutrality as British troops advanced on French strongholds. As British troops increasingly gained the upper hand, Laurentian Indigenous peoples began to consider neutrality, or even building new alliances with the British, as a necessary path forward. In 1760, after the fall of Quebec and as British troops descended on Montreal, the Wendat made their peace through treaty three days before the French capitulated.[24] Another treaty at Kahnawake on 15 and 16 September, made with the Seven Fires—a confederacy of Indigenous peoples living in the St Lawrence Valley—solidified this alliance.

Peace with the British resulted in little immediate change. The Wendat continued their moditional economy, anchored in hunting, fishing, agriculture, and artisanal craft production. Broader changes were afoot, however. The Jesuit presence in the community was under threat. During the 1760s and early 1770s, the British routinely discussed banning the Order, which was globally suppressed by the Vatican in 1773. The Jesuits' important role within Indigenous communities—often as agents of empire—meant that this wider context needed to be carefully negotiated. The British decided on compromise. Missionaries in place in 1760 would be allowed to remain, but no new recruits were welcomed. By 1800, the Order had been entirely removed from the colony.[25]

As Jesuit influence declined, Sawatanen and his brother Bastien left Lorette to seek out further education.[26] The Jesuit Order prized teaching and learning, and though it is difficult to be certain, with their impending demise it seems likely that the Wendat wanted this aspect of their relationship with the missionaries to continue. On their way to meet with Sir William Johnson about attending school, the boys met two missionaries from Moors Indian Charity School recruiting at the Mohawk village of Kahnawake. Together with eight others from that community,

Sawatanen and Bastien headed off to Moors Indian Charity School and Dartmouth College (an institution newly created from the Charity School for the purposes of higher education).[27] A few months after their arrival, the school's founder, Eleazar Wheelock, commended the two Wendat boys. Reflecting his own biases about Indigenous cultures, he praised their virtue and skill: "[they] appeared to have an uncommon thirst for Learning, have been diligent at their Studies, and have made good Proficiency for the Time therein. They appear to be rational. Manly Spirited, courteous, graceful and Obliging, far beyond What I have found common to Indians."[28]

Although Wheelock had only known Sawatanen a couple of months, his description was accurate. Sawatanen's linguistic abilities reveal that he was highly skilled and well trained. Sawatanen could read, write, and speak Wendat, Mohawk, Abenaki, English, and French. It is possible that Sawatanen developed these skills at Wheelock's schools, where he had the chance to learn European languages as well as interact with Indigenous peoples from elsewhere in the region. It is more likely, however, that he acquired them during his childhood. Not only might he have learned French from his mother and from French neighbours living near Lorette, but the village's relationship with the Jesuits and its role as part of broader Indigenous networks likely helped him to acquire Latin, and Iroquoian and Algonquian languages. When we add to this the languages he would have been required to learn at school, such as Greek and possibly Hebrew, it appears that Sawatanen was a polyglot with an unusual gift for languages. In an era when most people were illiterate, he was uniquely suited to move between Indigenous and French and English colonial worlds.

These skills were quickly put to work when war broke out again in the mid-1770s. During the American Revolution Sawatanen worked for the Continental Congress as an interpreter and ambassador. In 1776, he returned to the St Lawrence Valley with the two missionaries who had recruited him four years earlier to encourage the Seven Fires to side with the Congress.[29] In 1778, he was paid to interpret for representatives of the rebelling colonies and the Penobscot, Wulstukwuik, and Mi'kmaq along the Atlantic coast.[30] Given the role his grandfather had played in the region decades earlier, and Sawatanen's apparent facility in Algonquian languages, his work during the Revolution suggests that the Vincents had a long-standing relationship with these people.

Sawatanen continued his studies as warfare raged throughout the northeast. In 1781, he completed the college's academic program, becoming the first Indigenous student from the St Lawrence Valley and Lower Great Lakes to graduate from a colonial college, a rare accomplishment. By this time only 50 Indigenous people had even attended a colonial college; by 1800 only five had graduated.[31] Just before Sawatanen left the college for a final time, he met with George Washington to discuss the possibility of a military promotion. Washington used terms not all that different from Wheelock's earlier assessment. Washington was "Pleased with the Specimen [he had seen] in Mr Vincent, of the improvement and cultivation which are derived from an education in your Seminary of Literature [Dartmouth College]."[32] Sawatanen returned to the St Lawrence Valley—to Montreal—shortly after this meeting.

Sawatanen's return to Canada marks some important contrasts that resonate with the broader political changes taking place in the northeast. First, although he grew up in a Catholic mission, he married a Protestant woman, Marie-des-Anges Chalifour, in Montreal. Of even greater complexity, upon returning to the region, Sawatanen taught school in Montreal alongside the Anglican missionary John Stuart, who had recently moved into the area with the Mohawks from Canajoharie and Ticonderoga. Though Sawatanen had taken the Congress's side during the 1770s, Stuart was an ardent loyalist with strong links to both Thayandanegea (Joseph Brant), the well-known Mohawk leader, and Sir William Johnson, who was in a long-term relationship with Brant's sister, Koňwatsiātsiaiéňni (Molly Brant).[33] Four years later, Sawatanen accompanied the Mohawk (and the Stuarts) to the northern shores of Lake Ontario. There Stuart served as local priest to the new Loyalist colony begun at Cataraqui (Kingston, ON), while Sawatanen continued teaching school at the new Mohawk community on the Bay of Quinte.[34] It was at this time that Sawatanen and Stuart worked together on a Mohawk translation of the Gospel of Matthew. Decades earlier, Stuart had worked with another of Wheelock's students—Thayandanegea—on a translation of the Gospel of Mark.[35]

Sawatanen's life decisions during the 1770s and 1780s seem confusing. He was raised in a community allied to a Catholic mission, attended a Protestant school, married a Protestant woman, and worked with a Protestant missionary. Does this mean that he had a conversion experience? Likewise, the Wendat made peace with the British in 1760 and joined them during the American Revolution. Sawatanen's friends and relatives proudly received large silver medals from the colony's governor general acknowledging their important role in the fight against the "rebels."[36] Yet Sawatanen, as well as a number of others from the Seven Fires, sided with the Continental Congress. Does this mean he was a traitor—an outsider to his community—or that there was a broader political rift in the Confederacy?

Though we have little evidence to settle these questions definitively, the answer to both seems to be "no." Sawatanen took many decisions that do not align well with those he made at Lorette, but when peace returned to the northeast in the 1790s, he returned home and faced few challenges over his political and religious affiliations.[37] That the purportedly Catholic and revolutionary Sawatanen integrated so easily into a post-revolutionary Protestant and Loyalist world begs questions about how much weight we should accord to his religious and political allegiances. Rather than applying these Eurocentric identity markers to Sawatanen's belief system, we should instead look at how he applied them at Lorette during the 1790s. There, he used the knowledge and skills he had gained over the previous two decades for the community's benefit. Sawatanen's arrival home marked an important turning point in Lorette's history. Because of his advanced studies, which set him apart from most other community members and habitant neighbours, Sawatanen came to occupy a series of important positions within the village, including becoming a member of the village council, and the village's schoolmaster and interpreter.

A Return to Peace, a Return to Lorette

As the schoolmaster at Lorette, Sawantanen encouraged the community's youth to develop literacy skills. The few documents that describe the school show that it served between 25 and 30 students, both boys and girls, that is, most of the community's children under the age of 14.[38] By the 1820s, reflecting the village's regional social and political importance, a handful of Algonquin, Mohawk, Abenaki, Wustukwiuk, and Mi'kmaw students also attended.[39] Much like Sawatanen himself, his community school was unusual in the St Lawrence Valley. Not only did it draw from many northeastern Indigenous communities, but during this period, few Lower Canadian communities had similar institutions. It would be decades before an organized school system developed.[40]

Similarly, with ample knowledge of British political and judicial structures, Sawatanen served as an intermediary between the Wendat council (which he later joined in 1803) and colonial authorities. In this capacity he drafted petitions and official requests to the Crown, served as an interpreter at joint meetings, and fundamentally shifted the nature of Wendat land claims.[41] In fact, it was in 1791—just after his return—that the Wendat first sent a written petition to Lord Dorchester, the governor general of British North America. In this petition they demanded control over Sillery, a seigneury south of the village that the French Crown had granted to the Jesuit's Indigenous converts in 1651. They also sought access to the Petit Seminaire, the most prominent college in the colony.[42] This was a major shift in Wendat diplomacy. Until then, their concerns were always addressed orally with wampum and through an intermediary from the Indian Department.[43]

Much like that of others in his family, Sawatanen's life course, with its breadth of social and political networks forged during a period of profound change and extensive warfare, shaped these developments within the community. There is little doubt, for example, that his experience living with the Loyalist Mohawk along the Bay of Quinte immediately after the American Revolution helped him understand British law and its emphasis on compensation for lost, ceded, or stolen land. Indeed, the new British policy of negotiating territorial treaties and compensating Indigenous peoples for their lands was highly influential throughout the St Lawrence Valley. In the late 1780s, the Mohawk at Kanesatake demanded that their land be granted to them through the same procedures as those at Grand River and the Bay of Quinte.[44] Seeing the difference between their treatment and what occurred further west, Seven Fires delegates in the 1790s asked the Superintendent for Indian Affairs, "[W]hy does my father not love me like my brother [the Mississauga and Mohawk living north of Lake Ontario]."[45]

Like his experiences around Lake Ontario, the knowledge and relationships that Sawatanen developed during his time at Dartmouth, especially while serving as an interpreter between the Congressional troops and the Penobscot and Mi'kmaq, illustrated to him the importance of written text in British political culture. His knowledge of the British preference for textual over oral diplomacy, and his possible role at Lorette as a "man of memory," likely encouraged Sawatanen to both formulate written petitions to the Crown and to commit his community's history to paper.[46] In doing so, Sawatanen transposed the memories and experiences of his relatives, until then conveyed only orally, into a form that would give them greater authority in the eyes of the colonial commissioners.

Because of these decisions, Sawatanen's life provides a unique window onto the relationships between Indigenous societies and colonial powers, one that teaches us about the impact of Indigenous societies and their capacity for adaptation. More important, though, by employing a biographical approach that takes his community and extended family into account, we can see considerable continuity within the northeast. While France and Britain, and then Britain and the United States, fought over imperial and colonial borders, Sawatanen and others continued to live in a differently structured world. Although his, and his relatives', movements were shaped by the imperial events in which they themselves were deeply involved, from at least the 1740s to the 1820s, Sawatanen and the Wendat maintained connections with other Indigenous peoples living throughout the northeast and the lower Great Lakes. In doing so, this regional world shaped their decision-making and responses to the broader colonial transformations occurring within this violent period of imperial warfare.

Notes

1. A modified version of this essay originally appeared in Gaston Deschênes and Denis Vaugeois, *Vivre la Conquête*, Vol. 1 (Sillery: Septentrion, 2013), 204–14.

2. "Death Notices," *Salem Gazette* 39, 39, (17 May 1825), 3.

3. All genealogical information in this essay is from genealogist Serge Goudreau, an expert in Wendat family lineages (personal communication).

4. For texts covering early-Wendat history and migration see Kathryn Labelle, *Dispersed but Not Destroyed: A History of the Seventeenth-Century Wendat People* (Vancouver: UBC Press, 2013); Georges Sioui, *Les Hurons-Wendats: Une Civilisation méconnue* (Quebec: Presses de l'Université Laval, 1997); Bruce Trigger, *Children of Aataentsic: A History of the Huron People to 1660* (Montreal & Kingston: McGill-Queen's University Press, 1976).

5. For more on the Wendat/Algonquin alliance see Labelle, *Dispersed but Not Destroyed*, 68–82.

6. Labelle, *Dispersed but Not Destroyed*.

7. There may have also been a fifth group, the Ataronchronon (marsh), but their relationship to the confederacy is unknown. Bruce Trigger suggests that they may have been part of the Attignaouantan. See Trigger, 30.

8. "The Huron Mission at Notre Dame de Lorette," in Reuben Gold Twaites, ed., *The Jesuit Relations and Allied Documents*, Vol. 60 (Cleveland: Burrows Brothers, 1899), 25.

9. Léon Gérin, "Le Huron de Lorette," in Denis Vaugeois, ed., *Les Hurons de Lorette* (Sillery: Septentrion, 1996), 46.

10. John Lutz defines moditional economies as those that "combined the traditional modes of reproduction and production (for subsistence, prestige goods, and exchange—trade was always a part of the pre-European economy) with new modes of production for exchange in a capitalist market." John Sutton Lutz, *Makúk: A New History of Aboriginal–White Relations* (Vancouver: UBC Press, 2008), 23–4.

11. Charlevoix, *Journal d'un Voyage fait par ordre du Roi dans l'Amerique Septentionnale*, Vol. 5, (Paris: Rollins fils, 1744), 123; Peter Kalm, *Travels into North America* Vol. 2, 2nd edn, John Reinhold Forester, trans. (London: T. Lowdens, 1772), 307–9; Louis Franquet, *Voyages et mémoires sur le Canada,* (Québec: A. Côté & Cie, 1889), 102–8.

12. Jocelyn Tehatarongnantase Paul, "Le territoire de chasse des Hurons de Lorette," *Recherches Amérindiennes au Québec* 30, 3 (2000): 6; Thomas Peace, "The Slow Process of Conquest: Huron-Wendat Responses to the Conquest of Quebec, 1697–1791," in *Revisiting 1759: The Conquest of Canada in Historical Perspective*, John G. Reid and Phillip Buckner, eds (Toronto, University of Toronto Press, 2012), 116–19.

13. F.V. Melsheimer, *Journal of the Voyage of the Brun-swick Auxiliaries from Wolfenbuttel to Quebec,* (Quebec: "Morning Chronicle" Steam Publishing Establishment, 1891), 165.

14. August du Roi, *Journal of Du Roi the Elder*, Charlotte S.J. Epping, trans. and ed., (New York, University of Pennsylvania, 1911), 38 and 42.

15. Louise Vigneault and Isabelle Masse, "Les autoreprésentations de l'artiste huron-wendat Zacherie Vincent," *Journal of Canadian Art History* 32, no. 2 (2011): 65.

16. Vignault and Masse, 65; See also Fonds Propser Vincent, Centre de Référence de l'Amérique Française, P20.

17. Prosper Vincent was a key informant for Marius Barbeau and prominent member of the Wendat community at Lorette.

18. Franquet, *Voyages et mémoires*, 107.

19. Lettre de Beauharnois au ministre, 21 Sept 1741, C11A-75 fol. 138–42v; M. De Beauharnois to Count de Maurepas, in E. B. O'Callaghan, ed., *Documents Relative to the Colonial History of the State of New York (DRCHSNY)*, Vol. 9, (Albany, N.Y.: Weed, Parsons, 1855), 1069–70.

20. William Pote, *The Journal of Captain William Pote, Jr.* (New York: Dodd & Mead, 1896), 36.

21. Joseph Vincent à Matthew, Lord Aylmer, 1 Nov 1832, Library and Archives Canada (LAC), RG10, Vol. 85, p. 33791; *Journal of Indian Affairs,* 27 June 1763, *The Papers of Sir William Johnson,* Vol. 10 (Albany, University of the State of New York, 1951), 724–5; "Canada Indians to Western nations," 25 Aug 1763, *The Papers of Sir William Johnson*, Vol. 10, 793–4; Message of the Canada to the Western Indians, n.d., *DRCHSNY*, Vol. 7 (Albany, N.Y.: Weed, Parsons, 1856), 544–5.

22. Pierre-François-Xavier de Charlevoix, *Journal d'un voyage fait par ordre du roi dans l'Amérique septentrionale*, Pierre Berthiaume, ed. (Montréal: Presses de l'Université de Montréal, 1994), 452.

23. The concept of a Forty Years War is introduced by Jerry Bannister, "Atlantic Canada in an Atlantic World? Northeastern North America in the Long Eighteenth Century," *Acadiensis* 43: 2 (Summer/Autumn 2014): forthcoming.

24. James Murray to Hurons of Lorette, 5 Septembre 1760, Centre de référence de l'Amérique française, Faribault, no. 256; See also Denis Vaugeois, *Les Fins des Alliances* (Sillery: Septentrion, 1995); Vaugeois, *Les Hurons de Lorette*; Denys Delâge and Jean-Pierre Sawaya, *Les Traités des Sept Feux avec les Britanniques: droits et pièges d'un héritage colonial au Québec* (Sillery: Septentrion, 2001), Ch. 4.

25. See Peace, "The Slow Process of Conquest."

26. Eleazar Wheelock, *A Continuation of the Narrative of the Indian Charity School* (Portsmouth, NH: Daniel and Robert Fowle, 1772), 38. We do not know Bastien's Wendat name.

27. The best study on this subject is Colin Calloway, *The Indian History of an American Institution: Native Americans and Dartmouth* (Hanover, University Press of New England, 2010); See also Jean-Pierre Sawaya, "Les Amérindiens domiciliés et le protestantisme au XVIIIe siècle: Eleazar Wheelock et le Dartmouth College," *Historical Studies in Education/Revue d'histoire de l'éducation* 22 (Fall 2010): 18–38; and Mathieu Chaurette, "Les premières écoles autochtones au Québec: progression, opposition et luttes de pouvoir, 1792–1853," (MA thesis, UQAM, 2011).

28. From Eleazar Wheelock, 27 Feb 1773, *The Papers of Sir William Johnson*, Vol. 12 (Albany, The University of the State of New York, 1957): 1012.

29. Eleazar Wheelock to General Woster, 6 Feb 1776, Rauner Library and Special Collection, Dartmouth College (DCA), 776156.

30. John Wheelock's Petition to the Continental Congress, 3 Jan 1780, DCA, 780103.1; US National Archives and Records, Military Service Records, Louis Vincent, Bedel's New Hampshire Regiment.

31. Cary Michael Carney, *Native American Higher Education in the United States*, (New Brunswick, Transaction Publishers, 1999): 38.

32. To the Rev'd John Wheelock, 9 June 1781, *The Papers of George Washington*, series 3c, Varick Transcripts, Letterbook 4, 153; To General Bayley, 9 June 1781, *The Papers of George Washington*, series 3b, Varick Transcripts, Letterbook 13, 424.

33. T.R. Millman, "John Stuart," *DCB*.

34. Église d'Angleterre, Bibliothèque et Archives Nationales du Québec à Québec (BANQ-QUE), P1000, s3, d2735, p. 30; State of religion in Canada, n.d., LAC, Colonial Office 42, Vol. 72, p. 234; John Wheelock to John Forrest, 15 June 1785, DCA, 785365; "From Quebec to Niagara in 1794: Diary of Bishop Jacob Mountain," in *Rapport de l'archiviste de la province de Québec* (Roch Lefebvre, Imprimeur de Sa Majesté la Reine, 1959–1960), 164–5; John Wheelock to Jedidiah Morse , 25 Feb 1811, DCA, 811175.1.

35. Charles M. Johnston, "John Deserontyon," *DCB*.

36. du Roi, *Journal of Du Roi the Elder*, 38.

37. Thomas Peace, "Two Conquests: Aboriginal Experiences of the Fall of New France and Acadia," (PhD diss, York University, Toronto, 2011), 348–56.

38. Requête de Louis Vincent addressee aux commissaries des biens des Jésuites, 9 Dec 1800, BANQ-QUE, E21, s64, ss5, sss2, d1623; Catalogue de l'école Huronne, n.d., E21, s64, ss5, sss2, d2034; Nominal Census, 1784, BANQ-QUE, E21, S64, SS5, SSS1, D288.

39. J.G. Kohl, *Travels in Canada, and Through the States of New York and Pennsylvania*, Vol. I, Mrs. Percy Sinnett, trans. (London: George Manwaring, 1861), 177.

40. On the development of colonial schooling in the colony, see Bruce Curtis, *Ruling by Schooling:*

Conquest to Liberal Governmentality—A Historical Sociology (Toronto: University of Toronto Press, 2013).

41. À la demande des chefs hurons, Dec. 1803, LAC, RG10, Vol. 10, 9565; House of Assembly, Committee Room, Friday 29 Jan 1819. *Eighth Report of the Committee of the House of Assembly, on that part of the speech of His Excellency the Governor in Chief which relates to the settlement of the crown lands with the minutes of evidence taken before the committee*, (Quebec: Neilson & Cowen, 1824): 11.

42. At the Council Chambers in the Bishop's Palace, 15 Aug 1791, Centre de Référence de l'Amérique française, SME 1/2/12.

43. Peace, "The Slow Process of Conquest," 132.

44. Alain Beaulieu, *La question des terres autochtones au Québec, 1760–1860*, Report prepared for le Ministère de la Justice et le Ministère des Ressources naturelles du Québec, (Sept 2002), 111.

45. Recit du Conseil adressé à Monsieur le Colonel Campbell Surint Genl des Affaires Sauvages, 16 Dec 1791, LAC, MG 19 F35, Superintendent of Indian Affairs, series 2, lot 694. Denys Delâge, Jean-Pierre Sawaya and Alain Beaulieu have discussed the differences in how the British treated Indigenous peoples in each colony. See Delâge and Sawaya, *Les Traités des Sept Feux*, 227–33; Alain Beaulieu, "An equitable right to be compensated': The Dispossession of the Aboriginal Peoples of Quebec and the Emergence of a New Legal Rationale (1760–1860)," *The Canadian Historical Review* 94, 1 (March 2013): 1–27.

46. *Eighth Report of the Committee of the House of Assembly*, 12.

Primary Document

The Present State & Situation of the Indian Tribes in the Province of Quebec, May [20] 1779

Rauner Special Collections Library, Dartmouth College, 779301.

The Indian Tribes in Canada are an Object worthy our high attention, when we consider, together with their real strength, the influence that they have from the first preserved among the natives of our country. The ready communication of the western lakes with the river St Lawrence; the continual intercourse that has thereby been maintained between the Traders in that Province, & the Indians adjacent to the Lakes Superior, Ontario, & Huron, have familiarized the latter to those Tribes. When we in addition to this respect, that they have proved themselves to be enterprising & bold; and have every advantage of a national ferocity which they have practiced towards those against whom they were at war; that many of them moreover by the remarkable pains of Jesuits & Roman Priests, have attained to a knowledge of civilization, perhaps, unparalleled thro' all the Savages of America; One need not be at a loss for a reason of their importance not only among the Indians, but likewise the other Inhabitants of that Colony.

Their knowledge is really superior to that of the common people in the government who, however [reasonable?] it may appear, treat them with a degree of civility, this Indians are sensible of, & consequently the influence that they support.

But, to communicate a more distinct idea of the situation & importance of those Indians, I may Observe, that there are seven Tribes in Canada confederated much in the same manner as the Six Nations. The Kagnawaga Tribe, though not the largest, yet from its central situation, together with other reasons, maintains the greatest influence, much as the Mohawks have done in the former case. From the Mohawks, the Cagnawagas originated; a number of which . . . removed from their native country, about eighty years since, and settled at a place 9½ above Montreal on the south side of the river St Lawrence, which has been known from that time by the name of Kagnawaga, containing about an hundred families. Forty miles above this the Connasadagas live in two Villages, & are of the Kagnawaga race; but their land is chiefly owned by their two Priests, who purchased them with fraud & artifice. The Tribe of St. Francis are situate seventy miles below Kagnawaga on the river St. Francis three miles from its confluence with the river St. Lawrence, & an hundred & twenty above Loretto. The Tribe of Loretto are nine miles from Quebec, they, formerly lived on the ground where that City now stands: but the French traders when they settled in that country, at first had possession only of the Isle of Orleans, & gradually purchased the lands on the opposite shore by which means the Indians were obliged to move back four or five miles; 'till finally prostituting again their possession to the artifices of Traders they were necessitated to remove to the place, that they now inhabit. This intelligence I have received from particular Indians belonging to, & others that are acquainted with the Loretto Tribe, who preserve the account by tradition, it being the principle [sic.] history of their tawny race.

From Loretto to Penobscot may be an hundred & thirty or forty miles; but respecting the Penobscots, Mickmacks & St. John Indians, it is unnecessary to speak. It may be said with truth that the Eastern & northern Indians have in general preserved the greatest friendship; & if I mistake not the Penobscots & St. Francois have lately exchanged Belts of amity.

The Kagnawagas, as mentioned, have more influence than any in the Confederacy. This Tribe, that of St. Francois, & that at Loretto, are as nations well attached to the United States, which has not or little influenced the other Canadians. The Jesuit Priests in the two first Tribes are friendly, but the last is not esteemed as much . . .

[signature illegible]
May [20] 1779
The substance of the foregoing was delivered in writing to the hon Com[tee] for Ind[n] affairs

Questions for Consideration

1. What role did France's Indigenous allies—the Illinois, Ottawas, Ojibwa, Miami, and Hurons—play in the enslavement of the Fox in New France?
2. Why did the Fox become the implacable enemy of the Indigenous allies, with whom they shared a language and (to some degree) a culture? Why were the French allies of the Illinois, Ottawa, Ojibwa, Miami, and Huron allied with the French against the Fox Nation?
3. How many of the people listed in the baptismal register are identified as being from the Fox Nation? What roles did these individuals occupy in society? Why did they have these positions?

4. In what ways does Louis Vincent Sawatanen defy easy characterization?
5. What light does Louis Vincent Sawatanen's life story shed on the history of the Wendat?
6. In what ways is the document "The present State & situation of the Indian Tribes in the Province of Quebec, May [20] 1779" Eurocentric? What can we learn from this document?
7. To what degree did Indigenous peoples influence events as the French, British, and Americans expanded their territories? How did the creation of European nation-states in Turtle Island alter relationships between Indigenous peoples?

Further Resources

Books and Articles

Deloria, Philip. "What Is the Middle Ground, Anyway?" *William & Mary Quarterly*, 63, 1 (Jan. 2006): 15–22.

DuVal, Kathleen. *The Native Ground: Indians and Colonists in the Heart of the Continent*. University of Pennsylvania Press, 2006.

Edmunds, R. David, and Joseph L. Peyser. *The Fox Wars: The Mesquakie Challenge to New France*. Norman, OK: Oklahoma University Press, 1993.

Labelle, Kathryn Magee. *Disbursed But Not Destroyed: A History of the Seventeenth Century Huron-Wendat People*. Vancouver: UBC Press, 2013.

————. "'They are the Life of the Nation': Women and War in Traditional Nadouek Society," *The Canadian Journal of Native Studies*, 28, 1 (2008): 119–38.

Taylor, Alan. *The Divided Ground: Indians, Settlers, and the Northern Borderland of the American Revolution*. New York: Alfred A. Knopf, 2006.

————. *The Civil War of 1812: American Citizens, British Subjects, Irish Rebels, & Indian Allies*. New York: Alfred A. Knopf, 2010.

White, Richard. *The Middle Ground: Indians, Empires, and Republics in the Great Lakes Region, 1650–1815*. New York: Cambridge University Press, 1991.

Printed Documents and Reports

Snyder, Charles M., ed. *Red and White on the New York Frontier: A Struggle for Survival: Insights from the Papers of Erastus Granger, Indian Agent, 1807–1819*. Harrison, NY: Harbor Hill Books, 1978.

Thwaites, Reuben Gold, ed. *Collections of the State Historical Society of Wisconsin*, Vol. 16. Madison: State Historical Society of Wisconsin, 1902.

Films

Six Miles Deep. DVD. Directed by Sara Roque. NFB, 2010.
You are on Indian Land. DVD. Directed by Mort Ransen. NFB, 1969.

Websites

Archiving Early America: Full Text of the Jay Treaty
www.earlyamerica.com/milestone-events/jays-treaty/

The Mohawk Council of Akwesasne, "Aboriginal Border Crossing Rights and the Jay Treaty of 1794"
www.akwesasne.ca/node/119

Six Nations of the Grand River
www.sixnations.ca

The Fur Trade

Introduction

Early histories of the fur trade in North America, such as Harold Innis's 400-page tome, *The Fur Trade in Canada*, focused on the trade as integral to the economic development of the area that came to be known as Canada. European men figured prominently within this narrative of progress. Indigenous peoples, on the other hand, remained largely in the background, portrayed as pre-modern obstacles to the growth of the trade and eventually rendered obsolete and dependent on industrious Europeans for survival. Arthur J. Ray's work, *Indians in the Fur Trade*, refocused the lens of fur trade history onto Indigenous peoples to trace the roles they played in the establishment, success, and eventual decline of the trade. This picture has been further complicated by scholars such as Sylvia Van Kirk and Jennifer Brown, who both include women in their examinations of fur-trade history. Van Kirk, in particular, highlights the centrality of women's cultural knowledge and labour to the survival of European men. The significance of these two works is that they initiated a new perspective on the fur trade, portraying it as the beginning of a socio-cultural complex that drew on the traditions of both groups and produced its own unique culture and lifeways. Susan Sleeper-Smith's work expanded on the importance of women by looking at kinship relations and the significance of Indigenous women as "negotiators of change" both at the personal level through their marriages to fur traders and, more broadly, by mediating their community's relations with traders and the European economy.

The two articles in this section offer two more perspectives. The first, by Elizabeth Vibert, uses food as a lens through which to examine the role that the fur trade played, or in some cases did not play, in the lives of Indigenous people living in the Plateau region of present-day British Columbia. Instead, Vibert argues that historians need to read fur traders' texts as part of the meaning-making process that Europeans participated in when they came to Turtle Island and reimagined North America as something akin to their own homes and cultures in Europe. Moreover, Vibert asserts that the importance of the fur trade to Europeans should not lead historians to assume it had the same importance for Indigenous nations and communities. The second article, by Brian Gettler, looks at the Innu in northern Quebec and suggests that for some communities the fur trade played a central role in their economic, social, and political well-being. Gettler also observes that a regional examination of the fur trade is important because it illuminates how Indigenous nations participated differently in the fur trade economy and the strategies they used to remain successful and competitive long after the trade's decline, which occurred, according to most historians, in the late nineteenth century.

Chapter Objectives

At the end of this chapter, you should be able to

- understand the varied and vital roles that Indigenous peoples played in the fur trade;
- appreciate how region, identity, and gender affected the role the fur trade played in Indigenous peoples' lives;
- see the history of the fur trade from an Indigenous perspective; and
- understand how our picture of the fur trade changes when seen from an Indigenous rather than a European perspective.

Secondary Source

Wretched Fishers and Manly Men: The Meanings of Food in the Plateau Fur Trade

Elizabeth Vibert, University of Victoria

In 2013, historian Ian Mosby revealed disturbing details of nutritional experiments carried out in the 1940s and 50s on malnourished Aboriginal people. Government documents from the time show that over a period of 10 years, at least 1300 people in Aboriginal communities in the north and in residential schools across Canada were subjected, without their knowledge, to experiments involving such things as the deliberate withholding of adequate food. Many children died as a result. Scientists, doctors, and government officials were aware of the rampant hunger and malnutrition in the selected schools and communities, problems that were rooted in the long-term dispossession of Aboriginal land and resources by the state, economic depression, and more immediately, the often appalling food in the schools. Yet, rather than intervene to relieve their suffering, scientists and bureaucrats viewed Aboriginal bodies as "experimental materials" to advance the emerging science of nutrition (and their own careers).[1] Asked about "the Indian problem," these officials zeroed in on hunger and looked for technical fixes that would help bring Aboriginal communities to "modern" food practices.

Food has long been an essential way of marking the difference between "us" and "them." In the period of European colonialism beginning in the sixteenth century, food functioned as a principal grammar of difference, a crucial way of identifying who belonged to one's community and who did not; who was coming along on the forward march of modernity and who would be left behind. In this chapter I investigate the mechanisms by which food functioned as a boundary marker in a particular colonial encounter—the encounter between mostly British fur traders who established trading posts along the waterways of the Columbia Plateau in the early nineteenth century and the Indigenous peoples of this region west of the Rockies. Interactions in this era ranged from trade and intermarriage to conflict. Yet it is important not to overstate the impact of the fur trade on Aboriginal lifeways in the Plateau. The introduction of epidemic disease was a disastrous unintended effect, but in fact the Plateau peoples' involvement in the fur trade was limited, partly as a result of the scarcity of fur-bearing animals in the region and partly because the economic strategies of most of these peoples were based on fishing and gathering more than hunting and trapping. Generalizations are tricky—the peoples of the Interior Plateau include such diverse First Nations as the Okanagan, Secwepec (Shuswap), Ktunaxa (Kutenai), Walla Walla, Salish Flathead, and many others—but for the most part the Indigenous communities of the Plateau took what they wanted from trade (including useful goods such as iron tools, kettles, and guns) and held the traders and their demands at a distance.[2]

If the effects of the fur trade were limited, the impacts of the fur-trade documentary record have been more far-reaching. Often the first written accounts of interactions between Europeans and Indigenous peoples, fur-trade records have been mined for data in political negotiations and court cases seeking to determine Aboriginal entitlement to land and resources. When read uncritically, these records have resulted in grave misunderstandings of Aboriginal cultures. For instance, in an important decision in the British Columbia Supreme Court in 1991, the chief justice relied heavily on traders' writings to argue that Aboriginal peoples were "primitive" and lazy.[3] Fur-trade records have profoundly shaped subsequent understandings of Indigenous societies. Here I read those accounts closely, critically, and in context, in an effort to understand why traders viewed Indigenous cultural practices in the ways they did and how those views shifted, or not, over time. Where evidence permits, I offer alternative readings of the fur-trade record, readings that undermine the notion that Indigenous food practices were somehow deficient.

Starving Fishing Tribes

British fur traders arrived in the "unhallowed wilderness" of the Interior Plateau to find the Indigenous peoples living by fishing, gathering, and hunting—living, as one trader phrased it, and all presumed, in a "rude state of nature."[4] Traders' ideas about what constituted this "rude state," which they saw as so distinct from British and European lifestyles, turned on a complex interweaving of material and moral concerns. Yet even by the most mundane material measures—how many furs produced for trade, how much assistance offered to traders—all Indigenous peoples were not created equal in the eyes of fur traders. Traders elaborated a distinct hierarchy of Indigenous peoples in the Plateau. In this ranking, "salmon tribes" figured as the poor and "hunting tribes" the rich.[5] Traders wrote at length about the poverty of those they viewed as fishing tribes. The ultimate manifestation of their poverty was starvation. Cases of "starving" or "half starving" were reported with startling frequency throughout the era of the fur trade in this interior region. What did "starving" mean in this context? Why were those described by the traders as "fishing tribes" so often said to be starving, and why were "hunting tribes" so rarely depicted as hungry? A key part of the puzzle is traders' ideas about what constituted good food. Salmon did not rank highly, for a combination of historically specific and broader cultural reasons. Meat, on the other hand, was seen to make the man.

As anthropologist Mary Black-Rogers demonstrated years ago in a study of Algonquian and Athapaskan cultures, and as I have shown in my work on the Columbia Plateau, "starving" came in many varieties and often had little to do with lack of food.[6] Close analysis of traders' uses of the term, and of related concepts like "lazy" and "pitiful," reveals much about their perceptions of Indigenous sustenance methods, and about the interface between those views and their own business interests.[7] In 1810, Northwest Company trader and explorer David Thompson made the perceived link between a fishing way of life and deprivation explicit when he wrote of the Lower Ktunaxa (Kutenai) people that they were "living on Fish . . . their Poverty owing to a War broke out between them and the Peagans [Piegan]." Ross Cox, also with the Northwest Company, found these people the most wretched he had encountered: they had "no horses, are poor hunters, go nearly naked, and subsist principally on fish." The image of the famished, impoverished "fishing Indian" was persistent. A dozen years after Thompson, Alexander Kennedy wrote from Spokane House that the Lower Ktunaxa still did no business with the traders, and so remained fishermen, living "half starved and half naked."[8]

These are examples of what Black-Rogers classified as the technical usage of starving—technical in the sense that it had very specific fur-trade connotations. "Starving" used in this way did not mean literal starvation, that is, "dying of hunger or suffering from lack of food."[9] Rather, it often meant that people were not eating what the traders considered appropriate or adequate food. The principal message was that those in question were preoccupied with meeting their own food needs, leaving little time for other activities—including the activity of most concern to traders, the trapping of furs. This insight goes a long way towards explaining the exasperation of Simon McGillivray during his posting at Fort Nez Percés in the early 1830s. McGillivray's journal is spiced with references to people around the post "starving," "getting desperate," and "begging something to eat." By mid-March there was still no beaver trade, leading McGillivray to complain that "the tribes of the Columbia, *do nothing in winter*, but procure a livelihood, and the latter with a great deal of trouble."[10] There may well have been a food shortage involved, but McGillivray's central concern was clearly something other than hunger. Hudson's Bay Company Governor George Simpson, on his first visit to the Columbia District in the 1820s, was similarly perturbed with the Sxoielpi people near Kettle Falls. These people were "more wretched than any I had seen on the East side the Mountains," a phrase suggesting severe suffering. But he went on: the Sxoielpi were living on "rotten salmon" and did not have "a single article of British Manufacture in their possession but a Gun and Beaver Trap." The Sxoielpi were doubly wretched in Simpson's view: they were compromised by their need to procure food, and by their lack of British technology—not least the technology to procure the furs and hides that Simpson so avidly sought.[11]

Traders' writings from upstream locales like the Kootenays, Spokane, Colville, and Kamloops are full of references to Indigenous people collecting "rotten," "dead and dying," or "putrid" salmon. Fish collected on the lower Columbia River late in the season were described in similar terms. The consumption of fish in this state was often equated with starvation, and the people doing the eating were viewed as desperate "salmon eaters." Such observations must be understood in the context of salmon biology, season, and local cultural practice. In most cases these observations were recorded in autumn, after the main salmon runs were over. Salmon described as "putrid" would have been spawned-out or exhausted chinook or sockeye. Salmon do not feed during their migration to their natal streams and lakes, and the demands on their energy reserves for travel, maturation of gonads, spawning, and nest defence are great. Sockeye fat reserves, for example, are depleted by 90 per cent by the time they die at the spawning grounds. Yet one person's trash is another's treasure: lean fish are ideal for preserving by air drying. While fat Chinook and sockeye are delicious and sought after by Aboriginal people for eating fresh, their high water and oil content can make them prone to souring or bacterial infection when dried. Lean fish are best for preservation.[12]

Over time traders came to learn about the movements and use of salmon at different phases of the life cycle. Ktunaxa people explained to John Work that the fish were "remarkably fine" when they entered the Columbia from the sea; having seen the value of lean, spawned-out fish for drying purposes, Work was less dismissive of those who ate such fish. At Spokane House in 1822–23, Alexander Kennedy noted the complementary roles of "fine" and "bad" salmon in the local diet. During the summer, he observed, people set up villages at favourite fishing sites and caught and dried large quantities for winter use. In autumn, emaciated and battered salmon were collected "to be used when necessity requires." Regions farther inland received some high-quality fresh specimens early in the season, but at the best of times they had nothing like the quality and quantity of salmon available at favoured downstream sites like The Dalles and Kettle Falls.[13] Such differences in resource distribution were fundamental to Plateau social relations, making it necessary for communities to trade with each other and to gather, fish, and hunt in other groups' territories. The multi-ethnic fishery at Kettle Falls each summer, and the huge assemblage of people at "the big time" in Yakama territory, are examples of such collaborative use of favoured harvest sites.[14]

The use of undesirable fish "when necessity requires" indicates that the cushion for survival through the long winter was not overly generous.[15] The belief that salmon runs might inexplicably fail reinforced many traders' perception that the life of inland peoples was by nature precarious. In the summer of 1826, Hudson's Bay Company trader Samuel Black reported that the Cayuse and Walla Walla had left the river to go and harvest roots, "for this year there is no Salmon."[16] What did "no Salmon" mean? Shifts over time in Black's understanding of the food procurement strategies of local people provide insight. He made the "no Salmon" comment in his first year at Fort Nez Percés. He saw people leaving the river for the root grounds and concluded they were doing so because of the failure of the salmon run. By 1829, Black's fourth year in the district, he had come to recognize that "the great support of the Natives in this District is their Nutritive Roots . . . and a great Cause of their movements and residences at certain Seasons."[17] Black's observation is noteworthy for a couple of reasons. First, unlike many traders (and many scholars since), he recognized the centrality of gathered plant foods, produced by women, to Indigenous economies. Making the same point years later, Nlaka'pamux (Thompson River) elder and author Annie York told researchers that plant foods often saved the lives of Indigenous people: "They're very valuable food. . . . [During times of scarcity] cow-parsnip and spring beauty, avalanche lily, tiger lily . . . and Indian carrot and thistle . . . they eat that and they survive."[18] Second, trader Black was unusual in acknowledging the importance of gathered foods even to communities he and fellow traders classified as "hunting tribes." Buffalo hunters, those most revered by fur traders for their manliness and their contributions to trade, timed their hunts to allow them to "pass the Spring [on] the Root Plains."[19] Though they might be called hunters, in fact these communities on the eastern edge of the Plateau had a complex and varied seasonal round, harvesting plants like lomatium ("Indian celeries") and bitterroot in early spring, wild carrots later in the season, and camas (a plant commonly eaten by West Coast Indigenous peoples) in early summer. Berries and other gathered foods, freshwater fish, and other game rounded out the diet. Buffalo became a focal point for these eastern Plateau communities by the latter part of the eighteenth century, but meat did not supplant gathered foods and other elements of their seasonal round.[20]

The other point to bear in mind about "no Salmon" is that salmon runs rarely entirely fail. In the normal course of things, runs are subject to dramatic fluctuation, exacerbated by floods, drought, landslides, and variations in other natural conditions. (Nowadays stresses include overfishing and habitat destruction; research indicates that salmon runs will be severely affected by climate change, since small changes in water temperature can profoundly affect fish physiology). Sockeye exhibit a marked four- or five-year cycle, an aspect of their life history that never failed to baffle fur traders. Indigenous peoples of the Columbia Plateau exploited a wide range of salmon runs from spring through autumn, catching all five varieties of Pacific salmon as well as steelhead. Figures for commercial yields on the Columbia some decades after the fur trade show that the quantities available to Aboriginal populations would have been far more than they needed. They preserved enormous amounts for winter and enjoyed the health benefits of the high protein and healthy fats in dried salmon. So much for "starving fishing tribes" and "no Salmon."[21]

The Meaning of Meat

If Aboriginal peoples were rarely forced to do without fish—not to mention an array of plant foods—why did traders so commonly depict them as malnourished? An important piece of the puzzle is traders' perceptions of the relative merits of fish and meat. Prior to the twentieth century, meat occupied the paramount position in the food hierarchy of western cultures. In material terms, the status of meat derives from its relative scarcity, unpredictability, and difficulty of capture, as well as the high nutritional return per unit effort. The prestige, ritual, and myth that have grown up around hunting or herding animals in many cultures relate, in part, to such issues of costliness and unpredictability. However, the affinity for meat in a given culture is deep-seated and symbolically charged, and is far more than a question of costs and benefits. What is considered good to eat is also, to borrow a phrase, a matter of "value judgements . . . and phantasmic beliefs."[22]

In western cultures the luxury value of meat has long defined it as a kind of social cement, a measure of position in the social hierarchy and a means of reproducing that position. Historian Stephen Mennell has explored the social functions of food in England and France from the Middle Ages to the present. Meat has been a marker of social position throughout.[23] By the end of the eighteenth century, when many of the fur traders under study here were growing up in England, Scotland and the isles, and Lower Canada (present-day Quebec), class differences in meat consumption remained pronounced. The basic diet of working families consisted of masses of bread, porridge, and/or potatoes. Cheap cuts of meat or offal might be purchased from the butcher once a week if the family purse permitted. By the turn of the nineteenth century grow-ing numbers of well-paid artisans, professionals, and others—the burgeoning British middle class—could afford to buy meat, poultry, and fish on a regular basis. Those who could were sure to do so. As historian E.P. Thompson showed, meat was "one of the first items upon which any increase in real wages will have been spent."[24] In the fur trade, those at the top of the social hierarchy, company officers, generally reserved for themselves the fresh meat they obtained from Aboriginal hunters. The labouring men were left to eat dried fish and other dried rations.

A look at fur traders' perceptions of their own diet in fur-trade country helps to illuminate their impressions of Indigenous diets. Complaints were endless about the "horrid stuff" on which traders—especially those of the servant rank—were expected to subsist in the Plateau. Chief trader John Tod sympathized with the men who walked off the job in Kamloops in the early 1840s to protest the "privations" of a steady diet of dried salmon.[25] Traders at Kamloops were "always hammering about after salmon," making several trips a year to the Fraser River to trade for the 12,000 fish consumed annually at the post.[26] At Fort Okanogan in 1826, 3 officers, 12 working men, and their Aboriginal families ate over 18,000 dried fish in under ten months. A servant's daily ration was three fish, each weighing about a pound, plus two for his Aboriginal wife and one for each child. One and a half kilograms of dried salmon was considered the equivalent of 4.5 kilograms of fresh: in other words, a lot of fish. While a steady diet of dried salmon sounds challenging, it is hard to conceive of it as any worse than the standard diet in traders' home territories. According to one seasoned fur-trade observer, those from the Scottish isles "had Seldom, if Ever, Eat Any thing better than Pease or Barley Bread with Salt Sellocks [salt fish] and Kale."[27] The diet of those from Lower Canada appears to have been similar to that in England at the time—heavy in bread and dried pulses. Things may have been better in rural parishes, where people grew kitchen gardens, but estimates of wheat consumption of a kilogram per person per day suggest that flour was by far the dominant staple.[28]

The bias against fish was not confined to the Columbia Plateau. East of the Rockies, service at so-called "fish posts" was widely viewed as penance. At posts where meat was plentiful, fish often found its way to the dogs. In contrast to dried salmon, pemmican—the dried meat used widely as travel food and rations east of the moun-tains—was seen as "wholesome" and "well tasted."[29] While at times Plateau traders had little more than dried salmon to eat, the record shows that for the most part their diet was more varied. Officers ate best, as noted: when newly minted HBC Governor Simpson arrived for a visit in 1824 he was aghast at the volume of imported foods enjoyed by fur-trade gentlemen, from chocolate and coffee to fancy preserves. He cut back on the imports and company employees gradually settled into a hybrid dietary regime based on fish, game, and gathered foods, often acquired from Aboriginal people, as well as crops and livestock raised at new company farms.[30]

What is perhaps a universal cultural (not to mention nutritional) need for variety colours traders' complaints about a diet heavy in fish. The Indigenous peoples they called "salmon eaters" certainly ate far more than salmon. Oral histories and anthropological studies indicate that Interior peoples prior to and in the early decades of contact ate a highly varied diet over the year. Indeed, they tended to eat numerous different foods at each meal. A favourite Nlaka'pamux dish, for instance, was a mixture of prepared bitterroot, serviceberries, and deer grease that was rich in vitamins and minerals as well as protein and carbohydrate.[31] Although there was a superabundance of salmon in the region, there was a similar wealth of roots, berries and other plant foods, as well as diverse fish and game.[32]

Meat Makes the Man

Another aspect of traders' dim view of fish lies deep in British cultural traditions. Long-established popular wisdom and medical orthodoxy held that fish was a weak or even feminine food.[33] The power of such perceptions is clear in contemporary prescriptions for good health. In Britain the most influential household health manual was William Buchan's *New Domestic Medicine*, which went through myriad editions between 1769 and 1846. The manual advised that animal flesh, being "wholesome" and "solid, with a sufficient degree of tenacity," was the best food for men. "Laborious" men, in particular, needed adequate supplies of red meat to fuel their bodies. Those who "labour hard without doors" needed high-energy foods that were "almost indigestible" to town dwellers involved in commerce and other sedentary work.[34] The bodies of labourers, then, were adapted for red meat. Training diets for soldiers called for enormous quantities: men who carried arms for the nation were to protect the national vigour by eating plenty of meat.[35] There is a hint of eighteenth-century stadial theories of civilization here. Those closest to the land and nature had the highest requirement for animal foods; those who had evolved to a higher state—the apex in these theories being British commercial society—had achieved some distance from this physiological need.[36] Convictions about the indispensability of meat to hardy manhood had a broad reach. The British in India in the nineteenth century, for instance, came to view Hindu men as weakened and effeminate, the result of an array of cultural practices, including failure to eat sufficient meat.[37] Meanwhile, those of "delicate" constitution in Britain—meaning women, children, the old and infirm—were urged to choose lighter foods like chicken, fish, and eggs.[38] Such prescriptions speak to a highly gendered code of foods, one in which red meat grounded the masculine pole and pale or weak foods the feminine.

Although none made reference to Dr Buchan's advice, it is clear that traders in the Plateau were influenced by such orthodoxies on the physical effects of diet. Northwester Jules Quesnel lamented the effects of such *mauvaise nourriture* on the bodies of his once-robust colleagues. Thomas Dears complained that he had grown so emaciated he was in danger of "slipping through my Breeks [breeches]." Until traders got used to it, John McLean remarked, a steady diet of salmon went through them like a dose of laxative salts.[39] Not surprisingly, such views transferred to Indigenous peoples who were believed to subsist on a diet of fish. The Sanpoil of the Columbia River, living on dried salmon and roots, were said to be "meagre wretches" whose features would be improved by eating better food—that is, meat. When Alexander Ross met some Secwepemc (Shuswap) living on fish, roots, and berries he described their "wretched condition"—although paradoxically they also seemed "comfortable and happy." At a particularly good fishing site Indigenous people might appear to better advantage. Simpson found the people of Kettle Falls, for instance, to be "very good looking and generally stouter than the natives of the East side the Mountain." This view echoes other traders' depictions of coastal First Nations.[40]

Ordinarily in the Plateau, compliments about fine physiques were reserved for "hunting tribes." Describing the buffalo-hunting peoples of the eastern Plateau, Ross waxed lyrical. The men "were generally tall, raw-boned, and well-dressed . . . Their voices were strong and masculine . . . On the whole, they differed widely in appearance from the piscatory tribes we had seen along the river."[41] Appearances mattered. In the words of the founder of the new science of physiognomy, which was growing in popularity by the early nineteenth century, human physical form was an index not only of the emotions and intellect "but, most important, [of] the possibilities of moral life."[42] The racial science emerging in this era traded heavily in notions of the deeper meaning beneath surface markers like skin tone and hair.[43]

The fine physique Ross and his colleagues attributed to hunters was rooted, they were convinced, in diet. If fishing peoples were "wretched," hunters, who presumably could eat all the meat they wanted, were "tall, raw-boned," "fully formed," and "well made for activity."[44] Indigenous hunters in the Plateau—especially buffalo hunters—were admired for a range of manly virtues, including courage and sportsmanship, mastery of nature, and work ethic. I have examined traders' valorization of hunters elsewhere.[45] Suffice to say that buffalo hunters were quintessential "Indian men"—noble savages who rode on horseback and hunted big game at great risk and effort. Northwester Ross Cox, in characteristically purple prose, held up Salish Flathead and Upper Ktunaxa hunters for special praise:

> Their bravery is pre-eminent; a love of truth they think necessary to a warrior's character. They are too proud to be dishonest, too candid to be cunning. Their many avocations leave them no leisure for gambling; and their strict subordination, joined to the necessity of exerting all their energies against the common enemy, prevents them from quarreling.[46]

Here is the "noble savage" in all his glory: brave to a fault, morally upright, hard-working. So potent was the image of the horseback-riding buffalo hunter that by the late nineteenth century he had come to displace his Eastern Woodland cousins (Pocahontas, Hiawatha, and their vaguely Algonkian kin) as *the* Indian of the European-American imagination.[47]

The hardy and productive masculinity that traders imagined these buffalo hunters to possess was ambiguous, however. These hunters might be brave and martial, but they were still "savage." Describing an 1812 war expedition by a group of buffalo hunters into Siksika (Blackfeet) territory on the eastern flank of the Rockies, Thompson wrote approvingly of their "cautious boldness" and courage, and then moved on to describe "their wild war dance" and "wild war yell." The boundary between heroic hunter–warrior culture and savage nature, it seems, was a thin one in trader discourse. John Work made a similar slide in his account of the dress habits of Plateau hunters: the young men, he wrote, "occupy no inconsiderable portion of the morning decorating themselves[;] in point of time, and the degree of pains taken to ornament their hair, paint their faces &c they may compete with the more accomplished fops in the civilised world."[48] Such behaviour was at odds with traders' notions of their own respectable manhood. For aspiring middle-class men of "zeal and hard work," such affectations were a waste of time. "Fops" were the posers of their day—affluent, often aristocratic men of leisure (worse, they were frequently French) who spent their time socializing and preening. The masculinity of the middle-class British man of the early nineteenth century was defined quite distinctly, by a punishing work ethic, independence, sobriety, and dedication to family.[49]

Buffalo hunters might be real men, then, contributing vital supplies to the fur trade—from leather pack cords, portable hide lodges, and other items, to welcome infusions of dried meat—but they were *Indian* men. Elsewhere in fur-trade country the hunting way of life tended to be imagined as a backward state. "Indian hunters," it was widely believed, could not bear hard labour and would rather rove for hours on end than "work one hour with the pick axe and spade . . . the Indians are not industrious." The work of hunting did not stand up to agriculture, that art of "Civilized men."[50] Elsewhere in the Empire, British newcomers held similar views of Indigenous hunters. Mobile hunting and mixed subsistence patterns were widely viewed as a rejection or inversion of "civilized" ethics of self-discipline and hard work.[51]

Reduced to Roots

As shown above, Samuel Black was one of the few traders to describe the role of diverse foods in Indigenous diets. Many acknowledged the value of plant foods as supplements to meat or fish. Even on a trader's plate these unfamiliar tubers, "mosses," and the like might serve as potatoes, or the "rough bread of the country." Yet the assumption was that living on such foods was an option of last resort. Gabriel Franchère noted that the Salish Flathead, great buffalo hunters, were "reduced" to living on roots when kept from hunting by their foes from the plains. Moss (actually black tree lichen) always suggested starvation. Franchère found Sxoielpi living on lichen cakes to be "thin and gaunt, scarcely able to move"; they were "reduced" to this food in late winter when the hunting was poor and the salmon had not yet arrived. Thompson found the cakes "just nourishment [enough] to keep a person alive." He believed the Sanpoil to be in a particularly perilous state, deriving, he estimated, two-thirds of their sustenance from roots and berries.[52]

Thompson's two-thirds estimate is astute, given the findings of recent scholarship showing that vegetable foods accounted for one-third to as much as two-thirds of the calories consumed by Plateau peoples across the year.[53] The failure of many traders to recognize the value of gathered foods in local diets reflects both their cultural bias in favour of meat and their tendency to undervalue the activities of women and the foods women produced. The formal questionnaire on "Natural History" that the London Committee of the Hudson's Bay Company began circulating to trading posts in the 1820s speaks volumes about how gender structured contemporary British understandings of economy. The series of questions about the "usual occupations" of Indigenous people begins with the query "What are the usual occupations, besides hunting and fishing of the father and sons, in the family of an Indian?" Occupations, it seems, were the domain of men. Finally came a question about women: "Are they employed solely in household and culinary work or do they engage in hunting and fishing . . . or what are the usual occupations of the females?"[54] Production of vegetable foods is nowhere in the list.

The centrality of gathered foods to Indigenous diets in this region undermines labels like "hunting tribe" and "fishing tribe." Many scholars have argued that notations like "gatherer-hunter," "gatherer-fisher-hunter," or even "eclectic subsister" would more closely reflect the relative contributions of various methods of food production. Indigenous researchers and other scholars have described the often elaborate methods of cultivation and management used by women to produce plant foods.[55] The range of plant foods in use went well beyond the roots and mosses of "last resort" described by traders. Experts among the Nlaka'pamux, most notably female herbalists, named at least 350 species of native plants, over a hundred of which were eaten. Indigenous place names often speak to the vital foods produced there: even in the late twentieth century Sahaptin elders of the southern Plateau identified culturally important sites like "lovage place" and "place of yellow pond lily," where vast stores of vegetable foods were historically harvested. "Indian Heaven" was a place rich in the most delectable local variety of huckleberries.[56]

Aboriginal people themselves may have had a hand in traders' failure to grasp the central role of plant foods in their diets. Male informants may have emphasized hunting ability as an important symbolic expression of manhood. In many communities a young man's first kill was a rite of passage to adulthood and a prerequisite to marriage. On the other hand, ritual reinforced the value of *all* foods. In thanksgiving or "first foods" ceremonies in the communities of the middle Columbia, foods were traditionally presented in the following order: water, salmon, bitterroot, lomatium species (wild carrots and related herbs), and huckleberries. As anthropologist Eugene Hunn points out, salmon was first on the list after water, but the gathered foods so honoured were more numerous. Hunn's Indigenous research collaborator James Selam refused to rank these foods in order of importance, insisting "all the foods are most important."[57] Selam was unwilling to ascribe to food the kind of hierarchy that British fur traders took for granted.

Conclusion

Malnourished Aboriginal people in the 1940s and 1950s became unwitting subjects of nutritional experiments that ultimately did nothing to improve their circumstances. A century before the experiments, Indigenous people going about their lives in the Columbia Plateau were widely imagined as "hungry Indians"— "wretched," "lazy," and frequently "starving." A great deal happened in Indigenous–settler encounters between the fur-trade years of the early nineteenth century and the economic and social displacements of the twentieth. History does not produce many straight lines, and it is certainly not possible to draw a straight line from trader discourse to unethical experiments on Aboriginal bodies. However, those experiments were conceivable in part because of a deeply embedded and long-standing assumption—the assumption that Indigenous people's food practices were deficient. Just as the fundamental misconception that Indigenous people did not make proper use of the land helped to underwrite myriad acts of colonial dispossession, so did fundamental misunderstandings of Indigenous foodways help to fuel racism for years to come.

Notes

1. Ian Mosby, "Administering Colonial Science: Nutrition Research and Human Biomedical Experimentation in Aboriginal Communities and Residential Schools, 1942–1952," *Histoire sociale/Social History* 46, 91, May 2013: 145–72.

2. Elizabeth Vibert, *Traders' Tales: Narratives of Cultural Encounters in the Columbia Plateau* (Norman, OK: University of Oklahoma Press, 1997 and 2000).

3. *BC Studies* 95 (1992), special issue "Anthropology and History in the Courts."

4. Alexander Henry, *Journal,* in *New Light on the Early History of the Greater Northwest vol. 2,* ed. Elliott Coues. (Minneapolis: Ross and Haines, 1965). 707; Alexander Ross, *Adventures of the First Settlers on the Oregon or Columbia River* [London 1849] (Chicago: Lakeside Press, 1923), 158.

5. I explore this hierarchy in more detail in *Traders' Tales.*

6. Mary Black-Rogers, "Varieties of "Starving": Semantics and Survival in the Subarctic Fur Trade," *Ethnohistory* 33 (4), 1986; Vibert, *Traders' Tales.*

7. Vibert, *Traders' Tales,* Ch. 4; John S. Lutz, *Makúk: A New History of Aboriginal–White Relations* (Vancouver: UBC Press, 2008).

8. Catherine White, ed., *David Thompson's Journals Relating to Montana and Adjacent Regions* (Missoula: Montana State University, 1950); 97; Ross Cox, *The Columbia River, or Scenes and Adventures . . .* ed. E. I. Stewart and J. R. Stewart [London 1831] (Norman: University of Oklahoma Press, 1957), 251; Hudson's Bay Company Archives [HBCA], B.208/e/1, fos. 3–4.

9. *Oxford English Dictionary.*

10. Emphasis added. HBCA, B.146/a/2, entries for 20 Feb. and 17 Mar., 1832.

11. HBCA, D.4/122, fo. 21; Simpson, *Journal 1824–25, Remarks Connected with the Fur Trade . . .* in *Fur Trade and Empire: George Simpson's Journal,* ed. Frederick Merk (Cambridge, MA: Harvard University Press, 1968), 40.

12. Robert Burgner, "Life History of Sockeye Salmon," in *Pacific Salmon Life Histories,* eds C. Groot and L. Margolis (Vancouver: UBC Press, 1991), 15; Steven Romanoff, "Fraser Lillooet Salmon Fishing," *Northwest Anthropological Research Notes* 19 (2), 1985: 119–34.

13. British Columbia Archives and Records Service [BCARS], John Work Journals, Journal No. 1, fos. 40–41; HBCA B.208/e/1, fo. 2; see also BCARS, Thompson's River Post Journal, 1841–43, entries for 12–27 Aug. 1841.

14. Vibert, *Traders' Tales,* 140–42.

15. Eugene Hunn with James Selam, *Nch'i-Wana, "The Big River": Middle Columbia Indians and their Land* (Seattle: University of Washington Press, 1990), 132–4.

16. HBCA, D.4/119, fo. 6; BCARS, Work, Journal No. 4, fo. 113; HBCA, B.223/b/2, fo. 41.

17. HBCA, B.146/e/2.

18. Quoted in Nancy Turner et al., *Thompson Ethnobotany* (Victoria: Royal British Columbia Museum, 1990), 32; also Mary Ellen Kelm, *Colonizing Bodies: Aboriginal Health and Healing in British Columbia* (Vancouver: UBC Press, 1998), Ch. 2.

19. Vibert, "Real Men Hunt Buffalo: Masculinity, Race and Class in British Fur Traders' Narratives," *Gender and History* 8 (1), 1996; White, ed., *Thompson's Journals,* 102.

20. White, ed., *Thompson's Journals,* 36–9, 46, 58, 94, 102, 204, 213; HBCA, B.69/a/1, fos. 3, 6, 7; B.45/e/2, fo. 4; BCARS, Work, Journal No. 8, fos. 33, 38; Work, Journal No. 10, Pt. II, fo. 73; Nicolas Point, "Journals," in *Wilderness Kingdom: Indian Life in the Rocky Mountains, the Journals and Paintings of Nicolas Point,* ed. Joseph P. Donnelly (New York: Holt, Rinehart and Winston, 1967), 120–28, 163–66.

21. Hunn, *Nch'i-Wana,* 148–9; Hunn, "Mobility as a Factor Limiting Resource Use in the Columbia Plateau," in *Resource Managers: North American and Australian Hunter–Gatherers,* eds Nancy Williams and Eugene Hunn (Boulder: American

Association for the Advancement of Science, 1982), 31–2; T. Rivera, "Diet of a Food-Gathering People," in *Indians of the Urban Northwest* ed. M. W. Smith (New York: Columbia, 1949); James Teit, "The Thompson Indians of British Columbia," *Memoirs of the American Museum of Natural History* 2 (4), 1900: 252–3.

22. Nick Fiddes, *Meat: A Natural Symbol* (London and New York: Routledge, 1991); Maurice Godelier, *The Mental and the Material* (London: Verso, 1986), 135.

23. Stephen Mennell, *All Manners of Food: Eating and Taste in England and France* (Oxford: Blackwell, 1985).

24. E. P. Thompson, *The Making of the English Working Class* (London: Victor Gollancz, 1963), 348–49; Mennell, *All Manners*, 303, 310–15; Michael Payne, "Daily Life on Western Hudson Bay, 1714–1870: A Social History of York Factory and Churchill," PhD diss., Carleton University, 1989, 477–78.

25. HBCA, D.5/19, fo. 299.

26. James Gibson, *Farming the Frontier: The Agricultural Opening of the Oregon Country* (Vancouver: UBC Press, 1985), 24; HBCA, B.97/e/1, fo. 3; B.146/e/1, fo. 2; B.146/e/2, fos. 3, 9. Fish posts east of the Rockies: Payne, "Daily Life," 439.

27. Chief Trader Ferdinand Jacobs, quoted in Payne, "Daily Life," 475.

28. Allan Greer, *Fur Trade Labour and Lower Canadian Agrarian Structures.* Historical Papers, Canadian Historical Association, Toronto, 1981: 197–214; Dale Miquelon, *New France, 1701–1744* (Toronto: McClelland and Stewart, 1987), 223–4.

29. HBCA, F.3/2, fos. 125–26; B.97/a/1, fo. 5; UBC Special Collections Division, Edward Ermatinger Papers, 1820–74 [typescript], 288–90.

30. Cox, *Columbia*, 254; Simpson, *Journal 1824–25*, 48; Gibson, *Farming the Frontier*, 18–20 and Ch. 2; Richard Mackie, *Trading Beyond the Mountains: The British Fur Trade on the Pacific* (Vancouver: UBC Press, 1997); E.E. Rich, ed., *The Letters of John McLoughlin from Fort Vancouver to the Governor and Committee*, Vol. 1 (London: Hudson's Bay Record Society, 1941), 235; Simpson, *Journal 1824–25*, 86.

31. Teit, "Thompson Indians," 236.

32. Hunn, *Nch'i-Wana*, 148.

33. Douglas Hay, *Albion's Fatal Tree: Crime and Society in Eighteenth-Century England* (London: A. Lane, 1975).

34. William Buchan, *The New Domestic Medicine*, 14th edn (London: A. Strahan and T. Cadell, 1794), 71–2, 74.

35. Buchan, *New Domestic Medicine*, 19, 57, 65, 594.

36. Roxann Wheeler, *The Complexion of Race: Categories of Difference in Eighteenth-Century British Culture* (Philadelphia: University of Pennsylvania Press, 2000).

37. Parama Roy, "Meat-Eating, Masculinity, and Renunciation in India: A Gandhian Grammar of Diet," *Gender & History* 14, 1, 2002: 62–91.

38. Buchan, *Domestic Medicine*, 70–2, 74; Roy, "Meat-Eating," 75–6; Anita Guerrini, "A Diet for a Sensitive Soul: Vegetarianism in Eighteenth-Century Britain," *Eighteenth-Century Life* 23, 2, 1999: 35–7.

39. Quesnel to J. M. Lamothe, May 1809, in Simon Fraser, *Journal*, in *The Letters and Journals of Simon Fraser*, ed. W. Kaye Lamb, (Toronto: MacMillan, 1960), 262; UBC Sp. Coll., Ermatinger Papers, 288–90; John McLean, *Notes of a Twenty-Five Years' Service* [1849] ed. W.S. Wallace (Toronto: Champlain Society, 1932), 186.

40. Cox, *Columbia*, 251, 260; Edward Ermatinger, "York Factory Express Journal . . . 1827–28," *Transactions of the Royal Society of Canada* 6, 1912, sec. 2, 115; BCARS, Work, Journal No. 7, fo. 10; HBCA, B.146/a/1, entry for 7 April 1831; Alexander Ross, *Fur Hunters of the Far West* [1855], ed. Kenneth Spaulding (Norman: University of Oklahoma Press, 1956), 100; HBCA, D.4/122, fo. 121; Simpson, *Journal 1824–25*, 40.

41. Ross, *Adventures*, 137.

42. J.K. Lavater quoted in Billie Melman, *Women's Orients: English Women and the Middle East: Sexuality, Religion, and Work* (Ann Arbor: University of Michigan Press, 1992), 113.

43. Wheeler, *Complexion of Race*; Steven Shapin, "'You are what you eat': Historical changes in ideas about food and identity," *Historical Research* 87, 237, Aug. 2014: 377–92.

44. Ross, *Adventures*, 137; HBCA, B.45/e/2, fo. 12; Thompson, *Narrative*, 435; Fraser, *Journal*, 145.

45. Vibert, "Real Men Hunt Buffalo."

46. Cox, *Columbia*, 264, 267.

47. For discussion of traders' views of women, see Vibert, *Traders' Tales*, Chs. 4 and 7.

48. Thompson, *Narrative*, 548–52; HBCA, B.45/e/2, fo. 5.

49. Simpson, *Journal 1824–25*, 140.

50. Thompson, *Narrative*, 80; UBC Sp. Coll., Ermatinger Papers, 237–8.

51. J. M. Coetzee, *White Writings: One the Culture of Letters in South Africa* (New Haven: Yale University Press, 1988); Mary Louise Pratt, *Imperial Eyes: Travel Writing and Transculturation* (London: Routledge, 1992).

52. Franchere, *Journal*, in *Franchère's Journal of Voyage on the Northwest Coast of North America 1811–1814*, ed. W. Kaye Lamb and trans. W. T. Lamb (Toronto: Champlain Society, 1969), 155; Thompson, *Narrative*, 388–92, 474, 476, 484.

53. See Hunn, "Mobility as a Factor"; Nancy Turner, *Ancient Pathways, Ancestral Knowledge: Ethnobotany and Ecological Wisdom of Indigenous Peoples of Northwestern North America* (Montreal: McGill-Queen's University Press, 2014); Turner, *Thompson Ethnobotany*.

54. HBCA, PP 1828-1, Queries Connected with Natural History, fo. 1, queries 41–4.

55. Turner, *Thompson Ethnobotany*; Richard B. Lee and Richard Daly, eds, *The Cambridge Encyclopedia of Hunters and Gatherers* (Cambridge: Cambridge University Press, 2004).

56. Hunn, *Nch'i-Wana*; Turner, *Thompson Ethnobotany*, 13, 28.

57. Hunn, *Nch'i-Wana*, 208.

Primary Document

Report from Colvile District, "Answers to Queries on Natural History," 1829

John Work

Hudson's Bay Company Archives [HBCA], B.45/e/2, fos. 1, 4, 5, 12 [extracts]

[fo. 1] [The Colvile District is situated] West of the Rocky Mountains at the Kettle Falls on the Columbia [River], the highest establishment on the river, it is named Fort Colvile. I have been five years in the district, one at Spokane, one at the Flat Head [post] and three at this place. . . .

[The local Indigenous peoples include] The Columbia, the Pendant d'Oreille, the Kooteny [sic], and the Spokane with their branches. . . . [These communities' preferred names are Sinkiuse-Columbia, Pend d'Oreilles or Kalispel, Kootenai and Ktunaxa, and Spokane.]

[fo. 4] [They live] On the produce of the chase, the animals found in their forests and plains, and the fish of their rivers & lakes; And on roots and berries, the spontaneous produce of the earth. The only instance of agriculture I have heard of in the district is among the Kootanees where, with great ceremony, a small quantity of a kind of tobacco is raised. . . .

[fo. 5] A small portion of their time is taken up making their hunting and fishing implements, canoes &c, but the far greater part is employed gambling, in which both sexes and both old and young join, or loitered away in idlings. The young of both sexes but particularly the men, when not depressed in spirit for want of food or other causes, employ no inconsiderable portion of the morning decorating themselves; in point of time, and the degree of pains taken to ornament their hair, paint their faces &c they may compete with the more accomplished fops in the civilised world. The remainder of the day and often the night is spent, most frequently, gallanting, gambling & the like. Some occasionally employ themselves in trading excursions among their neighbours. They are also very fond of visiting & of making singing and dancing parties which are mostly of a religious nature. . . .

[fo. 12] They exchange furs, provisions and other articles, for arms ammunition, axes, kettles, knives, woolen goods, Trinkets &c with the Europeans. And with the neighbouring tribes a barter is carried on with articles as are wanted by the one and can be spared by the other.

Secondary Source

Innu Participation in the Saguenay-Lac-Saint-Jean Fur Trade, 1888–1950

Brian Gettler

In 1888, the first train arrived in Roberval, a small French-Canadian community on the shores of Lac-Saint-Jean, from Quebec City on the Quebec and Lake St John Railway. Three decades earlier, the United Province of Canada had decreed that roughly 3200 hectares be set aside at Pointe-Bleue (Mashteuiatsh), immediately adjacent to this newly founded town, for the creation of a reserve for the people then widely known as the Montagnais (Innu). The reserve was situated in the heart of the vast territory occupied by the Innu, who had lived along Lac-Saint-Jean, the Saguenay River, and the north shore of the St Lawrence since before the arrival of Europeans in the sixteenth century. Although minuscule when compared to this much larger region, Mashteuiatsh served as a home base from which Innu families continued through the mid-twentieth century to travel each year deep into the bush to earn a living. The reserve and its proximity to towns like Roberval also served to tie the Innu ever more closely to the capitalist market and non-Indigenous society. As communities across Quebec, Canada, and throughout North America struggled with the profound social and economic changes of the late nineteenth and the first half of the twentieth century, the Mashteuiatsh Innu struggled alongside them, altering their daily lives according to their specific cultural prerogatives so they could survive in this challenging environment.[1]

The arrival of the railroad allowed non-Indigenous sportsmen unprecedented access to the bush and its resources, accelerating changes in the Indigenous economy that had begun during the preceding decades. This chapter describes the process through which Innu society, like that of both Quebec and Canada, underwent significant change in the decades that followed, as families spent less time in the bush and more time on reserve, earning an increasing portion of their livelihood from wage work, agriculture, and other sedentary economic activities.[2] At the same time, families spent growing amounts of income securing material needs and desires through the market economy. The Great Depression and the collapse of fur prices at the end of the Second World War made this turn to the market for subsistence permanent, even as the provincial and federal states first tightened hunting and trapping regulations and then replaced private enterprise in the purchase and marketing of Innu furs.

Saguenay-Lac-Saint-Jean at the End of the Nineteenth Century

Saguenay-Lac-Saint-Jean roughly corresponds to the region drained by the Saguenay River, covering nearly 100,000 km^2 between the St Lawrence in the south and the height of land to the north, Mauricie (the area drained by the St Maurice River) to the west and the North Shore on the east. In the mid-seventeenth century, French officials had set aside Saguenay-Lac-Saint-Jean as part of the King's Domain or King's Posts, guaranteeing the Crown a monopoly on the region's fur trade. Through the mid-nineteenth century, French and later British officials maintained this privilege, most often leasing trading rights to private, profit-seeking companies while banning permanent settlement not linked to the fur trade or missionary work. In 1842, authorities in Canada East officially opened the region to colonization, accepting their inability to prevent the illicit settlement tied to commercial logging that had been taking place along the Saguenay since the late 1830s. Sixteen years later, the monopoly to the King's Posts fur trade, then held by the Hudson's Bay Company (HBC), expired, formally permitting competition in the region's fur-buying market for the first time in over two centuries. These changes combined to integrate Saguenay-Lac-Saint-Jean and its population into the political community centred on the St Lawrence Valley and the Lower Great Lakes, foreshadowing Canada's 1870 incorporation of Rupert's Land. Several developments contributed to remaking the region's politics and its economy: roads, and, later, railroads were created and maintained; the administrative apparatus of the state was imported; and standard weights and measures and an officially backed currency were imposed. These changes shifted the weight from monopolistic fur trade companies and their Indigenous trading partners to civil servants, businessmen, local professional elites, and a handful of prosperous farmers.[3]

The European-Canadian presence in the region boomed from this point. Prior to the 1830s, there were fewer than 150 Innu in Saguenay-Lac-Saint-Jean. By 1891 the Innu represented only 1.4 per cent of the region's total population of 29,000, a proportion that would grow slightly by 1951 to 4.3 per cent of the nearly 200,000 residents.[4] Furthermore, although initially restricted to the shores of the Saguenay River and Lac-Saint-Jean, non-Indigenous settlement had, by the mid-twentieth century, spread up to 40 kilometres into the interior in certain places, eliminating vast swaths of traditional hunting and trapping grounds.[5] As this process of dispossession and alteration of the landscape intensified, sportsmen and conservationists successfully pushed the province to begin eliminating exemptions previously granted First Nations for hunting, fishing, and trapping, further complicating Innu access to hunting territories and their resources.[6] These developments had profound impacts on Innu economic activity in general, and on the fur trade in particular.

Innu Trading Practice in the Context of Fierce Fur-Buying Competition

As had been the case for hundreds of years, the HBC, by far the largest purchaser of furs operating in the subarctic, based its profit model in the late nineteenth century on the mutually dependent annual cycle and debt system.[7] In theory, in late summer trappers purchased on credit the necessary provisions for life in the bush during the winter. By the beginning of the following summer, they returned to the post at which they had received credit and settled their debt by selling their furs to the company. If each trapper repaid his debt in full, the HBC turned a handsome profit both on the purchase of furs and the sale of provisions. Even in the best of economic times, however, Indigenous trappers, whether in Saguenay-Lac-Saint-Jean or elsewhere, were rarely debt-free.

Nineteenth-century colonization in the region reconfigured the debt system as the HBC lost its effective monopoly on both fur buying and the sale of provisions. With the increasing non-Indigenous population came a corresponding growth in the number of independent buyers. Most of these men purchased furs as a sideline, earning the majority of their income from other activities such as seasonal work in lumber camps. Since they had neither the capital nor the ability to manage the large stocks of trading goods on which fur companies had long relied, these men traded on a purely cash basis. At the same time, the Innu had increasing access to other retailers who happily accepted such money in exchange for goods. From the perspective of HBC management, these developments posed an enormous threat to the company's bottom line by potentially increasing outstanding debt and decreasing profits on both furs and provisions. However, its brief attempts during the late 1870s to end the use of credit in Saguenay-Lac-Saint-Jean proved ineffective, forcing the HBC to reverse course by the time the railroad arrived in Roberval, reinstating credit and beginning to use cash to secure Innu patronage.[8]

In the early years of the twentieth century, the HBC saw its declining portion of the Saguenay-Lac-Saint-Jean fur trade further eroded by the arrival of two major competitors. Revillon Frères, a nearly 200-year-old French manufacturer of luxury fur goods, began purchasing directly from trappers throughout the subarctic at the turn of the century, basing its buying operations on the HBC's centuries-old model. By 1906, the French company was operating a trading post on the opposite end of central Mashteuiatsh from the HBC, where it remained active until 1933, when it relocated to Roberval. Revillon Frères finally ceased all operations in 1936 when the HBC purchased its Canadian fur-buying operations.[9] At about the same time that Revillon Frères began operations in the region, Méridé Robertson opened a store in Mashteuiatsh, where he also purchased furs and sold provisions.[10] However, Robertson was not backed by international capital nor was he a newcomer to the region; he was a member of the Innu community who, along with his descendants, proved to be a particularly effective competitor of both the HBC and of Revillon Frères. Throughout the first half of the twentieth century, and indeed to the present day, the Robertson family continued to purchase furs and sell goods.[11] In addition to these major actors, several small buyers moved in and out of the fur market throughout this period. Most of these men travelled over relatively large areas to secure furs from a variety of sources, including the Saguenay-Lac-Saint-Jean Innu. In 1933, for example, only five of the eight buyers active in the region were permanently based there (Brassard in Roberval, Clément Dufour in Chicoutimi, and the HBC, Revillon Frères, and Méridé Robertson in Mashteuiatsh). The other three came from as far away as Montreal.[12]

As fur buyers proliferated in the region in the early twentieth century, the Innu enjoyed a flourishing market and good hunts over a series of years. Although it is difficult to conclusively correlate the arrival of new trading partners and Innu financial well-being, it is clear that the presence of Revillon Frères, Méridé Robertson, and others led to a seller's market in which the proliferation of buyers kept fur prices high. Indeed, in the years between the French company's arrival and the outbreak of the First World War, those Innu who engaged in trapping had "good" hunts and found "the price of furs very remunerative."[13] Moreover, competition between fur buyers pushed HBC regional management to abandon its preferential treatment of "loyal" trappers through the practice of paying higher prices for the purpose of debt reimbursement, to both pay and accept cash in any and all possible transactions, and to actively court the business of non-Indigenous people.[14] Although the outbreak of war radically altered the Canadian fur trade by rerouting furs from the traditionally dominant international auctions in London and Leipzig to competitors in New York, St Louis, and Montreal, this high-level change appears to have only marginally affected the Innu. Although the HBC initially refused to make the switch to North American auctions, as a result slashing cash purchases and the provision of credit, smaller traders continued their activities in much the same way as they had before the war, absorbing many of the furs the Innu would otherwise have sold to the HBC.[15] Given the paucity of sources for the Saguenay-Lac-Saint-Jean fur trade during the war and to independent fur buyers in the region in general, it is difficult to assess the impact of the war on Innu trappers' incomes.[16] Although trappers' combined revenue may have fallen by as much as 45 per cent between 1914 and 1916, half of this amount had been recouped by the end of the war.[17]

By the early 1920s, Innu income from the fur trade had rebounded to pre-war levels despite Canada's deep postwar recession.[18] Relatively high prices would continue in Saguenay-Lac-Saint-Jean throughout the 1920s, due in part to a powerful new marketing strategy adopted by the Innu during the decade to take advantage of fierce competition among fur buyers. Trappers organized what one HBC employee termed "auction sale[s]" where buyers proposed prices, with "the highest bid get[ting] the Furs."[19] Through this mechanism, in operation through at least the mid-1930s, trappers sold their catch on the open market and used the proceeds to reimburse whatever debt they had previously incurred.[20] The Innu generally held these auctions either on the reserve or in the neighbouring towns of Roberval and Saint-Félicien and invited all interested parties to attend to place bids. A June 1935 entry in the HBC's Mashteuiatsh post journal makes the practice's attractiveness to trappers clear: "Baptiste Philippe's fur was worth about $525.00. Brassard of Roberval bid $475.00[.] Clement Dufour bid $535.00 so [HBC employees] G. Fowlie & L.G. Tassé bid $550.00. Then the fun started and Dufour began bidding up the furs as he did on the Boivin deal. The Company's men were determined to purchase, on account of the moral affect [sic] on the Indians, and kept raising their prices until they got the lot at $620.00."[21] In this case, as in many others, auctioning furs allowed the Innu to earn amounts well above those they would have received from isolated buyers.[22] Although clearly wary of this practice, the HBC and other buyers adopted it since they felt that refusing to do so could lead trappers to neglect them altogether.

In an effort to increase its Innu patronage and presumably to decrease the amount of fur sold at auction, the HBC responded by re-introducing to the region a long-abandoned commercial technique: the outpost. During the 1920s, the company opened a post on the Ashuapmouchouan River under the management of Tom Moar, and established another trading site, most likely in the vicinity of Chibougamau, under Napoléon Bégin.[23] These outposts opened exclusively in the winter, conducting business in the heart of Innu hunting and trapping territory as a means of increasing the HBC's market share. Rather than the formal environment of the company's stores, the sites were essentially well-stocked winter camps, from which Moar, Bégin, and their families based their own hunting and trapping activities. The HBC's employment of Moar and Bégin, both of whom were members of the Mashteuiatsh band (though Moar was originally from Mistassini) of mixed Indigenous and European heritage, reflected its interwar practice of hiring precisely such men to manage its outposts throughout Canada.[24] The HBC outfitted such "independent" traders at advantageous prices in the hope that they would be able to protect the company's credit by collecting furs caught in the vicinity of their outpost.[25] Once again, though, the HBC's commercial strategy proved less than entirely successful. Though both Moar and Bégin successfully secured a portion of the Innu fur catch for the HBC, they refused to subordinate their own personal economic interests to those of the company. Although they had received their "goods for cost" from the HBC, both men sold their personal catch via auction, using the proceeds to repay the HBC in cash.[26] Moreover, rather than exclusively using these goods in their dealings with other Innu, both Moar and Bégin spent large amounts of cash on furs, thereby decreasing the company's profits.[27] Although such practices must have exasperated HBC staff, they do not appear to have been the cause of the decline and ultimate disappearance of both outposts during the 1930s.[28] Their closure can be explained in particular by the decade's twin shocks of economic and ecological disaster and, more generally, the unprecedented reordering of the Saguenay-Lac-Saint-Jean fur trade in the years leading up to mid-century.

The Péribonka Beaver Sanctuary and the State's Direct Market Intervention

The Great Depression marked a turning point for the Saguenay-Lac-Saint-Jean fur trade. Though the Innu managed to maintain their system of fur auctions through the middle of the decade, the economic downturn pushed many unemployed men to leave the cities of the south in the hopes earning a living through trapping in the subarctic. This movement resulted in the simultaneous loss of Indigenous trappers' income and the collapse and near extinction of the beaver population.[29] At the same time, fur prices on the world market, already declining during the late 1920s, fell to historic lows in the early 1930s, before briefly rebounding at the end of the decade and falling once more during the early years of the Second World War.[30] This Canada-wide phenomenon had become particularly troubling in Saguenay-Lac-Saint-Jean by the middle of the 1930s when, according to anthropologist Julius E. Lips, $500 in trapping income for an Innu family, including husband, wife, and three adult children constituted "a good average year."[31] From roughly $120 in 1866–67, the average Innu family earned, in its dealings with the HBC alone, approximately $230 in 1905, $550 five years later, and roughly $700 in 1924–25.[32] Since HBC numbers fail to account for all Innu revenue, this decrease would appear to be in line with the 44 per cent loss in income on average across Quebec and comparable to the average income earned by the lowest-paid, unskilled, non-Indigenous workers in the province.[33] After years of this unprecedented crisis, the provincial and federal governments intervened to encourage the re-establishment of the region's beaver population and what civil servants hoped would be the revitalization of the Innu economy.

In 1941, Ottawa and Quebec City created an approximately 32,630 square-kilometre beaver preserve on the Péribonka River north of Lac-Saint-Jean. It was divided into 28 sections, and one or several Innu tallymen were responsible for maintaining beaver counts and reporting poaching in each section. Authorities assigned 12 of these sections to residents of Mashteuiatsh and 16 to residents of Pessamit, a reserve community on the north shore of the St Lawrence whose members were also to have access to the sanctuary. Officials began by restocking each section with live-trapped beaver from elsewhere in the country. Then, over the course of nearly a decade, beaver trapping was proscribed by law, giving them time to reproduce in sufficient numbers to once again support commercial trapping. This project owed its existence not only to the Depression but also to the success of similar projects launched from 1929 in eastern James Bay, the region immediately north of Saguneay-Lac-Saint-Jean.[34]

Despite the creation of the beaver sanctuary, access to trapping grounds remained difficult for two reasons. First, the project required several years of closed trapping in which the beaver population could grow. Second, the region's relatively large non-Indigenous population had far more experience than the Innu in dealing with provincial bureaucracy, making them more adept at navigating provincial hunting, fishing, and trapping regulations. As a result, European-Canadians snapped up hunting leases on Crown lands while the Innu waited for officials to open the Péribonka preserve to trapping. Although powerless to change this situation, several residents of Mashteiuatsh made their dissatisfaction known to the Indian agent, who, given the tone of his correspondence with his superiors in Ottawa, fully shared both their attitude and their inability to inspire action from federal and provincial decision-makers.[35] The Innus' powerlessness in accessing the preserve even as late as the end of the decade and the limitations this placed on trappers' ability to function independently predictably produced resentment and resistance among some individuals.[36] Among other acts, several Innu defied the legal restrictions placed on trapping to continue their activities and earn a livelihood, in the process risking fines that could reach several hundred dollars.[37]

Regardless of written protests and willful acts of resistance, the Péribonka beaver sanctuary only opened for production during the 1949–50 season. From this point, married men could trap 20 beaver and single men were permitted 10 each, with previously appointed tallymen receiving priority to trap in their sections of the sanctuary. In contrast to earlier fur trade practice, private buyers such as the HBC did not have access to the harvested pelts. Instead, following an advance provided through local stores of up to $10, the Indian agent forwarded each Innu's harvest to provincial game officials who oversaw its sale at auction. Each trapper would then receive the difference between the final sale price and any advances he had received from Indian Affairs minus handling fees, state royalties, and 10 per cent tallymen wages on the price paid at auction.[38]

Despite the theoretical implementation of this system, the Indian Agent at Mashteuiatsh remained unaware of its details and his own role in purchasing and marketing furs even after trappers had begun returning to the reserve in December

1949 with their initial catch.[39] The preserve's management also experienced other major problems during its first year of operations. Although the Quebec government supplied Indian Affairs with the proceeds of its mid-January 1950 fur auction within a month, the staff at the federal agency's headquarters required a further month to inform its Quebec fur supervisor of the amount each trapper was to receive.[40] Due to this general lack of preparation, Indian Affairs' inability to publicize the preserve's opening, and the lethargic pace of payment, Péribonka's first season proved a dismal failure. Indeed, Innu from both Mashteuiatsh and Pessamit combined to trap only 210 of the 1000 beaver that the Quebec Fish and Game Department had authorized for the whole sanctuary during 1949–50.[41] Furthermore, although the incomplete archival record for Péribonka does not permit an in-depth analysis of fur prices, the contemporaneous case of the Kesagami beaver preserve near Moose Factory, Ontario suggests that they were most likely far below those paid before the Depression. In this sense, it would seem that the benefits of a renewed population of fur-bearing animals in Saguenay-Lac-Saint-Jean may well have been offset by low prices and the replacement of seasoned commercial fur buyers with often marginally competent and ill-informed civil servants.[42]

Conclusion

Between the end of the nineteenth and the middle of the twentieth century, the Saguenay-Lac-Saint-Jean fur trade underwent massive change in terms of both its structure and, when seen from the perspective of the trappers who supplied the vast majority of its labour, its profitability. This second shift explains concurrent developments in the Innu economy. Though the fur trade remained Mashteuiatsh's primary economic motor until the end of the Depression, it produced ever-diminishing returns, leading to the growth of other economic activities.[43] For most, this initially meant adopting seasonal wage labour, the manufacture for sale of traditional goods such as moccasins and snowshoes, and agriculture, alongside hunting, fishing, trapping, and gathering. However, as time went on, these other activities slowly displaced the fur trade and, by the mid-twentieth century, wage labour had come to dominate Mashteuiatsh's economy.

This move towards wage work had begun immediately following the railroad's arrival in Roberval. Innu men found abundant work guiding the sportsmen from southern Quebec and the United States who flocked to Saguenay-Lac-Saint-Jean where, according to an 1889 *New York Times* article, "The water is full of fish, the woods are full of game, and 100 miles around it, in any direction, you can go and stand where no white man ever stood before."[44] This sort of work, which resembled but was not identical to the fur trade of old, remained central to Mashteuiatsh's economy through mid-century and was joined by other activities, allowing the Innu to frequent the bush and to engage in animal stewardship as their ancestors had done for generations.[45] The manufacture for sale of traditional objects such as moccasins generated considerable income for women and girls, whether they spent the majority of their time in the bush with their family or lived year-round in Mashteuiatsh. Men, too, engaged in such work, although, rather than moccasins, they specialized in the production for sale of snowshoes.[46]

Until the Depression and the collapse of the fur market and the beaver population, such work complemented rather than replaced participation in the fur trade for most Innu. From the late 1930s and 1940s, though, Mashteuiatsh's economy underwent rapid change as ever-increasing numbers of Innu took year-round wage work in saw-mills, forestry, and mineral prospecting. In this sense, the state's intervention in fur conservation proved simply to be a case of too little, too late.[47] Indeed, in addition to the major problems associated with the opening of trapping on the Péribonka sanctuary, the large numbers who had already abandoned the fur trade as their primary source of revenue explain why the Innu harvested so few beaver in 1949–50.

By the middle of the twentieth century, then, the fur trade occupied a marginal position in the economy of Saguenay-Lac-Saint-Jean's Indigenous population. In some sense, it is remarkable that this change took so long to occur. European-Canadians had been flooding into the region since the end of the 1880s, establishing farms and clearing vast regions of what had until then been prime fur-producing areas. During the next 40 years, though, the Innu proved extremely adept at continuing their participation in the fur trade, whether as trappers who spent the majority of their year in the bush or, as in the case of Méridé Robertson and his descendants, as savvy, reserve-based businessmen. They adopted novel techniques for marketing their furs, benefiting from intense competition among fur buyers, while supplementing their income through allied activities. The Depression, though, spelled the end of this lifestyle for the vast majority of Innu, an end that a well-meaning, though ultimately ineffective, state program of fur conservation proved unable to avert.

Notes

1. Scholars have long underlined the importance of culture to the ways in which both First Nations and Canadians of European origin reacted to changing economic and social conditions. See, for example, Gérard Bouchard, *Quelques Arpents d'Amérique: Population, économie, famille au Saguenay, 1838–1971* (Montréal: Boréal, 1996) and John Sutton Lutz, *Makúk: A New History of Aboriginal–White Relations* (Vancouver: UBC Press, 2008).

2. Claude Gélinas, *Indiens, Eurocanadiens et le cadre social du métissage au Saguenay-Lac-Saint-Jean, XVIIe–XXe siècle* (Sillery, QC: Septentrion, 2011), 84–7.

3. On this process, see Brian Gettler, "Money and the Changing Nature of Colonial Space in Northern Quebec: Fur Trade Monopolies, the State, and Aboriginal Peoples during the Nineteenth Century," *Histoire sociale/Social History* 46, 92 (November 2013), 271–93.

4. For the 1831 population estimate, see "Indian Population of the King's Posts & Mille Vaches Seigniory, 1831," 1 August 1831, HBCA, E.20/1, reel 4M127, f. 83. For the other non-Indigenous figures, see Camil Girard and Normand Perron, *Histoire Du Saguenay-Lac-Saint-Jean* (Québec:

Institut québécois de recherche sur la culture, 1989): 144. In 1891, the Department of Indian Affairs reported 403 Innu living on the reserve, a figure that had grown to 860 in 1949. *Indian Affairs Annual Report, 1891*, 246 and Gélinas, *Indiens, Eurocanadiens et le cadre social du métissage*, 112.

5. Girard and Perron, Histoire Du Saguenay-Lac-Saint-Jean, 133.

6. On the history of the interaction of sportsmen's and conservationist groups and wildlife regulation in Quebec, see Darcy Ingram, *Wildlife, Conservation, and Conflict in Quebec, 1840–1914* (Vancouver: UBC Press, 2013).

7. On the debt system, see Toby Morantz, "'So Evil a Practice': A Look at the Debt System in the James Bay Fur Trade," in *Merchant Credit and Labour Strategies in Historical Perspective*, ed. Rosemary E. Ommer (Fredericton: Acadiensis Press, 1990), 203–22; On the nineteenth-century fur trade in Saguenay-Lac-Saint-Jean, see Gettler, "Money and the Changing Nature of Colonial Space."

8. Ibid.

9. The HBC had actually purchased a controlling stake in Revillon Frères in 1926. Although it

tried to keep this purchase secret in order to discourage new competitors in the fur trade, controlling fur prices, limiting debt, and lowering operating costs, information of the merger circulated widely and employees of the two companies continued competing, refusing to forget the hard feelings built up over decades. Lynda Harris, "Revillon Frères Trading Company Limited: Fur Traders of the North, 1901–1936" (n.p.: Ministry of Culture and Recreation for the Ministry of Natural Resources, Northern Region, Ontario, 1976), 65–82.

10. For the location of the Revillon Frères, HBC, and Méridé Robertson stores in 1910, see Stuart S. Oliver, "James' Bay and Eastern Railway. Plan shewing Indian Village, Pointe-Bleue," 21 September 1910, Bibliothèque et Archives nationales du Québec—Québec (BanQ-Q), CA301, S41, D45D.

11. Tommy Robertson, for example, ran the business by 1947. [J.N. Stevenson], "Report on Beaver Trapping Re Joseph Simeon," s.d. [17 November 1947], LAC, RG10, Vol. 6754, file 420-10-4-PE-1. On the family's present-day activities, see René Robertson Fourrures, www.fourruresrobertson .com/, retrieved 15 August 2014.

12. Tuesday, 1 June 1933, HBCA, B.329/a/16, p. 1, reel 1MA53. The number of fur buyers seems to have diminished during the Great Depression. During the 1920s, at least another local merchant, Alfred Drolet of Saint-Félicien, bought furs in his general store. Wednesday, 7 May 1924, HBCA, B.329/a/8, 36, reel 1MA53.

13. Armand Tessier, "Report on the Montagnais of Lake St. John," 11 June 1910, in *Indian Affairs Annual Reports*, *1910*, 50. Five years earlier, the Indian agent made nearly identical comments: "The hunt this year was very good for all, and the price obtained for the furs very remunerative." Alphonse Marcoux, Report on the Montagnais of Lake St. John, 25 September 1905, in *Indian Affairs Annual Reports*, *1905*, p. 46. The agent made similar remarks in 1913. Armand Tessier, Report on the Montagnais of Lake St John, 7 June 1913, in *Indian Affairs Annual Reports*, *1913*, 53.

14. C.G. Wilson to W.R. Hamilton, 30 November 1912, HBCA, B.329/c/3, f. 518-9, reel 1MB90.

15. Arthur J. Ray, *The Canadian Fur Trade in the Industrial Age* (Toronto: University of Toronto Press, 1990), 99–102. Although mentioning several "Quebec Dealers," HBC correspondence only refers to Vermette by name. C.G. Wilson to W.R. Hamilton, 28 November 1914, HBCA, B.329/c/4, f. 187, reel 1MB90 and C.G. Wilson

to W.R. Hamilton, 8 December 1914, Ibid., fo. 191.

16. Indian Affairs tabular statements, an imprecise yet still useful estimate of economic activity, is the only source allowing for some notion of the volume of Innu wartime fur sales. On their use as an historical source, see Appendix 2: "Reliability of Department of Indian Affairs Estimates" in Lutz, *Makúk*: 316–7.

17. In 1914, Indian Affairs reported that the "Lake St. John" band earned a total of $45,000 "by Hunting and Trapping." Table no. 12, "Sources and Value of Income," in *Indian Affairs Annual Report, 1916*: 123. Two years later, this figure had fallen to $25,000 before rebounding to $35,000 in 1919. Table no. 12, "Sources and Value of Income," in *Indian Affairs Annual Report, 1916*: 113 and Table no. 6, "Sources and Value of Income," in *Indian Affairs Annual Report, 1919, 78.*

18. In 1922, Indian Affairs reported Innu earnings of $43,000 from hunting and trapping over the preceding year. This figure is $2000 short of that reported in 1914. Table no. 6, "Sources and Value of Income," in *Indian Affairs Annual Report, 1922*, 56.

19. Tuesday, 26 May 1925, HBCA, B.329/a/9, 46, reel 1MA53.

20. The Clearys' 1925 sale illustrates the auction's use in this respect. According to the HBC's post journal: "Two of our Hunters arrived today, Wm. & Chs. Clarey. They will sell tomorrow, by auction. . . . We got the lots of Wm. & Charles Clarey this morning, Dufour's bid being lower than our's. 75 Beavers in that lot." Sunday 7 and Monday 8 June 1925, HBCA, B.329/a/10, p. 1, reel 1MA53. The Innu also continued to reimburse their debt in the "traditional" manner, through the use of furs not cash. "Eustache Robertson was in this morning with enough Furs to pay for his account." Wednesday, 5 January 1927, HBCA, B.329/a/11, fo. 21r, reel 1MA53.

21. Friday, 14 June 1935, HBCA, B.329/a/18, 5, reel 1MA53.

22. HBC archival sources make this process of bidding up prices abundantly clear. For example, the Pointe Bleue post journal notes: "Mr. Tassé and G. Fowlie made four or five trips to see fur of Baptiste Philippe. All the other buyers made bids and we finally secured it for $780.00." Tuesday, 6 June 1933, HBCA, B.329/a/16, 1, reel 1MA53.

23. The first reference to the outpost on the Ashuapmouchouan River in the Pointe Bleue journals dates to the fall of 1924. Thursday,

9 October and Friday, 10 October 1924, HBCA, B.329/a/9, 16, reel 1MA53. The HBC had also operated a post on the site, approximately 90 miles upriver from Lac St. Jean, prior to 1850. On the post's history, see J. Allan Burgesse, "The Unwanted Post," *Canadian Historical Review*, vol. 28, no. 4 (December 1947): 401–10. Between the early 1890s and 1903, the HBC again operated an outpost here, abandoning it when its manager, the Innu Charles Robertson, resigned. S.K. Parson, "Report: Rupert's River District, Mistassinni Post," 9 September 1891, HBCA, B.133/e/17, 12–3, reel 1M1257 and P. McKenzie to W.R. Hamilton, 14 March 1903, HBCA, B.329/c/2, f. 208, reel 1MB89. Information on the outpost near Chibougamau comes from several sources. In 1926, the Pointe Bleue post journal notes that, "Napoleon Begin left today, leaving Tom Moar the only one of our men to go now." Wednesday, 28 July 1926, HBCA, B.329/a/11, 5, reel 1MA53. Although he fails to mention the individual who ran the outpost, Burgesse, in his article on the history of the HBC's Ashuapmouchouan posts, refers to "a second establishment [that] was located at Chibougamau, a little further north" during the 1930s. Burgesse, "The Unwanted Post," 410.

24. Ray writes: "by 1919 'native' (mixed-blood) men managed a high proportion of its outposts." Although these men worked hard, their employment proved problematic from the HBC's perspective. "Most native men were illiterate and they had been given no training in simple bookkeeping. Even more troublesome, they extended credit too liberally to their kinfolk, and often they paid too much for their furs." Ray, *The Canadian Fur Trade in the Industrial Age*, 110.

25. Ibid., 76.

26. In 1931, for example, the company's Masteuiatsh post journal records that, "Tom Moar . . . had about $250.00 in furs which he left on his account and $130.00 his personal hunt which I paid in cash. There were four buyers there to see him besides me Meridy Robertson, Mr. Brousseau, A. Drolet, and Eugene Simard. Meridy Robertson bought a small lot from him." Wednesday, 1 April 1931, HBCA, B.329/a/14, 24, reel 1MA53. For Bégin's use of the auction, see Saturday, 8 June 1931, B.329/a/14, 39, reel 1MA53.

27. In the fall of 1925, for example, cash accounted for over 30 per cent of the value of Tom Moar's trade stock. The HBC would have preferred that Moar deal in goods and the repayment of debt alone. The company's Pointe Bleue post journal records that "Mr. Moor left this AM at 10, with about 700.00 Dollars of merchandise and 325.00 in Cash."13 October 1925, HBCA, B.329/a/10, 15, reel 1MA53.

28. J. Allan Burgesse, an employee of the HBC's Pointe Bleue post during the period, writes, based on his personal recollection, that both posts "disappeared quietly around 1937." Burgesse, "The Unwanted Post," 410.

29. Claude Gélinas, *Les Autochtones dans le Québec post-confédéral, 1867–1960* (Sillery, QC: Septentrion, 2007), 205.

30. Ray, *The Canadian Fur Trade in the Industrial Age*, 114.

31. Julius E. Lips, "Naskapi Law: (Lake St. John and Lake Mistassini Bands) Law and Order in a Hunting Society," *Transactions of the American Philosophical Society* 37, 4 (December 1947): 439.

32. For the 1866–67 numbers, see Gettler, "Money and the Changing Nature of Colonial Space," 288. The other estimates are based on the population figures reported by the Department of Indian Affairs, Lips' judgment that Mashteuiatsh's mid-1930s population of 776 individuals represented approximately 50 families that the HBC outfitted each year, and the HBC's valuation of its trade on the reserve. *Indian Affairs Annual Reports*, 1905, 1910, and 1924, Lips, "Naskapi Law": 451, and HBCA, A.74/15, fo. 31, A.74/20, f. 32, and A.76/40a, 151.

33. Sylvie Taschereau, "Les années dures de la crise," in *Histoire de Montréal et de sa région*, ed. Dany Fougères, vol. II: 1930 à nos jours (Québec: Presses de l'Université Laval, 2012): 807 and Andrée Lévesque, *Virage à gauche interdit: Les communistes, les socialistes et leurs ennemis au Québec 1929–1939* (Montréal: Boréal, 1984), 15.

34. On beaver conservation in eastern James Bay, see Toby Morantz, *The White Man's Gonna Getcha: The Colonial Challenge to the Crees in Quebec* (Montreal & Kingston: McGill-Queen's University Press, 2002), 158–75.

35. The clearly exasperated Indian agent asked his superiors whether "the Indians are allowed to trap there this year???? When? Are indians entitled to trap beaver??? How many per season???" Edgar Arsenault to Indian Affairs Branch, 15 November 1948, LAC, RG10, Vol. 6754, file 420-10-4-PE-1. This animated letter only managed to inspire the bland response that the sanctuary would remain closed during the 1948–49 season. H.R. Conn to E. Arsenault, 22 November 1948, LAC, RG10, Vol. 6754, file 420-10-4-PE-1.

36. David Massell, *Quebec Hydropolitics: The Peribonka Concessions of the Second World War* (Montreal & Kingston: McGill-Queen's University Press, 2011), 161.

37. On alleged Innu poachers in the Péribonka beaver sanctuary and in nearby Parc de la Manouane and Parc de la rivière modeste in the late 1940s, see LAC, RG10, Vol. 6754, file 420-10-4-PE-1. In one 1947 case, the court, following an investigation by Indian Affairs officials, RCMP officers, and the Quebec Department of Game and Fisheries, fined the accused $175 in addition to approximately $200 in legal charges.

38. H.R. Conn to Lucien Morisset, 26 October 1949, LAC, RG10, vol. 6754, file 420-10-4-PE-1 and Lucien Morisset, "Peribonka Beaver and Fur Preserve Annual Report, 1950," s.d. [14 October 1950], LAC, RG10, Vol. 6754, file 420-10-4-PE-3.

39. Edgar Arsenault to H.R. Conn, 13 December 1949, LAC, RG10, Vol. 6754, file 420-10-4-PE-1.

40. Lucien Morisset to H.R. Conn, 5 January 1950, Lucien Morisset to H.R. Conn, 25 January 1950, Lucien Morisset to H.R. Conn, 13 March 1950, and Hugh R. Conn to Lucien Morisset, 14 March 1950, LAC, RG10, Vol. 6754, file 420-10-4-PE-4.

41. Lucien Morisset, "Peribonka Beaver and Fur Preserve Annual Report, 1950," s.d. [14 October 1950], LAC, RG10, vol. 6754, file 420-10-4-PE-3.

42. On the Kesagami beaver sanctuary, see Brian Gettler, "Colonialism's Currency: A Political History of First Nations Money-Use in Quebec and Ontario, 1820–1950" (PhD Diss (History), Université du Québec à Montréal, 2011), 362–76.

43. Gélinas, *Indiens, Eurocanadiens et le cadre social du métissage*, 81–2.

44. "In the Canadian Wilds: The Hudson's Bay Company's Country. The Lake St. John Wilderness, the Montagnais Indians, and the Great Ouananiche Fishing," *New York Times*, 4 August 1889, n.p.

45. By 1950, numerous Innu engaged in wage work raising mink and other market-based activities such as gathering blueberries for sale. Lucien Morisset, "Peribonka Beaver and Fur Preserve Annual Report, 1950," s.d. [14 October 1950], LAC, RG10, Vol. 6754, file 420-10-4-PE-3.

46. Lips, "Naskapi Law," 450.

47. Gélinas, *Indiens, Eurocanadiens et le cadre social du métissage*, 85–7.

Primary Document

Annual Report of the Department of Indian Affairs for the Year Ended March 31, 1910

Dominion of Canada, PRINTED BY ORDER OF PARLIAMENT

Ottawa, Printed by C.H. Parmelee, Printer to the King's Most Excellent Majesty, 1910

Sessional Paper No. 27

Health and Sanitation.—There were no contagious diseases during the past year. Sanitary precautions have been observed. The houses as well as the surroundings are well kept.

Occupations.—The resources of the Indians are numerous. Several of them cultivate land, others work in the woods, load vessels, river-drive and act as guides to tourists. There is a good mill on the reserve, which gives employment as well as affording a convenience for their fire-wood.

Buildings.—The buildings are in general fairly good. The Indians have good houses, well furnished and well kept. They also have good barns and stables.

Stock.—Their stock is well kept. They have good horses, good cows and other stock.

Farm Implements.—Those who have sufficient land to cultivate are well supplied with farm implements. They know well how to use them and take good care of them.

Characteristics and Progress.—These Indians are good workers and command good wages, but some are still very improvident. However, I am pleased to observe that there is an improvement in this matter.

Religion.—All these Indians are Roman Catholics. The Capuchin Fathers are in charge of them and take great care of their spiritual and temporal welfare.

Temperance and Morality.—I regret to say that these Indians still have a very pronounced taste for liquor, which they procure very easily from neighbouring places in spite of the watchfulness exercised over them. Their morals are very good in general.

I have, &c.,

J. PITRE,
Indian Agent.

Province of Quebec,
Montagnais of Lake St. John,
Pointe Bleue, June 11, 1910.

Frank Pedley, Esq.,
Deputy Supt. General of Indian Affairs,
Ottawa.

Sir,—I have the honour to submit my report and statistical statement for the year ended March 31, 1910.

Tribe.—The Indians of Lake St. John belong to the Montagnais tribe.

Reserve.—This reserve is situated on the northwest shore of Lake St. John, in the county of Chicoutimi, province of Quebec, about 5 miles from the town of Roberval. It contains an area of 22,423 acres, comprising the whole of the township of Ouiatchouan, of which 19,525 acres has been surrendered by the band and sold for its benefit, which leaves for the use of the Indians an area of 2,900 acres. This part of Ouiatchouan township reserved for the Indians is known as Pointe Bleue, and is certainly, owing to its site, one of the prettiest and most healthful places of Lake St. John. From the top of the hill, a few yards from the shore, the view embraces a superb horizon. The soil is of superior quality, suitable for all kinds of cultivation, and, although this reserve is situated in the northern part of the province, its climate is magnificent.

Population.—The population of the reserve is 583.

Health and Sanitation.—The members of the band have as a rule enjoyed good health. They have not suffered from any epidemic disease during the course of the year. The laws of health appear to be better understood now by the Indians than formerly. In spring, when the weather gets warm enough, these Indians burn all the rubbish accumulated during the winter, and all make it a duty to ventilate their houses properly. The medical service is performed by Dr. J. Constantin, of Roberval, who discharges his duties religiously, one might say. All the sick Indians have been treated by him with care and diligence. Some of the Indians are extreme in their requirements, but rather than let them be discontented, the doctor, to my personal knowledge, has often complied with their caprices.

Occupations.—Two-thirds of the Indians of this reserve are hunters. Usually they leave the village in the beginning of September and go into the great forests of the north, whence they do not return as a rule until the end of June. Hunting has been good and the price of furs very remunerative. Other Indians live exclusively by the revenue of their lands, which they know how to cultivate with care. The lands, fences and ditches are well maintained. The taste for farming is certainly increasing among the Montagnais; they now take much more interest in agricultural matters than in the past. Finally these Indians are recognized as guides, canoemen, and experienced explorers. They are sought for as such and the revenue derived each year from this source is considerable.

Buildings.—The houses are sufficiently isolated from one another; they are suitable, comfortable, and kept with care by most of the Indians.

Stock.—The stock is well and regularly cared for, and there is a strong tendency towards improved breeding.

Farm Implements.—Those who engage in cultivation among the members of this band are well provided with modern farm implements. They make good use of them and take good care of them.

Characteristics and Progress.—As a rule the Montagnais are energetic and industrious. The number of the indolent, lazy and improvident is diminishing every year. They are intelligent and are not easily taken advantage of. Several of them have deposits in the banks at Roberval. There is certainly advancement in every respect.

Temperance and Morality.—In the matter of temperance things are going better than ever before, and this is the first time that I have not had to complain of the conduct of the Indians. They are beginning to understand that it is for their own good, for the good of their health and fortune, to abstain from intoxicating liquor. I have not had to deplore any serious abuse of liquor. I do not doubt that there is still much to be done; but a change for the better appears to have taken place, and disgraceful scenes, fights, and disputes among the Indians are things of the past.

Cases of immorality are very rare and in this respect the Indians equal the surrounding whites.

I have, &c.,

ARMAND TESSIER,
Indian Agent.

Questions for Consideration

1. How does looking at the history of the fur trade from an Indigenous perspective change traditional historical interpretations of it?
2. How important was the fur trade to the lives of Indigenous people on the British Columbian plateau? As students of history, what broader lessons about the fur trade does this convey to us?
3. In examining Hudson's Bay Company agent John Work's report from the Colvile District, how important does it appear the fur trade was in the lives of the Indigenous peoples he discusses? What biases are apparent in the source and how should students of history negotiate them?
4. What did the Innu of the Lac-Saint-Jean area do to remain prosperous and competitive in the fur trade well into the twentieth century?
5. How does the history of the Innu in the Lac-Saint-Jean area challenge stereotypes of Indigenous peoples and throw into question historians' interpretations of the fur trade?
6. What can we learn from the 1910 reports of the "Indian Agents" on the Innu ("Montagnais") of the Lac-Saint-Jean area? What might be of particular interest here to historians of the fur trade and why? In what ways are Innu activities hidden from the historian's sight in this document and why?
7. How has the historiography of the fur trade changed with time? What further changes to the history of the fur trade as told by historians do these articles imply are needed? Do you agree those changes are needed?

Further Resources

Books and Articles

Binnema, Ted. *Enlightened Zeal: The Hudson's Bay Company and Scientific Networks, 1670–1870*. Toronto: University of Toronto Press, 2014.

Moreau, Bill. "Fur Trade Letters of Willie Traill, 1864–1893" in *The University of Toronto Quarterly 79*, no. 1 (Winter, 2010): 573.

Podruchny, Carolyn. *Making the Voyageur World: Travelers and Traders in the North American Fur Trade*. Lincoln & Toronto: University of Nebraska Press & University of Toronto Press, 2006.

Ray, Arthur J. *Indians in the Fur Trade*, 2nd edn. Toronto: University of Toronto Press, [1974] 1998.

Sleeper-Smith, Susan. *Indian Women and French Men: Rethinking Cultural Encounter in the Western Great Lakes*. Amherst, MA: University of Massachusetts Press, 2001.

———. *Rethinking the Fur Trade: Cultures of Exchange in an Atlantic World*. Lincoln: University of Nebraska Press, 2009.

Van Kirk, Sylvia. *Many Tender Ties: Women in Fur Trade Society, 1670–1870*. Winnipeg: Watson & Dwyer, 1980.

Printed Documents and Reports

Rich, E.E., ed. *Minutes of the Hudson's Bay Company, 1671–74*. Toronto: Champlain Society, 1942.

Thwaites, R.G. *The Jesuit Relations and Allied Documents*, 71 vols. New York: Pagent Book Company, 1959. Available at http://puffin.creighton.edu/jesuit/relations/.

Films

Canada: A People's History. Episode 6. DVD. Executive produced by Mark Starowicz. CBC, 2000.

The Other Side of the Ledger: An Indian View of the Hudson's Bay Company. DVD. Directed by Martin DeFalco and Willie Dunn. NFB, 1972.

Websites

Canadiana.ca, "Exploration, the Fur Trade, and Hudson's Bay Company"
www.canadiana.ca/hbc/stories/aboriginals1_e.html

CBC, "Happy Birthday Hudson's Bay—From Canada's Indians," 12 Dec. 1970
www.cbc.ca/archives/entry/our-native-land-happy-birthday-hudsons-bay-from-canadas-indians

CBC, "Hudson's Bay Company Ends its Fur Trade," 30 Jan. 1991
www.cbc.ca/archives/entry/1991-hudsons-bay-company-ends-its-fur-trade

Hudson's Bay Company Heritage
www.hbcheritage.ca/hbcheritage/home

6

Locating Métis Identity

Introduction

The **Métis** past is contentious and no issue is more contentious than the question of Métis identity. As Métis scholar Paul Chartrand recently noted, although the Canadian Métis share many cultural attributes, they are a diverse group with varied histories and senses of identity. Moreover, it is not clear who is legally defined as "Métis" in the Canadian **Charter of Rights and Freedoms**, which recognizes the Métis as one of Canada's Aboriginal peoples. The definition reflects neither the heterogeneity of the community nor the historical elasticity of its boundaries.[1]

Historians have also grappled with this problem. In 1985, for example, Jacqueline Peterson and Jennifer S.H. Brown cautiously suggested using the term *Métis* to describe those descended from the "Red River Métis" and therefore belonging to the "Métis Nation" as defined by the Métis National Council, while designating others as lowercase métis. This practice, they argued, created a second "inclusive category" to describe all those of "mixed ancestry." Peterson and Brown's own book, however, made the difficulties of this distinction apparent, as the authors chose to stick to the latter spelling rather than "take it upon [themselves] to decide who belongs to socio-political categories that are still subject to redefinition and evolution."[2] A survey of the most recent literature shows that most scholars are similarly reluctant but prefer to use *Métis*.[3] This is the spelling we have chosen to use in this textbook.

As Peterson and Brown's conundrum suggests, one of the many distinctions among the Métis derives from the prominence of Red River in Métis history. This focus led Trudy Nicks and Kenneth Morgan to complain, in 1985, that historians were suffering from "Red River myopia," concentrating on the Red River Colony at the expense of Canada's many other Métis communities.[4] Answering Nicks and Morgan's call to correct this problem, many scholars (particularly Métis historians) have been busily unearthing the histories of the Métis beyond Red River. Ute Lischke and David McNab's recent edited collection, for example, includes articles focusing on the Métis in present-day Ontario, Alberta, and the United States.[5]

In this chapter, Geoff Read and Todd Webb look at the degree to which the wider western world recognized the Métis as a unique community and as a nation during the latter half of the nineteenth century. In the process, Read and Webb discover that, from 1869 to 1885, the Métis were widely discussed by commentators outside Canada's borders who largely defined the Métis by their status as a people of "mixed race." Their research also serves as a stark reminder of the colonial and racist confines within which the new nation had to act and sheds light on why the Canadian government treated Louis Riel and his followers so pitilessly. Adam Gaudry's article offers a counterpoint to definitions of Métis identity offered by historians like McNab. Gaudry argues that focusing on the "mixedness" of Métis reduces a culturally distinct and unique Indigenous people to a mere biological category. All societies include the offspring of the unions between people from different cultural and racial backgrounds, but as Gaudry points out, rarely if ever is it suggested that the descendants of such "mixing" constitute a nation. Instead, Gaudry argues that more inclusive definitions of Métis are merely a ploy by the federal government to deny Indigenous nationhood to those Métis who trace their ancestry and cultural heritage to the historic Métis Nation at Red River. These two articles force readers to consider how identity/nationhood is constituted and recognized, an issue that has been of particular significance for the Métis Nation and the Métis peoples of Canada, broadly understood.

Chapter Objectives

At the end of this chapter, you should be able to

- identify when, where, and how the Métis emerged and address the complexity of determining who "belongs" to the Métis community;
- understand the significance of debates about Métis identity;
- understand better how and why Indigenous peoples are often ignored in European/European–Canadian/state discussions and definitions of their own identities and fates.

Notes

1. John Giokas and Paul L.A.H. Chartrand, "Who are the Métis? A Review of the Law and Policy," in Paul L.A.H. Chartrand and Harry W. Daniels, eds, *Who Are Canada's Aboriginal Peoples? Recognition, Definition, and Jurisdiction* (Saskatoon: Purich Publishing, 2002), 83–125.

2. Jacqueline Peterson and Jennifer S.H. Brown, "Introduction," in Peterson and Brown, eds, *The New Peoples: Being and Becoming Métis in North America* (Winnipeg: The University of Manitoba Press, 1985), 6.

3. See, for example, Sarah Quick, "The Social Poetics of the Red River Jig in Alberta and Beyond: Meaningful Heritage and Emerging Performance," *Ethnologies* 30, 1 (2008): 77–101.

4. Trudy Nicks and Kenneth Morgan, "Grand Cache: The Historic Development of an Indigenous Alberta Métis Population," in Peterson and Brown, eds, *The New Peoples*, 163–81.

5. Ute Lischke and David T. McNab, eds, *The Long Journey of a Forgotten People: Métis Identities and Family Histories* (Waterloo: Wilfrid Laurier University Press, 2007). See also Heather Devine, *The People Who Own Themselves: Aboriginal Ethnogenesis in a Canadian Family, 1660–1900* (Calgary: University of Calgary Press, 2004); Brenda Macdougall, *One of the Family: Métis Culture in Nineteenth Century Saskatchewan* (Vancouver: UBC Press, 2009); Gwen Reimer and Jean-Philippe Chartrand, "Documenting Historic Métis in Ontario," *Ethnohistory* 51, 3 (Summer 2004): 567–607; Nicole St-Onge, *Saint-Laurent, Manitoba: Evolving Métis Identities, 1850–1914* (Regina: Canadian Plains Research Centre, 2004).

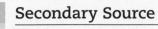

Secondary Source

Respecting Métis Nationhood and Self-Determination in Matters of Métis Identity

Adam Gaudry, University of Saskatchewan

> "*Métis have rights . . . not because we are of mixed Indian and European ancestry, but because we are descendant from distinct Métis communities . . . notably the historic Métis Nation community that emerged in the historic Northwest.*"[1]

This quote is taken from the Métis National Council's *Métis Registration Guide*, which acknowledges the Métis as a distinct national community with political, cultural, social, and economic boundaries. This Indigenous nation emerged in the nineteenth century in the historic "North-West," an area containing the Red River Settlement (now Winnipeg) and the northwestern Prairies to the Rocky Mountains.[2] Although more common definitions of Métis identity may include any mixed-race, non-status individual, this is the product of a century of Canadian government categorization, not a reflection of a cultural collectivity. As this chapter will show, the present-day descendants of "the historic Métis Nation" are the only political community that has inherited the name Métis—along with the responsibility for perpetuating the social, cultural, economic, and political institutions of our ancestors.[3]

While many still wish to apply the term *Métis* to any individual or community of mixed Indigenous-European lineage, a "Métis-as-mixed" definition, as Chris Andersen argues, actually undermines Métis nationhood, reducing a coherent Indigenous people to a state of mere biological mixedness.[4] Instead, we should see Métis people as an entity much like other Indigenous peoples, as possessing a common way of life, common language(s), common political and social institutions, common art forms, and most important, self-awareness as a people. As we will see, only the Métis Nation of the historical North-West fits these criteria, possessing both a historical *and* contemporary understanding of themselves as Métis.

Moving Away from a Mixed Definition of Métis Identity

Perhaps the root cause of this confusion stems from the fact that the discourse around Métis identity is coloured by more than a century of colonial government categorization and academic studies that omit the collective existence of a Métis people. Rather than recognizing the Métis as a political collective with which Canada must deal on a nation-to-nation basis—in other words, as a *people*—policy-makers and scholars have treated Métis as individuals of Indian descent who simply need special social services. Indeed, the expansion of Métis identity to include any mixed European-Indigenous population is in keeping with Canada's denial of a nation-to-nation relationship with the Métis people.

Canadian policy and academic scholarship has thus reinforced what Andersen calls a definition of Métis based on the assumption that Métis emerged from a social and biological process of mixture, ignoring the inherent mixedness present in *all* cultures and peoples. In other words, the Métis are not the only people who are culturally and biologically mixed: all cultures are, including "Indian" ones.[5] In fact, during the fur trade, when the Métis Nation rose to prominence, they were not the only community deeply influenced by intermarriage and cultural hybridity. Many "Indian" communities considered the mixed offspring of Indigenous women and fur traders to be, unproblematically, Cree, Assiniboine, Saulteaux, and so forth, rather than being Métis by virtue of their mixedness. Robert Alexander Innes notes, for example, that the famous Cree chief Poundmaker came from an extensive mixed lineage that situated him within a complex multicultural alliance network:

> Poundmaker was the son of an Assiniboine man and a Métis woman who had been adopted by Blackfoot Chief Crowfoot. Chief Big Bear's father is considered to have been a renowned Ojibwe medicine man named Black Powder, who was originally from Ontario and the chief of a mixed Cree and Saulteaux band.[6]

Even with his complex lineage, Poundmaker still identified as Cree. But this makes sense, as that is how he would have understood himself. Like the Métis, the Plains Cree inhabited a diplomatic structure where intermarriage with other people—Indigenous or European—produced political advantage for their people. In fact, on the Prairies, Indigenous peoples intermarried extensively as a way of ensuring a large network of relatives to support one another, form military alliances, and provide food and shelter in times of need.[7] Cross-cultural marriage alliances were nothing new to the fur trade; they were a long-standing Indigenous tradition readily adopted by European fur traders seeking new trading partnerships.[8] With cultural mixing, mixed marriages, and mixed offspring a long-standing reality, there is nothing inherently unique about Métis mixedness. Rather, all Indigenous peoples were influenced by intermarriage with Europeans, and many Indigenous bands were successful in establishing themselves as "middle men" in the fur trade, able to negotiate Indigenous and European cultural worlds.[9] This was by no means the exclusive purview of the Métis.

Where Métis mixedness has been interpreted as being foundationally different is when Métis are said to transcend the *racial* boundaries of Europeans and "Indians." The problem with this notion, however, is that outside of the social value we give to it, race does not actually exist. Race is a socially constructed phenomenon—that is, even though humans may have different physical characteristics, there is no link between race and social behaviour. Social behaviour is just that, social. It is determined by the complex interplay of life with other human beings, learned through experience rather than inherited genetically through one's "race." Indeed, aside from physical characteristics, race plays no determinable role in human behaviour.[10] Yet the ongoing fixation with Métis as a mixed-race people is rooted in a colonial fantasy of biologically pure races such as "white" and "Indian" and the belief that mixed offspring inherited behavioural traits from their parents' races.[11] However, since race is neither pure nor a determining factor in how humans live with one another, biological mixing alone cannot result in the formation of a distinct group of people—only social and political processes create new human communities.

Instead of rooting Métis identity in this mixing of "races" and cultures, Andersen argues that what created Métis peoplehood was their conscious self-identication as

Métis. That is, they applied the term to themselves to differentiate themselves from others.[12] Jacqueline Peterson has established a test for establishing whether or not a historical community understood itself as Métis, using the example of a mixed-descent fur trader in the Great Lakes region:

> Was Alexis Bailly a Métis? That is, did he view himself as such, and did he live and marry among other members of a distinct ethnic group bounded by a set of face-to-face communities, a shared language, culture, history, and sense of homeland? In Bailly's case, the answer is likely no. He did not move to Red River, and there is no evidence that he ever used the term Métis or *bois-brûlé* in reference to himself. Actually, there is no evidence that prior to, or even subsequent to 1815, mixed-descent residents of Great Lakes fur-trading communities had developed a separate ethnic identity or political consciousness even though many of the cultural characteristics of Great Lakes fur trade communities were similar to those seen among the Red River Métis.[13]

Peterson, like Andersen, looks to Métis *self-consciousness* as the basis for Métis identity, rather than "insert[ing] Métis consciousness into areas and eras where they did not previously exist."[14] Scholars like Andersen and Peterson have thus refocused discussion on Métis identity on historical self-ascription, political consciousness as Métis, and membership in a living Métis community as the basis for contemporary Métis identity. While this position is largely at odds with more recent attempts by various levels of government to define the Métis as a mixed, non-Indian community, it is nonetheless more consistent with traditional Métis identity boundaries that were rooted in kinship and collectivity rather than abstract notions of racial mixing.

From *Bois-Brûlés* to Métis: The Development of a Collective Consciousness

Scholars seeking to move beyond the notion that Métis are simply the mixed offspring of fur traders and Indian women tend to concentrate on the moment of Métis cultural birth, what is called *ethnogenesis*. Many scholars trace Métis ethnogenesis to a very specific time and place—the Battle of Seven Oaks near the Red River Settlement on 19 June 1816. Seven Oaks, which the Métis remember as *La Grenouillère,* was a short military encounter between Métis soldiers and a group of Scottish colonists at the nascent Red River Settlement.[15] This group, which referred to themselves as *Bois-Brûlés* until the 1820s, when they became the Métis,[16] opposed Scottish agricultural settlement in the region, seeing it as a threat to their economic livelihood. The *Bois-Brûlés* were the primary supplier of foodstuffs to the fur trade, and at Seven Oaks sought to defend their land and economy from strangers.[17] The *Bois-Brûlés* routed the Scots in a lopsided engagement, and the battle became a celebrated moment, a cultural touchstone shared by all *Bois-Brûlés*.

It was with their victory at *La Grenouillère* that the *Bois-Brûlés* first saw themselves as a collective entity, first by understanding that it was their corporate well-being (rather than their individual interests) that was under threat, and second by acting together to protect that collective interest.[18] This moment, forged as it was in blood and violence, signalled to the world—and more importantly to the

Métis themselves—that a "New Nation" had emerged on the prairies.[19] The night following the battle, a *Bois-Brûlé* soldier named Pierre Falcon composed a song, *La Chanson de la Grenouillère*, commemorating the victory, which spread rapidly through *Bois-Brûlé* camps. This song helped to cement this newly corporate spirit among the *Bois-Brûlés*. Its lyrics allowed the *Bois-Brûlés* to imagine themselves as a collective, contrasting the "foreigners . . . who'd come from Orkney . . . to rob our country" with the *Bois-Brûlé* singing "this song of praise for the victory *we* won this day."[20] This *chanson* allowed Métis to "become aware" of the thousands of others like them, connecting them through this popular narrative into "the embryo of the nationally imagined community."[21] This song of Métis national sentiment was passed down for generations and sung on the cart trails as the Métis moved throughout the Prairies chasing the buffalo. In 1864, a missionary in the company of a Métis hunting brigade complained that his guide "sang the song so often it got on his nerves," and during the Red River troubles of 1869–70, *La Chanson de la Grenouillère* was sung by the Métis soldiers to "generate fire and furor."[22] Seven Oaks thereby became a national epic, not unlike the Anglo-Saxon *Beowulf,* that moved Métis to imagine that the battle had been a victory for the entire Métis people, not just the few soldiers who fought there.

This imagined national community was reinforced over subsequent decades by the development of common political institutions, most notably the large-scale Métis buffalo hunts. The hunt grew rapidly in size in the 30 years following Seven Oaks.[23] In the hunt, Métis systematized the selection of their leadership and developed a shared process for collective decision-making. If Seven Oaks had allowed Métis to imagine themselves as a collective, the buffalo hunt brought the collective into actual existence.[24]

The buffalo hunt, with its elected chief and councillors, soldiers, and scouts, served as the constitutional basis of Métis political authority and was the basis for Métis political life. It determined how this authority could be legitimately expressed, and to whom it applied. The hunt also established specific laws that governed how Métis lived together, which included provisions against theft and outlined the punishment for those Métis who might hunt buffalo ahead of the rest of the party. Long after the Métis Nation had outgrown a single hunt, they nonetheless used a common constitutional process for selecting leaders and making decisions.[25] This allowed a fluid membership between hunting groups and forged a sense of community among Métis, including among those they had not met. The buffalo hunt persisted into the 1950s, and after the decline of the buffalo it was used to gather roots and berries on a smaller scale.[26] Even today, the Métis National Council and its provincial affiliates trace their origins to the buffalo hunt, drawing legitimacy from this traditional Métis form of governance, and instituting modern-day Laws of the Hunt to govern renewable resource harvesting.[27]

Alongside these political institutions, Métis established shared social practices as well. Métis liked to dance, especially during cold winter nights when people had more time on their hands. They developed a unique style of jigging, which spread through Métis settlements as Métis moved the fur trade north and west. They held "half-breed balls" full of food and dancing, which had detailed social etiquette and expectations:

The evening began with a feast. People outdid themselves to see who could serve the biggest meal. During the feast, there'd be a big singing contest and after that would come the dancing. Talk about every kind of reel and jig you can imagine! Fiddles, drums, accordions, guitars, jew's harps and mouth organs, anything was fine as long as it went along more or less with the rhythm. At a shindig like that it was always a contest to see who could play the best, and who could dance the best, who could sing the best, who could wear through his moccasins first, who'd be the first to cripple up with cramps in their legs.[28]

Though less common, such occasions still happen today. Métis jigging, fiddling, and parties are rooted in these old prairie parties, and both jigging and fiddling have become essential Métis art forms.

Like political life, social relations were structured by kinship responsibilities. Family determined social and political duties among families and individuals, and this great web of kinship was what bound the Métis people together.[29] The social responsibilities owed to relatives, what Brenda Macdougall calls *wahkootowin*,[30] allowed Métis to form "complex systems of relationships among each other based on family ties and shared homeland."[31] In particular, as Macdougall and Nicole St-Onge have demonstrated, Métis hunting brigades and Métis settlements tended to coalesce around female relatives—particularly sisters.[32] Métis family relatedness, *wahkootowin*, was thus firmly established as the criterion for belonging, and as Macdougall notes, "rights flowed from . . . membership in the family and, through that membership, a claim to being part of the land itself."[33] Family was what held Métis in place, and because family defined one's hunting group, it also played a central role in Métis political life. Métis did not see family in narrow terms, but had an expansive view of relatedness. The Métis trader Louis Goulet noted that, "family ties among the Métis could stretch to infinity, so to speak. If two grandfathers traded dogs one day, that was enough for their grandchildren to call themselves relatives. Children of cousins two or three times removed turned into uncles and aunts."[34] For Métis, kinship and membership in the nation was more or less the same thing. It defined political, social, and economic obligations—as well as land use rights and a stake in Métis territorial ownership.

With the value Métis put on family relatedness, it is tough to imagine that historic Métis communities would have seen non-kin as part of the Métis family. For the Métis of this era, membership in the Métis Nation was not determined by self-identification or distant genealogical descent, but by living within a kinship-based social, political, and economic system. Membership was retained by living up to the responsibilities expected from a good relative. Strangers, or non-kin, were potentially dangerous and therefore treated with caution.[35] All this is to say that nineteenth-century Métis did not see their national community as open access, with membership available to anyone of mixed descent. Rather, Métis have always understood that there were national boundaries that contained a large number of relatives who lived like them, thought as they did, told the same stories, sang the same songs, used the same political institutions, understood proper social etiquette, and believed in the same political community. And as the nineteenth century progressed, the understanding of Métis nationhood only became stronger—especially when strangers from the east arrived in 1869 saying that they owned the land, which Métis had lived on for generations.

Métis Resistance and Identity

While the Battle of Seven Oaks cemented a collective identity for Métis people in the early nineteenth century, two conflicts between the Métis Nation and the Dominion of Canada in the late nineteenth century reinforced it. In 1869, Métis learned that the Hudson's Bay Company, claiming ownership over the shared territories of the Métis, Plains Cree, Assiniboine, and Saulteaux, was preparing to sell its claimed territory to Canada. The Métis organized themselves using buffalo hunt protocols, expelled Canada's would-be governor from the Red River territory, and created a provisional government to negotiate a resolution to the situation.

These events, propelling Louis Riel into the ranks of Métis leadership, also signalled a strengthening of Métis national attachment. This resistance drew on a tradition of Métis national independence dating back to Seven Oaks, which empowered Métis to take up arms against the strangers from Canada. The Métis-run provisional government emphasized a Métis collective right *as a people* to "establish any form of government it may consider suited to its wants." It also rejected rule by "a foreign power," like Canada "which pretends to have a right to coerce us, and impose upon us a despotic form of government . . . contrary to our rights and interests."[36] This agitation led to a negotiated settlement between the Métis Provisional Government of Assiniboia and the Dominion of Canada that established a new province—Manitoba—in which one-seventh of the lands were set aside for Métis. This large Métis land reserve was intended to provide a permanent home for the people and allow Métis social, political, and economic institutions to persist in an era of rapid agricultural settlement on the Prairies. Ultimately, the influx of tens of thousands of Ontario settlers, coupled with the Dominion's refusal to protect the Métis land reserve from land-hungry settlers, pushed many of the Métis from Red River west into the Saskatchewan country and beyond.

The resulting Métis diaspora from Red River and their western kin were not finished agitating to protect their national rights, however. When Canadian settlement threatened to displace long-standing Métis communities in the South Saskatchewan River valley in 1884–85, the Métis again defended the Métis homesteads that dotted the Prairies. This time Canada sent its fledgling military and with physical violence subdued the central Saskatchewan Métis community of Batoche. The Métis leader, Louis Riel, was executed for treason a few months later. The year 1885 marks a turning point for the Métis Nation. What had once been one of the strongest political and military powers on the northern plains was increasingly disempowered; with most of their lands lost to dishonest dealings with Canadian government officials and land speculators, Métis were pushed to the margins and into the ever-growing Métis diaspora that now encompasses most of Western Canada.

Both the power of Métis resistance and the trauma of their defeat remain part of the Métis collective consciousness. Like Seven Oaks and Falcon's *La Chanson de la Grenouillère*, it was the Metis' "ability to force the Canadian government to halt, however briefly, its annexation of territories now known as western Canada" that served as a touchstone for

Métis understandings of their homeland, their national status, and the historical injustice that continues to affect Métis lives profoundly today.[37] These events, shared on some level by every Métis family, have only further strengthened the sense of Métis national belonging, and have served as a collective and unifying experience that other "Métis" communities lack, such as those in Ontario, the Far North, and British Columbia.

Government Compartmentalization of Métis Identity

The post-1885 period saw Métis identity increasingly redefined by Canadian policy-makers in a way that did not recognize the Métis as a people, but as racialized mixed-descent individuals. For over a hundred years, Canadian policy has defined Métis in a way that meets the needs of colonial management, rather than reflecting how Métis people understand themselves. And as the contributions in this volume on the Indian Act and treaty-making demonstrate, state policy, despite its many arbitrary distinctions, nonetheless possesses the "ability to legitimize, as obvious or natural, what are in fact historical and thus ultimately arbitrary visions of the world."[38] As a result, state policy-makers have recrafted Métis designations in ways nearly synonymous with racial mixing, despite the persistence of Métis objections. Canadian government policy has rejected the corporate existence of (and hence any responsibility to deal with) the Métis people, and instead has preferred to deal with Métis people individually, or as a racial group.

Following Canada's 1885 "Indian wars," a shift in political power from Indigenous to settler colonial institutions began to disrupt older Indigenous identities. When "Indian" took on specific legal meaning in Canadian law after the passage of the Indian Act (1876), "Métis" and "Half-breed" became public policy designations for Canadian government officials as well. "Half-breed" was used to denote those that the Canadian government considered part-Indian, regardless of how these families and communities understood themselves. Thus, like "Indian," the policy category of "Half-breed" was defined primarily by outside observers rather than those who populated the category itself.

From the perspective of the Canadian government, Half-breeds were in the "possible possession of Indian title," which Canada wished to extinguish.[39] Indian title was supposedly extinguished through treaty-making for those considered "Indians."[40] The status of Half-breeds' Indian title, however, was unclear; the government therefore sought to remove this potential obstacle to western settlement through a one-time cash or land grant called "scrip." After they took scrip, Canada considered those it defined as "Half-breeds" to be ordinary citizens with no special relationship with the Crown. So, from the government's perspective, while those categorized as Indians received ongoing benefits (however minimal) from Canada, Half-breeds received a one-time cash or land grant in exchange for the extinguishing of their traditional land use rights.

Over time, the overwhelming power of the state allowed "colonial codes" to seep into the everyday lives of Indigenous peoples, which "increasingly mediated decisions about belonging."[41] During the negotiations of the Numbered Treaties (1871–1921) individual families were given a choice: take treaty as an "Indian" or scrip as a "Half-breed." While Indigenous peoples still based their identities on kinship relations, the changing political dynamics of the settler-dominated West meant that they also needed to concern themselves with government categorizations. What served the family's long-term and short-term interests better: to be Indian or Half-breed? Was it better to take treaty or scrip? The choice that families made during this period had long-standing impacts for their descendants. Many Métis, regardless of their sense-of-self chose to enter treaty and became Status Indians, meaning that their descendants would be Status Indians, rather than Half-breeds. Conversely, even though they were eligible to become "Indians" through treaty, many families were categorized as Half-breeds, and were therefore excluded from any collective or individual benefits accorded to bands recognized by the Indian Act.[42] So although government categories of "Indian" and "Half-breed" used terms long in circulation in the West, they did not match the earlier meaning of the terms, and over time the gap between policy and everyday definitions diminished.

These categories were not static, and in the years immediately following the treaty negotiations, many families still migrated between these two government classifications, attempting to secure a future for their families during a time of rapidly deteriorating Indigenous economic prospects. Some of my relatives crossed the Indian/Half-breed categorical boundary several times. Gabriel Gaudry, also known by the Cree name Meskekeawahsis, was born to a Métis father and Plains Cree mother, making him a member of both communities. In 1872, he married a woman named Marie-Anne Kasapatjinan/Seeasakwachenin, who had a Plains Cree father and a Métis mother, and, like Gabriel, probably fit in easily in both Métis and Cree contexts. In 1876, Gabriel Gaudry was enrolled as a member of Strike Him on the Back River Cree Band, a signatory of Treaty 6. Gabriel fought with his Cree relatives at Cut Knife Hill in 1885, but, likely due to the restrictive policy changes of the Indian Act afterwards, left treaty in 1886. He and his wife both took scrip and each claimed 240 acres nearby, thus ceasing to be "Indian" and becoming "Halfbreed"—at least, on paper.[43] Despite this migration across government categories, the Gaudry family remained both Métis and Cree in their daily lives, situating their sense of identity in a much older way of thinking about belonging. As Gabriel and Marie-Ann's story demonstrates, how families chose to define their relationship with the Canadian government did not necessarily reflect how they understood their own identities. Just because the government labelled families as Half-breed or Métis for administrative purposes did not make them so. In fact, many of these families likely made this choice on the basis of a calculation of the material benefits of their options; this was, therefore, a way for families to express agency over a system designed to constrain and control them.

Despite an Indigenous preference for older ways of understanding their identities and relationships with one another, these outsider categorizations came with real benefits and consequences. Those categorized as Indians now had a protected land base for their exclusive use, however paternalistic its management, whereas those categorized as Half-breeds often lost their scrip lands to unreasonable government policy, corrupt speculation practices, or some combination of the two.[44] Therefore, being categorized as Indian or Half-breed had a major impact on whom one could live with, where one could live, which lands one could access, and what economic opportunities one had. Whereas in the 1880s kinship and close family relationships between Métis and Cree peoples allowed older Indigenous forms of belonging to trump outsider categorization, subsequent generations of bleak economic circumstances made attachment to Canadian government categories important for a family's livelihood and well-being. Families began to identify with these categories, sometimes more than their traditional attachments.

Over time, Canadian preference for the term *half-breed* waned, as many of the communities it was applied to saw it as derogatory. In an effort to be more respectful to these communities, policy-makers and scholars inserted the name "Métis" in its place. Although they avoided using a demeaning term, they now applied the term *Métis* to all Half-breeds regardless of their self-understandings, ignoring, as a result, many existing local identities used by these non-Métis peoples themselves. Names like "*chicot, voyageur, tripper*, or *Saulter*," terms by which many non-Métis "Half-breeds" identified themselves, were ignored, and "Métis" was applied instead, replacing one set of outsider names with another.[45] Compounding government categorization was an emerging academic discourse in the 70s and 80s that applied Métis-ness to a number of Great Lakes communities who never used the term themselves. This was a "clumsy" use of academic terminology, "used uncritically and ahistorically," confusing definitions of Métis identity.[46] According to Andersen, this policy and scholarly confusion over Métis identity has manifested itself in the many contemporary non-Métis communities who now "misrecognize" themselves as Métis because of their racial/cultural mixedness. These communities, due to policy and scholarly "clumsiness," now use a name that their ancestors would never have applied to themselves, and lack an attachment to the historic Métis Nation who did use the name.[47] The uncritical substitution of the term *Métis* in place of *Half-breed* has resulted in several groups of Indigenous people being imported into the Métis policy category, many of which have now adopted the term Métis to describe themselves.

This policy category, "Métis," was given more substantive content when it was included in section 35 of the *Constitution Act* in 1982, which recognized and affirmed the Aboriginal and treaty rights of "Indians, Inuit, and Métis peoples."[48] The constitutional protection of Métis Aboriginal rights—which until 1982 were presumed extinguished through scrip—caused a massive shift in thinking among the Métis people. However, as the Canadian governments and Aboriginal leadership failed to agree on what "existing aboriginal and treaty rights" actually meant and what exactly s. 35 protected, they also never established what "Métis" in s. 35 meant and to whom it referred. Was it the old government category of "Half-breed" with a politically correct title? Or, was it the Métis Nation who called themselves by that name? For many Métis, the answer is clear. Legal scholars Paul Chartrand and John Giokas argue that s. 35 protects the rights of "the people descended from this historic [Métis] nation that had political relations with the Crown,"[49] because the *Constitution Act* recognizes that "the source of Aboriginal rights lies in the political relationship between the Crown and historic nations. . . . [it] is not to be found in racist ideologies which attempt to classify human beings into biological categories."[50]

Despite the assertion by many Métis intellectuals that "Métis" in s. 35 refers only to Métis people, no political consensus has ever been reached on its meaning.

Like most s. 35 Aboriginal rights issues, political impasse has led to litigation, leaving judges to resolve matters. In defining s. 35 "Métis," the Supreme Court of Canada's 2003 *R. v. Powley* decision defines Métis identity, not on national self-awareness but on the problematic assumption of historical mixing. The *Powley* case involved two men, Steve and Roddy Powley, who were charged with shooting a moose without a provincial licence in Sault Ste Marie, ON. They successfully argued in court that they possessed the right as an Aboriginal to hunt as Métis. The Supreme Court's decision in their case focused on the crude "biological categories" that Chartrand and Giokas condemned. The decision states:

> The term "Métis". . . refers to distinctive peoples who, in addition to their mixed ancestry, developed their own customs, way of life, and recognizable group identity separate from their Indian or Inuit and European forebears.[51]

By choosing a definition rooted in colonial government categorization rather than the historical existence of a Métis people, the courts once again individualized what is a collective identity. Thus, like the government category of "Métis" used as a politically correct alternative to "Half-breed," the constitutional meaning of the term *Métis* has also been dislodged from its original meaning, and now applies to numerous communities that before *Powley* would likely never have identified as Métis.[52]

Putting into Practice a Respect for Métis Nationhood

That previously unrecognized communities may now be able to access Aboriginal rights is not in itself a problem, but what the proliferation of Métis identity claims does to the actual Métis Nation, is. The rapidly expanding self-identification of Métis individuals—especially in the Maritimes, southern Ontario, and Quebec, which have no historical Métis communities—impedes the ability of the actual Métis people to define their own membership, engage in public discussion about the future of their political community, and otherwise maintain the boundaries of their people. Since these activities are all key components of political self-determination, the simultaneous redefinition of the Métis people by Canadian scholars, jurists, and policy-makers, combined with the erroneous self-identification of non-Métis people as Métis, should be seen as a serious threat to Métis nationhood.

Although the Indian Act has, through its exclusionary membership criteria, unjustly and unilaterally excluded many Indigenous people from full participation in their ancestral communities, migration to an ahistorical "Métis" identity should be seen as problematic for two reasons. First, as Andersen has stated, "We are not the soup kitchen for those disenfranchised by past and present Canadian Indian policy and, as such, although we should sympathize with those who bear the brunt of this particular form of dispossession, we cannot do so at expense of eviscerating our identity."[53] Second, as non-Métis Indigenous people migrate to Métis-ness due to real material considerations like access to programs and services, it aids in the considerable depopulation of other Indigenous nations—a long-standing goal of Canadian Indian policy. While some may argue that Métis should look after those without an obvious home, I would argue instead that the obligation falls to their actual kin to bring disenfranchised community members back into the fold. Although this may seem harsh to some, a central, if not difficult, component of substantive decolonization is that Indigenous nations take responsibility for all of our people—even those who, through many different ways, have been cut loose, pushed out, or forcibly removed from our nations. Treating Métis as some sort of catch-all category for those who do not fall easily within other colonial categories does little to repopulate our nations and only serves to reinforce outsider control of our identities. The hard truth is that colonialism has been particularly effective at assaulting the boundaries of Métis identity that allow Métis to be a nation. What is needed is a long and critical dialogue over what those boundaries were and what they should look like now. It is difficult to foresee what will come of this debate, but it is clear that this needs to be a discussion on the terms of the Métis people themselves, one that is historically rooted and critical of the ongoing colonial interference in contemporary Métis identity.

Notes

1. Métis National Council, *Métis Registration Guide*, 2011, 2.

2. Now Manitoba, Saskatchewan, Alberta, North and South Dakota, and Montana.

3. Métis National Council, *Métis Registration Guide*, 2011, 2.

4. This argument is found in great detail in Chris Andersen, *"Metis": Race, Recognition, and the Struggle for Indigenous Peoplehood* (Vancouver: UBC Press, 2014).

5. Ibid., 7, 38.

6. Robert Alexander Innes, "Multicultural Bands on the Northern Plains and the Notion of Tribal Histories," in *Finding a Way to the Heart: Feminist Writings on Aboriginal and Women's History in Canada*, Robin Jarvis Brownlie and Valerie J. Korinek, eds (Winnipeg: University of Manitoba Press, 2012), 131.

7. Ibid., 123–4.

8. Michael J. Witgen, *An Infinity of Nations: How the Native New World Shaped Early North America*, 1st edn, Early American Studies (Philadelphia: University of Pennsylvania Press, 2012), 94.

9. Andersen, *"Metis": Race, Recognition, and the Struggle for Indigenous Peoplehood*, 7.

10. Ibid., 31.

11. See, for example, Marcel Giraud, *The Metis in the Canadian West* (Edmonton: University of Alberta Press, 1986), 346.

12. Andersen, *"Metis": Race, Recognition, and the Struggle for Indigenous Peoplehood*, 41.

13. Jacqueline Peterson, "Red River Redux: Métis Ethnogenesis and the Great Lakes Region," in *Contours of a People: Métis Family, Mobility, and History*, Nicole St-Onge, Carolyn Podruchny, and Brenda Macdougall, eds (Norman: University of Oklahoma Press, 2012), 39–40.

14. Ibid., 28.

15. J.M. Bumsted, *Trials & Tribulations: The Red River Settlement and the Emergence of Manitoba, 1811–1870* (Winnipeg, MB: Great Plains Publications, 2003), 56–7.

16. Literally "burnt wood," likely referring to their dark complexion.

17. Bumsted, *Trials & Tribulations*, 17.

18. Nicole St-Onge, "Uncertain Margins: Métis and Saulteaux Identities in St-Paul des Saulteaux, Red River 1821–1870" *Manitoba History* 53 (2006): 2.

19. Darren O'Toole, "From Entity to Identity to Nation: The Ethnogenesis of the *Wiisakodewininiwag*," in *Métis in Canada: History, Identity, Law & Politics*, Christopher Adams, Gregg Dahl, and Ian Peach, eds (Edmonton: University of Alberta Press, 2013), 172.

20. Pierre Falçon, *La Chanson de la Grenouillère*, 1816. Available from www.metismuseum.ca/media/document.php/12336.pdf. Emphasis added, accessed 31 August 2014.

21. Benedict Anderson, *Imagined Communities: Reflections on the Origin and Spread of Nationalism*. (London: Verso, 1991), 44.

22. Gerhard Ens, "The Battle of Seven Oaks and the Articulation of a Métis National Tradition, 1811–1849," in *Contours of a People*, St-Onge, Podruchny, and Macdougall, eds (Norman, OK: University of Oklahoma Press, 2012), 109.

23. Alexander Ross, *The Red River Settlement: Its Rise, Progress, and Present State* (Edmonton: Hurtig Publishers, 1972), 246.

24. Louis Goulet, *Vanishing Spaces: Memoirs of a Prairie Metis* (Winnipeg: Editions Bois-Brules, 1976), 17–19.

25. Ross, *The Red River Settlement*, 245–6, 251.

26. See Maria Campbell, "Changing the Way," in *Contours of a People*, St-Onge, Podruchny, and Macdougall, eds (Norman, OK: University of Oklahoma Press, 2012).

27. John Weinstein, *Quiet Revolution West: The Rebirth of Métis Nationalism* (Markham, ON: Fifth House, 2007), 166.

28. Goulet, *Vanishing Spaces*, 43.

29. See Nicole St-Onge and Carolyn Podruchny, "Scuttling Along a Spider's Web: Mobility and Kinship in Métis Ethnogenesis," in *Contours of a*

People: Family, Mobility and Territoriality in Métis History, Nicole St-Onge, Carolyn Podruchny, and Brenda Macdougall, eds (Norman, OK: University of Oklahoma Press, 2012), 62.

30. Brenda Macdougall, One of the Family: Metis Culture in Nineteenth-Century Northwestern Saskatchewan (Vancouver: UBC Press, 2010), 8.

31. Idem, "The Myth of Cultural Ambivalence," in Contours of a People, eds St-Onge, Podruchny, and Macdougall, (Norman, OK: University of Oklahoma Press, 2012), 449.

32. Macdougall, One of the Family, 57; Brenda Macdougall and Nicole St-Onge, "Rooted in Mobility: Métis Buffalo-Hunting Brigades," Manitoba History 71(2013): 21.

33. Macdougall, "The Myth of Cultural Ambivalence," 447.

34. Goulet, Vanishing Spaces, 43.

35. Liam J. Haggarty, "Métis Economics: Sharing and Exchange in Northwest Saskatchewan," in Métis in Canada: History, Identity, Law & Politics, Christopher Adams, Gregg Dahl, and Ian Peach, eds (Edmonton: University of Alberta Press, 2013), 210.

36. Provisional Government of Assiniboia, "Declaration of the People of Rupert's Land and the North-West," (Red River Settlement, 1869).

37. Andersen, "Métis": Race, Recognition, and the Struggle for Indigenous Peoplehood, 198.

38. Ibid., 95.

39. Gregg Dahl, "A Half-Breed's Perspective on Being Métis," in Métis in Canada: History, Identity, Law & Politics, ed. Christopher Adams, Gregg Dahl, and Ian Peach (Edmonton: University of Alberta Press, 2013), 101.

40. See Michael Asch, On Being Here to Stay: Treaties and Aboriginal Rights in Canada (Toronto: University of Toronto Press, 2014).

41. Michel Hogue, "The Montana Métis and the Shifting Boundaries of Belonging," in Contours of a People: Métis Family, Mobility, and History, Nicole St. Onge, eds (Norman, OK: University of Oklahoma Press, 2012), 320–1.

42. Bonita Lawrence, "Real Indians" and Others: Mixed-Blood Urban Native Peoples and Indigenous Nationhood (Vancouver: UBC Press, 2004), 88.

43. Lawrence J. Barkwell, Veterans and Families of the 1885 Northwest Resistance (Saskatoon: Gabriel Dumont Institute, 2011), 132.

44. Maria Campbell, Halfbreed (Toronto: McClelland and Stewart, 1973), 7–8.

45. Chris Andersen, "'Moya 'Tipimsook' ('the People Who Aren't Their Own Bosses'): Racialization and the Misrecognition of 'Métis' in Upper Great Lakes Ethnohistory," Ethnohistory 58 (2011): 43–4.

46. Macdougall, "The Myth of Cultural Ambivalence," 424.

47. See Andersen, "Moya 'Tipimsook."

48. Weinstein, Quiet Revolution West, 62.

49. Paul L.A.H. Chartrand and John Giokas, "Defining 'the Métis People': The Hard Case of Canadian Aboriginal Law," in Who Are Canada's Aboriginal Peoples? Recognition, Definition and Jurisdiction, Paul L.A.H. Chartrand, ed. (Saskatoon: Purich Publishing, 2002), 277.

50. Ibid., 283.

51. Powley, Paragraph 10. Quoted in Andersen, "Métis," 65.

52. Ibid., 168.

53. Chris Anderson, "I'm Métis, What's Your Excuse?: On the Optics and the Ethics of Misrecognition of Métis in Canada," Aboriginal Policy Studies 1 (2011): 165.

Primary Document

Métis Registration Guide: Fulfilling Canada's Promise

Métis National Council

All MNC Governing Members have adopted the MNC's Métis definition, which is now the citizenship definition specified in their respective Constitutions and By-Laws; and all have put into place a process to implement that definition; however each Métis Registry has its own specific requirements. Basically, you must apply to be included in the Registry; you must provide proof that you are who you say you are, such as government issued photo identification; you must provide your Long-Form Birth Certificate or Baptismal Record; and you must show that you are a descendant of the historic Métis Nation. You will also be required to provide passport quality photos to place on your new citizenship card.

To prove descent from the historic Métis Nation, applicants are required to furnish a genealogy showing their link to an historic Métis ancestor. Unlike the Indian Registry, which has been in operation for well over a hundred and twenty-five years, there exists no database listing all persons who were Métis in the past, so it is now necessary to reconstruct Métis ancestry through genealogical research. While this no doubt makes registration a more onerous process, it is important to note that production of a genealogy is a one-time event, since once you are recognized as Métis you should never be required to do it again. Moreover, your genealogy can, with your written consent, be used to help your children, siblings and close relatives obtain registration as Métis. In time, as more and more people register as Métis, the greater will be the chance that Métis Registries will already have your family tree information in their databases.

It is also important to understand that, to meet the requirements of the MNC'S Métis definition, you have to trace your ancestry back to the "historic Métis Nation." For Métis residing in the Prairie Provinces or whose family comes from the Prairie Provinces, this means tracing your ancestry to a person who received Métis scrip or Manitoba land grants or who is listed as Métis or Half-Breed in the 1901 Canadian Census, which was particularly thorough in identifying half-breeds. This can usually be accomplished by tracing your ancestry back about a hundred years, that is, four, five and perhaps six generations, depending on your age. For Métis whose ancestors did not receive scrip or who come from areas of the Métis Homeland where scrip was never issued, other documentation, such as census and trading records, often exist to identify a historic Métis ancestor.

The Supreme Court in Powley stressed the importance of providing "objectively verifiable" proof of descent from an historic Métis community. Métis Registries, as a consequence, do require applicants to furnish documentation, such as Long-Form Birth Certificates, marriage certificates or baptismal records, providing official proof of inter-generational links for each generation to your historic Métis ancestor, that is, of your parent, grandparent and sometimes great-grandparent on the Métis line. This is often the most difficult part of the genealogy, but most Métis Registries can assist you in obtaining these documents.

Secondary Source

Only Pemmican Eaters? The International Press and Métis Identity, 1869–85

Geoff Read and Todd Webb

Few episodes in Canadian history have received more attention than the "Riel rebellions" of 1869–70 and 1885.[1] Pitting the Métis peoples of the Prairies against the Canadian state, the Métis resistance to the colonization of the West has fascinated historian and citizen alike. This is, in part, because the resistance evokes fundamental divisions between Aboriginal and settler, French and English, Protestant and Catholic, and Liberal and Conservative.

The questions of Métis identity and nationhood are particularly contentious. Some historians, such as D.N. Sprague, have argued that, by the early nineteenth century, the Métis in the vicinity of Red River possessed a distinct identity and constituted a nation that was repeatedly wronged by the Canadian state.[2] The Métis themselves, particularly those tracing their ancestry to the Red River Métis, strongly support this perspective and forcefully assert their distinctiveness and nationhood in both the past and the present. For example, the Manitoba Métis Federation proclaims in boldface on its website that "Manitoba is the birthplace of the Métis nation."[3] Conversely, some anglophone historians have sought to undermine such assertions. Gerhard J. Ens has stated that when the fur-trade economy collapsed at Red River on the eve of the resistance of 1869–70, so too did any chance of creating a genuine Métis nation in what was to become Manitoba. Similarly, Tom Flanagan has asserted that the Métis currently have no claim to redress because they were fairly compensated in the Manitoba Act of 1870.[4]

While this article does not attempt to settle this dispute, it does seek to shed light on the debate from a new angle. A number of scholars have examined how the Métis resistance was depicted in the English- and French-Canadian press in order to explore the position of the Métis in the expanding dominion.[5] Likewise, many historians have examined Métis identity formation and ethnogenesis across present-day Canada and the northern United States. Their studies reveal an undeniably distinct community—within Red River and well beyond—manifesting a group consciousness roughly within the time frame outlined by Sprague and others.[6] The focus of research has, quite properly, been on the Métis themselves: Did they or did they not see themselves as a nation? However, this essay asks a different question: Did the trans-atlantic community recognize either a distinct Métis identity or Métis nationhood? As John E. Foster has pointed out, when determining "who is and who is not a member of a particular people" or nation, it is vital to consider the "views of the historical actors, both "insiders" and "outsiders." In other words, we need to determine not only "when a particular population saw itself" as Métis but also when, or even if, "outsiders shared this view."[7] The degree to which the broader international community acknowledged Métis claims and nationhood shaped the socio-political terrain upon which the Métis had to operate. A survey of the press coverage of the Métis resistance—particularly in newspapers in Canada, the United States, France, Great Britain, Ireland, and Australia—suggests that those "outsiders" had mixed views about what it meant to be Métis and the existence of a Métis nation in the West.

Underlying much of the discussion of Métis nationhood is the group's hybridity. As a people with both European and Indigenous heritage, the Métis occupied what Homi K. Bhabha would call "liminal space" between Indigenous and Euro-Canadian cultures.[8] While their cultural and ethnic duality marked the Métis as unique and as a people of interest among commentators in the transatlantic media, it also exposed them to the assertions that, on the one hand, they were "racially" and culturally inferior as an Indigenous people and, on the other, indistinct from French Canadians. Certainly, the Métis appear to fit theorist Gayatri Chakravorty Spivak's definition of the term *subaltern* as "the oppressed" whose "identity is its difference." Spivak also suggests that "there is no unrepresentable subaltern subject that can know and speak itself," and that the "subaltern cannot speak."[9] As a racialized minority standing in the way of Canadian expansion, the Métis, despite their constant efforts to make themselves heard and recognized, increasingly found their voices drowned out in the domestic and international press. This situation suggests that while Julie F. Codell and Alan Lester, both historians of British imperialism, are right to say that colonized peoples could, as Codell puts it, "write back," they did so under constrained circumstances and were often ignored.[10] The subaltern might have been able to speak, but that did not mean anyone was listening. In the Canadian context, this attitude translated into a federal government that wantonly trampled the Métis' rights and claims to nationhood while also stealing their land and attempting to obliterate their culture.

The Métis Nation

By the time Louis Riel was executed for treason in November 1885, the Métis had little doubt about their status as a distinct people or nation. Whether viewed in terms of race, culture, or language, the Métis were different from the Europeans and constituted an Aboriginal people in their own right. As their name suggests, the Métis were a "mixed-blood" community, the product of unions between Aboriginal women and European men. Some of the Métis were English-speaking and Protestant, but the majority were French-speaking and Catholic. For the most part, the latter group defined what it meant to be Métis. The Métis were neither exclusively European farmers nor Indigenous hunters. While most had farms that they worked for part of the year, they also played a major role in the buffalo hunt. Another indication of the Métis' status as a unique community was their dress. Métis women were masters of needlework, producing clothing for their families that combined European and Aboriginal elements. By the mid-nineteenth century, these Métis artisans were selling their handiwork to European travellers and settlers, and the clothes they produced were valuable precisely because there was nothing else like them. Even more significantly, some Métis developed their own language. Like almost everything else in Métis life, **Michif** was an Indigenous and European hybrid, mixing Cree verbs and French nouns.[11]

Between 1816 and 1885, the Métis articulated their nationhood in conflicts with European and Canadian groups. At the Battle of Seven Oaks in 1816 and at the trial of Métis fur trader Guillaume Sayer in 1849, the Métis of Red River defined and defended what they saw as their territory and rights against European interlopers and the trade monopoly of the Hudson's Bay Company (HBC). In both instances, the Métis' struggle created a sense of shared purpose in pursuit of their collective interests. That self-identification as a nation was articulated most clearly, however, when they resisted the expansion of the recently created Dominion of Canada in 1869–70 and 1885. In 1869–70, the HBC's sale of Rupert's Land to Canada threatened the Métis, who felt that their rights had been ignored in the transaction. In response, they seized control of Red River, formed their own provisional government, and commenced negotiations with the Tory government of Sir John A. Macdonald. The resulting Manitoba Act of 1870 brought Red River into Confederation as a province but failed to secure the Métis' future. As Riel stated in a letter to US President Ulysses S. Grant, the Métis entered "the Canadian Confederation, on the faith of a treaty which, Canada, as one of the two contracting parties, does not fulfil." Instead, the fate of the Métis in the Dominion was to suffer "prosecutions," "unwarranted arrests," "confinement in irons," "condemnation to death," "outlawry," and "the banishment of the Métis Leaders and representative men."[12]

Map 6.1 Great Lakes Metis Settlements, 1763–1830. (Source: The Metis Resource Centre of Canada Inc.)

Indeed, after the Canadian government sent an army to pacify the new province, many Métis fled further west, while Riel went into exile in the United States. Riel returned in 1884 to help the Métis press their ongoing grievances with the federal government. Thanks to the government's unresponsiveness, both the Indigenous people of the West and the Métis took part in related but separate armed uprisings in March 1885. The Métis went into battle declaring that "[i]f we are to die for our country, we will die together." Many of them did die during and after the Canadian army's suppression of this final episode of armed resistance. Riel was hanged at Regina on 16 November 1885. Even in defeat, however, the Métis saw themselves as a nation defending their territory,[13] and their leaders—including Riel's former lieutenants, such as Gabriel Dumont—continued to press their case with politicians both north and south of the border. In a letter, Dumont even assured his Métis brethren in Canada that he had enlisted the help of "an exalted person" in France, who "sympathizes with our cause."[14]

During the resistance, the Métis, with Riel as their spokesperson, attempted to make their voice heard in the press, both in Canada and abroad. In 1869–70, however, the Métis message was a mixed one—a reflection of Red River's unique political position as a former HBC settlement within the British Empire but not yet legally a part of Canada. In proclamations that were reprinted in the English-Canadian, French-Canadian, and American press, Riel declared that, in resisting the Canadian government, the Métis were defending both "the rights of nations and our rights as British subjects." He also described the West as "our country," though, given the fact that the **Red River Resistance** relied on the support of groups besides the Métis, his language was necessarily vague. That was no longer the case in 1885. During the **1885 Resistance** and in the months after his capture, Riel outlined the character and grievances of his followers in the clearest terms. In interviews first printed in the newspapers of Western Canada and then reprinted in Ontario and Quebec, Riel portrayed the Métis as an independent people who "never sold their rights, or agreed . . . to

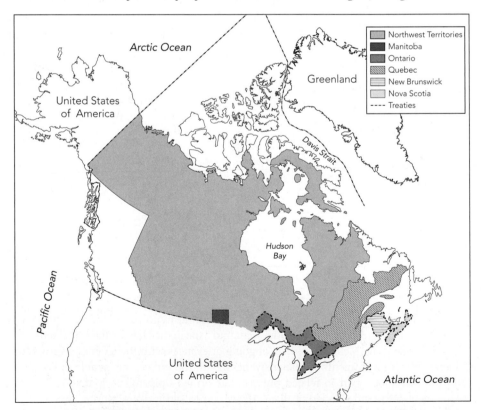

Map 6.2 Canada 1870, Territorial Evolution Map. (Source: Indian and Northern Affairs Canada.)

recognize the Dominion Government." "We did not rebel," he argued, "we defended and maintained rights which we enjoyed and had neither forfeited nor sold." On several occasions at his widely reported trial, Riel referred to the Métis as a "nation" with all the rights that such a description entailed.[15] In effect, he repeatedly made the case for a Métis nation in the most public forum available to him. But Riel could not control how either the Canadian or international press framed the Métis story.

The Anglophone World and the Métis

From the beginning, the English-Canadian and English press seemed determined to brush aside the idea that the Métis were a distinct nation. In this approach, Toronto's *The Globe*, the most influential English-Canadian newspaper of its time, set a pattern that others followed. Like the majority of English journalists on both sides of the Atlantic, *The Globe*'s editor, George Brown, firmly believed that Canada was destined to colonize the West and did not look kindly on anything that stood in the way. He consistently denied the Métis resisters' autonomy, stating that they were "a few desperadoes, reckless of bloodshed" driven on by Riel's despotic will or that of "some other evil genius behind him."[16] Reflecting the racist and colonialist mentality of their age, the rest of the English and English-Canadian press agreed that, even if the Métis were a separate people, they were dupes of Riel with no significant will of their own. They were "irresponsible demi-savages" and "ignorant half breeds" who were racially incapable of independent action, and had been delivered into Riel's hands by the HBC, the Catholic clergy, various American wire-pullers, or an incompetent Conservative government in Ottawa.[17] "Riel feeds them on **pemmican**," *The Globe* reported in April 1870, "and as long as they can get nothing better they will stick to him till they eat what he has."[18] The Métis might be linguistically and ethnically distinct and have some legitimate grievances, as the London *Times* and *The Anglo-American Times* noted, but they were considered a primitive people, somewhere "between French and Indians" who could not possibly "resist the British Empire."[19]

In 1885, the English-Canadian press appeared to be more willing to support the Métis argument that the Canadian government had treated them badly. Papers friendly to the Liberal Party, eager to strike a blow against Macdonald's Conservative government, stated regularly that the Métis were "neglected, despised, wronged."[20] Even the staunchly Conservative *Toronto Daily Mail* accepted this image of the Métis. They could "complain, and justly, that the Dominion has not treated them fairly," it noted. If the federal government had disrupted the Métis way of life, the *Mail* concluded, they certainly deserved "compensation."[21] And when Riel's Métis supporters adopted a revolutionary Bill of Rights in March, a correspondent from the *Mail* was present to record their actual thoughts that "the Government had for fifteen years neglected to settle the half-breed claims, though it had repeatedly . . . confessed their justice" and so a provisional government had become a necessity.[22] It had taken a decade and a half, but the English-Canadian press seemed ready to deal with the Métis with a measure of cultural sensitivity.

That possibility proved illusory as both Tory and Liberal papers resurrected the racist image of the Métis as simple savages in efforts to gain advantage over their political opponents, undercutting the Métis claim to nationhood in the process. The newspapers of English Canada stressed that the Métis were "a people who knew little of the world." They were a "peaceable" and "loyal people" who were "naturally easy-going."[23] It made political sense for editors, on both sides of the partisan divide, to describe the Métis as naive innocents. Doing so allowed Tory papers to depict them as fooled by Riel, thus exonerating the federal government. The Liberal papers, in contrast, portrayed the Métis as being taken advantage of by both Riel and the Conservatives, whose incompetence had delivered the resisters into Riel's hands.[24] According to the English-Canadian press, the Métis of 1885 were a unique but dependent group in the West whose ability to influence events was limited. They were the victims of Louis Riel, the federal government, or both. The Métis were not and could never be an autonomous force and, by implication, did not constitute a nation.

In 1885, the British imperial press was far more interested in the events unfolding in the Canadian West than it had been in 1869–70, though newspapers in England, Ireland, and Australia continued to follow the English-Canadian editorial lead. Editors across the British world suggested that the Métis were a unique group in Western Canada, distinct from the Native people and white settlers and divided into "Métis-Francais" and the "Métis-Anglais."[25] The imperial press also concurred that the "grievances of the half-breeds are undoubted" and sometimes blamed Canada's federal government for the uprising.[26] From there, however, editors in England and Australia attempted to fit the Métis into the wider context of British imperial affairs, the better to help their readers make sense of events in the Saskatchewan country. According to the London *Times*, the Métis were the Canadian equivalent of "the Boer adventurers of Bechuanaland," a reference to the Dutch settlers of Southern Africa who stubbornly resisted British rule in the 1870s and 1880s.[27] In Australia, the *Brisbane Courier* likened the Métis to the Maori of New Zealand, similarly determined opponents of British "land-grabbing." From this point of view, the Métis could not be dismissed as "only pemmican eaters": "[M]en fighting for their old free, open-air life of trapping will fight for what they hold to be their own, pemmican eaters or not. They are just as fond of their rights as if they had been nourished on the most delicate fare."[28]

In other words, both the English and Australian press characterized the Métis as one of the subject peoples of the British Empire, a rhetorical device that Riel himself employed.[29] However, this portrayal did not necessarily earn the Métis any respect. The *Brisbane Courier* denounced them as "little better than a pest," while papers in England and Ireland argued that they were under Riel's spell.[30] This confusion—the Métis were a proud and distinct people but also the simple-minded victims of Riel's plotting—reflected the reliance of the Empire's newspapers on their English-Canadian counterparts.[31] With little direct knowledge of Canadian affairs, the editors had to make sense of the partisan wrangling of the Canadian coverage. Under such circumstances, the resulting image of the Métis was bound to be contradictory.

Readers seeking more clarity would have found it in the American press, particularly the two leading newspapers of New York, *The New York Times* and the *New York Tribune*. In 1869–70, the New York newspapers provided their readers with a somewhat nuanced view of Red River and its people. According to the *Times* and the *Tribune*, the Métis were separate not only from various groups of Anglo-American settlers but also from "[t]he Scotch and English half-breeds."[32] Nor were the French and Catholic Métis to be confused with the Aboriginal peoples of the West.[33]

The American newspapers also had no time for the notion that the Métis were the puppets of some other more powerful group. In 1874, the *Times* published an account of the resistance from the Métis point of view to counteract English-Canadian and English claims that Louis Riel was "the leader of a mob of French half-breeds, whose chief purpose was plunder" and terror. It strongly suggested that the Métis constituted a nation, arguing that they were a people with genuine grievances, stemming from their deep roots in the region.[34]

But, influenced perhaps by a general hardening of American attitudes towards any obstacle to western expansion in the 15 years after the Red River Resistance, the New York newspapers were less uniformly supportive of the Métis cause in 1885 than they had been in 1869–70. Like editors in English Canada and the British Empire, New York journalists told their readers that the Métis had "suffered at the hands" of the Macdonald government "and inch by inch their land is slipping from them."[35] At the same time, however, the New York press drew on English-Canadian papers that argued that Louis Riel was "the cause of all the troubles."[36] At one extreme, the *Times* depicted the Métis as Riel's enraptured followers: "Of 30,000 half breeds he is the idol," it stated, "he has chained them to him by his gift of fiery eloquence and by his undaunted courage."[37] The *Tribune*, in contrast, was less sure. Taking up the role played by the *Times* in 1869–70, the *Tribune* stressed Métis agency. The aims of Riel and the Métis were not necessarily synonymous, it pointed out, and it might be possible to convince the latter that their leader "is standing between them and their interests." If that happened the Métis "would almost certainly abandon" Riel and "make terms for themselves." They would behave, in other words, as rational actors, even though they remained fundamentally a "half-savage people."[38]

This picture of Métis distinctiveness became muddied after the resistance collapsed and the Canadian army captured Riel. Observing the drama of Riel's trial, conviction, and execution from a distance, the *Tribune* noted that any idea of the Métis as a unique people in Canada was fading fast. As Riel's execution approached, the Métis became subsumed within a larger French-Canadian nation: Riel's fate became the fate of the Métis, and the fate of the Métis became that of French Canada as a whole.[39] At the moment of their greatest international notoriety, US commentators transformed the Métis' story into nothing more than

Louis Riel, a prisoner in the camp of Major F.D. Middleton, c. 16 May 1885, Batoche. (Library and Archives Canada/Frederic Hatheway Peters fonds/C-003450.)

another episode in the long battle between English and French Canada. Certainly, there was no evidence of a widespread understanding of or sympathy for Métis claims to nationhood.

The Francophone North Atlantic and the Métis

In French Canada and France, the story of the Métis nation followed a different trajectory. In the initial stages of the Red River Resistance, commentators shared George Brown's ignorance of the Métis. Although there was more sympathy for the Métis in francophone ranks, confusion reigned over what exactly bound the Métis together.[40] Montreal's Liberal paper *Le Nouveau Monde* listed traits that it thought typified the Métis, but these in no way distinguished them from French Canadians.[41] This uncertainty prevailed despite attempts by some Métis to outline their culture and lifestyle to Quebec newspapers and, through them, to French Canadians. For example, in response to a patronizing piece that appeared in *Le Nouveau Monde*, a Métis letter-writer underlined that the Métis enjoyed many of the accoutrements of European culture. Even "on the Mackenzie River, at Great Slave Lake," he remarked, "one can find pianos and musicians to play them. So don't be surprised if there's a piano at Fort Garry."[42]

Perhaps the most interesting coverage appeared in *Le Courrier de St. Hyacinthe*, an influential conservative paper published outside Montreal, which printed regular reports from a man in the field who identified with the resisters and was likely Métis. As he wrote on 1 March 1870, "Mr. Riel . . . is the leader of the nation, which recognizes him as such."[43]

In French Canada, and to a lesser degree in France, serious discussion of the issues behind the Red River Resistance transpired. This was particularly true of *Le Nouveau Monde*, in which editorials explained the Métis' assertion that, as they had not been consulted by either the HBC or the government over the sale of Rupert's Land, Canadian sovereignty in the region was null and void. The newspaper went so far as to suggest a referendum in Red River on joining Confederation.[44] Even Conservative Member of Parliament Joseph Édouard Cauchon allowed that government agents had run roughshod over the Métis' claims to the land and had been insensitive to their concerns; he urged an even-handed resolution to the conflict.[45] Thus, in French Canada, the commentariat understood Métis disquiet and conceded its legitimacy.

Eventually, what emerged in the francophone discussion of Red River was a construction of Métis identity that emphasized the purported rebels' French heritage and frontier lifestyle. Absent was any meaningful discussion of the Métis' Indigenous heritage: it was their European ancestry that allowed them to be seen as civilized and so worthy of recognition. In this instance, the Métis' hybridity worked to their advantage. The respected Parisian daily *Le Temps*, for instance, carried a lengthy discussion of the disturbance at Red River. "Most of the insurgents," noted *Le Temps*' Washington correspondent, "have French blood in their veins." They were "pioneers of civilization, simple and honest men." The author counted the Métis among the 20,000 "white" inhabitants of the Red River Valley and at one point even referred to them as "[French] Canadian peasant[s]."[46] Thus, the erasure of the Indigeneity of the Métis fostered sympathy for their cause.

In 1885, by contrast, French-language coverage of the resistance was much more extensive than in 1869–70 and was driven initially by an interest in the "red peril." Newspapers ran lurid accounts of "redskin" violence and alarmist reports of a mass uprising among western Aboriginal peoples. Even Paris's Marxist *Le Cri du Peuple*, later sympathetic to the Métis' plight, initially stoked the racist fears of its readers by predicting "a war between [the Indians] and the whites, which will be long and bloody."[47] This sensationalism reached a fever pitch following the kidnapping of two white women by Cree warriors in early April 1885. The spectre of white women under the control of Aboriginal men was, in the minds of French-Canadian and French journalists, beyond horrifying, and newspapers fuelled their readers' outrage with speculation that the leader of the Cree resisters, Big Bear, planned to take the captive Theresa Delaney as a wife.[48]

To the extent that such reporting reveals anything about the authors' perceptions of Métis identity or nationalism, it indicates incomprehension and a conflation of the Métis with their Cree allies, a pattern that persists to this day. Thus, whereas the Métis' French heritage had won them sympathy in 1869–70, in 1885 their Indigenous ancestry initially alienated potential supporters. However, understanding of the Métis did improve and the francophone press on both sides of the Atlantic made a substantial effort to inform their readers of Métis culture and grievances. For example,

Mistahi Maskwa (Big Bear). (Library and Archives Canada/C-001873.)

Montreal's papers attempted to distinguish the Métis from "the savages," insisting that only the former were "civilized."[49] Racist though this discourse was, it represented a step towards recognition of the Métis as a unique group by francophone journalists.

A further move in this direction came with the elucidation of the Métis' lifestyle. Many publications, for instance, underlined that the Métis were hunters and trappers; others emphasized their religiosity; and still others examined Métis appearance, dress, and history.[50] Oftentimes, these investigations were, to borrow Edward Said's term, Orientalist.[51] A peculiarly persistent tendency was to liken the Métis to Bedouins. Both groups, journalists informed their readers, possessed remarkable horseback riding and sharpshooting skills. Several publications, in both Canada and France, likewise compared Riel to another "rebel" of 1885: Muhammad Ahmad al-Mahdi, who led a Sudanese rebellion against Egyptian (and by extension British) authority.[52] Thus, the Métis became an exotic "other."

Others made more concrete attempts to educate the public about the Métis and their grievances. In France, *Paris-Canada* explained to its readers that the dispute was over the dispossession of the Métis' land, adding that the Métis were a culture apart, descended from Indigenous and French unions. The pro-Canadian bent of the publication, however, led the author to ascribe the Métis' plight to their supposed indolence. They had, he explained, "abandoned Manitoba for the North-West, meaning hard work and industry for hunting and fishing."[53] *Paris-Canada* thus constructed the Métis as separated from the Indigenous peoples by their French heritage and Catholic religion but, due to their Indigenous origins, unsuited to the "hard work" of modern life. In so doing, of course, the paper drew on the racist trope of Indigenous peoples as inherently lazy. As *Paris-Canada* stated condescendingly, "The population is nomadic, anxious, easily offended, [and] childlike."[54]

Commentators also made the Métis' racial hybridity a centrepiece of their coverage. A common theme was that the Métis played a role as intermediaries between "Indians" and whites in the Northwest.[55] Crude though this obsession with the duality of Métis identity was, it was often accompanied by serious consideration of the Métis' grievances. Paris's *Le Figaro*, for example, explained that the Métis' main sources of discontent were their being pushed off their land and "persecutions" at the hands of white settlers.[56] Perhaps the most comprehensive analysis came courtesy of Alexandre Taché, the Catholic archbishop of St Boniface, MB. Taché had a personal relationship with Riel and had been accused by the anglophone press of fomenting Métis unrest. Nevertheless, the archbishop bravely outlined the many ways in which the Métis' concerns had been ignored and concluded that the responsibility for the violence was widely shared among the government, the settlers, and the resisters themselves.[57] In short, sympathy for the Métis' plight, if not their violent actions, was nearly universal in the francophone North Atlantic. As left-wing firebrand Henri Rochefort wrote in Paris, the Métis were one of many "peoples enslaved, stripped [of their rights], and decimated by English oppression."[58]

Thus, within the French-language transatlantic conversation about the Métis in 1885, it is clear that commentators recognized the Métis' unique hybrid identity and conceded the legitimacy of their complaints. Did this constitute an international recognition of Métis nationhood? One searches in vain for any commentator not connected to the Métis who used the language of nation to describe them. Yet, particularly during the rigorous discussion of the justice of Riel's conviction and hanging, observers plainly viewed him as a defender of his "people." This was especially evident on the political left in both French Canada and France. The organ of the French Workers' Party described Riel as "the heroic leader of the rebellious Canadian Métis"; French liberal theorist Gustave de Molinari portrayed him as motivated by "patriotism"; and French-Canadian journalist P.-Ernest Tremblay dubbed Riel a "champion of the rights of an oppressed people."[59] Moreover, commentators of all political stripes cast the Métis leader as a martyr. For example, Charles Longuet, Karl Marx's son-in-law and a fervent Marxist, stated that Riel was a "prisoner of war" who was treated as a "criminal" and rendered a "martyr" by his executioners.[60] While there was no widespread recognition of Métis nationhood, at least some commentators on both sides of the Atlantic certainly recognized the Métis as an independent people.

The passionate defence of Louis Riel that arose in both French Canada and France also saw a repetition of the pattern of 1869–70. As authors came to identify with the Métis, they underscored their French heritage and conflated the Métis with French Canadians. Suddenly, just as the story of the resistance of 1885 reached its international climax with Riel's execution, the key theme became "the conquered [French] race against the conquering [English] one."[61] In an extreme case, the Parisian paper *Le Figaro* explained: "Riel . . . is a Métis, a half-Frenchman; but in Canada, where the love of the mother country, of France, is so deeply rooted in people's hearts, a half-Frenchman could pass for a Frenchman and a half. Thus, there, on the banks of the St. Lawrence, a Frenchman is in distress for having defended his home!"[62]

This metamorphosis resulted principally from the political purposes of francophone authors, always eager in both French Canada and France to rouse their readers against "the Ontarian devourers of priests" or "cowardly England."[63] Unfortunately, clarity over Métis identity fell victim to expediency. Once again, therefore, the Métis' hybridity shaped the recognition of their singular identity but paved the way for their effacement within a larger French-Canadian whole. That their effacement transpired despite the continued political activity of the Métis and their claims to be recognized as a distinct nation[64] illustrates all too clearly the hegemony of the predominant view of Indigenous peoples in the western world.

Conclusion

If the test of nationhood is domestic and international recognition, the Métis of 1869–70 and 1885 did not qualify, as transatlantic francophone and anglophone commentators did not extend such acknowledgement. On the whole, this indifference was unsurprising given that even the most radical commentators assumed the inevitability of the extension of Canadian colonialism in the West. That the grievances of a few thousand "mixed-race" farmers and hunters might prevent the forward march of "civilization" was unimaginable to the vast majority of western observers in the context of the day.

In their discussion of Riel's trial and execution, both francophones and anglophones increasingly referred to the Métis in terms synonymous with French Canadians. Thus, the hybridity of the Métis proved doubly disadvantageous. Their Indigeneity enabled their representation as "uncivilized," while their French heritage led to their distinctiveness being erased or overlooked.

Did this western inability to perceive the nationhood and political maturity of the Métis matter? Certainly, the Canadian government was sensitive to the criticisms of its conduct in the international community, as shown by its defence of its actions to the Committee of the Privy Council in Great Britain.[65] Had that community made the case for a Métis nation it might well have given Canada pause. More importantly, the pervasiveness of this mentality on both sides of the Atlantic offers a window into the western mindset of the late nineteenth century, a mindset that shaped Canadian policy and was hostile to the rights of Indigenous peoples. Alas, the climate of the times was such that John A. Macdonald confessed publicly without hesitation or shame that the Canadian government's chief aims in dealing with the Red River Métis were "to obtain possession of the country" and "the extinguishment of the Indian title."[66]

That does not mean, however, that the Métis did not possess a national identity or that the international press ignored them entirely. By the time Riel was hanged in November 1885, the Métis self-identified as a unique community in the Canadian West, and many Métis asserted their rights and nationhood in the strongest possible terms. As Riel proclaimed during his trial, the Métis were a "nation" possessing land—their "inheritance from God."[67] Moreover, despite the repression they suffered post-1885 at the hands of Canada, the Métis endured and their culture thrived. For their part, in 1869–70 and 1885 the transatlantic French community and the majority of the anglophones of the British Empire and United States portrayed the Métis as a distinct group, acknowledging, to varying degrees, the legitimacy of their grievances.

Notes

1. In this article, the rebellions will be referred to as Métis resistance because the legitimacy of Canada's sovereignty in 1869–70 is questionable and these incidents were part of a larger pattern of anti-colonial resistance.

2. D.N. Sprague, *Canada and the Métis, 1869–1885* (Waterloo: Wilfrid Laurier University Press, 1988).

3. www.mmf.mb.ca/, accessed 25 May 2011.

4. Gerhard J. Ens, *Homeland to Hinterland: The Changing Worlds of the Red River Metis in the Nineteenth Century* (Toronto: University of Toronto Press, 1996); Thomas Flanagan and Ens, "Métis Land Grants in Manitoba: A Statistical Study," *Histoire Sociale/Social History* 27, 53 (May 1994): 65–87.

5. See, for example, A.I. Silver, "Ontario's Alleged Fanaticism in the Riel Affair," *Canadian Historical Review* 69, 1 (1988), 21–50; Jennifer Reid, *Louis Riel and the Creation of Modern Canada: Mythic Discourse and the Postcolonial State* (Albuquerque: University of New Mexico Press, 2008), 72–158.

6. See, for example, Lawrence J. Barkwell, Leah Dorion, and Darren R. Préfontaine, eds, *Métis Legacy* (Winnipeg: Pemmican Publications, 2001); Ute Lischke and David T. McNab, eds, *The Long Journey of a Forgotten People: Métis Identities and Family Histories* (Waterloo: Wilfrid Laurier University Press, 2007).

7. John E. Foster, "Some Questions and Perspectives on the Problem of Métis Roots," in Peterson and Brown, eds, *The New Peoples*, 77.

8. Homi K. Bhabha, *The Location of Culture* (New York: Routledge, 1994), 3–9.

9. Gayatri Chakravorty Spivak, "Can the Subaltern Speak?" in C. Nelson and L. Grossberg, eds, *Marxism and the Interpretation of Culture* (Basingstoke: MacMillan Education, 1988), 271–313. See also pp. 69, 80, and 104.

10. See, for example, Julie F. Codell, "The Empire Writes Back: Native Informant Discourse in the Victorian Press," in Codell, ed., *Imperial Co-Histories: National Identities and the British and Colonial Press* (Madison: Fairleigh Dickinson University Press, 2003), 188–218; Alan Lester, *Imperial Networks: Creating identities in nineteenth-century South Africa and Britain* (London: Routledge, 2001), 5–8, 189–92.

11. Sarah Carter, *Aboriginal People and Colonizers of Western Canada to 1900* (Toronto: University of Toronto Press, 1999), 62–82; Gerald Friesen, *The Canadian Prairies: A History* (Toronto: University of Toronto Press, 1984), 91–7; Sherry Farrell Racette, "Sewing for a Living: The Commodification of Métis Women's Artistic Production," in Katie Pickles and Myra Rutherdale, eds, *Contact Zones: Aboriginal and Settler Women in Canada's Colonial Past* (Vancouver: University of British Columbia Press, 2005), 17–42.

12. Louis Riel to Ulysses S. Grant, 10–15 Dec. (?) 1875, in George F.G. Stanley, Raymond J.A. Huel, Gilles Martel, Thomas Flanagan, and Glen Campbell, eds, *The Collected Writings of Louis Riel* (Edmonton: The University of Alberta Press, 1985), 2: 6–7.

13. Michael Barnholden, trans., *Gabriel Dumont Speaks*, rev. edn (Vancouver: Talonbooks, 2009), See also Carter, *Aboriginal People and Colonizers*, 70–3, 105–11, 150–61; George F.G. Stanley, *The Birth of Western Canada: A History of the Riel Rebellions* (Toronto: University of Toronto Press, 1960).

14. Gabriel Dumont, quoted in George Woodcock, *Gabriel Dumont: The Métis Chief and his Lost World* (Edmonton: Hurtig Publishers, 1985), 240.

15. Stanley et al., eds, *Collected Writings of Louis Riel*, 1:77, 1:42–5, 3:521, 3:533, 3:543, 3:549–50.

16. "Affairs at Red River," *The Globe*, 12 Feb. 1870, 2; "'President' Riel's Latest," 26 Feb. 1870, 2.

17. "Who is Responsible?" *The Globe*, 4 Apr. 1870, 2; "The Expedition to Red River," *The Globe*, 4 Apr. 1870, 2; "The Red River Affair," (London) *Times*, 22 Apr. 1870, 5; *The Anglo-American Times*, 23 Apr. 1870, 10.

18. "The Nor'-West Trouble," *The Globe*, 28 Apr. 1870, 2.

19. "The Week," *The Anglo-American Times*, 2 Apr. 1870, 9; (London) *Times*, 6 May 1870, 9; "Canadian Affairs," *The Anglo-American Times*, 7 May 1870, 15.

20. "Riel Released," *Manitoba Free Press*, 17 Nov. 1885, 4.

21. "Riel," *Toronto Daily Mail*, 16 Mar. 1885, 4.

22. *Toronto Daily Mail*, 13 Apr. 1885, quoted in Maggie Siggins, *Riel: A Revolutionary Life* (Toronto: Harper Collins, 1994), 368.

23. "The Riel Case," *The Globe*, 14 Aug. 1885, 4; "The Government and the Rebellion," *Manitoba Free Press*, 27 Mar. 1885, 2; "The Rebellion," *Toronto Daily Mail*, 29 May 1885, 2.

24. "The Rebellion," *Toronto Daily Mail*, 29 May 1885, 4; "Riel's Diary," *The Globe*, 15 July 1885, 5; "Riel and Dewdney," *Manitoba Free Press*, 17 Apr. 1885, 2.

25. "The Week," *The Anglo-American Times*, 24 Apr. 1885, 13. See also (London) *Times*, 31 Mar. 1885, 9; *Northern Whig*, 22 Apr. 1885, 4; "The Rebellion in Canada," (London) *Times*, 16 May 1885, 7.

26. *Freeman's Journal*, 14 May 1885, 5; "The Uprising in Northwest Canada," *The Anglo-American Times*, 17 Apr. 1885, 8–9; "Canada," *Guardian*, 22 Apr. 1885, 580; "Riel and the Rebels," *Northern Whig*, 29 May 1885, 8.

27. (London) *Times*, 31 Mar. 1885, 9.

28. "The Insurrection in Manitoba," *Brisbane Courier*, 16 May 1885, 1.

29. Writing to Macdonald from his jail cell, Riel repeatedly compared the Métis' position in Canada to that of the Irish in the United Kingdom: Louis Riel to John A. Macdonald, 16 July 1885, in H. Bowsfield, ed., *Louis Riel: Rebel of the Western Frontier or Victim of Politics and Prejudice?* (Toronto: The Copp Clark Publishing Co., 1969), 144–5.

30. "The Canadian Disturbance," *Brisbane Courier*, 23 May 1885, 1; (London) *Times*, 3 Apr. 1885, 7; *Northern Whig*, 8 May 1885, 5.

31. Similar transatlantic networks have been explored in Alan Lester, "British Settler Discourse and the Circuits of Empire," *History Workshop Journal* 54 (2002), 24–48.

32. "The Red River Rebellion," *The New York Times*, 16 Jan. 1870, 5. See also *The New York Times*, 28 Dec. 1869, 1; *The New York Times*, 6 Feb. 1870, 1; "The Red River Council in Session," *New York Tribune*, 8 Feb. 1870, 1.

33. "A Winnipeg Policy," *New York Tribune*, 23 Apr. 1870, 6.

34. "Louis Riel," *The New York Times*, 11 May 1874, 2.

35. "Some Hit and Miss Chat," *The New York Times*, 5 Apr. 1885, 3; "The Canadian Revolt," *New York Tribune*, 3 Apr. 1885, 4.

36. *The New York Times*, 19 Oct. 1884, 2.

37. "Some Hit and Miss Chat."

38. "Negotiating with Riel," *New York Tribune*, 11 Apr. 1885, 4.

39. "The Conviction and Sentence of Riel," *New York Tribune*, 4 Aug. 1885, 4; "The Respite of Riel," *New York Tribune*, 23 Oct. 1885, 4; "The Hanging of Riel," *New York Tribune*, 17 Nov. 1885, 4.

40. "Bulletin du jour," *Le Nouveau Monde*, 19 Nov. 1869, 1.

41. "Editorial," *Le Nouveau Monde*, 15 Nov. 1869, 1.

42. Un Métis, "Le Piano dans le Nord-Ouest," *Le Courrier de St.-Hyacinthe*, 5 July 1870, 2.

43. "Lettre de la Rivière-Rouge," *Le Courrier de St. Hyacinthe*, 1 Mar. 1870, 2.

44. "La question du Nord-Ouest," *Le Nouveau Monde*, 30 Dec. 1869, 1. For the piece detailing the Métis' grievances in France, see "Lettres des États-Unis," *Le Temps*, 1 Apr. 1870, 2.

45. Joseph Édouard Cauchon, "Le Nord-Ouest: Détails intéressants," *Le Pionnier de Sherbrooke*, 6 May 1870, 1.

46. "Lettres des États-Unis."

47. "La révolte au Canada," *Le Cri du peuple*, 11 May 1885, 2.

48. "L'Insurrection du Nord-Ouest," *Le Courrier de St. Hyacinthe*, 9 May 1885, 1. See also Sarah Carter, *Capturing Women: The Manipulation of Cultural Imagery in Canada's Prairie West* (Montreal: McGill-Queen's University Press, 1997), 48–86.

49. "Trouble au Nord-Ouest," *La Minerve*, 24 Mar. 1885, 3; "Servilisme," *La Patrie*, 27 Apr. 1885, 1.

50. "La révolte du Nord-Ouest," *La Patrie*, 9 Apr. 1885, 1; "L'inhumation de Louis Riel," *Le Pionnier de Sherbrooke*, 24 Dec. 1885, 2; Edmond Johanet, "Riel: Le condamné à mort," *Le Figaro*, 13 Aug. 1885, 1.

51. Edward Said, *Orientalism* (New York: Vintage Books, 1979).

52. See, for example, "Les Métis," *La Minerve*, 7 Apr. 1885, 2; L. de L., "Mort de Riel," *Le Figaro*, 2 Dec. 1885, 3.

53. "Une révolte au Nord-Ouest," *Paris-Canada*, 1 Apr. 1885, 1–2.

54. "La fin de l'insurrection," *Paris-Canada*, 27 May 1885, 1.

55. "Trouble au Nord-Ouest," *La Minerve*, 24 Mar. 1885, 3.

56. "Bulletin de l'étranger," *Le Figaro*, 21 Apr. 1885, 2; L. de L., "Mort de Riel."

57. Mgr Alexandre Taché, "La Situation," *Le Manitoba*, 10 Dec. 1885, 2.

58. Henri Rochefort, "Riel et ses assassins," *L'Intransigeant*, 19 Nov. 1885, 1.

59. "L'Exécution de Louis Riel," *Le Cri du peuple*, 19 Nov. 1885, 2; "L'exécution de Riel jugée en Europe," *Le Pionnier de Sherbrooke*, 10 Dec. 1885, 2; P.-Ernest Tremblay, "Chronique: Riel," *La Patrie*, 21 Nov. 1885, 1.

60. Charles Longuet, "L'exécution de Riel," *La Justice*, 19 Nov. 1885, 1.

61. See, for example, Léon Millot, "Chronique: Louis Riel," *La Justice*, 25 Oct. 1885, 1.

62. Edmond Johanet, "Riel: Le condamné â mort," *Le Figaro*, 13 Aug. 1885, 1.

63. "Débats sur le Nord-Ouest," *Le Pionnier de Sherbrooke*, 13 May 1870, 2; Rochefort, "Riel et ses assassins."

64. For a discussion of this continued activity, see John Weinstein, *Quiet Revolution West: The Rebirth of Métis Nationalism* (Calgary: Fifth House, 2007), 24–5.

65. Bowsfield, ed., *Louis Riel*, 146–51.

66. *House of Commons Debates*, 6 July 1885, 3113.

67. Louis Riel, statement to the court, in Bowsfield, ed., *Louis Riel*, 156.

Primary Document

The Insurrection in Manitoba

Brisbane Courier, 16 May 1885

A telegram which we publish this morning from our correspondent at Montreal shows that the half-breed insurrection in the North-west of Canada has become very serious. On Thursday the insurgents gained a victory over the Government troops and police. A Canadian Cabinet Council has, our correspondent says, determined to send 2000 men against the rebel force. The question now agitating the Dominion is whether the Indians, some 16,000 in number, will join the rebels. If not, the rebellion will be easily crushed. If they do, the resources of Canada will be heavily taxed. Louis Riel, the half-breed leader, appears to have been making inflammatory speeches about the disabling effect of the dispute between England and Russia, while the Fenians along the American border are threatening to join in the fray. But we are certain that the crisis will be met with courage and coolness by our gallant fellow-subjects, and that Lord Lansdowne will not be wanting to the occasion. The origin of the insurrection is the same as it was in 1869. Everybody has heard of the Red River expedition and many people have a confused idea that some one up a river had to be "smashed," and that Colonel, now General Lord Wolseley smashed him. This conception of what occurred is wanted in exactitude. M. Louis Riel, who led the Red River insurgents, withdrew when Colonel Wolseley's men appeared on the horizon. But though he withdrew, M. Riel was not quite disposed of. He lived to fight another day; the other day has arrived, and his followers are formidable. "What they fought each other for?" is a question that has puzzled more mature historical inquirers than Southoy's little Peterkin. In ancient days men did battle for a woman, or a well, and things were intelligible. Now they grow too confusing, from the intricacy of tribal and national interests, and from the enormous distances of space still covered by our Empire. The causes of quarrel between M. Louis Riel and the British Government in 1870 may be gathered from Colonel Butler's very interesting book, "The Great Lone Land." The Red River Settlement was in insurrection under Riel, because of certain arrangements between the Governor of Canada and the Hudson's Bay Company. The dwellers on the Red River Settlement, the half-French, half-Indian people, wish themselves to be regarded as protesting against land-grabbing. That is really what their case comes to. Ever since English history begins we have been acquiring land, and the natives have protested. Sometimes they protested with polished, neolithic, stone-headed weapons. Sometimes, as when we took the isle of Albion, they protested with laments, which may be read in Gildas. When we occupied New Zealand, they appealed to green-jade axes and *patu patus*.

What was it which really occurred on the Red River? "The native," says Colonel Butler, "knew this land was his, and that strong men were coming to square it into rectangular farms, and to push him further west by the mere pressure of civilisation . . . What were these new people coming to do to him?" Manifestly to "eat him up," as the Zulus say. The plan to which the "rebels" under Riel objected transferred land in the Northwest from the Hudson's Bay Company to the Crown. It would have been a most commendable transfer, but there were 15,000 people living in the territory, and "they objected to have themselves and their possessions signed away without one word of consent or one note of approval." So the resisting natives got out their powder horns, put new flints in their old guns, and attacked the surveying parties. Louis Riel, who led freedom's battle, is occasionally described as a half-breed, but there seems to be a divergence of opinion about his lineage. French, or half French half Indian, his energy of character is highly spoken of by some of his biographers. He had rather an excellent opportunity, for no pains were taken by the Hudson Bay Company, or the Imperial Government, or the Dominion Government, to settle the rights and wrongs of the question on the basis of justice and honesty. The Metis the discontented half-breeds, were called "only pemmican eaters," and that was supposed to be a sufficient refutation of their claims. Now, men fighting for their old free, open-air life of trapping, will fight for what they hold to be their own, pemmican eaters, or not. They are just as fond of their rights as if they had been nourished on the most delicate fare. The Red River natives drove the Governor of the country appointed by Canada out of the frontier station at Pembina. They fortified the road between Pembina and Fort Garry. Lastly, they seized Fort Garry, which was their Khartoum, for there they found a battery of nine pounders, with musketry and ammunition. All this was done in a style admired by Colonel Butler. "One hates so much to see a thing bungled," says this distinguished officer, "that even resistance, though it borders upon rebellion, becomes respectable when it is carried out with courage, energy, and decision." All these qualities had, so far, marked the performances of M. Louis Riel.

Although Riel's conduct was at first bold and energetic, he had to be "smashed," or at the very least "disintegrated." Colonel Wolseley, with men in boats, was sent to smash, but only succeeded in disintegrating. The expedition drew near to Fort Garry; it was not fired upon, like that unhappy relief of Khartoum, but was welcomed by all the Scotch and English of the settlement. They were tired of Dictator Riel. Still Riel held out in Fort Garry, just when France was being driven back from her frontiers by the overwhelming weight of the German armies. Fort Garry was reached by our expedition, but there was no sign of hostile occupation. The banner of the insurgents did not flaunt the breezes; in fact there was no banner at all. The gate was open—anyone could go in. An officer of the Hudson's Bay Company was on the threshold to welcome Colonel Wolseley. M. Riel had made war-like preparations. His gallant force had loaded their rifles, and afterwards thrown them away, because they interfered with a speedy strategic movement to the American frontier. "Twenty hands, with an aggregate of perhaps two and a-half hearts among them, were all Riel had to depend on at the last moment." The Dictator, M. Riel, escaped with his life. But he has not forgotten, nor have his kindred forgotten, how they were disposed of, quite without a plebiscite, as Imperial France would have arranged their transfer. The Catholic clergy, no doubt, dislike the increase of Protestant or perhaps agnostic sheep in their fold. The Indians are restless. Then, across the frontier, are our old enemies, the American Irish, who are not likely to keep out of any fighting in which the United States permit them to take part. There is a blood feud between Louis Riel and civilisation. In 1870 he more or less judicially murdered one Thomas Scott, and Scott's slaying is unavenged. The state of things, as we have said, is grave. But we have the satisfaction of knowing that it is being faced with a thorough determination to protect Canadian territory from turbulent risings and lawless raids.

Questions for Consideration

1. In what period did a Métis national consciousness emerge? Where and why did this happen? What events are pointed to by historians and Métis nationalists as the seminal moments in the formation of Métis national identity?

2. Do you think that Adam Gaudry is right to argue that ascribing Métis identity to all peoples of "mixed" Indigenous and European ancestry denies the existence of a distinct Métis Nation at Red River and on the plains?

3. How does the Métis National Council determine who is and who is not Métis? How does this compare to how other nations determine inclusion in and exclusion from the nation?
4. During the periods of armed Métis resistance in Red River and the "North-West," did the international press recognize the Métis as possessing a distinct identity or nationhood? How might this treatment have affected the Métis resistance?
5. Does the perception of the Métis resistances of 1869–70 and 1885 in the trans-Atlantic world support the view that colonial subjects are silenced by the colonizing society? Why or why not?
6. In what ways does the article from the *Brisbane Courier* afford the Métis recognition of their distinct identity or nationhood?
7. When, where, and how did a Métis identity emerge? Who contributed to the construction of this emergent identity and who comprised the Métis community?

Further Resources

Books and Articles

Adam, Christopher, Gregg Dahl, and Ian Peach, eds. *Métis in Canada: History, Identity, Laws, and Politics*. Edmonton: University of Alberta Press, 2013.

Anderson, Chris. *Métis: Race, Recognition, and the Struggle for Indigenous Nationhood*. Vancouver: UBC Press, 2014.

Barkwell, Lawrence J., Leah Dorion, and Darren R. Préfontaine, eds. *Métis Legacy*. Winnipeg: Pemmican Publications, 2001.

Brown, Jennifer and Jacqueline Petersen, eds. *Being and Becoming Métis in North America*. Winnipeg: University of Manitoba Press, 1985.

Campbell, Maria. *Halfbreed*. Halifax: Seal Books Edition, 1973.

Lischke, Ute, and David T. McNab, eds. *The Long Journey of a Forgotten People: Métis Identities and Family Histories*. Waterloo: Wilfrid Laurier University Press, 2007.

Macdougall, Brenda. *One of the Family: Métis Culture in Nineteenth-Century Saskatchewan*. Vancouver: UBC Press, 2009.

Palmater, Pamela. *Beyond Blood: Rethinking Indigenous Identity*. Saskatoon: Purich Publishing, 2011.

Sprague, D.N. *Canada and the Métis, 1869–1885*. Waterloo: Wilfrid Laurier University Press, 1988.

St-Onge, Nicole, Carolyn Podruchny, and Brenda Macdougall, eds. *Contours of a People: Métis Family, Mobility, and History*. Norman: University of Oklahoma Press, 2012.

Printed Documents and Reports

Sprague, D.N., and R.P. Frye. *The Genealogy of the First Métis Nation: The Development and Dispersal of the Red River Settlement, 1820–1900*. Winnipeg: Pemmican Publications, 1983.

Stanley, George F.G., Raymond J.A. Huel, Gilles Martel, Thomas Flanagan, and Glen
    Campbell, eds. *The Collected Writings of Louis Riel*, 5 vols. Edmonton: University of
    Alberta Press, 1985.

Films

Canada: A People's History, Episode 10. DVD. Executive produced by Mark Starowicz.
    CBC, 2000.
Mémère Métisse/My Métis Grandmother. Directed by Janelle Wookey. Winnipeg Film
    Group, 2008.
Mistress Madeleine. DVD. Directed by Aaron Kim Johnston, NFB, 1986.
Places Not Our Own. DVD. Directed by Derek Mazur, NFB, 1985.
Richard Cardinal: Cry from the Diary of a Métis Child. DVD. Directed by Alanis Obomsawin.
    NFB, 1986.
Riel Country. DVD. Directed by Richard Duckworth. NFB, 1996.
We Are Métis. Web video. Directed by Stephen St Laurent. 2008. Available at http://
    vimeo.com/6216205.

Websites

Apihtawikosisan Blog
http://apihtawikosisan.com/

Manitoba Métis Federation
www.mmf.mb.ca

Métis Bill of Rights, 1869
www.canadahistory.com/sections/documents/thewest/metisbillrights.htm

Métis National Council
www.metisnation.ca/

The Virtual Museum of Métis History and Culture heritage exhibit
www.metismuseum.ca/exhibits/heritage

Federal and Provincial Indian Policy

Introduction

The British laid the foundations of Canada's Indian policy with the **Royal Proclamation of 1763**. In part, the Proclamation was an attempt to ensure peaceful co-existence between Indigenous and non-Indigenous peoples by creating guidelines to regulate trade, settlement, and land purchases. Over the next century, the focus of this policy changed drastically. In 1830, the Indian Department was transferred to civilian control in what would become Canada and partnerships were formed with various Christian churches to pursue a policy of "civilization and assimilation." The government and missionaries sought to isolate Indigenous peoples on reserves, "encourage" their adoption of European-style agriculture, and gradually assimilate them by inculcating the social and cultural values and practices of European-Canadians. The federal government expected that, as Indigenous peoples assimilated, the state would acquire their land and resources, and Indigenous peoples would cease to exist, either literally through death and disease or figuratively through assimilation and cultural annihilation.

As discussed by J.R. Miller in Chapter 3, in the 1850s fur trader and politician William B. Robinson negotiated what came to be known as the Robinson Treaties, which involved territories along the northern shores of Lake Huron and Lake Superior. These treaties signalled the beginning of a more formalized system of land surrender that continued to develop through the negotiation of the western numbered treaties during the 1870s. The 1850s also witnessed the passage of increasingly restrictive legislation that controlled all aspects of Indigenous peoples' lives, determining such things as where they could live; whom they could marry; what types of social, cultural, and religious beliefs were acceptable; and how their children would be educated. All legislation pertaining to Indigenous peoples was consolidated under the Indian Act in 1876, and the bureaucracy to manage "Indians" was created in 1880. Although the foundations of Indian policy were laid in the nineteenth century, the bureaucrats who came to work in the Department of Indian Affairs during the twentieth century continued to pursue policies of assimilation with vigour and enthusiasm, and, for the most part, they showed a complete lack of awareness of and disregard for Indigenous cultures and peoples.

In light of the coercive and draconian nature of much of Canada's Indian policy, it has been a long time since it has been described as benevolent by historians. There is general agreement that "Indian" policy was not only a failure but also constituted cultural genocide. However, the ongoing efforts of Indigenous peoples to challenge the policies and actions of the federal government, in conjunction with the success of decolonization movements within the former European empires after the Second World War, and the hard-fought gains of the civil rights movements of the 1960s and later, have created a popular perception that Indian policy after 1945 improved dramatically and was shorn of its most coercive practices. Hugh Shewell's article presents a welcome corrective to this assumption and provides a broad overview of Indian policy in the twentieth and early twenty-first centuries. Shewell argues that the goal of Canada's Indian policy—to, in the infamous words of Duncan Campbell Scott, "rid Canada of its Indian problem"—remains the same as it was at the turn of the century.[1]

Lori Chambers looks at how Indian policy has been implemented and shaped at the provincial level. Under section 91 subsection 24 of the *British North American Act* of 1867, all "Indians and lands reserved for Indians" are under federal jurisdiction. However, all health care, infrastructure (such as roads, bridges, airports, water and sewage treatment plants, and schools), natural resources, education, and child welfare, are under provincial jurisdiction. Revisions to the Indian Act in 1951 provided that "all laws of general application . . . in force in any province are applicable [on reserve] . . . except to the extent that such laws are inconsistent with this *Act*." Instead of this amendment extending the same necessary programs and infrastructure to reserve residents that all other Canadians enjoyed, the provincial government used it to extend provincial social welfare services onto reserves and remove children from their homes and communities. Chambers argues that the child welfare system that was employed in the 60s, 70s, and 80s by provincial governments served the same objective as federal residential schools had—to remove children from their homes and assimilate them into European-Canadian society. There are now more Indigenous children in care than was ever the case at any one time in the residential schools system.

Chapter Objectives

At the end of this chapter, you should be able to

- understand and explain the goals of Indian policy past and present;
- recognize the high degree of continuity in that policy;
- recognize the ideological framework underpinning Canada's Indian policy and identify the tactics used to carry it out;
- understand the "Sixties Scoop" and the role that provincial child services played in implementing policies of assimilation;
- appreciate Indigenous peoples' distrust of the Canadian state better.

Note

1. Duncan Campbell Scott in E. Brian Titley, *A Narrow Vision: Duncan Campbell Scott and the Administration of Indian Policy in Canada* (Vancouver: UBC Press, 1986), 50.

Secondary Source

Dreaming in Liberal White: Canadian Indian Policy, 1913–2013

Hugh Shewell, Carleton University

In this chapter, I explore Canadian Indian policy from 1913 to 2013. These 100 years represent the rise and entrenchment of the bureaucratic administration and management of First Nations in Canada beginning with the repressive administration of Duncan Campbell Scott and ending with the ironclad management of First Nations' affairs by the federal Conservative government of Stephen Harper. In addition to tracing the historical path of Indian policy during this period I will argue that the policy and its implementation, while appearing to be more progressive in the post–Second World War period, remained assimilationist, seeking to dissolve First Nations into white, liberal Canadian society.[1]

The roots of Canada's Indian policy can be found in the Royal Proclamation of 1763, the subsequent approach to Indigenous peoples adopted by the British Colonial Office up to the middle of the nineteenth century, and the eventual ascendancy of responsible government in the colonies of British North America.[2] The Proclamation was designed to maintain good relations with First Nations peoples and to manage relations between them and the rising numbers of settlers.[3] Thus, it sought first to recognize the First Nations peoples as the legitimate occupants of the land, and, second, to guarantee their continued use of it. Contrapuntally, while it "acknowledged some form of pre-existing Indian title," it asserted that "the Crown had acquired underlying title through discovery." The Proclamation provided a procedure by which lands could be ceded for settlement only to the Crown, "not to other imperial powers or to individual subjects of the Crown" and only with First Nations agreement.[4]

The Royal Proclamation thus provided the original constitutional framework by which British colonial authorities, well before Confederation, struggled with what was termed the "Native question"; what was to become of First Nations in British North America? While the plans differed somewhat from colony to colony, the ultimate solutions were roughly the same: "Indians" were to be assimilated into the broader Euro-Canadian society.[5] At first, assimilation was generally understood to mean that First Nations peoples would amalgamate with Euro-Canadian society and participate collectively in the developing market society, but would, broadly speaking, retain their autonomy.[6]

Central to liberalism is the belief that people are autonomous, self-contained, sovereign beings endowed with the right to own and exploit property.[7] This concept of the sovereign individual was contrary to nearly all First Nations' cultures and belief systems, that placed far greater emphasis on the collective society, on communal needs, and on maintaining a oneness with the land. Nonetheless, by the late 1840s the colonial legislatures began to see the solution to the "Native question" not in amalgamation but in individual enfranchisement, meaning that the Native peoples' "full civilization . . . could be achieved only when Indians were brought into contact with individualized property."[8] This required a revised constitutional relationship permitting a reconstruction of the Indian as an individual requiring development and acculturation to liberal values and behaviour.

To begin to acculturate First Nations as individuals, the legislature of the United Canadas passed the *Gradual Civilization Act* in 1857. This act formed the basis of the future Indian Act of Canada and the policies that flowed from it. The Gradual Civilization Act created an enduring paradox: its stated purpose was to civilize and integrate Indians into Canadian society and to make Indians legally indistinct from other Canadians but, at the same time, it separated them from Canadian society by defining who was an Indian and denying them the majority of legal rights accorded to Euro-Canadians.[9] Following Confederation in 1867, a new Indian Act in 1876, together with new measures (especially concerning the education of First Nations children), consolidated previous colonial legislation. The net effect was to deny Indigenous peoples of Canada a partnership in Confederation, to subjugate and strip them of their self-government and autonomy, and to devalue their cultures. They became dependent wards of the state—children in need of development.[10]

Subjugation, Repression, and Tutelage, 1913–45

How then did the federal government propose to assimilate these "uncivilized" peoples? The methods proposed were to confine them to reserves, morally elevate and educate their children, teach them to be agriculturalists, gardeners, mechanics, or domestic servants, and suppress or ban their cultural practices.[11] Accompanying this was a policy of chipping away at Indian lands by stealth or negotiated surrender so that settlement and commerce could proceed unimpeded.[12]

These policies were institutionalized by the time Duncan Campbell Scott became the Deputy Superintendent General of Indian Affairs in 1913. One of his first actions was to issue a lengthy policy statement to all the Indian agents in the field instructing them on 70 specific points covering nearly every aspect of the Indians' lives, including their subjection to "the ordinary law, both civil and criminal, except in so far as the Indian Act makes special provision for their exemption."[13] Scott was determined to run a parsimonious department that emphasized Indian individual self-reliance. "In whatever occupations the Indians are engaged," he wrote, "they should be encouraged in habits of industry and thrift."[14] In addition, the Indian agents were to assiduously pursue the education of Indian children to turn them away from their own cultures that "tend to destroy the civilizing influences of the education imparted" to them.[15] For Scott, the "civilizing" of Indians meant only one thing: their complete absorption and disappearance into the general population. In his view the "great forces of intermarriage and education will finally overcome . . . native custom and tradition."[16]

When Scott became deputy superintendent, Indian Affairs employed 651 "Indian agents" across the country.[17] Scott demanded absolute loyalty from them and suffered little criticism—like Indians, "good" agents were obedient agents. The agents developed a clear, paternalistic relationship with the Indians for whom they were responsible. Thomas Deasy, Indian Agent for the Queen Charlotte Islands, was a typical example. In 1920 he prepared a pamphlet for Scott that he thought might serve as an introduction to the role of the agent. He wrote, "Since the introduction of . . . Responsible Government," the authorities considered it advisable to appoint men . . . to educate, christianize (sic) and protect the tens of thousands of people emerging from the darkness of superstition, idolatry and self-constituted authority, through which all nations passed, in earlier stages of history."[18]

With respect to the "economic progress" of Indians, little was done to develop the economies of their communities outside of agriculture.[19] While the approach to Indian economic development was passive, Scott's administration continuously attempted to press Indians (mainly adult males) into employment and other forms of self-sufficiency by discouraging dependence on relief (welfare)—at that time issued only as food rations or clothing; hence, if relief was given it was so minimal as to act as a deterrent to remaining dependent on it.[20]

In addition to the three fundamentals of Indian policy—education, agriculture, cultural repression—Scott's administration focused on land surrenders and transfers to commercial and settler interests, compulsory enfranchisement, and the suppression of Indian resistance and political organizing. Scott had been directly involved in the negotiation of Treaty No. 9 (Northern Ontario, 1905) and influenced its final extension to other bands (1929–30). He also helped to frame Treaty No. 10 in northern Saskatchewan and Treaty No. 11 (the Mackenzie River Valley) in 1921–22.[21] In all cases he was determined to make the terms as advantageous to the federal and provincial governments as possible by limiting the payments to First Nations and by minimizing the ongoing obligations of the state. Certainly, the enormous profits subsequently realized by mining and forestry interests as well as the Canadian Pacific Railway and the government-owned Canadian National Railway far outstripped any benefits that accrued to the signatory bands. As Brian Titley notes, the profit realized by mining companies "makes it impossible to dispute that fraud of a high order was involved," in these land surrenders.[22]

Perhaps nothing irritated Scott more than "uppity" Indians. The example of the First World War and its aftermath illustrates this point. Although at the outset Indian Affairs did not think Indians could make a useful contribution to the war effort, by its mid-point Indian men were being actively recruited. Even before the administration's encouragement, Indian men enlisted in far greater proportion to their numbers than did non-Indians, a phenomenon that was repeated in the Second World War.[23] When the war ended, the formation of the League of Indians of Canada under the leadership of F.O. Loft, a Mohawk and war veteran, represented the first movement organized to unite Indians across Canada in resistance against federal Indian policies. The League strongly objected to federal policies that too readily permitted the surrender and sale of reserve lands and the discriminatory treatment of Indian veterans, who were denied benefits under the Soldier Settlement Act. These and other grievances fuelled much Indian discontent. Scott's response was to find ways to discredit the leadership of the League, to threaten leaders and followers alike with forced enfranchisement (and thus revocation of official Indian status), and, finally, in 1927, to engineer an amendment to the Indian Act that "forbade bands to pay lawyers or organizers to make claims against the government."[24] This last action had the temporary effect of rendering widespread Indian political resistance nearly impossible.

Scott's most enduring legacy of Indian policy, however, was the expansion of the Indian residential school system, especially in Western Canada.[25] Despite increasing evidence of the severe maltreatment of Indian children—including sexual abuse—and a scathing report by P.H. Bryce in 1909 on the poor health of the children at these institutions, Scott pressed on because he saw the schools as the most effective means of divorcing Indian children and youth from their societies and cultures.

The well-documented problems that existed in the residential schools sometimes divert attention away from their primary purpose: the cultural and social destruction of First Nations peoples. Unquestionably, Scott's administration viewed residential and day schooling as the main weapon in the state's arsenal to crush First Nations peoples' collective identities and to transform them into a readily available supply of cheap labour. Between 1912 and 1932—the year of Scott's retirement—the number of Indian students rose by 51 per cent, from 11,303 to 17,163, an increase aided by an amendment to the Indian Act in 1920 compelling Indian children to attend school. Yet, when the dust had settled on Scott's career there was no tangible evidence that Indian children had assimilated in any great numbers. Nevertheless, great damage had been done to First Nations cultures and societies as well to the individual students, the effects of which remain today.[26]

Dr Harold W. McGill, a crony of then Prime Minister R. B. Bennett, succeeded Scott in 1932 when the country was in the depths of the Great Depression. McGill's tenure lasted 12 years and his term was both the apex of the department's repressive measures and the beginning of their undoing. McGill continued Scott's parsimonious ways and greatly aggravated the effects of the Depression on First Nations peoples— average per capita relief expenditure on First Nations, for example, remained substantially below that provided to other Canadians and actually declined for three years as McGill sought to reduce Indian welfare rolls and save the Crown money.[27]

The Second World War heralded a shift in the government's approach to First Nations. For one thing, the active participation of First Nations militarily and on the home front raised public awareness of their presence and discriminatory treatment. More importantly, Indian political resistance reasserted itself in the face of an obdurate and repressive Indian administration. The suggestions by the Liberal government of Mackenzie King that First Nations might be subject to income tax and conscription propelled them into nation-wide resistance, culminating in the formation of the Committee for the Protection of Indian Rights, led by Chiefs John Tootoosis and Andrew Paull from Western Canada and Jules Sioui from Québec. The Committee staged two national conventions in Ottawa in 1943 and 1944, the latter attracting some 200 delegates despite McGill's efforts to subvert it.[28] Thomas Crerar, the Minister of Mines and Resources (the federal department then responsible for Indian Affairs) agreed to meet with the convention organizers. In addition, he spoke at length to the delegates and reminded Indians of their responsibility to become self-supporting and to be "useful citizens in our common country."[29] Crerar's speech foreshadowed postwar Indian policy while the convention itself gave rise to the formation of the North American Indian Brotherhood (NAIB) and served notice of a new Indian political consciousness.

Citizenship and Integration, 1946–68

Throughout the Great Depression and the Second World War, Canadians had begun to demand greater rights and entitlements by virtue of citizenship. The federal Liberal government responded by taking a more interventionist role in the economy, introducing modest welfare measures and passing a new citizenship act in 1946 that created

Canadian, as opposed to British, citizenship. Also in 1946, in response to public pressure, the federal government struck a joint parliamentary committee to investigate the Indian Act and the policies and practices that flowed from it. The committee sat for two years and proposed that a new Indian Act replace the act of 1876 to "facilitate the gradual transition of Indians from 'wardship to citizenship' and . . . help Indians to advance themselves."[30] Overall, the thrust of the committee's recommendations was to promote the fuller participation of Indian communities in the social, political, and economic life of Canada while permitting them to retain some political and cultural autonomy. In 1949, as if to affirm this new direction, the Indian Affairs Branch was transferred into the new Department of Citizenship and Immigration.

What did this really mean? Even as the committee met, changes were happening in the administration of Indian Affairs. R.A. Hoey, a former Manitoba minister of education, and progressive-minded, had replaced McGill.[31] Expenditures for Indian Affairs were rising; for example, a new housing program was introduced, better-qualified teachers were hired, and new classrooms built. With the rise of the NAIB, Indian Affairs instituted occasional consultation with Indian leaders to seek general advice on policy and on the proposed new Indian Act.[32]

The new Indian Act of 1951 rid Indian Affairs of many of the features of the 1876 act that had compelled the administration to vigorously pursue assimilation. Yet, the new act remained assimilationist. In John Tobias's words, it provided "a co-operative approach between government and Indians towards the goal of assimilation."[33] Moreover, the removal of the compulsory aspects of the old acts of 1876 and 1880 was illusory. Programs and strategies that fostered assimilation while ignoring legitimate concerns like land claims showed that the state remained determined to absorb First Nations peoples into Canadian society. To this end, the treatment of Indians was to be normalized and Indians were dealt with as though they were in transition to citizenship.

During the 1950s and early 1960s, this approach fell flat. Federal welfare benefits were extended to Indians on reserves while limited attempts were made to promote economic self-sufficiency. However, as their traditional economies continued to be undermined, Indians were encouraged to seek employment off reserves. Special employment placement offices as well as Indian Friendship Centres were established in major cities to foster integration into the Euro-Canadian mainstream.[34] Despite the branch's claims that progress was being made, the socio-economic conditions of First Nations peoples relative to other Canadians scarcely improved. Many issues continued to fester. A land claims commission recommended by the 1946 Joint Committee was never established, an omission that was a source of discontent among Indian leaders. The question of unconditional Indian enfranchisement—that is, the granting of full rights of citizenship without surrender of Indian status—also spurred criticism of the federal government both nationally and internationally.[35]

A new Progressive Conservative government under John Diefenbaker reacted to these criticisms, first by establishing a Joint Parliamentary Committee on Indian Affairs in 1959, and second, by unconditionally granting registered adult Indians the federal franchise in 1960. The committee sat for two years and, like its 1946 predecessor, received testimony from diverse constituencies. Although the committee heard many "expressions of Indian nationalist sentiment, as well as demands for greater autonomy and self-government," its final report essentially endorsed the integrationist principles of postwar Indian policy.[36] The upshot of the committee's recommendations was business as usual with one important exception: it again recommended the establishment of a land claims commission. The Diefenbaker government accordingly prepared legislation to do so. At the same time the government also approved a three-year independent study of the Indians in Canada to provide the information needed to raise their socio-economic status to the same level as other Canadians. The study was headed by Dr Harry B. Hawthorn, a professor of anthropology at the University of British Columbia. Shortly thereafter, however, the government fell, and while the Hawthorn study continued, the land claims commission legislation died.[37]

Lester B. Pearson's incoming Liberal government began an immediate reorganization of Indian Affairs. Pearson positioned Indian matters in the general "War Against Poverty," a mantra taken up from the American Kennedy and Johnson administrations of the 1960s.[38] The progressive R.F. Battle, who became director of Indian Affairs,[39] and his new deputy minister, Claude Isbister, introduced a community development program on the reserves to promote Indian responsibility for the management of their own affairs by providing "a framework for coordinating existing health, education, welfare, and economic development services on the reserves and . . . 'reduc[ing] costs in such palliative areas as welfare assistance payments.'" The government argued that this approach would lead to the full integration of Indian communities into their provincial and municipal jurisdictions.[40]

The Hawthorn Report appeared in 1966 and explored nearly every facet of civil, political, and economic life in Indian communities. In its recommendations it grappled with two fundamental issues: the rights of First Nations peoples as distinct from those of other Canadians and the marginalization and "structured poverty" of First Nations. Hawthorn's researchers recommended considerable direct economic investment in Indian communities and greater integration of them into provincial jurisdictions. However, they also recommended preserving and protecting Aboriginal cultures and their distinct rights; Indians were to be "citizens plus." Nevertheless, the progressive thrust of the report was offset by its assimilative and integrative approach to economic progress.[41]

The Hawthorn Report was well received by First Nations leadership, especially its recommendations for special status and increased autonomy. As for its reception in official circles, on the one hand, the Liberal government was not ready to entertain the idea of "citizens plus"; on the other, many of Hawthorn's recommendations influenced subsequent initiatives in welfare, education, skills training, and economic development. Finally, despite its liberality the report provided a cover for the branch—now part of the Department of Indian Affairs and Northern Development—to maintain control over the management of Indian lives.[42] Eventually the influence of the Hawthorn report led to the devolution of Indian program administration and to the replication of the Indian Affairs bureaucratic structure at the band level. Before this happened, however, two important events occurred: first, Pearson stepped down as prime minister and second, his successor, Pierre Elliot Trudeau, proposed a radically different solution to the "Indian problem" in Canada.

From Near Termination to Near Autonomy, 1969–83

Trudeau, who took power in 1968, was a champion of individual civil rights and promised a "just," participatory, and transparent government. He was anxious to end First Nations' marginalization as quickly as possible. Almost immediately upon taking power the new government, with a view to developing an entirely new Indian policy, engaged in a year-long process of consultation with Indian leadership. This, however, turned out to be "a dialogue of the deaf."[43] In 1969, Jean Chrétien, the Minister of Indian Affairs and Northern Development, announced the "Statement of the Government of Canada on Indian Policy" (commonly known as the White Paper) in the House of Commons. Chrétien outlined the government's intention to end the special legal status Indians enjoyed because that status had "kept the Indian people apart from and behind other Canadians."[44] The government argued that equal opportunity for First Nations could only be achieved by terminating their special status and by giving them control over their land as though it were private property. The Department of Indian Affairs would be shut down and Indians would access services like other Canadians. After a year of consultation in which they had expressed their aspirations for "economic and social recovery without losing their identity," First Nations peoples felt betrayed. By 1970 they had rejected the proposal and Trudeau had stated, "We won't force any solution on you." The White Paper was officially withdrawn in 1971 and the government announced an end to assimilation policy.[45]

The fallout from the White Paper was twofold: one, Indian leadership became more assertive in demanding self-government and advancing their peoples' rights, and two, the government transferred the administration of programs designed to foster integration to the bands while permitting First Nations to maintain their separate identities. Throughout the 1970s and early 1980s the Department of Indian Affairs and Northern Development (DIAND) began to offer a greater range of programs and services to Indian communities. Increasingly, the bands themselves administered these although Ottawa carefully controlled their design, objectives, and funding. In effect, band administrations became agents of the state.[46] Most prominent among these programs were social assistance and related services, economic development, and community infrastructure. Bands were funded to hire social workers to administer social assistance, adult care, and homemaker programs. A new Indian Economic Development Fund targeted investment in First Nations communities. Innovative programs began to create jobs on reserves and to stimulate on-the-job training. Other economic development initiatives led to community improvement projects like the building of new schools, recreation centres, band offices, and roads.[47] The idea behind devolution was to give the appearance that the government supported increased autonomy; at the same time the policy "shifted critical attention away from [Indian Affairs] to the local chief, council, and manager."[48] Devolution, rather than being a step towards self-government, can be understood as preparation to terminate the special relationship between First Nations and the Crown.[49]

Nevertheless, the Native Indian Brotherhood (NIB)—later to become the Assembly of First Nations—continued to press its case for greater autonomy and self-government. The NIB did so on two fronts during the 1970s: the establishment of a land claims process and the control of Indian education. Progress on land claims came with a landmark decision by the Supreme Court of Canada in 1973. Although the court narrowly ruled against the Nisga'a's claim to the Nass River Valley, it "recognized that Aboriginal title existed in Canadian law."[50] In the wake of this decision, the federal government finally established a land claims process that same year. Also in 1973, the government accepted an NIB position paper, "Indian Control of Education." First Nations rightly understood that their survival as autonomous peoples depended on schooling their children. Thus, beginning in the mid-1970s, they began to take control of their own education, designing and implementing curricula and training and hiring committed and qualified teachers.[51]

After a brief hiatus, Trudeau's return to power in 1980 provided further impetus to First Nations' demands for self-government. Trudeau immediately began to focus his energies on repatriating the constitution from Great Britain to Canada. The newly constituted Assembly of First Nations (AFN) recognized this as an opportunity to have Indigenous rights recognized in the constitution and to have their claim as a third order of government accepted. Reneging on a previous commitment, Trudeau did not include First Nations in the constitutional negotiations, but the AFN lobbied strenuously and successfully to have Indigenous rights entrenched in the new constitution. The details were, however, left to be determined at a series of three conferences following repatriation in 1982, involving the provincial and federal governments as well as Indigenous leaders. Trudeau urged the provincial premiers to recognize the principle of Native self-government but the western premiers refused.[52] In the meantime, however, a parallel process had been underway.

During the 1970s, DIAND officials had secretly been developing a new band government policy. First Nations, however, had rejected the proposal because it failed to recognize their inherent right to self-government and instead positioned the Canadian government as permitting First Nations to govern themselves.[53] The rejection of DIAND's proposal led to the creation of a House of Commons committee "charged with reviewing all legal and related institutional factors affecting the status, development, and responsibilities of band government on Indian reserves."[54] The committee submitted its report in 1983. Informally known as the "Penner Report" after the committee's chairperson, Keith Penner, the *Report of the Special Committee on Indian Self-Government in Canada* recommended that Indian self-government be recognized as an inherent right and entrenched in the Constitution.[55] Further, the report recommended that DIAND be dissolved and its functions taken over by First Nations governments. To replace DIAND, the report urged the creation of a new Ministry of State for First Nations Relations that would deal with First Nations on a government-to-government basis. Finally, the report also recommended that First Nations' land claims be accelerated and/or that their territories be large enough to be economically and jurisdictionally viable.[56] Most important, the report reflected the First Nations' point of view—it heard and endorsed their voice.

Although the Trudeau government did not accept the entire report, it began to prepare legislation to enable a new form of Indian self-government. Sadly, in its final incarnation, Bill C-52, An Act Relating to Self-Government for Indian Nations, was little better than the original DIAND proposal and died with the dissolution of Parliament in June 1984.[57] The failure to adopt at least aspects of the Penner Report remains a lost opportunity that could conceivably have resolved many of the persistent political grievances and social and economic problems of First Nations.

Back to the Iron Cage, 1984–2013

A new Progressive Conservative government led by Brian Mulroney was less interested in resolving the issue of Indigenous rights; the Mulroney government was mainly focused on establishing a free trade agreement with the United States and having Québec become a signatory to the Constitution. During negotiations with the provinces for the now infamous Meech Lake Accord of 1987, no attempt was made to bring Indigenous leadership to the constitutional table. This proved to be fatal when a First Nations member of the Manitoba Legislature, Elijah Harper, voted against the Accord, effectively killing its ratification.[58]

The Mulroney government policy for Indigenous self-government reverted largely to the pre-Penner era; through a new self-government sector, First Nations bands were encouraged to develop municipal-like governments and to implement departmental programs at the local level.[59] Overall Indian policy thus focused on developing band capacity for taking on limited forms of self-government both within and outside the Indian Act. For example, bands or tribal councils could enter into tripartite agreements with the federal and relevant provincial governments to administer some programs within provincial jurisdiction[60]—notably child welfare and education—in ways that gave First Nations communities more decision-making and made the programs more culturally responsive.[61]

Along with self-government, more emphasis began to be placed on economic development. Ironically, however, Ottawa determined what kinds of economic projects it would fund and First Nations bands or businesses then had to tailor their proposals accordingly.[62] In 1989, building on earlier policies and initiatives, the government introduced the Canadian Aboriginal Economic Development Strategy (CAEDS) which was intended both to stimulate individual commercial enterprise and create employment.[63] Moreover, through the 1980s, the department tried a variety of programs designed to create employment and enhance individual employability. These "make work" programs hired individual band members to work on community-based improvement projects and combined funds from Canada Employment and Immigration and individual social assistance entitlements to create a minimum wage. CAEDS was the first program to incorporate funding for economic development and employment creation. Despite these initiatives, however, unemployment and, particularly, social assistance dependency on reserves remained very high—usually well above 40 per cent.[64]

Meanwhile, land claims and resolution of the First Nations' demands for recognition of the inherent right to self-government and inclusion at the constitutional table continued to fester. In July 1990, a relatively small land claim issue in Kanesatake (Oka, Quebec) exploded into a major crisis. The town of Oka proposed to expand a golf course into a small wooded area historically claimed as a sacred burial ground by the Kanesatake Mohawk. Following the shooting of a Quebec police officer, an armed standoff ensued between Mohawk warriors and the Canadian army which finally ended the following September without further bloodshed. Although Mulroney termed the Mohawk claim to have sovereign title "bizarre," the crisis finally impelled the launch of a promised royal commission on Aboriginal issues in 1991, and together with the failure at Meech Lake hastened renewed attempts at a constitutional accord.[65]

Following more First Ministers conferences and considerable consultation across Canada, a new constitutional accord, known as the Charlottetown Accord, went to a national referendum in 1992. The accord contained a clause recognizing the inherent right of Indigenous peoples to self-government and entrenching it as a third order of government in the Constitution. At the same time it limited First Nations' powers of self-government. The accord was defeated in part because many First Nations did not agree to the limitations on self-government and because many Indigenous women feared that their rights as women would not be fully protected.[66]

The Royal Commission on Aboriginal Peoples (RCAP) reported in 1996, by which time a new Liberal government led by Chrétien was in power. Like Penner's, the report recommended a new Royal Proclamation and sweeping changes to Aboriginal governance, including abolition of the Indian Act, the formation of an Aboriginal parliament, the recognition of an Aboriginal order of government, and significant expansion of the Aboriginal land base.[67] The federal government released its official response, *Gathering Strength—Canada's Aboriginal Action Plan,* two years later in 1998. It began with statements of reconciliation and renewal, then presented a four-part action plan focused on renewed partnerships, strengthened Indigenous governance, new fiscal relationships, and support to communities, peoples, and economies. The government (without a formal apology) regretted the damage done by the residential school system and put in place funds for an Aboriginal Healing Foundation.[68] Nevertheless, the net effect of *Gathering Strength* was more of the same policy, with no steps taken to entrench the inherent right of self-government in the Constitution. Although it announced an end to its paternalistic relationship with First Nations, the federal government continued to exert ultimate fiscal and managerial control over their activities, and made only minor concessions, such as, in policy, recognizing an inherent but limited right to self-government.[69]

In 2003, Paul Martin succeeded Chrétien as leader of the Liberal Party and prime minister and briefly ushered in a revitalized relationship between Indigenous leadership and the federal government. Martin accorded First Nations matters a high priority. A controversial bill, C-7, The First Nations Governance Act, previously introduced by Chrétien in 2002 was withdrawn due to First Nations' opposition. In 2004, Martin instituted a Canada–Aboriginal Peoples Roundtable, a series of meetings between the prime minister, other federal ministers, and Aboriginal leadership that led to the First Nations–Federal Crown Political Accord in 2005. The Accord strengthened the idea of partnership with the federal government in advancing First Nations governance, and was committed to drawing on the Penner Report, RCAP, and the AFN's own document on self-government in developing future policy.[70] Following the Accord that same year, Martin convened a First Ministers Conference in Kelowna, BC to which Indigenous leaders were invited. There, an historic agreement was reached in which all parties agreed to and accepted the conditions of $5.1 billion in new money to be invested in Indigenous housing, health, education, and economic programs. It is fair to say that this agreement and the Accord together were milestones in achieving a blueprint for advancing, in a meaningful way, the principle of Indigenous self-government and self-sufficiency in ways of Indigenous peoples' choosing.[71]

Unfortunately, the agreement did not survive. Almost immediately upon being elected to office in 2006, the new Conservative government under Stephen Harper introduced a budget that reduced the Kelowna spending agreement by 91 per cent! Indeed, after Mr Harper took office, Indigenous—particularly First Nations (Indian)—policy reverted to the pre-Penner period. Despite making a formal apology in Parliament to First Nations for the terrible harm inflicted by the residential school system, the Conservative government showed little inclination to advance real self-government or to promote social and economic programs, in keeping with First Nations' unique societies and cultures.[72] Rather, programs continued much as they were in the 1980s and 1990s, along with encouraging the conversion of reserve land to private property and attempting to tie First Nations education to provincial standards. In addition, tougher controls and auditing processes were put in place, as though First Nations are not fully capable of managing their affairs. This repressive and actively assimilationist policy gave rise to proactive resistance in the form of the Idle No More resistance movement, a coalition of grassroots First Nations groups who felt that the AFN was too close to the government and not representing their communities' best interests.[73]

Strongly connected to the Harper government's regressive approach to Indian policy was its seeming indifference to the plight of murdered or missing Indigenous women and girls in Canada. According to recent statistics from the Royal Canadian Mounted Police (RCMP) there are 1181 police-recorded incidents of missing or murdered Indigenous women. Of these, 164 women are missing and the cases unresolved, and 1017 are homicides. Further, "[t]here are 225 unsolved cases of either missing or murdered Aboriginal females: 105 missing for more than 30 days as of November 4, 2013, whose cause of disappearance was categorized at the time as 'unknown' or 'foul play suspected' and 120 unsolved homicides between 1980 and 2012. The total indicates that Indigenous women are over-represented among Canada's murdered and missing women."[74] Despite demands by national Indigenous organizations and other public interest bodies for a public inquiry into this very troubling issue, the Harper government refused, describing it as merely a criminal police matter, not a sociological or systemic phenomenon,[75] and as "not really high on our [the government's] radar."[76] Not only do these statements reflect a profound ignorance of the issue, they represent a twenty-first-century manifestation of typical settler society attitudes and policy towards Indigenous peoples in Canada.

Finally, although limited progress has occurred in economic areas where different models of economic development and opportunities have been initiated,[77] some of these models derive from Supreme Court of Canada decisions that uphold Aboriginal rights and acknowledge title to the land. This has obliged resource-based corporations, for example, to enter into consent agreements with First Nations.[78] Nevertheless, under Harper, a policy of containment and integration or assimilation into the rest of Canada persisted; First Nations remained in the iron cage of wardship. For too many First Nations, their position at the margins of Canadian society remains deeply entrenched. The dilemma remains: if meaningful self-government is not an option, is the gradual absorption of First Nations into Canada's liberal society a just solution to their marginality—or is it the death knell of their unique societies and cultures?

Notes

1. By "liberal" I am not referring to the Liberal Party but to the liberal values that inform Canada's national ideology.

2. John L. Tobias, "Protection, Civilization, Assimilation: An Outline History of Canada's Indian Policy," in *As Long As The Sun Shines And Water Flows: A Reader in Canadian Native Studies*, Ian A.L. Getty and Antoine S. Lussier, eds (Vancouver: University of British Columbia Press, 1983), 40–1.

3. Brian Titley, *The Indian Commissioners: Agents of the State and Indian Policy in Canada's Prairie West, 1873–1932* (Edmonton: University of Alberta Press, 2009), 3.

4. Peter J. Usher, "Environment, race and nation reconsidered: reflections on Aboriginal land claims in Canada," The Wiley Lecture, in *The Canadian Geographer/Le Geographe canadien* 47, 4 (2003), 377.

5. David T. McNab, "Herman Merivale and Colonial Office Indian Policy in the Mid-Nineteenth Century," in *As Long As The Sun Shines*, 85–7.

6. See, for example, John S. Milloy, "The Early Indian Acts: Developmental Strategy and Constitutional Change," in *As Long As The Sun Shines*, 56, 59.

7. C.B. Macpherson, *The Political Theory of Possessive Individualism: Hobbes to Locke* (Oxford: Oxford University Press, 1964), 263–71.

8. John S. Milloy, "The Early Indian Acts," 58. Enfranchisement generally refers to full citizenship together with the right to vote, a right which, at that time, was generally restricted to men of property.

9. Tobias, "Protection, Civilization, Assimilation," 42.

10. Milloy, "The Early Indian Acts," 62–3.

11. Titley, *The Indian Commissioners*, xi, 4, 9; Hugh Shewell, *"Enough to Keep Them Alive": Indian Welfare in Canada, 1873–1965* (Toronto: University of Toronto Press, 2004), 13–16.

12. E. Brian Titley, *A Narrow Vision: Duncan Campbell Scott and the Administration of Indian Affairs in Canada* (Vancouver: University of British Columbia Press), 1986, 41.

13. LAC, RG-10, Red Series, Vol. 3086, File 279, 222-1A, General Instructions to Indian Agents in Canada, issued by Duncan Campbell Scott, Ottawa, 25 October 1913. Cited in Hugh Shewell, *"Enough to Keep Them Alive,"* 95–6.

14. Ibid.

15. Ibid., 97.

16. Duncan Campbell Scott, cited in E. Brian Titley, *A Narrow Vision*, 34.

17. Hugh Shewell, *"Enough to Keep Them Alive,"* 94, 109.

18. Thomas Deasy, "Civilizing Influences," in LAC, RG-10, Black Series, Vol. 4093, File 570,970. Circa December, 1920.

19. One exception to this was the Home Industry Program initiated in 1926. It promoted the making and sale of Indian handicrafts for tourists—especially in more northern areas. See Hugh Shewell, *"Enough to Keep Them Alive,"* 125.

20. See, for example, Robin Jarvis Brownlie, *A Fatherly Eye: Indian Agents, Government Power, and Aboriginal Resistance in Ontario, 1918–1939* (Toronto: Oxford University Press, 2003), 106.

21. E. Brian Titley, *A Narrow Vision*, 67–73.

22. Ibid., 73.

23. Hugh Shewell, "An Examination of Aboriginal–State Relations in Canada and Their Possible Implications for Aboriginal Participation in the Canadian Armed Forces." Paper commissioned by the Royal Military College, Kingston, Ontario and presented to the Inter-University Seminar on Armed Forces and Society, Ottawa, October 2006, 7–9.

24. Shewell, *"Enough to Keep Them Alive,"* 157.

25. J.R. Miller, "Canada and the Aboriginal Peoples, 1867–1927," in *Reflections on Native–Newcomer Relations: Selected Essays* (Toronto: University of Toronto Press, 2004), 183–4.

26. Titley, *A Narrow Vision*, 90–1, 93.

27. Shewell, *"Enough to Keep Them Alive,"* 114–15.

28. Hugh Shewell, "Jules Sioui and Indian Political Radicalism in Canada, 1943–1944," *Journal of Canadian Studies* 34, 3 (1999): 227.

29. LAC, RG-10, Red Series, Vol. 3212, File 527,787–4, Transcript of Speech Delivered by the Minister, T. A. Crerar, to the Convention of Indians, Ottawa, 7 June 1944.

30. John F. Leslie, "Assimilation, Integration or Termination? The Development of Canadian Indian Policy, 1943–1963," PhD Dissertation (Ottawa: Carleton University, 1999), 177.

31. Ibid., 102.

32. Leslie, "Assimilation, Integration or Termination?," 174, 179, 181.

33. Tobias, "Protection, Civilization, Assimilation," 52.

34. Shewell, *"Enough To Keep Them Alive,"* 238, 262–3.

35. Leslie, "Assimilation, Integration or Termination?," 286–300.

36. Ibid., 387–8.

37. John F. Leslie, "The Policy Agenda of Native Peoples from World War II to the 1969 White Paper," in *Aboriginal Policy Research: Setting the Agenda for Change*, Vol. 1, Jerry P. White, Paul Maxim and Dan Beavon, eds (Toronto:

Thompson Educational Publishing, 2004), 18–19.

38. Ibid., 21.

39. Canada, Department of Citizenship and Immigration, Indian Affairs Branch, *Annual Report, 1959–1960* (Ottawa: The Queen's Printer, 1960), 46.

40. LAC, RG-10, CR Series, Vol. 8194, File 1/29-6, Part 3, Memorandum to Cabinet, "Community Development, Indian Affairs Branch, item 5, February, 1964. Cited in Shewell, *"Enough to Keep Them Alive,"* 310. For a more complete discussion of the Community Development Program see, Hugh Shewell, ""Bitterness behind Every Smiling Face": Community Development and Canada's First Nations, 1954–1968." *Canadian Historical Review* 83, No. 1 (2002): 58–84.

41. Shewell, "Rassembler nos forces," 44–6.

42. Ibid.

43. J.R. Miller, *Skyscrapers Hide the Heavens: A History of Indian–White Relations in Canada,* 3rd edn (Toronto: University of Toronto Press, 2000), 329.

44. Canada, Department of Indian Affairs and Northern Development, *Statement of the Government of Canada on Indian Policy* (Ottawa: Indian Affairs, 1969).

45. Sally M. Weaver, *Making Canadian Indian Policy: The Hidden Agenda, 1968–1970* (Toronto: University of Toronto Press, 1981), 187.

46. James S. Frideres and René R. Gadacz, *Aboriginal Peoples in Canada*, 9th ed. (Toronto: Pearson/Prentice Hall, 2012), 175–7.

47. Hugh Shewell, "Rassembler nos forces, ou recourir encore à l'aide sociale? La situation socio-économique des premières nations avant et après la Commission royale," *Recherches amérindiennes au québec*, Vol. XXXVII, 1, 2007, 46–7.

48. Frideres and Gadacz, *Aboriginal Peoples in Canada*, 177.

49. Shewell, *Enough to Keep Them Alive,* 310.

50. Miller, *Skyscrapers Hide the Heavens*, 343.

51. Ibid., 341.

52. Ibid., 350–1.

53. Frideres and Gadacz, *Aboriginal Peoples in Canada*, 327.

54. Ibid.

55. Ibid.

56. Sally M. Weaver, "A Commentary on the Penner Report," in Paul Tennant, Sally M. Weaver, Roger Gibbins and J. Rick Ponting, "The Report of the House of Commons Special Committee on Indian Self-Government: Three Comments," *Canadian Public Policy—Analyse de Politiques*, X, 2, (1984): 217–18.

57. Frideres and Gadacz, *Aboriginal Peoples in Canada*, 327–8.

58. Miller, *Skyscrapers Hide the Heavens*, 374–7.

59. Ibid., 361–2.

60. Frideres and Gadacz, *Aboriginal Peoples in Canada*, 177.

61. See, for example, Hugh Shewell and Annabella Spagnut, "The First Nations of Canada: social welfare and the quest for self-government," in *Social Welfare with Indigenous Peoples,* John Dixon and Robert P. Scheurell, eds (London: Routledge, 1995), 1–53.

62. Frideres and Gadscz, *Aboriginal Peoples in Canada*, 349.

63. Shewell, "Rassembler nos forces," 47–8.

64. Ibid., 46–7.

65. Miller, *Skyscrapers Hide the Heavens,* 377–8, 380–4.

66. Ibid., 378–9.

67. Frideres and Gadscz, *Aboriginal Peoples in Canada*, 180–1; Miller, *Skyscrapers Hide the Heavens,* 385.

68. Frideres and Gadscz, *Aboriginal Peoples in Canada*, 184; Wayne Warry, *Ending Denial: Understanding Aboriginal Issues* (Toronto: University of Toronto Press, 2007), 60–1.

69. Miller, *Skyscrapers Hide the Heavens,* 388; Frideres and Gadscz, *Aboriginal Peoples in Canada*, 331–2.

70. Warry, *Ending Denial*, 171–2.

71. Ibid., 173,179.

72. Ibid., 179–80; Frideres and Gadscz, *Aboriginal Peoples in Canada*, 333.

73. Gyasi Ross, "The Idle No More Movement for Dummies (or, "What The Heck Are All These Indians Acting All Indian-Ey About?")," http://indiancountrytodaymedianetwork .com/2013/01/16/idle-no-more-movement-dummies-or-what-heck-are-all-these-indians-acting-all-indian-ey, retrieved 12 Nov. 2014; Aboriginal Peoples Television Network, "AFN's fault lines magnified by Idle No More movement, Attawapiskat Chief Spence's protest," 15 January 2013, http://aptn.ca/news/2013/01/15/afns-fault-lines-magnified-by-idle-no-more-movement-attawapiskat-chief-spences-protest/, retrieved 12 Nov. 2014.

74. Canada, Royal Canadian Mounted Police, *Missing and Murdered Aboriginal Women: A National Operational Overview (2014).* www .rcmp-grc.gc.ca/pubs/mmaw-faapd-eng.pdf, retrieved 22 Jan. 2015.

75. CBC News, "Harper rebuffs renewed calls for murdered, missing women inquiry," 21 August 2014. www.cbc.ca/news/canada/manitoba/harper-rebuffs-renewed-calls-for-murdered-missing-women-inquiry-1.2742845, retrieved 22 Jan. 2015.

76. Ibid., "Full text of Peter Mansbridge's interview with Stephen Harper," 17 December 2014. www.cbc.ca/news/politics/full-text-of-peter-mansbridge-s-interview-with-stephen-harper-1.2876934, retrieved 22 Jan. 2015.

77. Frideres and Gadscz, *Aboriginal Peoples in Canada*. See Chapter 11 for an excellent discussion of the various models and strategies, 340–72.

78. Sean Fine, "Supreme Court expands land-title rights in unanimous ruling." *Globe and Mail*, 14 June 2014. www.theglobeandmail.com/news/national/supreme-court-expands-aboriginal-title-rights-in-unanimous-ruling/article19347252, retrieved 12 Nov. 2014.

Primary Document

Civilizing Influences

A proposed pamphlet by Thomas Deasy, Indian Agent, 1920

The Indian Agent is much misunderstood, by both Whites and Indians. His duties call for more than those of any other class of officials. Usually, his home is on a main reserve, among the people under his care. He is not there as a "mentor," or to interfere with the rights and privileges of the individual. The Indians, as "Wards," should look upon their Agent more in the light of a "father." It is true that the Indian Agent is clothed with the powers of a Magistrate, in certain cases, and requires compliance with the rules of law and order. He is governed, in his public acts, by the "Indian Act," which is carried out for the betterment of all concerned. It is not his privilege, or his duty, to enter into the private life, of a well-meaning member of the Bands, or to interfere with the conduct and management of those who comply with the law and engage in lawful occupations. His advice should be sought, on any question, public or private, which can be elucidated through channels that are not open to the residents of outside localities, sometimes far removed from the course of their advice, legal or otherwise.

It is a mistaken idea, of many of the Indians, that an Indian Agent represents only the powers that control him. His duty should be to forward the work of civilization, in a straightforward, honest, manner. The "Wards of Government" are approaching the day when they will be thrown on their resources. The majority of them are no longer in a condition where they will need direct guidance in all of their affairs. They must take their places, as men and women, capable of adjusting their own lives, free from direct supervision. Over fifty years of education, and the aid of self-sacrificing missionaries, should be sufficient, to lead a people from "wardship," to an understanding of what is required of them, not only for the good of themselves; but also for the public good.

The only law, differing from that controlling the other residents of the localities is one for the good of the Indian, in the prohibition of spirituous and intoxicating liquor and ingredients. Prohibition has been found of benefit to the Indian, to prevent degradation and crime. In no other way are the Indians restricted more than their other neighbours. Indulgence in intoxicants, without restraint, has been the curse of every country. If the individual cannot restrain himself, the government introduces laws, on many other matters, which govern the individual. It is safe to assert that the restriction of the sale and use of intoxicants has been the salvation of the Indians, in this country.

Long experience, with the Indians of a particular Province, shows that the natives have not, as a general rule, advanced as they should. The fault may be theirs, or it may be with those associating with them. No race of people will advance until they comply with the laws of God, and with the laws promulgated for health and sanitation. Education of the mind should mean observance of the law of God, and natural laws of health. It is of little use to store the mind with grammatical phrases, and overlook the betterment, by practice, of the interests of soul and body. "Cleanliness is next to Godliness" is an old adage. Outward appearance, in the way of gaudy clothing, may cover a body contaminated by lack of bathing and need of underclothing free from dirt. The body, like the soul, must not be contaminated, if health is desired.

Secondary Source

Indigenous Children and Provincial Child Welfare: The Sixties Scoop

Lori Chambers, Lakehead University

The treatment of Indigenous[1] children in Canada "is part of a longer story of massive social upheaval caused by colonial imposition, dispossession, and oppression."[2] The history of residential schools, and the responsibility of the federal government for such policies, has been the subject of significant protest and scholarly attention;[3] as a result, in 2008 the federal government belatedly, but officially, apologized for the residential school debacle.[4] Much less talked about, however, is provincial responsibility for rates of apprehension under child welfare regulations and the "Sixties Scoop," the deliberate placement of Indigenous and Métis children in white families in the 1960s, 1970s, and early 1980s.[5] The "Sixties Scoop" raised profound questions for (settler) law.[6] If adoption represented an absolute severance of the relationship between birth parent(s) and child, did children lose Indian status on adoption? The legality of formal adoption (at least in the eyes of settler society and the government), and the fact that the child would retain Indian status, was confirmed by the Supreme Court of Canada in 1976. Ultimately, however, Indigenous opposition to non-Indigenous adoption placements led, in 1984, to an amendment to the law of adoption in Ontario. This amendment required that courts determining custody under the best interests approach[7]—a new child-centred approach to child welfare which emphasized the needs of the child, not the rights of the parent—must, when dealing with Indigenous children, take into account "the uniqueness of Indian and native culture, heritage and traditions" and the goal of "preserving the child's cultural identity."[8] In this context, Indigenous child welfare services were created and rates of adoption out of communities declined dramatically. However, while governments and courts now recognize the problems inherent in out-adoption, resources have not been invested in Indigenous child welfare on reserve, "devolution of services . . . did not . . . address . . . material conditions of poverty"[9] and Indigenous children continue to be "institutionalized through long term foster care"[10] in disproportionate numbers. This chapter traces the history of legal responses to the adoption of Indigenous children out of their communities, from a time when such adoptions were wrongly believed to be beneficial to children, to the present context in which a class action suit alleges that adoptions caused enormous harm to individual children and to First Nations communities.

Under section 91 subsection 24 of the British North America Act, 1867, all "Indians and lands reserved for Indians" were placed under federal jurisdiction.[11] The federal government was committed to assimilation, encouraged primarily through religious day schools, attendance at which became mandatory for children age 7–15 in 1920.[12] Until the 1950s, the provinces provided no social welfare services on reserve. In 1951, however, revisions to the Indian Act provided that "all laws of general application . . . in force in any province are applicable [on reserve] . . . except to the extent that such laws are inconsistent with this Act";[13] this measure was explicitly intended to help extend provincial social welfare services onto reserves. No money, however, was forthcoming, and it was only in the 1960s that the federal government provided a mechanism for allocating money to provincial social service agencies.[14]

The arrival of white social workers from provincial agencies represented a new mode of intrusion into reserve and family life, rendering communities vulnerable to child apprehension. Social workers coming onto reserves brought with them middle-class, white notions of the proper family: "the white social worker, following on the heels of the missionary, priest, and the Indian agent, was convinced that the only hope for the salvation of the Indian people lay in the removal of their children."[15] Social workers also failed to recognize that Indigenous communities took wider communal responsibility for child-rearing, a lack of cultural understanding that may be "the greatest failing of the child protection system."[16] The net result of their interventions was that "the proportion of First Nations children in care began to increase dramatically across the country."[17] Child welfare experts note that, historically and in the present, First Nations children "are not removed from their parents because of higher rates of physical, sexual or emotional forms of abuse"; instead, it is "the persistent systemic and structural factors of poverty" and colonization that put Indigenous children at risk.[18]

In response to the fact that large numbers of First Nations, Inuit, and Métis children were in limbo in foster care, Adopt Indian Métis (AIM) was created in 1967 by the Saskatchewan government, initially as a pilot project to find adoptive homes for Indigenous children. In policies modelled on AIM, the Ontario government also deliberately undertook to place Indigenous children off-reserve in the late 1960s; although some effort was made to place children with Indigenous families off-reserve, many were adopted by white families.[19] By the late 1970s the number of Indigenous children adopted by non-Indigenous parents had increased fivefold.[20] As one social worker and advocate of Adopt Indian Métis asserted,[21]

> a concentrated educational program must be developed in order that the community no longer turns its back on the Métis and Indian child. The 32.3 per cent of children in care who are of Métis or Indian extraction have proven that they are no different from the other 67.7 per cent except for the color of their skin. All children have one common denominator, they need secure homes. These children are being denied that basic human right.

As this quotation illustrates, not only were Indigenous children disproportionately likely to be removed from their homes and placed in care, the motives behind the push for formal adoption were paternalistic. While the parenting skills of Indigenous peoples were denigrated, the adoption of First Nations, Inuit, and Métis children was simultaneously motivated by a liberal, naive belief that ethnicity and race were irrelevant if children were raised with love. Neither social workers nor adoptive parents, many of whom acted in good faith, recognized that "denigration of Aboriginal cultures and racism abound in both subtle and blatant ways for Aboriginal people. For Aboriginal adoptees, in particular, these experiences may be a harsh contrast to their experience of a safe, privileged non-Aboriginal environment."[22] Such contrasts could, and did, create identity confusion and anomie for many adoptees. Too often, adopted children grew up "being so dislocated in terms of their race, their family, that they ha[d] no clear sense of their identity and no home to which they can return: the circle has been broken."[23] As Fournier and Crey recognized in 1997, foster care and adoption may be even more harmful than residential schools:

> Residential schools incarcerated children for 10 months of the year, but at least the children stayed in an Aboriginal peer group; they always knew their First Nation of origin and who their parents were and they knew that eventually they would be going home. In the foster and adoptive system, Aboriginal children typically vanished with scarcely a trace, the vast majority of them placed until they were adults in non-Aboriginal homes where their cultural identity and legal Indian status, their knowledge of their own First Nation and even their birth names were erased, often forever.[24]

Numerically, AIM and other efforts to promote the adoption of Indigenous children were strikingly successful. However, despite these efforts, more First Nations, Inuit, and Métis children remained in foster care than were adopted. Ironically, this was (and is) in part because racism in Canada proved intransigent despite the optimism expressed by groups like AIM. The numbers of Indigenous children in foster care were also high because of disproportionate apprehension rates. By the 1970s, "1 in 3 Aboriginal children in Canada were separated from their families of birth through adoption or fostering."[25]

In this context of rapidly rising rates of adoption of Indigenous children by white families, the first issue that the courts had to consider was whether or not, under the Indian Act, the adoption of a status Indian child by any non-status family was legally possible, since adoption was under provincial jurisdiction but Indigenous children on reserve were the responsibility of the federal government. Did adoption thereby deny children Indian status, and was adoption legislation not applicable to First Nations and Inuit children? In *Natural Parents v. British Columbia* (Superintendent of Child Welfare) (1976), the Supreme Court of Canada found that it was legal to adopt a status Indian child and that the child did not lose his or her status as a result of being adopted. The Supreme Court of Canada, with the majority opinion delivered by J. Laskin,[26] found in favour of the adoptive parents and the child welfare regime, asserting that it would be undesirable to exclude "Indian children from possible adoption . . . outside of the Indian community."[27] Laskin cited the best interests of the child doctrine in asserting that the boy had to "be considered as an individual," which required thinking of him as "not part of a race or culture."[28] By this decision, the adoption would proceed and the child could claim Indian status upon reaching the age of majority.

The obvious question that emerged from this case was this: If a child retains his or her status, but has no knowledge of, or contact with, his or her birth parents or his or her Indigenous community, how will this status be recognized? Would the child be involuntarily enfranchised? In the wake of the Natural Parents decision, the federal government acted to encourage parents who had adopted status Indian children to apprise the children of their right to claim status. In a guidebook for adoptive parents, the government provided a very basic, condescending, and homogenizing history of First Nations and Inuit peoples in Canada pre- and post-contact and urged parents to be aware of the status rights of their adopted children. The pamphlet explained that the adopted child remained registered on his or her band list of birth, but reassured parents that identifying information about the birth parents was excised from the band records to ensure confidentiality. At the age of majority the child could claim his or her status.[29] The Department of Indian and Northern Affairs took the position that their "lawful obligations under treaty" to status children adopted by non-status parents [were] met by the adoption itself"[30] because the adoption was intended to meet the material and developmental needs of the child.

In this context, in which the Supreme Court of Canada had given clear support to out-of-community adoption, First Nations, Inuit, and Métis communities took aim at such policies. As Ovide Mercredi and Clem Chartier, prominent Indigenous leaders in Canada, asserted, "the increase in adoption has been viewed by Indian people as a form of assimilation and genocide, however the courts have attempted to negate them by ruling that an Indian child does not lose his/her status upon adoption."[31] The theft of Indigenous children in Canada was first labelled the "Sixties Scoop" by Patrick Johnson in 1983. He took this name from the remorseful words of a British Columbian child protection worker who admitted that workers had "scoop[ed] children from reserves on the slightest pretext."[32] The name reflected both the "notable increases in Aboriginal child apprehensions" and the fact that the children were "literally apprehended without the knowledge or consent of families and bands."[33] Despite protest from Indigenous peoples, however, the apprehension of Indigenous children in Canada continued unabated. For example, by 1980, 85 per cent of the children in care with the Kenora District Children's Aid Society were of Indigenous descent.[34] Against this backdrop of large numbers of children in care and growing Indigenous protest, individual adoption cases were challenged in (settler) courts.

The Supreme Court of Canada case that set the tone for many decisions to come, *Racine v. Woods*, heard in 1982, denigrated the importance of cultural connection in favour of the bonding that had occurred between the adoptive parents and the child; in fact, this was a landmark case accepting "psychological bonding—a relatively new concept in social science."[35] At the level of the Court of Appeal, Judge Matas had expressed concern that the white foster mother could never provide the modelling necessary for the child.[36] He asserted that the foster father was Métis and had an understanding of racism; however, he did not explore "whether the adoptive father would be able to provide [the child] with any exposure to the Ojibway language and culture that were her heritage."[37] While Matas was more sensitive to the issues of culture and ethnicity than the Supreme Court would prove to be, he relied nonetheless on an image of the homogenized Indian in failing to differentiate between a person of Métis descent and an Ojibway person. The Supreme Court of Canada deemed that the best interests of the child would be served by leaving her with the adoptive parents with whom she had bonded.[38] Beyond ignoring mounting evidence of the harm inflicted on Indigenous children by severing their cultural connections and ignoring racialized identities and experiences, this decision denigrated the intense healing work that the birth mother had undertaken, ridding herself of addictions, obtaining an education, and finding employment, all with the intention of reclaiming her child.[39] The birth mother explicitly asserted that the adoption of her child outside of her First Nations community reflected "systemic political oppression of native peoples."[40] The Court did not consider the issue of Indigenous culture any further, although the fact that the little girl would not lose her Indian status through adoption was cited as essential to the decision.[41] It should be noted that the Supreme Court refused to even consider the possibility, raised at the Court of Appeal, that the adoption be open and that the birth mother be granted access.

In response to *Racine v. Woods*, in December 1983 Chief Dave Ahenakew, speaking for the Assembly of First Nations (AFN), announced that the AFN planned to inform all adopted children of their Indian status and, if necessary, to challenge the confidentiality provisions for adoption under the Charter.[42] In this context, and perhaps fearing the consequences of such a challenge for adoptions that did not involve Indigenous children, the Ontario government took action.[43] In 1984, an amendment to Ontario adoption regulations required for the first time that, with regard to Indigenous children, courts employing the best interests approach must consider "the uniqueness of Indian and native culture, heritage and traditions" and the goal of "preserving the child's cultural identity."[44] Further, the Ontario Child and Family Services Act, which replaced the Child Welfare Act in 1985, explicitly set out under s. 1 (e) that it must be a priority of Child and Family Services to "respect cultural, religious and regional differences" and in s. 1 (f) acknowledged that Indigenous people are "entitled to provide their own child and family services." Independent First Nations child welfare services were established in communities with large First Nations populations, such as Northwestern Ontario. Priority was given to family and community placements under s. 53 (5) and bands were given a 30-day window in which to contest any agency plan for child placement and to come up with an alternative proposal. The reforms "delegated authority given by the provincial government . . . and tie First Nations people to the child protection standards of the provincial Child Welfare Act instead of letting them establish their own standards."[45] First Nations communities thereby became responsible for imposing settler law on their own children and communities.

Bands, as well as individual parents, contested the new adoption regime. Although the 1976 decision in Natural Parents had confirmed that adoption by non–First Nations families was legal, and despite the reforms of 1984, in 2004 the Algonquins of Pikwàkanagàn First Nation challenged out-of-community adoptions as a violation of the Charter.[46] The Ontario Superior Court of Justice, Toronto, had to consider the question of whether or not the placement of First Nations children for adoption outside their reserve violated their s. 7 rights to liberty and security of the person. Each of the siblings had been apprehended at birth, starting in 2000, and the Children's Aid Society had presented the band with their plans for the children in a timely manner, according to the requirements of legislation. These plans included the adoption of one of the children by an aunt who was First Nations and another child by a long-term foster parent. The band did not respond.[47] Although the parents had initially consented to the children becoming Crown wards, the father later became "concerned that the children would not all be placed with Native families."[48] The court asserted that "the band [had] received appropriate notice throughout. It was free to exercise any or all of these rights, within the same time constraints as a natural parent. That they chose not to is hardly a breach of any Charter right."[49] The court dismissed the assertion that the children's liberty interests included a right to be raised in a First Nations home:

> if that were so, then Native children could only be adopted by Native families or bands. The facts of this case highlight the lack of such homes for Native children. The applicant's interpretation would leave Native children in adoption limbo, waiting for Native placement . . . and would be contrary to the requirement that all Crown wards be placed for adoption within a reasonable period of time.[50]

The legality of out-of-community adoption was again affirmed by this decision.

Such adoptions, while legal, are less common than in the past. Apprehensions, however, have not decreased. Indigenous children remain disproportionately vulnerable to apprehension. Children's Aid Society complaints against Indigenous families occur at a rate "4.2 times that for non-aboriginal children (140.6 per 1000, vs. 33.5)."[51] There is little doubt that racism motivates this over-investigation and over-representation: colonization and resultant poverty and community disruption put Indigenous children at risk of being found to be neglected, but Indigenous parents are statistically less likely to be violent with children than white middle-class parents.[52] Apprehensions of Indigenous children are disproportionate. Currently, while out-of-community placements are viewed as a last resort, without adequate or appropriate supports on reserve for families of origin or for potential adoptive parents, it has become the reality for far too many children. In Ontario, 21 per cent of children in care are Indigenous, but Indigenous children constitute only 3 per cent of the child population.[53] Fostering does not solve underlying problems of poverty, social dislocation, colonialism, and racism; moreover, Indigenous children in the foster care system are not guaranteed access to their home communities or cultures. Ironically, we are now in much the same situation, with high rates of apprehension and an over-representation of Indigenous children in foster care, that prompted the creation of AIM and the promotion of the adoption of such children off-reserve in the 1960s.

It is in this context that the Assembly of First Nations and the First Nations Child and Family Caring Society of Canada (FNCFCS) filed a complaint with the Canadian Human Rights Commission over the lack of funding for Aboriginal child welfare in 2007. Initially the case was dismissed by the Human Rights Tribunal because there is no comparator group "as the government of Canada does not provide welfare funding for any other children." The Federal Court set aside this decision as "substantively unreasonable" and the hearing of evidence began on 25 February 2013. The federal government again attempted to halt proceedings through an appearance at the Federal Court of Appeal on 6 March 2013, but the right of the appellants to proceed was confirmed. The decision dismissing the appeal was released on 11 March 2013.[54]

The evidence amassed by the litigants, including reports from the auditor general in 2008 and 2011, from the Standing Committee on Public Accounts in 2009 and 2012, and the United Nations Committee on the Rights of the Child, is overwhelming and the Tribunal has the authority to make a finding of discrimination. The litigants seek equitable funding for child welfare and a trust fund of $112 million to assist the children and families who have already been harmed by government negligence.[55] The federal government has spent millions of dollars trying to avoid this hearing since proceedings were launched in 2007. Nonetheless, on 25 February 2013 the Human Rights Commission began hearing evidence.[56]

The legality of the Sixties Scoop is also being directly challenged. In *Brown v. Attorney General (Canada)*, Marcia Brown-Martel and Robert Commanda have initiated a class action suit against the federal government on behalf of all First Nations[57] children in Ontario who were adopted out of their communities and thereby lost their connections, not only to their biological families, but also to their cultures and languages during the period between 1965 and 1984. They allege that the federal government failed in its fiduciary duty to care for First Nations people and "wrongfully delegated its exclusive responsibility as guardian, trustee, protector, and fiduciary of aboriginal persons by entering into an agreement with Ontario that authorized a child welfare program that systemically eradicated the aboriginal culture, society, language, customs, traditions, and spirituality of the children." They assert that their loss and suffering, and that of other class litigants, is worth $50,000 a person, and also that the government owes fostered and adopted children an apology, much like that given to the victims of the residential schools tragedy.[58]

Brown and Commanda are of Ojibway ancestry and were themselves "scooped."[59] Their application is supported by a resolution from the Chiefs of Ontario. Both Brown and Commanda had unhappy childhoods with significant instability with their foster and adoptive parents; both tried, but found it very difficult, to reintegrate into First Nations society and their reserves of origin; and both suffered depression and anxiety as a result, they believe, of cultural dislocation.[60] For adopted Indigenous children who have suffered identity confusion and anomie, repatriation efforts are challenging beyond the issues inherent in an ordinary adoptive search for roots. In this context, Judge Perell found that while the pleadings as presented were flawed, there was a fundamental issue amenable to a class action decision, as follow:[61]

> In Ontario, between December 1, 1965 and December 31, 1984, when an aboriginal child was placed in the care of non-aboriginal foster or adoptive parents who did not raise the child in accordance with the child's aboriginal customs, traditions, and practices, did the federal Crown have and breach a fiduciary or common law duty of care to take reasonable steps to prevent the aboriginal child from losing his or her aboriginal identity?

Perell accepted the temporal limitations for the class action as proposed, 1965–84, the period during which the federal government funded provincial welfare measures that facilitated apprehension, foster care, and adoption, and before the provincial government officially recognized the importance of maintaining the Indigenous identity of children.[62] Perell also found, despite the assertion of the federal government, that the case should be a test case only,[63] that there was common ground for a class action suit.[64] Although he required amendments to the pleadings, he found that the action could be certified as a class action suit under the requirements of the *Class Proceedings Act, 1992*, S.O. 1992, c. 6.[65] Similar pleadings have since been initiated in British Columbia,[66] Saskatchewan,[67] Alberta, and New Brunswick.[68]

In January of 2012, the federal government won its appeal of this decision in Divisional Court; the ruling also ordered Brown and Commanda to pay $25,000 in costs.[69] The costs awarded against Brown and Commanda were then set aside by the Court of Appeal on 17 January 2013; the court found not only that costs were unfair because the case "raises novel points of law. The treatment of Aboriginal children in Ontario's child welfare system and Canada's responsibility for what occurred are matters of public interest,"[70] but also that the plaintiffs would have another opportunity to certify their pleadings. Justice Belobaba of the Ontario Superior Court of Justice certified the class action on terms very similar to Perell's on 27 September 2013.[71] The government was granted leave to appeal this certification by Justice Matheson on 11 March 2014,[72] but the appeal was dismissed. Judge Nordhemer determined that while the pleadings with regard to fiduciary duty might not be perfect they were "sufficient to get the respondents over the relatively low threshold for defeating a motion [to dismiss]."[73]

Although *Brown v. Attorney General (Canada)* highlights the injustices perpetuated against Indigenous children and communities via adoption, neither compensation nor an apology will solve the current problems that plague Indigenous child welfare. Indigenous child welfare is underfunded on-reserve, and Indigenous children across the country are disproportionately likely to be apprehended and remain in foster care. Disturbingly, however, the Harper government spent enormous sums litigating instead of apologizing and actively working to improve the prospects of Indigenous children, particularly those living on-reserve. Such policies are not only unjust, but also short-sighted because "First Nations represent the fastest growing population of young people in Canada" and the World Health Organization has clearly illustrated that "one of the best investments governments can make is in children's programs."[74] Justice for Indigenous children requires much greater investment in services for their families.

Notes

1. The term *Indigenous* is employed throughout this chapter to refer to First Nations, Inuit, and Métis peoples, except when direct reference is being made to the Indian Act. Indigenous people are correct in critiquing the government's use of the word *Indian* and the classification systems that have emerged from this term. "This expression 'Indian' [as defined by the federal government in the Indian Act] is an alien one. It is a term imposed by the colonial governments. It is not a First Nations term. First Nations people have their own words for themselves in their various languages": Mary Ellen Turpel-Lafond, "Patriarchy and Paternalism: The Legacy of the Canadian State for First Nations Women," in Andrews and Rogers, eds, *Women*

and the Canadian State (Montreal & Kingston: McGill-Queen's University Press, 1997), 66. The term *Indian* both homogenizes the wide variety of cultures and nations that occupied the territory we now refer to as Canada, and divides and conquers based on status and non-status divisions within and among Indigenous communities because the Indian Act relies upon blood quantum definitions for status. When referring to particular communities, or only to those who have Indian status as a result of government policy, the term *First Nation* is used.

2. Hadley Friedland, "Tragic Choices and the Division of Sorrow: Speaking About Race, Culture and the Community Traumatization in

the Lives of Children," *Canadian Journal of Family Law* 25 (2009), 223–56, para. 1.

3. Mandatory English-language instruction, religious indoctrination, and often harsh punishment and sometimes violence and sexual abuse, have made the residential schools infamous. In 2008, the federal government belatedly, but officially, apologized for the residential school debacle and its long-term negative impact on Indigenous communities and individuals.

4. *House of Commons Debates*, No. 110 (11 June 2008) at 1519 (Hon. Peter Milliken).

5. Raven Sinclair, "Identity Lost and Found," *First Peoples Child and Family Review* 3, 1 (2007), 66.

6. I use the term *settler law* because this legal system has been imposed on First Nations, Inuit, and Métis communities without their consent.

7. The best interests of the child standard replaced parental rights as the guiding concept in child welfare litigation in the 1970s. The emphasis on the needs of the child overturned the historical notion of children as property and was based in part on the work of John Bowlby in the 1950s, which emphasized the early bonding of children with their caregivers, and reflected both the growing influence of child psychology in the courts and the work of advocates of children's rights who argued that bonding must be a guiding principle in custody contests: M. Woodhead, "Psychology and Social Construction of Children's Needs," in James, A and A Prout eds, *Constructing and Reconstructing Childhood: Contemporary Issues in the Sociological Study of Children* (London: Falmer Press, 1990, 2nd edn, 1997); Michael Wald, "Children's Rights: A Framework for Analysis," *University of California Davis Law Review* 12 (1974), 255.

8. *An Act Respecting the Protection and Well-Being of Children and their Families*, Part VII, Adoption, S.O., 1984, 704.

9. Friedland, "Tragic Choices and the Division of Sorrow," at para. 19.

10. Sinclair, "Identity Lost and Found," 68.

11. Constitution Act, 1867 (U.K.), 30 & 31 Vict., c. 3, reprinted in R.S.C. 1985, App. II, No. 5.

12. *An Act to Amend the Indian Act*, 1920, A10.

13. *Indian Act*, 1952, s. 88.

14. H.P. Hepworth, "Trends in Provincial Social Service Expenditures, 1963–1982," in J.S. Ismael, ed., *Canadian Social Welfare Policy: Federal and Provincial Dimensions* (Montreal & Kingston: McGill-Queen's University Press, 1985), 140–1. *Canada Assistance Plan* 1966–1967, c. 45, s. 1.

15. Sinclair, "Identity Lost and Found," 67.

16. Philip Zylerberg, "Who Should Make Child Protection Decisions for the Native Community?" *Windsor Yearbook of Access to Justice* 11 (1991), 77.

17. Marlee Kline, "Child Welfare Law: Best Interests of the Child Ideology and First Nations," *Osgoode Hall Law Journal,* 30 (2) (1992), 387.

18. Kathryn Irvine, "Supporting Aboriginal Parents: Teachings for the Future," *National Collaborating Centre for Aboriginal Health,* 2009, 12.

19. Saskatchewan, Department of Welfare. Child Welfare Branch, *Annual Report* (1964–1965), 17.

20. Hepworth, *Foster Care and Adoption*, 120.

21. Saskatchewan, Department of Welfare. Child Welfare Branch, *Annual Report* (1964–1965), 17.

22. Sinclair, "Identity Lost and Found," 78.

23. Emily Carasco, "Canadian Child Welfare Laws: Have Canadian Child Welfare Laws Broken the Circle?" *Canadian Journal of Family Law* 5 (1986), 4.

24. Fournier, Suzanne and Ernie Crey, *Stolen from our Embrace: The Abduction of First Nations Children and the Restoration of Aboriginal Communities* (Vancouver: Douglas and McIntyre Ltd., 1997), 81.

25. Ibid., 64.

26. All judges are referred to here in the correct manner employed in legal writing, with J. standing for Justice and J.A. for Justice in Appeal.

27. *Natural Parents v. British Columbia (Superintendent of Child Welfare)* [1976] 2 S.C.R. 751 at 766.

28. Ibid. at 768. Philip Girard has argued that "in other decisions dealing with the rights of native peoples, Laskin displayed either a neutral or an overtly hostile approach to the whole system of Indian status created by the Indian Act: Philip Girard, *Bora Laskin: Bringing Law to Life* (Toronto: University of Toronto Press and the Osgoode Society for Legal History, 2005), 396.

29. Indian and Northern Affairs Canada, *Adoption and the Indian Child.* (Ottawa, ON: Minister of Indian Affairs and Northern Development, 1981).

30. Anne McGillivray, "Transracial Adoption and the Status Indian Child," *Canadian Journal of Family Law* 5 (1986), 445.

31. Ovide Mercredi and Clem Chartier, "The Status of Child Welfare Services for the Indigenous Peoples of Canada: The Problem, the Law and the Solution," presented at the National Workshop on Indian Child Welfare Rights, March 1981, 45. Ovide Mercredi is Cree and has been the Chief of the Assembly of First Nations of Canada. Clem Chartier has served as president of the Métis National Council and the International Council of Indigenous Peoples.

32. Patrick Johnson, *Native Children and the Child Welfare System* (Ottawa: Canadian Council on Social Development, 1983), 23.

33. Sinclair, "Identity Lost and Found," 66.

34. Carasco, "Canadian Native Children," 112.

35. Ellen Anderson, *Judging Bertha Wilson: Law as Large as Life* (Toronto: University of Toronto Press and the Osgoode Society for Legal History, 2001), 190.

36. *Racine v. Woods* (1982) [1983] 2 C.N.L.R. (Man. C.A.), 157 at 187.

37. Kline, "Child Welfare Law," 402.

38. *Racine v. Woods* [1983] 2 S.C.R. 173 at 185. While the concerns about respect for Aboriginality might have greater weight given statutory reform since 1983, *Racine v. Woods* has yet to be overturned by the Supreme Court. See, Tae Mee Park, "In the Best Interests of the Aboriginal Child," *Windsor Review of Legal and Social Issues* 16 (2003), 43.

39. Anderson, *Judging Bertha Wilson,* 189.

40. Ibid., 190. Marlee Kline asserted that this case reveals a fear of a successful activist First Nations woman "who acknowledged, confronted and attempted to resist what she perceived as harsh treatment of herself and her people by the child welfare system": Kline, "Child Welfare Law," 409.

41. Ibid., 190.

42. McGillivray, "Transracial Adoption and the Status Indian Child," 466.

43. These concerns helped to prompt the investigation of adoption disclosure laws undertaken by Ralph Garber for the Ontario government: Ralph Garber, *Disclosure of Adoption Information* (Report of the Special Commissioner to the Honourable John Sweeney, Minister of Community and Social Services, Government of Ontario, November 1985).

44. *An Act Respecting the Protection and Well-Being of Children and their Families*, Part VII, Adoption, S.O., 1984, 704.

45. Jocelyn Downie, "A Choice for K'aila: Child Protection and First Nations Children," *Health Law Journal* 2 (1994), 99–120 at para. 40.

46. *Algonquins of Pikwakanagan First Nation v. Children's Aid Society of Toronto* [2004] 3 C.N.L.R. 1 (Ont. Ct. J.) Court File Number: 04-FA-12584 Toronto at para. 1.

47. Ibid., at paras. 4–6.

48. Ibid., at para. 15.

49. Ibid., at para. 42.

50. Ibid., at para. 44.

51. Vandna Sinha and Anne Kozlowski, "The Structure of Aboriginal Child Welfare in Canada," *The International Indigenous Policy Journal* 2, 2 (2013), 2.

52. Irvine, "Supporting Aboriginal Parents," 12.

53. Assembly of First Nations, *Kiskisik Awasisak: Remember the Children*: www.cwrp.ca/ at 5. And Ontario's rate is considerably lower than those of the Prairie provinces where upwards of 50 and even 75 per cent of Indigenous children are in care.

54. AFN press release on decision: www.afn.ca/index.php/en/news-media/latest-news/afn-welcomes-federal-court-of-appeal-decision-to-continue-chrt.

55. Andy Cosby, "Human Rights Tribunal Hears Indigenous Child Welfare Case to the Ire of Harper Government," *The Leveller*, 12 March 2013: www.leveller.ca/2013/03/human-rights-tribunal-hears-indigenous-child-welfare-case-to-the-ire-of-harper-government//.

56. www.fncaringsociety.ca/I-am-witness. According to *The Globe and Mail*, as of 1 October 2012, the federal government had spent more than $3 million in its "unsuccessful attempts to keep a high-stakes battle over first nations child welfare out of the courts": Heather Scoffield, "Ottawa spends $3 million to battle first nations child welfare case," *Globe and Mail*, 1 October 2012: www.theglobeandmail.com/news/national/ottawa-spends-3-million-to-battle-first-nations-child-welfare-case/article4581093//.

57. The term *First Nations*, not *Indigenous*, is used here because the arguments in the class action suit apply only to status First Nations people who were apprehended from reserves.

58. *Brown v. Attorney General (Canada)* [2010] O.J. No. 2253 at para. 3.

59. Ibid., at para. 2.

60. Ibid., at paras. 49–51.

61. Ibid., at para. 82.

62. Ibid., at paras. 155–67.

63. The practical impact of making the case a test case, instead of a class action suit, would be to limit its impact and to require all other potential litigants to sue independently. With a class action suit hearings are much shorter and individual evidence is taken in a context in which, if the class action has been successful, the merits of the wider issue do not have to be reproven in each case by individual litigants. Instead, they only have to prove that they are members of the affected class.

64. *Brown v. Attorney General (Canada)* at para. 184.

65. Ibid., at para. 9. Under this *Act*, the court shall certify a class action suit only if: " (a) the pleadings disclose a cause of action; (b) there is an identifiable class; (c) the claims of the class members raise common issues of fact or law; (d) a class proceeding would be the preferable procedure; and (e) there is a representative plaintiff who would adequately

represent the interests of the class without conflict of interest and who has produced a workable litigation plan": at para. 71. The pleadings were to be limited to issues of failure of protection and negligence on the part of the federal government.

66. www.kleinlyons.com/class/aboriginal-sixties-scoop/.

67. www.ammsa.com/publications/saskatchewan-sage/class-action-lawsuit-filed-behalf-%E2%80%9860s-scoop%E2%80%99-children.

68. Linda Diebel, "Legal setback for Ontario aboriginals taken from their families during the 'sixties scoop,' *The Star*, 25 January 2012: www.thestar.com/news/canada/2012/01/25/legal_setback_for_ontario_aboriginals_taken_from_their_families_during_the_sixties_scoop.html.

69. Ibid/.

70. http://sixtiesscoopclaim.com/2013/02/07/update-on-the-decision-from-the-court-of-appeal/.

71. *Brown v. Canada (Attorney General)* 2013 O.N.S.C. 5637 (Ont. C.A. 27 September 2013).

72. *Brown v. Canada (Attorney General)* 2014 O.N.S.C. 1583 (Divisional Court File No. 523/13).

73. *Brown v. Canada (Attorney General)* 2014 O.N.S.C. 6967 (Divisional Court File No. 523/13), at para. 29.

74. Paul Martin, "Opinion: Shortage of funds, surplus of suffering," *The Toronto Star*, 22 November 2009: www.thestar.com/opinion/2009/11/22/opinion_shortage_of_funds_surplus_of_suffering.html.

Primary Document

A Legacy of Canadian Child Care: Surviving the Sixties Scoop

Christine Smith (McFarlane)

I'm sitting at a long brown table, a table scratched and worn by the god-knows-how-many people who have sat here before me. My feet barely touch the floor. An older lady, my lawyer, sits beside me.

My heart is thumping as I look out over the huge expanse of brown carpet to the large desk where the judge sits.

I glance up and see my adoptive father striding across the floor. He stares ahead, careful not to look over at me, and then sits down at the court officer's request.

The fear inside me pushes my heart into my throat and I take a huge gulp of air, willing my heart to slow down.

I don't remember much about what was said that day in court, decades ago. Everything that happened went over my 10-year-old head. But, I do remember the devastation I felt when I heard the words, "Christine is not wanted. We want to give her up to the care of the Children's Aid Society."

I remember walking out of the courtroom to the elevator with my lawyer. We were both quiet. I wanted to cry but couldn't. My little fists were clenched at my sides. My insides were in turmoil, and all I could think was, "I don't have parents anymore: I am an orphan."

My life as I knew it changed that day, but the course I was on had started much earlier. I was a child caught in the Sixties Scoop.

The Sixties Scoop refers to the period of Canadian history from 1960 through the mid-1980s when thousands of First Nations children were taken from their homes and communities and adopted by non-Native families.

Figures from Aboriginal Affairs indicate that at least 11,132 status children were adopted in this period. Determining a precise number is all but impossible because adoption records rarely indicated Aboriginal status as they are now required to do.

In the Kenora, Ont., region in 1981, 85 per cent of the children in state care were First Nations children, though First Nations people made up only 25 per cent of the population. The number of First Nations children adopted by non-Native parents increased fivefold between the early 1960s and late 1970s, with 78 per cent of the adoptions of First Nations children going to non-Native families.

Disconnection

My experience with the Sixties Scoop began when my three siblings and I were removed from our mother's care in the early 1970s in Winnipeg. My older brother was put into an institution because of developmental issues, but at ages three and four, my biological sister and I were adopted out into a non-Native home in Ontario. My younger brother's whereabouts are still unknown.

My sister and I were obviously different from the rest of our adoptive family. For the first couple of years, our situation seemed okay: there were no outright displays of abuse towards us, or none that I can recall. But once we started school, the emotional and physical abuse began. We were separated from our culture, kept from knowing our own language or traditions.

Our adoptive parents believed that because we were First Nations we were genetically predisposed to obesity. Their obsession with fat led them to withhold adequate food from us. They would lock me in the backyard, crying from hunger, with the family pets. When I was allowed to eat, I was given bland foods or small portions. My sister would convince me to go down to the kitchen late at night and sneak us some food even though it meant getting beaten if I was caught.

Physical and emotional abuse were a part of my daily life. I was called insulting and degrading names and, towards the end of my time with my adoptive family, I was locked in my bedroom and only allowed out to go to school. I reacted to this abuse by acting out and running away from home. At the age of 10, I was taken to a girls' residence, and within months of arriving there, I found myself sitting in that courtroom hearing the words "you are not wanted."

When I was returned to the care of the child welfare system, I was separated from my sister, my last connection to my birth family, for the next seven years. My experience was not exceptional. Breakdowns in adoptive families were common. Seventy per cent of Aboriginal children adopted into non-Native homes as part of the Sixties Scoop were returned to the care of the Children's Aid Society.

The forced removal of First Nations children from their families and communities in this period had various consequences. Many children grew up without knowing about their culture, language, or traditions. The Canadian government's colonialist policies made First Nations children feel something was wrong with them. This led to loss of identity, separation from birth families, and difficult reunions with birth family members in later years. Children had to fight to learn the ways of their people, often from outside their adoptive families and communities.

Métis historian Olive Patricia Dickason has said that "for aboriginal peoples the experience of externally enforced assimilation was a national one, as were its consequences: rising rates of substance abuse, with physical and health problems; psychological and sexual abuse; broken families, community dysfunction and soaring suicide rates." The policy of "killing the Indian in the child" resulted in adults who were "disconnected from their communities, in turn mistreating their own children in a cycle that has passed from generation to generation."

Without Apology

I did not know that the turmoil and pain I was suffering were connected to the way that many other First Nations children in similar situations felt. The practice of adopting First Nations children into non-Native households had intense identity consequences for the objects of interracial adoptions. The adoptions, like the residential schools before them, created a deep and unhealed pain in First Nations communities. Jeannine Carrière, a Métis adoptee and adoptive parent and a social work instructor, describes the Sixties Scoop as the "most comprehensive assault on Indigenous families following that of sending Indigenous children to residential schools."

As a ward of the state, I felt an immense loss that I could not explain to others around me. When I spoke of the loss I felt from being taken from my birth family and then my adoptive home, I felt worthless. I felt that if my own biological parents and, subsequently, my adoptive parents, did not want me, there must have been something fundamentally wrong with me. There were many times I did not think I would survive and times I did not want to live.

In the child welfare system, I struggled in my foster homes because I believed that I was not worth caring for. I stayed longest in my third foster home, where the foster parents let me know from the beginning that, no matter what I did, they wanted me. Although I had this assurance from them, my self-esteem was so low that I continued to act out in their care. I had shut myself down. I turned my pain, hurt, and sadness inwards and became anorexic. My teenage years were fraught with confusion and pain no matter what others did or where I landed.

After my third foster home, I moved into an independent living home run by the Roman Catholic Children's Aid Society that was supposed to help me learn to live on my own. I lived with several other girls and one staff member and had a semblance of support and routine, but my transition was difficult. I had been thrust into an environment I wasn't prepared for. I had no one watching out for me when it came to the eating disorder, and my self-harm escalated. When I moved out on my own at 17, I was still a small child at heart.

Ultimately, my struggles with identity and eating disorders, and my numerous suicide attempts, landed me in an intensive care unit. I was in and out of psychiatric hospitals until I was well into my 20s. The hospital became a safe haven, a place that could protect me from myself and the emotional pain I felt. All I saw was a darkness from which I did not think I could ever rise.

It wasn't until I entered post-secondary education at the University of Toronto in my early 30s that I learned about the Sixties Scoop and its effects on First Nations people. In learning about First Nations peoples and history, I also learned about the role of child welfare in the history of adoption in First Nations communities. For the first time, I realized my story was not unique and that other First Nations people were struggling with the same pain.

The Canadian government has made two apologies to the First Nations people of Canada. The first was on 7 January 1998, when then-Indian Affairs minister Jane Stewart singled out Indian residential schools as the most reprehensible example of Canada's degrading and paternalistic Indian policies. The second was when Prime Minister Stephen Harper stood before Parliament on 11 June 2008, and offered an apology to former students of Indian residential schools.

Though Harper stated that the treatment of children in residential schools was a sad chapter in Canada's history, I questioned why he didn't also apologize for the systematic adoptions of First Nations children into non-Native homes, a central practice of the Sixties Scoop.

Where I Am

The Canadian government's attempt to assimilate First Nations children through adoption continues, but, since the time of the Sixties Scoop, there have been some important changes to child welfare policy. Beginning in the 1980s, the provinces and territories amended adoption laws to prioritize adoption placements that would keep children within their extended families or with other Native families. In 1990, Indian and Northern Affairs Canada created the First Nations Child and Family Services program which transferred the administration of child and family services from the province or territory to the local band. In many provinces and territories across Canada, children are now entitled to know their cultural background.

That said, in 2013, there are more First Nations children in state care than ever before. The estimated 27,000 First Nations children in child welfare account for 48 per cent of children in care even though they represent less than 5 per cent of the child population of Canada. These numbers reveal a colonial system that thousands of Indigenous children and families still endure.

Many First Nations adoptees from the era of the Sixties Scoop still fight feelings of shame and low self-worth. It has taken me many years to get to where I am, and I recognize that I am fortunate. I am doing what I love the most: writing. I know that I no longer have to destroy myself. It is within me to address the wrongs that were done to me and to change the legacy of my family and community, one step at a time, by making my voice heard. I want others to know they can fight too—and be survivors.

Source: *Briarpatch Magazine*, 1 September 2013. http://briarpatchmagazine.com/articles/view/a-legacy-of-canadian-child-care.

Questions for Consideration

1. What was the goal of Canadian Indian policy between 1913 and 1983? What sorts of measures did the Canadian government use in pursuit of this objective?
2. In Shewell's view, what ideological framework underpinned (and underpins) Canada's Indian policy? Do you agree with his assessment? Why or why not?
3. How is Thomas Deasy's vision of the ideal Indian agent consistent with Shewell's interpretation of the goals of Indian policy? How is it inconsistent?

4. What was the Sixties Scoop? Would you describe the goals of government agencies and agents who "scooped" Indigenous children as benevolent, assimilationist, or some combination of the two?

5. Does Lori Chambers's study support or contradict Hugh Shewell's conclusions about the goals and design of federal "Indian" policy?

6. What evidence of the assimilationist aims of the Sixties Scoop do you perceive in the testimony and experiences of survivor Christine Smith? Based on her comments, do you believe the Sixties Scoop and the widespread adoption of Indigenous children by non-Indigenous Canadian families thereafter should be seen as representing a departure from or a continuation of the residential schools system?

7. How would you characterize federal Indian policy? How did Indigenous peoples resist and/or react to federal Indian policy?

Further Resources

Books and Articles

Getty, Ian and Antoine Lussier, eds. *As Long as the Sun Shines and the Water Flows: A Reader in Canadian Native Studies*. Vancouver: UBC Press, 1983.

Harris, Cole. *Making Native Space: Colonialism, Resistance, and Reserves in British Columbia*. Vancouver: UBC Press, 2002.

Shewell, Hugh. *"Enough to Keep Them Alive": Indian Welfare in Canada, 1873–1965*. Toronto: University of Toronto Press, 2004.

Titley, E. Brian. *The Indian Commissioners: Agents of the State and Indian Policy in Canada's Prairie West, 1873–1932*. Edmonton: University of Alberta Press, 2009.

Printed Documents and Reports

Aboriginal and Northern Affairs Canada, Indian Affairs Annual Reports, 1864–1990. www.bac-lac.gc.ca/eng/discover/aboriginal-heritage/first-nations/indian-affairs-annual-reports/Pages/introduction.aspx.

Canada, *Statement of the Government of Canada on Indian Policy: The White Paper, 1969*, www.aadnc-aandc.gc.ca/eng/1100100010189/1100100010191.

Canada, *Social Affairs Division, Aboriginal Self-Government, 15 December 2009*, www.parl.gc.ca/Content/LOP/ResearchPublications/prb0923-e.htm.

Canada. *Royal Commission Report on Aboriginal Peoples, 1996*, www.aadnc-aandc.gc.ca/eng/1307458586498/1307458751962.

Venne, Sharon Helen, and Gail Hinge, eds. *Indian Acts and Amendments 1868–1975, An Indexed Collection*. Saskatoon: University of Saskatchewan Native Law Centre, 1981.

Films

Dancing Around the Table. DVD. Directed by Maurice Bulbulian. NFB, 1987.

Duncan Campbell Scott: The Poet and the Indians. VHS. Directed by James Cullingham. NFB, 1995.

Qimmit: A Clash of Two Truths. DVD. (Documentary). Directed by Ole Gjerstad and Joelie Sanguya. Piksuk Media Inc. and NFB, 2010.

Websites

First Nations Child and Family Caring Society of Canada
www.fncaringsociety.com/

The Sixties Scoop (Scoopster's): Connecting the 60s and 70s Scoop with Information
https://scoopsters.wordpress.com/tag/canada/

Text of the 1985 Indian Act
http://laws.justice.gc.ca/eng/acts/I-5/

Survivance, Identity, and the Indian Act

Introduction

The previous chapter dealt generally with Indian policy in Canada and its goal of assimilating Indigenous peoples into European-Canadian society. As we discussed, the strength of Indigenous peoples and the contradictory nature of this policy ensured the failure of this objective. Nevertheless, government policy has had far-reaching and unexpected consequences on the lives of Indigenous peoples. This chapter examines some of its more insidious costs.

Two of the most significant pieces of legislation affecting the identity of Indigenous peoples were passed in Upper and Lower Canada in 1850. These statutes set a precedent—for the first time, non-Indigenous people determined who was and was not considered an "Indian" in Canada and enshrined that definition in law. The acts were called An Act for the Better Protection of the Lands and Property of Indians in Lower Canada (a similarly entitled one was passed in Upper Canada) and the Gradual Civilization Act. The colonial practice of categorizing Indigenous peoples continued thereafter. In 1876, all legislation pertaining to Indigenous peoples in Canada was consolidated into the Indian Act, a document that still plays a significant role in the daily lives of Indigenous peoples today. As Bonita Lawrence addresses in her article, this legislation—in combination with traditional and stereotypical ideas of what consti tutes an authentic Indigenous identity—shapes how Indigenous peoples interact with each other and with European-Canadian society. According to Lawrence, the need to claim an identity based on legal and cultural stereotypes has led to a feeling of superficiality for some Indigenous peoples who do not feel "Indian enough" and has caused many to jostle one another for access to rights. Moreover, the artificial permanency of these legal categories ignores the fluidity of identity evident within Indigenous societies before contact with Europeans.

Jaime Cidro's article addresses similar themes by using the tools of gender analysis. Though roles in Indigenous communities were organized along gender lines, the nature of these divisions was not the same as in European-Canadian society. In an effort to ensure patriarchy in Indigenous communities, the government passed statutes in 1868 and 1869 that gave Indigenous women fewer rights under the law than Indigenous men. Furthermore, the Indian Act meant different things for women than it did for men. The most damaging discrepancy was found in section 12(1) (b) (often referred to as the "marrying out clause"), which stipulated that any "Indian" woman who married a "non-Indian" man or Non-Status "Indian" lost her "Indian" status. Notably, Indigenous men retained their status no matter whom they married, and their non-Indigenous wives acquired "Indian" status. Cidro explores this piece of legislation, the struggles of Indigenous women to address its unfairness, and the damage it has caused them, their families, and their communities. She also outlines the impact of **Bill C-31**, an amendment passed in 1985 that allowed for the reinstatement of Indian status, and the most recent efforts of the federal government in 2011 to legislate identity through Bill C-3: Gender Equity in Indian Registration Act.

Chapter Objectives

At the end of this chapter, you should be able to

- discuss the logistical and ethical complexity of the federal government's attempts to define who is and who is not an Indian;
- discuss the impact of this strategy on different communities and individuals, both in the past and in the present;
- identify the ways that the 1876 Indian Act created artificial but harmful divisions between communities;
- consider whether pursuing recognition under the Indian Act is a positive and fruitful strategy for Indigenous people, nations, and activists; and
- identify how federal Indian policy has discriminated against Indigenous women as *women* and discuss how Indigenous women have resisted this discrimination.

Secondary Source

Identity, Non-Status Indians, and Federally Unrecognized Peoples

Bonita Lawrence

The foundation of any Indigenous nation is its cultural identity. Traditionally, this has been maintained through language, spirituality, connection to land, and kinship networks. However, colonization was has so profoundly assaulted these parameters that it has radically transformed Indigenous cultural identity. While such transformations are remarkably uneven, depending on the community's experience, in all cases there has been a fundamental fragmentation in world view, as Leroy Littlebear has described it, below:

> Colonization created a fragmentary worldview among Aboriginal people. By force, terror, and educational policy, it attempted to destroy the Aboriginal worldview—but

failed. Instead, colonization left a heritage of jagged worldviews among Indigenous people. They no longer had an Aboriginal worldview, nor did they adopt a Eurocentric worldview. Their consciousness became a random puzzle, a jigsaw puzzle that each person has to attempt to understand . . . Aboriginal consciousness became a site of overlapping, contentious, fragmented, competing desires and values.[1]

A crucial step in this fragmentation process for many communities has been their legal transformation from sovereign nations to "Indian bands." This subordination, brought about by the very treaty process that Indigenous nations usually entered into to protect their lands and assure their futures, introduced controls over kinship patterns, marriage, and access to land; the suppression of ceremonies; and the imposition of residential schooling and the child welfare system. These policies caused profound chaos within communities, including the fracture of family ties; the loss of knowledge of language, ceremonies, songs, and rituals; and the demise of a daily living relationship to the land.

The result has been individuals who know they are "Indian" but who no longer have clear knowledge of what it means to be Indigenous. Yet the imposition of a hegemonic understanding of the Indigenous self as Indian has sparked significant resistance. This is not, in a sense, surprising when we take into consideration how hegemony works:

> I propose that we use the concept [of hegemony] not to understand consent but to understand struggle, the ways in which the words, images, symbols, forms, organizations, institutions and movements used by subordinate populations to talk about, understand, confront, accommodate themselves to, or resist their domination are shaped by the process of domination itself. What hegemony constructs, then, is not a shared ideology but a common material and meaningful framework for living through, talking about, and acting upon social orders characterized by domination.[2]

For many communities, being Indian and confined to a reserve has become a primary site of resistance to the colonial process, insofar as the relative isolation of reserve life can enable communities to recoup some aspects of traditional identity and cultural knowledge. In many communities, then, pride in "being an Indian" has become central to resistance.

In such a context, losing or being denied Indian status has severe repercussions. When Indianness becomes the framework through which cultural resistance and the reclaiming of an Indigenous self are organized, the colonial refusal to acknowledge individuals or whole communities as Indian negates any possibility of Indigenous counter-hegemonic struggle. Yet those citizens denied recognition as Indians experienced much of the same cultural dissolution as those who were recognized, having been forced off their land by settlers or resource development. Being rendered landless, many non-recognized communities have become fragmented because their members are forced to scatter just to survive. With the loss of connection to community comes the loss of Indigenous languages, as well as knowledge of cultural and spiritual practices related to living on the land. Although both citizens who are recognized as Indian and those who are not have both suffered the loss of traditional cultural knowledge, the latter group has also been deprived of the means to participate in the resistance and cultural reclamation that is organized through an Indian identity.

This essay focuses on the ways that Indian status was denied or removed from communities and individuals, as well as the various efforts of both to challenge this lack of federal recognition. This discussion will, of necessity, involve engaging in a basic overview of the issues rather than an in-depth exploration of specific kinds of non-status experience. The essay examines how Canada asserted control over Indigenous identity by replacing "the nation" with "the Indian." It also explores the ways in which Canada subverts efforts to address denial of Indian status and suggests that pursuit of federal recognition may not always be the most useful path for Indigenous peoples to follow. Indeed, efforts at cultural revival can be sidetracked by the quest for recognition.

Becoming a Status Indian: Regulation by Gender and Blood

Although Indigenous identities are traditionally constructed through kinship practices and networks, being subordinated under the Indian Act forced powerful constraints on Indigenous communities that gradually transformed Indigeneity into Indianness. Moreover, the treaty process—particularly the numbered treaties—played a key and sometimes decisive role in shaping whether individuals could either acquire or maintain their Indianness.

The 1876 Indian Act consolidated previous legislation on Indigenous peoples and regulated matters such as land and money. Most significantly, the Act also determined who could and who could not be recognized as Indian. In this article, the Indian Act is understood as a colonial mechanism of control that not only subverted and transformed how communities lived in relation to the land but was also created with the goal of forcing an entirely new understanding of identity onto Indigenous nations. The primary means by which the Act pursued this objective was by reducing Indigenous peoples to a singular racial category: Indian. Indeed, whether this category is replaced with other generic categories in the hopes of appearing less openly colonial—whether it is called "Native," "Aboriginal," or even "First Nation citizen"—the fact that any such label refers to a singular category discounts and denies the diversity of Indigenous nationhood.[3]

This process of denying Indigenous nationhood happened at both the local and national levels. Although most of the pre-Confederation treaties did not actively deny nationhood, they were signed with communities that had already been fragmented by over a century of the fur trade, missionary pressure, waves of disease, and colonial warfare.[4] Post-Confederation, the nascent Canadian state negotiated treaties that specifically categorized individuals as Indians in ways that denied their Indigenous nationhood discursively and limited it practically.

Legislation passed in Upper and Lower Canada in the 1850s attempted to define the term *Indian* as someone of Indian descent or as a woman who was married to a male Indian. Responsibility for Aboriginal people was officially assigned to the federal government in the British North America Act of 1867, but it was another two years before the Gradual Enfranchisement Act was passed, giving the superintendent of Indian Affairs (or his agent) extremely wide powers over almost every aspect of Indigenous life. In terms of regulating identity, section 6 of this Act began a process of defining Indianness based on gender that would not be definitively changed until 1985. Under this section, Indian women were declared "no longer Indian" if they married anybody who lacked Indian status. On marrying an Indian from another "tribe, band or body," an Indian woman and her children belonged to her husband's tribe only.[5] As Kathleen Jamieson notes, the Act was initially created to control those Indigenous communities in Eastern Canada that had already been induced into farming in settled communities by a combination of missionary programs and settler competition for resources.[6] As Canada pushed north and west into Ojibway and Cree territory, however, the legislation imposed controls on Indigenous patterns of land use, residential practices, and kinship relations. Moreover, with the numbered treaties, Canada began defining individuals as "non-Indian" not only on the basis of gender but also of "blood."

Externalizing the "Half-Breed"

In 1870, Canada acquired Rupert's Land, the massive territories previously claimed by the Hudson's Bay Company and encompassing the lands west of Lake Superior to the Rocky Mountains and north to the Arctic. From this point on, the definition of Indianness by blood took on increased importance, given that the legacy of the fur trade had produced unprecedented levels of migration and hybridity among the Indigenous peoples of the territory. This resulted in myriad forms of Indigenous communities that included not only "full-blood" and "mixed-blood" peoples but also detribalized and transient individuals whose ties to their communities had gradually attenuated through a lifetime engaged in the fur trade. In this complex world of what would soon be designated the Northwest Territories, the status of so-called half-breeds (subsequently known as "Métis") became a central concern of the Canadian government.

It is important to emphasize that "Métisness" has never been simply a matter of blood, as Canadian authorities asserted. Theda Perdue and Eva Marie Garroutte demonstrate that, in most Native communities, kinship ties were the definitive factor in a person's belonging. Thus, the mixed-blood children of Indigenous women remained part of their tribal communities; moreover, many people who self-segregated as Métis were acknowledged as relatives by their tribal communities; then, as now, Métisness is a matter of shared cultural identity, rather than blood.[7]

With Canada's acquisition of Rupert's Land, however, surveyors began encroaching on lands around the Red River that were farmed by mixed-bloods who self-identified as Métis. Through their resistance, the Red River Métis had been successful in forcing Canada to create a new province, Manitoba, that included recognition of their Indian title, which was to be established not through treaty but through setting aside 1.4 million acres for Métis families to settle on.[8] Subsequently, with the signing of Treaties 1 and 2 in the area, the mixed-blood members of Ojibway and Cree bands who regarded themselves, and were regarded as, Indians, were included in the Indian treaties, with the proviso that they relinquish any rights as half-breeds.[9] However, the signing of Treaty 3 with the Saulteaux in Northern Ontario in 1873 brought the issue of half-breed exclusion from treaties to the forefront. It was clear that the Saulteaux viewed Canada's desire to segregate mixed-bloods from full-bloods as a strategy to divide Indigenous resistance. Treaty 3 was anomalous in that the Saulteaux were negotiating from a position of relative strength—Canada's ability to access the Red River Settlement depended on passageway through their lands. Negotiations for the treaty took an unprecedented three years, and the Canadian government was forced to concede the inclusion of the Métis in its provisions in 1875.[10]

The rigidity with which the government insisted upon a strict racial classification based on blood in the framing of the subsequent numbered treaties revealed the colonial belief that "race" was crucial in both defining and maintaining control of colonial subjects. Even so, Canadian views of half-breeds and Indians varied over time. On the one hand, Indigenous people were often viewed as "noble savages" existing in a "pure" primitive state that racial mixing would destroy. On the other hand, they were frequently seen as brutish savages who needed civilizing, which intermarriage could facilitate. But whether half-breeds were seen as inferior or superior to their full-blooded relatives, treaty negotiators were firm in their conviction that they were immutably different from Indians and that blood was the true measure of Indigeneity. Accordingly, when the Indian Act was passed in 1876, it contained a provision that excluded anybody who was not considered to be "pure Indian" from Indianness. The Act stated, "No half-breed head of a family (except the widow of an Indian, or a half-breed who has already been admitted into a treaty) shall be accounted an Indian, or entitled to be admitted into any Indian treaty."[11]

It is clear that, despite the Canadian insistence that all half-breeds were irrevocably distinct from all Indians, both groups were ultimately viewed as premodern and as impediments to the development of modern Canada. Furthermore, the nearly absolute dispossession of Métis people from their lands demonstrates that classifying Indigenous people as non-Indian was a powerful tool deployed by the Canadian state in suppressing anti-colonial resistance.

Externalizing Federally Unrecognized Communities

If the treaty process enabled thousands of individuals to be classified as half-breeds and therefore non-Indian, other communities were denied federal recognition simply by oversight, by lack of a treaty, or by having traditional territories that were bisected by Canadian and provincial borders. The Indian Act not only determined that half-breeds would not be registered as Indian in Western Canada, it also limited what communities would be acknowledged as Indian in Canada. This legislation narrowed federal recognition of Indianness to Indigenous people living in areas under Canadian control who already lived on recognized reserves or belonged to recognized Indian bands.[12]

This denial of recognition has come about in a variety of ways. For example, some small nations that occupied land spanning the Canadian–American border (such as the Passamaquoddy Nation of New Brunswick or the Sinixt Nation in British Columbia) have been dispossessed in Canada by policies that effectively prevent individuals enumerated as Indians in the United States from "counting" as Indians in Canada. As a result, these nations are federally recognized in the United States but not in Canada. Other bands are federally unrecognized because Canada has refused to honour historic relationships or has disregarded the traditional boundaries of Indigenous nations.[13]

However, most federally unrecognized bands or nations were created by the treaty process itself. After the 1850s, most treaties were generally not negotiated on a nation-to-nation basis but with multiple Indigenous bands of different nations for large areas of land. Other bands were excluded from the treaty process because they were overlooked by treaty commissioners or were absent when the commissioners arrived to negotiate.[14]

The experiences of federally unrecognized nations have varied depending on the extent to which they faced mining, hydro development, clear-cutting, or direct settler incursion on their lands. In places where resource development has occurred, Indigenous peoples faced the combined efforts of police and natural resource personnel forcing them away from their settlements, in some cases through violent coercion. For many, the ongoing risk of settler violence has meant that speaking Indigenous languages was dangerous and therefore discouraged. Some individuals have adopted the identity of the dominant culture and severed their ties to Indigenous communities altogether, while many others have simply made efforts to hide their Indigeneity to protect themselves and their families.[15] Elders from these federally unrecognized communities may retain a strong sense of cultural identity; however, as the suppressed culture becomes increasingly inaccessible to later generations and phenotypic markers of Indianness are lost, many Indigenous people feel that they are "not really Indian" or "not Indian enough."[16] Although some communities are focusing on cultural revival to address this phenomenon, it is typical for Indigenous identities in federally unrecognized communities to be in flux.

Making Status Indians into Non-Indians

The final means through which people become federally unrecognized is by having their Indian status rescinded because of the identity section within the Indian Act. As the treaties and the Indian Act whipsawed their way across "Indian country," gendered racial categories that were tremendously destructive to Indigenous communities, as well as legislation forcing enfranchisement upon individuals and their families, made it difficult for any individual who engaged too successfully in the world outside the reserve to remain an Indian. The 1876 Indian Act dictated, for example, that any Indian who became a professional—a lawyer, doctor, or minister of religion—or who gained a university degree was automatically enfranchised and so lost their status.[17]

The effects of these regulations enforcing loss of status were devastating. On the one hand were the men who were enfranchised—frequently war veterans who returned from serving their country only to find themselves classified as "no longer Indian." But of far greater impact in terms of sheer numbers were the women who married non-Indians, for the Indian Act, like the Gradual Enfranchisement Act before it, dictated that Indigenous women who married non-status men forsook their Indian status and could not pass their status on to their descendants.[18] If their marriages broke up, such women frequently found themselves excluded from both white society and their own communities. In many cases, unable to find work or to access welfare, these women squatted at the edges of their former reserves, living in shacks and eking out their living through fishing, cutting wood to sell, or other marginal activities.

Jamieson has documented the extensive economic and cultural losses, as well as the profound isolation and psychological burden suffered by these women, who were sometimes considered "traitors to their race" for marrying non-Indians.[19] The children of those who returned home and squatted on-reserve were excluded from the most basic rights: they could not attend cultural events in the community, attend reserve schools, or be bused to off-reserve schools (so non-status children walked for miles daily just to attend school). They were also frequently taunted by Indian children as being non-Indian because they lacked Indian status. Conversely, those who grew up in primarily white urban environments faced discrimination for being Indian. Understandably, many of these children experienced a profound confusion about their Native identity, which persisted long after their status was reinstated in 1985 under the provisions of Bill C-31.[20]

The intense struggle waged by a number of individuals, organizations, and communities to reverse over a century of gender discrimination in the Indian Act has been well documented.[21] However, the passing of Bill C-31 did not end this form of bias. This amendment actually makes it easier for Indian people to lose their status by creating what is known as "partial status." Individuals registered under section 6(2) of the Indian Act have only one recognized Indian parent; if these individuals marry non-Indians, their children lose status. With this legislation, intermarriage now represents a "ticking time bomb" in that anybody who has only partial or "half" status cannot pass status on to his or her children unless the other parent is a Status Indian. Indeed, many reserve communities have large numbers of members with only half status so it is highly likely that increasing numbers of band members will be born without Indian status.[22]

Struggles for Federal Recognition as Indian

Struggles to gain or regain federal recognition have been fraught with different pitfalls. Even successful outcomes have had unexpected negative implications that serve the very government agendas that people sought to challenge by winning recognition. One example of this situation is the Métis' efforts to gain status in the 1970s. Although it is unclear whether those who thought of themselves as historical Métis sought Indian status, it is evident that, during this time in Ontario, anyone who lacked Indian status was commonly referred to, by Canadians and by other Indigenous peoples, as Métis. Indeed, in Western Canada today, individuals of Métis heritage represent a broad mixture: those who see themselves as essentially "Indians without status cards," those who are Métis because their Cree grandmothers lost Indian status and married Métis men, and those who see their lineage as pure Red River Métis. Furthermore, many who first expressed themselves as Métis in the late 1970s have begun to refocus their cultural identity on their Indigenous heritage.[23]

The 1982 **Constitution Act** changed the official understanding of Métis identity. After a century of designating Métis people as non-Indian, the government formally recognized them as Aboriginal. However, the Act did not challenge the legal distinction between Indian and half-breed. Instead, disregarding how Métis land rights had been conceptualized as the settling of their Indian title, it defined Métis as irrefutably and perpetually distinct from Indian. As a result, the mutable nature of Métis as a category, which intersected with Indianness and was often indistinct from the category of **Non-Status Indian**, was replaced by a hard-and-fast Métisness entirely discrete from Indianness. The Indian Act created the legal fiction of Indianness to reduce citizenship in multiple Indigenous nations to a singular racial category, and subsequent legislation divided those whose experience of colonization had differed into the categories of Indian and not Indian. Rather than destroying the colonial categories dividing these individuals, the Constitution Act established a new legal fiction, namely that there are and always have been rigid and clear distinctions between Indians and Métis.

The recognition of the Métis as an Indigenous people has allowed them to claim certain rights previously denied to them. Most recently, the 2003 Powley decision extended hunting rights to Métis people that Indians have generally enjoyed as part of their Aboriginal and treaty rights.[24] However, recognition has also resulted in a drive within Métis organizations to determine who can be considered Métis and an insistence that Métisness is categorically different and distinct from Indianness. One particularly extreme example occurred in September 2002, when the Métis National Council adopted a new definition of Métisness, restricting membership in the Métis Nation to individuals who could claim descent from the historic Red River community.[25] Another sign of this policing of boundaries has been an explosion of scholarship that defines Métisness as "distinct" from Indians. Unfortunately, much of this scholarship focuses only on defining relations between Métis and Canada, not between Métis and Indians. The cost of recognition for Métis, then, has been permanent segregation from Indianness and a hardening of what was once a mutable and shifting identity.

Non-Status communities have only limited ways to gain federal recognition. Some can attempt recognition as an Indian band on the basis of distinct historical circumstances (such as the Mi'kmaq of Newfoundland, the Passamaquoddies of New Brunswick, and the Beaverhouse Algonquins in Northern Ontario). Others, in areas where no treaties have been signed, can participate in a **comprehensive land claims** process, as the Algonquins in Ontario did. Both methods are fraught with difficulties, and the costs are high. It is precisely through the process of seeking federal recognition that the informal boundaries maintaining "insider" (Indian) and "outsider" (non-Indian) status in federally unrecognized communities become formalized. For this reason, it is important to take into consideration the very real problem highlighted by anthropologist Bruce Miller: How is membership within federally unrecognized communities to be understood, given the intensity of colonial contact which assaults and fragments Indigenous identities?[26] Because of the massive cultural disarray created in many Indigenous communities, particularly by residential schooling, there is no consensus about what makes a person Indigenous.

Colonial policies have therefore created profound confusion in many communities about the boundaries between who is Indigenous and who is not. As a result, disputes about identity claims frequently arise and divide families and communities.[27] In this respect, Métisness may be more acceptable to Status Indians than the identity claims of their non-status relatives, insofar as the term now represents a different kind of Indigeneity than Indianness and, as such, does not create the potential threat to the identities of Status Indians that claims of Non-Status Indians to Indianness represent. For example, Kirby Whiteduck, chief of Pikawakanagan First Nation, warned the Assembly of First Nations that, while definitions of Métisness were now definite and sufficiently distinct from Indianness not to threaten Status Indian rights, Non-Status Indian identity was too nebulous and ill-defined and so jeopardized the "distinctness" of Status Indian identity.[28]

Finally, for individuals with reinstated Indian status, a significant problem is that, even as attempts are made to address gender biases, the federal government appears determined to maintain racial categories. With the McIvor decision, for example, the gender discrimination inherent in the "second-generation cut-off" is deferred by at least a generation; however, nothing prevents future losses of status due to intermarriage. (Further discussion of the McIvor case is included in endnote 29.) Sharon McIvor attempted to broaden the question to address this racial context, but her appeal was denied.[29] Indianness now stops inexorably at the "one grandparent" cut-off; gendered categories may be rendered more flexible but racial categories are firmly fixed.

Cultural Identity Rather than Federal Recognition

Glen Coulthard suggests that there are inherent dangers in casting self-determination efforts in the language of recognition, as has been the practice for the past 30 years. His concern is the manner in which Indigenous peoples seeking federal recognition are forced to accommodate the colonialist state so that their collective rights and identities are recognized only if they do not obstruct the imperatives of the state or capital. The other crucial problem is that struggles for recognition do not allow for revisiting traditional teachings and Indigenous paradigms but frequently demand that individuals institute further changes to accommodate state categories.[30] For example, to be defined as Métis according to the Constitution Act requires the descendants of diverse populations of mixed-blood, detribalized, half-breed, and Métis peoples, who traditionally existed in some form of relationship to their Indigenous nations of origin, to actively prove their difference from Indianness to assert Métis distinctiveness. Métis cultural regeneration must involve reclaiming the heritage of the Indigenous nations that constitute part of their Métisness; however, current definitions of the term militate against doing so.

Furthermore, when recognition is negotiated without accommodating the need of the nation involved to pursue cultural regeneration, the terms of recognition often reflect Canada's colonialist agenda.[31] Given that recognition projects in the form of land claims involve the surrender of Aboriginal rights, it is highly dangerous to undertake these projects without first re-envisioning Indigeneous nationhood. The fundamental question that must be addressed relates to the reason for pursuing federal recognition of Indianness. Many pursue recognition solely for the services and benefits that accrue from it. Although poverty is a constant reality in Indigenous communities, Taiaiake Alfred warns against allowing Indigenous vulnerability to facilitate the colonialist project. He suggests that, given the reality of these communities' utter economic dependence on the state for their survival, their resulting susceptibility to paternalistic economic development schemes, and the very limited forms of self-government "allowed" to communities by the federal government, Indigenous peoples need to think hard about what problems their communities face and whether the status quo can actually address them. He writes:

> The problems faced by Onkwehonwe have very little to do with the jurisdiction and financing of band councils or even with high unemployment rates. The real problems

are the disunity of our people, the alienation of our youth, our men disrespecting our women, the deculturing of our societies, epidemic mental and physical sicknesses, the lack of employment in meaningful and self-determining Indigenous ways of working, the widespread corruption of our governments and the exploitation of our lands and peoples—all of which most of our current leaders participate in, rather than resist.[32]

Indeed, both Coulthard and Alfred believe that true empowerment for Indigenous peoples involves working to diminish their dependence on the colonial state, moving towards transformative self-empowerment, and turning away from the assimilative lure of settler-state recognition, which comes at such a cost. Although the temptation to pursue the acquisition or recuperation of Indianness (or, equally, Métisness) for those who are not federally recognized is undeniably powerful, their energies are perhaps better spent pursuing the Indigenous identities that classification as Indian attempted to foreclose generations ago.[33]

Notes

1. Leroy Littlebear, "Jagged Worldviews Colliding," in Marie Battiste, ed., *Reclaiming Indigenous Voice and Vision* (Vancouver, Toronto: UBC Press), 84–5.

2. William Roseberry as quoted in Jeffrey L. Gould, *To Die in This Way: Nicaraguan Indians and the Myth of Mestizaje, 1880–1965* (Durham and London: Duke University Press, 1998), 12.

3. Wendy Cornet, *Executive Summary: First Nation Identities and Individual Equality Rights: A Discussion of Citizenship, Band Membership, and Indian Status* (Prepared for the National Aboriginal Women's Organization, 26 Jan. 2003).

4. Bonita Lawrence, "Rewriting Histories of the Land: Colonization and Indigenous Resistance in Eastern Canada," in Sherene Razack, ed., *Race, Space and the Law: Unmapping a White Settler Society* (Toronto: Between the Lines, 2002), 27–9, 36–41.

5. Kathleen Jamieson, *Indian Women and the Law in Canada: Citizens Minus* (Ottawa: Canadian Advisory Council on the Status of Women and Indian Rights for Indian Women, 1978), 29–30.

6. Ibid., 25.

7. Theda Perdue, "Race and Culture: Writing the Ethnohistory of the South," *Ethnohistory* 51, 4 (Fall 2004): 701–02; Eva Marie Garroutte, *Real Indians: Identity and the Survival of Native America* (Berkeley: University of California Press, 2003), 118–19.

8. Brad Milne, "The Historiography of Métis Land Dispersal, 1870–1890," *Manitoba History* No. 30 (Autumn 1995).

9. Wayne E. Daugherty, "Treaties and Historical Research Centre, Self-Government," Indian and Northern Affairs Canada, 1986. Available at www.ainc-inac.gc.ca/al/hts/tgu/pubs/t3/tre3-eng.asp, accessed 27 Mar. 2010.

10. Ibid.

11. As quoted in James Waldram, "The "Other Side": Ethnostatus Distinctions in Western Subarctic Native Communities," in Laurie Barron and James B. Waldram, eds, *1885 and After: Native Society in Transition* (Regina: University of Regina, 1986), 281.

12. Larry Gilbert, *Entitlement to Indian Status and Membership Codes in Canada* (Scarborough: Carswell, 1996), 15.

13. The Caldwell band in Ontario is an example of the former and the MoCreebec Council of the Cree Nation in Quebec and Ontario the latter. See D. Smoke, "Caldwell War Underway," *Turtle Island Native Network News* (April 2001). Available at www.turtleisland.org/news/news-smokecaldwell.htm (accessed 7 Mar. 2010); R. Kapashesit, "Misiwa Chiwaacheyemitinwaa," *MoCreebec Council of the Cree Nation 25th Anniversary Commemorative Report* (MoCreebec Council of the Cree Nation, 2004).

14. For example, the Teme-Augama Anishnabai in central Ontario were left out of the Robinson Huron Treaty in 1850, whereas the Lubicon Cree of northern Alberta were not included in Treaty 8 in 1899. Because these groups did not sign treaties with the Crown, they have not extinguished their Aboriginal rights. As a result, the federal and provincial government do not acknowledge their existence as nations or their Aboriginal rights. In other words, the Teme-Augama Anishnabai and Lubicon Cree were administratively eliminated as recognized groups, despite the fact that both had asserted their rights over their traditional territories for generations and at times had been acknowledged by representatives of the federal

governments to have those rights. For the Teme-Augama Anishnabai, see D. McNab, "Who Is on Trial? Teme-Augama Anishnabai Land Rights and George Ironside, Junior: Re-Considering Oral Tradition," *The Canadian Journal of Native Studies* 18, 1 (1998): 117–33; and G. Potts, "Teme-Augama Anishnabai: Last-Ditch Defence of a Priceless Homeland," in Boyce Richardson, ed. *Drumbeat: Anger and Renewal in Indian Country* (Toronto: Summerhill Press and the Assembly of First Nations), 201–28. For the Lubicon Cree, see Richardson, "Wrestling with the Canadian Legal System: A Decade of Lubicon Frustration," in *Drumbeat: Anger and Renewal in Indian Country*, 229–64; and Bruce Miller, *Invisible Indigenes: The Politics of Nonrecognition* (Lincoln and London: University of Nebraska, 2003), 146–52.

15. B. Lovelace, "An Algonquin History," www.aafna.ca/history.html (accessed 10 Mar. 2010); Marijike E. Huitema, "'Land of Which the Savages Stood in No Particular Need': Dispossessing the Algonquins of South-Eastern Ontario of Their Lands, 1760–1930" (MA thesis, Department of Geography, Queen's University, 2000), 170, 174–8; Rose Cunha, interview with author, Sept. 1998.

16. Art Cota III, interview with author, 4 Nov. 2007.

17. Jamieson, *Indian Women*, 44.

18. Ibid., 30.

19. Ibid., 72. However, as Jamieson's work shows, it is the personal and cultural losses of losing status that Indian women have most frequently spoken about. Some of the costs have included being unable to participate with family and relatives in the life of their former communities, being rejected by their communities, being culturally different and often socially rejected within white society, being unable to access cultural programs for their children, and, finally, not even being able to be buried with other family members on the reserve.

20. Bonita Lawrence, *"Real" Indians and Others: Mixed-Blood Urban Native People and Indigenous Nationhood* (Vancouver: UBC Press, 2004), 143–51.

21. See, for example, Lawrence, *"Real" Indians*.

22. Stewart Clatworthy, "Roundtable on Citizenship and Membership Issues," *Summary of the 2nd Institute on Governance Roundtable Series* (Ottawa, Oct. 2004).

23. For example, Maria Campbell, author of *Halfbreed*, the definitive work addressing Métis identity, in many respects focuses on Cree cultural heritage rather than the notion of building a "national" identity as "Métis." Meanwhile, one of the crucial figures in the Métis revival of the 1970s, Duke Redbird (whose master's thesis, "We Are Métis," is an impassioned history of the Métis), now focuses primarily on his Saugeen Ojibway heritage. And Lee Maracle, who in the 1970s referred primarily to her mother's Métis heritage, now refers primarily to her Sto'lo heritage.

24. "Métis Nation of Ontario Harvesting News." Available at www.metisnation.org/harvesting/the-powley-story, accessed 26 Jun. 2015.

25. Paul Barnsley, "New National Métis Organization Forming," *Windspeaker* (Feb. 2003), 15.

26. Miller, *Invisible Indigenes*, 20.

27. Ibid., 24.

28. Kirby Whiteduck, "Pikwakanagan's Presentation to the Assembly of First Nations Renewal Commission," 26 Feb. 2004. Available at www.afn.ca/afnrenewal/ottawa.pdf, accessed 10 Mar. 2010.

29. Sharon McIvor regained her Indian status in 1985. McIvor's children also have status even though their father is a "non-Indian." Her son Charles married a non-Indian woman. As a result of what has been dubbed the "second generation cut-off," Charles's children do not have Indian status. Conversely, the children of Charles's sister have status because their father is an Indian. McIvor claims that the denial of status to Charles's children is discriminatory on the basis of gender. The problem arises from the 1985 amendments, which reinstated women who lost their status as a result of marrying non-Indian men (Indian men who married non-Indians kept their status and their wives gained status as well). The second generation cut-off therefore operates differently for those who trace their Indian heritage maternally versus those who trace it through their paternal lineage. See John Rowenski, "Indian Status: Changing the Status Quo," Media K-Net, 2009. Available at http://media.knet.ca/node/7330, accessed 29 Mar. 2010.

30. Glen Coulthard, "Beyond Recognition: Indigenous Self-Determination as Prefigurative Practice," in Leanne Simpson, ed., *Lighting the Eighth Fire: The Liberation, Resurgence, and Protection of Indigenous Nations* (Winnipeg: Arbeiter Ring Publishing, 2008), 199.

31. Ibid., 194.

32. Taiaiake, Alfred, *Wasase: Indigenous Pathways of Action and Freedom* (Peterborough: Broadview Press, 2005), 44.

33. Bonita Lawrence, "Gender, Race, and the Regulation of Native Identity in Canada and the United States," *Hypatia: A Journal of Feminist Philosophy* 18, 2 (2003): 25.

Primary Document

Indian Act, 1876, Sections 3(3)–3(6)

1. The term "Indian" means—
    First. Any male person of Indian blood reputed to belong to a particular band;
    Secondly. Any child of such person;
    Thirdly. Any woman who is or was lawfully married to such person:
    (a) Provided that any illegitimate child, unless having shared with the consent of the band in the distribution moneys of such band for a period exceeding two years, may, at any time, be excluded from the membership thereof by the band, if such proceeding be sanctioned by the Superintendent-General:
    (b) Provided that any Indian having for five years continuously resided in a foreign country shall, with the sanction of the Superintendent-General, cease to be a member thereof and shall not be permitted to become again a member thereof, or of any other band, unless the consent of the band with the approval of the Superintendent-General or his agent to be first had and obtained; but this provision shall not apply to any professional man, mechanic, missionary, teacher or interpreter, while discharging his or her duty as such:
    (c) Provided that any Indian woman marrying any other than an Indian or a non-treaty Indian shall cease to be an Indian in any respect within the meaning of this Act, except that she shall be entitled to share equally with the members of the band to which she formerly belonged, in the annual or semi-annual distribution of their annuities, interest moneys and rents; this income may be commuted to her at any time at ten years' purchase with the consent of the band:
    (d) Provided that any Indian woman marrying an Indian of any other band, or a non-treaty Indian shall cease to be a member of the band to which she formerly belonged and become a member of the band or irregular band of which her husband is a member:
    (e) Provided also that no half-breed in Manitoba who has shared in the distribution of half breed lands shall be accounted an Indian; and that no half-breed head of a family (except the widow of an Indian, or a half-breed who has already been admitted into a treaty), shall, unless under very special circumstances, to be determined by the Superintendent-General or his agent, be accounted an Indian, or entitled to be admitted into any Indian treaty.
2. The term "non-treaty Indian" means any person of Indian blood who is reputed to belong to an irregular band, or who follows the Indian mode of life, even though such person be only a temporary resident of Canada.
3. The term "enfranchised Indian" means any Indian, his wife or minor unmarried child, who has received letter patent granting him in fee simple any portion of the reserve which may have been allotted to him, his wife and minor children, by the band to which he belongs, or any unmarried Indian who may have received letters patent for an allotment of the reserve.
4. The term "reserve" means any tract or tracts of land set apart by treaty or otherwise for the use or benefit of or granted to a particular band of Indians, of which the

legal title is in the Crown, but which is unsurrendered, and includes all the trees, wood timber, soil, stone, minerals, metals, or other valuables thereon or therein.

Secondary Source

Stuck at the Border of the Reserve: Bill C-31 and the Impact on First Nations Women

Jaime Cidro

In the 30 years since the passing of Bill C-31, An Act to Amend the Indian Act, the effects of this legislation on the daily experiences of First Nations women, as well as the implications for the sustainability of First Nations communities and memberships, have become clear. The amended Indian Act highlights some of the persistent identity issues facing First Nations women, which are set to dramatically change the face of First Nations communities in Canada. Many judicial scholars, politicians, and academics are wading through the contemporary interpretations of the Indian Act and trying to systematically reconcile its utility in a modern context.

The Indian Act is a foundational piece of Canada's legislation that provides the framework for the colonial establishment and expansion of newcomers across the country. Although many sections within the Act are no longer relevant, the Act continues to determine the relationship between the Canadian government and First Nations people. This legislation has been a long-standing centre of controversy between Canada and First Nations communities. As First Nations scholar Bonita Lawrence describes:

> [T]o treat the Indian Act merely as a set of policies to be repealed, or even as a genocidal scheme that we can simply choose not to believe in, belies how a classificatory system produces a way of thinking—a grammar—which embeds itself in every attempt to change it.[1]

The implications of the Indian Act and Bill C-31 for First Nations women have been profound. The dislocation of women from their home communities because of who they married has resulted in identity trauma that has trickled down to First Nations children. Although the amendment ended the most blatant gender discrimination against First Nations women, gender bias in the Indian Act remains. This article discusses the history of the Indian Act and Bill C-31, the effects of the latter on First Nations women's identity, the anticipated future of Indian status, and contemporary court challenges to the Indian Act.

The History of the Indian Act and Bill C-31

The Indian Act of 1876 consolidated all legislation pertaining to First Nations people in Canada and created the legislative framework for Indian policy that was applied more or less uniformly across the country. It granted considerable power to the superintendent-general and his representatives and ensured that Indians were increasingly subjected to bureaucratic regulation.[2] This Act also determined who was legally able to register as Indian. It decided who was eligible to live on reserves; how those lands were managed, protected from encroachment, disposed, or leased; and how land revenues were invested. The Indian Act also controlled what cultural/social practices could be carried out and how people would be educated.[3] Significantly, this legislation was designed to replicate the gender relations of white society and the nuclear family, in which the male was the head of the household. As a result, many components of the Indian Act focus on creating distinctions in rights based on gender. For example, when the federal government passed legislation that divided reserves into residential lots in 1869, widows were unable to inherit their husbands' lots.[4]

At the end of the 1940s, a joint committee of the Senate and the House of Commons was established to examine policy related to Indian people. The committee recommended broad changes to the Indian Act; however, beliefs about European-Canadian civilization and assimilation philosophy continued to inform those changes. In 1951, major amendments were made to the Indian Act, including the removal of bans on customs such as **potlatches**, powwows, and other ceremonies. Other changes granted women the right to hold office and vote in band council elections.

Although the 1951 amendments were an important step in dismantling some of the worst transgressions of the Indian Act, little changed for women. Arguably, these amendments further entrenched the more problematic gender inequities of the Act. For example, before 1951, Indian women who lost status due to the death or desertion of their husbands were given "red tickets." These identity cards provided women with access to treaty moneys and, in some cases, the right to continue living on reserves, despite having lost their Indian status. After 1951, these women were compulsorily enfranchised, and their access to band assets, treaty monies, and the right to live on reserves terminated.[5]

The next major amendment to the Indian Act did not occur until 1985, with the passage of Bill C-31. This bill ended the process of enfranchisement,[6] or the removal of Indian status through marriage under section 12(1) (b) of the Act. The fight to repeal this section, which ultimately led to the passage of Bill C-31, began in 1971 with Jeanette Corbière-Lavell of the Wikwemikong Unceded Indian Reserve. After her name was removed from the band list for marrying a non-Indian man, Corbière-Lavell brought a court action against the federal government under the Canadian Bill of Rights.[7] During the same period, Yvonne Bédard challenged her band's (Six Nations of the Grand River) refusal to allow her to live in a house on-reserve following her separation from her non-Aboriginal husband, despite the fact that her mother had bequeathed the house to her.[8] Both Corbière-Lavell and Bédard lost their cases. The Supreme Court ruled that the Indian Act did not discriminate against Indian women because, in losing status, they gained rights as white women.[9] Corbière-Lavell's case served as the catalyst for the formation of the Native Women's Association of Canada (NWAC) in 1974. Its mandate was to achieve equality for all Aboriginal women in Canada.

In 1977, a Maliseet woman named Sandra Lovelace filed a complaint with the United Nations Commission on Human Rights under the Optional Protocol to the International Covenant on Civil and Political Rights because she lost her status when she married a non-Indian man in 1970. After her divorce, she attempted to return to her reserve, the Tobique in New Brunswick, but was forbidden. Lovelace contended that section 12(1) (b) represented a major loss of identity, emotional ties to friends and relatives, and the cultural benefits of living in an Indian community. Lovelace's only recourse was to take her case to the international level. Her lack of options was caused in part by the opposition of the National Indian Brotherhood (NIB) to any revision of section 12(1) (b). The NIB also held a seat on the Joint Committee for Indian Act Policy Changes. Later, the NIB became the Assembly of First Nations (AFN). In 1978, the committee dissolved over conflict around education rights, and the NIB withdrew. First Nations women's rights, however, remained unresolved. As a result, Lovelace's complaint stayed with the UN because the Canadian government was unable to address her complaint at the national level.

While Lovelace's case was being considered, First Nations women became more organized and the NWAC grew stronger. In 1976, the organization recommended to the federal government that sections 12(1) (a) (iv) and 12(1) (b) be temporarily suspended at the request of individual First Nations. In 1980, the Ministry of Indian Affairs agreed. By 1982, 285 bands had suspended section 12(1) (a) (iv) (the double mother clause, which removed status from children once they reached the age of 21 if their mother and paternal grandmother were Non-Status Indians) and 63 had suspended section 12(1) (b).[10] Because any amendment to the Indian Act would require going through the Joint Committee for Indian Act Policy Changes (which still existed but was no longer operating), the federal government also exempted the Indian Act from the application of the Canadian Human Rights Act (CHRA), closing the door for any challenges based on the CHRA. Although this was supposed to be a temporary suspension, it persists to this day.

In 1978, the Canadian Advisory Council on the Status of Women published the first major study of discrimination against First Nations women. Written by Kathleen Jamieson, *Indian Women and the Law in Canada: Citizens Minus* outlined how "the deleterious effects of this oppressive legislation on the Indian woman and her children materially, culturally and psychologically could be very grave indeed."[11] Following the release of this report, a march from the Tobique Reserve to Ottawa took place to protest housing conditions for women on the reserve. This march culminated in a historic rally on Parliament Hill on 21 July 1979. Two years later, the UN reached its decision on the Lovelace case: it found Canada to be in violation of Article 27 of the Covenant because it denied Lovelace the right to live in her community and, thus, access to her culture, religion, and language. The federal government stated its intention to amend these sections, and a standing committee of the House of Commons was struck to review all "legal and related institutional factors affecting the Status, development and responsibilities of band governments on Indian reserves and a study on Aboriginal self-government."[12]

The 1982 enactment of the Charter of Rights and Freedoms left little time to postpone an examination of gender discrimination under the Indian Act. In 1984, the Liberal government put forth Bill C-47 in an attempt to address the issue. The amendment did not pass Parliament, partially because of the different interpretations of the Charter by groups such as the AFN. The AFN argued that the Charter did not apply to the Indian Act because it focused on individual rights rather than collective rights, which was inconsistent with the right to self-government provided in the 1982 Constitution Act. Bill C-31 passed in 1985, under Brian Mulroney's Conservative government. Along with ending the process of enfranchisement, Bill C-31 provided First

Nations people who had lost their status with options to regain it (called reinstatement). Aboriginal Affairs and Northern Development Canada (AANDC) estimates that since Bill C-31 was enacted, 117,000 people who had lost their Indian Status have regained or acquired status (DIAND 2009). The resulting increase from Bill C-3 was estimated at 45,000 people in 2009 with approximately 6 per cent living on-reserve. This number is set to peak at 66,881 in the year 2059, with the majority of individuals living off-reserve (DIAND, 2010).

The influx of reinstated First Nations women and children stretched the resources of many First Nations communities without corresponding increases in federal funding. There has been a general reluctance to accept new band members because most bands were already unable to meet basic needs with their current resources.[13] Although this reluctance continues, the reality is that few reinstated band members have returned to their communities, a trend that is estimated to continue.[14]

Bill C-31 also allowed individual bands to control their own membership lists by developing membership codes specific to the demands of the community. This change meant that people could acquire Indian status under the Indian Act (be put on the general roll) but be denied band membership by their communities. The criteria of individual bands' membership codes also varies dramatically, ranging from a degree of legal descent of 50 per cent (previously, AANDC required only 25 per cent), to parental residency requirements and moratoriums on services and rights to reinstated persons.[15] However, the federal government cannot remedy any exclusionary criteria of bands because First Nations are not subject to the CHRA. Section 67 of the CHRA provides that nothing in the Act "affects any provision of the Indian Act or any provision made under or pursuant to that Act."[16] People who are denied reinstatement must seek remedy through the courts because there is no process for review or appeal under AANDC.

With the passing of Bill C-31, disclosing paternity has also become a crucial issue. For many First Nations women, revealing paternity "can place them in social jeopardy, perhaps endanger them, and at the very least cause social conflicts where a man either denies paternity or refuses to acknowledge it to state authorities."[17] Another problem is that, since 1985, unknown or unacknowledged paternity affects the status of future generations. Statistics indicate that this issue is significant: from 1985 to 1999, there were 37,300 births to women with 6(1) Indian status with unstated paternity.[18] These children have 6(2) Indian status, which means they will be unable to extend Indian status to their descendants. The intricacies of Bill C-31 also dictate an even more fundamental change to the Indian Act: the slow removal of status from First Nations people in subsequent generations through mixed parenting or "exogamous parenting"[19] (marriage or parenting with Non-Status Indians) and the eventual extinction of Status Indians.

Bill C-31 sparked debate among many First Nations and Métis organizations and governments across Canada. The AFN, in particular, declared that membership/citizenship were First Nations matters and could not be dictated by the federal government.[20] This argument was similar to the position that the organization put to the Standing Committee on Aboriginal Affairs in 1982: "As Indian people we cannot afford to have individual rights override collective rights . . . if you isolate the individual rights from the collective rights, then you are heading down another path that is ever more discriminatory. . . .

The Canadian Charter is in conflict with our philosophy and culture."[21] The conflicts between individual rights, as guaranteed by sections 15(1) and 28 of the Charter, and collective rights, those sought through the process of self-government, became the mask that the AFN used to oppose the amendment of section 12(1) (b). The result was to separate the issues of Indian status, band membership, and who can and cannot pass status on to children. This new policy created four types of Indians in Canada: status with band membership, status with no band membership, no status with band membership, and no status with no band membership.[22]

The Impact of Bill C-31 on First Nations Women

Policies are the product of negotiation and compromise, and Bill C-31 is no exception. This amendment was never considered a panacea for the flaws of the Indian Act but a temporary solution to deal with the glaring inequities facing First Nations women who had lost their status, and with the outdated provisions of the Act. However, these biases were inadequately dealt with in the bill and have persisted.[23] Women continue to face prejudice and inequities in their communities due to the process of reinstatement and the gender discrimination embedded in the Indian Act. Specifically, this treatment consists of community-based lateral violence for Bill C-31 reinstatees, statistical extermination, and family and community fragmentation.

Community-Based Lateral Violence

The experiences of many Bill C-31 reinstatees and their descendants in First Nation communities can be characterized by the term *lateral violence*. Psychiatrist Wolfgang Jilek describes lateral violence as a perceived behaviour in reaction to alienation from history and culture; feelings of frustration, defeat, and discouragement, and low self-esteem associated with aggressive behaviour against oneself and/or others or moral disorientation; and alcohol abuse.[24] For First Nations women, the experiences of lateral violence are closely connected to identity because of their reliance on external validating sources (i.e., family, community members, and political leaders).

The historical use of degree of descent can also foster intra-group conflict, discrimination, or hostility when it is internalized by First Nations people.[25] Criminologist Wenona Victor notes that "internal colonialism and internal racism is crippling many Indigenous communities. Lateral violence is endemic."[26] The effect of lateral violence on communities and individuals cannot be underestimated. Victor states, "Aboriginal communities that have been traumatized (due to colonial processes) display fairly predictable patterns of collective dysfunction," which are expressed through gossip, perpetual social and political infighting, political corruption and lack of accountability and transparency in governance, suspicion and mistrust of others, and an inability to work together to solve community-based problems. These factors result in a lack of progress and capacity-building.[27]

The outcomes associated with feeling "inauthentic" as a First Nations person are far-reaching. The loss of power that a First Nations person can experience might result in multiple and overlapping issues such as depression, anxiety, suicide, and feelings of rejection. For First Nations communities, promoting the notion of "inauthenticity" through the poor treatment of returning community members can also result in a diminished human resource capacity by forcing members to live and work outside the community. The struggle with not feeling "Indian enough" serves only to obfuscate "the real sources of oppression—colonialism and global capitalism."[28] A "shared peoplehood" should be the goal as communities work towards sovereignty and self-determination rather than dividing people into self-imposed categories that perpetuate lateral violence.

Statistical Extermination of Status Indians

The number of First Nations people seems to be growing. According to AANDC's *Registered Indian Population Projections for Canada and Regions from 2000–2021*, the Registered or Status Indian population is expected to rise from 690,000 (in 2001) to 940,000 (in 2021).[29] However, upon closer examination, the rate of growth including and excluding Bill C-31 registrants has declined and will continue to do so. According to projections, "sometime around the end of the fifth generation (of descendants of Bill C-31 reinstated members) no further children would be born with entitlement to Indian registration."[30] This conclusion is based on scenarios that assume consistent out-marriage or exogamous parenting and includes factors such as "higher attendance at post-secondary institutions and increasing employment off reserve," resulting in more social interaction between Status Indians and non-Indian populations and subsequently growing out-marriage.

Figure 8.1 shows that the number of individuals who trace their ancestry entirely through the pre-Bill C-31 population are expected to increase from the current level of 540,800 to 864,800 over the next two generations. Over the course of the following two generations, this segment of the Registered Indian population is expected to decline to approximately 550,000 people. The Bill C-31 population (and those who trace their ancestry through Bill C-31) is anticipated to increase slightly for about a decade, before, after years of slow decline, reducing to only 7900 people in the fourth generation.[31] Projections also show that the registered Indian population will begin to decrease in 50 years.[32]

An even closer look reveals that Bill C-31 registration has steadily decreased since 1993. Predictions show that the total population of survivors and descendants is likely to increase to slightly more than 2 million within four generations. What is most ironic about the struggles presented by Bill C-31 and the tensions that arise between Status, Non-Status, and Reinstated Status Indians is that, if population forecasts are accurate, "there may be few Status Indians left and the entire landscape of federal government–First Nations relations that has been built on the basis of Status and non-Status distinctions so carefully maintained through Bill C-31 will have changed beyond recognition."[33]

The implications of statistically exterminating Status Indians are tremendous for sustaining rural reserve communities. To live on-reserve, a person must be a band member or married to a band member. Although many communities now face huge housing shortages because of an exploding population, such demands will decrease as the number of people eligible to live on reserves declines. These consequences have further implications for land claims suits, access to treaty rights, and the provision of benefits such as the Post-Secondary Student Support Program and the Non-Insured Health Benefits Program. The inability

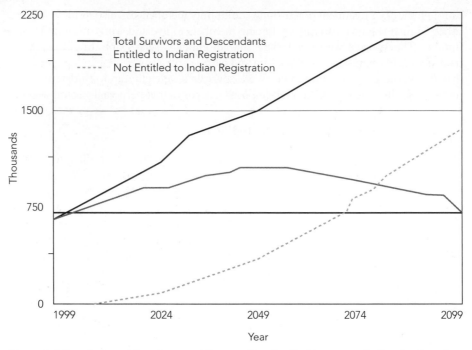

Figure 8.1 Population of Survivors and Descendants by Entitlement to Indian Registration, Canada, 1999–2099. (Source: Clatworthy, Stewart. Indian and Northern Affairs Canada. Policy and Strategic Direction. Research and Analysis Directorate. Re-assessing the Population Impacts of Bill C-31. Ottawa: Indian and Northern Affairs Canada, 2004. figure 17, 39.)

of communities to sustain their populations has clear implications: First Nations people are part of a system that will statistically and legally eliminate them. The socio-economic situation of many First Nations people in Canada has placed them in an untenable position where long-term strategic planning is problematic.

Fragmentation of Families and Communities

Statistics aside, the impacts of Bill C-31 are very real within the family homes and the borders of First Nation communities. The fragmentation that exists politically at the community level and even more so at the national level reduces the sustainability of First Nation communities in Canada. The family and community tension towards Bill C-31 reinstatees can affect personal identity because of the initial rejection of one family member by another. A study by the Aboriginal Women's Action Network (AWAN) found that internalized racism and lateral violence absorbed at the reserve level from the larger non-Indigenous society result in attitudes against reinstated band members as not being "real Indians" or "pure Indians" and perceptions that women left the reserve "voluntarily" and want "something for nothing."[34]

When the ability of a woman to pass on her rights and band membership to her children is lost, her ability to give her children an identity will be destroyed. Being rejected by an entire band is especially difficult for adolescents to endure.[35] Subsequently, these youth may feel alienated and turn to high-risk behaviours (such as solvent and drug abuse), attempt or commit suicide, and abandon education. The internal conflict of legally belonging to an ethnic group with a distinctive culture but not being accepted by those group members has a negative effect on these individuals. Pamela Palmater describes the effect of losing status and access to culture and language:

> [I]f a grandmother lost her status by marring a non-Indian, and she and her children are then separated from the community, the child may not learn his Indigenous language. Several decades later, when one or both are reinstated, the children and grandchildren have missed out on learning their language and can't pass it to future generations.[36]

Community members who are raised in off-reserve and urban communities can often feel a sense of being inauthentic, and these negative feelings are often validated by their family members who grew up in the First Nations community. A high proportion of Bill C-31 reinstatees live in urban centres, where they are further disconnected and alienated from their families and First Nations communities. In 2001, 72 per cent of Aboriginal women lived off-reserve.[37] Feelings of disconnection, isolation, and alienation can be mitigated when people become involved in their own urban Aboriginal community because there are many people who have a diminished sense of connection to their First Nation.

Eva Marie Garroutte, a Cherokee scholar, discusses the tie to socially constructed determinants of identity through one of her research respondents (Billy S).[38] This respondent felt that knowing your language, songs, and culture is what makes a person an Indian:

> Because it [identity] is not just a legal document; it's a way of life, it's a way of thinking, a way of living, a way of worship that you can't instill on someone with a notarized legal documentation. And I feel that too many times we get into looking at things from a legalistic standpoint and really lose the idea of what it is to be Native.[39]

The resistance and tension that surround Bill C-31 reinstatees within families and communities revolves around the availability of already scarce resources. Fighting for the limited resources offered by the federal government affects the ability of people to grapple with the bigger picture. The political tension and conflicts between "automatic" band members and incoming reinstated band members is a very real situation. The effect on some First Nations, especially those with few resources, could be severe and lead to serious conflicts if their need to preserve their social and cultural integrity is disregarded.[40] These tensions exist even within the same family units because brothers and sisters have unequal abilities to pass on status to their descendants. All of these inequalities contribute to strife and division within families and communities. The results are and continue to be devastating to adults and children alike.[41]

Bill C-31 remains a colonialist act, "not even as an event based project with a beginning and an end, but as a contemporary process that is still energized by the particular history and experience of racialized and gendered exclusions in Canada."[42] Whether or not one can still belong to the group without being a Status Indian remains a difficult question:

> [L]iving, feeling citizenships, may not be institutionally recognized, but are socially and politically recognized in everyday life of the community and that people get called

out on them. The challenge to the community is to harden the possibilities into membership policy that may accommodate the simultaneity of these experiences, these different transhistoric discourses (and people), so that these "feeling citizenships" may then become lived citizenships.[43]

Urban and off-reserve Indigenous people also struggle with their identity as they attempt to assimilate into communities with many different cultures that may not reflect their own heritage, history, and value systems. Urban and rural communities are demonstrating the new ways in which First Nations communities are developing outside reserve boundaries: "[S]ome Aboriginal people experience marginalization in urban centres, others experience success. Many Aboriginal people maintain strong connections with their rural communities of origin, but many do not."[44] This is especially true for First Nations women, who continue to be discriminated against and marginalized because of their Indian status. As "cultural carriers," it is important for First Nations women to have a positive sense of identity so that they can pass it on to future generations.

Contemporary Dialogue on Bill C-31

Today we look to Sharon McIvor as the new champion for First Nations women's rights in Canada. A Nlaka'pamax woman from the lower Salish community in the Lower Nicola Valley First Nation in British Columbia, McIvor has fought the federal government in the courts for decades, challenging the sexual discrimination of the Indian Act. In 1985, McIvor and her children applied for membership with the Lower Nicola Valley First Nation. Whereas McIvor was reinstated as a Status Indian according to Bill C-31, her grandchildren could not have status because their paternal grandfather and their mother were not Status Indians (the "second generation cut-off"). McIvor, a lawyer, launched a Charter challenge, alleging that the status provisions of the Indian Act preferred descendants who traced their status through their paternal side.

After 20 years, the government reversed its decision and granted McIvor's children Indian status on the grounds that McIvor was considered to be an illegitimate child. (The pre-1985 rules indicate that illegitimate children were assumed to be Indian.) However, the issue of status was not resolved. Due to the fact that McIvor had married and had children with a non-status man, her children would be unable to pass their status onto their children. Despite the concessions of the government, McIvor continued her court challenge for her grandchildren and all other descendants of First Nations women who have also lost status. In 2007, the BC Supreme Court judge agreed with McIvor, finding that the Indian Act provisions contravened the Charter by directly discriminating based on sex. The judge called for the immediate registration of all descendants of women who had married non-Indians prior to 1985. The federal government believed that it was impossible to implement this broad remedy and sought an appeal based on the argument that, in fact, the Charter could not be applied retrospectively.

In April 2009, the BC Court of Appeal found that section 6 of the Indian Act was indeed discriminatory but in a more limited way than the Supreme Court of British

Columbia did. It concluded that the source of the discrimination was the way in which the amended Indian Act dealt with the transition from past registration rules to the future non-discriminatory system. Specifically, the Court was referring to the double mother clause. Bill C-31 eliminated the clause; however, the Court found that, by doing this, a new inequity that disfavoured Sharon McIvor and her descendants followed. The Court of Appeal decision provided a diagram depicting a hypothetical brother and his ability to transmit status as being enhanced by the 1985 amendment (see Table 8.1).

The diagram shows how, prior to 1985, the grandchild of the hypothetical brother would have lost his or her Indian status at the age of 21. With the 1985 amendment to the Indian Act, the grandchild would be entitled to registration. What the Court of Appeal explained is that Sharon McIvor's grandchild cannot be registered and that "this distinction was not justified by the objective of preserving existing rights because Bill C-31 enhanced the existing "age-limited" right to transmit status to the ability to transmit it for life."[45]

Although the Court of Appeal declared that the amendment to the Indian Act was contrary to the Charter, it chose to leave it to Parliament to determine a resolution, setting a time limit of one year. The deadline ended in April 2010, but the Court allowed for an extension until January 2011. After seeking advice from various stakeholders, the federal government tabled Bill C-3, the Gender Equity in Indian Registration Act, which came into force on 31 January 2011. However, this Act does not address the long-standing issue of First Nations sovereignty over citizenship. Mary C. Hurley and Tonina Simeone (2014) describe the responses from First Nations organizations as disappointment and critical about the federal government's lack of full and substantive consultation. Bill C-3 was viewed as an "inadequate redress to historic discrimination in the Act's registration scheme, as raising a number of implementation and resource issues, and in particular, as continued interference with and failure to acknowledge First Nations jurisdiction over citizenship matters."[46]

Table 8.1 Situation under Old Legislation and Situation under 1985 Statute

Situation Under Old Legislation	Situation Under 1985 Statute
Hypothetical Brother Status Indian (s. 11 (e) of pre-1985 Act) Marries non-Indian Maintains Status	Hypothetical Brother Status Indian (s. 11 (e) of pre-1985 Act) Marries non-Indian Maintains Status
Child born—Child entitled to Status	Child born—Child entitled to Status
	1985 Act Comes Into Force
Grandchild of hypothetical brother loses Indian status at age 21 (s 12(1)(a)(iv) of pre-1985 Act) (Double mother rule)	Grandchild of hypothetical brother entitled to Indian status (s. 6(2))
Assume child marries a non-Indian and has children	Assume child marries a non-Indian and has children

Source: Indian and Northern Affairs Canada, "Changes to the Indian Act Affecting Indian Registration and Band Membership: *McIvor v. Canada*" (Discussion paper) (Ottawa: Ministry of Indian and Northern Affairs, 2009). Available at www.aadnc-aandc.gc.ca/eng/1100100032487/1100100032489.

Conclusion

Although First Nations identity is inextricably tied to the Indian Act, this archaic legislation has clearly become irrelevant to the needs of First Nations people and is hindering the ability of First Nations communities to plan strategically for long-term sustainability. Bill C-31 has also done little to improve the lives of the First Nations women it sought to help. Despite years of negotiation and lobbying by Aboriginal women's groups and individual claimants, the Indian Act continues to be a blemish on Canada's reputation.

Reinstated members continue to experience lateral violence in their communities as they attempt to access benefits, and are often characterized as "half Indian" or a "new Indian." They often feel ostracized because of the reluctance of already economically marginalized communities to accept new members. Alarming trends indicate that, because of the rules of the Indian Act, Indian status will become statistically extinct, which means that the fate of First Nations communities is uncertain. As Sharon McIvor has shown us, Bill C-31 not only failed to stop the loss of Indian status based on gender discrimination, it also provided new ways for First Nations women to experience differential treatment under the Indian Act. In many cases, a family in which both grandparents hold Indian status may have some grandchildren with Indian status and others without. The result is that some family members can access benefits and rights of Status Indians, including living in the First Nations community, and some cannot. As Palmater states,

> First Nations have also recognized that the Indian Act creates artificial divisions between siblings, families and communities, and removes tens of thousands of Indigenous peoples from their Nations. As long as the Indian Act remains in existence, then it must be amended to comply with domestic and international Indigenous rights related to non-discrimination.[47]

Because Indian status is so closely linked to identity, the ways in which people consider themselves to be "authentic" are often intimately connected to government-imposed definitions of self. There are some possibilities for opening up the rigid requirements of the Indian Act through Bill C-3; however, the long-standing issues of who determines membership and citizenship will remain, and the ability of First Nations communities to be self-determining will continue to be limited. As Cannon argues, the McIvor case had the opportunity to correct the history of gender-based discrimination, but it failed. Martin Cannon states that Bill C-3 has in fact "(re-)told a raceless story of sexism as well as an original Eurocentric fiction that separates "woman" from "Indian," which in turn prevents society from "seeing the inequality of treatment that indigenous women and their descendants—indeed, all status Indians—face as racialized people."[48] McIvor disagrees with the adoption of Bill C-3, claiming that it "will have the effect of perpetuating discrimination in the status registration provisions. This fact makes the government's proposal unacceptable."[49] We can continue to look to First Nations women such as McIvor and the women who came before her to ensure the sustainability and perpetuation of First Nations families and communities in Canada, and we can embrace new ways of feeling authentic that have nothing to do with a plastic card issued by the federal government.

Notes

1. Bonita Lawrence, "Gender, Race, and the Regulation of Native Identity in Canada and the United States," *Hypatia: A Journal of Feminist Philosophy* 18, 2 (2003): 25.

2. E. Brian Titley, *A Narrow Vision: Duncan Campbell Scott and the Administration of Indian Affairs in Canada* (Vancouver: UBC Press, 1988).

3. J.R. Wunder, *Native Americans: Interdisciplinary Perspectives* (New York: Garland Publishing, 2003), 24.

4. Bonita Lawrence, *"Real" Indians*, 51.

5. Ibid., 50.

6. Enfranchisement was a legal process in which Status Indians lost their status under the Indian Act. The term refers to both voluntary and involuntary enfranchisement, which primarily affected women with Indian status who married non-status men. Enfranchisement was considered by the government as an opportunity for Aboriginal peoples to assimilate into Canadian society.

7. Native Women's Association of Canada (NWAC), *Aboriginal Women and the Implementation of Bill C-31* (Ottawa: Native Women's Association of Canada, 1991), 8.

8. Ibid., 8.

9. Lawrence, "Gender, Race, and the Regulation of Native Identity," 13.

10. Joan Holmes, *Background Paper – Bill C-31, Equality or Disparity? – The Effects of the New Indian Act on Native Women* (Ottawa: Canadian Advisory Council on the Status of Women, 1987), 6.

11. Kathleen Jamieson, *Indian Women*, 1.

12. NWAC, *Aboriginal Women and the Implementation of Bill C-31*, 11.

13. James Frideres and René R. Gadacz, *Aboriginal Peoples in Canada* (Toronto: Pearson Prentice Hall, 2008), 28.

14. Ibid., 30. DIAND. Estimates of Demographic Implications from Indian Registration Amendment— McIvor v. Canada. Ottawa, March 2010.

15. Holmes, *Background Paper*, 37.

16. Canadian Human Rights Act, "Expanding Knowledge National Aboriginal Initiative," Canadian Human Rights Commission, 8 Sept. 2010. Available at www.chrc-ccdp.ca/.

17. Joanne Fiske and Evelyn George, *Seeking Alternatives to Bill C-31: From Cultural Trauma to Cultural Revitalization through Customary Law* (Ottawa: Status of Women Canada, 2006), v.

18. Stewart Clatworthy, *Factors Contributing to Unstated Paternity* (Ottawa: INAC Strategic Research and Analysis Directorate, 2003), 2.

19. Stewart Clatworthy, *Indian Registration, Membership and Population Change in First Nations Communities* (Ottawa: Indian and Northern Affairs, 2005), 17.

20. Holmes, *Background Paper*, 37.

21. NWAC, *Aboriginal Women and the Implementation of Bill C-31*, 5.

22. Frideres and Gadacz, *Aboriginal Peoples in Canada*, 30.

23. Joanne Fiske, "Political Status of Native Indian Women: Contradictory Implications of Canadian State Policy," *American Indian Culture and Research Journal* 19, 2 (1995): 2.

24. Wolfgang Jilek, "Culture and Psychopathology Revisited," *Culture* 3,1 (1983), 51.

25. Patricia Barrios and Marcia Egan, "Living in a Bicultural World and Finding the Way Home," *Affilia* 17, 2 (2002): 212.

26. Wenona Victor, *Indigenous Justice: Clearing Space and Place for Indigenous Epistemologies* (Vancouver: National Centre for First Nations Governance, 2007), 13.

27. Ibid.

28. Sandy Grande, *Red Pedagogy: Native American Social and Political Thought* (Maryland: Rowman and Littlefield Publishers, 2004), 92.

29. INAC, *Registered Indian Population Projections for Canada and Regions from 2000–2021* (Ottawa: INAC, 2001), 4.

30. Ibid., 42.

31. Stewart Clatworthy, *First Nations Membership and Registered Indian Status: Southern Chiefs Organization, Manitoba* (Ottawa: Indian and Northern Affairs Canada, Research and Analysis Directorate, 2001), 39.

32. John Giokas and Robert K. Groves, *Who Are Canada's Aboriginal Peoples?: Recognition, Definition and Jurisdiction*, Paul Chartrand, ed. (Saskatoon: Purich Publishing, 2002), 68.

33. Ibid., 73.

34. NWAC, *Bill C-31 Amendment*, 14.

35. Holmes, *Background Paper*, 37.

36. Pamela Palmater, "Genocide, Indian Policy, and Legislated Elimination of Indians in Canada," *Aboriginal Policy Studies*, 3, 3 (2014): 42–3.

37. Statistics Canada, *Women in Canada: A Gender-based Statistical Report* (Ottawa: Statistics Canada, 2006), 185.

38. Garroutte, *Real Indians*.

39. Ibid., 99.

40. Holmes, *Background Paper*, 35.

41. Ibid., 38.

42. Audra Simpson, "To the Reserve and Back Again: Kahnawake Mohawk Narratives of Self,

Home and Nation" (PhD dissertation, McGill University, 2003), 240.

43. Ibid., 249.

44. Evelyn J. Peters and David Newhouse, *Not Strangers in These Parts: Urban Aboriginal Peoples* (Ottawa: Policy Research Initiative, 2003), 9.

45. INAC, "Changes to the Indian Act Affecting Registration and Band Membership McIvor v Canada," Indian Affairs and Northern Development, 11 Mar. 2010. Available at www.aadnc-aandc.gc.ca/eng/1100100032501/1100100032506.

46. Mary C. Hurley and Tonina Simeone, "Legislative Summary of Bill C-3: Gender Equity in the Indian

Registration Act," *Aboriginal Policy Studies*, 3, 3 (2014): 159.

47. Palmater, "Genocide, Indian Policy, and Legislated Elimination of Indians in Canada," 45.

48. Martin Cannon, M.J. "Race Matters: Sexism, Indigenous Sovereignty, and McIvor," *Canadian Journal of Women and the Law*, 26, 1 (2014): 23.

49. Sharon McIvor, "Sharon McIvor's Response to the August 2009 Proposal of Indian and Northern Affairs Canada," 6 Oct. 2009. Available at www.socialrightscura.ca/documents/legal/mcivor/McIvorResponse.pdf.

Primary Document

Excerpt from an Interview with Life History Respondent 12

Interview by Jaime Cidro, 28 July 2008

I think that there was one thing that kept me in these relationships; I wanted my kids to have status. Once I learned about what all of that meant, I wanted them to get status. It's extremely hard to find a Native man who does not have alcohol problems. With the current guy I'm with, he's Bill C-31 too, so our kids have status. It's been really hard to find a good guy.

When I [. . .] tried to change things, I always heard, "You didn't grow up here, you're not from here, and you don't know what it's like to grow up on the rez." That was something I'd heard for so many years, but we had been coming there for many years. That was part of the thing I had a problem with, the inequality.

Questions for Consideration

1. What were the consequences of the federal government's attempts to define who is and who is not an Indian?

2. Why does Lawrence disagree with the strategy often pursued by Indigenous groups to obtain recognition of their Indian status? What do you think of this tactic?

3. In what ways does the 1876 Indian Act create artificial but harmful divisions between Indigenous peoples?

4. How have the Indian Act and Bill C-31 shaped Indigenous women's lives and identities?

5. How have Indigenous women resisted the discriminatory or injurious provisions of the Indian Act and Bill C-31? Why, in 2011, did the federal government continue to pass legislation like Bill C-3?

6. Based on the life history respondent's testimony, how have the provisions of Bill C-31 influenced Indigenous women's decisions about their personal relationships?

7. What has been the long-term impact of the Indian Act? What, if anything, should be done with the Act now?

Further Resources

Books and articles

Carlson, Nellie, and Kathleen Steinhauer. *Disinherited Generations: Our Struggle to Reclaim Treaty Rights for First Nations Women and their Descendants*, as told to Linda Goyette. Edmonton: University of Alberta Press, 2013.

Chartrand, Paul, ed. *Who Are Canada's Aboriginal Peoples? Recognition, Definition and Jurisdiction*. Saskatoon: Purich Publishing, 2002.

Cherubini, Lorenzo. "Aboriginal Identity, Misrepresentation, and Dependence: A Survey of the Literature." in *The Canadian Journal of Native Studies*, 28, 2 (2008): 221 39.

Frideres, James. "Aboriginal Identity in the Canadian Context" in *The Canadian Journal of Native Studies*, 28, 2 (2008): 313–42.

Garroutte, Eva Marie. *Real Indians: Identity and the Survival of Native America*. (Berkeley: University of California Press, 2003.

Lawrence, Bonita. *Fractured Homeland: Federal Recognition and Algonquin Identity in Ontario*. Vancouver: UBC Press, 2012.

Palmater, Pamela D. "Matnm Tel-Mi'kmawi: I'm Fighting for My Mi'kmaw Identity," in *The Canadian Journal of Native Studies*, 33, 1 (2013): 147–67.

———. *Beyond Blood: Rethinking Indigenous Identity*. Saskatoon: Purich Publishing, 2011.

Retzlaff, Steffi. "What's in a Name? The Politics of Labelling and Native Identity Constructions," in *The Canadian Journal of Native Studies*, 25, 2 (2005): 609–26.

Printed Documents and Reports

Cornet, Wendy. *Executive Summary: First Nation Identities and Individual Equality Rights: A Discussion of Citizenship, Band Membership, and Indian Status*. Prepared for the National Aboriginal Women's Organization, 26 Jan. 2003.

Dead Dog Café Comedy Hour, Vols 1–4 (CD).

Jamieson, Kathleen. *Indian Women and the Law in Canada: Citizens Minus*. Ottawa: Advisory Council on the Status of Women, 1978.

Simpson, Leanne, ed. *Lighting the Eighth Fire: The Liberation, Resurgence, and Protection of Indigenous Nations*. Winnipeg: Arbeiter Ring Publishing, 2008.

Films

As I Am. DVD. Directed by Nadia Myre. NFB, 2010.
Between: Living in the Hyphen. DVD. Directed by Anne Marie Nakagawa. NFB, 2005.
Club Native. DVD. Directed by Tracey Deer. NFB, 2006.

Websites

The 1491s
www.youtube.com/user/the1491s

Aboriginal Affairs and Northern Development Canada, "Basic Departmental Data"
www.aadnc-aandc.gc.ca/eng/1100100016873/1100100016874

AANDC, "Gender Equity in Indian Registration,"
www.aadnc-aandc.gc.ca/eng/1308068336912/1308068535844

Assembly of First Nations, "Gathering Voices: A First Nations Dialogue on Citizenship"
www.afn.ca/index.php/en/policy-areas/citizenship

Canadian Feminist Alliance for International Action
www.fafia-afai.org/

Canadian Human Rights Commission's "National Aboriginal Initiative"
www.chrc-ccdp.ca/

Residential Schools

Introduction

Residential schools embody some of the most brutal, dehumanizing, and destructive elements of Canada's colonial project. The school system, in accordance with the general direction of the government's Indian policy outlined in Chapter 7, was designed to assimilate Indigenous children by removing them from the care of their families and communities at a very young age and placing them in boarding schools to receive a European-Canadian education. These schools were funded and run by the state and various church organizations, with very little sympathy for the children in their custody or consideration for their welfare. In fact, given the high death rates of students and graduates of the schools, the degree of sexual, physical, and emotional abuse that occurred within the schools, and the failure of the state or churches to resolve problems even after they became aware of them, it is very clear that the federal government was at best indifferent to the suffering of residential school students. Dr Peter H. Bryce, in his position as chief medical officer of the Department of Indian Affairs (DIA), revealed in a 1906 report that the government's annual expenditure of $2 million on education was largely a waste because almost 75 per cent of residential school students died before they reached the age of 18.[1] Bryce's report was neither the first nor the last document that detailed the horrible conditions rampant in the schools. Even more disturbing is that, after the horrendous conditions of these schools were brought to the DIA's attention, they continued to run for almost another century. This system was inherently violent, for at its very core lay the "intention to 'kill the Indian' in the child for the sake of Christian civilization."[2]

Both articles in this chapter seek to re-centre the history of residential schools by positioning it at the heart of Canada's national history rather than as an unfortunate aberration in an otherwise admirable past. They also emphasize that, given its centrality to Canadian history, the residential school system should be of concern to all Canadians, not just to the victims and their families. Finally, these articles assert that the history of residential schools remains a contemporary concern. According to Celia Haig-Brown, residential schools are part of *our* heritage—"Aboriginal, newcomer, and long-time settler alike"—and everyone must remember and acknowledge them.

Lorena Sekwan Fontaine addresses the silence that continues to haunt communities and mask not only the experience of residential schools but also their legacy. Fontaine argues that the violence played out on the bodies and minds of Indigenous children did not end when they left the schools: "I realized that the violence that my family had experienced in the schools had been brought into our home." She further states that "shame is arguably the most enduring intergenerational impact left by residential schools." This shame, coupled with the sense of not feeling "Indian enough" as outlined by Bonita Lawrence in Chapter 8, can produce a profound sense of cultural dislocation and alienation. Acknowledging this reality is an important part of addressing the shameful legacy of the residential school system.

Chapter Objectives

At the end of this chapter, you should be able to

- trace the history of the residential school system, including its goals and the methods used to accomplish them;
- recognize the long-term consequences of the residential school system, including the intergenerational impacts;
- recognize the complexity of students' responses—including forms of resistance—to the schools' assimilationist project;
- understand the implications of student-on-student violence;
- evaluate the mandate of the Truth and Reconciliation Commission and the positive and negative consequences of restorative justice; and
- consider and debate the place of the residential school system in Canadian history.

Notes

1. Canadian Tuberculosis Association, Annual Reports, 1906, 26–7, LAC, Records of the Canadian Tuberculosis Association, Vol. 23.
2. John S. Milloy, *A National Crime: The Canadian Government and the Residential School System, 1879 to 1986* (Winnipeg: University of Manitoba Press, 1999), v.

Secondary Source

Always Remembering[1]: Indian[2] Residential Schools in Canada

Celia Haig-Brown

Introduction

> Three things stand out in my mind from my years at school: hunger; speaking English; and being called a heathen because of my grandfather.
>
> —George Manuel, 1974[3]

The word or the name "Spanish" might seem to be no more filled with menace than any other word; but it inspired dread from the first time we Indian boys heard it . . . we knew that "Spanish" was a place of woe for miscreants, just as hell and purgatory were for sinners. . . . "Spanish" for us came to mean only one thing: "the school," known as St. Peter Clavier's Indian Residential School and then later, from 1945, as the Garnier Residential School.

—Basil Johnston, 1988[4]

I am holding the Talking Stick. I have been talking about the Indian Residential School in Shubenacadie for many years, and I still don't understand why the hurt and shame of seeing and hearing the cries of the abused Mi'kmaw children, many of them orphans, does not go away or heal. I hope the act of writing it down will help me and others to come up with some answers.

—Isabelle Knockwood, 1992[5]

From the early seventeenth century to the late twentieth, missionaries and governments sought to "Christianize and civilize" the Indigenous peoples of what we now call Canada by establishing various forms of industrial, boarding, and residential schools and hostels. Amazingly, however, we have entered the second decade of the twenty-first century with many Canadians not remembering—or even knowing about—the role that Indian residential schools played in the colonization of this country. Year after year, university students are shocked to hear the extent of the schools' reach. Considering the continuing publicity regarding the schools, the 1996 Royal Commission on Aboriginal Peoples, and the creation of the Aboriginal Healing Foundation in 1998 and the **Truth and Reconciliation Commission** (TRC) in 2009, one is tempted to attribute this oversight to a form of studied amnesia. Those who do know about the residential schools but believe that they belong to a very distant past may be shocked to learn that the last one closed in 1997.

Some people refer to the legacy of residential schools as a dark chapter in Canadian history. Historian John Milloy agrees:

The system is not someone else's history, nor is it just a footnote or a paragraph, a preface or a chapter, in Canadian history. It is *our* history, *our* shaping of the "new world"; it is *our* swallowing of the land and its First Nations peoples and spitting them out as cities and farms and hydroelectric projects and as strangers in their own land and communities.[6]

This article makes visible the history of residential schools and their impacts through its re-presentation of fragments of a story that stretches from ocean to ocean to ocean within this country. It insists on the importance of remembering this heritage for all Canadians: Aboriginal, newcomer, and long-time settler alike.

Origins

The origins of residential schools lie in the philosophies of missionaries who came from Europe seeking to "Christianize and civilize" the peoples they encountered. The **Récollets**, an order of Franciscan monks, were among the first missionaries to come to the land now called Canada. As the Récollets ministered to the **Innu** on the northern shores of the St Lawrence River in the early 1600s, they were "[d]isturbed by the ability of Native adults to accept Christianity whilst retaining their own cultural and religious framework."[7] Thus, the missionaries turned their attention to establishing boarding schools offering religious training and French education to children, believing that they would more easily accept a substitute and, in European eyes, superior civilization. These missionaries were the first to separate children from their families and communities. While their schools ultimately failed, a precedent had been set for removing children from community influences to hasten assimilation and Christianization. Schooling became a fundamental tool of colonization of the minds, souls, and territories of the Indigenous peoples in North America.

Extending the Reach

Traditional Indigenous education focuses on lifelong learning with no separation of children from adults. Learning takes place in everyday contexts through watching, listening, and then doing. While some Indians initially saw benefits in sending their children to school, such as learning to read, write, and do mathematics in order to prosper within colonial society, many withdrew their support as they recognized government and missionary rejection of all Indian ways.[8] Historian Robin Fisher comments: "Because missionaries did not separate Western Christianity and Western civilization, they approached Indian culture as a whole and demanded a total transformation of the Indian proselyte. Their aim was the complete destruction of the traditional integrated Indian way of life."[9]

Sporadic and geographically focused efforts to use schools to influence Aboriginal children were developed from the 1600s, but it was not until the mid-1800s that British North America undertook a systematic investigation into the use of residential schools to serve the goal of assimilation. In 1847, the Province of Canada published a report based on the ideas of Egerton Ryerson, setting future directions in Indian education policy.[10] Ryerson clearly expresses his belief in the superiority of Western European cultures and the need "to raise [Indians] to the level of the whites," as well as the goal of seizing control of Indigenous peoples' land. This aim was implicit in the recommendation that efforts be continued to resettle Indigenous peoples in easily accessible communities to facilitate "Christianization." In addition, missionaries were to establish schools focused on teaching menial skills and furthering the assimilationist project. Specifically, "their education must consist not merely of the training of the mind, but of a weaning from the habits and feelings of their ancestors, and the acquirements of the language, arts, and customs of civilized life."[11]

Following Confederation in 1867 and the consolidation of existing legislation into the Indian Act in 1876, Regina MP Nicholas Davin was commissioned by the federal government to report on schools for Indians in the United States. In his introduction, Davin references President Ulysses Grant's policy on the so-called Indian question: "The Industrial school is the principal feature of the policy known as 'aggressive civilization.'"[12] Reiterating early missionaries' sentiments, Davin wrote,

> [T]he experience of the United States is the same as our own as far as the Indian adult is concerned. Little can be done with him [sic]. . . . The child, again, who goes to a day

school learns little, and what he learns is soon forgotten, while his tastes are fashioned at home and his inherited aversion to toil is in no way combated.[13]

Recommending the establishment of residential schools in Canada, Davin concluded: "if anything is to be done with the Indian, we must catch him very young." Clearly, the lessons of the Récollets' failures were long forgotten. Davin's recommendations were widely and quickly implemented. Financed by the federal government, the schools were managed by the churches. This mutually beneficial relationship created a source of funding and a captive audience for the churches and, for the government, made it easier to assimilate Indigenous peoples and take over their lands.[14] This initiative proved long-lasting and affected thousands of First Nations, Métis,[15] and Inuit children across the developing nation.

By 1920, amendments to the Indian Act included compulsory school attendance for children and boarding schools as the best option. That same year, in a parliamentary discussion concerning revisions to the Indian Act, Deputy Superintendent General Duncan Campbell Scott made his now infamous comment: "Our object is to continue until there is not a single Indian in Canada that has not been absorbed into the body politic and there is no Indian question, and no Indian department."[16] Between 1838 and 1985, from British Columbia to Nova Scotia and north to the Yukon and Northwest Territories, over 150,000 students attended 134 schools for Indian, Inuit, and Métis children.[17]

Residential School Life

No matter which schools one considers,[18] the accounts of former students resonate with one another. Memories begin with journeys away from home and family, and arrivals at alien institutions. Daily routines were highly structured: early mornings, prayers, morning "mush," chores, a few hours of school, more chores, more prayers, unappetizing suppers, homework, prayers, and bed. Scattered throughout these endless days are some good memories: learning to read and write; success at sports, dancing, and other competitions; kindnesses of certain staff; and friendships with other children. Many more speak of bad memories arising from the imposition of a foreign culture: general confusion about how things worked; the dehumanization of institutional life; punishments; loneliness; illnesses; all imaginable forms of abuse; and fundamental disrespect. The Government of Canada acknowledges that "while some former students have spoken positively about their experiences at residential schools, these stories are far overshadowed by tragic accounts of the emotional, physical and sexual abuse and neglect of helpless children, and their separation from powerless families and communities."[19] Let us hear what those who attended the schools have to say in their own words.

Arriving

Leaving home and coming to a huge foreign institution stand out in the minds of many residential school students:

I was five years old and my sister, Mavis, was nine years old when we were sent from home to Edmonton Residential School. Dad took us to Prince Rupert on the freight boat. . . . [There] we were put on a train to Edmonton. At first I found this exciting. . . . But as the train took us farther and farther away I began to feel afraid. At each stop more and more Native children were put on the train. . . . All around there were other children like us, looking and feeling afraid. . . . Finally we stopped in Edmonton; a place far away from home, a place I had never heard of, a place I had never seen. We were crowded into buses which took us into the country. . . . We stopped in front of a huge red brick building full of windows.

—Rosa Bell[20]

All of a sudden, here we come in front of this building [Kamloops Indian Residential School]. And after being told to be afraid of white people, you can imagine the feeling we had. . . . We were all standing there, my sister and I hanging on to each other. We were already so scared. . . . Why did my mother and father send us away? Then all of a sudden, we seen somebody coming down the hallway all in black and just this white face and that's when I started just shaking and we all started crying and backing up.

—Sophie (pseudonym)[21]

Then one day a "flyable" took me away from our world through the sky to a dark and desolate place. I do not remember having time to say goodbye to Cyril, my soul mate. I do not remember having time to say goodbye to the puppies or the bright environment before we boarded the RCMP Single Otter to go to Chesterfield Inlet Residential School. . . . Entering "the hostel," it was impossible to ignore all your senses. Strange voices and languages could

Work and Play, Residential School in Fort Resolution, NT. (PA-048021. Library and Archives Canada.)

be heard in the distance, strange new smells permeated the air at the doorway, and everything was painted in white, in contrast to the people in black.

—Jose Amaujak Kusugak[22]

Haircuts and uniforms were standard welcomes:

In keeping with the promise to civilize the little pagan, they went to work and cut off my braids, which, incidentally, according to Assiniboine traditional custom, was a token of mourning—the closer the relative, the closer the cut. After my haircut, I wondered in silence if my mother had died.

—Dan Kennedy[23]

Then they brought me to this one room and I had long hair, my hair was really long. And that lady, it was a nun, she said we all have to take a shower. While they were filling the tub up for me, they told me how much I stank. Then they grabbed my hair and told me to sit on a stool. So I sat on it and then they started cutting my hair and I didn't know what was going on. . . . They took me in where the bathroom was. That lady bathed me, and they told me my number was thirteen. That's when they gave me my number and my clothes. It was their clothes and we all had numbers.

—Anonymous[24]

Residential School Curriculum

Educationalist Elliot Eisner[25] writes of the three curricula that all schools teach: the implicit, the explicit, and the null. The implicit includes the transmission of attitudes and beliefs, as well as the use of discipline and surveillance to produce what French philosopher Michel Foucault would call normalized behaviours. The explicit refers to the official curriculum, subjects such as reading, writing, and arithmetic. The null curriculum is everything that schools do not teach.

In the residential schools, one day was much like another: the implicit curriculum consumed much of the students' lives. Although students who could afford it and whose homes were close by went home for the summer and winter holidays, others (especially those without families) spent their childhoods in the institution. For them, the days proceeded for years on end with no breaks. Former students speak eloquently of the dehumanizing monotony of their daily routines:

6:15 A.M. Clang! Clang! Clang! I was nearly clanged out of my wits and out of bed at the same time. Never had anything—not wind, not thunder—awakened me with quite the same shock and fright. . . . Clank! Clank! Clank! went the washbasins as they were flipped right side up on the bottom of a long shallow sink that resembled a cattle feeding trough. . . . Clank! Hiss! Gargle! Scrub-a-dub! Scrape! Choo-choo-choo! were the only sounds from the washing area. . . . Clang! Clang! Clang! "Line up!" Two serpentine columns of listless boys formed.

—Basil Johnston[26]

Inuit children who lived too far away and had to stay at school during the summer. Anglican Mission School, Aklavik, NT, c. 1941. (PA-101771. Library and Archives Canada.)

First thing in the morning, we were awakened by the nun's clapping. Then we'd hit the cold floor and say our morning prayers. Then we'd get ready for Mass which lasted for an hour. This was 365 days a year with no let-up.

—Betsey Paul[27]

We spent over an hour in the chapel every morning, every blessed morning. And they interrogated us on what it was all about being an Indian. . . . [The priest] would get so carried away: he was punching away at that old altar rail. . . to hammer it into our heads that we were not to think or act or speak like an Indian. And that we would go to hell and burn for eternity if we did not listen to their way of teaching.

—Sophie[28]

As for the explicit curriculum, the emphasis in the early years was on learning English: "The study of the first importance in these schools, for the Indian child, is the acquisition of the English vernacular," wrote Inspector Martin Benson in 1897. "Then should follow Reading, Writing, Arithmetic and Hygiene for the needs of the skilled Indian life, some Geography and History, so that he may know something of the world in which he lives and especially the empire of which he forms a part."[29] By 1910, there was a shift in emphasis. As Deputy Superintendent General Scott explained, religious instruction was the key priority. A clearly gendered division of labour within the school came next.[30] Finally, the teaching of "the ordinary branches of an English education" was addressed. Jack Funk speaks of 1930s L'École St Henri (Delmas Boarding School) in similar terms, "The school curriculum had three parts to it. Religious instruction was the first priority, work training was a second while academic studies was a distant third."[31] Until the 1950s, despite paying lip service to having Aboriginal people become part of "white stream" Canada, most schools emphasized skills that, at best, equipped students for menial jobs. This explicit curriculum influenced the implicit. Students learned quickly that all things related to their own civilization were not tolerated. Not being allowed to speak their language, especially the lasting impact that this loss of language had on family relationships, is a dark memory many shared:

> Neither me nor Teresa could speak a word of English because at home we had spoken all Indian—our native tongue. So they started off with an interpreter who was one of the older kids who told me if I was caught talking Indian again I was to be beaten and that sort of put a fright into me. . . . So inside of four or five years, I forgot all my Indian. . . . Well, just think, it was pounded out of me with a few strappings from the nuns.
>
> —Peter Julian[32]

Agnes Grant says that "the most frequent punishments were for speaking a Native language."[33] Isabelle Knockwood comments:

> Not only were little children brutally punished for speaking their mother tongue, reducing them to years of speechlessness, but the Mi'kmaw language was constantly referred to as "mumbo-jumbo" as if it were some form of gibberish. . . . The punishment for speaking Mi'kmaw began on our first day at school, but the punishment has continued all our lives as we try to piece together who we are and what the world means to us with a language many of us have had to re-learn as adults.[34]

Marlene Starr recalls her exposure to the implicit and explicit curricula in this way:

> My formal schooling began in Sandy Bay Residential School in 1963. I did my time for seven years, and there were four significant lessons I learned in that institution. I learned how to be silent and how to be obedient to authority. I learned that being "Indian" is to be inferior. I also learned to read and write.[35]

In terms of the null curriculum, most students were rarely exposed to traditional knowledge, language, or Indigenous thought within the school.[36] Even now, Indigenous thought is given short shrift in most schools and many post-secondary institutions.

Balancing "Act"

Emotions run high in contemporary accounts of residential schools, with good reason. For some, the schools hold nothing but negative memories; others seek to redeem some dimensions of their experiences. The accounts vary widely, which is understandable given that there were so many institutions, so many children, so many years, and so many teachers and administrators. In working with former students of St Mary's Indian Residential School near Mission, BC, non-Aboriginal author Terry Glavin seeks a balance.[37] Bill Williams, a former student, says,

> I don't think any of the histories that have been written about the residential schools so far tell the whole story. There is no balance. But in Glavin's work, it is there. . . Chiefs,

councillors, band managers, and professional staff, we all learned skills important for our people. . . . I've come out of there with more than I had. I learned how to retain my language and culture in my own way.[38]

Glavin expresses the turmoil even he felt about the school: "It was an evil place. It was a beautiful place."[39] In contrast, Bev Sellars, who attended St Joseph's Mission in Williams Lake, BC, stated unequivocally in her speech to the First National Conference on Residential Schools that

Another comment I have heard is that . . . the schools produced the Native artists, Native leaders, and other Native people who are successful in today's world. Today's successful Native people are proof of the power of Native spirit, and are not as a result of the residential schools. They exist in spite of the residential schools.[40]

Former chief of the Assembly of First Nations (AFN) Phil Fontaine reiterates the tensions characterized above:

My experiences at residential school taught me to be insecure, to be unsure of myself, to be uncertain of me. I would never send my children to residential school. Further, some people think that residential school was the best thing they could have had because it taught them to work, it taught them discipline, and it helped establish friendships. For those people, I think residential school represented an important part of their lives and one shouldn't take that away from them. . . . But for many others that remember residential schools for the hell-holes they were, they should be given an opportunity to re-examine those negative experiences so they can put them to rest. When you put something to rest it doesn't mean you forget about it. You remember it in different ways, in ways that give you strength.[41]

These "hell-holes" were places of extreme punishment and, in many cases, sexual abuse. Students talk of the liberal administration of the strap for a variety of offences. "Pulling ears, slapping heads, and hitting knuckles"[42] were par for the course. Others recount stories of bedwetters being forced to stand with their wet sheets over their heads as a form of public ridicule. One former student speaks of an adolescent girl who was forced to put her bloody underwear on her head.[43] Another recalls hospitalization after being strapped 128 times.[44] Every history of residential schools includes descriptions of harsh physical abuse.

Sexual abuse is also clearly documented. Fontaine is one public figure who speaks openly about the abuse he suffered. Randy Fred writes of his abuse first by an older student and then by a supervisor.[45] In the last few decades, numerous prosecutions have been documented in the media. In 1989 and 1991, an Oblate priest and an Oblate brother who had worked at St Joseph's Residential School in Williams Lake pleaded guilty to sexual assault of 13 boys and sexual abuse of 4 more.[46] In 1995, a former supervisor from the Port Alberni, BC, school was sentenced to 11 years for sexually assaulting boys attending the school between 1948 and 1968. The sentencing judge referred to him as a "sexual terrorist."[47] The TRC has heard many more such stories.

There was also death in the schools. Children died from physical illnesses, such as tuberculosis and blood poisoning. Some people say that children died of heartbreak.

Boys standing in front of buildings, Tsuu T'ina (Sarcee) Reserve, Alberta, c. 1920. Back row (L–R): Fred Sarcee (Tsuu T'ina) Woman, Reggie Starlight, George Big Plume, Tom Many Horses. Front row (L–R): Stanley Big Plume, Paul Crowchild, Jimmy Big Woman, Alec Big Plume, Edward One Spot, Joe Tony, Pat Dodging Horse, Dick Big Plume. Note that some boys are wearing bandages for tuberculosis. (Glenbow Archives NA-192-13.)

Others died while trying desperately to run away from the schools and go home, sometimes in the freezing temperatures of mid-winter.[48]

Despite their environment, students found creative ways to survive and flourish. Almost every text on the schools includes a description of students' resistance to authority.[49] They found places to speak their languages and sources of food and fun, built lasting friendships, and cared for one another. Some runaways made it home, where their relatives hid them. Families also intervened, hiding their children when the agents came to collect them, appearing at schools to insist that conditions ranging from bad food to harsh punishments be improved, and even having staff dismissed. Rather than simply existing as passive victims of a huge bureaucracy, students and parents found ways to push back as active agents.

The Teachers

Who were the teachers and administrators of the schools? Grant states that they fall into one of two categories: "those who are remembered because they were kind or were particularly effective teachers and those who inspired fear and anger."[50] As early as 1891, a former residential school principal wrote of his doubts about the schools:

> How would we white people like it if . . . we were obliged to give up our little children . . . KNOWING that they were taken away from us for the *very purpose* of weaning them away from the old loves and old associations—if we found they were most unwillingly allowed to come back to us for the short summer holidays, and when they came were dressed in the peculiar costumes of our conquerors, and were talking their language instead of the dear old tongue.[51]

While critical of teachers' cruelty, former students also acknowledged the difficulties they faced. Mary John of Lejac School says, "I'm sure they never expected to end up as teachers in the wilds of British Columbia." Chief John Tootoosis's biographers write:

> His initial impressions of the nuns soon developed into an adversary relationship. Pious and dedicated they were, but also human, and they were almost continually irritated and impatient with their doggedly silent and unresponsive pupils. More and more frequently this continued passive resistance to their efforts exploded into open resentment and anger.[52]

Fontaine acknowledges, "In spite of all my bad memories, I still end up going to visit the nuns who once taught us at residential school. . . . I need to show them I turned out pretty good in spite of what they thought."[53]

A recent article tells the story of one teacher and the process of healing with her student. Florence Kaefer, now 75 and never an abuser, found herself increasingly reluctant to speak of her residential school teaching, especially as revelations of sexual abuse were publicized. Recently, she reconnected with a student who had been abused. Kaefer participated with him in a healing circle as they worked together to reconcile their relationship. Former student and country singer Edward Gamblin described this process as "reconciliation on a one-to-one basis. That's the only way healing can work."[54]

Residential Schools in the Twenty-First Century

The fate of residential school buildings exemplifies the current relationship between the school system and its former students, their relatives, their offspring, and their memories. Some buildings are now controlled by local First Nations and are hives of activity. For example, the Woodland Cultural Centre in Brantford, ON—which features a museum, research library, and language department—sits on the site of the former Mohawk Institute. Museum Director Tom Hill comments:

> We are probably the only Cultural Centre in Canada that has had to establish a support counseling program for past students of the Mohawk Institute returning to our site to convince them that they are welcome to come in to see an exhibit, share a public program, visit our library or just browse our Gift Shop.[55]

Certain parts of the school remain untouched, including the carved names and messages of former students that are still visible on the bricks at the back of the building.

The last residential school in existence, the Prince Albert Indian Student Education Centre, operated for a time under the direction of the Chiefs' Council. In 1985, the Council took control of the school as others across Canada were either closing or undergoing a radical transformation of purpose. In the face of increasing public criticism of residential schools generally and the withdrawal of federal funding, the centre finally closed its doors in 1997, despite the protests of First Nation parents.

In another show of the power of community action, administration of the Blue Quills Residential School in eastern Alberta was transferred to the First Nations people of the surrounding territories. When the federal government decided to close the school in 1971 without their input, community members and supporters occupied the school and its grounds: "the old buildings were ringed with tents, hunting parties were sent out for deer, Saskatoon berries and rhubarb, and children went fishing. Elders moved into the gym."[56] As a result of the occupation, not only did Minister of Indian Affairs Jean Chrétien capitulate, but turned over 23 other schools to the management of "properly constituted Indian groups" in 1973.[57] Blue Quills became an adult education centre and eventually an accredited college.

Other buildings remain empty or were burned. The empty Shubenacadie Residential School, like others over the years, burned to the ground in 1968. Rumours circulated that "Indians" had started the destructive blaze. Former students gathered to cheer the building's demolition. "There was no sadness, no tears at seeing the building finally being punished and beaten for having robbed so many Indian children of the natural wonders and simple joys of being alive and being Native."[58] L'École St Henri had burned in 1948 while active. As they watched the fire, "the nuns cried but the children did not."[59] The Port Alberni building was torn down by former students, and the rubble remained for several years as a reminder of its horrors. Nothing marks the locations of some schools, though curious visitors comment that strange feelings emanate from the sites.

Always Remembering

Reconciliation, healing, always remembering. Residential schools in Canada are a controversial and complex part of all those who dwell in this land. Grant writes: "As the twenty-first century begins, it is possible to examine the era, talk about it freely, and seek redress and healing. Though public understanding, formal apologies, and compensation payments are helpful, it is only from within the cultures that real healing will come."[60]

Greg Younging makes clear that Canadians need "to undergo a micro-reconciliation within themselves":

> The present generation of Canadians need to face up to what has been done in their name, and they must own it as being part of who they are. . . . Canadian reconciliation must begin with: 1) throwing out all the historical disassociations and denials, and 2) getting out of prevailing generation-centric headspace.[61]

Mi'kmaw Sister Dorothy Moore comments, "It is not where we are that counts; it is where we are going that matters."[62]

First Nations, Métis, and Inuit people have more than survived the colonial assault exemplified by the residential schools of Canada. They have resisted all efforts to assimilate into the "white" majority. As Chief Shane Gottfriedson said to the crowds at the 2010 Kamloopa Powwow, "They didn't succeed: we are still here." Indigenous peoples across the nation are recreating their traditional civilizations in the contemporary context of Canada on their own terms. They are strong leaders, doctors, lawyers, artists, and educators *in spite* of efforts to annihilate them. Certainly, many former students and their families are still reeling from the intergenerational effects of residential schools; others have found ways to cope. The lessons of the schools and all that they represent remain for those who consider themselves Canadian, Indigenous and non-Indigenous peoples.

The previous and (especially) current work of our government and our churches is the collective responsibility of all Canadians. We will always remember, and now we must find the best ways to move into honourable relations with one another—First Nations, Métis, Inuit, long-time settler, and recent immigrant alike.

Notes

1. Colleen Seymour, Secwepemc friend and former student of the Native Indian Teacher Education Program, ends all her correspondence with these words.

2. The term *Indian* is used for individuals designated Indian under the Canadian Indian Act. This Act remains in force as this chapter is being written. Reference to Inuit, Métis, and First Nation refer to groups now recognized either by the Constitution of Canada and/or by formal organizations within Canada. Use of the word *Native* indicates this is in original text. In some parts of Canada, the word *Aboriginal* is considered to include all individuals with ancestry related to the original peoples of Canada. *Indigenous* is another term for the original peoples of a particular land (i.e., those who can trace ancestry to the time before written records often through oral histories); it is often used in international contexts.

3. George Manuel and Michael Posluns, *The Fourth World: An Indian Reality* (New York: The Free Press, 1974), 63.

4. Basil H. Johnston, *Indian School Days* (Toronto: Key Porter Books, 1988), 6.

5. Isabelle Knockwood, *Out of the Depths: The Experiences of Mi'kmaw Children at the Indian Residential School at Shubenacadie, Nova Scotia* (Lockeport, NS: Roseway Publishing, 1992), 7.

6. John Milloy, *A National Crime*, xviii.

7. Emma Anderson, "Between Conversion and Apostasy: The Religious Journey of Pierre-Anthoine Pastedechouan," *Anthropologica* 49, 1 (2007): 17–34.

8. See Agnes Grant, *No End of Grief: Indian Residential Schools in Canada* (Winnipeg: Pemmican Publications, 1996), 59.

9. Robin Fisher, *Contact and Conflict* (Vancouver: UBC Press, 1977), 144–5.

10. Alison L. Prentice and Susan E. Houston, *Family, School and Society in Nineteenth-Century Canada* (Toronto: Oxford University Press, 1975), 218.

11. Ibid., 220.

12. Nicholas F. Davin, *Report on Industrial Schools for Indians and Halfbreeds* (Ottawa: 14 Mar. 1879). PABC, RG 10, Vol. 6001, File 1-1-1, Pt.1.

13. Ibid., 2.

14. See also Noel Dyck, *Differing Visions: Administering Indian Residential Schooling in Prince Albert, 1867–1995* (Halifax: Fernwood, 1997), 96. "Underlying denominational and government educational programs for Indians in Saskatchewan and elsewhere was the firm belief that Aboriginal cultures and modes of social organization were 'primitive' and 'inferior' to those of Euro-Canadians. This racist belief had, of course, provided the justification for appropriating Aboriginal lands across Canada."

15. Rita Flammand recounts her Métis mother's time in residential school, pointing out that she was there to fill the quota "while they were in the process of rounding up the Treaty Indian children from the north." Greg Younging, Jonathan Dewar, and Mike DeGagné, eds, *Response, Responsibility, and Renewal: Canada's Truth and Reconciliation Journey* (Ottawa: Aboriginal Healing Foundation, 2009), 74.

16. Miller, in Celia Haig-Brown, *Resistance and Renewal: Surviving the Kamloops Indian Residential School* (Vancouver: Tillicum Library, 1988), 30.

17. See Aboriginal Healing Foundation, *Directory of Residential Schools in Canada* (Ottawa: Aboriginal Healing Foundation, 2003).

18. People from locations as diverse as Nigeria and Wales speak of the resonances of their experiences in colonially controlled boarding schools with those of students in Canada. See also Randy Fred's reference to the Coorgs, Indigenous people of India. Foreword to Haig-Brown, *Resistance and Renewal*, 15.

19. Text accessed from www.shannonthunderbird.com/residential_schools.htm, 9 Aug. 2010.

20. Rosa Bell, "Journeys," in Linda Jaine, ed., *Residential Schools: The Stolen Years* (Saskatoon: University of Saskatchewan Extension Press, 1993), 8–9.

21. Sophie, in Haig-Brown, *Resistance and Renewal*, 50–1.

22. Jose Amaujaq Kusugak, in Younging et al., *Response, Responsibility and Renewal*, 19–20.

23. Dan Kennedy, in Grant, *Grief*, 19 (n.p.).

24. Anonymous, in Agnes Jack, ed., *Behind Closed Doors: Stories from the Kamloops Indian Residential School* rev. edn (Kamloops: Secwepemc Cultural Education Society, 2006), 47.

25. Elliot Eisner, *The Educational Imagination: On the Design and Evaluation of School Programs* 3rd edn (New York: Macmillan College Publishing, 2001).

26. Johnston, *Indian School Day*, 27–8.

27. Betsey Paul, in Knockwood, *Out of the Depths*, 31.

28. Sophie, in Haig-Brown, *Resistance and Renewal*, 59.

29. Grant, *Grief*, 163–4.

30. Ibid., 164–5.

31. Jack Funk, "Une Main Criminelle, L'École St. Henri—the Delmas Boarding School," in Jaine, ed., *Residential Schools*, 73.

32. Peter Julian, in Knockwood, *Out of the Depths*, 34.

33. Grant, *Grief*, 189.

34. Knockwood, *Out of the Depths*, 98.

35. Marlene Starr, "Foreword," in Agnes Grant, *Finding My Talk: How Fourteen Native Women Reclaimed Their Lives after Residential School* (Calgary: Fifth House, 2004), vii.

36. One example of a notable exception is Emmanuel College's Principal Mackay, who became a fluent Cree speaker, speaking it with students. See Dyck, *Differing Visions*, 23.

37. Although a number of critics of the existing literature suggest that they over-emphasize the bad stories, when one reads closely, they almost all document positive moments and aspects. However, the weighting most often favours the negative: perhaps because those who enjoyed their experiences feel they have little to contribute or because there simply were more negative than positive ones.

38. Bill Williams, "Foreword," in Terry Glavin and Former Students of St Mary's, *Amongst God's Own: The Enduring Legacy of St. Mary's Mission* (Mission: Mission Indian Friendship Centre, 2002), 10.

39. Ibid., Introduction, 11.

40. Bev Sellars, "Opening Address to the First National Conference on Residential Schools, 18 June 1991," in Elizabeth Furniss, *Victims of Benevolence: The Dark Legacy of the Williams Lake Residential School* (Vancouver: Arsenal Pulp Press, 1995), 125. Emphasis in original.

41. Phil Fontaine, "We Are All Born Innocent," in Jaine, ed., *Residential Schools*, 63.

42. "Bear," in Dyck, *Differing Visions*, 45.

43. Starr, in Grant, *Finding*, viii.

44. Grant, *Grief*, 225.

45. "Foreword," in Haig-Brown, *Resistance and Renewal*, 21.

46. Furniss, *Victims*, 115.

47. Grant, *Grief*, 229.

48. For examples, see Dyck, *Differing Visions*, 17; Funk, in Jaine, ed., *Residential Schools*, 84; Furniss, *Victims*, 62; Haig-Brown, *Resistance and Renewal*, 110; Knockwood, *Out of the Depths*, 108.

49. See, for example, Grant, *Grief* ; Haig-Brown, *Resistance and Renewal*; Agnes Jack, ed., *Behind Closed Doors: Stories from the Kamloops Indian Residential School* (Penticton: Theytus Books, 2006).

50. Ibid., 141.

51. David Nock argues convincingly that these are the words of E.F. Wilson, former principal of Shingwauk and Wawanosh schools. In David Nock, *A Victorian Missionary and Canadian Indian Policy: Cultural Synthesis vs Cultural Replacement* (Waterloo: Wilfrid Laurier Press, 1988), 165. Emphasis in original.

52. Cited in Grant, *Grief*, 145.

53. Jaine, ed., *Residential Schools*, 63.

54. Patrick White, "Together they've turned shame into pride," *The Globe and Mail*, 18 June 2010, A10.

55. Patrick White, "Healing Comes Full Circle," *The Globe and Mail*, 17 June 2010. Accessed. www.theglobeandmail.com/news/national/healing-comes-full-circle/article4322344/

56. Grant, *Finding*, 171–2.

57. Ibid., 172.

58. Knockwood, *Out of the Depths*, 132.

59. Funk, in Jaine, ed., *Residential Schools*, 86.

60. Grant, *Finding*, 209.

61. Gregory Younging, "Inherited History, International Law, and the UN Declaration," in Younging et al., *Response, Responsibility, and Renewal*, 327.

62. Ibid., 85.

Primary Document

Program of Studies for Indian Schools, 1897

The Programme of studies herein prescribed shall be followed by the teacher as far as the circumstances of his school permit. Any modifications deemed necessary shall be made only with the concurrence of the department.

Subject	Standard I	Standard II	Standard III	Standard IV	Standard V	Standard VI
English	Word recognition and sentence making. Simple sounds of letters of alphabet. Copying words	Sounds continued. Sentence making continued. Orthography, oral and written. Dictation of words learnt of and of simple sentences.	Sounds completed. Simple homonyms explained. Orthography, oral and written. Sentences dictated. Composite sentences about objects and actions.	Sounds reviewed. Sentence enlargement. Orthography, oral and written. Letter-writing. Simple composition, oral and written, reviewing work on general knowledge course.	Enlargement and correction of sentences continued. Orthography, oral and written. Letter-writing continued. Easy oral and written, composition, reviewing general knowledge course.	Analysis of simple sentences. Parts of speech. Orthography, oral and written. Letter-writing continued. Oral
General Knowledge	Facts concerning things in school. Develop what is already known. Days of week, month.	The seasons. Measures of length and weight in common use. Colours. Commence animal and vegetable kingdoms, their parts and uses, cultivation, growth, &c. Things in about the school and their parts.	Animal and vegetable kingdoms continued. Money. The useful metals.	Animal, vegetable and mineral kingdoms continued. Uses of railways and ships. Explain manufacture of articles in common uses. The races of man.	Same enlarged. Laws regarding fires, game, &c. of daily use	Social relations. Seats of Government in Canada. System of representation and justice. Commerce and exchange of products.
Writing	Elementary strokes and words on slates. Large round hand.	Words, &c., on slates. Large round hand.	Slates and copy-book No. 1. Medium round hand	Copy-books Nos. 2 and 3. Medium round hand.	Copy-books Nos. 4 and 5. Small round hand	Copy-books Nos. 6 and 7. Small round hand.

Subject	Standard I	Standard II	Standard III	Standard IV	Standard V	Standard VI
Arithmetic	Numbers 1 to 10: their combinations and separations, oral and written. The signs +, −, ×, ÷. Count to 10 by ones, twos, threes, &c. Use and meaning of one-half, one-third, one-tenth. Making and showing one-half, one-fourth, one-eights, one-third, one-sixth, one-ninth, one-fifth, one-tenth, one-seventh (no figures). Simple problems, oral.	Numbers 10 to 25: their combinations and separations (oral and written). Count to 25 by ones, twos, threes, &c. Use and meaning of one-half, one-third, one-fourth, &c., to twenty-fifth (no figures). Relation of halves, fourths, eighths, thirds, sixths, twelfths, ninths (no figures). Simple problems, introducing gallons in peck, pecks in bushels, months in year, inches in foot, pound, current coins up to 25c. Addition in columns, no total to exceed 25.	Numbers 25 to 100: their combinations and separations, oral and written. Count to 100 by ones, twos, threes, &c., to tens. Use and meaning of one-twenty-sixth, one-twenty-seventh, &c., to one-hundredth (no figures). Addition, subtraction, division, and partition of fractions of Standard II. Roman numerals I to C. Simple problems, introducing seconds in minutes, minutes in hours, hours in day, pounds in bushel, sheets in quire, quires in ream.	Numeration and rotation to 10,000. Simple rules to 10,000. Addition, subtraction, division and partition of fractions already known (figures). Introduce terms numerator, denominator. &c. Roman notation to 2,000. Graded problems, introducing remaining reduct on tables. Daily practice in simple rules to secure accuracy and rapidity.	Notation and numeration completed. Formal reduction. Vulgar fraction to thirtieths. Denominate fractions. Daily practice to secure accuracy and rapidity in simple rules. Graded problems. Reading and writing decimals to thousandths inclusive.	Factors, measures and multiples. Vulgar fractions completed. Easy application of decimals to ten-thousandths. Easy application of square and cubic measures. Daily practice to secure accuracy and rapidity in simple rules. Easy application of percentage. Graded problems.

Subject	Standard I	Standard II	Standard III	Standard IV	Standard V	Standard VI
Geography			Development of geographical notions by reference to geographical features of neighbourhood. Elementary lessons on direction, distance, extent.	(a) Review of Standard III. Lesson to lead to simple conception of the earth as great round ball, with surface of land and water, surrounded by the air, lighted by the sun, and with two motions. (b) Lessons on natural features, first from observation, afterwards by aid of moulding-board, pictures and blackboard illustrations (c) Preparation for and introductions of maps. (Review of lessons in position, distance, direction with representation drawn to scale). Study of map of vicinity drawn on blackboard.	Simple study of the important countries in each continent. Province in which school is situated and Canada to be studied first. The position of the country in the continent; its natural features; climate, productions, its people, their occupations, manners, customs, noted localities, cities, &c. Moulding-boards and map-drawing to be aids in the study. Simple study of the important countries in each continent, &c., &c.	(a) The earth as a globe. Simple illustrations and statements with reference to form, size, meridians and parallels, with their use; motions and their effects, as day and night, season, zones, with their characteristics, as winds and ocean currents, climate as affecting the life of man. (b) Physical features and conditions of North America, South America and Europe, studied and compared. Position on the globe; position, relative to other grand divisions, size, form, surface, drainage, animal, vegetable life, resources, &c.

Subject	Standard I	Standard II	Standard III	Standard IV	Standard V	Standard VI
				Maps of natural features drawn from moulded forms. Practice in reading conventional map symbols on outline maps. (d) General study from globe and maps. The hemisphere, continent, oceans and large islands, their relative positions and size. The continents: position, climate, form, outline, surroundings, principal mountains, rivers, lakes; the most important countries, productions, peoples, interesting facts and associations.		Natural advantages of the cities. (c) Observation to accompany the study of geography-apparent movements of the sun, moon and stars, and varying times of their rising and setting; difference in heat of the sun's rays at different hours of the day; change in the direction of the sun's rays coming through the school-room window at the same hour during the year; varying length of noon-day shadows; changes of the weather, wind and seasons.
Ethics	The practice of cleanliness, obedience, respect, order, neatness.	Right and wrong. Truth. Continuance of proper appearance and behaviour.	Independence. Self-respect. Develop the reasons for proper appearance and behaviour.	Industry, Honesty. Thrift.	Citizenship of Indians, Patriotism. Industry. Thrift, Self-maintenance. Charity. Pauperism.	Indian and white life. Patriotism. Evils of Indian isolation. Enfranchisement. Labour the law of life. Relations of the sexes as to labour. Home and public duties.

Subject	Standard I	Standard II	Standard III	Standard IV	Standard V	Standard VI
Reading	First Primer	Second Primer	Second Reader	Third Reader	Fourth Reader	Fifth Reader
Recitation		To begin in Standard II, are to be in line with what is taught in English, and developed into pieces of verse and prose which contain the highest moral and patriotic maxims and thoughts.				
History			Stories of Indians of Canada and their civilization.	History of province in which school is situated.	Canadian History (commenced).	Canadian History (continued).
Vocal Music			Simple songs and Hymns. The subjects of the formers to be interesting and patriotic. The tunes bright and cheerful.			
Calisthenics				Exercises, frequently accompanied by singing, to afford variation during work and to improve physique.		
Religious Instruction				Scripture Reading. The Ten Commandments. Lord's Prayer. Life of Christ, &c., &c.		

Note: English. – Every effort must be made to induce pupils to speak English and to teach them to understand it; unless they do, the whole work of the teacher is likely to be wasted.

Reading. – Pupils must be taught to read loudly and distinctly. Every word and sentence must be fully explained to them, and from time to time they should be required to state the sense of a lesson or sentence, in their own words, in English, and also in their own language if the teacher understands it.

General. – Instruction is to be direct, the voice and blackboard being the principal agents. The unnecessary use of text books is to be avoided.

N.B. – It will be considered proof of the incompetency of a teacher, if pupils are found to read in "parrot fashion" only, i.e., without in the least understanding of what they read. And the following remark applied to all teaching, viz.:- Everything must be thoroughly understood, before a pupil is advanced to further studies.

Secondary Document

Reflections on the Post–Residential School Settlement Agreement: Expressions of Reconciliation—Looking Back Forward Looking

Lorena Sekwan Fontaine

Expressions of reconciliation have emerged since Canada's Residential School Settlement Agreement of 2006 (the Agreement). Profound work in the areas of truth-telling, testimony, healing, resiliency, and relationship-building is attempting to transcend physical, sexual, cultural abuses, death, and illness often associated with the residential school court claims. A section of the Agreement provided opportunities for Aboriginal peoples to examine, assess, and reflect upon their residential school experiences through the mandate of the Truth and Reconciliation Commission of Canada (TRC). The TRC process also set the stage for both Aboriginal peoples and Canadians to consider other possible avenues to reconcile a shared history. Many people involved with the TRC have characterized the relationship between Aboriginal peoples and Canada as fundamentally flawed, but remain hopeful for reconciliation. Others remain skeptical. This chapter examines the complexities of reconciliation that the TRC has encountered over the past few years which affect Aboriginal peoples and all Canadians. The inspiration for this article comes from my mother's courage to publicly speak about her experiences in the schools. It is also in honour of my late father, Lawrence Edward Fontaine, who passed away a few years before residential schools were publicly discussed. I know they both struggled tremendously as parents because of the abuse they experienced in the schools and I am forever grateful for their resilience. I recognize that they, as well as so many other residential school survivors, suffered silently.

Looking Back—Forward Looking

Over the past six years, TRC Commissioners Justice Murray Sinclair, Wilton Littlechild, and Marie Wilson chaired several national and community events in which thousands of residential school survivors and their families came forward. Their presentations disclosed the horrific and unimaginable treatment of children (some as young as three) and the effect this has had on their families and communities. Many testimonies reveal haunting experiences but are also telling because they relate to the challenging issues Aboriginal communities face on reserves and within urban settings. Within these reconciliation processes a door has opened for individuals to come forward and have their experiences acknowledged. The TRC forums also offered opportunities for others to become aware of the healing work that has changed the lives of Aboriginal peoples affected by the residential schools.

I have witnessed several survivors' testimonies over the past four years while attending four TRC gatherings (Halifax, Vancouver, Edmonton, and Saskatoon). Their stories have changed my life. I will never see this country in the same way again. I now recognize the devastation the schools caused from a broader context and the government's culpability. The images of Aboriginal children being abused, neglected, harmed, and denigrated is firmly etched in my memory. While my heart has been broken by the thought of these experiences, I have also been inspired by the survivors' resilience, their bravery, and the ability of many to make a life for themselves in spite of ongoing struggles.

I have also witnessed skeptical attitudes being transformed during TRC events. These people spoke candidly to me in between TRC sessions and confessed to being overwhelmed by what they had heard. Others said that they had no idea how terribly Aboriginal children were treated in the schools. Others expressed extreme anger and disillusionment that a country like Canada could have let the residential schools go on for so long. In almost every case, I saw major shifts in the human spirit as a result of hearing survivors' public statements.

In 2013, my mother provided a private statement to the TRC in Saskatoon that resulted in an unexpected shift in my life. For months leading up to my mother's statement, I felt her restlessness. She was extremely anxious. Due to her nervous energy, I was worried about the effect that providing her statement would have on her health. During this time, my thoughts turned to survivors who have had heart attacks and others who passed away shortly after providing their statement. I recognized that there was a great deal of emotional trauma involved in coming forward. Knowing this made me very afraid for my mother so I was relieved the day she completed her testimony, with a great deal of support from family, TRC staff, cultural support workers, and our traditional medicines. As people were getting ready to leave, my mother turned to my brother and I and said that she was sorry that she was not able to be the best mother. The simple acknowledgement that our family life was complex and often uncertain provided me with an opportunity to reconcile with my family's experience and the legacy we carry. It was truly an inspiring occasion but also emotionally draining. I had a choice in that moment to accept what had happened and then let it go or I could continue to let the past influence my life. The most important part of that day, however, was that my mother was okay.

As well as the thousands of statements provided to the TRC, there are a variety of views on reconciliation. A common perspective held by those directly involved is that more time is required for reconciliation to occur. Others advocate for restitution of the theft of land and resources before they reconciliation can be considered. Still others seek restitution by having Canada recognized as a country that has committed cultural genocide against Aboriginal peoples. Then there are many survivors who would simply like to move on with their lives without ever having to look back again; to them this would result in reconciliation. In addition to the varied views held by Aboriginal peoples, Canadians also have a role to play in reconciliation.[1]

Many Canadians remain ignorant of residential school history and its legacy. These individuals will first need to learn about residential school history so reconciliation can become a possibility. In my experience as a professor, people are not always moved by facts and figures. At the worst end of the spectrum, I have heard comments such as: "Why can't Aboriginal peoples just get over it?" To my knowledge, every person who has had an opportunity to hear survivors speak firsthand has changed their pessimistic attitudes. It is the human connection that seems to create empathy among the general public.

In 1998, the Aboriginal Healing Foundation (AHF) began its work to educate Canadians and Aboriginal peoples on the legacy of the residential schools. Initially, $350 million in funding was allocated. The goal was also to encourage and support community-developed and culturally based programs directed towards healing from the effects of the residential school system. Then, in 2007, the Indian Residential Schools Settlement Agreement provided another $125 million in funding for five more years, allowing for a research series on reconciliation from the perspectives and experiences of survivors and family members as well as the Canadian public. There were also 134 contribution agreements for community healing projects that targeted the intergenerational legacy of the residential schools.

In August 2014, the AHF released *Full Circle: the Aboriginal Healing Foundation and the Unfinished Work of Hope, Healing and Reconciliation*. This publication reveals the experiences of the AHF and the significant initiatives that resulted from its mandate. AHF president Georges Erasmus expressed pride in its accomplishments: "The work of healing and reconciliation is by no means complete. But the past years show us what we can do by working together, and so I urge the public to support survivors by supporting this work of healing and reconciliation."

With the closing of the Aboriginal Healing Foundation (AHF) and the completion of the TRC's mandate at the end of June 2015, one wonders what will replace their important work. What will happen next? Although the AHF and TRC provided structure for healing, education, and reconciliation, does momentum exist to carry on their work? Where does this leave Aboriginal peoples and Canadians today? Although at different stages, a segment of the non-Indigenous population is currently engaged in a period of reflection. At the same time, legacy issues continue to affect the lives of Aboriginal peoples and require Canada's immediate attention.

Legacy Issues

One glaring example of the damage the schools has created is the over-institutionalization of Aboriginal peoples. Many people argue that the child welfare and justice systems have simply replaced the residential school system. It is estimated that there are 27,000 Aboriginal children now in care, more than at the height of the residential school system.[2] A recent human rights complaint made by the Assembly of First Nations and the First Nations Child and Family Caring Society of Canada chronicles the discriminatory treatment of Aboriginal children while linking it as a legacy of the residential schools.[3] Another significant issue was reported on 7 March 2013 by the Correctional Investigator, *Spirit Matters: Aboriginal People and the Corrections and Conditional Release Act* acknowledging the over-representation of Aboriginal peoples in the federal corrections system. Currently 23 per cent of the federal incarcerated population is Aboriginal. Alarmingly, since 2005–06 there has been a 43 per cent increase in the Aboriginal inmate population.[4] One of the major contributions to the high rate of incarceration is the legacy of the residential schools and inadequate initiatives to deal with related issues that continue to affect the Aboriginal community.

Violence against young Aboriginal girls and women is also an issue associated with the residential school era. A 2014 House of Commons Parliamentary Report, *Invisible*

Women: A Call to Action, reveals that the impact from the residential schools is a living legacy that is evident in high rates of domestic violence against Aboriginal women. The report concludes that, among other issues, there are not enough culturally appropriate services for Aboriginal women in urban areas. Racism also continues to affect the way Aboriginal women are portrayed and ultimately treated by members of society.[5]

Another issue that goes to the heart of Aboriginal culture and identity is the loss of Aboriginal languages. It is predicted that only three of the original 52 Aboriginal languages will survive. The 2005 Task Force on Aboriginal Languages and Cultures attributed the endangered state of all Aboriginal languages to the government's blatant attempt to eradicate Aboriginal languages in the residential schools.[6] Aboriginal children were repeatedly punished for speaking their mother tongue. Aboriginal culture was ridiculed and children were made to feel ashamed of their Aboriginal identity. The rippling impacts from these experiences are now evident in the small number of speakers of Aboriginal languages, with the majority of speakers now over the age of 60.[7] With few resources being directed towards Aboriginal language revitalization efforts and inadequate support from the government for immersion programs, there is cause for alarm. No Aboriginal community in Canada has not been affected by the damage the schools did to Aboriginal languages and cultural identities.

In the midst of these daunting legacy issues, there have been a number of initiatives that are paving a new path for change. In 2012, the TRC released an interim report, *They Came for the Children,* which issued 20 recommendations for action at the federal and provincial level, including the creation of educational materials about the residential schools and the establishment of parenting programs and trauma therapy centres. Additional recommendations are for compensation to day school students, who are currently excluded from the residential school agreement settlement, as well as increased funding for archiving historical residential school records.[8] Although none of these and other TRC recommendations has been adopted to date, they provide direction on what needs to be done.

On 17 September 2013, approximately 70,000 people, guided by 450 volunteers, demonstrated their support for reconciliation in Vancouver, British Columbia in a Walk for Reconciliation. The organization responsible for the walk, Reconciliation Canada, was founded in 2012 to create opportunities to build better relationships between Aboriginal and Canadians. The vision of the organization is that

> through a better understanding of our shared history as Canadians, and the values we share, we can build a new relationship between Aboriginal and non-aboriginal Canadians, built on a foundation of openness, dignity, understanding and hope.[9]

One organization tasked with carrying on the TRC's important archival work is the National Research Centre (NRC). The NRC will be a vehicle to inform Canadians and others about what happened in the residential schools system. Thousands of transcripts, and audio- and video-recorded statements will be permanently housed in the NRC's collection at the University of Manitoba. Millions of archival documents and photographs from the Government of Canada, church organizations, art work, artifacts, research, and other expressions of reconciliation presented during TRC events will be included in the collection. The NRC will house archival material so that what happened in the schools will never be forgotten. This brings some peace of mind to many survivors.

A recent innovation that will leave a lasting imprint is the production of a ballet on the residential schools, with Joseph Boyden as the scriptwriter. *Going Home Star* was performed by the Royal Winnipeg Ballet in October 2014. The story is about two young Aboriginal people, Annie and Gordon. Annie lives a challenging life in the city; Gordon is a former student at a residential school. Their meeting results in profound change and healing in each others' lives. Their love empowers Gordon to move towards a healing. Robert Enright of the CBC characterized the production as an unqualified success that "promises a legacy of light, understanding and hope."[10]

As well as the reconciliation work from the arts community, a new organization called *Canadians for a New Partnership* was recently formed. Aboriginal and non-Aboriginal leaders are examining ways to tackle the challenges Aboriginal peoples face by calling on Canadians to act on Aboriginal issues. The group consists of former politicians such as Paul Martin and Joe Clark, as well as former National Chief of the Assembly of First Nations Ovide Mercredi; former Inuit Tapiriit Kanatami Leader Mary Simon; former premier of the Northwest Territories Stephen Kakfwi; and former auditor general of Canada Sheila Fraser. The organization advocates for change through education and discussion while creating better economic opportunities for Aboriginal peoples. Ovide Mercredi says the organization will be aimed at reconciliation: "Part of the reconciliation that needs to happen, clearly, is to deal with the treaties and the Constitution but not to stop there, because people need help right now for basic things like better education, better health care and so on."[11]

In the midst of these important and challenging initiatives there have been some setbacks. Many survivors of the schools are very concerned about the fate of the records that were generated from their hearings during the Independent Assessment Process (IAP). In this process, former students of the schools are seeking compensation for more severe cases of physical and sexual abuse. The head of the IAP, Dan Shapiro, wants the records from the hearings and any additional materials destroyed. The federal government's position is that censoring documents is a standard process of protecting the privacy of those involved and claims that it would be too cumbersome to black out all the names or identifying characters, so all the hearing records must be destroyed. Another argument is that the thousands of testimonies already collected by the TRC are enough for Canada's historical record. Currently 800,000 documents and 19,500 written decisions have been generated from the IAP.

Michael Cachagee, a 75-year-old survivor from a residential school in Ontario, questions the motives behind this action. He wonders who is being protected by the destruction of the records. Cachagee's view is that the destruction of the records is protecting the perpetrators and that the government does not "want the public to see the devastation and ugliness of what happened, under the guise of protecting my innocence."[12] Many former students share Cachagee's concern and are against the idea of destroying any of their records. One former student says that in destroying these records,

[w]e lose a section of history. We lose the ability to understand why people are the way they are. We lose the ability to learn from our own mistakes and try to treat each other equally. Our children must be able to see these documents, understand us and understand how policy can affect generations of people.[13]

In addition to losing an important part of our history, we need to honour the wishes of those survivors who want their records kept. It is, after all, their story, their experiences, and their legacy.

Expressions of Reconciliation

In spite of the current setback with the government's position on IAP records, there are Canadians who are trying to advance a reconciliation agenda. People like Shelagh Rogers, an honorary witness to the TRC and radio broadcaster at the Canadian Broadcasting Corporation, says that "until we come to some understanding of how Canada has gotten to where it is now with the Residential School and the legacy it has imprinted on country, the future between Aboriginal and non-Aboriginal peoples looks uncertain at best."[14] Rogers recognizes the role that colonization has played in the destruction of relationships on many levels:

> Colonialism is not over. Its tentacles reach into the present, and it is the greatest stain on Canada. The journey from truth (hearing the stories) to reconciliation (fixing what is broken and building and re-building) will involve taking apart a whole system of colonialism and entrenched relationships—personal, political and philosophical.[15]

Aboriginal peoples have made a number of significant statements regarding reconciliation over the past few years that are critical to understanding the responsibility that lies ahead in working towards reconciliation. The former lieutenant-governor of British Columbia, the Honourable Steven Point offers wisdom on forgiveness, truth, and the barriers to reconciliation:

> And so many of you have said today, so many of the witnesses that came forward said, "I cannot forgive. I'm not ready to forgive." And I wondered why. Reconciliation is about hearing the truth, that's for sure. It's also about acknowledging that truth. Acknowledging that what you've said is true. Accepting responsibility for your pain and putting those children back in the place they would have been, had they not been taken from their homes. . . .
>
> What are the blockages to reconciliation? The continuing poverty in our communities and the failure of our government to recognize that "Yes, we own the land." Stop the destruction of our territories and for God's sake, stop the deaths of so many of our women on highways across this country. . . . I'm going to continue to talk about reconciliation, but just as important, I'm going to foster healing in our own people, so that our children can avoid this pain, can avoid this destruction and finally, take our rightful place in this "Our Canada" (*Final Report of the Truth and Reconciliation Commission of Canada*, 14)[16]

Patsy George, an Honorary Witness to the Truth and Reconciliation Commission, acknowledges the significance of Aboriginal women and children in the process of reconciliation:

> Women have always been a beacon of hope for me. Mothers and grandmothers in the lives of our children, and in the survival of our communities, must be recognized and supported. The justified rage we all feel and share today must be turned into instruments of transformation of our hearts and our souls, clearing the ground for respect, love, honesty, humility, wisdom and truth. We owe it to all those who suffered, and we owe it to the children of today and tomorrow. May this day and the days ahead bring us peace and justice (*Final Report of the Truth and Reconciliation Commission of Canada*, 11).[17]

The summary of the Final Report of the Truth and Reconciliation Commission of Canada provides important remarks to residential school survivors and their families, government, churches, schools, and all Canadians of what is required in order to practice reconciliation in our daily life:

> For many Survivors and their families, this commitment is foremost about healing themselves, their communities, and nations, in ways that revitalize individuals as well as Indigenous cultures, languages, spirituality, laws, and governance systems. For governments, building a respectful relationship involves dismantling a centuries-old political and bureaucratic culture in which, all too often, policies and programs are still based on failed notions of assimilation. For churches, demonstrating long-term commitment requires atoning for actions within the residential schools, respecting Indigenous spirituality, and supporting Indigenous peoples' struggles for justice and equity. Schools must teach history in ways that foster mutual respect, empathy, and engagement. All Canadian children and youth deserve to know Canada's honest history, including what happened in the residential schools, and to appreciate the rich history and knowledge of Indigenous nations who continue to make such a strong contribution to Canada, including our very name and collective identity as a country. For Canadians from all walks of life, reconciliation offers a new way of living together. (*Final Report of the Truth and Reconciliation Commission of Canada*, 21–21)[18]

One of Canada's leading intellectuals and an advocate for reconciliation is John Ralston Saul. In his latest book, *The Comeback*, he points out that "we haven't ever had a government that has put its mind to trying to understand what the concept of reconciliation means, let alone how to transform."[19] Saul suggests "[I]f we start down a road of shared reconciliation and restitution, we will have taken a crucial step in building a sense of ourselves and the country. It is a matter of being true to where we are, to what is fair and possible here. That consciousness, that sense of ourselves, will solidify our ability to live together and to do in an atmosphere of justice."[20] What Saul and others suggest is that Canada still has a great deal of work to do on reconciliation.

It is important to recognize that reconciliation is also not confined to Canada. Indigenous communities globally struggle with the impact of state action that has attempted to eradicate Indigenous peoples culturally and linguistically through the removal and treatment of children. The effect of this history stretches to places such as the United States (Adams), New Zealand (Waitangi Tribunal) and Australia (Australian Human Rights Commission), among other countries. In her comparative study to the United Nations Permanent Forum on Indigenous Issues, Andrea Smith concludes that boarding schools have been used as a tool for cultural assimilation and have greatly infringed on Indigenous peoples' right to self-determination.[21] Smith also states that "These schools have resulted in cultural alienation, loss of language, disruptions in family and social structures, and increased community dysfunction. Many schools were exceedingly brutal places where children were physically, sexually and emotionally abused."[22] Smith suggests that educational systems may provide opportunities to reverse the harm that the boarding schools have created.

Whatever the solutions are, reconciliation is now a global issue. Indigenous peoples around the world have been affected by boarding school systems but now have a right to determine their own futures. An important stepping-stone towards reconciliation is exemplified in the principles in the UN *Declaration on the Rights of Indigenous Peoples* which countries need to recognize and advance.

Concluding Remarks

Although it is evident that reconciliation is complex and uncertain at this stage, it is certain that it will not be achieved overnight. The TRC commissioners have emphasized that it took over one hundred years to cause the damage and it will likely take at least that long, if not longer, to repair the damage and require a great deal of effort on many fronts. Reconciliation is not a defined process nor is it a one-size-fits-all outcome. It does not necessarily mean forgiveness or instantaneous healing. It will mean different things to different people depending on the context of their relationship to the residential school legacy. Many Aboriginal peoples have stated that they will never forgive or heal but that they are determined to move towards healthier lives for their children and grandchildren. Others have reconciled by letting go of the past as a result of healing work they have done over the years. It is my hope that a significant step towards reconciliation will occur in my lifetime.

Notes

1. Paulette Regan, *Unsettling the Settler Within* (Vancouver: UBC Press, 2010).
2. Aboriginal Affairs and Northern Development Canada, "First Nations Child and Family Services Program," www.aadnc-aandc.gc.ca/eng/1334326697754/1334326744598, accessed 2 August 2015.
3. First Nations Child and Family Caring Society of Canada, i am a witness. Canadian Human Rights Tribunal, 2015, www.fncaringsociety.ca/i-am-witness, accessed 2 August 2014.
4. Correctional Investigator's Report, *Spirit Matters: Aboriginal People and the Corrections and Conditional Release Act*, 22 October 2012, www.oci-bec.gc.ca/cnt/rpt/oth-aut/oth-aut20121022-eng.aspx, accessed 2 August 2014).
5. Parliament of Canada, the Special Committee on Violence Against Indigenous Women, *Invisible Women: A Call to Action*. 41st Parliament, Second Session, March 2014. www.parl.gc.ca/HousePublications/Publication.aspx?DocId=6469851, accessed 30 August 2014.
6. Canadian Heritage, *Towards a New Beginning: A Foundational Report for a Strategy to Revitalize First Nation, Inuit, and Métis Languages and Cultures*. Report to the Minister of Canadian Heritage by the Task Force on Aboriginal Languages and Cultures, June 2005. Catalogue no. CH4-96/2005 (Ottawa: Canadian Heritage, 2005).
7. Statistics Canada, Aboriginal Languages in Canada, Language 2011 Census of Population, Catalogue no. 98-314-X20110003. 2011,

www12.statcan.gc.ca/census-recensement/2011/as-sa/98-314-x/98-314-x2011003_3-eng.cfm.

8. Truth and Reconciliation Commission of Canada. *They Came for the Children.* Library and Archives Canada, 2012. www.trc.ca/websites/trcinstitution/index.php?p=580, accessed 1 September 2014.

9. Reconciliation Canada. http://reconciliationcanada.ca, accessed 10 September 2014.

10. Robert Enright, "RWB's *Going Home Star—Truth and Reconciliation* is inspired and inspiring." CBC News, 2 October 2014, www.cbc.ca/news/canada/manitoba/rwb-s-going-home-star-truth-and-reconciliation-is-inspired-and-inspiring-1.2785096, accessed 3 October 2014.

11. "Former Politicians and Aboriginal Leaders Announce New Partnership," CBC News, 4 September 2014. www.cbc.ca/news/aboriginal/former-politicians-and-aboriginal-leaders-announce-new-partnership-1.2754758, accessed 3 October 2014.

12. Tim Alamenciak. "Survivors of Residential Schools Push Back Against Document Destruction." *Toronto Star*, 20 June 2014. www.thestar.com/news/gta/2014/06/20/survivors_of_residential_schools_push_back_against_document_destruction.html, accessed 1 September 2014.

13. Ibid.

14. Shelagh Rogers, Mike DeGagne, and Jonathan Dewar, *Speaking My Truth, Reflections on Reconciliation & Residential School* (Ottawa: Aboriginal Healing Foundation, 2012), 5.

15. Ibid., 8.

16. TRC, AVS, Steven Point, Statement to the Truth and Reconciliation Commission of Canada, Vancouver, British Columbia, 20 September 2013, Statement Number: BCNE304, cited in *Final Report of the Truth and Reconciliation Commission of Canada, Volume One Summary, Honouring the Truth, Reconciling the Future.* Toronto: James Lorimer and Company, 2015.

17. TRC, AVS, Patsy George, Statement to the Truth and Reconciliation Commission of Canada, Vancouver, British Columbia, 21 September 2013, Statement Number: BCNE404, cited in *Final Report of the Truth and Reconciliation Commission of Canada, Volume One Summary, Honouring the Truth, Reconciling the Future.* Toronto: James Lorimer and Company, 2015.

18. *Final Report of the Truth and Reconciliation Commission of Canada, Volume One Summary, Honouring the Truth, Reconciling the Future.* Toronto: James Lorimer and Company, 2015.

19. John Ralston Saul, *The Comeback* (Toronto: Penguin, 2014), 120.

20. Ibid., 170.

21. Andrea Smith, Indigenous Peoples and Boarding Schools: A Comparative Study, for the Secretariat of the United Nations Permanent Forum on Indigenous issues. E/C.19/2009/CRP.1, 26 January 2009, 49. www.un.org/esa/socdev/unpfii/documents/E_C_19_2009_crp1.pdf, accessed 6 June 2014.

22. Ibid., 49.

Primary Document

Excerpt from the Indian Residential Schools Settlement Agreement, May 2006

Schedule "N"

Mandate for the Truth and Reconciliation Commission

Terms of Reference

1. Goals

    The goals of the Commission shall be to:
    - (a) Acknowledge Residential School experiences, impact and consequences;
    - (b) Provide a holistic, culturally appropriate and safe setting for former students, their families and communities as they come forward to the Commission;

(c) Witness,[1] support, promote and facilitate truth and reconciliation events at both the national and community levels;

(d) Promote awareness and public education of Canadians about the IRS system and its impacts;

(e) Identify sources and create as complete an historical record as possible for the IRS system and legacy. The record shall be preserved and made accessible to the public for future study and use;

(f) Produce and submit to the Parties of the Agreement[2] a report including recommendations[3] to the Government of Canada concerning the IRS system and experience including: the history, purpose, operation and supervision of the IRS system, the effect and consequences of IRS (including systemic harms, intergenerational consequences and the impact on human dignity) and the ongoing legacy of the residential schools;

(g) Support commemoration of former Indian Residential School students and their families in accordance with the Commemoration Policy Directive (Schedule "X" of the Agreement).

Notes

1. This refers to the Aboriginal principle of "witnessing."

2. The Government of Canada undertakes to provide for wider dissemination of the report pursuant to the recommendations of the Commissioners.

3. The Commission may make recommendations for such further measures as it considers necessary for the fulfillment of the Truth and Reconciliation Mandate and goals.

Questions for Consideration

1. When was the residential school system established? When was it dismantled? What were its goals?

2. What methods did residential schools employ in pursuit of their goals? How did Indigenous children react to and/or resist these methods?

3. Why does Haig-Brown believe it is essential for all Canadians to remember the residential schools? Do you agree? Why or why not?

4. What were the goals of the Department of Indian Affairs' program of studies for residential schools?

5. What are the long-term consequences of the residential school system?

6. Did the Truth and Reconciliation Commission provide an appropriate forum for dealing with the legacies of student-on-student abuse? If so, why? If not, what would be the best way to deal with these legacies?

7. To what extent did non-Indigenous Canadians participate in the Truth and Reconciliation process? Do you think non-Indigenous Canadians see the history of the residential schools as integral to Canada's history as a nation? Why or why not?

8. Has the federal government lived up to the terms of the Truth and Reconciliation Commission?

Further Resources

Books and Articles

Chrisjohn, Roland. *The Circle Game: Shadows and Substance in the Indian Residential School Experience*. Penticton, BC: Theytus Books, 2006.

Churchill, Ward. *Kill the Indian, Save the Man: The Genocidal Impact of American Indian Residential Schools*. San Francisco: City Lights Publishing, 2004.

Henderson, Jennifer and Pauline Wakeham, eds. *Reconciling Canada: Critical Perspective on the Culture of Redress*. Toronto: University of Toronto Press, 2013.

Knockwood, Isabelle. *Out of the Depths: The Experiences of Mi'kmaw Children at the Indian Residential School at Shubenacadie, Nova Scotia*. Lockeport, NS: Roseway Publishing, 1992.

MacLean, Hope. "Ojibwa Participation in Methodist Residential Schools in Upper Canada, 1828–1860," *The Canadian Journal of Native Studies* 25, 1 (2005): 93–137.

Miller, J.R. *Shingawauk's Vision: A History of Native Residential Schools*. Toronto: University of Toronto Press, 1996.

Milloy, John S. *A National Crime: The Canadian Government and the Residential School System, 1879 to 1986*. Winnipeg: University of Manitoba Press, 1999.

Mosby, Ian. "Administering Colonial Science: Nutrition Research and Human Biomedical Experimentation in Aboriginal Communities and Residential Schools, 1942–1952," *Histoire sociale/Social History*, 46, 91 (2013): 145–72.

Niezen, Ronald. *Truth and Indignation: Canada's Truth and Reconciliation Commission on Indian Residential Schools*. Toronto: University of Toronto Press, 2013.

Regan, Paulette. *Unsettling the Settler Within: Indian Residential Schools, Truth Telling, and Reconciliation*. Vancouver: UBC Press, 2011.

Younging, Greg, Jonathan Dewar, and Mike DeGagné, eds. *Response, Responsibility, and Renewal: Canada's Truth and Reconciliation Journey*. Ottawa: Aboriginal Healing Foundation, 2009.

Printed Documents and Reports

Canada. *Royal Commission on Aboriginal Peoples: Residential Schools, Vol. 10*. Ottawa: Queen's Printer, 1996. www.collectionscanada.gc.ca/webarchives/20071124130216/; www.ainc-inac.gc.ca/ch/rcap/sg/sgm10_e.html.

Jack, Agnes, ed. *Behind Closed Doors: Stories from the Kamloops Indian Residential School*, rev. edn. Kamloops: Secwepemc Cultural Education Society, 2006.

Truth and Reconciliation Commission of Canada. *Canada, Aboriginal Peoples, and Residential Schools: They Came for the Children*. Winnipeg: Truth and Reconciliation Commission of Canada, 2011.

Truth and Reconciliation Commission of Canada. *Truth and Reconciliation Commission of Canada: Interim Report*. Winnipeg: Truth and Reconciliation Commission of Canada, 2012.

Truth and Reconciliation Commission of Canada. A *Honouring the Truth, Reconciling for the Future: Summary of the Final Report of the Truth and Reconciliation Commission of Canada*. TRC: June 2015. www.trc.ca/websites/trcinstitution/File/2015/Exec_Summary_2015_06_25_web_o.pdf.

Films

The Fallen Feather: Indian Industrial Residential Schools. DVD. Directed by Randy N. Bezeau. Fallen Feather Productions, 2007.

Muffins for Granny: Exposing the Restlessness of an Ancient Sadness. DVD (Documentary). Directed by Nadia McLaren. Feather Productions, 2007.

Older Than America. DVD (drama). Directed by Georgina Lightning. Tribal Alliance, 2008.

Rabbit-Proof Fence. DVD (drama). Directed by Phillip Noyce. HanWay Films, 2002.

We Were Children. DVD. (documentary). Directed by Tim Wolochatiuk. National Film Board, 2012.

Where the Spirit Lives. Film (drama). Directed by Bruce Pittman. CBC, 1989.

Websites

Lenore Keeshig-Tobias: "Stop Stealing Native Stories"
http://web.uvic.ca/vv/stolo/2015/Tobias.pdf

The Bryce Report
https://archive.org/stream/storyofnationalc00brycuoft/storyofnationalc00brycuoft_djvu.txt

Assembly of First Nations
www.afn.ca/index.php/en/policy-areas/indian-residential-schools-unit

Hidden from History
www.hiddenfromhistory.com

Prime Minister Stephen Harper's apology for the residential school system
www.cbc.ca/news/canada/story/2008/06/11/pm-statement.html

Truth and Reconciliation Commission
www.trc.ca/websites/trcinstitution/index.php?p=3

Where are the Children? Healing the Legacy of the Residential Schools
www.wherearethechildren.ca

Religion, Culture, and the Peoples of the North

Introduction

This chapter focuses on the Inuit and First Nations people living in present-day Northern Canada. The North is often characterized as geographically isolated and forbidding, a myth that is, in part, a product of the fact that non-Indigenous peoples initially expressed little interest in the North. Until the early twentieth century, few outsiders lived in the North except for fur traders and trappers, missionaries, and the North-West Mounted Police (after 1919, the RCMP). As a result, historical research on the North and its peoples typically focuses on one of the following topics: European exploration, the missionary encounter, or the exploitation of natural resources. At the heart of each of these topics lies a fascination with Inuit and First Nations societies in transition. The entry of missionaries into the North and the establishment of permanent missions has been of particular interest. However, most of this literature tends to be one-sided, and written from the missionaries' perspective. These conventional narratives focus on the heroic nature of the men and women who travelled north to convert Indigenous peoples. More recent histories are much more critical of the missionary endeavour, locating it as part of the colonial project; however, the focus of such works continues to be somewhat Eurocentric. In these narratives, Indigenous communities are most often described as timeless and previously unchanged societies whose interactions with Christianity and European society and technology led to cultural decline.

Recent examinations of the missionary encounter offer a more sophisticated analysis of the reactions of Indigenous peoples to these meetings. In the first article, Cornelius H.W. Remie and Jarich Oosten provide a new perspective on missionaries and contact in the North. By examining the formative years of the Catholic mission at Pelly Bay (in present-day Nunavut), the authors suggest a different and more complex interpretation of the role played by missionaries and missions in Inuit society. They propose that the mission served more than a religious function; it fit into the social, cultural, and economic contours of the community in complex ways. Inuit incorporated

Catholicism into their own world views and used the mission itself as a way of accessing goods and services otherwise unavailable to the community during certain periods of the year. Indigenous peoples did not indiscriminately adopt Christianity; they "selectively adapted to or rejected features" of it in accordance with their own needs, desires, and interests.

The period after the Second World War witnessed renewed public and private interest in the North; the federal government in particular came to covet the region's natural resources and see them as a potential source of wealth and prosperity. To consolidate its presence and sovereignty the government initiated a series of housing programs to "modernize" the North: the Eskimo Housing Loan Program, the Canada Mortgage and Housing Corporation (CMHC), and the National Housing Act (NHA). In the second article Robert Robson outlines how western-style houses were built without due care given to the needs of their inhabitants. For the Inuit, this meant overcrowded, unaffordable, and short-term housing conditions. Today, the consequences of these ill-conceived and paternalistic housing programs are readily apparent. Currently, almost 50 per cent of Inuit live in overcrowded homes.[1] Good housing is one of the major determinants of health and well-being. Poor and overcrowded housing leads to higher incidences of colds and influenza, respiratory illnesses, tuberculosis, and skin problems, as well as an increased risk for chronic stress and depression. Instead of helping local populations to obtain appropriate housing, the federal government, as Robson illustrates, served its own needs and has left Inuit to deal with the failures of these programs.

Chapter Objectives

At the end of this chapter, you should be able to

- understand how and why Indigenous peoples of the North adopted and used western religion, customs, culture, and technologies;
- identify ways in which Inuit modified Christianity to suit their own spiritual and religious needs;
- understand and explain why federal and territorial public housing initiatives largely failed in the Northwest Territories; and
- see how the failure to build adequate housing in the Northwest Territories was connected to the federal government's goals and priorities, especially its "Northern Initiative."

Note

1. "Nunavik Housing Shortage a 'Crisis': Inuit," *CBC News*, 18 March 2010 www.cbc.ca/news/ canada/montreal/nunavik-housing-shortage-a-crisis-inuit-1.937118, accessed 19 May 2015.

Secondary Source

The Birth of a Catholic Inuit Community: The Transition to Christianity in Pelly Bay, NU, 1935–50

Cornelius H.W. Remie and Jarich Oosten

In this article, we will examine the formative years of the Catholic mission post in Pelly Bay. The paper is based on literary and archival sources and on interviews with one of the Oblate missionaries who spent 27 years in Pelly Bay, Father Franz Van de Velde. With the exception of some brief autobiographical notes, there are no written sources in Inuktitut for the period under scrutiny. The Inuit views of Christianization we discuss are there-fore largely inferred from *Qallunaat* (non-Inuit) data and research carried out elsewhere in Nunavut. In the next few years, we hope to supplement these data with interviews with older informants from Pelly Bay. Such interviews are indispensable to obtaining a more balanced understanding of the transition to Christianity in Pelly Bay.

The *Codex Historicus* of the Pelly Bay mission[1] is an important source for this paper. It was written by the resident missionaries and gives an account of the daily events at the mission post. But the *Codex* is by no means a private diary. We hear little about the private thoughts and the feelings of the missionaries or their views of the Inuit. Neither is it an ethnographic account. We find hardly any references to conver-sations with Inuit or descriptions of events in the Inuit camps themselves.

Another important source for our paper is the oral comments on the *Codex* by Father Van de Velde, recorded in 1982 by the first author. These comments provide a wealth of detailed explanations of the entries in the *Codex* of Pelly Bay and of the culture of the Nattilingmiut[2] in general.

Oblate Plans and Inuit Strategies

The foundations of [Catholic] missionary expansion [in the far north] were laid by Father Arsène Turquetil, who established the first Oblate mission in Chesterfield Inlet in 1912. The northern move by the Oblate Fathers was a reaction to the expansion of Anglican missionary activities to the Keewatin district.[3]

The first Inuit were converted and baptized in 1917. The Oblates consolidated their position at Chesterfield Inlet and only expanded their missionary activities in the late 1920s, when Anglican pressure on the Keewatin increased. Their strategy aimed at ensuring control of the land before the Anglicans arrived.[4] In only a little over 10 years, 6 new mission posts were established, [including,] in 1933 and 1935, the posts of Repulse Bay and Pelly Bay.

The Repulse Bay mission soon developed into an important logistic centre for the northern missions of the Hudson Bay vicariate. In the first two years of its exist-ence, the Pelly Bay mission was a dependency of Repulse Bay. On 23 August 1937, on the occasion of the vicarial synod held in Chesterfield Inlet, it was recognized as an independent mission. On that same occasion, Father Franz Van de Velde, a newly arrived Flemish Oblate, was appointed socius of [the resident missionary,] Father Henry and joined him in 1938.[5]

The decision to open a mission post at Pelly Bay was taken after a request by converted Pelly Bay people who were living temporarily in the Aivilik [Repulse Bay] area. They belonged to a substantial group of Nattilingmiut who had migrated south at the end of the nineteenth or the beginning of the twentieth century.[6] This migration of about 40 per cent of the total Nattilik population had far-reaching effects. It boosted the female infanticide ratio and manifested latent factionalism.[7] Such factionalism was quite marked among immigrants from the eastern branch of the Nattilingmiut who had their traditional hunting grounds around Arviligjuaq (Pelly Bay). Within this community existed two groups, the so-called Kukigarmiut, and the Irmalingmiut, named after the protagonists of a feud that probably dates back as far as the end of the eighteenth century.[8]

Among the 36 persons baptized prior to the founding of the Pelly Bay mission, only 6 were Irmalingmiut, whereas 26 were of Kukigaq extraction.[9] Apparently, Kukigaq leaders realized the potential benefit of being Catholic earlier than their Irmalik counterparts and made the tactical move to side with the missionaries. This interpretation of the differential rates of baptisms prior to 1935 is further substantiated by the behaviour of Qaqsuvik, the leader of the Kukigarmiut. Not only did he request a missionary to come and live with them, but he also attempted to influence where the missionary would live. Father Henry noted in the *Codex*:

> Sudden departure of K'arsuvik for Igluriarjuk. Despite their beseeching, I do not want to follow them. I have found an ideal spot to settle in front of the little hill between the river and the sea. I have decided to build a winter house of stone and clay here. Against the approval of my Eskimos who encourage me to settle down farther North.[10]

The reasons for his decision are clear: Father Henry wanted to be independent, whereas his Inuit guides preferred him to go with them. We do not know how Qaqsuvik and the other members of the Kukigaq faction took his decision. A comment by Father Van de Velde suggests that it took them quite a while to accept the independent position of the mission:

> Father Henry wanted to be independent in order to be the priest of all and not just the priest of one group. The Father had to be handy, tactful and sometimes firm to express his independence [. . .]. It is only after my arrival in 1938 that the Father was able to make them finally understand that the Mission was there for all.[11]

Thus the Oblate missionaries were not the only ones planning their moves; Inuit also had their own strategies. Although these plans and strategies sometimes conflicted, they often reinforced each other: when the request for a resident missionary in Pelly Bay was made, it was quickly granted because it fitted into the general Oblate strategy of occupying what they considered to be a religious *terra nullius*.

The Founding of the Pelly Bay Mission

In 1934, Father Henry expressed the wish to found a mission at Pelly Bay. Father Clabaut [at Repulse Bay] was only prepared to let him go if a family invited him for instruction, a family that would supply him with the seal blubber for the lamp which was needed to survive. Once these conditions were met, Father Henry set out on his journey on 26 April 1935. He travelled with the family of Qaqsuvik, the oldest Christian family at Pelly Bay.[12] [Jean Philippe, OMI,] records a brief dialogue between the old Qaqsuvik and the missionary. One evening Qaqsuvik asked him, "Why are you going to Arviligjuaq (Pelly Bay)?" The missionary answered, "To tell you about the good God, whom you do not know. . . ." The old man answered, "You will often be hungry at Ar-vi-lee-goo-ar."[13]

This brief dialogue reflects the encounter of two worlds: the ambitions of the missionary and the concerns of the Inuit. Both were concerned with each other's welfare: the missionary with the spiritual welfare of the Inuit, the old Inuk with the well-being of the foreign missionary who did not know the land.

After a difficult journey by dog sled, Father Henry arrived at the mouth of the Kuugaarjuk River on 1 June. Almost immediately Father Henry started building a stone house annex chapel, a project that would take several months to complete. In the meantime he had to hunt and fish for his own subsistence. Food was a continuous problem.[14]

By the end of November, Inuit [had] built an igloo for him, as living in the stone house was impossible because of the cold. Qaqsuvik supplied him with oil for the lamp during the winter.[15] Weeks of preparations followed for baptisms that would take place at Christmas when most inhabitants of the area would gather at the mission. At the first Christmas celebration in Pelly Bay, 40 Nattilingmiut attended the festivities.[16] A few days later they departed for their seal hunting camps on the sea ice of Pelly Bay.

In January, February, and March 1936, Father Henry occasionally visited the Inuit in these camps and instructed his catechumens, heard confessions, celebrated Mass, and distributed Communion. In March, preparations for Easter started. At Easter, Inuit from all over Pelly Bay would gather at Kuugaarjuk, as at Christmas. After that, some Inuit would travel to the Hudson's Bay Company (HBC) store in Repulse Bay to trade; others would trade at Gjoa Haven on King William Island, whereas those who stayed behind would engage in various hunting activities. In June and July 1936 Father Henry was engaged in further building activities and, after break-up, in netting seals and fish in the Kuugaarjuk River.

The presence of a resident missionary in Pelly Bay did have considerable demographic effects. In November 1935, the total population of Pelly Bay consisted of only 54 individuals. A year later their number had risen to 83[17] and in February 1937 there were 89 people.[18] In subsequent years this number would further expand until it reached an average of about 125 in the early 1950s.[19]

The Growth of the Mission

In the summer of 1937, the Hudson's Bay Company had established a post at Fort Ross on the south end of Somerset Island.[20] To counter possible Anglican influence, Father Henry visited the Inuit at Iktuaqturvik and Ikpik (Thom Bay) and quickly instructed and baptized a sick Inuk whom he had met earlier in Pelly Bay.[21]

He was barely back in Kuugaarjuk when his socius, Father Van de Velde, arrived. Father Henry expressed his joy at having a fellow missionary after almost four years of solitude.[22] Father Van de Velde was a young Flemish missionary and his energy and skills proved a great help to Father Henry at the mission. Together they started new building activities and took turns visiting Inuit camps to baptize older catechumens and newborn children. Over the next 12 years, Father Henry and Father Van de Velde worked together to develop the mission.

Social and Economic Role of the Mission

Economic Functions

From its very beginning the Pelly Bay mission played an important part in local economics. Since Pelly Bay was landlocked and not accessible by boat, the Roman Catholic mission depended upon bulk freighting by dog sled for its own logistics. Freighting was done on a voluntary basis by Inuit, who often combined the trip with some trading of their own. The compensation for such freighting trips varied over the years and was regularly adapted to price standards. In 1950, Pelly Bay Inuit received $60 for a round trip to Repulse Bay to bring in 363 kilograms of freight.[23] At that time, this was sufficient to buy 24 average-sized seals for dog food, 181 kilograms of caribou meat, or 4 male dogs.[24] In the early years of the mission, Inuit were also compensated for supplying the mission with country food (seals and fish), for assisting in construction work, and for acting as guides during the missionaries' visits to Inuit camps in the area.

Since its foundation, the Pelly Bay mission had operated a small mission store. Through that store, Inuit could obtain scarce commodities when the HBC stores at Repulse Bay and Gjoa Haven were inaccessible as a result of limited mobility, from June till the end of October. Tea, tobacco, flour, sugar, sewing materials, and ammunition were sold at the mission store. Another important product was caribou skins for winter clothing. At the time the Roman Catholic mission was established, caribou were scarce at Pelly Bay. They had disappeared from Simpson Peninsula and could only be hunted far to the south and southwest. To alleviate the problem of deficient winter clothing, the mission bought caribou skins by the hundreds and sold them locally.[25]

The mission also bought products from the Inuit such as seals for dog food, fish, and pelts of arctic foxes. Trapping was a marginal activity in Pelly Bay, and the number of fox pelts bought by the Pelly Bay mission never exceeded 200 in any of the years under review in this paper. The pelts were transported south and sold to the HBC at Repulse Bay or sent to Churchill, where the economic affairs of the vicariate were handled.[26]

The mission store had considerable advantages for the Pelly Bay Inuit. Pricing was fair and in tune with Repulse Bay prices, and basic commodities were accessible during periods of the year when they would otherwise have been out of reach. But the mission store had some disadvantages too. These did not stem from the store itself, but from the way its fiercest competitor, the Hudson's Bay Company, perceived it. When the HBC trading post at Fort Ross was closed and moved to Spence Bay in 1949, the new post manager did everything to discourage the Nattilingmiut from trading at the mission. According to Van de Velde, when Catholics from Pelly Bay came to trade at Spence Bay, they were treated condescendingly and their furs were systematically depreciated. Counter slips of their purchases were withheld so that they had no way of complaining when items they had ordered and paid for were missing when they collected their goods at the post.[27] The manager even called in the RCMP to get the Pelly Bay mission store closed. Father Van de Velde protested vigorously against what he considered to be an injustice. The final result of his protests was that the Pelly Bay mission store received a formal outpost licence in 1952.

Taking Care of the Sick

Until the early 1950s the Oblate mission at Pelly Bay was the only *Qallunaaq* organization that did take care of the sick on a daily basis. The missionaries had received some elementary training in dealing with illnesses; they were equipped with a medical handbook and had some basic medicines at their disposal.[28] When the Oblate mission started using a radio in December 1944,[29] the [missionaries] could contact the doctor at the mission hospital at Chesterfield Inlet for further advice. If necessary, the missionaries were entitled to send patients to the mission hospital or, at the end of the 1940s when planes made their appearance on the northern scene, to call upon the RCMP or the Hudson's Bay Company to arrange for a medical evacuation.

Freighting to Repulse Bay, Gjoa Haven, and Spence Bay increasingly led to out breaks of small epidemics of flu, as did contact with outside parties that visited the Pelly Bay mission by plane in the 1940s. As communication with the outside world intensified, more epidemics spread. Some were of an increasingly aggressive nature such as the 1949 polio epidemic in the Central Arctic that claimed the lives of many Inuit. In Pelly Bay, only one case occurred, but that same year an influenza epidemic claimed the lives of five victims.[30] In 1953 and 1954 eight patients were evacuated because of tuberculosis and two because of tuberculosis of the dorsal spine.[31]

Religious Life

Religious Feasts and the Celebration of Sunday

The mission post in Pelly Bay immediately became a religious centre in the area as Inuit began to convene at the mission to celebrate the Christian holy days, notably Christmas and Easter. At the Christmas celebrations in 1935, 40 people were present and in 1936, Christmas was celebrated in grand style.[32] A big igloo was built. Sixty people were present. At eight o'clock the vigil started. Every hour, songs were chanted and exhortations made. Games were played. At eleven o'clock the *Veni Creator* was sung, and at midnight six adults were baptized. A mass was celebrated followed by grace and a meal. At 11 in the morning, another mass was celebrated, followed by a copious meal of fish, caribou, and biscuits. After four o'clock various competitions were organized.[33]

The combination of Christian rituals, competitive games, and great meals was characteristic of Inuit Christmas celebrations in northeast Canada and proved very successful in Pelly Bay. In the 1940s, the number of participants gradually increased and at the end of the decade more than 100 people might have be present. In 1949 the Christmas meal required 60 fish, 25 gallons of caribou meat and boiled rice, tea, and five biscuits for each participant. Games such as *nugluktaq* (thrusting a stick through a small hoop) and archery were practised. In many respects Christmas seems to have replaced the traditional Inuit winter feasts, of which drum dances were an essential element.[34]

The celebrations of Easter were less well attended [and] we do not find many references to other feasts. All Saints did not appear to be an important holiday. [On] 1 November 1950, the *Codex* states: "Poor Sunday of All Saints. It is as if it were an ordinary day." For Epiphany it seems to have been the same: 6 January 1941, "Epiphany. Seven people present at Holy Mass." Efforts by the missionaries to turn Assumption (15 August) and Immaculate Conception (8 December) into feast days also do not seem to have been successful.[35]

Like anywhere else in the Catholic world, Inuit were expected not to work on Sunday.[36] However, hunting often occurred.[37] In practice, the Roman Catholics were less strict about hunting and travelling on Sundays than the Anglicans. Thus Father Henry arrived at the mission on Sunday, 25 November 1939.

Sacraments

Baptism had a central place in the program of the Oblates in the Hudson Bay vicariate. Through baptism a person was saved, and he or she became a new being, expressed in the adoption of a new name. The name already had a central place in pre-Christian Inuit cosmology as it was assumed that a deceased namesake lived on in persons named after him or her. The Inuit continued this practice and retained their Inuit names beside their Christian names, combining shared identities with their deceased namesakes with the new Christian identity.

According to Catholic custom, newborn children were preferably baptized immediately after birth. Fathers Henry and Van de Velde took great pains to baptize infants once they learned about their birth. Concern about the possibility that infants might be killed made them act quickly.[38] A child whose life was in danger could be baptized without instruction. It had to be baptized, even if the parents were opposed.[39]

According to Catholic belief, baptized children who died became little angels watching and protecting people. We find at least five references in the *Codex* that express this idea.[40] It may have been picked up easily by the Inuit who strongly believed in the efficacy of protective spirits.

To ensure that newborn children could become little guardian angels, the missionaries taught Inuit how to baptize. Sometimes an invalid baptism occurred:

> The wife of Paul has delivered a premature boy of seven months, alive, at nine in the evening. Paul has baptized him. The child died this morning at ten. Was the baptism performed well? He has said: "Kobverivagit Ernernerub Anernealub atingni." It is a pity.[41]

The fact that Paul baptized the child in the name of the Son and the Holy Spirit but not of the Father, is decisive: the child is lost.

This strict adherence to ritual formulas probably appealed to the Inuit who were well aware of the power of magic words. Missionaries and Inuit shared a strong belief in the miraculous power of prayer. In a number of [*Codex*] entries this power is emphasized as a means of healing.[42] Inuit used prayer in much the same way, as can be inferred from the following entry in the *Codex*: "Little Jacques was born in the autumn on the river. Konwaksiut almost lost her life in bringing him into the world. Only the incessant prayers of the Inuit miraculously saved her."[43]

Individual confession, another important aspect of the Catholic dogma, did not present a major problem for Inuit in the transition to Christianity. Father Van de Velde argued that Inuit were accustomed to making public confessions during shamanic séances:

> During the general sorcery séances, the sorcerer usually demanded a general confession from all those present. The Eskimos accused themselves of their most hidden failures and omissions as well as of the most intimate faults of which they were guilty. These self-accusations were public, made in the presence of the entire community young and old alike. . . .[44]

Confession in the Catholic Church is not a public affair. This confidential nature of the confession must have implied a great change in religious life. On the one hand, shamanism became a tradition that was practised in secrecy; on the other hand, confession itself became a confidential matter thus changing the traditions of sharing knowledge.

In contrast to confession, Communion was a public affair. It is general practice in the Catholic Church for young children to receive their first Communion when they reach the age of reason (i.e., when they are about seven years of age). Pelly Bay was no exception. In the *Codex* we find seven entries referring to First Communion and in all cases it concerned the First Communion of young children.[45] Adults received their first Communion at the time of their baptism.

As a rule a bishop administered confirmation. In the case of Pelly Bay, problems of communication with the outside world sometimes called for another solution. Thus, in 1937, Mgr Turquetil sent Father Clabaut by dog sled to Pelly Bay to confirm 42 Christians. On later occasions, in March 1944, in April 1949, and in May 1950, Bishop Turquetil's successor, Mgr Lacroix, came by plane to Pelly Bay to administer confirmation. The *Codex* mentions only one case in which the missionary confirmed a dying child. This case may have contributed to the perception that confirmation was a *tuqunaqsiuti*, a "means that makes one die." [Cornelius] Remie refers to two other cases in which confirmation was seen this way.[46] Van de Velde confirmed that this Inuit view of the sacrament existed.[47]

[When] people died in the vicinity of the mission, they were buried at the nearby cemetery. This sometimes gave rise to avoidance behaviour since Inuit believed that the spirits of the dead would stay around and could cause harm and spread sickness. The frequent occurrence of small or greater epidemics at the mission post was attributed to the spirits of the dead.[48]

Control of Moral Attitudes and Conduct

As religious leaders, missionaries had to see that their parishioners persevered in their conviction and observed the moral standards set by the Catholic faith. The missionary strategy was to never ridicule Native customs. Instead, according to Turquetil, missionaries should try to point out to Inuit in a benign and kind-hearted way what their shortcomings were and how these could be mended.[49]

The purpose of control of moral attitudes and conduct was to keep the flock religiously on track and prevent them from abandoning the Church. But such control, and in particular reprimand, was not always appreciated by the Inuit, as is clear in the case of Iksivalitaq, the son of the famous shaman Alakkannuaq. Iksivalitaq, a shaman who wore the *kigluraq*, a little tattoo between the eyebrows that signified that he had slain a *tupilaq* (evil spirit), constantly challenged the religious authority of Father Henry. Finally, he renounced the Catholic faith by saying that he did not want to be reprimanded by [the missionaries].[50]

Missionary attempts to control the moral attitudes and conduct of their parishioners did not mean that Inuit easily gave up their customs and beliefs. Although we find very few references to religious continuity in the first volume of the *Codex*, we do learn that some Inuit still practised *sakkajuq*[51] and *tuumgijuq*,[52] used amulets,[53] [and] believed that illness was caused by evil spirits.[54] Testimonies by Elders such as Aupilaarjuk from Rankin Inlet and Victor Tungilik from Naujaat, both of Nattilik origin, reflect Inuit perspectives on the religious changes that occurred. Aupilaarjuk remembers the void created by the rejection of traditional beliefs and customs by the missionaries:

> . . . The Catholic priest said that our Inuit ways were evil, and only the ways of God, Jesus and Mary were good. If he had told us that we had to follow the *maligait* [dicta] of Jesus, then I would have understood. We were only told to abandon our Inuit *maligait*, but they did not give us anything to replace them. For example, I would no longer *anijaaq*, go out early in the morning. I felt like I was in a void. I no longer wanted to follow what my parents had taught me. If I did something wrong or something shameful, I did not need to tell anyone about it. I did whatever I wanted. I did not tell anyone if I did something wrong. Before that, we had *angakkuit* [plural of shaman] who could see if we had done something wrong. . . .[55]

The conversion to Christianity often implied a deprivation of cultural traditions that is still resented by Elders. Aupilaarjuk observed:

> I had a lot of *aarnguat* [amulets]. They were taken away by the Catholic missionaries when we were baptized. Now we see a lot of *Qallunaat* in important positions wearing necklaces. The *Qallunaat* took them away because they thought they were evil, but they were not evil. Through the help of the *aarnguat* and through the protection provided by my mother, I have been able to live a long life.[56]

Conflicts between Inuit traditions and the new religions were hard to solve for individual Inuit. Victor Tungilik from Naujaat practised as a shaman for several years. In his youth his parents instructed him not to become an *angakkuq*:

> When my parents started following the Anglican faith, they told me that I was going to be following the Catholic religion. I was told that when they accepted religion. They

told me to let go of the ways of the *angakkuq*, because the ways of the *angakkuq* were not compatible with religion. . . .[57]

During his youth, Tungilik heard a sermon about Judgment Day in Igluligaarjuk that influenced his decision to let go of shamanism:

> If I continued to be an *angakkuq*, I would end up in hell in the great fire. Because I didn't want this to happen I let my *tuurngait* [helping spirits] go [. . .]. When my two in-laws died I regretted having let my *tuurngait* go. Although I knew that I might not have been able to heal them, I still thought that maybe I should have hung on to my *tuurngait* a little longer and not sent them away right away. . . .[58]

Such testimonies are not preserved in the *Codex Historicus*. However, a striking example of cultural continuity, related in the *Codex* entries of 8–14 September 1944, is the death of old Alakkannuaq, the famous shaman. Alakkannuaq was baptized on 2 February 1937 and learned syllabics in order to read the Catholic prayer books. Yet, he committed suicide with the help of two of his sons in accordance with traditional Inuit customs and beliefs. Father Henry wrote a brief account:

> . . . Ovide Allakatnuar, aged 70, suffered a stroke, thus losing the power of speech and part of the use of his limbs. However, his mental capacities stayed intact. . . . Because the camp had to break up and move inland for the caribou hunt, and because the old Allakatnuar had become invalid and an obstacle to break up, Niptayok and Kayaitok decided to make an end to the life of their father, believing that by doing so they would respond to the wishes of their old father. The two sons, aged 50 and 40, prepared a gallows equipped with a rope with a noose outside the tent. Then they brought the sick man there. In a sitting position, he put his head through the noose and let himself fall to strangle himself. . . .[59]

When Father Henry learned about Alakkannuaq's death, he exclaimed, "But what kind of Christians are we raising?" In a conversation with the first author in the summer of 2001, [Father Van de Velde] emphasized that from an Inuit point of view, Alakkannuaq had sacrificed himself. He wanted to end his days so that the younger generation could move inland to hunt caribou and survive: "His deed was in fact an altruistic one. Therefore, we should not judge too harshly." And pointing his finger to heaven, he added, "You will be surprised whom you will see up there!"

Conclusions

The Oblate fathers attempted to secure the Central Arctic for the Catholic Church and to block the westward expansion of Anglicanism. In doing so they appear to have been much more concerned with the containment of Anglicanism than with the survival of paganism. Whereas preventing the former was seen as an urgent necessity, the replacement of the latter by Catholicism was perceived as a long-term process.

The way the transition to Christianity in Pelly Bay has usually been described fails to appreciate the role of Inuit in this process. A number of Nattilingmiut had already been baptized before the opening of the mission post at Pelly Bay in 1935. These converted Inuit asked for a missionary to come and live with them. The request fitted well into the Hudson Bay vicariate's policies and was granted. The Oblates were not aware that the vast majority of early converts belonged to one of the two major factions of the Pelly Bay community, the Kukigarmiut. The latter apparently had their own agenda and tried to use the missionaries' presence to strengthen their own position. But [Father Henry] took an independent stance, chose his own location for the mission post, and thereby laid the foundation for what was to become the permanent settlement of Pelly Bay in the late 1960s.

Once the Pelly Bay mission was established, the Oblate missionaries quickly assumed tasks that transcended the boundaries of their religious occupations. In the economic field they incorporated Inuit in the mission post's logistics, introducing paid labour and initiating the production of carvings to be sold on foreign markets. The small mission store facilitated access to *Qallunaaq* products.

The missionaries also assumed responsibility for the treatment of the sick. In the absence of good and quick means of communication with the outside world, health care had to remain elementary. Outside assistance only arrived around 1950.

The missionaries gave the religious guidance Inuit had requested. They served the religious community, expanded it in a concerted effort, and wherever possible established religious routines. As in most Inuit communities, Christmas became the most important religious feast, in many respects replacing the old traditions of the Inuit winter feasts. In the delivery of sacraments, the Oblate fathers adhered to strict norms of ritual correctness, a regime that may well have appealed to the Inuit, who were accustomed to the importance of strictly observing ritual rules.

Like shamans, missionaries assumed leadership roles in many fields. Yet, they were often not aware to what extent Inuit continued their traditional practices. Neither were they aware of the extent to which Inuit integrated these practices into Catholicism, thus developing a form of religiosity that responded to their own existential and cultural needs. The missionary perspectives still have to be complemented by the recollections of Inuit Elders participating in the process of transition to Catholicism. Only the Pelly Bay Elders can tell us why and how they decided to make the transition to Christianity.

Notes

1. *Codex Historicus* (hereafter *Codex*), Mission Pelly Bay, I, 26 April 1935–31 Dec. 1950, (manuscript).

2. In this article, we use the term *Nattilingmiut* to refer to the group classified by Knud Rasmussen as the Netsilik Eskimos. See Knud Rasmussen, *The Netsilik Eskimos. Social Life and Spiritual Culture*, Copenhagen, Report of the Fifth Thule Expedition, 1921–24, 8, 1 (1931).

3. Esquisse synthétique sur la Baie d'Hudson, Document LCB3.C56Rl, Archives Deschâtelets, Ottawa (typescript), 4–5.

4. Ibid., 9.

5. *Codex*, Aug. 1937. A socius was an associate.

6. See Susan Rowley, "Population Movements in the Canadian Arctic," *Études/Inuit/Studies* 9, 1 (1985): 3–21.

7. See Cornelius H.W. Remie, "Culture change and religious continuity among the Arviligjuarmiut of Pelly Bay, NWT, 1935–1963," *Études/Inuit/ Studies* 7, 2 (1983): 53–77; and Cornelius H.W. Remie, "Towards a new perspective on Netjilik Inuit female infanticide," *Études/Inuit/Studies* 9, 1 (1985): 67–75.

8. See Guy Mary-Rousselière, "The Grave of Kukigaq," *Eskimo* 57 (1960): 18–22; Cornelius H.W. Remie, "Ermalik and Kukigak: Continuity and Discontinuity in Pelly Bay, Northwest Territories, Canada," in C. Buijs, ed., *Continuity and Discontinuity in Arctic Cultures: Essays in Honour of Gerti Nooter, Curator at the National Museum of Ethnology, 1970–1990* (Leiden, The Netherlands: Centre of Non-Western Studies, 1993), 78–90; Geert van den Steenhoven, *Leadership and Law among the Eskimos of the Keewatin District, Northwest Territories* (Rijswijk: Excelsior, 1962).

9. Franz Van de Velde, Statistiques objectives sur la population Netjilique, Vols. I–IV, Hall Beach, NT, 1979, 1980, 1981, 1984 (typescripts).

10. *Codex*, 6 Mar. 1935.

11. Van de Velde, Statistiques objectives, 1979, 69.

12. *Codex*, 2 Feb. 1937.

13. Jean Philippe, OMI, "Realizing a dream," *Eskimo* (May 1946), 6.

14. See *Codex*, 2 Sept. 1935.

15. *Codex*, 27 Jan. 1936.

16. *Codex*, 27 Dec. 1935.

17. *Codex*, 7 Nov. 1936.

18. *Codex*, 4 Feb. 1937.

19. See Franz Van de Velde, O.M.I. Trinette S. Constandse-Westermann, Cornelius H.W. Remie, and Raymond R. Newell, "One hundred and fifteen years of Arviligjuarmiut Demography, Central Canadian Arctic," *Arctic Anthropology* 30, 2 (1993): 12.

20. See Ronne Heming, ed., *NWT Data Book 1986–87: A Complete Information Guide to the Northwest Territories and its Communities* (Yellowknife: Outcrop, 1986), 210.

21. *Codex*, 13 Feb. 1938.

22. *Codex*, 23 Apr. 1938.

23. See Simon et Fabien, Cie de transport pour R.B. Document LCB330.C56R4, Archives Deschâtelets, Ottawa (manuscript).

24. See R.C. Mission Pelly Bay, N.W.T., Invoice to R.C.M. Police, G Division, Ottawa, Ont., Document LCB321.C56R7, Archives Deschâtelets, Ottawa (typescript).

25. Van de Velde, Comments on the *Codex Historicus*, Part 2.

26. Ibid.

27. Ibid.

28. Ibid., Part 1.

29. *Codex*, 16 Dec. 1944.

30. See Van de Velde et al., "One hundred and fifteen years of Arviligjuarmiut," 13.

31. Ibid., 5.

32. Franz Van de Velde, OMI, Comment la traite se faisait-elle dans le temps? Miscellaneous notes compiled by Father Franz Van de Velde, Hall Beach, N.W.T., Volume A: 178–80, 1982 (typescript).

33. *Codex*, 25 Dec. 1936.

34. In the *Codex*, we found two entries where drum dances are mentioned as part of the Christmas celebrations: 26 déc. 1930, 25 Dec. 1940.

35. *Codex*, 15 août 1940, 15 août 1944, 15 Aug. 1950, 8 Dec. 1941.

36. The Inuktitut name for Sunday is *sanattaili*, i.e., day on which manual work is forbidden. See Lucien Schneider, O.M.I, *Ulirnaisigutiit: An Inuktitut-English Dictionary of Northern Quebec, Labrador and Eastern Arctic Dialects (with an English-Inuktitut Index)* (Québec: Les Presses de l'Université Laval, 1985), 339.

37. *Codex*, 27 sept. 1941 and 27 juin 1948; Van de Velde, Comments on the *Codex Historicus*, Part 2.

38. Van de Velde, Comments on the *Codex Historicus*, Part 2. It has been suggested that female infanticide quickly disappeared under the influence of the Pelly Bay mission; Asen Balicki, "The Netsilik Inuit Today," *Études/Inuit/Studies* 2,1 (1978): 113.

39. In volume 1 of the *Codex* of Pelly Bay, we find one entry by Father Henry that refers to such a case: 2 June 1948.

40. *Codex*, 10 Feb. 1942; 11 Dec. 1946; 25 Feb. 1947; 1 juil. 1948; 9 Dec. 1949.

41. *Codex*, 10 Feb. 1946.

42. See *Codex*, 4 June 1935; 30 Oct.1936.

43. *Codex*, 18 Jan. 1938.

44. Franz Van de Velde, OMI, "Religion and Morals among the Pelly Bay Eskimos," *Eskimo* 39 (1956): 8.

45. *Codex*, 4 Jan. 1937; 12 Aug. 1945; 9 Sept. 1945; 8 Dec. 1945; 23 Mar. 1946; 18 Aug. 1946; and 12 Jul. 1947.

46. Remie, "Culture Change and Religious Continuity," 68.

47. Van de Velde, Comments on the *Codex Historicus*, Part 2.

48. Remie, "Culture change and religious continuity," 68.

49. Turquetil, Textes des résolutions, 22–3.

50. Franz Van de Velde, OMI, Statistiques objectives sur la population Netjilique, Vol. III, 241; Van de Velde, Comments on the *Codex Historicus*, Part 2.

51. *Sakkajuq* means "performs witchcraft over a sick person," See Lucien Schneider, OMI, *Dictionnaire esquimau-français du parler de l'Ungava et contrées limitrophes* (Québec: Les Presses de l'Université Laval, 1970), 308.

52. *Tuumgijuq* means "invokes the (protective) spirits." See ibid., 370.
53. *Codex*, 9 Aug. 1949.
54. *Codex*, 19 Jan. 1940.
55. Jarich Oosten, Frédéric Laugrand, and Wim Rasing, eds, *Perspectives on Traditional Law: Interviewing Inuit Elders*, Vol. 2 (Iqaluit, Nunavut Arctic College, 1999), 22–3.
56. Ibid., 29.
57. Jarich Oosten and Frédéric Laugrand, eds, *The Transition to Christianity: Inuit Perspectives on the 20th Century*, Vol. 1 (Iqaluit: Nunavut Arctic College), 63.
58. Ibid., 111.
59. Notes sur le suicide d'Allakatnuar, Document HEF3244.F83D.6, Archives Deschâtelets, Ottawa (undated manuscript).

Primary Document

Excerpt from Codex Historicus, 25 December 1940[1]

The missionaries at Pelly Bay kept a journal detailing the activities at the mission. The following is an excerpt describing the Christmas celebrations in 1940.

94
1940

21 – Arrival of Niptayok with his entire family for Christmas. Yesterday evening, return of Julien, Zacharie, Bernard and Dominique with a large catch of fish. Quiet time. Construction of 2 naves at the main igloo of K'agorangoar: Julien and Zacharie.

22 – Sunday, low mass at 8 o'clock and high mass at 10 in the house.

23 – 38 C below (A; very cold, very little wind; construction of porches on the 3 naves, magnificent view. Dimensions of "naterk": 6 m 2 (about 18 feet) from the entrance i.e., from the "kattar" to the bed of K'agortangoar, and 7 m (21 feet) wide i.e., from Julien's bed to Zacharie's. The tower's peak is definitely 15 feet from the ground (4 m). Today, arrival of Anemilik, Adgonerk, Paul, K'avik, Papik: 5 initiates.

24 – Mass with the Esk. under the new dome; 6 new initiates present: Padlak, K'épigayok, Taleriktok, Charley, Joani, Kokowak. In total, 16 initiates participating in Christmas celebrations; 48 in attendance, 10 absences due to lack of warm clothes.

The evening, presided over by R. Father VdV [Father Van de Velde]. Opening at 81-.. [SIC]; the evening took place in the following order: speech; surprises; distribution of the party prizes; some entertainment . . . the chair game, rifle shooting; the candy rain, etc. etc. At 6 o'clock, there was singing, the rosary and a sermon by Father Henri. At midnight, Father Henri sang high mass followed by 2 other masses; finally, Christmas Eve dinner of oatmeal and brioches, cacao.

25 – mass at 11 o'clock by Father VdV who had already celebrated two masses at the house; at about 2 o'clock, lunch: fish and a bouillabaisse of caribou, rice and peas; self-serve brioches and tea. Various games followed: rifle-shooting, archery. Dancing to drums.

26 – Big gun shooting after the St. Etienne high mass; sack race; candy rain. Tug of war: 5 on each side; imitation games, etc.

27 – During the Christmas celebrations, it was extremely cold dropping to 39.1 C below zero.

Note

1. This entry was translated by Geoff Read.

Secondary Source

Housing in the Northwest Territories: The Postwar Vision

Robert Robson

The traditional pattern of community and community development in the Northwest Territories (NWT) was dictated by the immediate needs of the local population. The traditional community was a flexible response to the community needs of the resident population: it reflected the culture and heritage of the residents as well as the wide-ranging variations in the local economy, the changing seasonal and/or climatic conditions of the northern community, and even the ecological balance of the northern ecosystem. Sometimes seasonal, sometimes temporary, and sometimes permanent, northern settlements have followed patterns of growth and decline. These patterns, however, dramatically changed in the post–Second World War era when community and community development became an integral part of the government's newly defined northern vision.[1]

The northern vision was undertaken for many reasons: to capitalize on the resource potential of the Canadian north, to address the sovereignty issues of the postwar era, to rationalize northern administration, to modernize northern infrastructure, and, perhaps most pointedly, to reinforce the metropolitan relationship typical of the north–south experience. Under the rubric of the northern vision, northern development was a government-contrived expansionary program of resource development schemes, road-building projects, military defence operations, and government services, including a variety of community development and redevelopment programs. This initiative not only facilitated growth and expansion, it also provided for an increasingly visible government presence in the Canadian north.

It was at the community level that the effect of the northern initiative was most obvious.[2] As there was little or no opportunity for northern residents to participate in the planning process, the community initiative was a government-orchestrated affair that reflected its agenda of expansion. The end results were prefabricated dwelling units, wide winding streets, a host of utility services, and communities that reflected the linear spatial orientation of government planners. Unfortunately for the local population, this often meant overcrowded, inappropriate, unaffordable, and short-term housing.[3]

Both the federal and the territorial governments eventually assumed central roles in providing housing. In most respects, however, housing conditions did not improve dramatically, regardless of which level of government was involved. Indeed, by consolidating the units in selected communities, introducing monthly payment schedules, and incorporating southern designs and building techniques, the initiatives adopted by the two levels of government actually made what was already a bad situation worse.

Although the process of providing housing for territorial residents was undoubtedly difficult, the two senior levels of government never adequately understood the unique housing needs of the northern community.[4] Compounding these difficulties was the fact that building conditions were often precarious. In the semi-permafrost region, the climate was unforgiving, the shipping season was short, storage facilities were non-existent, indigenous building materials were in short supply, skilled labour was generally unavailable, and local capital finance was limited. In the end, the housing that the various government programs delivered in the NWT was usually inferior in design, poorly constructed, expensive, small, and often without services like running water and electricity.

Although housing programs in the NWT were initially delivered through specialized programs such as the Eskimo Housing Loan Program, and the Canada Mortgage and Housing Corporation (CMHC), applying the National Housing Act (NHA), it was the two senior levels of government, federal and territorial, that coordinated much of the post–Second World War housing construction in the territorial north. The territorial government entered the housing process in 1972, with the creation of the Northwest Territories Housing Corporation (NWTCH) when it started a fast-track housing program that was intended to resolve the territories' housing problems. Eventually the government of the NWT, like the federal government, would offer a wide range of housing programs, but in neither case did the housing activity pursued by the two senior levels of government meet the long-term housing needs of the local population.

While the two senior levels of government were building houses that were too small, too costly, and too drafty, a third force emerged as a significant participant in northern housing. Evolving in part because of the inadequacies of government program initiatives, organizations such as community-based housing authorities, housing associations, or the Inuit Tapirisat came to assume a major role. The community-based organizations responded more specifically to the unique housing needs of the northern population. They allowed the local population to be more involved and recognized the unique housing needs for northern conditions.

Housing in the Northwest Territories: The Formative Era

The Eskimo Housing Loan Program was the first significant housing program introduced by the federal government in the territorial north. It was intended to provide the opportunity of home ownership to "Eskimo" families who had the perceived financial capacity for it. It was also intended to meet the mandate of the northern vision. The government deemed home ownership to be the means of stabilizing the northern community. In place from 1959–65, the Program delivered approximately 1200 housing units across the north.[5]

Originally introduced in the Eastern Arctic, the Eskimo Housing Loan Program was actually a rental–purchase program, which offered residents the opportunity to own a home if they were deemed capable of making regular monthly payments. The payment scale, however, was prohibitively high.[6] Indeed, as D.K. Thomas and C.T. Thompson argue, the select few who could actually benefit from the program "could only afford the smallest house of 280 square feet."[7] Largely because of the cost of home ownership, the majority of units delivered under the program remained as rental stock. In many cases, even nominal monthly rental payments were not made.

The original units delivered by the initiative were much-maligned one-room "matchbox" structures.[8] Prefabricated wood-panel homes, the matchbox units were "ill-conceived structures" that offered few, if any, comforts to the northern household.[9] Although the matchbox units would eventually be augmented by rigid-frame and/ or Angirraq houses (prefabricated low-cost housing developed for the Department of Northern Affairs and National Resources), none of the units delivered under the Eskimo Housing Loan Program met the housing needs of the NWT population. They were "drafty, cramped, unsafe and totally unsuited" to the northern lifestyle.[10] Indeed, as suggested by the Inuit Non-Profit Housing Corporation, the units "meant the perpetuation of many of the health and over-crowding problems that the houses were intended to alleviate."[11]

In an effort to remedy some of the deficiencies of the Eskimo Housing Loan Program, the Department of Indian Affairs and Northern Development launched a "five-year crash program aimed at providing low-cost rental housing to the Eskimo population of the NWT."[12] Established in 1965, the Eskimo Rental Housing Program reintroduced the home-ownership stock of the Eskimo Housing Loan Program as rental stock. The decision to end the housing loan program was based on the results of two surveys of housing need conducted by the federal government in 1965,[13] which underscored the inappropriateness of the federal government's early attempts to encourage home ownership in the NWT.

The Eskimo Rental Housing Program was clearly a more realistic housing initiative than the Housing Loan Program. Not only did the new program offer recipients a rent-geared-to-income payment schedule but it also made a variety of housing types available, and provided numerous rental services such as fuel, electrical servicing, and household furnishings. In the end, however, even when a rental rate of 20 per cent of family income was applied by the federal government or when fuel quotas were made available, or when the newly introduced, three-bedroom "Urquaq" was erected, the Rental Housing Program still did not meet the housing needs of the local population. The 20 per cent of income payment schedule was particularly difficult for a population whose income was seasonally based. Fuel quotas, which were determined on the basis of house size, were generally inadequate given the wide-ranging variations in temperature, wind chill, and snow conditions. Even the Urquaq or the "370" house type as provided by the new program, did not meet the much-sought-after communal space requirements or the storage facilities the local population demanded. The new program, however, did meet the larger program goals of government. By focusing the program on the Eastern Arctic, the federal government attempted to centralize the local population in Frobisher Bay (Iqaluit) and Baker Lake. The goals of government were reinforced by the number of houses made available in the Eastern Arctic region (roughly 83 per cent of the total stock), the number of houses constructed in Frobisher Bay and Baker Lake (roughly 23 per cent of the total stock), and by the various housing services that were made available through the program.[14]

Over the course of its mandate (1965–69), the Eskimo Rental Housing Program delivered 864 units.[15] Seven-hundred-and-eighty-four of the houses were constructed in the NWT, with the remainder erected in Nunavik (Arctic Quebec). Of the 784 units built in the NWT, 655 were delivered to the Eastern Arctic districts of Frobisher Bay and Keewatin, with Frobisher Bay receiving 101 and Baker Lake receiving 79 units.[16] For the most part, the houses were two- or three-bedroom units of approximately 60–67 square metres that were constructed almost entirely from prefabricated plywood panels. The vast majority of them offered little in the way of basic amenities such as running water or sewage disposal.

By 1967–68, in response to the broader issues of community well-being, the northern housing initiative began to change. As can be seen in the 1967 Territorial Ordinance designed to "Promote the Development of Housing and Living Conditions in the Northwest Territories," (renamed in 1968 the Territorial Purchase Program and the Northern Rental Purchase Program, housing had become one component of a strategy to improve the living conditions of northern residents. Indeed, as suggested in the government-generated *Final Report of the Special Committee on Housing*, the post-1967 thrust of northern housing was to provide "adequate, affordable accommodation to all northerners."[17]

The Northern Rental Purchase Program is perhaps the best example of the new initiative. Cited by government personnel as a "major step toward the goal of integrating all housing programs in the north along non-ethnic lines," the Northern Rental Purchase Program was an ambitious attempt to provide greater equity in the housing process.[18] Its initial mandate called for the delivery of 1558 three-bedroom dwellings in 43 northern settlements.[19] The program actually delivered 1378 houses.[20] A sampling of the units and the communities to which they were delivered, shows that the initiative was not that different from its predecessor. One noticeable difference, however, was the shifting regional focus. With the target group of the Northern Rental Program expanded to include the Dene population, the rental initiative moved west. The total number of rental units constructed under the new program in the Keewatin District declined significantly when compared with the Eskimo Housing Loan Program and, conversely, the number of units delivered in the Yellowknife District increased by almost 100 per cent.[21] Although there was little actual difference between the type of housing delivered under the two programs, the Northern Rental Program clearly broadened the rental mandate in the NWT.

The purchase option of the Northern Rental Purchase Program was designed so that tenants could apply rental payments towards the purchase price of a house; the program was an innovative response to both the home-ownership and rental needs of the NWT. It was also an innovative response to the needs of government. Indeed, much of the motivation to provide the home ownership option was based upon the government assessment that home ownership met the larger goals and objectives of the decision-making process. For example, home ownership was perceived as the means of providing a permanently settled population in selected communities.

The rental–purchase program provided NWT residents with the opportunity to purchase what had formerly been rental stock. The sale price of each unit was based on the original construction cost. This price was then reduced by an additional 5 per cent per year based on the age of the unit. As well, the cost of the house was adjusted to reflect both improvements and the general condition of the unit.[22] The problem with the program was not so much the sale price but rather the outstanding rehabilitation and maintenance work required on each individual house. Most of the houses had suffered through several years as rental stock and in some areas the costs of rehabilitation averaged out to $76,000 per dwelling.[23] Even when the houses were properly prepared for occupancy, the nagging question of operating and maintenance costs remained unresolved. As argued by Gordon Wray, one-time NWT Minister responsible for Housing, "those houses are in such poor shape that most people could never hope to run them because of the high cost of fuel and power."[24]

In any event, some clients did opt for the purchase program and in certain circumstances it did meet the community's needs. Both the administration and management responsibilities for the program were turned over to local authorities and, while the cost burden was assumed by the two senior levels of government, the initiative provided a vehicle for a community-oriented, housing program.

According to figures compiled by Bushey et al., some 700 units were turned over through the rental–purchase option.[25] But the actual number of units delivered under the purchase option appears to be considerably less. Indeed, the 700 figure is about seven times the number of units made available.[26] During the years 1979–84, approximately 91 houses were sold under the purchase program.[27] By 1987 the purchase option of the rental–purchase program had run its course. With the total number of units purchased under the program hovering around the 100 mark, few, if any, houses left were worth recycling.

Three other programs relevant to the early period of housing activity in the North are the non-profit and territorial and federal employee housing programs. These programs delivered a significant proportion of the total housing stock available in the NWT. Indeed, based on the NWT Housing Corporation's "Comparative Analysis of Housing Stock," by 1972 NWT Employee Accommodations accounted for 19 per cent, Federal Employee Accommodation 9 per cent, and Non-Profit Housing 5 per cent of the total NWT housing stock.[28]

The staff housing initiative was an outgrowth of the federal government's northern living allowance program which was introduced, in part, to attract and maintain a stable and skilled workforce in isolated regions. The community of Inuvik offers one of the best examples of the staff housing initiative. The entire "pool" of housing in the serviced section of the community (occupied primarily by non-Inuit), with the exception of two privately owned houses, was government built and maintained.[29] Erected between 1959 and 1961, the full complement of married staff dwellings in Inuvik consisted of 84 row and 52 detached houses with 32 one-room apartments for single men.[30] In both married and single staff quarters, a nominal rental fee, which included the cost of heat, light, power, furniture, and appliances, was charged to the occupant. Ranging from a low of $90 per month for a three-bedroom row house to a high of $122 for a four-bedroom detached unit, the government housing program not only provided inexpensive accommodation for government employees but also created a hierarchy of housing within the community.[31]

GNWT (Government of the Northwest Territories) staff housing, which accounted for a large portion of the total territorial housing stock, was introduced to the territory in 1969.[32] The government's rationale in creating the staff housing program was summarized in 1985 with the notation "that quality housing was required to attract teachers, administrators and other government of the NWT staff to the North."[33] By 1972, the employee program offered approximately 580 units to government personnel.[34] Included in the program were a monthly housing and household allowance, fuel subsidies, and furniture allocations. At the same time, however, the staff housing, with its subsidy support programs, tended to accentuate the inequities of NWT housing stock. Whereas the policies for territorial staff housing changed over time, the dichotomy between employee housing and non-employee housing remained. As argued in the brief submitted from the Baffin–High Arctic region to the government task force on housing: "The rules and rents are different for government employees living in staff housing than for people living in public housing and this causes resentment."[35]

The non-profit initiative was typified by the activity of the Inuit Non-Profit Housing Corporation (INPHC). Operating under section 56.1 of the *National Housing Act*, the INPHC provided subsidized rental housing for a low-income clientele. By 1987 a total of 16 dwellings had been erected under the INPHC program.[36] Six units were built in Rankin Inlet, a five-plex consisting of two three-bedroom and three one-bedroom apartments, and a three-bedroom "dome"; a six-plex of one-bedroom units was constructed in Tuktoyaktuk; two three-bedroom dwellings were built in Cape Dorset; and two four-bedroom units were delivered at Lake Harbour.[37]

Housing in the Northwest Territories: The Modern Era

In 1972, the GNWT established the Northwest Territories Housing Corporation (NWTCH) as its housing agent. Although the NWTCH quickly moved into the housing business, it was not until 1976 that the Corporation offered a clear policy statement, entitled *An Integrated Housing Policy for the Northwest Territories*. This statement was described by the NWTCH board of directors as a "comprehensive integrated housing policy proposal, satisfying the needs of all northerners, including renters and homeowners."[38] The objectives of the NWTCH as established by the policy statement were to ensure that NWT residents had access to an adequate supply of reasonably priced housing.[39]

Although the NWTCH was charged with the responsibility to rehabilitate and maintain existing housing, produce social housing, and develop a shelter support system, the main focus of the Corporation's activity, in reality, was public housing.[40] Over the ten-year period from 1974 to 1984 the Corporation erected approximately 2700 public housing units.[41] Offering subsidized rental units to a low-income clientele, the program, which included family, single-person, and senior-citizen accommodations, was a joint CMHC/NWTCH endeavour. Financed under the NHA cost-sharing agreement, the public housing initiative provided everything from row-housing in the larger communities to prefabricated single family dwellings in smaller, more isolated settlements. The flurry of construction that accompanied the public housing initiative gave rise to an "unprecedented" building boom in many NWT communities.[42]

The rental scale as established by the joint public housing initiative was based on the CMHC national scale.[43] Responding to the call for a "more appropriate" rental scale, the NWTCH rewrote its rental payment schedules in 1977 and attempted to apply a more equitable rental scale.[44] The system adopted on 1 April 1978 attempted to respond to the regional needs of the client group.[45] The NWTCH encountered the same problems with the new rental scale: a low-income clientele living in a high-cost environment.

In 1982, a local task force was charged with the responsibility of investigating NWT rental scales. In September 1982, the Task Force tabled its *Final Report* with the Housing Corporation. Based on its recommendations, the NWTCH adopted a new scale in January 1983. This scale was based not only on what the Housing Corporation called "Family Assessable Income" but also on "cost zones."[46] Based on the Department of Social Services' basic living allowances and the location of the community, six NWT "cost zones" were developed. Each was allotted a standard factor of rent adjustment that was then cross-tabulated with family size to arrive at an assessed rent reduction. The use of the cost zones, which ranged from the central Zone 1 communities of Hay River and Yellowknife to the more isolated Zone 6 settlements of Grise Fiord or Sachs Harbour, provided for variations in cost of living, economies of scale, and the changing circumstances of community in the NWT. A family of four, for example, living in Hay River with a NWTCH-determined monthly "living allowance" of $440, would receive no rent reduction whatsoever, whereas a similar-sized family living in Grise Fiord with a living allowance of $622 would receive a reduction of $38.

The 1983 rental scale, like its predecessor, eventually came under attack for its failure to adequately meet the housing needs of the NWT. With the declared aim of reducing "the incidence of arrears" and making the rental scale more comprehensive, the Housing Corporation evaluated the rental program in February 1985.[47] Arguing on the one hand that it was "the right of all families in the NWT to have affordable and suitable housing regardless of the amounts of money a family can pay" and, on the other, that the aim of the overall housing policy was to "move rental tenants with adequate incomes towards this goal of home ownership," the NWTCH set out a series of rental scale objectives:

> Stimulate the private rental market.
> Make suitable, affordable rental housing available to all NWT residents who need housing.
> Provide incentives to encourage continued employment.
> Provide incentives for home ownership.
> Encourage less dependency on government.
> Pay shelter subsidies only.
> Reflect the size and condition of the unit.
> Be simple.[48]

Although the Housing Corporation had defined the mandate of the rental scheme, senior management had doubts about whether the rental scale would work. The broadening debate eventually spawned the creation of an independent Cost of Living Inquiry. The Inquiry was authorized to make a "comprehensive" study of the rental scale proposal, but the recommendations of the Housing Corporation received little attention.[49] The immediate impact, however, of the Inquiry's work was to implement a user-pay program for electricity, intended to "reduce waste, give public housing tenants the opportunity of benefitting from their own initiatives and ensure that all tenants are treated uniformly and equitably."[50]

The user-pay alternative was incorporated across the NWT on 31 May 1985. The program—known locally as the "2 cents/3 cents" program—implemented electrical rates of 2 cents per kilowatt hour in areas above the treeline and 3 cents per kilowatt hour for those below the treeline, in an effort to cut operating costs and instill a sense of responsible electrical power consumption.[51]

The Low Rental Housing Program, introduced by the NWTCH in the post-1972 era, was a further attempt by the territorial government to meet the special needs of the NWT's low-income population, who are predominantly Inuit. Although the defined goal of the program was to "provide low rental housing units to individuals or families of low income," when it was applied, it would appear as though the program was initially directed at corporations' housing needs.[52] Although the NWTCH owned the structures, they were rented to various companies across the NWT who in turn offered them to their employees. There were six such projects in the territory, with a total of 155 units. They were "built in large working centres or were built and made available under an agreement to companies in an attempt to guarantee local hiring and encourage native people to enrol in apprenticeship programs."[53]

All in all, although the program did indeed provide housing units, it did not necessarily provide units for low-income families. As suggested by NWT Housing Corporation personnel, the units that were constructed were turned over to the various enterprises in the selected communities at a specified cost.[54] The companies themselves assumed the responsibility for rental rates, tenant selection, and the general administration of the housing stock.

The Small Settlement Home Assistance Grant (SSHAG) Program was another program introduced by the NWT Housing Corporation in the mid-1970s. The SSHAG initiative was designed to assist "people who required housing with low incomes in communities where rental housing was either unavailable, restricted, or not desired by the majority of community residents."[55] In its earliest configuration the program was applied only in communities below the treeline, but with the introduction of "frame" designed units it was adopted in all six NWT districts. In its most recent form as the Homeownership Assistance Program, the scheme came to apply to all NWT communities, with the exception of Yellowknife.

The SSHAG program offered a $10,000 grant to residents to help defray the costs of home ownership.[56] This was intended to help the homeowner buy building materials and to offset incremental costs such as transportation. First made available in the Mackenzie Valley region, the NWTCH amended the SSHAG program to broaden its application. Retitled the Homeownership Assistance Program (HAP), the new initiative not only extended the geographic region in which the program was applied but it also expanded its loan capacity. Under the HAP mandate every NWT community, with the exception of Yellowknife, qualified for NWTCH housing assistance. Described as "the most popular of the homeownership programs in the NWT," the HAP alternative offered homeowners a maximum forgivable loan of approximately $40,000.[57] Thirty thousand dollars was provided in the form of a "material package" and an additional $10,000 was made available for freighting, site development, and other sundry costs.

The HAP initiative was instituted to provide financial assistance to clients interested in constructing their own homes. The specific program objectives ranged from stimulating housing construction to making capital available for the construction of new housing units.[58] For an applicant who had not previously received a Housing Corporation grant or subsidy, who held title to a leased lot within recognized municipal boundaries, who was over 19 years of age, and who met the Housing Corporations' "greatest need" criteria, the HAP option was a viable form of home-ownership assistance.[59]

Initially undertaken as an entirely NWTCH endeavour, the HAP was eventually partially funded by the CMHC and the Canada Employment and Immigration Commission (CEIC).[60] With a yearly budget in the neighbourhood of $2.5 million, the Homeownership Assistance Program delivered over 189 units across the NWT.[61] Although there were ongoing problems with needs assessment and the "one size fits all" approach of the homeownership program, the program did nonetheless fill a void in home ownership programming in a limited way, and established housing-program precedents that were closely followed elsewhere.[62]

The fourth housing program of the modern era, the Rural and Remote Housing Program (RRHP), was a joint federal–territorial undertaking from the beginning. Operating under section 40 of the NHA, RRHP was a 75–25 per cent cost-shared arrangement between CMHC and NWTCH. Directed at a clientele with enough income to maintain a home, but who, for whatever reason, could not afford or obtain mortgage financing, the program was intended to "provide safe, adequate, modest housing at an affordable price to low income families in rural communities, and . . . to increase the privately owned housing stock, thereby helping to create a private housing market."[63]

Using the NWTCH criteria of "greatest need," the Housing Corporation based its prioritization of RRHP clientele on a worst-first housing scenario. The larger the family, the lower the income, or the more remote the community, the better chance an individual had of obtaining assistance under the Remote and Rural Program.[64] When and if assistance was granted, it took the form of a subsidized mortgage, balanced with a low down payment requirement. The total cost to the homeowner was a $500 down payment, a monthly mortgage payment of 25 per cent of the gross family income, and a continuing commitment to operating and maintaining the unit.[65]

Between 1977 and 1983, approximately 42 houses were either built or purchased under the Rural and Remote Program.[66] Most of these units represented the purchase of existing stock, so although the program was meeting the objective of providing housing, it was not stimulating construction. As a result, NWTCH, with the agreement of CMHC, redrafted its RRHP mandate to include the "speculative delivery" of low-income housing.[67] In 1984, after the program revisions were implemented, approximately 25 additional units were delivered. With a declared budget of $2.5 million, the joint low-income program tentatively began to address the housing needs of the NWT.[68]

Although the Rural and Remote Housing Program provided housing stock, it did not necessarily meet the needs of a low-income clientele. Even with a mortgage payment of 25 per cent of income, the program requirements were often well beyond the clientele's capabilities. As a result, approximately 70 per cent of the RRHP clientele were in arrears.[69] In 1984, in a sample of 50 households, the total amount owing on mortgage payments was well over $100,000.[70]

Although the home ownership and rental housing programs offered by the NWTCH formed the crux of the territorial housing initiative, also important were the variety of capital improvement programs introduced by the Corporation. Based on figures supplied by the Housing Corporation itself, roughly 24 per cent of the total budget in any given year was committed to maintenance.[71] At the same time, total expenditures, when broken down to a per-unit cost, were only a nominal amount. For the year 1974–75, for example, the per-unit repair expenditures amounted to $225, which, as suggested by the Special Committee on Housing, "does not go far."[72]

Conclusion

The housing process in the Northwest Territories in the post–Second World War era offers an intriguing overview of government activity. The federal and territorial governments both became major participants in the housing process. Each level of government used the opportunity of providing for the housing needs of the local population in an attempt not only to improve the quality of life for northern residents, but also to assert governmental authority in the north. At various times housing was a symbol of government sovereignty, a tool of modernization, a catalyst for economic growth, and, above all else, a strong statement of government's newly defined northern initiative. As a result, the effort to provide for the accommodation needs of territorial residents was often deferred to the broader issues of the decision-making process, which were always connected to the south's vision of northern development.

Yet the housing initiatives pursued in the NWT seldom met the ongoing needs of the local population. This was best articulated by one-time president of the Inuit Tapirisat, Michael Amarook, in his 1980 address to the Inuit Non-Profit Housing Corporation:

> We have often thought how lucky we have been to get all these houses from the government. But over the years our gratitude has changed gradually to anger. We have seen how housing which was provided to us was very inferior. We were told that running water and more space per person were impossibly expensive. And yet at the same time we saw government employees in ever increasing numbers arriving in our communities and being provided with high quality housing, with running water, furniture and lots of space often at lower rents. . . .[73]

The houses were inferior, expensive, small, and not constructed to meet the housing needs of the local population. As a result, the living space was compartmentalized, there was no work space within the unit to clean or prepare meat or fix snow machines, little thought was given to storage areas, and the cold porch was still very much a thing of the future. Beyond structural problems, there were also difficulties with rigid payment schedules, inadequate maintenance programs, operational deficiencies, and the enforced permanency created by home ownership. In the end, the housing programs made available in post–Second World War NWT redefined community in the NWT. Further, these programs allowed government to consolidate its position as the centralizing authority in the North.

Notes

1. For a discussion of the post–Second World War northern vision, see Richard J. Diubaldo, *The Government of Canada and the Inuit, 1900–1967,* (Ottawa: The Branch, 1985).

2. To one degree or another, the community-based northern initiative was applied across the north, from the territorial north of the Northwest Territories and the Yukon to the provincial north of Saskatchewan and Quebec.

3. For a discussion of northern housing, see E. Buchanan, "Arctic Housing: Problems and Prospects," MA thesis, University of British Columbia, 1979.

4. Peter Dawson argues that the "alien spatial environment" provided by government housing programs contributed to "increasing gender asymmetry, a transformation of social relations through the delayed resolution of interpersonal conflicts, confusion over how, when, and where to conduct various household activities, and a loss of cultural identity." Peter C. Dawson, "Unsympathetic Users: An Ethnoarchaeological Examination of Inuit Responses to the Changing Nature of the Built Environment," *Arctic,* 48, 1 (March 1995): 71–80.

5. Government of the Northwest Territories (GNWT), Task Force on Housing, *Task Force Report on Housing* (Yellowknife, 1972), 12.

6. GNWT, Legislative Assembly, *The Final Report of the Special Committee on Housing,* 1985, 36.

7. D.K. Thomas and C.T. Thompson, *Eskimo Housing as Planned Cultural Change* (Ottawa: Information Canada 1972), 10.

8. Larsson Consulting, *Development Strategy for Guideline Documents for Northern Residential Construction,* A Report Prepared for Canada Mortgage and Housing (Ottawa, 1985), 4.

9. "Housing By and For Inuit," *Inuit Today,* 5, 10 (November 1976), 25.

10. Ibid.

11. *An Introduction to Housing Conditions in Canada's Arctic and to The Inuit Non-Profit Housing Corporation,* A Report Prepared for the Inuit Non-Profit Housing Corporation, n.d, n.p.

12. C.T. Thompson, *Patterns of Housekeeping in Two Eskimo Settlements* (Ottawa: Department of Indian Affairs and Northern Development, 1969), 1.

13. Northwest Territories Housing Corporation, *Housing Needs and Delivery in the Northwest Territories,* 1984, n.p.

14. See Frobisher Bay in Moshe Safdie and Associates, *General Development Plan, Municipality of Frobisher Bay, NWT,* Interim Report (Montreal, 1977); and Baker Lake in J.K. Stager, *Baker Lake, NWT, A Background Report of Its Social and Economic Development,* A Report Prepared for the Settlement Council of Baker Lake and the Polar Gas Project, 1977.

15. GNWT. See the graphic "Northern Rental Housing Program," Thompson, *Patterns of Housekeeping.*

16. See Frobisher Bay in Safdie and Associates, *General Development Plan,* and Baker Lake in Stager, *Baker Lake.*

17. GNWT, *The Final Report of the Special Committee on Housing,* 25.

18. GNWT, *Task Force on Housing,* 2.

19. Ibid.

20. GNWT, *The Final Report of the Special Committee on Housing,* 57.

21. This has been extrapolated from Thompson, *Patterns of Housekeeping.*

22. R. Bushey, E. Bhajan, and R. Stevenson, *Task Force Report on Home-Ownership in the MacKenzie Valley* (Yellowknife, 1977), 16.

23. GNWT, *The Final Report of the Special Committee on Housing,* 57.

24. Ibid.

25. Bushey et al., *Task Force Report,* 16.

26. Northwest Territories Housing Corporation, "Northwest Territories Housing Corporation's Programs," (Mimeo), n.d., n.p.

27. Ibid.

28. GNWT, Task Force on Housing, *Task Report on Housing,* n.p.

29. J.R. Lotz, "Inuvik, NWT, A Study of Community Planning Problems in a New Northern Town," 23.

30. Ibid., 23–6.

31. Ibid., 24.

32. GNWT, Task Force on Employee Housing, *Task Force Report on Employee Housing* (Yellowknife, 1979), 15.

33. GNWT, *The Final Report of the Special Committee on Housing,* 72.

34. GNWT, Task Force on Employee Housing, *Task Force Report on Employee Housing,* 28.

35. GNWT, *The Final Report of the Special Committee on Housing,* 142.

36. Northwest Territories Housing Corporation, "Northwest Territories Housing Corporation's Programs" (Mimeo), n.d., n.p.

37. Northwest Territories Housing Corporation, *Capital Assets, Inventory Report,* December 1987, n.p.

38. GNWT, *An Integrated Housing Policy for the Northwest Territories,* i.

39. Ibid., 1.

40. Ibid.

41. Northwest Territories Housing Corporation, "Northwest Territories Housing Corporation's Programs" (Mimeo), n.d., n.p.

42. GNWT, *The Final Report of the Special Committee on Housing*, 27–8.

43. GNWT, Task Force on Employee Housing, *Task Force Report on Employee Housing*, 19.

44. Northwest Territories Housing Corporation, "1983 NWTCH Rent Scale" (Mimeo), n.d., n.p.

45. GNWT, *The Final Report of the Special Committee on Housing*, 38.

46. Ibid.

47. Ibid.

48. Ibid., 42.

49. Northwest Territories Housing Corporation, "1983 NWT Rent Scale" (Mimeo), n.d., n.p.

50. GNWT, *The Final Report of the Special Committee on Housing*, 45.

51. Ibid., 45–6.

52. Northwest Territories Housing Corporation, "Northwest Territories Housing Corporation's Program" (Mimeo), n.d., n.p.

53. Ibid.

54. This information is based on a telephone conversation with the NWTCH Program's division staff.

55. GNWT, *The Final Report of the Special Committee on Housing*, 53.

56. R. Bushey et al., *Task Force Report*, 15.

57. GNWT, *The Final Report of the Special Committee on Housing*, 53.

58. Northwest Territories Housing Corporation, "Northwest Territories Housing Corporation's Programs" (Mimeo), n.d., n.p.

59. Ibid.

60. GNWT, *The Final Report of the Special Committee on Housing*, 54.

61. Northwest Territories Housing Corporation, *Housing Needs and Delivery in the Northwest Territories*, 19.

62. GNWT, *The Final Report of the Special Committee on Housing*, 56.

63. Northwest Territories Housing Corporation, "Northwest Territories Housing Corporation's Program" (Mimeo), n.d., n.p.

64. GNWT, *The Final Report of the Special Committee on Housing*, 49.

65. Northwest Territories Housing Corporation, "Northwest Territories Housing Corporation's Programs" (Mimeo), n.d., n.p.

66. Ibid.

67. Ibid.

68. GNWT, *The Final Report of the Special Committee on Housing*, 50.

69. Ibid., 51.

70. Ibid.

71. Northwest Territories Housing Corporation, *Housing Needs and Delivery in the NWT*, 1984, 28.

72. GNWT, *The Final Report of the Special Committee on Housing*, 65.

73. T.S. Carnegie, "Inuit Builders: A Case for Grass Roots Development in Canada's Eastern Arctic," 4.

Primary Document

Royal Commission on Aboriginal Peoples: Presentation

Pia Kooneelusie, Pangnirtung Housing Association (via Translator)

May 28, 1992

. . . The major concerns that we have—I'm sure that you have a document in front of you in respect to that. I'd like to start with the amount of rent that is required by tenants to pay. Since the start of the community in 1960 when they were being brought from the outpost camps, the Federal Government provided housing in the community and they weren't paying any rent.

And so in the 1960s they started asking for rent at a start of from $2 to $15 per month. Per month. And they told us that they would raise the arrears and since then it has gone up to $32 to $532 per month and there's also a new scale to be used in 1993 from $32 to $1400 per month.

And once we started using this, up to $1400 a month, we don't agree with that amount of money that it is to be paid for rent and we, as Inuit, it is going to be very difficult for most Inuit to pay that amount of money per month just to live in a house. We know that everything is—the prices are always changing and continuing to rise and if we're going to start paying $1400 per month it is going to be very difficult for most Inuit, especially for the hunters.

The hunters—hunting equipment, snowmobiles, boats, are very expensive and if they're going to be paying that amount of money just for rent. . . .

And also I'd like to say that the older houses are up for sale and we'd like to know that if we can—the newer houses for sale rather than the old, battered ones so that more people will be able to buy their own houses in the community rather than trying to sell off the old houses and especially if a household has a great number in each family, in each household, and I'm sure most of their children would like to have their own houses and provide for their own family.

Most of them don't apply for housing because they aren't able to pay that amount of rent per month. If I didn't have a house I wouldn't even think of applying for a house.

Also, if we did get single-room units starting this year, and I think this is the last year that they'll build single-family units and if we continue to be short of housing in the community there's a bit of—quite a number of people on the waiting list for a single-family unit and if we're going to move, I mean, to a two-bedroom—even if they had asked for a single-family unit and they would have to end up paying a lot more for the amount of space that they require.

There's a lot of social problems involved with overcrowding and not good housing. No running water, no septic tanks, things like that we're running into.

A lot of problems with overcrowding. Two and three families living together in one house. People sleeping on the floors because there's no bedrooms, things like that. . . .

there are seven houses coming in the next year. It doesn't help when you've got 69 people on a waiting list. Seven is a drop in the bucket.

Questions for Consideration

1. Why did Inuit convert to Catholicism in Pelly Bay between 1935 and 1950?
2. Discuss the ways that some Inuit preserved their previous beliefs and traditions after converting to Catholicism.
3. What does the excerpt from the *Codex Historicus* tell us about life at the Pelly Bay mission? What light does it shed on the reasons for Inuit converting to Catholicism?
4. What was the Northern Initiative? How did it shape federal and territorial housing policies and programs?
5. Why has the housing constructed under government programs been inadequate and why does housing continue to be a problem plaguing Indigenous peoples in the North?

6. What problems related to housing in Pangnirtung does Pia Kooneelusie identify? How well does this accord with the analysis of housing in the North provided by Robert Robson?

7. How does ignoring Indigenous voices prevent a better understanding of the past and present, especially for urgent social issues such as housing?

Further Resources

Books and Articles

Adelson, Naomi. *"Being Alive Well": Health and the Politics of Cree Well-Being* (Toronto: University of Toronto Press, 2000).

———. "Discourses of Stress, Social Inequities, and the Everyday Worlds of First Nations Women in a Remote Northern Canadian Community," *Ethos* 36, 3 (2008): 316–31.

Blaisel, Xavier, Frédéric Laugrand, and Jarich Oosten. "Shamans, Leaders and Prophets: Parousial Movements among the Inuit of Canada," *Numen* 46 (1999): 370–411.

Debicka, Elizabeth and Avi Friedman. "From Policies to Building: Public Housing Canada's Eastern Arctic 1950s to 1980s," *Canadian Journal of Urban Housing Research*, 18, 2 (2009): 25–39.

Gray, Susan. *I Will Fear No Evil: Ojibwa-Missionary Encounters Along the Berens River, 1875–1940* (East Lansing: Michigan State University Press, 2007).

Morantz, Toby. *The Whiteman's Gonna Getcha: The Colonial Challenge to the Crees in Quebec* (Montreal: McGill-Queen's University Press, 2002).

Robson, Robert. "Suffering an Excessive Burden: Housing as Health Determinant in the First Nations Community of Northwestern Ontario," *Canadian Journal of Native Studies*, 27, 1 (2008): 71–87.

Rutherdale, Myra. *Women and the White Man's God: Gender and Race in the Canadian Mission Field* (Vancouver: UBC Press, 2002).

Schiff, Rebecca and Fern Brunger. "Northing Housing Networks: Building Collaborative Efforts to Address Housing and Homelessness in Remote Canadian Aboriginal Communities in the Context of Rapid Economic Change," *Journal of Rural and Community Development*, 10, 1 (2015): 1–18.

Tester, Frank. "Iglutaasaavut (Our New Homes): Neither 'New' nor 'Ours.'" *Journal of Canadian Studies*, 43, 2 (2009): 137–58.

Printed Documents and Reports

Inuit Tuttarvingat. *If not now . . . when? Addressing the Ongoing Inuit Housing Crisis in Canada* (Ottawa: National Aboriginal Health Organization, 2011).

National Aboriginal Health Organization. *Homelessness and Housing Realities for Inuit* (Ottawa: Inuit Tuttarvingat, 2008).

Office of the Auditor General of Canada. "Chapter 6—Federal Government Support to First Nations—Housing on Reserves," *2003 April Report of the Auditor General of Canada*, www.oag-bvg.gc.ca/internet/English/parl_oag_200304_06_e_12912.html.

Oosten, Jarich, and Frédéric Laugrand, eds, *Inuit Perspectives on the 20th Century*, 4 vols (Iqaluit: Nunavut Arctic College, 1999–2002).

Films

Atanarjuat: The Fast Runner. DVD (drama). Directed by Zacharias Kunuk. Isuma Igloolik Productions, 2001.

CBQM. DVD. Directed by Dennis Allen. NFB, 2009.

The Challenges in Old Crow. DVD. Directed by George Payrastre. NFB, 2006.

Christmas at Moose Factory. Film. Directed by Alanis Obomsawin. NFB, 1967.

The Experimental Eskimos. DVD. Directed by Barry Greenwald. White Pine Pictures, 2009.

Nanook of the North: A Story of Life and Love in the Actual Arctic. DVD. Directed by Robert J. Flaherty. Les Frères Revillon/Pathé Exchange, 1922.

The People of the Kattawapiskak River. DVD. Directed by Alanis Obamsawin. National Film Board of Canada, 2012.

Television Programs on Housing. Aboriginal People's Television Network. http://aptn.ca/news/tag/housing/

Websites

âpihtawikosisân, "Attawapiskat: A Study in the Need to Openly Address Misunderstandings," blog, August 2012.
http://apihtawikosisan.com/2012/08/attawapiskat-a-study-in-the-need-to-openly-address-misunderstandings/

Aboriginal Affairs and Northern Development Canada, "First Nation Housing,"
www.aadnc-aandc.gc.ca/eng/1100100010715/1100100010719

Canadian Mortgage and Housing Corporation, "About First Nation Housing,"
www.cmhc-schl.gc.ca/en/ab/abfinaho/index.cfm

Grand Council of the Crees
www.gcc.ca/cra/cranav.php

A Guide to Inuit Culture by the Inuit Women of Canada
www.pauktuutit.ca/pdf/publications/pauktuutit/InuitWay_e.pdf

Inuit Circumpolar Council
http://inuitcircumpolar.com

Inuit Tapiriit Kanatami heritage
www.itk.ca/publication/5000-years-inuit-history-and-heritage

The Economy and Labour

Introduction

Conventional economic and labour histories of Canada overlook the roles of Indigenous peoples in the economy and workforce. This oversight is not because Indigenous peoples did not participate in the capitalist economy, trade unions, or the labour force; it is a function of persistent misconceptions about Indigenous peoples themselves. Stereotypes of them being lazy, dependent, marginalized, or remnants of the past capable only of European-Canadian conceptions of "traditional" Indigenous work make Indigenous people appear out of place in the "modern" capitalist economy. This misconception is perpetuated by historians who tend to emphasize the importance of Indigenous people's labour within the fur and robe trade and imply that the decline of that trade marked the growing irrelevance of Indigenous peoples to the Canadian economy, particularly the industrial economy.[1] Acknowledging the contribution of Indigenous peoples to the industrialization and modernization of the Canadian economy makes it harder for European-Canadians to rationalize the exclusion of Indigenous peoples from the benefits of the prosperity that accompanied that process, particularly in the post–Second World War period. Recognizing that Indigenous workers of both sexes played vital roles in Canada's emerging industrial economy is not to suggest that they did not experience racism or that they were not subject to exclusionary policies, formal and informal, that barred them from many workplaces. It is meant to acknowledge that, as historian Mary Jane McCallum argues, "marginalization and displacement could and did exist simultaneously with other experiences, and . . . a history of decline or persistence, coercion or autonomy, difference or accommodation cannot adequately represent our past."[2]

The articles in this chapter look at the wage-for-pay of Indigenous peoples at two historical moments in the twentieth century: the turn of the century and the 1950s. In examining the former, John Lutz attempts to understand the processes by which Indigenous peoples in British Columbia went from being central actors in the province's economy to being invisible. According to Lutz, "ignoring Aboriginal participation in the workforce misses the role that wage labour played in the "peaceful subordination" of Canadian Aboriginal peoples and the establishment of modern Canada."[3] Overlooking these processes, which also made Indigenous peoples one of the most impoverished segments of BC society, disregards the actions of the state that regulated (and reduced) the place of Indigenous labourers in crucial (and lucrative) segments of the economy, such as resource extraction.

In the post–Second World War period, the federal government sought to "save" Indigenous women from "failing reserves" through labour placement programs, which were designed to allow Aboriginal women to enjoy the benefits of the modern economy and urban living. These programs also facilitated the assimilationist project outlined by Hugh Shewell and others in this volume. Joan Sangster explores these labour placement programs and the reasons they failed to achieve the goals of the Indian Affairs Branch. While the federal government responded in part to Aboriginal leaders and communities' calls for economic development, it failed to address the economic and ideological legacies of colonialism. As a result, the government ensured the failure of its half-hearted attempts at stimulating economic development for Indigenous peoples.

Chapter Objectives

At the end of this chapter, you should be able to

- recognize the roles that Indigenous workers have played in Canada's modern economy;
- understand the goals of the labour placement programs for Indigenous workers in the postwar period and how they fit in with the broader goals of federal Indian policy;
- understand how economic policies contributed to the poverty experienced by Canada's Indigenous peoples; and
- understand how gender shaped Indigenous peoples' experiences of the labour market and Canadian labour policy.

Notes

1. Mary Jane Logan McCallum, "Labour, Modernity, and the Canadian State: A History of Aboriginal Women and Work in the Mid-Twentieth Century" (PhD dissertation, University of Manitoba, 2008), 4.
2. Ibid., 16.
3. John Lutz, *Makuk: A New History of Aboriginal–White Relations* (Vancouver: UBC Press, 2008), 8.

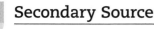

Secondary Source

Vanishing the Indians: Aboriginal Labourers in Twentieth-Century British Columbia

John Lutz

Visitors to British Columbia in the late nineteenth century were surprised by what they saw. In 1886, famous anthropologist Franz Boas recorded his observations about Indigenous people in Victoria: "We meet them everywhere. They dress mostly in

Ts'msyen Chief A.S. Dudoward's house, 1905. (Residence of A.S. Dudoward, Indian Chief, Port Simpson, BC. Library and Archives Canada.)

European fashion. . . . Certain Indian tribes have already become indispensable on the labour market and without them the province would suffer great economic damage."[1] At the turn of the century, settlers and visitors were astonished not only at the number of Aboriginal people in the province's workforce but also at how wealthy they were. This wealth was sometimes reflected in large Victorian homes, such as Ts'ymsan Chief Dudoward's in Port Simpson, but it was more often noted at potlatches.[2]

Historians have not generally noticed that Indigenous people were wealthy in the nineteenth century, but consider the evidence from around Victoria, BC. *The British Colonist* estimated that, at a potlatch in April 1869, the Lekwungen people gave away an astounding $20,000 in goods and cash to 700 assembled guests. In April 1874, "the grandest affair of that kind that has been held upon Vancouver Island for many years, came off . . . at Victoria," hosted by Chief Sqwameyuks (Scomiach) of the Lekwungen. Sqwameyuk personally distributed over $1000 worth of blankets to the 2000 assembled there, and the total value of goods given away by all the families during that week amounted to between $8000 and $10,000. The next year, a week-long potlatch saw a similar distribution among a crowd of the same size. Two years later, at a potlatch given by the neighbouring Wsanec people, the Indian superintendent saw "three members of one family (brothers) give away 3,500 blankets, no doubt the savings of many years. . . . Goods to the value of $15,400 were distributed ere the affair ended."[3] Such amounts would be considered large even today. In the mid- to late nineteenth century, when Aboriginal workers made 50 cents to 1 dollar per day and white labourers made 2 dollars, these sums represent an incredible accumulation of wealth. A sum of $15,000 in 1870 would be the equivalent of more than $315,000 today.[4]

In 1884, a delegation of Nuu-chah-nulth chiefs from Vancouver Island's west coast expressed their views: "We work for our money and like to spend it as we please, in gathering our friends together; now whenever we travel we find friends; the 'potlatch' does that."[5] Like Aboriginal people in many parts of the region, they made wage labour work for them, not the other way around. This concept is borne out by Helen Codere's study of the Kwakwaka'wakw on northeastern Vancouver Island, which shows that work for wages and the production of goods for sale increased the frequency of potlatches, the number of guests,

Potlach Gifts at Albert Bay, 1910–12, photographed by A.M. Wastrell. City of Vancouver Archives, IN P1192. (City of Vancouver Archives, In P119.2.)

and the wealth distributed. She calls the period between the founding of Fort Rupert in 1849 and 1921 "the potlatch period. . . ."[6]

Historian Robin Fisher has argued that "the effect of frontier settlement was to diminish Indian wealth," but Superintendent of Indian Affairs I.W. Powell finished his 1881 overview with the observation that "there was never a time in the history of the Province when the Indians have been so prosperous as during the present year."[7] Apparently, Aboriginal people eagerly participated in the foreign economy because they had well-developed potlatch economies of their own. However, instead of hoarding wealth, status in Northwest Coast cultures was achieved by hosting a potlatch and giving away all of one's wealth.

When historians write about British Columbia's Aboriginal peoples, they generally use one of three broad storylines. While each metanarrative has contributed to erasing the history of Aboriginal workers, the earliest and most enduring casts "Indians" as obstacles to economic development, or "progress." This perspective, although found in early-twentieth-century Canadian texts,[8] is best exemplified in the work of an American, Frederick Jackson Turner. His *The Significance of the Frontier in American History* argues that the destruction of Indigenous peoples is part of the trial by fire from which a new nation and people were born.[9] Another "progressive" variant of this argument states that Aboriginal peoples should exchange their "primitive existence" for "civilization" under the guiding hand of the missionary, teacher, or government agent. Although now out of fashion in the scholarly world, these ideas still have wide currency. As recently as 1991, they formed the basis for a major legal decision that rejected Aboriginal land claims.[10]

A second metanarrative can be summed up by the term *fatal impact*. In other words, trade and contact between an avaricious European world and an (often romanticized) Aboriginal culture resulted in the destruction of the latter. The reasons usually given for this outcome are superior European technology, Aboriginal passivity, and the inherently static nature of "primitive societies." Such an explanation is often a thinly veiled critique of a capitalist society that has flattened Indigenous cultures that stood in its path. This metanarrative frequently devalues contemporary Aboriginal society as being only the "debris" of an idyllic Aboriginal past. Both versions portray

Aboriginal peoples as victims of superior force and deny them a role in the making of their own history.[11]

The third metanarrative is more subtle. Best known in British Columbia from Fisher's work, it considers the period following first contact as one of cultural florescence. Sometimes called the "enrichment thesis," this storyline argues that Aboriginal people had a great deal of control over the fur trade and were able to choose the aspects of the immigrant culture they wished to adopt, thereby enriching their own culture. This narrative temporarily restores agency to Aboriginal peoples. The fatal impact of European settlement, it seems, was not averted but only delayed:

> The fur trade had stimulated Indian culture by adding to Indian wealth and therefore to the scope of Indian creativity. Settlement, on the other hand, often had the effect of subtracting from Indian wealth and this tended to stultify Indians . . . The Indians had been able to mould the fur trade to their benefit, but settlement was not malleable; it was unyielding and aggressive. It imposed its demands on Indians without compromise.[12]

Thus, settlement, not contact, marked the demise of Aboriginal culture and history.

If Aboriginal people were labouring "in the sawmill, the logging camp, the field, the store, in fact in every department where labour is required . . ."[13] in the 1870s and 1880s, what became of them? Did they continue to work in these enterprises into the twentieth century? If they vanished from the workforce, when did this happen? For the answers to these questions, we can look to the autobiographies written by Aboriginal people during this period. These stories are supplemented by more routine sources generated by an increasingly bureaucratic government. From the mid-1880s to the 1940s, the Department of Indian Affairs (DIA) expanded the types of information it gathered about Registered Indians, including estimated annual incomes.[14] Beginning in the late 1870s, the federal Department of Fisheries (DOF) expanded its collection of data on matters relating to fur sealing, fishing, and canning, with a view to regulating and allocating access to marine resources. Different agencies of the provincial government also became involved in gathering information on Aboriginal people. In 1926, the province established the Game Laws Enforcement Branch, with wardens stationed around the province enforcing hunting and trapping regulations. Due to a general labour shortage during the Second World War, the provincial labour department began an annual count of Aboriginal people. In fact, we have quite a bit of data on the "invisible Indian."

The Industrious Indian

Both the autobiographies and government records allow us to see what was happening in many of the sectors that were major employers of Aboriginal people, including trapping, commercial fishing, and agriculture. The autobiographies show that trapping was the first activity that brought most Aboriginal people into contact with the non-Aboriginal economy.[15] Like sealing, fishing, and other industries employing concentrations of Aboriginal people, trapping was a seasonal industry. By the 1920s, it remained the main source of income only in the northern part of the province.

However, the fur industry was not an entirely reliable source of income because prices and supply fluctuated widely from year to year (see Figure 11.1). Nor were prices the only problem. In his annual report for 1892, the superintendent of Indian Affairs wrote that, for the first time, Aboriginal people were facing significant competition from non-Aboriginal trappers. This situation was exacerbated in 1926, when the provincial government required traplines to be registered. Many Aboriginal people found that the traplines that their ancestors had worked for generations had been registered by non-Aboriginal people.

While the decline of the trapping industry was felt primarily in the north, changes in the commercial fishing industry affected much larger numbers. Commercial fishing was concentrated in coastal regions, but people from as far inland as Lillooet (on the Fraser River), Kispiox (on the Skeena River), Telegraph Creek (on the Stikine River), and the Chilcotin Plateau as far east as Kluskus Lake migrated seasonally to participate.[16] Coupled with the existing concentration of Aboriginal people on the coast, these migrations meant that the fishing industry was the largest employer of Aboriginal labour from the 1880s through to the 1960s. The canneries employed 1400 fishermen in 1882; by 1929, that number had grown to 12,675. Between 1925 and 1940, the fishing fleet was 30 to 40 per cent Aboriginal. The cannery labour force grew as well and, by 1929, the DIA estimated that 11,488 Aboriginal people (or 41 per cent of the Aboriginal population in British Columbia) "engage in the several branches of the commercial fishing operations."[17]

The importance of the fisheries is also reflected in the autobiographies of Aboriginal people. All but one of the coastal men who wrote their stories fished commercially. Several owned their own fishing boats.[18] The Aboriginal cannery workforce was heavily dominated by women. Children also contributed to the family income by

Daniel Wigaix (Big Wings), Gistskan, with winter's catch of furs, 1923. (Marius Barbeau, 1923 Canadian Museum of History, 59501.)

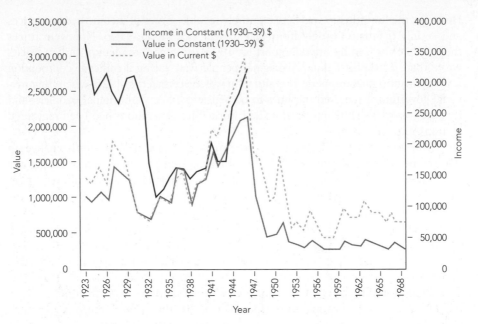

Figure 11.1 Value of Fur Trapped in British Columbia, 1923–70, and Registered Indian Income from Trapping, 1923–46.
Source: Department of Indian Affairs Annual Reports.

finding employment there: Florence Davidson recalls starting work in the canneries at age 11 and James Sewid and Ed Sparrow started at age 8.[19]

The fishing industry and the canneries that employed such a large percentage of Aboriginal people were, however, in decline over the latter part of the period under study. Several factors, including technological change and financial consolidation, contributed to this decline. The introduction of gas-powered boats in the 1920s meant that greater distances could be travelled faster. In the 1930s and 1940s, refrigeration allowed for fish to be transported over longer distances. Previously, fish had to be processed within a day of being caught, requiring many small canneries close to the prime fishing sites—sites that Aboriginal people had identified centuries before and established as village locations. Keeping fish fresh for longer periods meant that canneries could be consolidated into large operations located in two main centres: Vancouver and Prince Rupert. Figure 11.2 shows the rise and fall of the cannery industry.[20]

Cannery closures affected both the cannery labour force and the fishermen. Many canneries provided boats to Aboriginal fishermen on a share basis, boats that were no longer available when the canneries closed. At Klemtu, George Brown noted,

> [w]e have about sixty families in the village; only nine or ten people own a fishing boat. When the cannery was still open, our men fished on company boats. The ones that didn't go fishing worked in cold storage. All the women worked during canning season. But the plant closed in 1968. For forty years we had got used to working all the time. Then they closed her down, quit operating. That's when things went from

James Sewid and crew of his fish boat, Twin Sisters, 1963. (Canadian Indians Today, 1963.)

bad to worse. . . . Prices here are about double Vancouver's. Many people are on welfare; that's why it hits us so much.[21]

A different comparison illustrates the same trend. In 1892, 16 Fraser River canneries employed between 640 and 800 Aboriginal women. By 1953, that number was down to 10 canneries and a total of 91 Aboriginal women and men.[22]

Other changes also affected Aboriginal people's involvement in the fishing industry. A long-term decline in the number of fishing licences held by Aboriginal men, discernible from 1925, was temporarily reversed by the internment of Japanese-Canadians during the Second World War, allowing Aboriginal fisherman to benefit from high prices and reduced competition. After the war, the decline continued. Between 1948 and 1953, the number of Aboriginal fishermen fell even though the total number of fishermen increased. In his autobiography, Harry Assu observed that "the number of our native people fishing in their own waters here on the coast has fallen off with poor harvests and the restrictions on fishing. While our people lost out in many places, the number of non-Indian "fishermen" buying seiners on these waters built up" (see Figure 11.3).

Although fishing's contribution to Aboriginal income rose during the war years, by 1954 it was in decline. In the northern fishing district, Aboriginal fishermen held their relative position a decade longer, but after 1964 the share of licences going to Aboriginal people in this district also fell off.[23] The year-to-year decline was often small, but the long-term effect was striking. In 1883, the canneries of the Fraser River area alone employed 1000 to 1200 Aboriginal fishermen.

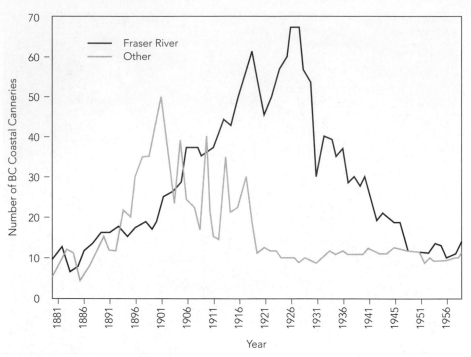

Figure 11.2 Number of BC Coastal Canneries, 1881–1959.
Source: Cicely Lyons, *Salmon: Our Heritage* (Vancouver: British Columbia Packers Ltd. and Mitchell Press, 1969.)

Seventy years later, fewer than 100 were employed in fishing in the whole lower coast area.[24]

Another main employer of Aboriginal people was agriculture. Some raised crops and stock as farmers and ranchers, for both the commercial and domestic economies. A larger number worked as wage or piece-rate labourers for other farmers. Despite the characterization of British Columbia's Aboriginal people as non-agricultural, this sector at the beginning of the century and between 1910 and 1926 supplied more income to British Columbia Indigenous people than any other. In the latter part of the period studied, farming declined in importance as a source of income for Aboriginal people, though, even in 1961, it remained the third largest employer after fishing and forestry.[25]

Although agriculture was concentrated in the southern interior and the coastal river valleys of British Columbia, many Aboriginal people from other parts of the province expanded their seasonal migrations to participate in seasonal paid labour in the Fraser Valley and Puget Sound. Over half of the existing work histories of Aboriginal people describe this practice. A seasonal migration to the hop fields of the area was part of Charley Nowell and John Fornsby's experiences in the 1880s.[26] John Wallace was born at the Hulbert's Hop Yard in the Fraser Valley on 25 September 1905 while his family was working there. Around the same time, Henry Pennier worked nearby at a single hop farm employing 700 "Indians from all over the [province]. . . . They'd bawl me out in their own languages and I'll bet my last bale of hay that there were seven or eight different Indian languages there."[27]

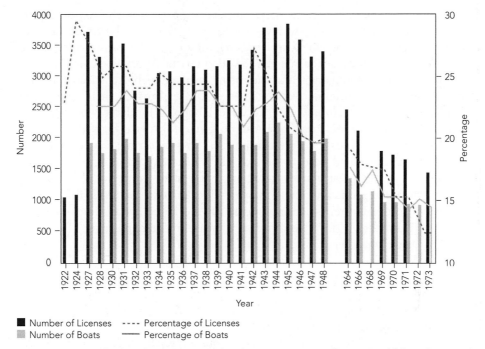

Figure 11.3 Number and Percentage of Fishing Licences and Boats Held by Aboriginal People, Selected Years, 1922–73.
Source: Fisheries and Oceans Canada. This does not constitute an endorsement by Fisheries and Oceans Canada of this product.

Some calculations suggest that the peak years for the migrations may have been the late nineteenth century.[28] In the summer of 1912, however, a Vancouver newspaper estimated that 1500 Aboriginal hop pickers were employed in the Fraser Valley alone. This figure shows the continued importance of seasonal agricultural labour for many Aboriginal people. Indian agents' reports reveal that, while seasonal agricultural labour remained a source of Aboriginal income, its importance was dwindling by the early 1950s. The Canadian Regional Employment Offices placed the average number of Aboriginal people migrating to the United States during this time at 1800 men and 1555 women. Most of this group were agricultural labourers from British Columbia. The offices also estimated that a similar number migrated within the province to engage in seasonal agricultural labour. But by 1957, only 300 Aboriginal people from British Columbia were participating in the hop harvest in the province and in the United States.[29]

The third main employer of Aboriginal people was the forest industry. However, an overall picture of Aboriginal labour in forestry is hard to come by. We do know that all of the 12 Aboriginal men who left work histories (and who were from all parts of the province) worked at some time as loggers, wood cutters, boom men, sawmill labourers, or pole cutters. Charles Jones turned to logging at the turn of the nineteenth century (when the sealing industry shut down) and was a logger for the rest of his life, though "when the jobs in the logging industry were scarce, I often went fishing."[30] Although logging activity was widely distributed throughout the province, it was most intensively pursued in the coastal regions. Helen Codere's study of the Kwakwaka'wakw and James Pritchard's of the Haisla found widespread involvement in hand-logging during the early twentieth century. This is probably true for many of the other coastal Aboriginal communities.[31]

When legislative changes and increasing regulation forced an end to hand-logging in 1910, Aboriginal people, in several cases, formed their own logging companies or found employment as wage labourers for larger logging firms. Pritchard found that the peak of Haisla logging took place between 1917 and 1924, although the Haisla people continued as loggers during the Second World War and the immediate postwar period. There are two indicators of the relative significance of the forestry sector to Aboriginal people. First, the decennial census (1931–61) suggests an increase in the importance of the forest industry and a decline in agriculture. Second, a survey of Aboriginal occupations conducted by Harry Hawthorn in 1954 confirms an increase in the importance of the forest industry as an employer.[32]

Based on the autobiographies and the Indian agents' reports, it is possible to say that the forest industry continued to be a major employer of Aboriginal people in the province. However, it is difficult to chart changing patterns of Aboriginal employment. Interviews with Aboriginal men in the coastal towns of Queen's Cove, Kingcome, and Owikeno show that, while logging employed a part of the male labour force formerly engaged in fishing, the employment was tenuous, especially once the local area was logged out.[33]

The only local study of an Aboriginal economy centred on logging is Douglas Hudson's survey of the Carrier people in North Central British Columbia. Based on

Aboriginal hop pickers, Chilliwack, BC. (Chilliwack Museum and Archives, P1622.)

interviews with a forestry employer, Hudson argues that the period from 1946 to 1964 marked the boom years for logging operations in that area and the peak years of Aboriginal employment in the sector. In the following years, the small local logging operations and local sawmills that employed most of the Aboriginal forest workers were displaced by multinational firms, who brought in workers from "outside."[34] Although Aboriginal people were engaged in a wide variety of non-forestry occupations, these comprised a relatively small part of the workforce.

Boom and Bust Cycles

While they do not often appear in our histories of the two world wars and the Great Depression, Aboriginal people were dramatically affected by these major events. The First World War created a massive demand for workers to supply the war industry and replace the enlisted men. Like other Canadians, Aboriginal people benefited from the increase in wartime employment. In 1918, the annual report of the DIA recorded the following:

> The past year has been one of great prosperity for the Indians of southwestern British Columbia, . . . [due to] the extraordinarily high price paid for all kinds of fish, and the great scarcity of unskilled labour. Never in the history of the Pacific Coast have such high prices been paid for fish as during the past year. . . . On the West Coast some Indians are known to have earned as much as $1,000 in a single week.[35]

The following year, the DIA's annual report stated, "The prevailing wage paid for farm labourers and for work in the saw mills and logging camps was higher than at any time previous . . . In the lumbering industry wages were exceptionally high and Indians engaged in that work earned from five to eight dollars per day."[36] Yet, despite the rising wages, wartime inflation caused a decline in real income. Following the war, real income rose, returning to pre-war levels in 1929–30 before plummeting during the Depression.[37]

Carrier-Dene Mary John described the effect of the Depression on her community: "Our hard life became harder. . . . Employment for our men became scarce and finally non-existent. By the end of the Depression the only work available for the men was relief work. . . . Many times relief money was the

Hank Pennier, *Stó:lō logger*. (Photo 2003.39.7, courtesy of the Chilliwack Museum and Archives.)

only cash which was circulating on the reserve." Other evidence indicates that her experience was widely shared among Registered Indians in British Columbia. They rode the roller coaster of the national and international economy along with other Canadians, experiencing the sharp dips in 1914, 1924, and 1927 and the full impact of the Great Depression.[38]

Similarly, recollections of increases in wages and employment levels during the Second World War are dramatically reflected in the income statistics and other information gathered by the provincial Department of Labour. These data indicate that Aboriginal people were hired in industries and occupational categories outside the range of where they had previously been concentrated. Hundreds of British Columbia's Aboriginal men also joined the military and fought in the war. Employment in these enumerated industries doubled between 1940 and 1941 and almost doubled again to a peak in 1942, when it started to decline.

The plentiful supply of wartime work was used as an excuse by the DOF to further reduce Aboriginal access to food resources. The Chief Inspector of Fisheries wrote the following to one of the Indian agents: "It is felt that Indians engaged in the commercial fishing during the height of the season do not require food permits."[39] But when growing numbers of Aboriginal people returned to the relief–subsistence combination after the war, the DOF still withheld fishing permits. In 1955, Andy Paull, editor of *Indian Voice* magazine, told a conference that conditions were better earlier in the century: "At least then a hungry Indian could go down to the creek and hook a salmon—now they have to watch the salmon swimming by."[40] Hunting regulations also limited Aboriginal people's ability to hunt food. By the 1950s, the state had game wardens enforcing the law in much of the province. Clam digging remained one of the few means by which the coastal people could still harvest food without restriction for food and sale. However, this freedom lasted only until 1960, when the DOF instituted an annual closed season for commercial harvesting of clams between June and November. Lekwungen Chief Albany considered it another step in the federal government's appropriation of Aboriginal resources:

Okanagan men in uniform. (O'Keefe Historic Ranch, F30-6.)

Now through regulations, it [the season for digging clams] is only seven months. They tell us the clams are no good from June to November, but Indians feel the clam is really at its prime then. Those are the months

Indians used to put up their food for the winter. For many hundreds of years Indians were eating clams in those months.

Albany noted that, because Aboriginal people could not sell the clams in order to buy other food, the shellfish was about all they would have to eat. In Victoria, the newspaper headlines on 18 October 1960 read "Indians Face Starvation."[41]

The gradual erosion of Aboriginal access to subsistence resources increased their dependence on the wage economy. However, several factors limited Aboriginal success in the capitalist economy: the province and municipalities refused to hire them for public works; the Forest Service refused to give them timber leases; the DOF limited the kinds of fishing licences they could have; the Lands Branch gave whites preferential access to irrigation water and range land; the Indian Act criminalized the sale and possession of alcohol by Aboriginal people, which cut them out of the restaurant and hotel business altogether and made running a store less profitable; and the reserve system made it difficult for Aboriginal people to acquire capital for a business because they could not use their homes or land as security to get a loan. More personal kinds of racism, including white customers' refusal to be served by Aboriginal people, meant that they were not hired in restaurants or retail stores, and low educational levels kept them out of white-collar professions. When the wage economy contracted, as it did after the Second World War, the government's alternative to the subsistence economy was the expansion of the welfare system.

At the turn of the nineteenth century, Indian agents estimated that less than 1 per cent of Aboriginal income came from the government. This figure rose to 4 per cent during the Depression and to 17 per cent by 1954. In 1966, 25.4 per cent of the on-reserve Aboriginal population in British Columbia received financial assistance, more than eight times the provincial average. By 1972–3, the percentage of British Columbia's Aboriginal people dependent on social assistance had increased to 47 per cent.[42]

Conclusion

In the twentieth century, several simultaneous processes affected Aboriginal people's ability to earn a living. First, industry and seasonal work, the main employers of Aboriginal people, were in decline. Second, while educational levels for Canadians and the percentage of jobs requiring high-school and post-secondary education were rising rapidly, this was not the case for Aboriginal people. In residential schools, Aboriginal people were

Indigenous girls trained to be servants at All Hallows Residential School, Yale, BC. (Annual report of the Department of Indian Affairs for the year ended June 30 1902. COP.CA.CI.1 1902 Copy 1 [AMICUS 90778].)

educated for menial, low-paying jobs, many of which were also in decline due to mechanization. Third, the land and sea that Aboriginal people had turned to in the past could no longer provide as good a living as a result of competing economic activities such as logging and commercial fisheries, as well as state regulations that limited hunting and fishing. Fourth, an influx of settlers from Eastern Canada and Europe reduced Aboriginal people to a minority in the province. These immigrants produced and supported racist ideologies that characterized Aboriginal people as lazy and worthless, preventing employment in many service industries. Finally, at the beginning of the twentieth century, laws against the potlatch began to be enforced. Because earning wealth to potlatch had been one of the key motivations for Aboriginal people to join the capitalist economy, the government discouraged them from working for their own reasons.

In the latter half of the twentieth century, Aboriginal people vanished from the workforce and became one of the most impoverished segments of British Columbia society through a process of increasing state regulation and anti-conquest narrative. This latter approach had different fronts: residential schools, missionaries, literary and media constructions, and derogatory stereotypes. The anti-conquest narrative also existed in workplaces, where Aboriginal people were inundated with capitalist values, and in the regulations that denied Aboriginal people access to their subsistence and capitalist economies. Lekwungen Elder Joyce Albany recognized the challenge. "Believe me," she told the *Colonist* in 1973, "we very often sit down and talk about the White Problem."[43]

Notes

1. Franz Boas, *The Ethnography of Franz Boas: Letters and Diaries of Franz Boas Written on the Northwest Coast from 1886–1931*, ed. Ronald Rohner, trans. Hedy Parker (Chicago: University of Chicago, 1969), June 1889. I use the terms *Aboriginal peoples*, *Indigenous people*, and *Native people* to describe the descendants of the pre-European population in the Americas. For one suggested usage, see Greg Younging, "Talking Terminology: What's in a Word and What's Not," *Prairie Fire* 22, 3 (2001): 130–40.

2. Potlatch refers to a variety of feasts held by Northwest Coast Indigenous peoples. While the feasts might mark weddings, deaths, or the passing of titles or ownership to rights or resources, the common feature was that the hosts fed visitors—sometimes numbering in the thousands—and provided goods as gifts to all that attended. The higher status a guest, the more valuable the gift.

3. Reverend H.B. Owen in "Reports of the Rev. H.B. Owen . . . to the United Society for the Propagation of the Gospel," Rhodes House Library, Oxford, as cited in Grant Keddie, *Songhees Pictorial: A History of the Songhees People as Seen by Outsiders, 1790–1912* (Victoria: Royal British Columbia Museum,

2004); *British Colonist*, 23 and 28 Apr. 1874; *Victoria Daily Standard*, 22 Apr. 1874; see also W.W. Walkem, *Stories of Early British Columbia* (Vancouver: News Advertiser, 1914), 114–15; I.W. Powell, Department of Indian Affairs Annual Report (DIAR), 1877, 32–4.

4. From 1870 to 1975, adjusted by F.H. Leacy, *Historical Statistics of Canada* (Ottawa: Statistics Canada, 1983), Index K44–6; and from 1975 to 2008, adjusted by the Consumer Price Index historical summary from Statistics Canada, http://www.40.statcan.ca/cstolecon46.htm (site now discontinued; see new summary tables site at www.statcan.gc.ca/tables-tableaux/sum-som/l01/cst01/econ46a-eng.htm).

5. DIAR, 1882, 160, 170; DIAR, 1885, 101; J.H. Van Den Brink, *The Haida Indians: Cultural Change Mainly between 1876–1970* (Leiden, The Netherlands: E.J. Brill, 1974), 42.

6. Helen Codere, *Fighting with Property: A Study of Kwakiutl Potlatching and Warfare, 1792–1930* (Seattle: University of Washington Press, 1972), 126.

7. I.W. Powell in DIAR, 1882, 130–60; Robin Fisher, *Contact and Conflict: Indian–European Relations in British Columbia*, 2nd edn (Vancouver: UBC

Press, 1992), 111. This pattern differs from the experience in the rest of Canada, but wherever you look, Indigenous peoples' poverty worsened as areas were settled by Europeans.

8. F.W. Howay and E.O.S. Scholefield, *British Columbia from the Earliest Times to the Present* (Vancouver: S.J. Clarke, 1913); E.O.S. Scholefield and R.E. Gosnell, *Sixty Years of Progress: A History of British Columbia*, 2 vols (Vancouver, Victoria: British Columbia Historical Association, 1913); see also H.H. Bancroft, *History of British Columbia, 1792–1887* (San Francisco: History, 1887).

9. Frederick Jackson Turner, *The Frontier in American History in 1920* (New York: Holt, Rinehart and Winston, 1962). See also Richard Slotkin, *Regeneration through Violence: The Mythology of the American Frontier, 1600–1860* (Middleton, CT: Wesleyan University Press, 1973).

10. In April 1991, Justice McEachern, in *Delgamuukw v. BC*, took this position in denying the claim. See *BC Studies* 95 (1992) and Dara Culhane, *The Pleasure of the Crown: Anthropology, Law, and First Nations* (Vancouver: Talonbooks, 1998).

11. An example of this perspective is Peter Carstens, *The Queen's People: A Study of Hegemony, Coercion and Accommodation among the Okanagan of Canada* (Toronto: University of Toronto Press, 1991).

12. Fisher, *Contact and Conflict*, 111, 211.

13. James Lenihan, Canada Sessional Papers, (Cda. S.P.) 1876, 56; see also Indian Superintendent Powell, Cda. S.P. 1877, 33–4.

14. Library and Archives of Canada, (LAC) RG 10 Vol. 1350 file: Cowichan Agency Departmental Circulars, 1892–1910, A.W. Vowell, 9 Mar. 1896.

15. James Spradley, ed., *Guests Never Leave Hungry: The Autobiography of James Sewid, a Kwakiutl Indian* (Kingston: McGill-Queen's University Press, 1989), 27; Bridget Moran, *Stoney Creek Woman: The Story of Mary John* (Vancouver: Tillacum Library, 1988), 29, 78, 81; Beth White in Yukon Archives (YA), Yukon Women's Project Sound Recording (Transcripts) file 13-5; Margaret Blackman, *During My Time: Florence Edenshaw Davidson, A Haida Woman* (Vancouver: Douglas and McIntyre, 1982), 109; Harry Assu, *Assu of Cape Mudge: Recollections of a Coastal Indian Chief* (Vancouver: UBC Press, 1989), 62; Leona Marie Sparrow, "Work Histories of a Coast Salish Couple" (Master's thesis, University of British Columbia, 1976), 263.

16. Maureen Cassidy, *From Mountain to Mountain: A History of the Gitksan Village of Ans'payaxw* (Kispiox: Ans'payaxw School Society, 1984), 39; DIAR, 1901, 285; Joan Skogan, *Skeena: A River Remembered* (Vancouver: British Columbia Packers, 1983), 77.

17. Department of Fisheries, *Annual Report*, 1929–30, 105; M.C. Urquhart and K.A.H. Buckley, *Historical Statistics of Canada* (Toronto: MacMillan, 1965), 396.

18. Sayachi'apis, John Fornsby, August Khatsahlano, George Swanaset, John Wallace, and James Spradley fished but do not mention owning their own boats.

19. Sparrow, "Work Histories," 30; Spradley, *Guests*, 58; Blackman, *During My Time*, 82; Collen Bostwick, "Oral Histories: Theresa Jeffries," *Labour History*, 2, 3 (1980): 8–15.

20. John McMullan, "State, Capital, and the B.C. Salmon Fishing Industry," and Keith Warriner, "Regionalism, Dependence, and the B.C. Fisheries: Historical Development and Recent Trends," in Patricia Marchak, Neil Guppy, and John McMullan, eds, *UnCommon Property: The Fishing and Fish-Processing Industries in British Columbia* (Toronto: Methuen, 1987), 107–52, 326–50; Dianne Newell, *Tangled Webs of History: Indians and the Law in Canada's Pacific Coast Fisheries* (Toronto: University of Toronto, 1993).

21. Ulli Steltzer and Catherine Kerr, *Coast of Many Faces* (Vancouver: Douglas and McIntyre, 1979), 46, 49.

22. British Columbia, *Sessional Papers* (BC S.P.), 1893, "Report of the British Columbia Fishery Commission" estimated that canneries employed an average of 40–50 Aboriginal women; 1953 figure from H.B. Hawthorn, C. Belshaw, and S.M. Jamieson, *Indians of British Columbia: A Study of Contemporary Social Adjustment* (Toronto: University of Toronto Press, 1959), 113.

23. Hawthorn et al., *Indians of British Columbia*, 115; M.J. Friedlaender, *Economic Status of Native Indians in British Columbia Fisheries* (Vancouver: Environment Canada, Fisheries Operations Branch, Technical Report Series PAC/T-75-25, 1975).

24. *Resources of British Columbia*, 1, 4 (June 1883), 4; Cda, S.P. 1886, Vol. 4, 84; Hawthorn et al., *Indians of British Columbia*, 114.

25. Lutz, *Makúk*, Table VII.

26. Clellan S. Ford, *Smoke from Their Fires: The Life of a Kwakiutl Chief* (Hamden, CT: Archon, 1968), 133–4; June Collins, "John Fornsby: The Personal Document of a Coast Salish Indian,"

in Marian Smith, ed., *Indians of the Urban Northwest* (New York: Columbia University Press, 1949), 329; Oliver Wells, *The Chilliwacks and Their Neighbours* (Vancouver: Talonbooks, 1987), 197; Harry Robinson, *Write It on Your Heart: The Epic World of an Okanagan Storyteller*, ed. and comp. Wendy Wickwire (Vancouver: Talonbooks/Theytus, 1989), 11.

27. Henry Pennier, with Herbert L. McDonald, *Chiefly Indian: The Warm and Witty Story of a British Columbia Half Breed Logger* (Vancouver: Graydonald Graphics, 1972), 57.

28. James Burrows, "'A Much Needed Class of Labour': The Economy and Income of the Southern Interior Plateau Indians, 1897–1910," *BC Studies* 71 (Autumn 1986): 27–46; DIAR, 1886 Vol. 4, 81, 84.

29. LAC, Department of Citizenship and Immigration, RG 26 Vol. 106 file: 1/1-15 part 8: "Indian Migrant Workers," Report for the International Labour Organization, Oct. 1953; LAC, RG 10, Vol. 8423 801/21-1, reel C-13835, W.S. Arneil to Indian Affairs Branch, 27 May 1957.

30. Charles Jones with Stephen Bosustow, *Queesto, Pacheenaht Chief by Birthright* (Nanaimo: Theytus, 1981), 91.

31. Frank Fuller, "Gilbert Joe," *Labour History* 2, 3 (1980): 16–19; Blackman, *During My Time*, 109; Jones with Bosustow, *Queesto*, 90–1; Interviews with Dave Dawson at Kingcome and Charlie Johnson at Owikeno, in Steltzer and Kerr, *Coast of Many Faces*, 68, 82, 135.

32. Hawthorn et al., *Indians of British Columbia*, 113.

33. Helen Codere, *Fighting With Property: A Study of Kwakiutl Potlatching and Warfare, 1792–1930* (Seattle: University of Washington, 1972), 43–8; Blackman, *During My Time*, 109; Assu, *Assu*, 66; Spradley, *Guests Never Leave Hungry*, 75; Pritchard, "Economic Development and the Disintegration," 122–7; Jones with Bosustow, *Queesto*, 94.

34. Douglas Hudson, "Traplines and Timber: Social and Economic Change among the Carrier" (PhD dissertation, University of Alberta, 1983), 145.

35. DIAR, 1918, 38.

36. DIAR, 1919, 52–3.

37. Ibid.

38. Moran, *Stoney Creek Woman*, 77–81; see also Pennier, *Chiefly Indian*, 58; Assu, *Assu*, 66; Spradley, *Guests Never Leave Hungry*, 95; Blackman, *During My Time*, 120; Lutz, *Makúk*, Figure VII.

39. LAC, RG 10, Vol. 11,147 file: Shannon "Fishing 1914–41," J.A. Motherwell, Chief Supervisor of Fisheries to M.S. Todd, M.S. Indian Agent, Alert Bay, 20 May 1940; LAC, RG 10, Vol. 11,147 file: Shannon "Fishing 1914–41," W.M. Halliday to W.E. Ditchburn, 16 June 1919.

40. LAC, RG 10, Vol. 8570, file: 901/1-2-2-2, Andy Paull speaking at a conference on the Indian Act, 20–1 July 1955.

41. Albany claimed clam digging and commercial fishing accounted for 80 per cent of their livelihood, *Colonist*, 18 Oct. 1960, 1; LAC, RG 10, Vol. 9,170 file: Cowichan Agency General B-45 Lizzie Fisher to H. Graham, Cowichan Indian Agent, Aug., 1932; Charles to H. Graham, 6 Aug. 1932; Robbie Davis to H. Graham, 8 Dec. 1934.

42. D.B. Fields and W.T. Stanbury, *The Economic Impact of The Public Sector Upon the Indians of British Columbia* (Vancouver: University of BC, 1973), 46; Andrew Siggner and Chantal Locatelli, *An Overview of the Demographic, Social and Economic Conditions Among British Columbia's Registered Indian Population* (Ottawa: Research Branch, Corporate Policy, Department of Indian Affairs and Northern Development, 1981), 39.

43. *Colonist*, 30 Jan. 1973.

Primary Document

Excerpts from the Diary of Arthur Wellington Clah

Introduction by John Lutz

Arthur Wellington Clah (1831–1916) was a Ts'msyen man who led a varied and rich life as a trader, an Aboriginal healer, a Christian teacher, and a labourer. He mixed his traditional spiritual, family subsistence, and economic practices with those of the immigrant society.[1] In 1857, Clah met William Duncan, a missionary, in Fort Simpson (now Port Simpson) on the BC coast. The two men taught each other their native languages, although (as you will see) Clah's English is very much his own version. As a result of this encounter, Clah kept a daily diary from 1858 to 1916. Because few Aboriginal people could write in English in this period and journal writing was not one of their practices, Clah's diaries are an extremely rare kind of primary source—a view of the nineteenth-century world through the eyes of an Aboriginal man.

What follows are excerpts from Clah's diary from the spring and summer of 1860. We have kept his spelling but have indicated places where we are unsure of his intentions with [?] and placed suggested words in square brackets. The original diaries are housed at the Wellcome Institute in London, England (MS American 140).

5th Months May had 31 Days 1860
Morning and I begin work [?] at New Westminster and of Fraser River 14 of May 1860
I had 15 Days of working at New Westminster an of Fraser River for in May 1860

24th May 1860
Queen is Born[2]

Steamer Wilson G. Hunt started for New Westminster about 7 o'clock on Thursday night the 15 of May 1860. Capt. Wellice Commante [in command?] and Clah going the same steamer Wilson G. Hunt go all night. 9 hours gone an he in New Westminster and Clah Shew [?] in Fraser River on Wednesday morning

6th Months June had 30 Days 1860
I begin work.

Victoria V.I. friday june 29th 1860. I bought a revolver from soldiers and I pay 2 of silver him standing by Sawchuck [?] Indian.
I left New Westminster on Saturday morning on Steamer Wilson G. Hunt.

Steamer Wilson G. Hunt arrived at New Westminster at Fraser River on the 20th

Arthur Wellington Clah. (Apostle of Alaska/ Wikipedia.)

June 1860. And I heard some bad news. I hear my brother has been shoot. Blessed are those who die in the Lord and I am very Sorry for my Brother Die. My Brother also was name Wallice Brother of Clah: this man who shooting brother of Clah also name Cayqun [of layqun?] he is Bad Man killing my Brother.

Cayqun [?] him over
Bad Man be his
Place Name
Yellow Jaw [?]
Cay Qun Killing
3 men in one day an in one hour.
On man killing another
day 4 men all together
Wallice Shu claks [?] weth [with] my [me].

7th Months July has 31 days 1860
I had in that month good working do Some things and every Day.

7 of July 1860 and I went Down Victoria on Saturday evening and on steamer hunt and steamer hunt arrived on Sunday morning 8 inst. [inst. meaning of this month] with 9 hours from at Fraser River an at New Westminster.
And 13 at inst. and the same steamer started for New Westminster.
And he arrived at place on Saturday morning carry good lot men.
8th Month August had 31 days 1860

Westminster Fraser River August 6th 1860
Monday morning I have been working for week and when I am done working and I going back in my house and I shew [saw] one large deer swim an in the River. To when I shew [show] deer them I called Charry [Charley?] he had a little boat uset [used] for carry loaves Bread at Bank and of Soldiers Camp. Clah an them I called Charrly 2 of men siting in little boat and after that one indian came coming to 2 indian sitting an 2 indian first killing Deer and was [?] catching Deer from indian Charrly Tuked [took] Deer in is boat an he going to Shore and all whit [whites?] coming together and some men has knive in them hand to cuting Deer is meat an all the men cuted [cutted]

an Deer is fresh cuted there in pieces an Tooked [taken] away and Charrly angry with them all men and Charrly fighting with one man. fighting for deer

Notes

1. To learn more about Arthur Wellington Clah, see Robert Galois, "Colonial Encounters: The Worlds of Arthur Wellington Clah", *BC Studies* 5–6 (Autumn–Winter 1997/98): 105–47.

2. [Clah is noting the celebration of the Queen's birthday, Victoria Day.]

Secondary Source

Colonialism at Work: Labour Placement Programs for Aboriginal
Women in Postwar Canada

Joan Sangster

During the 1950s, the Department of Indian Affairs' newsletter *The Indian News* featured optimistic stories of Aboriginal[1] women's successful integration into the world of steady wage labour. "Indian Girls Achieve Successful Careers—Pave the Way for Others," reprinted on pages 302–4, was typical of these expositions. Another article highlighted "Treaty Indian" women who had migrated to the city from reserves and had conquered many obstacles to became stenographers, hairdressers, and office workers. Their personal stories projected a positive message: persistent women could overcome time in a sanatorium, rural isolation, or lack of education and triumph in the world of work.[2] In contrast, popular exposés of Indigenous women's downward spiral into poverty and criminality also emerged in the mainstream press, not unlike some of the recent "sensational" stories of Indigenous women adrift in the city.[3] These women were often portrayed as refugees from dying reserves. In one well-publicized story, two young girls from God's Lake, MB, were sent to Vancouver on a trip funded by MacMillan Bloedel, in the hopes that they would imbibe the benefits of further education and pursue careers as typists. Instead of joining the modern life of "airplanes, appliances, and bathtubs" that they experienced in the city, the girls returned to the "futility, despair, unemployment" of the reserve. The article suggested that it was the responsibility of Canadian society to aid and uplift Aboriginal people like these, who were attempting to move from traditional to modern lives by escaping failing reserves.[4]

Aboriginal women's experiences of life and labour were far more complex than these stark morality tales would suggest. While there is no doubt that some faced increasing material and social marginality in the postwar period, their actual labour was misrepresented in this dualistic narrative of moving either up or down the ladder of modernity. At the same time, these narratives do reflect some of the popular prejudices and state perspectives of the postwar period. The Indian Affairs Branch (IAB), under the purview of the Department of Citizenship and Immigration during the 1950s, believed that Aboriginal women would increasingly migrate to urban areas, that they should be integrated into permanent wage labour in service and clerical jobs (at least until marriage), and that expert guidance from the state was necessary as Aboriginal women made the transition from "traditional" modes of living to modern employment. This article explores the genesis in the 1950s of federal labour placement programs for Aboriginal women, how these programs were actually implemented on the Prairies, and why they failed to achieve the stated goals of the IAB.[5] Although these programs had some limited successes, they were unable to effectively reverse Aboriginal women's economic marginalization. Indeed, they might simply have modernized or reinvented colonial relationships. This is not to say that Aboriginal peoples had no interest in such initiatives; on the contrary, in testimony before Senate and House of Commons committees, Aboriginal organizations often called for more training, better education, and greater wage labour opportunities, especially for their youth. However, the calls of Aboriginal organizations for employment justice were wider ranging and encompassed a much broader program of economic development, while state-initiated programs were narrowly designed and ultimately unable to address the more pervasive economic and ideological legacies of colonialism.

Labour historians often designate the post–Second World War period as that of the "Fordist accommodation," a tacit pact between organized labour, capital, and the state that offered labour new legal protections in exchange for increased production and regulation of the workplace. While this agreement may have increased economic security for unionized workers, it did not apply to a "second tier" of the labour force, including many women, immigrants, and non-white workers who faced a gendered and racialized division of labour, less job security, and more limited (if any) unemployment benefits. Not only was Fordism a term that had little resonance for Indigenous peoples, but many Aboriginal communities actually experienced intensified economic marginalization in the postwar period; the Royal Commission on Aboriginal Peoples (RCAP) refers to this as a "dark era of increased dependency."[6] The legacies of this economic marginalization remain visible today. The high levels of urban poverty, racism, criminalization, and violence that Aboriginal women face must be seen in the context of the postwar era of deepening "dependency," a process that labour placement programs were unable to address effectively.

In order to understand the context and rationale for labour placement programs, the questions posed by feminist labour history and political economy are useful starting points. How did men and women sustain themselves as the material conditions around them changed? How did they negotiate, accommodate, and resist economic and social changes, drawing on the cultural resources at hand and, in turn, reshaping their cultures? How did women's role in social reproduction shape daily life and wage labour? What was the role of the state in shaping gender and racial divisions of labour? In this story, life and labour, colonialism and class, gender and race become inseparable categories; the denigration of Indigenous cultures and the racialization of Aboriginal women cannot be separated from their economic exploitation. However, even if hard economic times defined Aboriginal women's lives in the postwar decades, they did not determine them. Women's own accounts indicate how they negotiated the changing economic situation with their own courageous strategies for individual and family survival. Some embraced the possibility that labour placement programs seemed to offer, even if the overall impact of these programs was far less than Aboriginal peoples had hoped.

Context for Labour Placement Programs

Historically, it is difficult to disentangle Aboriginal women's work from family and community or to separate their paid and unpaid labour, especially for those peoples combining different kinds of work, including seasonal and casual wage labour, permanent wage labour, bush production for use, and bush production for market exchange.

As one study of Manitoba First Nations concluded, most families on reserves and in rural areas were enmeshed in a family economy that involved multiple earners and multiple occupations, what Jean Legassé labelled a "cycle economy."[7] Aboriginal economies also varied considerably in strength and affluence (or poverty) across the Prairies, but there are still good reasons for the RCAP's negative characterization of this period, even though for some communities a downward slide had started in the 1930s. In northern Manitoba, for instance, Aboriginal peoples had been adjusting their labour to new markets and resource extraction for decades. However, changes in the fur trade, a decline in fur prices, the dispossession of Aboriginal land title, the incursion of new resource industries, and the loss of casual work that had been essential for Aboriginal families combining multiple forms of labour for survival all made this adaptation more difficult. As Frank Tough concludes, there was "an intensified integration of Indigenous communities into the capitalist market on terms very unfavourable to them."[8]

There are six brief points to make about the intensification of hard times on the Prairies after the war and the context in which labour placement programs emerged.[9] First, economic changes always interacted dynamically and often negatively with other social and cultural assaults on Indigenous life, such as the legacy of violence and cultural denigration associated with residential schooling. Second, economic problems were particularly difficult for those involved in the production of commodities such as fish and fur and for those engaged in multiple occupations or a seasonal cycle of jobs. Because many waged jobs were decasualized in northern areas and given to white people, Indigenous families were forced to rely more heavily on trapping at a time of declining fur prices.[10] In northern Saskatchewan, for instance, some families combined trapping with what little wage labour or welfare could be secured, eking out an existence on $300 to $400 a year, an income that was undoubtedly "Third World" in nature.[11]

Third, in many expert studies by social scientists and in the eyes of IAB, women in these economies were secondary workers, who, for example, might help to bring in extra money as handicraft producers but were not the primary earners. Even researchers who recognized that they were dealing with a "colonial" economy in northern Saskatchewan still referred to Aboriginal "male breadwinners" as being responsible for all the trapping "income," while women were responsible for "domestic affairs."[12] The interdependent nature of the family economy was thus misread, and women's unpaid labour, essential to family survival, was rendered invisible. Yet, in their autobiographical accounts, Métis and Indian women recall how they produced food for survival, cared for the family, collaborated in the fishing industry, and were part of a chain of production in fur, skinning and creating a pelt for sale in a process that was itself highly skilled and "artisanal." Increasingly, Aboriginal women also had to find more wage work to aid the family economy.

Fourth, the state's response to these economic difficulties was often stop-gap and based on decidedly colonial views of Indigenous labour. One example was the sugar beet program in southern Alberta, which employed Indigenous families from across the Prairies who were denied welfare payments in their home reserve if they refused to migrate to the beet fields for summer work. IAB pushed Aboriginal people into seasonal fieldwork during the 1950s because it saw them as well-suited for migrant, temporary, physical, low-paid work; moreover, it knew that practices of family-based labour were easily incorporated into the regime of agricultural work.

Fifth, Aboriginal people tried to offer their input on economic development and labour policies. To note only one example, many bands and Indian organizations provided briefs or gave testimony on these issues to federal parliamentary committees in 1947–48 and again in 1959–60. Although the 1947–48 hearings on the Indian Act focused more on issues such as education, treaty rights, and health, these were not completely distinct from economic development. In its submission, the Le Pas Indian Band argued that "economic conditions are at the heart of the whole problem [of Indian life] . . . without a decent income, the average Canadian, Indian or otherwise, will not be healthy. Only by raising living standards through cooperative industrial development, will there be the basis for a healthy and virile people."[13] During the 1959–60 joint Senate and House of Commons hearings into Indian Affairs, more calls were made by Aboriginal groups for expanded wage employment in concert with demands such as the protection of trapping rights, the establishment of make-work projects on reserves, and job training off the reserves. In the groups' view, respecting the treaties and protecting the right to subsistence were quite compatible with more education and paid work, but many politicians tended to see an either/or choice for Indigenous peoples: either "traditional" trapping or "modern" work roles. Finally, these calls for economic development and justice, while challenging a racial division of labour, did not question the existing gendered division of labour. Chiefs, bands, and advocacy groups generally assumed that women needed access to home aide, clerical, and nursing aide jobs. This is hardly surprising, given the tenacious persistence of a sex-segregated labour market for all Canadian women and the glaring lack of any jobs for Indigenous women in many communities.

Labour Placement Programs

It was precisely these difficult conditions that led to Aboriginal women's increased mobility and search for new economic options in the postwar period. Moreover, leaving reserves allowed Aboriginal people to escape the often invasive and moralistic surveillance of the Indian agent.[14] The high number of women moving to urban areas was also a result of the Indian Act's infamous "marrying out" clause (section 12(1) (b)), which stated that "Indian" women lost their status and right to live on the reserve when they married a non-Indian.[15] Like their Métis counterparts, these women were then disadvantaged because they were officially disqualified from participating in the IAB's education and labour placement programs. Whether status or non-status, many Aboriginal women who were new to urban areas had difficulties finding jobs and housing, coping with low wages, and handling the isolation from their communities. The 1957 Labour Placement and Relocation Program (shortened to Labour Placement Program) was supposed to address at least some of these problems: the solution to Aboriginal economic development, the state reasoned, was "full time jobs, steady incomes . . . and integration into the industrial economy of Canada."[16] Initiated with placement officers located in four large cities (three in the Prairie West), the program sought to provide employment counselling, liaison with unions and businesses, on-the-job training, help finding jobs, and loans and aid with relocation. The IAB identified the need for "general" placements in casual jobs and "permanent" placements for which the candidate might need more training, though it clearly saw more hope in the latter. Although there were some rural dimensions (resource work) to the program, it was generally assumed that relocation to towns and cities would be necessary, especially for female-typed jobs. The program was not unlike the American relocation program begun by the Bureau of Indian Affairs a few years earlier, which encouraged (indeed, pushed) American Indians to leave reservations and relocate in urban centres, where blue- and white-collar jobs were more plentiful.[17]

In developing the program, the IAB could point not only to Aboriginal demands for more employment opportunities but also to contemporary social science experts, many of whom urged greater wage employment as a key solution to the poverty on reserves. The implicit assumption was that Native poverty was the product of their failure to embrace wage labour rather than the result of colonialism and capitalist underdevelopment.[18] Moreover, the IAB chose selectively from the experts. Anthropologist Harry Hawthorn's extensive investigation of contemporary Indian life opened by rejecting the "assimilation and integration" of Indians as a state objective, yet he also tended to fall back on a model that posited a linear progression from failing subsistence economies to jobs within industrial capitalism; progress was equated with higher-paying wage labour, enhanced skills and training, acceptance of new forms of work discipline, and, importantly, the male breadwinner family. Hawthorn believed that this strategy would aid, not destroy, Aboriginal cultures, stemming the tide of "personal and social disorganization" plaguing Indigenous communities.[19] Hawthorn's anthropological perspective on cultural preservation was not embraced by the IAB, which was more inclined to favour integration as a means of replacing what it saw as problematic Aboriginal cultural practices with new ones better suited to the "modern" workplace.

Labour placement programs had two gender tracks: men were moved into resource work or into (generally) blue-collar jobs in urban areas, while women were trained for white-collar and service occupations.[20] These parallel streams were linked ideologically through the ideal of the "family wage";[21] women's job options were often predicated on the belief that they would eventually become part of a male breadwinner household. While our historical focus has understandably been on forms of political discrimination against Aboriginal women encoded in the Indian Act, it is important to remember that the state's active promotion of this male breadwinner model was also instrumental in both encouraging patriarchal ideologies in Indigenous families and communities and offering lessons in racialized and gendered labour.

Unfortunately, one of the IAB's longer-standing work solutions for Aboriginal women, long before 1957, was domestic service, which was integrated into new placement programs even though some Indian agents admitted that it was not always popular or permanent work for women. Girls coming out of residential schools were presumed to be especially well-suited for such work because domestic training was an important part of the curriculum, because girls were forced to perform domestic labour within the schools, and because some girls had worked in domestic placements during their summers.[22] Domestic service was supposed to provide young women with a preliminary introduction into the world of wage labour and serve as the first step towards employment in service or factory jobs. Indeed, in its list of public achievements, the IAB pointed to the domestic courses it offered Aboriginal girls as signs of its success.

The IAB also promoted domestic jobs as a means of preventing female juvenile delinquency, claiming that they kept young women, susceptible to immoral influences, off the streets. Like earlier generations of working-class women, these domestic workers were viewed as morally fragile and susceptible to the "wrong kind of influence."[23] However, race and the racialization of urban space were also at issue. Aboriginal women's presence in the city was viewed as alien to the natural Indian character; they were literally out of place in urban spaces or, worse, viewed as "trespassers" in white space, a colonialist view that exposed women to the threat of racism and violence.[24] As one well-intentioned Winnipeg reformer put it, Aboriginal women are "displaced persons in their own land, trying to bridge the gap between generations when their proud race was *left behind*."[25] This image of a "race left behind" may have inspired the pity of some, but it also encouraged contempt from others, an invitation for discrimination and violence.

Theoretically at least, there was supposed to be more emphasis on training women for jobs in the white- and pink-collar sectors: clerical, hospital, and hairdressing work were three hopeful areas for female employment. The IAB also assumed that many Indigenous people needed cultural makeovers if they were to move into jobs requiring "white" standards of work discipline, as if Aboriginals had had no previous experience with wage labour. Cultural explanations were often used to explain the dissonance between "Indian" and "modern" work and as a rationale for special "catch up" economic aid for Aboriginals. Bush production may have imposed a different timetable and culture of work, but to see it only as intermittent or as a choice that allowed one to escape working year round missed the structured imperatives of the cycle economy in which many Aboriginal communities were enmeshed. The IAB's attempts to educate the public in this regard are revealing. Its widely circulated pamphlets on Indian life argued that Aboriginal peoples needed sympathy and aid in securing new employment since white incursions onto their land had "knocked [Aboriginal] cultures off balance . . . leading Indians feeling lost, bewildered and hopeless" and since they now faced "social and cultural intolerance."[26] Yet this modicum of sympathy and responsibility was negated by descriptions that made Indigenous peoples sound like "primitives" needing paternal aid: they were people whose idea of making a living was to "live only for today"; "they lived by the sun, moon and tides rather than by the clock or calendar"; and "nothing in their experience has taught them to deal with crises they now faced."[27]

The implication that Aboriginal cultures were, by their very definition, incompatible with the rhythms of modern wage labour was also potentially dangerous. Taken in one extreme direction, this determinist view of culture became a rationale for simplistic prejudices. In Winnipeg, a local committee with state, labour, and business participants was set up to help to integrate Indians into urban jobs. A garment manufacturer told the first meeting that there were many jobs available but that Aboriginal women had problematic work habits. The union representative agreed: "Indian women could be absorbed into the needle trades, dry cleaning, and other service jobs" if only their work habits and "social adjustment" improved.[28]

Given the IAB's notion that there was an "Indian" employment personality, placement officers were required to assess not only candidates' formal education and language skills but also their character traits before enrolling them in the program. Since life in the city was assumed to involve stressful cultural adaptation, only those with "stable" personalities who were able to "mix with non-Indians" and withstand pressure without "losing control or resorting to alcoholism" were to be selected. Particular hope was placed on the young, who were seen to be more malleable. "With considerable guidance," it was believed that "this younger element could eventually integrate into the non-Indian communities." Integration, however, was just another word for assimilation.

For some Aboriginal women, hairdressing was a step up from domestic work; however, it was not necessarily work that could sustain a household. In her autobiography, *Halfbreed*, Maria Campbell recalls getting a job in a beauty salon after taking a hairdressing course. Within two weeks, it was clear that the "wages were so poor" that she could not support herself and her children. She had no choice but to head to the welfare office.[29] The number of women trained to be hairdressers, however, paled beside those who ended up in service jobs and domestic work. When Jean Lagassé did his survey of Aboriginal employment in Winnipeg, he found that the largest groups of women who came to the city found their first job in "restaurant kitchen work" (38 per cent) and their second in housework (38 per cent), with a much smaller group (4 per cent) in nurse's aide positions. Aboriginal women's wages put them at the bottom of the economic scale, followed closely by Métis women—statistics that remain similar today.[30]

Lagassé, like many other well-meaning liberals, called for an end to racial discrimination and special supports for Métis and Aboriginal families, but he too saw permanent and skilled work for men as *the* solution. Women's economic fate was largely determined by their ties to men. While recognizing that Aboriginal women had their own employment dreams, such as nursing jobs, he pointed out that they—unlike Aboriginal men—could always marry a white man and therefore "move up" the social ladder. Some urban Aboriginal women, he said, already "pass," importing a term usually applied to African Americans. These women did not need special programs since they "already fit into urban Canada as contributing members."[31] Who, then, were the non-contributing members: Indigenous women who valued their heritage but were still employed washing dishes? Lagassé implied that these "passing" women were the successful ones, but the response of one such woman who was interviewed was a horrific comment on the pervasiveness of racism: "My husband would kill me [if he knew I was an Indian]," she said.[32]

One of Lagassé's recommendations, supported not only by the IAB but also groups such as Indian and Métis friendship centres, was that girls should be taught typing and other commercial skills because these jobs were seen as better opportunities for young urban women. The IAB developed an in-house placement experiment for such women, costing the department a mere $10,000 a year. It had to lobby strenuously to increase funding and expand the program to 22 placements. Status Indians with high-school or commercial college education but still unable to find employment were given jobs in IAB offices in order to provide them with experience, letters of reference, and extra training. Workers received a weekly allowance but not actual wages, so they were ineligible for unemployment insurance, leaving them vulnerable after the program ended. Moreover, there was no question that the government saw this as a program for single women rather than female "breadwinners."

Given the focus on clerical jobs, there was a certain bias towards women, and there were some small but noticeable increases in the number of Aboriginal women in white-collar work by the end of the 1960s. Again, however, a cultural makeover was part of women's training, for the women were often seen as too insecure, shy, reclusive, and quiet for the work world and not the kind, one IAB pamphlet informed the public, "likely to sparkle in an interview."[33] The IAB solution was to require the women to take the federal civil service exam after a period of training, so that they could move beyond the supposed "safety" of the IAB offices to other jobs. Perhaps a more pressing problem than "personality" was the limited nature of these in-house programs: 22 jobs do not solve an unemployment problem, let alone address larger issues of economic justice. Even the larger placement program dealt with only about 300 to 600 people a year.[34] One Saskatchewan assessment of labour placement programs in 1969 provided a dismal picture: 79 per cent of the women could only obtain jobs as domestics or waitresses, and the majority of women placed were in "temporary" positions. Placement officers, according to the assessment's radical author, helped employers fulfill hiring targets, while, in private interviews, employers admitted they did not think that "the vast majority of Indians employed would remain on the job."[35]

As these labour placement programs were developed, an anxious discourse about the "problem" of the "Indian in the City" was emerging, a fearful response on the part of whites to the increased urban migration of Indigenous peoples and a clear instance of how space was racialized according to colonial ideologies. While the debate at the time about "the urban Indian" is a topic onto itself, one aspect of it is important to a discussion of Aboriginal women workers: the preoccupation of experts and reformers alike with Aboriginal women's morals. In the Lagassé report, to cite only one example, an interview section that presented various "typical" experiences of women coming to Winnipeg to work was excessively preoccupied with their morality. The interview section discussed the discrimination that Aboriginal women faced in the labour market, their naïveté, and their (often) tragic downward spiral into crime. In one story, a young woman wishing to make good after getting into trouble as a teenager came to the city to find work in the needle trades. Despite her training in this area, she faced discrimination in her job searches. The result: because she was easily led astray by companions, she was soon in conflict with the law.[36] Stories of naive Aboriginal women tricked, led, or forced into prostitution shared parallels with white slave narratives concerning working-class women that circulated at the turn of the nineteenth century; however, the "promiscuity" of Indian women was sometimes taken as a given and equated with the behaviour of "lower-class" white women.[37] This image of an available, promiscuous Indian woman was a staple of racist ideology, and it became a licence for violence perpetrated against Aboriginal women.[38] While decrying discrimination on the one hand, racist stereotypes were thus perpetuated on the other hand in this report; any critique of Aboriginal women's imprisonment in low-wage job ghettos was compromised by recasting the issue as one of morality. These anxieties and stereotypes were replicated in the popular media in more lurid, sensational, and deterministic terms, intensifying the antipathy to Indigenous women's presence in the city. The material exploitation and sexual condemnation of Aboriginal women were thus closely intertwined; therefore, the appropriation of women's labour cannot be separated from the appropriation of their sexual dignity.

Conclusion

In the 1950s and 1960s, Aboriginal women increasingly migrated to urban centres in search of work or to escape conditions on reserves, sometimes making use of the few labour placement programs that existed to retrain, find work, or start new lives. Like many working-class women, they were in search of economic survival and new opportunities; however, many Aboriginal women were often already burdened with an inadequate education geared towards cultural assimilation, and they encountered profoundly racist views of their culture, ability, and morality.

The increasingly interventionist role of the state in managing and reorienting Aboriginal labour is an important theme in this period, one that was fundamentally gendered, both in the conceptualization of the problem and in the creation of policy solutions. Informed in part by social science studies of the time—but also by prevailing idealized images of the white middle-class family—politicians and policy-makers often assumed a male breadwinner family as the ideal. Women were seen as *ancillary* earners who only worked when they were young and single, even though that had never been the case in most Aboriginal communities based on a family economy of pooled resources.

Labour placement solutions to the economic problems faced by Aboriginal peoples took two gender paths: relocation programs to place male breadwinners in blue-collar jobs or job training geared towards a small range of gender-specific jobs for single women. The latter avenue involved both a continuation of earlier efforts to place Aboriginal women in domestic jobs and some new programs intended to foster skills necessary for pink- and white-collar jobs, and it was probably in the second category that some small successes were attained. A similar gendered division of labour was taken for granted by Aboriginal groups lobbying Parliament for more and better labour placement programs; however, their presentations differed from the views of politicians, experts, and bureaucrats in other ways. They did not see an irrevocable choice between bush production and "modern" wage work but promoted a more comprehensive, holistic vision of economic justice for Indigenous peoples.

The programs developed, however, were very limited and often reproduced lessons in gendered and racialized labour that left Indigenous women at the bottom of the employment ladder. Non-Aboriginal women were similarly channelled into a very restricted range of sex-typed jobs by the state, and working-class and poor white women experienced similar efforts to patrol their sexual morality. However, the moral and cultural explanations offered for Aboriginal women's supposed inability to adapt to wage labour, their poverty, or their criminalization were also racialized arguments, even if they were dressed up as cultural difference and paternalist protection. As a consequence, Aboriginal women were especially vulnerable to both material disadvantage and racist denigration as supposedly more "primitive" women. This designation also left them vulnerable to the hostility and violence that we have seen repeatedly directed against Aboriginal women in the most vicious way, from the case of Betty Osborne, murdered in northern Manitoba in November of 1971, to the hundreds of Aboriginal women who have disappeared from Canadian city streets over the past two decades.[39]

While scholarship has understandably focused on the Indian Act's discriminatory "marrying out" clause, this legislation, as Bonita Lawrence argues, was part of a much larger "regulatory regime . . . a way of seeing life . . . that ultimately forms an entire conceptual territory on which knowledge is produced and shaped." The state's image of women as ancillary workers in need of moral protection and its active promotion of a patriarchal male breadwinner model were also ingredients of this regulatory regime. Moreover, Lawrence adds that these ways of thinking often come to "permeate how Indigenous peoples think of themselves. . . . [and] even [their] attempts to change the system itself."[40] To focus on this regulatory regime is, admittedly, only one part of the story of Aboriginal women and paid work in this period, obscuring themes of agency and resistance. As Heather Howard-Bobiwash indicates in her study of the Toronto Indian and Métis Friendship Centre, some women who migrated to urban areas to seek out new employment developed strategies for survival, drawing on kin and community and building organizations to aid other women who came after them.[41] By concentrating on state-initiated programs, however, I have tried to emphasize that political choices were made by the IAB that rested not only on cultural and racial assumptions about the Aboriginal character but also on suppositions about how the capitalist market should work. More specifically, it relied on the theory that it did work—and for the better—allowing all working people, regardless of race and class, to move up the employment ladder. The story of labour placement programs for Indigenous women suggests the opposite: economic justice was not to be found in piecemeal programs or cultural makeovers but through a more comprehensive challenge to the legacies of colonialism on Aboriginal life.

Notes

1. I use *Aboriginal* here in the inclusive way that the RCAP did, to include Métis, Status, and Non-Status Indians. *Indigenous* is sometimes used as a synonym. Federal programs were generally directed at "Status Indians." When referring to documents of the time, I sometimes use their terms: e.g., *Indian*.

2. "Indian Girls Achieve Successful Careers—Pave the Way for Others," *Indian News*, June 1958, 6–7.

3. Dara Culhane, "Aboriginal Women in Eastside Vancouver: Emerging Into Invisibility," *American Indian Quarterly* 27, 3&4 (2003): 593–606.

4. AM, Hudson's Bay Company Records (HBC), RG 7/1/760, Reports from Posts, Newspaper clippings, 12 and 20 July 1966.

5. For a more detailed analysis of women's work in this period, see Mary Jane McCallum, "Labour, Modernity and the Canadian State: A History of Aboriginal Women and Work in the Mid-Twentieth Century," (PhD Dissertation: University of Manitoba, 2008).

6. Canada, *Royal Commission on Aboriginal Peoples*, Vol. 2 (Ottawa, 1996), 777.

7. Jean Lagassé, *The People of Indian Ancestry in Manitoba*, Vol. 3 (Winnipeg: Dept. of Agriculture and Immigration, 1959), 54.

8. Frank Tough, *As Their Natural Resources Fail: Native Peoples and the Economic History of Northern Manitoba, 1870–1930* (Vancouver: UBC Press, 1996).

9. For more on context, see Joan Sangster, *Transforming Labour: Women and Work in Postwar Canada* (Toronto: University of Toronto Press, 2010), Ch. 6.

10. Arthur Ray, *I Have Lived Here Since the World Began* (Toronto: Key Porter Books, 1996), 291.

11. P.M. Worsely, Helen.L. Buckley, and A.K. Davis, *Economic and Social Survey of Northern Saskatchewan* (Saskatoon: Centre for Community Studies, University of Saskatchewan, 1961).

12. J.M. Kew, *Cumberland House, 1960, Report #2, Economic and Social Survey of Northern Saskatchewan* (Saskatoon: Centre for Community Studies, University of Saskatchewan, 1962), 31, 90.

13. Canada, Senate and House of Commons Joint Committee on the Indian Act (JCI Act), 1947–48, #15, 665.

14. Joan Sangster, *Regulating Girls and Women: Sexuality, Family and the Law in Ontario, 1920–1960* (Toronto: Oxford University Press, 2000), Ch. 6; Robin Jarvis Brownlie, "Intimate Surveillance: Indian Affairs, Colonization, and the Regulation of Aboriginal Women's Sexuality," in Katie Pickles and Myra Rutherdales, eds, *Contact Zones: Aboriginal and Settler Women in Canada's Colonial Past* (Vancouver: UBC Press, 2006), 169–79.

15. Nancy Janovicek, "Assisting Our Own: Urban Migration, Self-Governance, and Indigenous Women's Organizing in Thunder Bay, Ontario, 1972–1989," *American Indian Quarterly* 27, 3&4 (Summer–Fall, 2001): 548–65.

16. Canada, Dept. of Citizenship and Immigration, *The Indian in Transition: The Indian Today* (Ottawa, 1962), 10, 15.

17. James Lagrand, *Indian Metropolis: Indigenous Americans in Chicago* (Urbana: University of Illinois Press, 2002); Kathryn MacKay, "Warriors into Welders: A History of Federal Employment Programs for American Indians, 1898–1972" (PhD dissertation, University of Utah, 1987).

18. See Hugh Shewell, *"Enough To Keep Them Alive" Indian Welfare in Canada, 1873–1965* (Toronto: University of Toronto Press, 2004).

19. Indian and Northern Affairs Canada, *A Survey of the Contemporary Indians of Canada Economic, Political, Educational Needs and Policies: Part 2* (The Hawthorn Report), (Ottawa, Indian Affairs Branch, 1967), 127.

20. There were distinct programs for Aboriginal nurses. See Mary Jane McCallum, *Twice As Good: A History of Aboriginal Nurses* (Ottawa: Aboriginal Nurses Association of Canada, 2007).

21. Michele Barrett and Mary McIntosh, "The Family Wage: Some Problems for Socialists and Feminists," *Capital and Class* 9, 1/2 (Summer 1980): 51–72.

22. LAC, RG 10, Vol. 8415, 1/ 21-1, Summer Placement from Mohawk Residential School, 1961.

23. LAC, RG 10, Vol. 8413, 1-21-1, Hilda Holland to Mr Matters, Indian Affairs, 18 Mar. 1948.

24. Evelyn Peters, "'Urban' and 'Aboriginal': An Impossible Contradiction?," in J. Caulfield and L. Peake, eds, *City Lives & City Forms: Critical Research & Canadian Urbanism* (Toronto: University of Toronto Press, 1996), 47–62; Sherene Razack, ed., *Race, Space and the Law: Unmapping a White Settler Society* (Toronto: Between the Lines, 2002).

25. AM, Beatrice Brigden Papers, P 820, f 2, clipping, *Winnipeg Free Press*, 18 Jan. 1958 (my emphasis).

26. The pamphlet distinguished the latter from "racial intolerance." George Mortimer, *The Indian in Industry: Roads to Independence* (Ottawa: Dept. of Citizenship and Immigration, 1965), 9.

27. *The Indian in Transition*, 6, and George Mortimer, *The Indian in Industry*, 7, 4.

28. LAC, RG 10, Vol. 8574, 1/1-2-2-17, 14 Feb. 1963.

29. Maria Campbell, *Halfbreed* (Toronto: Seal Books, 1973), 154.

30. Lagassé, *The People of Indian Ancestry*, 65; Linda Gerber, "Multiple Jeopardy: A Socio-Economic Comparison of Men and Women Among the Indian, Métis and Inuit Peoples of Canada," *Canadian Ethnic Studies* 22, 3 (1990): 69–84.

31. Lagasse, *The People of Indian Ancestry*, 129.

32. Ibid.

33. George Mortimore, *The Indian in Industry*, 7.

34. In 1959, it was reported that 262 Indians were established in urban employment as a result of the efforts of placement officers. The numbers did increase, but not dramatically. LAC, RG 10, Vol. 8414, file 1/21-1, pt 6, introduction, placement manual.

35. Edgar Dosman, *Indians: The Urban Dilemma* (Toronto: McClelland and Stewart, 1972), 133. Only 12 of 216 women in the sample had obtained permanent jobs. He did note that the "best off" were women with some high-school education who secured white-collar jobs.

36. Lagassé, *The People of Indian Ancestry*, 111–12.

37. Lagassé makes this equation more than once in *The People of Indian Ancestry*.

38. Andrea Smith, *Conquest: Sexual Violence and American Indian Genocide* (Boston: South End Press, 2005).

39. Amnesty International, *Stolen Sisters: A Human Rights Response to Discrimination and Violence Against Indigenous Women in Canada*, Oct. 2004. Available at www.amnesty.ca/sites/default/files/amr200032004enstolensisters.pdf.

40. Bonita Lawrence, "Gender, Race, and the Regulation of Indigenous Identity in Canada and the U.S.: An Overview," *Hypatia* 18, 2 (Spring 2003): 3–31.

41. Heather Howard-Bobiwash, "Women's Class Strategies as Activism in Indigenous Community Building in Toronto, 1950–75," *American Indian Quarterly* 27, 3&4 (Summer–Fall, 2001): 566–82.

Primary Document

Indian Girls Achieve Successful Careers—Pave Way for Others

Indian News, June 1958

Indian News was a newsletter published by the Department of Indian Affairs.

In recent years numbers of Indian workers have been finding their way to Winnipeg. Many who have settled there have found work to suit their abilities and are happy in their new life. Among those who have become successfully employed are young women working in homes and offices.

Miss Rose Bear came to Winnipeg five years ago from the Pequis Indian reserve near Dallas, Manitoba. At first she worked as a ward aid in a city hospital, later obtained employment with a wholesale firm doing general office work. With financial assistance obtained from the Indian Affairs Branch she studied comptometry at night school for 10 months and now utilizes her skill, coupled with switchboard operating, at the wholesale house.

The loneliness felt by a stranger in an unfamiliar city she allayed by joining a church choir, by going bowling with friends, by visits to relatives and occasional trips back to her home.

Another Treaty Indian girl to take advantage of assistance offered by the Indian Affairs Branch is Mrs. Gordon MacKay who left her home at Cross Lake two years ago to take a course in hair dressing at the Manitoba Technical Institute. She is now employed in a Sargent Avenue beauty salon, and is married to another Treaty Indian employed by a city department store. Between them they are saving to establish a home in the city.

Two teenagers, Ruth Le Tandre of Fairford and Frances McCorrister of Hodgson, attended high school together and came to Winnipeg to complete their education. They have been studying stenography at the Manitoba Technical Institute and learning to like the life of the city where they hope to earn their living.

Another successful migrant from the reserve to the city is young Lorna Kirkness of Koostatak, north of Fisher River. Though she was forced to spend several months in a sanatorium, she afterwards came to Winnipeg to temporary employment with the Manitoba Sanatorium Board. She took a course in shorthand at the Manitoba Technical Institute, with government assistance, and now is a stenotypist in the Board's new office.

Each day more Indian girls from reservations and rural points make their way into Canadian cities, seeking further education and jobs. Many succeed in their quest, thus bridging the gap successfully between an old and a newer life. And, in doing so, they pave the way for others of their race to take their place in Canadian society.

Frontier Nurse

A Treaty Indian, the first in Saskatchewan to be placed in charge of an outpost nursing station, is at work at La Range in the northern section of the province.

She is Jean Cuthland, 29 years of age, and a Registered Nurse. The new head nurse was born on the Little Pine Indian Reserve, just west of North Battleford, attended school at the Reserve, later in Saskatoon, and took her nurse's training at Holy Family Hospital in Prince Albert.

Before taking charge of the La Ronge nursing station, Miss Cuthland served in the Indian Hospital in Fort Qu'Appelle, and is anxious to continue as a "frontier nurse." Her example gives further evidence of the growing responsibility which Indian young people are taking in the country's social life.

Winnipeg Attracts Indian Workers

More Indians now live in Winnipeg than on any single reserve in Manitoba—and the movement is growing.

This surprising fact was revealed by Jean Lagassé, chairman of the housing committee of the fourth annual conference on Indians and Métis, held in Winnipeg in January. A survey had shown that more than 2000 Indians lived in Winnipeg while the largest reserve in Manitoba—Island Lake—was inhabited by 1620.

Resolutions presented at the conference stressed the need for increased education, recreation, housing, counselling and improved employment. It was also suggested that a referral service for Indian and part-Indian newcomers to Winnipeg should be established to counsel strangers on matters of employment, housing, education, health, and other community services, that Indians who had adjusted successfully to urban life should be enlisted to aid other Indians.

Questions for Consideration

1. How does Lutz's view of Indigenous peoples and labourers in the late nineteenth and early twentieth centuries challenge the usual historical view?
2. What, in Lutz's view, explains the marginalization of Indigenous peoples in British Columbia and their corresponding impoverishment?
3. What can the excerpts from Arthur Wellington Clah's diary teach us about the following: a) the labour market for Aboriginal workers; b) Clah's lifestyle and the lifestyles of other Indigenous peoples and workers; and c) settler–Indigenous relations on the west coast in 1860?

4. What were the goals of the labour placement programs for Indigenous workers in the postwar period? How did they fit with the goals of federal Indian policy more broadly, as outlined by Shewell in Chapter 7, and with the objectives of the residential schools, as discussed by Haig-Brown and Sekwan Fontaine in Chapter 9?

5. In what ways were the federal government's attempts to integrate Indigenous workers into the "modern" industrial economy gendered and/or racialized?

6. What lessons does the author of the article from *The Indian News* want readers to learn from the examples of "successful Indian girls" that he or she provides?

7. How integral have Indigenous workers been to the modern economy? How would you explain the poverty of Indigenous peoples in Canada and their exclusion/marginalization from the economy?

Further Resources

Books and articles

Fisher, Robin. *Contact and Conflict: Indian–European Relations in British Columbia*, 2nd edn. Vancouver: UBC Press, 1992.

Laliberte, Ron. "The "Grab-a-Hoe" Indians": The Canadian State and the Procurement of Aboriginal Labour for the Southern Alberta Sugar Beet Industry," *The Prairie Forum* 31, 2 (Fall 2006): 305–24.

Lutz, John. *Makuk: A New History of Aboriginal–White Relations*. (Vancouver: UBC Press, 2008).

McCallum, Mary Jane Logan. *Indigenous Women, Work, and History, 1940–1980* (Winnipeg: University of Manitoba Press, 2014).

Parnaby, Andrew. "The Best Men That Ever Worked the Lumber: Aboriginal Longshoreman on Burrard Inlet, B.C., 1863–1939," *Canadian Historical Review* 87, 1 (2006): 53–78. (online)

Williams, Carol. *Indigenous Women and Work: From Labour to Activism* (Urbana: University of Illinois Press, 2012).

Wright, Eric. "Indigenous Women and Work: From Labor to Activism," *The Canadian Journal of Native Studies* 33, 2 (2013): 192–4.

Printed Documents and Reports

Canada. Department of Indian Affairs, *Annual Reports*, 1864–1990. www.bac-lac.gc.ca/eng/discover/aboriginal-heritage/first-nations/indian-affairs-annual-reports/Pages/introduction.aspxCanada. Employment and Immigration Canada.

The Development of an Employment Policy for Indian, Inuit, and Metis People. Ottawa: Employment and Immigration Canada, 1978.

Canada. *Report of the Royal Commission on Aboriginal People*, Vol. 1–5 (Ottawa: Canada Communications Group Publishing, 1996).

Indian and Northern Affairs Canada. *A Survey of the Contemporary Indians of Canada: Economic, Political, Educational Needs and Policies: Part 2* (The Hawthorn Report). Ottawa: Queen's Printer, 1967. Available at www.aadnc-aandc.gc.ca/eng/12918324 88245/1291832647702.

Films

Broke. DVD. Directed by Rosie Dransfeld. ID Productions, 2009.
César's Bark Canoe. DVD. Directed by Bernard Gosselin. NFB, 1991.
High Steel. DVD. Directed by Don Owen. NFB, 1965.
Mohawk Girls. DVD. Directed by Tracey Deer. NFB, 2005.

Websites

Aboriginal Professional Association of Canada
www.aboriginalprofessionals.org/

BC Stats' statistics on Aboriginal peoples in the province
www.bcstats.gov.bc.ca/StatisticsBySubject/AboriginalPeoples.aspx

First Nations Employment Society
www.fnes.ca

Human Resources and Skills Development Canada, "Indicators of Well-Being"
www4.hrsdc.gc.ca/.3ndic.1t.4r@-eng.jsp?iid=16

Statistics Canada, "Aboriginal Peoples in Canada's Urban Area"
www.statcan.gc.ca/pub/81-004-x/2005003/8612-eng.htm

12

Indigenous Women, Strength, and Resilience

Introduction

In Canada, Indigenous women face a double bind—they experience discrimination not only as a function of patriarchy but also as a result of the intersection of colonialism, racism, and sexism. Under the auspices of the Canadian nation-state, Indigenous women are subject to disproportionate surveillance, restraint, and violence. Jaime Cidro's article in Chapter 8 outlines some of the structural sexism and racism Indigenous women face under the Indian Act due to the "marrying out clause." Beginning with legislation passed by the province of Canada in 1868 and 1869, Indigenous women were assigned far fewer rights under the law than Indigenous men. For instance, until 1951 Indigenous women were prohibited from holding elected positions as band council members or chiefs (this included voting in elections as well); married women could not possess land or marital property; and a widow could only inherit familial property upon her husband's death if it was willed to her and if the Indian agent deemed her to be of sound moral character. Such legal prohibitions ran contrary to the social, economic, and political practices of many Indigenous nations and were intended to make Indigenous peoples more like European-Canadians.

The systemic racism and sexism experienced by Indigenous women has taken many forms, but perhaps the most alarming is the disappearance and murder of Indigenous women, which has become epidemic in Canada. In 2004, Amnesty International published *Stolen Sisters: Discrimination and Violence against Indigenous Women in Canada*. The report revealed that young Indigenous women are five times more likely to die as a result of violence than any other women of the same age.[1] A 2014 RCMP report found that the "total number of murdered and missing Aboriginal females exceeds previous public estimates."[2] Although these are horrifying statistics, the depressing reality is that the evidence of this phenomenon is all around us. For example, the Highway of Tears (Highway 16) in northern British Columbia, Vancouver's Downtown Eastside, and the

"Killing Fields" outside Edmonton are all spaces of murderous sexual violence that target Indigenous women either disproportionately or exclusively.

The violence that Indigenous women experience today cannot be disassociated from the colonial past. Andrea Smith argues that violence, especially sexual violence, towards Indigenous women is part of a colonial strategy that seeks to "not only destroy people, but to destroy their sense of being a people."[3] The first article in this chapter, by Sarah Carter, outlines how Indigenous women were marginalized in Western Canada's nascent white settler society during the late nineteenth and early twentieth centuries. For instance, municipalities passed bylaws that prohibited Indigenous women from traversing urban areas without passes, and stereotypes that portrayed them as lascivious and sexually available made them appear threatening to the white body politic. Such stereotypes remain shockingly persistent. The dehumanization and objectification of Indigenous women makes the violence and murder perpetrated on their bodies appear normal and acceptable. According to Carter, the marginalization of Indigenous women, the sexualization of their bodies, and the violence done to their persons were essential to Canadian nation-building and to assuring "Euro-Canadian newcomers [of] their belief that their cultural and moral superiority entitled them to the land that had become their home."

Recent scholarship seeking to make the experiences and roles of Indigenous women more visible has also complicated the ways in which Indigenous women have responded to structural racism, sexism, and colonialism. In spite of the best efforts of the settler state, Indigenous women were and continue to be vital to the well-being and persistence of their families, communities, and cultures. Indigenous women have also stood at the forefront of demanding change—we need only to consider recent events: Christi Belcourt's founding of Walking With Our Sisters; the establishment of Idle No More in 2011 by three Indigenous women; the efforts of Chief Theresa Spence, and many other women like her in their communities across Turtle Island, to address the housing crisis in Attawapiskat First Nation; or the iconic image of Amanda Polchies, member of the Elsipogtog First Nation, who knelt down in the middle of a roadblock with an eagle feather while the RCMP advanced.

Such examples clearly show, as Sylvia Maracle and others emphasize, that although Indigenous women were victims of oppression, they were also strong and resilient, and, in countless instances, led and continue to lead their communities' attempts to overcome colonial legacies.[4] Lianne C. Leddy's piece looks at the efforts of Indian Affairs to impose European-Canadian domestic normativity on Indigenous women through the creation of Homemakers' Clubs on reserves. Although the clubs were intended to make Indigenous women more like European-Canadians, the women who joined them used the clubs for their own purposes, especially before 1951 when the Indian Act precluded Indigenous women from participating in more formal political structures. The final article in this chapter, by Cora Voyageur, examines Elsie Knott, the first woman to become a chief under the revised Indian Act of 1951. According to Voyageur, Knott's life is a testament to the strength, courage, and intelligence of Indigenous women in the face of overwhelming obstacles. Dedicated to improving the lives of the people in her community, Knott stands in the tradition of the many strong Indigenous women who have played central roles in their families and societies.

Chapter Objectives

At the end of this chapter, you should be able to

- identify some of the most common stereotypes associated with Indigenous women and explain how these labels helped further the colonial project;
- explain some of the ways that Indigenous women have resisted these stereotypes;
- identify some strong Indigenous women; and
- discuss the career of Curve Lake First Nation Chief Elsie Knott.

Notes

1. Amnesty International, *Stolen Sisters: A Human Rights Response to Discrimination and Violence Against Indigenous Women in Canada*. Oct. 2004. Available at www.amnesty.ca/research/reports/stolen-sisters-a-human-rights-response-to-discrimination-and-violence-against-indig, accessed 30 June 2015.

2. RCMP, *Missing and Murdered Aboriginal Women: A National Operational Overview* (Ottawa: 2014), 3.

3. Andrea Smith, *Conquest: Sexual Violence and American Indian Genocide* (Cambridge, MA: South End Press, 2005), 3.

4. Sylvia Maracle, "The Eagle Has Landed: Native Women, Leadership and Community Development," in Kim Anderson and Bonita Lawrence, eds, *Strong Women Stories: Native Vision and Community Survival* (Toronto: Sumach Press, 2003), 70–1.

Secondary Source

Categories and Terrains of Exclusion: Constructing the "Indian Woman" in the Early Settlement Era in Western Canada

Sarah Carter

In 1884, Mary E. Inderwick wrote to her Ontario family from the ranch near Pincher Creek, AB, where she had lived with her new husband for six months.[1] The letter provides a perspective on the stratifications of race, gender, and class that were forming as the Euro-Canadian enclave grew in the district of Alberta. Mary Inderwick lamented that it was a lonely life, as she was 22 miles from any other women, and she even offered to help some of the men near them to "get their shacks done up if only they will go east and marry some really nice girls." She did not consider the companionship of women such as "the squaw who is the nominal wife of a white man near us," and she had dismissed her maid, who had become discontented with her position as a servant. Inderwick had disapproved of a ball at the North-West Mounted Police (NWMP) barracks at Fort Macleod, despite the fact that it was "the first Ball to which the squaws were not allowed to go, but there were several half breeds." Commenting on the Aboriginal population that still greatly outnumbered the new arrivals, Inderwick wrote that they should have been "isolated in the mountains," rather than settled on nearby reserves, and that the sooner they became extinct the better for themselves and the country.

At the time of Mary Inderwick's arrival in the West the consolidation of Canada's rule was not yet secure. The Métis resistance of 1885 fed fears of a larger uprising, and an uncertain economic climate threatened the promise of a prosperous West. There was a sharpening of racial boundaries and categories in the 1880s and an intensification of discrimination in the Canadian West. The arrival of women immigrants like Mary Inderwick after the Canadian Pacific Railway was completed through Alberta in 1883 coincided with other developments such as the railway itself, the treaties, and the development of ranching and farming that were to stabilize the new order and allow the recreation of Euro-Canadian institutions and society. The women did not introduce notions of spatial and social segregation, but their presence helped to justify policies already in motion that segregated the new community from Indigenous contacts.[2] The Canadian state adopted increasingly segregationist policies towards the Aboriginal people of the West, and central to these policies were images of Aboriginal women as dissolute, dangerous, and sinister.

From the earliest years that people were settled on reserves in Western Canada, Canadian government administrators and statesmen, as well as the national press, promoted a cluster of negative images of Aboriginal women. Those in power used these images to explain conditions of poverty and ill health on reserves. The failure of agriculture on reserves was attributed to the incapacity of Aboriginal men to become other than hunters, warriors, and nomads.[3] Responsibility for a host of other problems, including the deplorable state of housing on reserves, the lack of clothing and footwear, and the high mortality rate, was placed upon the supposed cultural traits and temperament of Aboriginal women. The depiction of these women as lewd and licentious, particularly after 1885, was used to deflect criticism from the behaviour of government officials and the NWMP and to legitimize the constraints placed on the activities and movements of Aboriginal women in the world off the reserve. These negative images became deeply embedded in the consciousness of the most powerful socio-economic groups on the Prairies and have resisted revision.

The images were neither new nor unique to the Canadian West. In "The Pocahontas Perplex" Rayna Green explored the complex, many-faceted dimensions of the image of the Indian woman in American folklore and literature. The beautiful "Indian Princess" who saved or aided white men while remaining aloof and virtuous in a woodland paradise was the positive side of the image. Her opposite, the squalid and immoral "Squaw," lived in a shack at the edge of town, and her "physical removal or destruction can be understood as necessary to the progress of civilization."[4] The "Squaw" was pressed into service and her image predominated in the Canadian West in the late nineteenth century, as boundaries were clarified and social and geographic space marked out. The either/or binary left newcomers little room to consider the diversity of the Aboriginal people of the West or the complex identities and roles of Aboriginal women.

Euro-Canadian Settlement of the West

Following the transfer of the Hudson's Bay Company territories to the Dominion of Canada in 1870, the policy of the federal government was to clear the land of the Aboriginal inhabitants and open the West to Euro-Canadian agricultural settlement. To regulate settlement, the North-West Mounted Police was created and 300 of them were dispatched west in 1874. A "free" homestead system was modelled on the American example, and a transcontinental railway was completed in 1885. To open up the West to "actual settlers," seven treaties with the Aboriginal people were negotiated from 1871 to 1877, and through these the government of Canada acquired legal control of most of the land of the West. In exchange, the people received land reserves, annuities, and, as a result of hard bargaining by Aboriginal spokesmen, commitments to assist them to take up agriculture as their buffalo-based economy collapsed. A Department of Indian Affairs, with headquarters in Ottawa, was established in 1880, and in the field an ever-expanding team of Indian agents, farm instructors, and inspectors were assigned to implement the reserve system and to enforce the Indian Act of 1876. The people who had entered into treaties were wards of the government who did not have the privileges of full citizenship and were subject to a wide variety of controls and regulations that governed many aspects of life.

Much to the disappointment of the federal government, the West did not begin rapid development until the later 1890s. There were small pockets of Euro-Canadian settlement, but in 1885 in the district of Alberta, for example, the Aboriginal and Métis population was greater than 9500, whereas the recent arrivals numbered only 4900.[5] All seemed hopeless, especially by the mid-1880s, when immigration was at a near standstill. Years of drought and frost and problems finding suitable techniques for farming the northern Plains account in part for the reluctance of settlers, and the 1885 resistance of the Métis in present-day Saskatchewan did little to enhance the image the government wished to project of the West as a suitable and safe home.

Development of Stereotypes

Particularly irksome to many of the recently arrived "actual settlers" was the Aboriginal competition they faced in the hay, grain, and vegetable markets. Despite obstacles, many Aboriginal farmers had produced a surplus for sale. Settlers' particularly vocal and strident complaints led the government to curtail farming on reserves. To explain why underused reserves had become pockets of rural poverty, Indian Affairs officials claimed that Aboriginal culture and temperament rendered the men unwilling and unable to farm.

Plains women were also responsible: according to government pronouncements they were idle and gossipy, preferring tents to proper housing because tents required less work to maintain and could be clustered in groups that allowed visiting and gossip. Reports of the superintendent general of Indian Affairs claimed that Indians raised dust with their dancing and the women's failure to clean it up spread diseases such as tuberculosis. Administrators blamed the high infant mortality rate on the indifferent care of the mothers. The neglected children of these mothers grew up "rebellious, sullen, disobedient and unthankful."[6] Whereas men were blamed for the failure of agriculture, women were portrayed as resisting, resenting, and preventing any progress towards modernization. As an inspector of Indian agencies lamented in 1908, "The women, here, as on nearly every reserve, are a hindrance to the advancement of the men. No sooner do the men earn some money than the women want to go and visit their relations on some other reserve, or else give a feast or dance to their friends. . . . The majority of [the women] are discontented, dirty, lazy and slovenly."[7]

The unofficial and unpublished reports of reserve life show that officials recognized that problems with reserve housing and health had little to do with the preferences, temperament, or poor housekeeping abilities of women. Because of their poverty the people were confined in large numbers in winter to what were little better than one-room and one-storey huts or shacks that were poorly ventilated and impossible to keep clean, as they had dirt floors and were plastered with mud and hay. Tents and tipis might well have been more sanitary and more comfortable. One inspector of agencies noted in 1891 that women had neither soap, towels, wash basins, nor wash pails, and no means with which to acquire these.[8] Officials frequently noted that women were short of basic clothing but had no textiles or yarn to work with. Yet in official public statements, the tendency was to ascribe blame to the women rather than to draw attention to conditions that would injure the reputation of government administrators.

"Licentiousness" and Government Officials

Officials propagated an image of Aboriginal women as dissolute, as the bearers of sinister influences, to deflect criticism from government agents and policies. This image was evoked with particular strength in the wake of an 1886 controversy that focused upon the alleged "brutal, heartless and ostentatious licentiousness" of government officials resident in Western Canada.[9] The remarks of Samuel Trivett, a Church of England missionary on the Blood Reserve in present-day southern Alberta, became the focus of the controversy. To a special correspondent for *The Mail* of Toronto, Trivett said that Indian women were being bought and sold by white men who lived with them without legally marrying them and abandoned the offspring to life on the reserve.[10]

Trivett strongly hinted that some government agents were involved in licentious behaviour, an accusation seized upon by critics of the administration of Indian Affairs in Western Canada. In the House of Commons in April of 1886, Malcolm Cameron, Liberal member of Parliament, delivered a lengthy indictment of Indian Affairs in the West, focusing upon the unprincipled and unscrupulous behaviour of officials of the Indian department. Cameron quoted Trivett and further charged that agents of the government, sent to elevate and educate, had instead acted to "humiliate, to lower, to degrade and debase the virgin daughters of the wards of the nation." He knew of one young Indian agent from England, unfit to do anything there, who was living on a reserve in "open adultery with two young squaws . . . reveling in the sensual enjoy-ments of a western harem, plentifully supplied with select cullings from the western prairie flowers."[11]

Cameron implicated members of the NWMP in this behaviour, wondering why it was that over 45 per cent of them were reported to have been under medical treatment for venereal disease. Cameron was not the first to raise the matter of police propriety in the House. Concern about possible improper relations between the police and Aboriginal women long predated the Trivett scandal and was one aspect of a larger debate in the press and in the House in the late 1870s over char-ges of inefficiency, lack of discipline, high desertion rates, and low morale in the force. Lieutenant-Governor of the North-West Territories David Laird alerted NWMP Commissioner James Macleod in 1878 that reports about immoral conduct were in circulation:

> I fear from what reports are brought me, that some of your officers at Fort Walsh
> are making rather free with the women around there. It is to be hoped that the good
> name of the Force will not be hurt through too open indulgence of that kind. And
> I sincerely hope that Indian women will not be treated in a way that hereafter may
> give trouble.[12]

Although Macleod and Assistant Commissioner A.G. Irvine denied that there was "anything like "a regular brothel" about the police posts, such reports persisted. In the House of Commons in 1880 Joseph Royal, a Manitoba member of Parliament, claimed that the NWMP was being accused of "disgraceful immorality" all over the West. Royal had been informed that "many members of the force were living in concubinage with Indian women, whom they had purchased from their parents and friends."[13] In 1886, public attention was once again drawn to police behaviour. *The Mail* informed its readers that between 1874 and 1881 the police had "lived openly with Indian girls purchased from their parents" and only the arrival of settlers had compelled them to abandon or at least be "more discreet in the pursuit of their profligacy."[14]

There is little doubt that Trivett and other critics based their accusations of both the police and government officials on some foundation, but remaining evidence is scanty and scattered. Missionaries depended to a large extent on the goodwill of gov-ernment and were rarely as outspoken as Trivett or John McLean, a Methodist mission-ary on the Blood Reserve near Fort Macleod, who in 1885 characterized many reserve employees as utterly incompetent and urged the government to employ only married men, "of sterling Christian character."[15] But missionaries were instructed in 1886 by Edgar Dewdney, lieutenant-governor of the North-West Territories, not to voice their accusations to the newspapers "even if allegations against public officials were true," as this would do more harm than good, would affect mission work, and could be used to stir up political strife.[16] Government officials generally investigated reports of gov-ernment misconduct themselves and this functioned to cover up or to mitigate such allegations. Similarly, members of the NWMP themselves looked into any complaints about the force's behaviour.

Tahnoncoach, believed to be a niece of Sitting Bull, was the Lakota wife of George Pembridge, NWMP, Fort Walsh, c. 1878. (Glenbow Archives NA-935-1.)

Marriages of Aboriginal Women and NWMP Members

There were members of the NWMP, especially among the earliest recruits of the 1870s and early 1880s, who formed relationships with Aboriginal and Métis women, as did a great many other male immigrants of these years. Some of these were marriages of long standing, sanctioned by Christian ceremony or customary law. Other relationships were more temporary. Cecil Denny, for example, while a sub-inspector at Fort Macleod, had a daughter with Victoria Mckay, a part-Peigan woman who was the wife of another policeman, Constable Percy Robinson.[17] Denny was forced to resign from the force in 1881 as a result of his involvement in a series of court cases that Robinson brought against him for "having induced his wife to desert him and also having criminal connections with her."[18]

D.J. Grier, who served three years with the NWMP beginning in 1877 at Fort Macleod, married Molly Tailfeathers, a Peigan woman, and together they had three children.[19] By 1887, however, Grier had remarried a white woman. For a short time the children from his first marriage lived with their mother on the Peigan Reserve, but the two eldest were taken from her and placed in the care of Grier's parents. Grier was one of the most prominent men of the West. Renowned as the first commercial wheat grower in Alberta, he also served as mayor of Macleod for 12 years, from 1901 to 1913.

Abuse of Aboriginal Women

John O'Kute-sica wrote at length about one unsuccessful Wood Mountain customary marriage, that of his aunt Iteskawin and Superintendent William D. Jarvis. According to O'Kute-sica, his aunt consented to marry Jarvis because he promised that her brothers and sisters would have something to eat twice a day, and all of her people were in want and suffering. After only a few weeks of marriage, Jarvis, in a jealous rage, publicly assaulted Iteskawin at a Lakota "Night Dance," an incident that strained relations between the two communities, and she immediately left him.[20] On most of the few occasions that Aboriginal women laid charges against policemen for assault or rape, their claims were hastily dismissed.[21]

Some government employees resident on reserves clearly abused their positions of authority. In 1882, Blackfoot Chief Crowfoot and his wife complained that the farm instructor on their reserve demanded sexual favours from a young girl in return for rations, and when an investigation proved this to be the case the man was dismissed.[22] Both the documentary and oral records suggest that several of the government employees that the Crees killed at **Frog Lake** and Battleford in the spring of 1885 were intensely resented because of their callous and at times brutal treatment of Aboriginal women. The farm instructor on the Mosquito Reserve near Battleford, James Payne, was known for his violent temper—he once beat a young woman and threw her out of his house when he found her visiting his young Aboriginal wife. The terrified and shaken woman, who was found by her father, died soon after, and her grieving father blamed Payne, whom he killed in 1885.[23] As a Touchwood Hills farm instructor told a visiting newspaper correspondent in 1885, the charges of immorality among farm instructors on reserves were in many instances too true, as "the greatest facilities are afforded the Indian instructor for the seduction of Indian girls. The instructor holds the grub. The agent gives him the supplies and he issues them to the Indians. Now you have a good idea of what semi-starvation is. . . ."[24]

Blaming Aboriginal Women

The most vocal response to the accusations of Trivett and other critics was not to deny that there had been "immorality" in the West but to exonerate the men and blame the Aboriginal women, who were claimed to have behaved in an abandoned and wanton manner and were supposedly accustomed to being treated with contempt, to being bought and sold as commodities, within their own society. In defending the NWMP in 1880, the Toronto *Globe* emphasized that Aboriginal women had "loose morals" that were "notorious the world over" and that "no men in the world are so good as to teach them better, or to try to reform them in this respect." The editor of the Fort *Macleod Gazette*, a former member of the NWMP, argued that whatever immorality there might have been came from the women themselves and from the customs of their society. They were prostitutes before they went to live with white men, who did not encourage this behaviour but were simply "taking advantage of an Indian's offer." *The Mail* told readers that Aboriginal males had sold their wives and children in the thousands to soldiers and settlers since the time of the French fur trade in exchange for alcohol, and that with the arrival of the police a great deal had been done to end this situation.[25]

The *Gazette* stressed, incorrectly, that there was no marriage in Plains societies, simply a little lively bartering with the father and a woman could be purchased for a horse or two. The argument that Aboriginal women were virtual slaves, first to their fathers, and then to their husbands, was called upon by all who wished to deflect criticism from government officials and the NWMP. In the House of Commons in April 1886, Sir Hector Langevin claimed that to Indians marriage was simply a bargain and a sale and that immorality among them long predated the arrival of government agents in the North-West.[26]

The government published its official response to the criticisms of Indian affairs in the North-West in an 1886 pamphlet entitled "The Facts Respecting Indian Administration in the North-West." A government official had again inquired into accusations about the misconduct of employees of the Indian department and, predictably, had found no evidence. The investigator, Hayter Reed, assistant commissioner of Indian Affairs, was one of those unmarried officials who had been accused of having Aboriginal "mistresses" as well as a child from one of these relationships.[27] The pamphlet boldly asserted that Trivett was unable to come up with a shred of actual evidence, although the missionary vehemently denied this.[28] The pamphlet writer admitted that some men had acquired their wives by purchase, but claimed that this was the Indian custom, and that "no father ever dreams of letting his daughter leave his wigwam till he has received a valuable consideration for her." If the government stopped this custom, there would be loud protests, over and above the Indians' "chronic habit of grumbling." "The Facts" insisted that it was not fair to criticize the behaviour of the dead, such as Delaney and Payne, who had "passed from the bar of human judgment."[29]

Constraints on Aboriginal Women

It was the image of Aboriginal women as immoral and corrupting influences that predominated in the non-Aboriginal society that was taking shape. Authorities used this characterization to define and treat Aboriginal women, increasingly narrowing their options and opportunities. Both informal and formal constraints served to keep Aboriginal people from the towns and settled areas of the Prairies and their presence there became more and more marginal.[30] Their presence was seen as incongruous, corrupting, and demoralizing. Classified as prostitutes, Aboriginal women were seen as particular threats to morality and health. An 1886 pamphlet of advice for immigrants entitled "What Women Say of the Canadian Northwest" was quick to reassure newcomers that Aboriginal people were seldom seen. The 320 women who responded to the question "Do you experience any dread of the Indians?" overwhelmingly replied that they rarely saw any. Mrs S. Lumsden, for example, thought they were "hundreds of miles away with sufficient force to keep them quiet."[31]

Following the events of 1885, government officials as well as the NWMP made strenuous efforts to keep Aboriginal people on their reserves. A pass system required all who wished to leave to acquire a pass from the farm instructor or agent declaring the length of and reason for absence. A central rationale for the pass system was to keep away Aboriginal women "of abandoned character who were there for the worst purposes" from the towns and villages.[32] Classified as prostitutes, Aboriginal women could be restricted by a new disciplinary regime. Separate legislation under the Indian Act, and, after 1892, under the Criminal Code, governed Aboriginal prostitution, making it easier to convict Aboriginal women than other women. As legal historian Constance Backhouse has observed, this separate criminal legislation, "with its attendant emphasis on the activities of Indians rather than whites, revealed that racial discrimination ran deep through the veins of nineteenth century Canadian society."[33]

The pass system was also used to bar Aboriginal women from the towns for what were invariably seen as "immoral purposes." Women who were found by the NWMP to be without passes and without means of support were arrested and ordered back to their reserves.[34] In March of 1886 the Battleford police dealt with one woman who refused to leave the town by taking her to the barracks and cutting off locks of her hair. Two years later the Battleford paper reported that "during the early part of the week the Mounted Police ordered out of town a number of squaws who had come in from time to time and settled here. The promise to take them to the barracks and cut off their hair had a wonderful effect in hastening their movements."[35]

Accustomed to a high degree of mobility about the landscape, Aboriginal women found that the pass system not only restricted their traditional subsistence strategies but also hampered their pursuit of new jobs and resources. Government officials further limited the women's employment and marketing opportunities by advice such as that given by one Indian agent, who urged the citizens of Calgary in 1885 not to purchase anything from or hire Aboriginal people, so as to keep them out of the town.[36] The periodic sale of produce, art, and craftwork in urban or tourist areas could have provided income to women and their families, as did such sales for Aboriginal (and European-Canadian) women in Eastern Canada.

Murders of Aboriginal Women

Community reactions to the poisoning of one Aboriginal woman and the brutal murder of another in the late 1880s in southern Alberta reflect the racial prejudices of many of the recent immigrants. In 1888, Constable Alfred Symonds of the NWMP detachment of Stand Off was accused of feloniously killing and slaying a Blood woman by the name of Mrs Only Kill by giving her a fatal dose of iodine. The woman had swallowed the contents of a bottle given to her by Symonds that apparently held iodine and had died the next morning.[37] In his report on the case, Superintendent P.R. Neale of the NWMP wrote to his superior, "I do not think any Western jury will convict him." Symonds appeared before Judge James F. Macleod, former commissioner of the NWMP, in August of 1888 but the Crown prosecutor made application for "*Nolle Prosequi*," (abandoning a legal action) which was granted, and the prisoner was released.[38]

During the 1889 trials of the murderer of a Cree woman identified only as "Rosalie," who had been working as a prostitute, it became clear that there were many in Calgary who felt "Rosalie was only a squaw and that her death did not matter much."[39] Instead the murderer gained the sympathy and support of much of the town. The murder was a particularly brutal one, and the accused, William "Jumbo" Fisk, had confessed and given himself up to authorities, yet there were problems finding any citizens willing to serve on a jury who might convict a white man for such a crime. The Crown prosecutor stated that he regretted having to conduct the case, as he had known the accused for several years as a "genial accommodating and upright young man."[40] Fisk was a popular veteran of 1885, and he was from a well-established Eastern Canadian family. At the end of the first of the Rosalie trials, the jury, astoundingly, found the accused not guilty. Judge Charles Rouleau refused to accept this verdict and he ordered a re-trial at the end of which Rouleau told the jury to "forget the woman's race and to consider only the evidence at hand," that "it made no difference whether Rosalie was white or black, an Indian or a negro. In the eyes of the law, every British subject is equal."[41] It was only after the second trial that Fisk was convicted of manslaughter and sent to prison for 14 years at hard labour. The judge intended to sentence him for life, but letters written by members of Parliament and other influential persons who had made representations to the court as to his good character, combined with a petition from the most respectable people of Calgary, persuaded him to impose the lesser sentence.

The people of Calgary tried to show that they were not callous and indifferent towards Rosalie by giving her "as respectable a burial as if she had been a white woman," although several months later the town council squabbled with the Indian Department over the costs incurred, as the department did not think it necessary to go beyond the costs of a pauper's funeral. As a final indignity, Rosalie was not allowed burial by the priests in the mission graveyard, although she had been baptized into the Roman Catholic Church, because they regarded her as a prostitute who had died in sin. The lesson to be learned from the tragedy, according to a Calgary newspaper, was "keep the Indians out of town."[42]

Haunted by an Image

Negative images of Aboriginal women proved extraordinarily persistent. Their morality was questioned in a number of sections of the Indian Act. As late as 1921 the House of Commons debated a Criminal Code amendment that would have made it an offence for any white man to have "illicit connection" with an Indian woman. Part of the rationale advanced was that "the Indian women are, perhaps, not as alive as women of other races in the country to the importance of maintaining their chastity." The amendment was not passed, as it was argued that this could make unsuspecting white men the "victims" of Indian women who would blackmail them.[43] By contrast, any critical reflections upon the behaviour of early government officials and the police in Western Canada did not survive beyond the controversy of the 1880s. Ideological constraints, combined with more formal mechanisms of control such as the pass system, succeeded in marginalizing Aboriginal women and in limiting the alternatives and opportunities available to them.

Local histories of the Prairies suggest that by the turn of the century many of the settlements of the West had their "local Indian" who was tolerated on the margins or fringes of society and whose behaviour and appearance was the subject of local anecdotes. A solitary Indian woman known only as Liza camped on the outskirts of Virden, MB, for many years until her disappearance sometime in the 1940s. She lived winter and summer in an unheated tent by the railroad tracks although she spent the long winter days huddled in the livery stable and also at times crept into the Nu-Art Beauty Parlour, where she sat on the floor in front of the window, warming herself in the sun. Liza smoked a corncob pipe as she shuffled about the streets and lanes of Virden, rummaging in garbage tins. She bathed under the overflow pipe at the water tower, sometimes clothed and sometimes not, and dried off by standing over the huge heat register in Scales and Rothnie's General Store. To an extent she was tolerated and even assisted; town employees shovelled out a path for her when she was buried under snow, and it was thought that the town fathers supplied her with food from time to time.

The presence of Liza, and the stories told about her, served to sharpen the boundaries of community membership and to articulate what was and what was not considered acceptable and respectable.[44] Liza was the object of both fascination and repugnance as she violated norms of conventional behaviour, dress, and cleanliness, representing the antithesis of "civilized" Prairie society. Although economically and socially marginal, Liza was symbolically important. Her role attests to the recurrent pattern through which the new society of the West gained in strength and identity and sought to legitimate its own authority by defining itself against the people who were there before them. Liza was a real person, but what she represented was a Euro-Canadian artifact, created by the settlement. The narratives circulated about Liza were not those she might have told herself—of the disasters that had stripped her of family and community, or perhaps of her strategies in adopting the character role—and this folklore reflected less about Liza than about the community itself. Her solitary life was unique and in contrast to the lives of Aboriginal women; Liza was not representative of a Lakota woman within Lakota society. Yet her presence on the margins of the settlement was tolerated and encouraged in a way these women were not, as she appeared to fit into the well-established category of the "squaw" which still served to confirm the Euro-Canadian newcomers in their belief that their cultural and moral superiority entitled them to the land that had become their home.

Notes

1. Mary E. Inderwick, "A Lady and Her Ranch," in Hugh Dempsey, ed., *The Best from Alberta History* (Saskatoon: Western Producer Prairie Books, 1981), 65–77.

2. See Margaret Strobel, *European Women and the Second British Empire* (Bloomington: Indiana University Press, 1991). See also Ann Laura Stoler, "Carnal Knowledge and Imperial Power: Gender, Race, and Morality in Colonial Asia," in Micaela di Leonardo, ed., *Gender at the Crossroads of Knowledge: Feminist Anthropology in the Postmodern Era* (Berkeley: University of California Press, 1991), 51–101, and Stoler, "Rethinking Colonial Categories: European Communities and the Boundaries of Rule," in Nicholas B. Kirks, ed., *Colonialism and Culture* (Ann Arbor: University of Michigan Press, 1992), 319–52.

3. See Sarah Carter, *Lost Harvests: Prairie Indian Reserve Farmers and Government Policy* (Montreal & Kingston: McGill-Queen's University Press, 1990).

4. Rayna Green, "The Pocahontas Perplex: The Image of Indian Women in American Culture," in Ellen Carol DuBois and Vicki Ruiz, eds, *Unequal Sisters: A Multicultural Reader in U.S. Women's History* (New York: Routledge, 1990), 15–21, 5.

5. P.B. Waite, *Canada, 1874–1896: Arduous Destiny* (Toronto: McClelland and Stewart, 1971), 149.

6. Canada, *Sessional Papers*, Annual Report of the Superintendent General of Indian Affairs for the year ending 20 June 1898, xix. For the year ending 31 Dec. 1899, xxiii, xxviii, 166; The *Toronto Mail*, 2 Mar. 1889; Pamela Margaret White, "Restructuring the Domestic Sphere—Prairie Indian Women on Reserves: Image, Ideology, and State Policy, 1880–1930" (PhD dissertation, McGill University, 1987); W.H. Withrow, *Native Races of North America* (Toronto: Methodist Mission Rooms, 1895), 114 (quoted).

7. Canada, *Sessional Papers*, Annual Report of the Superintendent General of Indian Affairs for the year ending Mar. 1908, 110.

8. Inspector Alex McGibbon's report on Onion Lake, Oct. 1891, Library and Archives of Canada (LAC), Record Group 10 (RG 10), records relating to Indian Affairs, Black Series, Vol. 3860, file 82, 319-6.

9. *The Globe* (Toronto), 1 Feb. 1886.

10. *The Toronto Mail*, 23 Jan. 1886.

11. Canada, *House of Commons Debates*, Malcolm Cameron, Session 1886, Vol. 1, 72021.

12. E.C. Morgan, "The North-West Mounted Polic: Internal Problems and Public Criticism, 1874–1883," *Saskatchewan History* 26, 2 (Spring 1973): 56–9, Laird quoted 56.

13. Canada, *House of Commons Debates*, 21 Apr. 1880, Joseph Royal, Fourth Parliament, Second Session, 1638.

14. *The Toronto Mail*, 2 Feb. 1886.

15. John Maclean, "The Half-breed and Indian Insurrection," *Canadian Methodist Magazine* 22 (1 July 1885): 173–4.

16. Edgar Dewdney to the Bishop of Saskatchewan, 31 May 1886, NA, RG 10, Vol. 3753, file 30613.

17. *Blackfeet Heritage: 1907–08* (Browning: Blackfeet Heritage Program, n.d.), 171.

18. A.B. McCullough, "Papers Relating to the North West Mounted Police and Fort Walsh," Manuscript Report Series no. 213 (Ottawa: Parks Canada, Department of Indian and Northern Affairs, 1977), 132–3.

19. Personal interview with Kirsten Grier, great-grandaughter of D.J. Grier, Calgary, 19 May 1993. See also *Fort Macleod—Our Colourful Past: A History of the Town of Fort Macleod from 1874 to 1924* (Fort Macleod: Fort Macleod History Committee, 1977), 268–9.

20. John O'Kute-sica Correspondence, Collection no. R-834, file 17b, p. 3, Saskatchewan Archives Board (SAB).

21. S.B. Steele to Commissioner, Fort Maclod, 20 July 1895, LAC, RG 18, Vol. 2182, file RCMP 1895 pt. 2, and Gilbert E. Sanders" Diaries, 20 Oct. 1885, Edward Sanders Family Papers, M1093, File 38, Glenbow Archives, 26.

22. F. Laurie Barron, "Indian Agents and the North-West Rebellion," in F. Laurie Barron and James B. Waldram, eds, *1885 and After: Native Society in Transition* (Regina: Canadian Plains Research Centre, 1986), 36.

23. Norma Sluman and Jean Goodwill, *John Tootoosis: A Biography of a Cree Leader* (Ottawa: Golden Dog Press, 1982), 37.

24. Newspaper clipping, "Through the Saskatchewan," n.p., n.d., William Henry Cotton Collection, SAB.

25. *The Globe* (Toronto), 4 June 1880; [Fort] *Macleod Gazette*, 23 Mar. 1886; *The Toronto Mail*, 2 Feb. 1886.

26. Canada, *House of Commons Debates*, Session 1886, Vol. 1, 730.

27. William Donovan to L. Vankoughnet, 31 Oct. 1886, LAC, RG 10, Vol. 3772, file 34983.

28. *The Globe* (Toronto), 4 June 1886.

29. Department of Indian Affairs, "The Facts Respecting Indian Administration in the North-West" (Ottawa: Department of Indian Affairs, 1886), quoted 9, 12.

30. David Hamer, *New Towns in the New World: Images and Perceptions of the Nineteenth Century Urban Frontier* (New York: Columbia University Press, 1990), 17, 213.

31. "What Canadian Women Say of the Canadian North-West," *Montreal Herald*, 1886, 42–5.

32. L. Vankoughnet to John A. Macdonald, 15 Nov. 1883, LAC, RG 10, Vol. 1009, file 628, no. 596-635.

33. Constance B. Backhouse, "Nineteenth-Century Canadian Prostitution Law: Reflection of a Discriminatory Society," *Histoire sociale/Social History* 18, 36 (Nov. 1985): 420–2.

34. Canada, *Sessional Papers*. Annual Report of the Commissioner of the North-West Mounted Police Force for the Year Ended 1889, reprinted in *The New West* (Toronto: Coles Publishing Company, 1973), 101.

35. *Saskatchewan Herald* (Battleford), 15 Mar. 1886, 13 Mar. 1888.

36. *Calgary Herald*, 5 Mar. 1885.

37. *Macleod Gazette*, 18 July 1888.

38. R.C. Macleod, *The North-West Mounted Police and Law Enforcement, 1873–1905* (Toronto: University of Toronto Press, 1976), 145; see also LAC, RG 18, Vol. 24, file 667-1888.

39. Donald Smith, "Bloody Murder Almost Became Miscarriage of Justice," *Herald Sunday Magazine*, 23 July 1989, 13.

40. James Gray, *Talk to My Lawyer: Great Stories of Southern Alberta's Bar and Bench* (Edmonton: Hurtig Publishers, 1987), 7.

41. Rouleau, quoted in Smith, "Bloody Murder," 15.

42. *Calgary Herald*, 24 July, 10 Sept., 27 Feb., and 8 Mar. 1889.

43. Canada, *House of Commons Debates*, Session 1921, Vol. 4, 26 May 1921, 3908.

44. Diane Tye, "Local Character Anecdotes: A Nova Scotia Case Study," *Western Folklore* 48 (July 1989): 196.

Secondary Source

"Mostly Just as a Social Gathering": *Anishinaabe Kwewag* and the Indian Homemakers' Club, 1945–1960[1]

Lianne C. Leddy

The post–Second World War era has usually been described as a period of decolonization in Canada, with historians emphasizing changes in Canadians' consciousness about Indigenous issues, the appointment of the first Indigenous senator, James Gladstone, and the extension of the franchise to Status Indians.[2] Yet, scholars are now increasingly challenging that view of the period. Between 1950 and 1965, jurisdiction over Indigenous affairs fell to the Department of Citizenship and Immigration, making it easier for the Department to target Indigenous peoples for services similar to those for new immigrants to Canada, thereby undermining not only their cultures and languages, but also their Indigeneity. As Heidi Bohaker and Franca Iacovetta argue, as this next phase of assimilation dawned, the Department's aim was to "Canadianize" Indigenous peoples through the use of social science theory and practice.[3]

An example of this policy in action was the Indian Homemakers' Club, an organization encouraged by the Department, and aimed at Indigenous women. Hugh Shewell argues that the Indian Homemakers' Clubs and Leadership Training Programs, as well as other social science-influenced Indian policies, were designed to "facilitate economic dispossession and social displacement." He continues, "the cultural banners of humanitarianism and the applied reason of social science were mere masks obscuring the real task, which was capitalist expansion."[4] But, as in many aspects of the colonial relationship, Indigenous peoples did not necessarily interpret the clubs as simple tools of Canadian colonialism. As Kathryn Magee argues in her examination of Indian Homemakers' Clubs in Alberta, local organizations made it easier to deliver services and educational opportunities, leading Indigenous women to engage in political activism, including in their relations with the province.[5] Indeed, this chapter argues that while many reserve communities in Ontario formed such groups to encourage domestic and charitable pursuits, *Anishinaabe kwewag*[6] took leadership roles in Indian Homemakers' Clubs and made them their own, focusing their efforts on issues that they deemed important. The clubs were not solely tools of colonialism, but rather worked towards decolonization in unexpected ways. The club can be used to examine the postwar experience of *Anishinaabe kwewag* in Ontario, and question whether Indigenous women internalized 1950s ideals of domesticity, from which they were often excluded. In some cases, the club reinforced traditional community and kinship social support practices, and allowed women to exert their Indigenous gender roles. In fact, the women used community organizations to subvert the postwar feminine ideal and the colonial influences of the Department, and some reinforced their own political and social status in First Nations communities through their involvement in the Club.

The Indian Homemakers' Club was first established in 1937 in Saskatchewan by Thomas Robertson, the Inspector of Indian Agencies,[7] and the numbers of active clubs varied from year to year. In order to encourage the proliferation of these clubs, and the domestic work they were meant to value, the Department provided a sewing machine and $50 worth of supplies to new clubs. In some cases, women from active clubs would be sent, using Departmental funds, to other communities to gauge interest, establish new clubs, and provide introductory training. However, as Brendan Frederick R. Edwards argues, "the most remarkable trait associated with the Indian Homemakers' clubs was that although the movement was promoted by Indian Affairs, by the department's own admission they were organized 'with little departmental assistance or supervision' and were present in communities across the country."[8] At the same time, the Department tried to shape club activities, in particular the ways in which those activities and meetings were carried out. Indian Affairs Branch employees disseminated a club constitution that was adopted across the country, using one model for each organization. Its origin and purpose section indicated that its purpose was "to improve living conditions in Indian communities by co-operating in all projects which have as their objective a *better* life."[9] Of course, *better* was often defined by social workers and Department of Citizenship and Immigration employees in gendered and racialized terms. On the surface, certainly, the Indian Homemakers' Club as an institution aimed to mitigate Indigenous women's influence—often seen as potentially dangerous, unclean, or damaging[10]—by encouraging them to assimilate to white norms in the postwar period. The logo, [figure X] features a Eurocentric depiction of an "Indian maiden" and the motto "for home and country." This portrayal belies the disenfranchisement of Anishinaabe women federally and locally because, until 1960, First Nations women with Indian status could not vote in federal elections, nor could they participate in band elections or public meetings prior to the 1951 revisions to the Indian Act.[11] Even so, the organization as conceived by the federal government placed the women at the forefront of service for a community and country that excluded them from the most basic form of political participation.[12]

Despite these contradictions, such organizations provided an opportunity for women to become politically active in their communities, and allowed them to harness service opportunities for that purpose. When it came to the Club itself and the running of the organization, the documentary evidence suggests that the Department expected women to adopt the framework and meeting rules laid out by the constitution. The Indian Superintendent commented hopefully on the ability of the women of the Shawanaga Homemakers' Club to adopt western meeting and service practices: "[w]hile progress has been rather slow, we believe that through time their standards of procedure and their work on the reserve will show much improvement."[13] The concern for procedural rules of order, evident in the constitution and Indian Affairs Branch correspondence, was an attempt to impose a civilizing model that contained a strict speaking and motion policy. As such, it was inconsistent with *Anishinaabe* political and diplomatic protocols, which had been developed over centuries.

Further, the women who joined the Clubs were less concerned with procedure than with the actual work that needed to be done. Indeed, one handwritten report from the Saugeen Homemakers' Club listed their activities, which included sewing work, fundraising and organizing social evenings, as well as planting a garden. The report's author included one telling line about the nature of their meetings, highlighting the differences between Department and *Anishinaabe* protocols: "so far we have had 14 meetings mostly just as a social gathering."[14] These women had clearly been busy in the community re-establishing their club, raising funds, and securing food, but did not see the need to formalize their meetings in such a way as to slow down their work, which was tied to socializing and visiting. In other words, service work and social protocols were not distinct entities, but rather part of a comprehensive community role that did not necessitate the Department's definition of formalized meeting rules and regulations. While the Club members may have adopted its constitution, logo, and name, they concentrated on the work that needed to be done, and proved unwilling to have their meetings shaped by Departmental procedure.

Despite its intended purpose as a colonizing tool, Indigenous women used the Indian Homemakers' Club to harness community power and, in some cases, to reassert traditional social and political roles. Kim Anderson has reminded us that in most Indigenous societies "women were recognized for their unique contribution in the life-giving process" and that gender complementarity has been essential to community wellness and healing.[15] In the hands of Indigenous women, the Homemakers' Club became a mechanism for ensuring a healthy community in the face of colonial changes to gender complementarity and the financial restrictions imposed by the Indian Act. Oral history from Serpent River First Nation documents the work done by women in the Homemakers' Club and the Women's League. Knowledge holders still recount their memories of female leadership through fundraising, picnics, and dances. Frank Lewis recalled that the women's league supported the Serpent River First Nation baseball team through fundraising activities like box socials, where a boxed meal would be made and raffled off.[16] As sports such as baseball were very important to youth in the community,[17] women worked hard to secure equipment through fundraising, because efforts to access band funds for such purposes were not always successful.

Such a case occurred in April 1955, when the Chief and Council passed a resolution to spend $50 on the ball park and $146.35 on new equipment such as balls, bats, mitts, a catcher's mask, and a backstop. While the Indian agent, R.P.G. Laurence, agreed that the repairs to the ball field were justified, he sent the resolution on to the Department, noting his displeasure about the use of funds for equipment, feeling instead that "the ball club should try and obtain the money for equipment some other way than from Band funds."[18] F. Matters, the regional supervisor, agreed with the agent's assessment about the equipment, noting that he had already told the community that the "ball club should find some way to provide their own equipment and that the Branch did not think it advisable to use Band Funds for this purpose." His paternalistic disapproval of the elected leadership's use of money did not stop there, and he went on to extol the value of hard work: "if they work to acquire the equipment, they will take far greater care of it."[19] The fundraising work of the Homemakers' Club was therefore essential to the viability of recreational programs for community youth.[20] The Indian Act prevented political leaders from having control over financial decisions, and women's community organizations needed to supplement funding for community events and activities through sewing, box socials, and picnics.

Indigenous women carried out this work in reserve communities throughout the province, but the group's efforts went beyond sports and fundraising to community wellness stewardship. In one "real friendly letter," as the recipient noted, Mrs Simpson of the Georgina Island reserve wrote a report about her activities: "an indigent man, who did not have a relative in the world, he lived in a small house alone and then he went blind [. . .] The council never paid any attention, nor would pay him one cent [. . .] So, I am trying to do a little welfare work as I see the need. His name was [X] A member of our band. . . ."[21] It is unclear from the letter if the council had the money to pay for the Elder's care. Nevertheless, the Club worked to provide the relief necessary to ensure his health and well-being on their own initiative. Mrs Simpson was lauded for her "interesting welfare activities" and for her "kindness in looking after [X] to ensure that he had adequate care in comfortable surroundings to spend his last days and also making funeral arrangements. . . ." Colonel H.M. Jones of Indian Affairs then went on to say, "Thank you again for letting me know about your activities and my best wishes for continued success in any welfare work you may undertake."[22] It is unlikely that Jones realized that while the club's activities seemed harmless and domestic in the western sense, they also fulfilled traditional expectations in the community. The club at Georgina Island had worked to accomplish what the Department would not and was recognized for it.

In Shawanaga, the Homemakers' Club was pursuing similar wellness work in the face of budgetary restrictions. The Homemakers' Club there had "gathered together a second-hand cook stove, bed, spring and mattress, some curtains and other odds and ends to help make an old widower's house a little more homelike. The members cleaned his house and put things in order for him."[23] The Club's care for an elderly community member, as well as the care it provided to sick children, shows that the Homemakers' Club supplemented services provided by government agencies. Perhaps more significantly, it also reflects Indigenous concerns for youth and elders—traditional community responsibilities—that had been reframed in institutional ways. Band funds were not only in short supply for elder care, but also for initiatives for children. In Shawanaga, the club's report stated that in addition to having made quilts to sell to purchase more meeting materials, club members were also sponsoring a concert and preparing Christmas treats for ailing children. Their actions, in short, ensured adequate community care at a time when supplements to Departmental services were necessary. That is to say, women had always been responsible for this work and *Anishinaabe kwewag* used the Homemakers' Club as a continuation of, rather than a break from, past practices.

Community political leadership clearly valued the contributions made by these Clubs and were willing to fund them out of their own limited means. As has been mentioned above, until 1951 the Indian Act prevented Indigenous women from voting in community elections, and after 1951, Indigenous women were very new to the imposed formalized political process. However, it is clear that they had influence in other ways and were recognized for their community work. In 1954, the Chief and Council of Christian Island set aside a sum of $127.61 for the Homemakers' Club.[24] In 1956, a Parry Island Band Council Resolution (BCR) granted 19 square metres of shoreline to the Homemakers' Club. This was done "to promote summer picnics and other festivities during the summer months with which to raise funds for the Club." In fact, the area was to be surveyed for such a purpose.[25] It is clear that in these instances, the Homemakers' Club had the support of male-dominated community leadership in the form of the Chief and Council, and perhaps women members were working through their male elected representatives to secure these things for the community.

The political influence of women in local governance, despite their relatively recent enfranchisement under the Indian Act can be seen in the oral history from Indigenous knowledge holders at Serpent River First Nation. Marella Schofield recalled that women were present at political meetings, and described the active participation of Agnes Commanda and Agnes Meawasige, among others, at such meetings.[26] Women voiced their opinions about what needed to be done in the community, and while they may not have had the right to vote in elections or run for council before 1951, they certainly participated in political decisions, even in the presence of the Indian agent.[27]

Indigenous women used organizations such as the club to voice dissent and provide a "check" for elected band council representatives. In the case of Serpent River First Nation, *Anishinaabe* women were instrumental in securing safe recreational spaces and activities for themselves and their children. It is very clear that they did so by corresponding with Department officials, and by putting pressure on their own local government to act in accordance with their wishes. In October 1949, Mrs Commanda wrote to R.P.G. Laurence, the Indian superintendent, to report that the club had voted to request that the old school be kept for their use.[28] Laurence recommended that the request be approved, which it was, by the Department of Mines and Resources Indian Affairs Branch by the end of that month.[29]

Five years later, the community identified the need to have repairs done on the club house. A BCR was passed to that effect on 5 February 1956, but in May there was still no movement on the repairs, and Serpent River First Nation women had to write the Department again. In a letter dated 9 May 1956, the secretary of the Homemakers' Club, Mrs Meawasige—who was no longer the chief's secretary and whose husband was no longer chief—wrote to John O'Neil, the Indian Superintendent, asking about the status of the BCR:

> Some time ago last fall the Homemakers' Club asked and it was granted by the Indian Affairs Branch for $200 for the repairs of the Club House. The Homemakers' Club have decided to have a convention here this summer or fall if it is approved at North

Bay and we would be very pleased to have material to that amount for repairs on the club house. The resolution was signed according to one of the councillors but I never knew whether it had ever been sent. The resolution was signed between January and March as the Chief was told the money had to be spent before the end of March. Then again from different sources the chief did not want the Club House fixed as we were getting a basement in our church for social purposes. In any event it will take years before we will be able to make use of the church basement. My point in bringing the subject out is all the clubs make good use of the club house and there should be some repairs done now more so if we are to have the conference here.[30]

By writing this letter, Mrs Meawasige and the Club were acting independently of the Chief and Council to ensure that the repairs were carried out. Adequate space reserved for women and girls was important to the club and its members, and its secretary was willing to work around local leadership if necessary. Agnes was just one of the women who balanced familial, community, and work responsibilities, and it is not surprising, then, that some women would go on to secure formal political positions in band governance and paid administrative work once their children were older.[31]

In this respect, the term *homemaker* was actually a misnomer. While the Department wanted to encourage gendered domestic responsibility and western ideals for proper homes and families, homemaker may be more of a reflection of desired norms than reality for Indigenous women. This was evident as early as 1947 when the Indian agent at the Rama Agency, H.J. Featherston, mentioned that the president of the community club found it "hard to get the women to take an interest." He went on to explain that "Our Indians, generally speaking, are not hard up as Indians go, they gad around a lot, are more inclined to discard worn clothing than make it over or repair it." This was mainly due, with few exceptions, to the fact that "[f]or quite a few years now, all able bodied Indians have been quite able to make a living and I have purposely refrained from handing out something for nothing. They have lost some of their 'gimme' habits and are more self reliant."[32] Certainly, the rhetoric lauding self-sufficiency in the face of government handouts reflects Indian agents' views of *Anishinaabe* work and participation in the capitalist economy. Featherston related the image of the "lazy Indian" "gadding" about, but this time *Anishinaabe* men and women were engaged in the wage economy.

Featherston's letter revealed an internal contradiction between two Department policies. Namely, while he was pleased that community members were employed and self-reliant because of their relative close proximity to and participation in the paid workforce, Featherston bemoaned the women's limited interest in practising their homemaking skills in their leisure time. The fact that the women (or at least their husbands) had the ability to work and raise money for themselves and their families meant that they had less interest in mending and sewing. His solution, therefore, was to place a sewing machine in the room used for Sunday school, and encourage women to train in dressmaking and similar pursuits.[33] It is implicit in his letter that by formalizing this sewing experience, he was attempting to bridge the gap between Indigenous industry and female domestic responsibility.

Many of these women were not homemakers in the common definition of the word, or at least not all the time. While 1950s domestic ideals relegated white middle-class women to their homes for the support of their families, this was not possible, or perhaps even desirable, for many *Anishinaabe* women. The report of the Shawanaga Homemakers' Club stated that they "did not meet during the summer months as most of the members are away working."[34] In an accompanying letter, Indian Superintendent Ward L. Leroy further explained, "during the summer months when employment is good, the majority of the women leave the reserve for various tourist centres to be with their husbands and families or to obtain employment."[35] First Nations women in this case worked in the seasonal Central Ontario tourism industry, and this was not lost on the superintendent.

The Department's gradual acknowledgment of Indigenous women's paid labour affected their scheduling of the annual Homemakers' Convention. Each club would send delegates to the annual convention, which was organized by region, where they would be exposed to a number of presentations and lectures on homemaking skills, arts and crafts, and parenting tips. At the 1957 convention at Golden Lake, the business meeting notes show that some of the participants asked that the convention be held at a different time because they were "busy working in tobacco and elsewhere, therefore it was very difficult for the clubs to send delegates to the convention."[36] They thus voted to change the date. A 1961 report submitted by the Indian superintendent on behalf of all the clubs in the Parry Sound area requested that the annual Homemakers' Convention, which had usually been held in the summer, be moved to the fall or spring. This was justified by the fact that "there would be a better opportunity for them to attend, as most of them are working during the summer months and are in no position to pass up any opportunities for employment."[37] Once again, *Anishinaabe* women's participation in the paid labour force conflicted with the largest gathering in the province of delegates from Indian Homemakers' Clubs.

The regional conventions were also an opportunity for Indian Affairs, through its social worker, Helen Martins, to introduce delegates to the importance of Canadian values, particularly in the area of motherhood and housekeeping. At the 1957 southern Ontario convention in Golden Lake, the speakers, ranging from social workers to Indian Affairs representatives, principals, and priests, emphasized the roles of Indigenous mothers in preventing juvenile delinquency, disease, and unemployment. Education and employment were high on the list of desirable outcomes for children, and it was the responsibility of Indigenous mothers to ensure that they did not squander the opportunities that came with Canadian citizenship. The regional supervisor, J.E. Morris, addressed the delegates and encouraged them to embrace education and training because it would make their "girls and boys better fitted to accept higher salaried positions which are available." Keeping in mind that Indian Affairs was a branch of the Department of Citizenship and Immigration, it was clear that Morris did not see the difference between Indigenous peoples and new Canadians: "Many people from Europe are coming to this country and settling right in your own neighbourhoods. In a very short time they are gainfully employed and contributing considerably to the community as happy Canadians. Our girls and boys, if properly trained, can get their share of good jobs and they too will enjoy this better way of life which we as Canadians are so proud of."[38] Of course, the use of the terms *our* and *we* belied the political disenfranchisement of Indigenous peoples subject to the Indian Act, as well as the colonial processes of dispossession. But more than that, Morris's speech to the attendees showed that the Club was part of a larger colonizing and "Canadianizing" mission, and that it was up to Indigenous women to heed the call for the good of their children.

Martins, for her part, said that this process of "Canadianization" should start at an early age, and encouraged safe play for improved child development. She too failed to see the historical roots of social challenges in Indigenous communities, and went so far as to state that "the reason why so many men and women do drink and get into trouble is because they never learned how to play when they were young. They never learned how to enjoy themselves and have a good time." She went on to explain the dangers of substance abuse, particularly seeing alcohol as "a very poor substitute. It causes parents to neglect themselves and their children." Martins emphasized the very real consequences of this neglectful parenting: "If nothing can be done about such conditions, the children are either sent to residential school or grow up like their parents—ignorant of making a living and of properly raising their families."[39] The participants were clearly being called upon as mothers of the nation to keep their children, and by extension, their communities, out of trouble. At the same time, Indigenous motherhood was targeted as dangerous without the outside influence of the Department and its social workers.[40] The negative consequences of Indigenous parenting were already clear, and the state took measures to counter it: generations of children had already been removed to residential schools, and the Sixties Scoop (which was already underway in the late 1950s) threatened community cohesion anew. Clearly, the problem was not as simple as an absence of play in Indigenous childhoods. In fact, many groups in Ontario had already been fostering sports and leisure among their youth. Serpent River First Nation, though not located in southern Ontario where this convention took place, supported long-established sports teams, and the community had already built a playground and a hockey rink.[41] Indigenous communities had historically engaged in games and sports as part of their everyday lives, and such activities were often central to children's upbringing.[42] In other words, the notion that children should play was not a new concept to Indigenous peoples, but rather one that was formalized by social workers, government officials, and urban planners in the postwar context.[43]

Although convention participants were expected to listen a great deal of the time, they did contribute to problem-solving discussions based on questions prepared by conference organizers. Women were split into groups and asked to share ideas about the availability of employment, as well as possible answers to social problems. When asked what could be done about the absence of an Indigenous social worker in the community, one group suggested that they could "appoint a good person from the reserve as a social worker. One who is capable and can offer such service to the people." The same group also suggested organizing a social services committee. Mr Bonnah, the assistant regional supervisor of the Southern Ontario Region, replied, "social workers are not manufactured like saucers; [. . .] there is more to such a job than meets the eye." He recommended that, in keeping with the overall message of the convention, formal education and training was important, and some of the youth should be encouraged to pursue a career in social work.[44] While encouraging the further education of Indigenous youth was certainly a noble goal, the Department's response rejected the participants' ideas out of hand. The women in the group clearly had certain community members in mind to address the need for social workers. Anderson has documented that in the *Anishinaabe* context, an Elder or "crier" would reprimand bad behaviour as part of a community-wide process.[45] In actual fact, the organizers gave the question to the group, thereby pathologizing their communities, rather than providing an opportunity for participants to frame and answer a question on their own. To them, community capacity in the area of social improvement already existed. In other words, a "good person" with this capability would not necessarily need to have the formalized training envisioned by the Department, and a committee would ensure that there was not just one person with this responsibility. The group's suggestion encouraged a unified, community-based model that reflected their own cultural and historical ways of moving forward, which was consistent with the work Indian Homemakers' Clubs had been doing throughout the province.

In conclusion, the Homemakers' Club in Ontario, although instigated and strongly encouraged by the Department of Citizenship and Immigration, was also an organization Indigenous women used for their own purposes: whether it was reinforcing traditional kinship and generational roles, community fundraising, or securing space for themselves, it is clear that they were not simply reinforcing dominant postwar gender norms. Members of the Indian Homemakers' Clubs did not just meet "mostly just as a social gathering," but rather, they were finding their own ways to serve "home and country" when they were either new to—or completely excluded from—overt political participation.

Notes

1. This research was supported by a SSHRC Insight Development Grant and Memorial University. The author wishes to thank Marc Brouillette, Trevor Ford, Lyndsay Rosenthal, and Aileen Worrall for their research assistance, and the editors for their comments.

2. See, for example, R. Scott Sheffield, *The Red Man's on the Warpath: The Image of the "Indian" and the Second World War* (Vancouver: University of British Columbia Press, 2004); Hugh Dempsey, *The Gentle Persuader: A Biography of James Gladstone, Indian Senator* (Saskatoon: Western Producer Prairie Books, 1986); Ruth Gorman, *Behind the Man: John Laurie, Ruth Gorman, and the Indian Vote in Canada*, Frits Pannekoek, ed. (Calgary: University of Calgary Press, 2007).

3. Heidi Bohaker and Franca Iacovetta, "Making Aboriginal People "'Immigrants Too': A Comparison of Citizenship Programs for Newcomers and Indigenous Peoples in Postwar Canada, 1940s–1960s," *The Canadian Historical Review* 90, 3 (September 2009): 427–61.

4. Hugh Shewell, *"Enough to Keep them Alive": Indian Welfare in Canada, 1873–1965* (Toronto: University of Toronto Press, 2004), 262–3.

5. Kathryn Magee, "For Home and Country: Education, Activism and Agency in Alberta Native Homemakers' Clubs, 1942–1970," *Native Studies Review*, 18, 2 (2009): 27–49.

6. *Anishinaabek* refers to the Council of Three Fires, which comprises Ojibway, Pottawatomi, and Odawa peoples and their allies. *Anishinaabe* is the singular adjective, while *Anishinaabek* refers to the people as a whole. *Kwewag* is the *Anishinabemowin* (*Anishinaabe* language) word for women. In cases where a more inclusive term is needed, I have chosen to use *First Nations* or *Indigenous peoples*.

7. Indian Affairs Branch, Department of Citizenship and Immigration, *Constitution and Regulations for Indian Homemakers' Clubs* (Ottawa: King's Printer, 1951), 5.

8. Brendan Frederick R. Edwards, *Paper Talk: A History of Libraries, Print Culture, and Aboriginal Peoples in Canada before 1960* (Toronto: the Scarecrow Press, 2005), 145. The author is quoting the *Report of the Indian Affairs Branch for 1943*, 151.

9. *Constitution and Regulations for Indian Homemakers' Clubs*, 5. Italics by author.

10. See, for example: Jean Barman, "Taming Aboriginal Sexuality: Gender, Power and Race in British Columbia, 1850–1900," *BC Studies* 115–16 (Fall/Winter 1997–98): 237–66.

11. See Kathleen Jamieson, *Indian Women and the Law in Canada: Citizens Minus* (Ottawa: Advisory Council on the Status of Women, 1978).

12. Works on Indigenous women's political and social activism include Kim Anderson, *A Recognition of*

Being: Reconstructing Native Womanhood (Toronto: Canadian Scholars' Press, 2001); Kim Anderson and Bonita Lawrence, eds, *Strong Women Stories: Native Vision and Community Survival* (Toronto: Sumach Press, 2003); Janet Silman, *Enough is Enough: Aboriginal Women Speak Out* (Toronto: Women's Press, 1987); Lina Sunseri, *Being Again of One Mind: Oneida Women and the Struggle for Decolonization* (Vancouver: University of British Columbia Press, 2011); Cora J. Voyageur, "The Community Owns You: Experiences of Female Chiefs in Canada," in Andrea Martinez and Meryn Stuart, eds, *Out of the Ivory Tower: Feminist Research for Social Change* (Toronto: Sumach Press, 2003), 228–47 and "They Called Her Chief: A Tribute to Fort MacKay's Indomitable Leader, Dorothy McDonald," in Sarah Carter et al., eds, *Unsettled Pasts: Reconceiving the West Through Women's History* (Calgary: University of Calgary Press, 2005), 355–61; Cora Voyageur, *Firekeepers of the Twenty-First Century: First Nations Women Chiefs* (Montreal & Kingston: McGill-Queen's University Press, 2008).

13. Library and Archives Canada (LAC), RG 10, Vol. 8483, file 475/24-5, reel C-13817, letter from Ward L. Leroy, Indian Superintendent, 3 May 1955.

14. LAC, RG 10, Vol. 8483, file 478/24-5, Reel C-13817, report of the Saugeen Homemakers' Club, 28 August 1952.

15. Kim Anderson, "Affirmations of an Indigenous Feminist," in *Indigenous Women and Feminism: Politics, Activism, and Culture*, Cheryl Suzack, Shari M. Huhndorf, Jeanne Perreault, and Jean Barman, eds (Vancouver: University of British Columbia Press, 2010), 82.

16. Interview with Frank Lewis, Serpent River First Nation, 16 May 2014.

17. Interviews with Marella Schofield, Frank Lewis, Orval Commanda, and one Elder who preferred to be unnamed between 16–23 May 2014 all attest to baseball—both organized and after school—as being an important pastime.

18. LAC, RG 10, Vol. 11356, file 13/24-4-8, R.P.G. Laurence to Indian Affairs Branch, Department of Citizenship and Immigration, 18 April 1955. The resolution was passed on 14 March 1955.

19. LAC, RG 10, Vol. 11356, file 13/24-4-8, F. Matters to Indian Affairs Branch, Department of Citizenship and Immigration, 5 April 1956.

20. A later superintendent for the agency, J. O'Neill, often supported resolutions to use band funds for equipment, but it is unclear if this was due to his exercising his personal prerogative or indicative of a wider change within the Department as a whole in the late 1950s. LAC, RG 10, Vol. 11356, file 13/24-4-8.

21. LAC, RG 10, Vol. 8483, file 475/24-5, reel C-13817, Mary Jane Simpson (Mrs Al) to Col. H.M. Jones, 2 April 1961. The name of the man has been redacted to protect his privacy. Most of the women corresponding with the Department used their husband's first names, as was common in the 1950s, and were listed as such in reports.

22. LAC, RG 10, Vol. 8483, file 475/24-5, reel C-13817, Mr Jones, Director, to Mrs Simpson, 8 May 1961.

23. RG 10, Vol. 8483, file 475/24-5, reel C-13817, report of the Shawanaga Homemakers' Club, 31 December 1954.

24. LAC, RG 10, Vol. 8483, file 475/24-5, reel C-13817, Band Council Resolution [hereafter BCR], 13 September 1954.

25. LAC, RG 10, Vol. 8483, file 475/24-5 reel C-13817, Re: Resolution No. 7, Parry Island Band, 16 May 1956. The memo outlining the BCR is written by Ward L. Leroy and stamped with "recommended for approval."

26. Interview with Marella Schofield, Serpent River First Nation, 16 May 2014.

27. Ibid.

28. LAC, RG 10, Vol. 11357, file 13/24-5-8, Mrs. Commanda to Superintendent Laurence, 5 October 1949. Chief Meawasige also wrote to request that the school be set aside for the Club.

29. LAC, RG 10, Vol. 11357, file 13/24-5-8, Departmental correspondence from October 1949.

30. LAC, RG 10, Vol. 11339 part 1, file 13/7-2-7, Mrs Meawasige to Superintendent O'Neil, 9 May 1956.

31. By the 1970s, Serpent River First Nation had elected its first woman chief, Lorena Lewis, and other women were politically active as councillors, committee members, and employees.

32. LAC, RG 10, Vol. 8483, file 475/24-5, Reel C-13817, H.J. Featherston to Indian Affairs Branch of the Department of Mines and Resources in Ottawa, 29 March 1947.

33. Ibid.

34. LAC, RG 10, Vol. 8483, file 475/24-5, reel C-13817, report of the Shawanaga Homemakers' Club, 31 December 1954.

35. LAC, RG 10, Vol. 8483, file 475/24-5, reel C-13817, letter from Ward L. Leroy, Indian Superintendent, 3 May 1955.

36. AANDC Library, *Summary of Proceedings: Homemakers Convention*, 1957, 47-48.

37. LAC, RG 10, Vol. 8483, file 475/24-5, reel C-13817 "Extract from '"Welfare' Section of Quarterly Report—Parry Sound" dated 4 August 1961. Judging from other documents within the same file, this was probably written by E.H. Paterson.

38. AANDC Library, *Summary of Proceedings: Homemakers Convention*, 1957, 4.

39. Ibid., 3.

40. For works on Indigenous motherhood, see, for example: D. Memee Lavell-Harvard and Jeannette Corbiere Lavell, eds, *"Until our Hearts are on the Ground': Aboriginal Mothering, Oppression, Resistance and Rebirth* (Bradford: Demeter Press, 2006).

41. LAC, RG 10, Vol. 11356, file 13/24-4-8. Correspondence from 1954 to 1959 outlines the various youth activities in the community.

42. Philip J. Deloria, *Indians in Unexpected Places* (Lawrence: University Press of Kansas, 2004), 112–25; Greg S. Place and Jennifer Livengood, "Youth Leisure in a Native North American Community: An Observational Study," *The Canadian Journal of Native Studies* 30, 1 (2010): 117–41; Janice Forsyth, Audrey R. Giles, eds, *Aboriginal Peoples and Sport in Canada: Historical Foundations and Contemporary Issues* (Vancouver: UBC Press, 2013).

43. Shirley Tillotson, *The Public at Play: Gender and the Politics of Recreation in Post-War Ontario* (Toronto: University of Toronto Press, 2000).

44. AANDC Library, *Summary of Proceedings: Homemakers Convention*, 1957, 43.

45. Kim Anderson, *Life Stages and Native Women: Memory, Teachings, and Story Medicine* (Winnipeg: University of Manitoba Press, 2011), 77.

Primary Document

Constitution and Regulations for Indian Homemakers' Clubs

Department of Citizenship and Immigration

Constitution

Article 1. NAME:

The organization shall be known as The .... Homemakers' Club of .... Agency.

Article 2. OBJECTIVES:

(a) To assist Indian women to acquire sound and approved practices for greater home efficiency.

(b) To help the aged and less fortunate, and improve living conditions on the Reserve.

(c) To discover, stimulate, and train leadership.

(d) To sponsor and actively assist in all worthwhile projects for the betterment of the community.

(e) To develop better, happier, and more useful citizens.

Article 3. MOTTO:

"For Home and Country."

Article 4. BADGE:

Maple leaf with Indian woman's head.

Article 5. COLOURS:

Red, white, and blue.

Article 6. REQUIREMENTS:

The organization shall be non-sectarian, open to all Indian women.

Article 7. MEMBERSHIP:

Women and girls, (16 years of age and over), shall be eligible for membership on payment of the annual fee. An honorary life membership may be granted to an active member with the unanimous approval of the club to which she belongs.

Article 8. OFFICERS:

The executive officers shall be: The President, one or more Vice Presidents; a Secretary; a Treasurer; (the positions of Secretary and Treasurer may be combined).

Article 9. COMMITTEES:

The organization shall appoint such standing committees as may be required to operate in an effective manner. Each standing committee shall be headed by a Convener, who will be responsible for calling meetings of the committee and submitting reports of its activities to the general body; suggested committees:—Sick Visiting, Entertainment, etc.

Article 10. MEETINGS:

(a) A club shall meet at least once in each month.
(b) An annual general meeting shall be held once each year in December at which the work of the year shall be reviewed, and the officers elected. Minutes of the annual meeting shall be read and approved at the next regular club meeting, and will also be read for reference at the next annual meeting.

Secondary Source

Making History: Elise Marie Knott—Canada's First Female Indian Elected Chief

Cora Voyageur

When political neophyte Elsie Marie Knott threw her hat into the political ring for the Mississaugas of Mud Lake Indian Band's election in 1952, little did she know that, if elected, she would be making history. The 500 band members of the now Curve Lake

First Nation[1] broke the gender barrier for Indian chiefs in Canada by electing Chief Knott. Until that time the patriarchal Indian Act,[2] enforced from 1876, had banned women from both voting in or running for elected office in band elections. The amalgamated Indian Act was then created until amendments to the gender ban were made in 1951. After winning that historic election, Chief Knott would go on to win seven more campaigns, lasting 16 years, from 1952 to 1962, and then from 1970 to 1976. She was defeated by only 12 votes in her last run for office.[3]

In this chapter, I recount Chief Elsie Knott's personal and professional experiences in her history-making role, drawing on newspaper and magazine articles, diaries and personal papers, family interviews, and other published works to tell her story.[4] This energetic woman was not only Canada's first female Indian Act chief but a person who was deeply committed to improving the lives of band members. She was also an entrepreneur who was determined to overcome her own financial uncertainty. Through Elsie's concerns and experiences the reader gets a glimpse of the historical, social, economic, and political conditions of the First Nations population in postwar Canada.

Elsie Marie Taylor was born on 20 September 1922 to Esther Mae and George Henry Taylor. The Taylors were a large, well-established family in the Mud Lake Reserve community and Elsie enjoyed the benefits of a large, traditional, and extended family. As a child she was exposed to band politics, community issues, and social matters by her father, who was the caretaker of the band office. The young Elsie often accompanied him to band meetings and community events where she learned about the struggles faced by First Nations people.

Early on, Elsie sensed that as an Indian she was different from other Canadians. She knew that as wards of the government they were isolated from the outside world and subjected to oppressive rules. At this time in Canadian history, Indians were warehoused on reserves and thought by mainstream society to be a "vanishing race" that would simply disappear over time. Their mobility was strictly limited by an Indian Affairs policy that prohibited them from leaving the reserve without a pass from the Indian agent. Such policies meant there was little interaction between Indians and non-Indians. As a result of this isolation, the young Elsie was afraid of "white" people. It did not help matters any when her parents would scare her into going to bed by telling her to go to sleep because the "white man" was coming.[5]

The level of formal education that Elsie attained was low by today's standards, though on a par with that of other First Nations people at the time. The government's assimilation policy[6] dominated the curriculum and practices at Indian schools. While at these institutions, Indian children were expected to cast off all notions of Indian identity and culture, and speak only English. Elsie recalled that when she started school, speaking "Indian" was strictly prohibited. The names of those students "caught talking Indian" were listed on the blackboard with big Xs beside them.[7] Proponents of the assimilation policy thought that allowing traditional languages in schools would slow the assimilation of Indian children into mainstream society—the goal of the policy. Most reserve students ended their education at grade 8 since the nearest high school was 16 miles away in Lakefield and no transportation was provided for them to attend school there.

Married Life

Elsie grew up at a time when most people believed that women should marry, have children, and stay at home to care for their family's needs.[8] Elsie's parents had this scenario in mind for her when they arranged her marriage to a fellow band member, Cecil Knott, when she was 15 years old. Cecil Knott was 12 years her senior and suffered from tuberculosis for their entire marriage; he was often unable to work. Elsie soon became a mother and had three children in five years.

At the age of 20, Elsie was disheartened to find herself living on welfare. Although her husband found seasonal guiding employment in the summer and fall, mainly for hunters from the United States, they relied on the 12 dollars a month they received from social assistance. Kathleen Taylor, her relative, remembered, "Elsie's late husband was never really healthy. So I suppose, someone had to be the breadwinner and so Elsie took it upon herself to support the family."[9]

Cecil's sickness and the family's dire financial circumstances forced Elsie to look for work. She was not above doing menial work to support her family; early in her marriage she dug worms and caught minnows to sell to fisherman for bait. Her first paying job was berry picking in a town outside Toronto. The job paid poorly and after five weeks she had barely made enough money to get herself back home. Elsie's other jobs included working as a chambermaid at the Lakefield hotel and sewing pajamas for children in federal Indian hospitals for 35 cents a pair. Importantly, Elsie was creative, and had an entrepreneurial spirit and a keen sense of what services were in demand— traits that manifested themselves throughout her life.

Elsie's first opportunity to make a steady income on the reserve came by chance. Five children wanted to continue their education beyond grade 8 at the Lakeview School and the Indian agent hired a local man, at three dollars a day, to drive the students to and from the main highway, where they were picked up by the county school bus. Before long the man forgot to pick up the children after school and they had to walk the 8 kilometres home. The Indian agent then approached Elsie about driving them until he could find someone else. This enterprising woman saw an opportunity and established Knott Bus Service.

At first she drove the children to school in the family car but it soon became too small as the number of students attending the Lakefield School grew. She applied for a bank loan but was turned down.[10] So Elsie convinced the Indian agent to cosign a loan for $200 and bought an old hearse, converting it into a school bus by placing bench seats on the floor.[11]

Knott Bus Service eventually grew to include two 78-passenger school buses and remains in operation today. Elsie drove a school bus for the next 31 years (including when she was chief). In 1978 she received an award from the then Minister of Indian Affairs, the Honourable Hugh Faulkner, for her 25 years of accident-free driving.[12] She retired from driving in 1993 at the age of 71, only two years before her death.[13]

Political Life

Elsie ran for office because there were many things about reserve life that she wanted to change. For example, she did not agree that the federal government should have total control over Indian people; she believed that communities needed autonomy and control over their own affairs. She thought reserve children should be successful in school.[14] Previously, Indian children were not accepted at the Lakeview School and this made her unhappy. When there finally was school integration the town's children taunted the reserve students by calling them names and throwing rocks at their school bus.[15] Despite these challenges, some of the children she drove to school became successful professionals.

In newspaper interviews, Elsie described herself as shy and slightly afraid when she entered the political world. Being unsure of herself, she thought it was "the biggest joke ever when community members asked her to run for chief."[16] In her first election, she ran against two other candidates, including the incumbent, Dan Whetung. Even Elsie was not sure that she could beat the two men running against her. But she liked a challenge and it seemed that people were ready for a change in leadership. Her eldest son, Edward, then a teenager, was so afraid his mother would lose that he crossed the lake in a boat to avoid hearing the election results.[17] She won and someone had to get her son from the island. Elsie stated, "When I went in by a real big landslide it never dawned on me that I was making history."[18] Further, she commented, "I think women can be good at politics. They are more demanding. Everyone helps a woman."[19]

After the election, Elsie felt that she had a heavy burden on her shoulders. At 31, she was the elected leader of a 500-member band and worked with five band councillors. The community wanted a leader who would produce results. This was a daunting task because band elections were held every two years and producing tangible results in such a short time was difficult. Those in leadership usually need the first year to familiarize themselves with the job and the community, assess the issues, and become fully informed. The second year might be spent trying to address programming, and at the end of the second year there was another election. The short office term was a significant challenge for Elsie.

Knott found that when she became chief that one of her biggest obstacles was public speaking. Besides the fear of being in front of a crowd, Ojibway was her first language and she did not believe that she had a good command of English, "I could explain myself better in Indian than in the white language. I would think in Indian and it was hard to translate that in my head. I was afraid to make a mistake in English. I used to start off my talks with a joke. When you have them laughing you know they have accepted you and it used to give me a good feeling and then I'd lose my shyness right off."[20] As time went on, Elsie became more comfortable with public speaking and ultimately became a good orator.

As the excitement of winning the election began to wane, Chief Knott knew that she had a lot of work ahead of her. The reserve was mired in poverty and solutions to this situation had to be found. Band secretary Hannah Johnson recalled, "Elsie always seemed to know what she wanted and she seemed to know how to get it. And she wasn't afraid of saying what she wanted. She was a real worker too."[21] Elsie had lived her entire life in the community and knew what needed to be changed. Her daughter Rita Rose said, "I think her main goal seemed to be helping the Indian people have a better life. She did not like it when a lot of them were poor and abusing alcohol."[22] Elsie focused a great deal of effort on these social issues, and later prohibited the sale and consumption of alcohol on the reserve through a referendum.

As Elsie became more active in politics and community activities, life in her household changed. Her husband did not cope well with her success and was envious that she was young and full of energy. Rita was 11 when her mother became chief and she recalled, "I guess we were expected to do more housework. I cooked a lot when I was young."[23] All the children were expected to support Elsie by helping out at home.

Her husband also helped with running the household and taking care of the children, allowing Elsie to concentrate on band issues. Rita said that her mother either worked around the children's schedules or took them along with her to meetings.[24]

In 1962, Cecil died after a stroke at the age of 51. At 39, after 24 years of marriage, Elsie found herself a widow. She never remarried but kept herself busy with family, community issues, and political advocacy.

The Years in Office

During her tenure as chief, Elsie dealt with many barriers and hardships but she never viewed being a woman as a disadvantage. During an interview with a British newspaper in September 1973, Chief Knott said, "I think I can honestly say I never encountered discrimination because I was a woman. I didn't think about it really. I wanted to play my part."[25] Those who worked with Elsie tended to disagree with that view and believed that gender did play a role in her political life. Although some people thought a woman should not be chief, she persevered and proved that a woman could carry out all the duties of a chief. Her nephew, artist Norman Knott, said of his aunt, "[S]he had enough spunk to get out there and she was right for the job. That's the way they thought in those days. She made a lot of people realize that women can do a lot of things that men can do . . . she opened our eyes."[26]

Elsie was politically astute and was able to quickly identify the power brokers. She developed a good rapport with the Indian agent, A.E. Adams, who worked out of the Peterborough Indian Affairs office. It was important for her to cultivate this relationship because the Indian agent wielded a tremendous amount of power. His stamp of approval was required for every decision made about reserve life. She earned the agent's respect and was able to claim him as an ally.

Newspaper accounts of Elsie's early years in office portrayed her as a housewife who took on community duties but had not lost sight of her responsibilities to home and family. She was shown heading a variety of social activities, such as fish fries or corn roasts. A 1955 photograph shows her canning preserves while another undated photo captured her wearing a headdress, reading to children.[27] She was portrayed as a benevolent, affable individual who was not in any way threatening towards mainstream society.

Over time Elsie's meek and mild demeanour changed. In later years she became more outspoken and radical in her opinions and did not shy away from controversy. Rita Rose remembers her mother publicly burning the 1969 White Paper on Indian Policy introduced by the Trudeau government. After burning the White Paper, Chief Knott danced on the ashes. This incident occurred at the opening of the annual Curve Lake powwow. Then local Member of Parliament Hugh Faulkner was present and later downplayed her actions by saying, "[T]he incident was done in good fun."[28]

The White Paper said, "The Government believes that its policies must lead to the full, free and non-discriminatory participation of the Indian people in Canadian Society. Such a goal requires a break from the past. It requires that the Indian people's role of dependence be replaced by a role of equal status, opportunity and responsibility, a role they can share with all other Canadians."[29] To fulfill the plan, the government proposed to eliminate the unique status of Indian people and integrate services provided to Indian people with those of mainstream society.[30] These proposed actions touched off a firestorm of Indian protests across the country. Indian people responded to the White Paper with Citizens Plus (also known as the Red Paper), which was created under the guidance of the Indian Association of Alberta in 1970. The Red Paper suggested that the government abandon all plans to renege on treaty promises and eliminate Indian status and focus instead on improving living conditions in the communities and promoting economic development.[31] The White Paper was eventually withdrawn, in 1971.

On another occasion in 1975, Elsie led a protest against provincial legislation that encroached on Treaty Indians' rights to hunt and fish. Three band members had been charged by provincial wildlife authorities for fishing out of season. More than 200 people representing 10 First Nations in Ontario and the Union of Ontario Indians participated in the protest. A newspaper account described the incident:

> They fished through half a dozen holes in the ice in open defiance of provincial wild-life authorities who witnessed the four-hour demonstration from shore . . . The 200 year old Indian Act, and revisions in 1923 [under the terms of the Williams Treaty] give native people rights to self-determination including control over the wildlife and band members' use of it. Fisheries legislation of 1951 gives the provinces power to control, among other things, fishing seasons. Ontario has recently started enforcing the fishing laws, claiming they supersede the Indian Act.[32]

Elsie, along with other First Nations individuals, chose civil disobedience to defend their treaty rights.

Being an Indian chief and the first female Indian chief in Canada brought Elsie into some exclusive circles. She met every prime minister from John Diefenbaker to Jean Chrétien. While on vacation in England in June 1973, she was invited to a luncheon with Queen Elizabeth II and Prince Philip. The event was covered by the *West Sussex County Times*, in an article that described Chief Knott as, "an energetic, exuberant, and most exceptional woman."[33] Although delighted to meet the Queen and Prince Philip, she was less impressed with the spartan meal she was served: a little piece of filet mignon, three tiny potatoes, and two slices of fried cucumber. On the way home, she stopped for a Denver sandwich because she was still hungry.[34]

Elsie remembered England as a beautiful place. She loved the country's history, the flowers and the gardens, and the hospitality she received from the British people. While there, however, she felt out of sorts because she was homesick and unaccustomed to leisure time. She was so used to being busy that having free time made her uneasy. She was happy to get back to work, family, and community.

Contributions to Community Life

Elsie took steps throughout her political career to heighten cultural awareness both on the reserve and in the surrounding area by getting people involved in the community. In her first year in office, Elsie revived cultural events, such as the community pow-wow. She viewed the cultural activity as a means of upgrading the reserve and preserving its culture. The proceeds from the powwow helped to fund Christmas hampers for needy families.[35] Since the powwow was open to people from outside the community it also served as an opportunity for non–First Nations people to experience First Nations culture in a welcoming and non-threatening way.

Elsie was involved in a variety of community, regional, provincial, and national organizations. On the reserve she was a dedicated community worker, organizer, and fundraiser, using the funds raised through dances, regattas, and other activities to buy groceries for the entire village. She wanted to get everybody involved in some form of community activity and organized everything from Boy Scouts and Girl Guides for the children to men's baseball tournaments. She was an avid sports fan who loved baseball and, in fact, pitched for the married women's baseball team for many years.[36] Later she served as the sports representative for the southeastern region of the Union of Ontario Indians and helped to host a Native hockey tournament, with participants from 60 Ontario reserves.[37] For the women, she organized the Curve Lake Homemakers' Association, which had been created in the 1930s by the Indian Affairs Branch to promote home economics. Under Elsie's guidance, this club became a breeding ground for political activism for Indian women,[38] giving Elsie and other reserve women an opportunity to discuss women's issues and community politics.

At the provincial level Elsie was involved in the Union of Ontario Indians while she was chief, and later as its Southeastern Region Elder. The Union was formed in 1890 on the New Credit Reserve near Brantford in southern Ontario to address matters within the Indian Act and to win Indian representation in the House of Commons. The Union was reorganized in 1969 with an extended mandate that included protecting the culture and heritage of Ontario's First Nations people.[39] This organization mirrored Elsie's concerns about the loss of culture and language among her community members, leading her to hold Ojibway language instruction classes for children in the community school, and in the evenings for community members and other interested people.

On the national level, she served on the board of directors of the National Indian Brotherhood, the forerunner to the Assembly of First Nations. Elsie also pushed for universal franchise for Indians. She said "that Indians felt left out of things as long as they could not vote,"[40] referring to Governor General George Vanier's Throne Speech at the opening of the second session of the 24th Parliament on 14 January 1960, when he said, "Legislation will be introduced to give Indians the franchise in Federal elections."[41]

Improving Community Life

Elsie wanted better living conditions for reserve residents. Negotiating with the government and obtaining funding for reserve programs were difficult tasks. There was never enough money to do what was needed and it was hard work to find funds for even the most basic needs. When she took office there were no wells, the roads were poor, and the houses were mostly run down. Housing was a major concern for Elsie, and in five years she was able to obtain the resources to have 45 new houses built on the reserve.[42] She worked to bring better roads, streetlights, new wells, and better social services. "I took advantage of money available. The government wanted to improve the reserves so there were lots of grants out there. We took everything they handed out."[43] Further, she noted, "I had a new daycare centre built when I was chief."[44] Elsie believed that a daycare centre would enable the community women to go out to work or go to school to improve their education to help them get better employment.[45]

Chief Knott started a number of community initiatives. One example was Decoration Day, which she started the year she was elected. It was a day of beautification that got community members together to clean up the cemetery, plant flowers, and paint. Afterwards, the community members had a picnic and fish fry and the Salvation Army band from Peterborough performed. It was a great community-building effort that brought the people closer together. Elsie initiated many community efforts that drew on volunteers, and not money.

Elsie was concerned about the loss of Ojibway culture due to the assimilation efforts of church, school, and Indian Affairs. She brought traditional teachers to the reserve to help the people relearn drumming, dancing, and singing, and to make their own regalia. As mentioned earlier, with Gladys Taylor, Elsie taught weekly Ojibway language classes on the reserve. Ojibway language classes were also included in the schools as part of the educational curriculum for children. Elsie also translated 14 Christmas carols for children to sing at a concert.[46] Adult Ojibway language classes had about a dozen participants at any given time and continued for about two years.[47]

Elsie believed in education. She wanted reserve children to succeed in school, and she helped them in a variety of ways. Referring to Elsie's strong leadership, artist Randy Knott said, "I was so scared to leave the reserve and go to the other school. But through her we all got brave."[48] Former student Winston Taylor recalled, "Her example inspired me when I went back to school. She was that kind of lady who made up her mind to do something and she just did it."[49] Judge Tim Whetung often stopped to visit Elsie and thank her for having driven him to school when he was a boy.[50]

Political Defeat

Elsie Knott was chief for 16 years. Though it was long, her political career was not easy and she had her critics. Hannah Johnson, the band secretary, said that people had strong feelings about her.[51] In 1976, Elsie lost to Doug Williams by 12 votes. Williams was critical of Elsie and her council, saying,

> the council she was heading then was a "yes" council. It was practicing nepotism at this time. A lot of grants were forthcoming and many on the council were getting jobs. I was just clearly dissatisfied with the way things were going. I ran because I wanted to let Elsie know there were ill feelings on the reserve.[52]

Chief Williams also claimed that Elsie had taken the election loss hard and that she was vengeful.[53] Elsie took Williams's criticism personally. "I worked hard for the little I got. Some say I got ahead too fast."[54]

She was disappointed at losing the election and losing her role as chief. She commented,

> I should have given it up instead of losing it. I think that was a shock. Afterwards, I didn't know who my friends were. I didn't trust anyone. My nerves bother me sometimes. I took things personally. If someone criticized me just a little bit of what I did or didn't do—it would bother me for a night. I would toss and turn just thinking about that one subject. But I think I did my best anyway.[55]

Elsie believed she had lost the election because "the old people did not come out to vote. My supporters thought I would win by a landslide and thought that their votes would not be needed. The young people were pushing for the other guy."[56] She said, "[T]he first thing that Williams guy did was change the law that you could not work for the band and run for public office. I could not run as long as I have [sic] the bus contract for the band."[57] When asked if she would run again she said she would have to think twice about it. Given her long stint in public office, the electorate wanted a change in leadership.

Later in life, Chief Knott received accolades and recognition from across the country and she was the subject of many newspaper and magazine articles. In 1980, Lois Franks, of Boston University, wrote a play about her called, "Elsie, Indian Chief, Bus Driver, Shopkeeper, Grannie."[58] In 1975, International Women's Year, she was named one of Ontario's 25 outstanding women, along with geneticist Irene Ayako Uchinda, women's advocate Grace Hartman, and academic librarian Margaret Beckman. Elsie Marie Knott died on 3 December 1995 at the age of 73, with three children, ten grandchildren, and 13 great-grandchildren to mourn her passing. Honouring her in the Ontario legislature, Member of the Legislative Assembly R. Gary Stewart described her as, "a friend, mother, and leader of a community that benefited from her hard work and love of life."[59]

She was an unlikely political leader. She started out as a shy woman married to an ailing older man. Over the years she transformed herself into an effective leader and community advocate who worked hard to improve the lifestyles and living conditions of her community members. Financial circumstances caused her to move beyond her comfort zone and take chances that she might not ordinarily have taken. Dalton Jacobs said, "She was someone with tenacity and a strong work ethic. She would have done well in any community but I am just happy that she was part of my community."[60] Community members remembered her fondly and commented on her community work. "She was a pioneer and she made real accomplishments" according to band member Margaret Spencely.[61]

In the early years of her leadership, Elsie was singled out continually as the "woman chief." This was both a blessing and a curse. The recognition that came with the position of chief could work to one's benefit because, as Elsie mentioned, people were more likely to help a woman and less likely to refuse her requests for assistance. Elsie was portrayed in the media as a community worker but also as a woman who maintained the traditional care-giving role of wife and mother. She appeared to have simply increased her family size to include the entire band when she became chief. She was non-threatening as an Indian leader. This characteristic would have comforted local non–First Nations people who had limited contact with, and knowledge of, First Nations people.

Being the sole woman in a man's environment was isolating and lonely. Elsie's fame and her deep sense of duty meant giving up much of her privacy. Her work impinged on family time and occasionally caused resentment among family members. It also left little personal time for her to rejuvenate and reflect. Elsie dedicated her adult life to the community. Many opportunities presented themselves she acted on them. She worked as a domestic, postmistress, bus driver, store owner, and church superintendent. For Elsie, these jobs represented financial security. In a community with high unemployment, however, some people saw her as an elected person seizing opportunities for herself and her family instead of allowing others to compete for those jobs. She was accused of conflict of interest, nepotism, and benefiting from confidential information.

In short, her multiple jobs caused resentment in the community, and this was the basis of her political defeat.

Unfortunately, Elsie Knott did not have the opportunity to leave community politics on her own terms. She was forced out. Her final campaign was bitter and she was hurt by allegations that her financial assets had been gained by less than honourable means. The defeat took a huge personal toll on her and she was shaken to her core. She suffered both physically and emotionally from the loss, having trouble sleeping, and suffering from anxiety, and she felt betrayed by the community she had worked so hard for. For Elsie Knott, being chief was more than just a job. It had served as a means of transforming herself from a shy young woman into a respected and confident leader. She used her skills and her innovative ideas to bring improved living conditions and upgraded services to her community. The job kept her busy and helped her cope after the death of her husband. As chief, she moved from anonymity to fame. In his eulogy, Father Paul Heffernan intimated that sometimes one person can make a difference in a community. Summing up Elsie's character, he said, "With Elsie, the difficult was easy, the impossible took a little longer."[62]

An earlier version of this paper was published by the author in, Firekeepers of the 21st Century: First Nations Women Chiefs *(Montreal & Kingston: McGill-Queens Press, 2008).*

Notes

1. The Mississaugas of Mud Lake/Curve Lake First Nation is an Ojibway band in southeastern Ontario with a land base of about 1600 acres in the area covered by the Williams Treaty of 1923. It is on a peninsula surrounded by Buckhorn and Chemong Lakes about 32 kilometres from Peterborough, Ontario, Canada.

2. The Indian Act was amalgamated in 1876 to consolidate all government legislation pertaining to Indian people in Canada. It governs virtually every aspect of Indian life from cradle to grave.

3. "Williams Upsets Knott at Curve Lake Election," *Cortaid News*, 4, 13 1976, 28.

4. Other published works include an unpublished master's thesis by C.A. Franks from Boston University 1980, newsletters, and obituary notices.

5. C.A. Franks, *Elsie, Indian Chief, Bus Driver, Shopkeeper, Grannie.* Unpublished Master's thesis, Boston University, 1980

6. In 1920 Deputy Superintendent General Duncan Campbell Scott, an advocate of assimilation, stated, "I want to get rid of the Indian Problem. Our object is to continue until there is not a single Indian in Canada that has not been absorbed in the body politic and there is no Indian question and no Indian Department." Titley 1986, 50. The intent of the policy was to eliminate the "Indian Problem" by eliminating the Indians, their culture, and their language. In Duncan Campbell Scott's time,

Canada's Indian population numbered a mere 113,724—an all-time low.

7. L. Post, "Honouring the Memory of Elsie Knott," *Anishinabek News*, retrieved 28 May 2004 from http://tyendinaga.net/amsp/2nd/story/story8.thm1.

8. "Canada's First Woman Chief," *Indian Life*, (1996): 12.

9. Franks, 1980.

10. "Canada's First Woman Chief," 1996.

11. "Elsie Marie Knott, Enterprising Woman First Female Chief," *The Globe and Mail*, 1995, E6.

12. "She Has Driven Bus for Twenty-Five Years. Curve Lake Honours Elsie Knott," *Peterborough Examiner* (9 May 1978):8.

13. Personal interview, Rita Rose, Curve Lake First Nation, August 2002.

14. Post, 1998, 2.

15. Ibid.

16. Ibid., 8.

17. "Elsie Knott: A Curve Lake Elder and Crusader, Prime Time," *Peterborough County's Newspaper for People Fifty-Plus* (May 1995), 5.

18. Franks, 1980, 8.

19. Secretary of State, *Speaking Together: Canada's Native Women* (1975), 100.

20. Franks, 1980, 59.

21. Ibid., 8.

22. Personal interview, Rita Rose, Curve Lake First Nation, August 2002.

23. Telephone interview with Rita Rose, 2005.

24. Ibid.

25. "For a Start: Grannie is a Real Chief," *West Sussex County Times*, 7 September 1973, 21.

26. Post 1998, 3.

27. *Peterborough Examiner*, 1955, n.p.

28. Post, 1998, 3.

29. Canada, House of Commons, *Statement of the Government of Canada on Indian Policy (White Paper)*, (Ottawa: Supply and Services, 1969), 2.

30. Ken Coates, *The Marshall Decision and Native Rights* (Montreal & Kingston: McGill-Queen's University Press, 2000), 76.

31. Laurie Meijer-Drees, *The Indian Association of Alberta: a History of Political Action* (Vancouver: University of British Columbia Press, 2002).

32. P. Armstrong, "100 Indians Break the Ice in Fish Fight," *Peterborough Examiner*, 10 February 1975, n.p.

33. "For a Start," 1973, 21.

34. "Elsie Knott," 1995.

35. Franks, 1980.

36. Rose, 2005.

37. D. Clifford, "Indians 5000 Strong Coming to Peterborough," *Peterborough Examiner*, 9 March 1977, 9.

38. Canada, *Royal Commission on Aboriginal Peoples*, 1996.

39. Union of Ontario Indians, 2005.

40. "Indians Want Vote Rights," Governor General George Vanier's Speech from the Throne. Ottawa: 1960.

41. House of Commons, 1960.

42. Franks, 1980.

43. Ibid.

44. cited in Post, 1998, 3

45. Canada, Secretary of State, 1975.

46. Interview with Rita Rose, 2005.

47. Ibid.

48. Post, 1998, 2.

49. Ibid.

50. Ibid.

51. Franks, 1980.

52. Franks, 1980, 65.

53. Ibid.

54. Ibid., 70.

55. Ibid.

56. Ibid.

57. Ibid., 68.

58. "Elsie Marie Knott," 1995.

59. Ontario, Legislative Assembly, 1995.

60. Father Heffernan, "Elsie Knott's Legacy is One of Community First and Foremost," *Peterborough Examiner*, 15 December 1995, 15.

61. Franks, 1980, 67.

62. Heffernan, 1995, 15.

Primary Document

Excerpt from the Indian Act, 1951

Election of Chiefs and Band Councils

73.(1) Whenever he deems it advisable for the good government of a band, the Governor in Council may declare by order that after a day to be named therein the council of the band, consisting of a chief and councillors, shall be selected by elections to be held in accordance with this Act.

(2) The Council of a band in respect of which an order has been made under subsection (1) shall consist of one chief, and one councillor for every one hundred members of the band, but the number of councillors shall not be less than two nor more than twelve and no band shall have more than one chief.

(3) The Governor in Council may, for the purposes of giving effect to subsection (1), make orders or regulations to provide

(a) that the chief of a band shall be elected by

(i) a majority of votes of the electors of the band

or

(ii) a majority of the votes of the elected councillors of the band from among themselves, but the chief so elected shall remain a councillor,

(b) that the councillors of a band shall be elected by
- (i) a majority of the votes of the electors of the band

or

- (ii) a majority of the votes of the electors of the band in the electoral section in which the candidate resides and that he proposes to represent on the council of the band,

(c) that a reserve shall for voting purposes be divided into not more than six electoral sections containing as nearly as may be an equal number of Indians eligible to vote, and

(d) for the manner in which electoral sections established under paragraph (c) shall be distinguished or identified.

74.(1) No persons other than an elector who resides in a section may be nominated for the office of councillor to represent that section on the council of the band.

(2) No person may be a candidate for election as chief or councillor unless his nomination is moved and seconded by persons who are themselves eligible to be nominated.

75.(1) The Governor in Council may make orders and regulations with respect to band elections, and without restricting the generality of the foregoing, may make regulations with respect to

(a) meetings to nominate candidates,

(b) the appointment and duties of electoral officers,

(c) the manner in which voting shall be carried out,

(d) election appeals, and

(e) the definition of residence for the purpose of determining eligibility of voters.

(2) The regulations made under paragraph (c) of the subsection (1) shall make provision for secrecy of voting.

76.(1) A member of a band who is of the full age of twenty-one years and is ordinarily resident on the reserve is qualified to vote for a person nominated to be chief of the band, and where the reserve for voting purposes consists of one section, to vote for persons nominated as councillors.

(2) A member of a band who is of the full age of twenty-one years and is ordinarily resident in a section that has been established for voting purposes is qualified to vote for a person nominated to be councillor to represent that section.

77.(1) Subject to this section, chiefs and councillors hold office for two years.

(2) The office of chief or councillor becomes vacant when

(a) the person who holds that office
- (i) is convicted of an indictable offence
- (ii) dies or resigns his office, or
- (iii) is or becomes ineligible to hold office by virtue of this Act; or

(b) the Minister declares that in his opinion the person who holds that office
- (i) is unfit to continue in office by reason of his having been convicted of an offence,

         (ii) has been absent from meetings of the council for three consecutive meetings without being authorized to do so, or

         (iii) was guilty, in connection with an election, of corrupt practice, accepting a bribe, dishonesty or malfeasance.

  (3) The Minister may declare a person who ceases to hold office by virtue of sub-paragraph (iii) of paragraph (b) of subsection (2) to be ineligible to be a candidate for chief or councillor for a period not exceeding six years.

78.(1) The Governor in Council may set aside the election of a chief or councillor on the report of the Minister that he is satisfied that

    (a) there was corrupt practice in connection with the election

    (b) there was a violation of this Act that might have affected the result of the election, or

    (c) a person nominated to be a candidate in the election was ineligible to be a candidate.

79.(1) The Governor in Council may make regulations with respect to band meetings and council meetings and without restricting the generality of the foregoing, may make regulations with respect to

    (a) presiding officers at such meetings,

    (b) notice of such meetings,

    (c) the duties of any representative of the Minister at such meetings, and

    (d) the number of person required at the meeting to constitute a quorum.

Questions for Consideration

1. What negative images of Indigenous women did the Canadian government and European-Canadian newcomers promote and why?

2. Why did the accusations of missionary Samuel Triviett about the improprieties of government officials and members of the North-West Mounted Police cause such a scandal in 1886? Who was blamed for the alleged misbehaviour and why?

3. What were the Homemakers' Clubs? Why did the Canadian government establish these clubs?

4. How did the Indigenous women Lianne Leddy examines reshape the Homemakers' Clubs? Should this be understood as a form of resistance to Canadian colonialism?

5. What does the model constitution for Homemakers' Clubs reveal about the goals of the Canadian state for the Clubs? How does gender inform this document? Are the gender ideals revealed in the document Eurocentric?

6. Discuss the historical significance of Elsie Knott's life.

7. How did Elsie Knott's leadership benefit the people of Curve Lake First Nation?

8. According to the excerpt from the 1951 Indian Act, who could become chief of an "Indian" band? Under what circumstances could a chief be removed by the Governor in Council? Was the retention of this power to intervene in bands' affairs justified? Why or why not?

9. To what roles has the Canadian state attempted to consign Indigenous women? In what ways have Indigenous women adopted and resisted these roles?

Further Resources

Books and Articles

Acoose, Janice Pelletier. *Iskwewak Kah'Ki Yaw Ni Wahkomakanak: Neither Indian Princesses Nor Easy Squaws*. Toronto: Women's Press, 1995.

Anderson, Kim. *A Recognition of Being: Reconstructing Native Womanhood*. Toronto: Sumach Press, 2001.

———. *Life Stages and Native Women: Memory, Teachings, and Medicine*. Winnipeg: University of Manitoba Press, 2011.

——— and Bonita Lawrence, eds. *Strong Women Stories: Native Vision and Community Survival*. Toronto: Sumach Press, 2003

——— and Patricia McCormack, eds. *Recollecting: Lives of Aboriginal Women of the Canadian Northwest and Borderlands*. Edmonton: Athabasca University Press, 2011.

Carter, Sarah. *Capturing Women: The Manipulation of Cultural Imagery in Canada's Prairie West*. Montreal & Kingston: McGill–Queen's University Press, 1997.

Miller, Christine, and Patricia Chuchryk, eds. *Women of the First Nations: Power, Wisdom and Strength*. Winnipeg: University of Manitoba Press, 1996.

Green, Joyce, ed. *Making Space for Indigenous Feminism*. Halifax: Fernwood Publishing, 2007.

LaRocque, Emma. *When the Other is Me: Native Resistance Discourse, 1850–1990*. Winnipeg: University of Manitoba Press, 2010.

Maracle, Lee. *Bobbi Lee, Indian Rebel*. Toronto: Women's Press, 1975.

Smith, Andrea. *Conquest: Sexual Violence and American Indian Genocide*. Cambridge, MA: South End Press, 2005.

Printed Documents and Reports

Amnesty International. *Stolen Sisters: A Human Rights Response to Discrimination and Violence against Indigenous Women in Canada.* 2004.

Human Rights Watch. *Those Who Take Us Away: Abusive Policing and Failures in Protection of Indigenous Women and Girls in Northern British Columbia, Canada*, 13 February 2013. www.hrw.org/report/2013/02/13/those-who-take-us-away/abusive-policing-and-failures-protection-indigenous-women

Jamieson, Kathleen. *Indian Women and the Law in Canada: Citizens Minus*, Ottawa: Canadian Advisory Council on the Status of Women and Indian Rights for Indian Women, 1978.

Native Women's Association of Canada. *Aboriginal Women and the Implementation of Bill C-31*. Ottawa: Native Women's Association of Canada, 1991.

O'Donnell, Vivian and Susan Wallace. *First Nations, Métis, and Inuit Women: A Gender-based Statistical Report*. Ottawa: Statistics Canada, July 2011. www.statcan.gc.ca/pub/89-503-x/2010001/article/11442-eng.pdf

Troian, Martha. "Mikmaq Anti-Fracking Protest Bring Women to the Front Lines to Fight for Water," *Indian Country*, 10 November 2013. http://indiancountrytodaymedianetwork.com/2013/11/10/mikmaq-anti- fracking-protest-brings-women-front-lines-fight-water-152169

RCMP. *Missing and Murdered Aboriginal Women: A National Operational Overview.* Ottawa: 2014. www.RCMP-grc.gc.ca/pubs/mmaw-faapd-eng.pdf

Films

Finding Dawn. DVD. Directed by Christine Welsh. NFB, 2006.
Nose and Tina. DVD. Directed by Linda Bailey. NFB, 1980.
Places Not Our Own (part of the *Daughters of the Country* series). DVD. Directed by Derek Mazur. NFB, 1986.
Senorita Extraviada, Missing Young Woman. DVD. Directed by Lourdes Portillo. Independent Television Services, 2001.
The True Story of Linda M. DVD. Directed by Norma Bailey. NFB, 1995.

Websites

Amnesty International's No More Stolen Sisters
www.amnesty.ca/our-work/campaigns/no-more-stolen-sisters

Assembly of First Nations Women's Council
www.afn.ca/index.php/en/policy-areas/afn-womens-council

Curve Lake First Nation
www.curvelakefirstnation.ca

Indigenous Feminism Without Apology
www.newsocialist.org/689-indigenous-feminism-without-apology

A Short Course on Indigenous Feminism
https://bermudaradical.wordpress.com/2011/01/24/indigenous-feminism/

Native Women's Association of Canada
www.nwac.ca

Lee Maracle, "Connection between Violence against the Earth and Violence against Women"
www.youtube.com/watch?v=VdxJYhbTvYw

Lynn Gehl's Website on Unknown and Unstated Paternity and the Indian Act
www.lynngehl.com/unknown--unstated-paternity--the-indian-act.html

13

Health, the Environment, and Government Policy

Introduction

Many factors shape and determine the health and well-being of individuals and their communities. In Chapter 1, Betty Bastien shows how the Blackfoot (and many other Indigenous cultures) place a great deal of value on their interconnectedness with their environment. This relationship sustains the people, so, accordingly, environmental degradation represents profound cultural distress. Central to the decline of health and well-being in Indigenous communities was the gradual erosion of access to aspects of life that ensure both physical and spiritual well-being. For instance, Indigenous peoples (at different times and to differing degrees depending on location) experienced declining access to hunting and harvesting resources as a result of forced settlement on reserves and provincial hunting laws. These and other restrictions limited and in some cases criminalized Indigenous peoples' hunting, frequently in clear violation of the treaties they had signed with the Crown. As anthropologist Naomi Adelson writes, "[H]ealth and identity are linked as part and parcel of the ongoing struggle for voice and endurance in a world that has, over the years, muted and disenfranchised Native people's existence."[1]

The state, and other Euro-Canadian institutions, like the Hudson's Bay Company, damaged the health and well-being of Indigenous peoples and their communities in other ways as well. Although established in 1880, ostensibly to manage the state's relationship with Indigenous peoples, the Department of Indian Affairs (DIA) was slow to develop a health bureaucracy. Instead, it was churches and missionary organizations that first provided health care to Indigenous peoples by establishing hospitals on reserves and infirmaries in residential schools in the 1870s and 1880s. Not until 1904 did the DIA hire Dr Peter Bryce to be the first "federal official responsible for Indian health."[2] Even so, it was only after 1915 that the DIA began to provide medical services systematically. Historians such as Maureen Lux and Mary-Ellen Kelm have clearly outlined Indigenous peoples' separate and unequal access to medical and health care. Instead of serving as sites of health care, Lux finds that Indian hospitals operated as "sites of confinement and control and worked to isolate disease and continue the state's assimilationist agenda."[3] This chapter looks at the interconnections between environment, capitalism, and government policy as well as Indigenous peoples' varied responses and strategies in the shaping of health and well-being in their communities.

As Elizabeth Vibert reveals in Chapter 5, historians have paid disproportionate attention to the role that the fur trade played in the lives of Indigenous peoples. Indeed, historians have too frequently identified the decline of the fur trade as a main cause of ill health and starvation among Indigenous peoples. As a result, the historiography has neglected the importance of the aquatic environment in the lives of Indigenous peoples and thus the devastating impact of declining access to water resources and pollution. In the first article, Liza Piper emphasizes the consequences that the degradation of Indigenous people's connection to the aquatic environment has had on their health. Piper argues that the rise of industrial fisheries, the imposition of the interests of capital, and the increasing presence of European-Canadians on Indigenous waterways have fundamentally transformed the relationship among fish, people, and freshwater ecosystems. Contaminated water caused outbreaks of illnesses such as typhoid, and the depletion of fish stocks eroded people's abilities to sustain their families and communities.

The second piece, by Laurie Meijer Drees, seeks to understand how Indigenous peoples experienced the Canadian health care system and and how they resisted it. Drees refocuses historians' attention, showing how Indigenous peoples, despite being forced to remain in Indian hospitals for long periods, continued to practise their culture and pursue their own understandings of health and well-being—often while doctors and nurses remained dismissive or unaware of these efforts. Next, Kristin Burnett, Travis Hay, and Kelly Skinner look at government policy and corporate practices in Indigenous communities in Northern Canada. Using food as a lens, the authors explore how the federal government, in concert with the Hudson's Bay Company, has manufactured food insecurity in Indigenous communities, thus eroding the ability of Indigenous peoples to ensure their own well-being. In 2012, the United Nations' Special Rapporteur on the Right to Food, Olivier De Schutter, visited Canada and reported that 60 per cent of on-reserve Indigenous households in northern Manitoba were food insecure, as were 70 per cent of Inuit adults in Nunavut, "represent[ing] the highest documented food insecurity rate for any Indigenous population in a developed country."[4] The Auditor General of Canada raised concern over access to affordable and nutritious food for northern Indigenous communities again in November 2014 when he released his review of Nutrition North Canada, a federal program intended to subsidize the high cost of foods in northern communities. Food remains an ongoing concern for northern communities.

Chapter Objectives

At the end of this chapter, you should be able to

- recognize the interconnectedness of environmental health and personal well-being;
- understand the important role that the aquatic environment and fisheries played in the economic and personal lives of many Indigenous communities;
- recognize how the Canadian government used health care services as part of the wider colonial project;
- understand how Indigenous peoples used and continue to use the health care system without abandoning their traditional health practices; and
- appreciate how government policy in Northern Canada has caused and continues to cause widespread hunger and malnutrition in northern Indigenous communities.

Notes

1. Naomi Adelson, *"Being Alive Well": Health and the Politics of Cree Well-Being* (Toronto: University of Toronto Press, 2000), 110.

2. James Waldram, D. Ann Herring, and T. Kue Young, *Aboriginal Health in Canada: Historical, Cultural, and Epidemiological Perspectives*, 2nd edn (Toronto: University of Toronto Press, 2006), 188.

3. Maureen Lux, "Care for the Racially Careless": Indian Hospitals in the Canadian West,

1920–1950s," *Canadian Historical Review* 91, 3 (2010): 407–34.

4. UN Human Rights Council, "Report of the Special Rapporteur on the Right to Food, Olivier de Schutter: Addendum, Mission to Canada," 24 December 2012, A/HRC/22/50/Add.1, 16. www.refworld.org/docid/511cb0422.html, accessed 3 January 2015.

Secondary Source

Industrial Fisheries and the Health of Local Communities in the Twentieth-Century Canadian Northwest

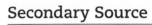

Liza Piper

Fish are neglected creatures in Canadian, Indigenous, and environmental histories. Although Harold Innis's *The Cod Fisheries* (1940) is a much more effective and comprehensive statement on the role of staples in Canadian history, his earlier *The Fur Trade of Canada* (1930) is far better known. In *Traders' Tales* (1997), Elizabeth Vibert explores European cultural preferences for animal flesh, noting explorer and cartographer David Thompson's explicit contrast that fish "can never compensate the want of Deer, Sheep, and Goats."[1] That animals occupied the pre-eminent position in western food hierarchies meant that European observers often discounted the value and importance of fish to Indigenous populations and livelihoods—a bias reproduced by historians who have foregrounded fur over fin. The lower status of fish in history is not only a product of culture but also of environment. As mammals, we share our environment most immediately with other warm-blooded terrestrial creatures. Because aquatic environments, whether freshwater, marine, or in-between (such as estuaries, marshes, and mangroves), are much less familiar to us, we have, throughout history, remained much more ignorant of aquatic character and complexity.[2]

At the heart of this essay lies the integral role of fish in western Canadian Indigenous history. Fish were an essential part of healthy freshwater ecosystems across Canada's Northwest, a region extending from Lake Winnipeg to the Mackenzie Delta. The area encompasses four of Canada's largest lakes—Lake Winnipeg, Lake Athabasca, Great Slave Lake, and Great Bear Lake—among countless mid-sized and small lakes, rivers, marshlands, bogs, creeks, sloughs, and ponds. A saturated place with extreme temperature variations, the Northwest historically offered an immense rich habitat for a range of fish species. Before the late-nineteenth-century rise of industrial fisheries, these fish were central to Northwest Indigenous and non-Indigenous peoples' subsistence practices, and, by extension, human health. Fish were ultimately transformed into a commercial export product by the early twentieth century. Part of this transformation involved commercializing fisheries and establishing hatcheries and fish farms, thereby separating fish in the public mind from the livelihoods, health, and well-being of Indigenous peoples. This essay uses the example of the Dauphin River hatchery in Manitoba to explore the health consequences of this transformation and, in particular, of the separation of fish, water, and people. Before we can discuss the specific case of Dauphin River, we need to briefly examine the longer history of freshwater fisheries in the Northwest and the relationship among fish, Indigenous and non-Indigenous peoples, and the health of freshwater ecosystems.

Pre-Contact and Colonial Fisheries

In the pre-contact era, freshwater fish flourished in the waters that run across the Precambrian Shield and in the Assiniboine, Red, and Saskatchewan Rivers, which cross the western interior. In summer, fish could easily be taken from parkland waters, and the autumn spawning runs provided opportunities to harvest concentrated fish populations on the boundaries between the parkland and the shield.[3] In certain places, as in the radial arms of Great Bear Lake, year-round fishing sites provided a greater, more reliable source of nutrition than could be harvested from the land. Indigenous technologies and cultures demonstrate the importance of freshwater fishing to pre- and early contact Indigenous populations west of Lake Superior. The **Dene** of the Northwest and the Ojibwe and Saulteaux of Lake Winnipeg employed the widest range of fishing tools, including traps, spears, hooks, nets, and weirs. Gillnets, nets used to catch larger fish by the gills, predated the arrival of European technology. Aboriginal nets, woven using willow bast, had to be kept moist and required more maintenance than those made of Italian twine, which were introduced later. For Cree and Ojibwe living near Lake Winnipeg, the lake sturgeon figured as a prominent spirit in their cosmology.

With the arrival of Europeans, sturgeon shifted from the spiritual to the earthly realm, marking the onset of the colonial era (contact to c. 1880) fishery.[4] Freshwater fish of all kinds, particularly inconnu, whitefish, and sturgeon became essential energy sources for the missions and the fur trade. Freshwater fish suited Catholic and Anglican endeavours because it was a reliable source of nutrition and it met with Christian dietary restrictions for Lent. The persistent regularity of fishing in fur-trade records signals its importance to the dominant commerce of the eighteenth- and nineteenth-century Northwest. For example, the Hudson's Bay Company (HBC) hired Orkneymen as expert fishermen. The HBC and its competitors also situated their posts at productive fish sites and kept stores of fish through the winter months. During the winter of 1820, George Simpson (then HBC governor-in-chief and overwintering in the Northwest) described regular work at the Old Fort Fishery on Lake Athabasca.[5] Late-nineteenth-century journals from Norway House describe an annual cycle of harvesting pike in spring, sturgeon in the summer, and whitefish in the fall and winter.[6] Yet the HBC was only ever interested in the fisheries as a support to its fur business, never as a resource opportunity in and of itself. In 1841, Simpson ordered a halt to an export fishery established at Fort William (Thunder Bay) by retired company servants. He expressed concern that local Indigenous peoples "expected to be supplied with agricultural implements, seed, [and] permanent occupation as fishermen and otherwise."[7] Not wanting to divert effort from the fur trade or to become responsible for the maintenance of settlements oriented around other resource pursuits, Simpson and the HBC encouraged fishing only insofar as it fuelled hunters, traders, their families, and their dogs.

The advent of the colonial period of freshwater fish exploitation changed how many and which species of fish were harvested across the Northwest. Nevertheless, there is little evidence to suggest widespread unsustainable relationships with freshwater ecosystems before 1880. As Shepard Krech has argued, the sustainability of freshwater ecosystems had less to do with the place of fish in Indigenous cosmologies than with their material relationships with the rest of nature.[8] In the colonial era, as before, freshwater fish consumption remained within the region. Increased exploitation reflected demographic changes and shifts in the consumption of fish products across the Northwest. For example, fisheries facilitated more permanent settlements during the colonial era. Where previously a large Indigenous population might have met seasonally to harvest a rich fishery, by the eighteenth and nineteenth centuries many of these same sites were sustaining year-round harvesting. To understand this shift, we can visualize fur trade and mission posts as places of intensified fishing activity. Local depletion at these sites meant that residents increasingly relied on fish from nearby areas and that the harvesting pressures created by colonial era fisheries increasingly radiated outwards from the posts. After 1850, the adoption of dogs—fed, and therefore fuelled, with fish—as a principal means of winter transportation also significantly increased demand. Collectively, these circumstances meant that freshwater fish populations were more widely and more regularly harvested and that a greater variety of fish species were heavily exploited compared to the pre-contact period, when greater harvests occurred locally and varied over the course of the year and across a given region.

Industrial Fisheries After 1880

The rise of industrial export fisheries in the late nineteenth century significantly changed relationships between fish, people, and freshwater ecosystems across the Northwest. The new industrial fisheries had a much more immediate and negative impact upon freshwater ecosystems than their predecessors. Signs of depletion and ecological damage appeared within a few years of the new fisheries opening, while more serious problems manifested within decades. Lake Winnipeg was the first northwest lake where freshwater fish were caught for export markets in the 1880s. Harvesting from Lake Winnipeg reached a historic peak in 1904–05. The harvests crashed shortly after, recovered during the 1910s and 1920s, and collapsed again during the 1930s, never to wholly revive. Lake Winnipeg's neighbour, Lake Winnipegosis, also showed signs of overfishing in the opening decades of the twentieth century. By 1930, the Dominion Fisheries inspector, J.B. Skaptason, observed that there "can be no doubt" that Lake Manitoba, the third of Manitoba's largest lakes, was "being fished beyond its capacity."[9] From the intensification of local harvesting that characterized the colonial era, the industrial export era vastly increased the scale of production across the region. Industrial fishers would identify lakes that had yet to be commercially exploited, harvest the "virgin" waters until depletion led to decreasing returns, and then move on.

Industrial fisheries affected the health of freshwater ecosystems in a number of ways. Commercial harvesting changed fish populations in lakes and rivers. Gillnet fisheries, which prevailed across the Northwest, preferentially harvested large, heavy, fast-growing fish. As a result, slow-growing smaller fish were able to thrive. In some places, an alteration in lake demographics led to the extirpation of commercial species (most notably lake sturgeon) and the loss of genetic diversity in freshwater environments. In addition to direct impacts on fish species, industrial harvesting generated enormous quantities of waste, including fish guts (offal), spoiled fish, and "rough" fish (non-commercial species), that further affected freshwater ecosystems. The majority of this waste was simply dumped back into the lakes or rivers from where the fish were taken. In the 1950s, one federal scientist argued that the waste acted as a fertilizer to help younger generations of fish. Experienced fishermen thought otherwise. According to Fred Fraser, a local government official from the Northwest Territories, "Old experienced fishermen, who have worked Lake Winnipeg, Winnipegosis, Lesser Slave and Athabasca, are unanimous, and vociferous in condemning the dumping of dead fish or offal in lake water. They blame that practice for the deterioration of fishing in all lakes . . . the rotten offal spreads disease and death."[10] Rotten fish offal had direct health consequences; not only did it leave the water oily and tasting like fish, but it could also cause gastroenteritis (an inflammation of the gastrointestinal tract leading to acute diarrhea). Fish offal dumped directly offshore at fish-packing sites across the Northwest also led to local eutrophication, with the additional organic nutrients infused into the lake waters.[11] This change in trophic conditions drove whitefish away from the shallow waters.

Across the Northwest, Indigenous people were repeatedly the first to notice and protest the degradation of freshwater environments. For example, Great Slave Lake had been closely monitored by scientists and bureaucrats from the Fisheries Research Board (FRB) since it was opened to commercial fishing in 1945. However, it was local, predominantly Indigenous, populations that first identified signs of depletion. It took six years of calling for the restriction of industrial operations before the FRB finally confirmed their findings and responded.[12] In Great Slave Lake and other areas, local Indigenous people were directly involved in industrial harvesting but lacked sufficient control over resource exploitation to effectively adjust harvesting practices to minimize depletion. Instead, they had to press provincial and federal authorities to make the necessary changes.

Early responses to overfishing focused on using fish hatcheries as the best means of restoring populations or of introducing commercial or sport fish into new waters. George Colpitts noted that the Department of Marine and Fisheries began working with fisheries scientists and local protective associations to advance a larger program of fisheries conservation.[13] The department also opened a large whitefish hatchery in Selkirk, just south of Lake Winnipeg, in 1893. Initial hatchery work in the Northwest was focused in Manitoba, with several more hatcheries for whitefish and pickerel opened on lakes Winnipeg, Manitoba, and Winnipegosis after 1907. The federal government built hatcheries further west: in Banff in 1913 and Fort Qu'Appelle in 1915. As one hatchery superintendent, George Butler, reported in 1930, "The principal work of the Prairie hatcheries has been to replenish the supply of whitefish and pickerel on the large commercial fishing lakes, although of late years increasing attention has been paid to sport fishing lakes and the propagation of sport fish."[14]

The Manitoba freshwater fish hatcheries reveal the industrial fisheries' significant effect on environmental health in the Northwest. The need for hatcheries to "restock" commercial populations on the largest lakes in Manitoba exposed the ill health of freshwater ecosystems caused by rapidly intensified harvesting. Fish populations—particularly the most sought-after commercial species, such as lake whitefish, gold-eye (*Hiodon alosoides*), sturgeon, pickerel (or walleye, *Stizostedion vitreum*), and lake trout (*Salvelinus namaycush*)—suffered directly from the new character of the fisheries. People who depended on these fish populations as part of their regular diet, especially people who lived along the lake shores and fished either for subsistence or as part of the commercial industry, faced seasonal malnutrition or had to adjust their diets in light of the scarcity of once-common fish.

Hatcheries and Health on the Dauphin River

There was more to the role of hatcheries in Indigenous health than matters of nutrition. One of the richest fishing sites in Manitoba was located where the Dauphin River flowed into Lake Winnipeg, connecting Lake Manitoba to its larger neighbour. Important whitefish and pickerel spawning grounds in this area ensured plentiful harvests. Lake whitefish usually spawned in shallower, inshore waters with hard or stony bottoms. Spawning occurred in the fall, when the eggs were "deposited more or less randomly over the spawning grounds by the parents."[15] The eggs remained on the spawning ground until hatching in April or May. Pickerel spawned in the spring or early summer, on coarse-gravelled lake bottoms or in river pools. Unlike whitefish, they moved into tributary rivers (such as the Dauphin River) as soon as the river was ice-free, which preceded the break-up of ice on the lake. They spawned at night in large numbers; eggs would hatch within a few weeks, but the young stayed in deep crevices until late summer.[16] Spawning grounds across the Northwest acted as important harvesting sites: fish congregated there to spawn, and predators (including adults of the same species that cannibalized their young) gathered to feast on the large numbers of juvenile fish. That pickerel and whitefish typically sought shallower waters near the shore for spawning also facilitated harvesting from shore or in smaller boats than those required to sail the often stormy and turbulent waters of the largest lakes.

Indigenous people returned to the mouth of the Dauphin River annually as part of their seasonal harvesting patterns. The richness of the site also attracted commercial operators. The first export-oriented commercial fishing company on Lake Winnipeg, Reid and Clarke, set up their first commercial operation at this site in 1881.[17] With the construction of the Gull Harbour hatchery (close to Hecla) in 1914, the government maintained a spawn camp at the Dauphin River to supply the new hatchery. Eggs were transported on a government steamer, the *SS Bradbury*. Unfortunately, many eggs did not survive the journey, and the Gull Harbour hatchery was replaced with a new operation at the Dauphin River itself in 1936. Fisheries officials relied on Indigenous knowledge of the Dauphin River area to help assess where and when to harvest spawn. As Skaptason wrote to his superior, A.G. Cunningham, "We were informed at Dauphin River by Indians that there is a considerable run of fish up the River the latter part of August, but that is entirely too early for our purpose."[18] By the 1940s, Indigenous people from the St Martin, Fairford, and Dauphin River reserves, as well as nearby communities, such as Gypsumville and Sandy Bay, had acquired fishing licences (another twentieth-century regulatory measure introduced to control fishing and address problems of overharvesting) to fish at this site. Some Indigenous people came to be characterized not as fishers but as "poachers" because they continued their long-standing harvesting activities in waters now re-defined as closed to fishing.[19]

Locating a hatchery at Dauphin River, a rich fishing site and seasonal gathering place, was not, of course, a coincidence. Both hatchery work and subsistence harvesting depended on the same environmental opportunities. There is no evidence to suggest that provincial fisheries officials saw any conflict between the hatchery and harvesting at the same site. Indeed, the hatchery superintendent was also responsible for distributing fishing licences. Local Indigenous men and women were hired to work at the hatchery, in fisheries-related tasks (e.g., collecting spawn), or as cooks, maids, and casual labourers. The hatchery thus became integrated into the social life of the region. Likewise, the buildings and equipment were connected to the physical environment. The hatchery and a neighbouring residence were constructed from nearby timbers. Local wood resources supplied the fuel for the SS *Bradbury* and the hatchery buildings. Local men submitted tenders to cut jackpine, tamarack, and poplar for cord wood.[20] Hatchery work also relied on the provision of water, which closely bound the hatchery to the immediate physical environment. An intake pipe continuously drew "a large volume of water" from the Dauphin River. This water was essential for the hatchery operations, where eggs, fry, and fingerlings had to be kept submerged in moving water. It was "also used as a supply for the plumbing systems in both buildings [the residence and the hatchery], and, in addition to being used for ordinary domestic purposes, may also be used for drinking."[21] Thus, the hatchery became intricately caught up in the hydrological system connecting the Dauphin River with Lake Winnipeg.

In November 1943, word reached the Game & Fisheries administration in Winnipeg of a serious epidemic at Dauphin River. George Butler, now supervisor of Fisheries, was consulted about the history of epidemics at this site. Butler, who had worked at Dauphin River "spawn-taking" since 1923, remarked that, over the years, he had experienced repeated "periods of distress and slight dysentery that I attributed to something in the water."[22] During construction of the new hatchery in 1936, many of the men working on the building had also contracted dysentery, a general term for a range of gastrointestinal disorders that involve the inflammation of the intestine, leading to bloody diarrhea and, possibly, death. Where dysentery is caused by bacteria, it can spread easily through contaminated water. Butler observed that "after freeze-up it usually passed away" and attributed the ailment to decomposing algae or "liberating toxins or poisons in the water."[23] Indeed, he considered it to be a "seasonal sickness" and hence was unsurprised by the prospect of serious illness in November. Ultimately, the reports of an epidemic in 1943 seemed exaggerated as there was no further news of sickness. The deaths of three small children were confirmed but were ascribed to "under-nourishment and lack of medical attention, rather than from any epidemic."[24]

While the absence of further evidence prevents conclusive analysis, it is noteworthy from an environmental health perspective that, during a period when the region's fish populations suffered from overharvesting, malnutrition and limited access to health care may have played a role in the deaths. Moreover, malnutrition at Dauphin River would have made the people in this community more vulnerable to other kinds of infections. That said, the characterization of Indigenous people as unwilling to use Western medicine and unable to feed their children properly reflected widely held attitudes among the dominant society in this period. By 20 November 1943, with no one else apparently ill, the medical director of health deemed the matter closed.[25]

During the following winter, families from the nearby reserves of St Martin, Fairford, and Dauphin River made their usual journey to fish on Lake Winnipeg. By March, over 300 people had been living at Dauphin River for several months and about 100 fishing licences were issued. The families lived in 20 or more log cabins along the riverbanks and in the bush. They carried water from the river to the cabins for food and washing. Food was harvested from the bush and the lake, although at least one cow and one goat were also kept in the community for milk, and some staple foods could be purchased from a small store situated on the hatchery property. Frequent dances and box socials were held. People fished both for themselves and commercially, with a large fish shed serving as the packing plant for the commercial fishery.

Although the fishing was good that winter, there were tragic consequences. One hatchery worker, a non-Treaty Indigenous man who lived just outside the northern limit of the Dauphin River Reserve, died from tuberculosis in early April. His death was followed by that of two small girls. In short order, an epidemic broke out—another 26 people fell ill either at Dauphin River or after their return to their own reserves.[26] Among those affected, 16 were under the age of 20 (and half of those were under the age of 10), nine were adults between the ages of 20 and 50, and only one was over 50.

The epidemic was confirmed as typhoid, an acute, highly infectious disease caused by the bacillus *Salmonella typhi*. Transmitted primarily through contaminated food and water, the disease manifests as a high fever, headache, diarrhea or constipation, coughing, and rose-coloured spots on the skin. Intestinal hemorrhaging can also occur, although it is relatively rare. Before effective antibiotics were available, approximately 10 per cent of those infected with the bacillus died. These antibiotics were available in North America by 1942; however, more remote communities in the Northwest had only limited access to them.

Investigations into the outbreak focused on two key features of the local environment: living conditions at Dauphin River and the character of the hatchery and settlement water supplies. In their reports, Chief Sanitary Inspector John Foggie, L.J. Hunter (one of Foggie's employees), and Director of Health C.R. Donovan concentrated first on the living conditions. This focus reflected in part the character of the outbreak. Because women and children were the most significantly affected, it was thought that the typhoid was food-borne rather than water-borne. However, widely held racist attitudes towards Indigenous people also significantly influenced what the inspectors saw and reported. Donovan and Hunter each drew attention to the "extremely overcrowded" conditions at Dauphin River. Hunter specified that "during the fishing and trapping seasons, many families move in [sic] the Dauphin River mouth district. As this migration or trek is annual, the over-crowded living conditions are present every year during certain seasons. It, therefore, follows that each family should provide their own shelter in this area."[27] This attitude spoke to commonly held attitudes among government officials who, since the nineteenth century, had endeavoured to force Indigenous people to change how they lived to meet the expectations of the settler society. In this instance, communal housing was seen as a menace to public health— even if it was only for the few months when people came to Dauphin River to fish. Hunter and Foggie characterized general sanitary conditions as "filthy," "ill-kept," and "careless." As the inspectors' reports made their way through the bureaucracy, greater attention was paid to the issue of living conditions. A.G. Cunningham, the director of Game and Fisheries, wrote to Deputy Minister D.M. Stephens, foregrounding how "[l]iving conditions among Indians on the Dauphin River reservation are extremely unsanitary and conducive to the breeding of infectious and contagious diseases."[28] Cunningham wanted this matter brought to the attention of the federal Department of Indian Affairs. He also implied that the presence of the Indigenous fishing camp posed a potential hazard to the health of hatchery employees (those for whom Cunningham himself was directly responsible).[29]

Only after the living conditions at Dauphin River were addressed was close attention given to the water supply itself. It became evident that there were serious issues with sanitation at both the hatchery and in the settlement. At the latter, there was no well; water for drinking and washing was taken from the Dauphin River in galvanized pails without subsequent treatment or boiling. Nine earth pit privies were located along the river banks. By contrast, the hatchery itself and the adjacent manager's residence each had a bath, wash basin, and toilet. The residence also had an additional sink. Water for the residence was taken from a wood-cribbed well with a wooden cover, located about 70 feet (21 metres) from the river. In the hatchery, water was used both in the building's operations and plumbing. This water was drawn directly from the river, 30 feet (9 metres) out from the bank. A log-pile crib, filled with stones and gravel, acted as a filter before the water entered the hatchery. While the waste from the privies remained in the soil, waste water from the hatchery and residence septic systems was dumped straight into the river. Thus, as Hunter observed in his report, "the water used by the Indians living between the fish hatchery and the river mouth could be polluted."[30] Also problematic was the fact that the water intake pipe for the hatchery, which supplied the building's toilet, bath, and basin, was situated downstream from where waste from the residence was discharged. The currents in the river contributed to a situation where "effluent from the septic tanks, even in small quantities, may quite readily be passed into the hatchery."[31]

The design of the hatchery's sanitation system points to some serious human errors. However, it also illuminates attitudes towards the hatchery and its purpose and towards Indigenous people and their use of the lake. Those who designed and constructed the hatchery (including George Butler) viewed it as a space for fish, fish management, and fish science. It was a work space, not a living space. This perspective did not take into account that Indigenous people living in the area and working in the hatchery would be using the water, an oversight that is apparent in the separation of the hatchery buildings and residence and even more so in the sequence of the pipes. If the hatchery intake was intended only for fish, it would not have mattered (at least to government and hatchery workers) if it took in polluted river water.

Indigenous uses of the lake appeared to be even further from the minds of those who designed the hatchery. As twenty-first-century observers, we might initially be struck most by the disparity between the availability of treated water at the reserve settlement and the hatchery. In effect, the fish got plumbing, but the reserve did not. However, we should also be mindful that this inequity is not exclusive to the past, as seen in the ongoing issues regarding the availability of clean water on First Nations reserves, particularly in the North.[32] What we can see with the benefit of hindsight is the compartmentalization of the different lake functions. The reports from the typhoid outbreak consistently separated the issue of the settlement (and sanitary conditions there) from the hatchery. As previously mentioned, many of those who lived in the settlement also worked in the hatchery; the families purchased goods at the hatchery store; and those who fished in the lake used the hatchery as headquarters. The hatchery was integrated socially and physically into the life of the Dauphin River community because both the community and the hatchery took advantage of the same environmental opportunities. For those from outside the community (the sanitary inspectors and Winnipeg bureaucrats), there was no such integration. The community was separate; the harvesting of the lake waters (even though providing fish to harvest was the very reason for the hatchery) was separate; and the people who lived in the community and harvested the lake were also separate—clearly othered in the reports on the typhoid outbreak, with responsibility for their well-being passed off onto the federal government. As Foggie noted, "[t]he Dauphin River . . . may be a hasard [sic] by virtue of the somewhat insanitary conditions that exist at habitations along the banks, and their methods of waste disposal, apart, altogether, from direct discharge of sewage from buildings."[33] The hatchery and the habitations were two separate things, even though they had been intimately bound together by the rise and intensification of industrial and commercial activity across the Northwest.

These disparities speak to the environmental injustice at work in the Northwest at mid-century. Particularly given that regulations under the provincial Public Health Act required that "*all surface waters* be regarded with suspicion, and that they be treated or sterilized before being used for drinking or domestic purposes," it is not coincidental that the Indigenous settlement did not have access to treated water. It does, however, demonstrate the segregation of Indigenous and non-Indigenous spaces and the different wealth, opportunity, and services available in these spaces.[34] Ultimately, the distance between the imagined separation and the actual integration created fertile ground for the typhoid bacillus.

Conclusion

The twentieth-century rise of industrial fisheries across the Canadian Northwest undermined the health of freshwater ecosystems and Indigenous people across this region. Industrial harvesting depleted fish stocks, altered freshwater fish demographics, and led to the dumping of wastes that affected nutrient levels and degraded freshwater habitats. Some of these changes to freshwater ecosystems also affected human health. The depletion of the ecosystems contributed to the marginalization of commercial fishing, and it was primarily Indigenous people who suffered the economic consequences. To the extent that health is linked to economic well-being through, for instance, access to appropriate health care, Indigenous health can also be seen as indirectly related to the deterioration of freshwater environments. For those people who relied on freshwater fish in their diet, the depletion of fish stocks also contributed to malnutrition well into the mid-twentieth century. In the construction of the Dauphin River hatchery, government officials failed to recognize the ways in which commercial fishing, hatchery operations, freshwater environments, and daily sustenance were all intimately linked. These associations led directly to a typhoid epidemic in the early 1940s, just one instance of how ill health is sometimes a direct consequence of our interconnection with and impacts on the wider, natural world.

Notes

1. As cited in Elizabeth Vibert, *Traders' Tales: Narratives of Cultural Encounters in the Columbia Plateau, 1807–1846* (Norman: University of Oklahoma Press, 1997), 172.

2. It is only in the twenty-first century that scientists have engaged in a wholesale census-taking of marine life. See Census of Marine Life, www.coml.org/ (accessed 1 Sept. 2010).

3. Arthur J. Ray, *Indians in the Fur Trade: Their Role as Trappers, Hunters, and Middlemen in the Lands Southwest of Hudson Bay, 1660–1870* (Toronto: University of Toronto Press, 1974), 27–32 and figure 15, 47.

4. Christopher Hannibal-Paci, "Historical Representations of Lake Sturgeon by Native and Non-Native Artists," *Canadian Journal of Native Studies* 18, 2 (1998), 214–24.

5. E.E. Rich, ed., *Journal of Occurrences in the Athabasca Department by George Simpson, 1820 and 1821, and Report* (London: Hudson's Bay Record Society, 1938), 197, 3 n. 5, 110, 139. See also George Colpitts, *Game in the Garden: A Human History of Wildlife in Western Canada* (Vancouver: UBC Press, 2002), 21.

6. Frank Tough, *"As their Natural Resources Fail": Native Peoples and the Economic History of Northern Manitoba 1870–1930* (Vancouver: UBC Press, 1996), 175.

7. George Simpson to the Governor, Deputy Governor, and Committee of the Honourable Hudson's Bay Company, 20 June 1841, in Glyndwr Williams, ed., *London Correspondence inward from Sir George Simpson, 1841–42* (London: Hudson's Bay Record Society, 1973), 25–6.

8. Shepard Krech, *The Ecological Indian: Myth and History* (New York: W.W. Norton & Company, 1999).

9. Manitoba, Department of Mines and Natural Resources, Annual Report, 1930.

10. Fred Fraser to C.H. Herbert, 25 June 1951, file 40-6-4B, part 2, Vol. 249, series 1-A-a, RG 22, Library and Archives Canada (hereafter LAC).

11. Eutrophication refers to the process whereby a body of water receives excess nutrients, which in turn can promote the excessive growth of aquatic plant life.

12. For more on this case study, see Chapter 7 in Liza Piper, *The Industrial Transformation of Subarctic Canada* (Vancouver: UBC Press, 2009).

13. George Colpitts, "Science, Streams and Sport: Trout Conservation in Southern Alberta, 1900–1930" (MA thesis: University of Calgary, 1993).

14. G.E. Butler, "Fish Culture in the Prairie Provinces, and Some of Its Results," *Transactions of the American Fisheries Society* 60, 1 (Jan. 1930): 119–20.

15. W.B. Scott and E.J. Crossman, *Freshwater Fishes of Canada* (Ottawa: Fisheries Research Board of Canada, 1973), 269–77.

16. Scott and Crossman, *Freshwater Fishes*, 767–74.

17. Tough, *As Their Natural Resources Fail*, 177.

18. J.B. Skaptason to A.G. Cunningham, Re Airplane Patrol to Dauphin River, 28 Oct. 1935, GR1600 G4555, Archives of Manitoba (hereafter AM).

19. Skaptason to Cunningham, 28 Oct. 1935. For the historiography of this transition, see Karl Jacoby, *Crimes Against Nature: Squatters, Poachers, Thieves and the Hidden History of American Conservation* (Berkeley: University of California Press, 2003) and J. Sandlos, *Hunters at the Margin: Native Peoples and Wildlife Conservation in the Northwest Territories* (Vancouver: UBC Press, 2007).

20. A.G. Cunningham to Capt. P.M. Pearson, 18 Sept. 1935; A.G. Cunningham to C.H. Attwood, 31 Oct. 1936; C.H. Attwood to A.G. Cunningham, 2 Nov. 1936, all in GR1600 G4555, AM.

21. J. Foggie, Chief Sanitary Inspector, Report of Inspection, Water Supply—Fish Hatchery, Dauphin River, Manitoba. 29 July 1944, GR1600 G4555, AM.

22. G.E. Butler to A.G. Cunningham, 3 Nov. 1943, GR1600 G4555, AM.

23. Ibid.

24. A.G. Cunningham to J.G. Cowan, 11 Nov. 1943, GR1600 G4555, AM.

25. C.R. Donovan to J.G. Cowan, 20 Nov. 1943, GR1600 G4555, AM.

26. J.G. Cowan to A.G. Cunningham, 25 Apr. 1944; G.E. Butler to A.G. Cunningham, 26 Apr. 1944; C.R. Donovan, Investigation of Typhoid Fever, 25 May 1944, all in GR1600 G4555, AM.

27. L.J. Hunter, Sanitary Inspector, "Sanitary survey following Typhoid Fever Investigation," 4 May 1944, GR1600 G4555, AM.

28. A.G. Cunningham to D.M. Stephens, 19 June 1944, GR1600 G4555, AM.

29. For a discussion of how non-Indigenous people perceived Indigenous people and communities as repositories for disease, see Maureen Lux, *Medicine that Walks: Disease, Medicine and Canadian Plains Native People, 1880–1940* (Toronto: University of Toronto Press, 2001).

30. Hunter, "Sanitary Survey."

31. Foggie, "Report of Inspection."

32. See, for example, CBC News, "Kashechewan: Water Crisis in Northern Ontario," 9 Nov. 2006. Available at www.cbc.ca/news2/background/aboriginals/kashechewan.html; CTV News, "Concerns over water on reserve ignored for years," 27 Oct. 2005. www.ctv.ca/servlet/ArticleNews/story/CTVNews/20051027/aboriginal_water_feature_051027/20051027/; Indian Affairs and Northern Development, "Progress on Kashechewan Action Plan," 3 Nov. 2005. www.ainc-inac.gc.ca/ai/mr/nr/s-d2005/2-02730-eng.asp.

33. Foggie, "Report of Inspection."

34. As cited in Foggie, "Report of Inspection."

Primary Document

Letter from Chief Pierre Freezie to S.J. Bailey, 9 October 1950

Rocher River, N.W.T.
9th October, 1950.
S.J. Bailey, Esq.,
Room 204,
Norlite Building,
Ottawa, Ont.

Dear Sir,
We, the undersigned, being residents and trappers of the settlement of Rooher River in the Northwest Territories do hereby tender this petition to stop further commercial fishing on Great Slave Lake.

Due to extensive commercial fishing it is becoming more difficult to catch sufficient fish for ourselves and our dogs. Fish is the staple food of dogs and when we do not get enough to feed them it is very difficult for us to travel about the country to visit our trap-lines. Trapping is our only means of livelihood.

Since commercial fishing started a few years ago on Great Slave Lake, we have noticed the fish getting more scarce each year, the quality is also poorer.

During the last two years we have had difficulty in obtaining sufficient fish for ourselves and dogs when we set our nets in the Taltson River which flows in to the Lake. For this reason we have tried setting our nets out in the Lake under the ice during the winter months but this idea has not been successful. It is becoming increasingly difficult for us to live off the country and when we get a year the caribou pass us up, it seems to all of us that certain steps should be taken to safeguard the little that is left.

We beg that the Government should put a stop soon to this extensive commercial fishing on this Lake, because the people living here are going to be in need and may become a Government liability.

Yours truly,
his
mark
Pierre Freezie
(Chief)

Secondary Source

Our Medicines: First Nations' Medical Practices and the Nanaimo Indian Hospital, 1945–75[1]

Laurie Meijer Drees

Introduction

In the mid-twentieth century, Canada's federal Indian Health Services (IHS) operated a network of hospitals, clinics, nursing stations, and travelling health units in an attempt to address health issues in Indigenous communities, especially those of registered Indian people. Before 1945, the Department of Indian Affairs operated various hospitals in conjunction with missionary and other non-denominational organizations. After 1945, the ravages of tuberculosis (TB) epidemics in northern and western Indigenous communities spurred the federal government's sense of moral duty and public safety enough to drive the creation of a separate bureaucracy and machinery to deal with Indigenous health: the IHS division, which was later housed within Canada's Department of Health and Welfare.

In creating this new system, Canada's federal government circumvented the previously central role of various Christian churches delivering Western medical care to Indigenous peoples. The history of the IHS and its predecessors has been dealt with, in broad strokes, by several important histories.[2] At the same time, there is little research to shed direct light on the actions and perspectives of Indigenous peoples within—and on—the IHS.[3] How did Indigenous peoples experience IHS? What impact did the IHS have on Indigenous medical practices?

The Indian hospital system run by the IHS was especially significant because it pushed the Canadian government's influence into Indigenous lives further than ever before. As historian Mary-Ellen Kelm points out, the IHS—even prior to 1950—aimed to legitimize colonial relations and encourage the assimilation of Indigenous peoples, in this instance at the level of Aboriginal bodies.[4] The federal government devised laws and policies designed to enforce the treatment of Indigenous patients with formal Western medicines. Drawing on the governing structures of Indian Affairs, including the residential school system, Ottawa ensured that Canada's formal Western medical system had access to Indigenous patients, with or without the patient's consent. Similarly, Kathryn McPherson identifies how the IHS and its staff of doctors and nurses, from 1945 to 1970, continued to operate as a colonizing force in Indigenous communities. In her view, IHS undermined traditional Indigenous medical traditions, offered contradictory services in Indigenous communities, underfunded its system, and as a form of coercive "charity," maintained relatively strict authoritarian control over its clients and their bodies.[5] As both writers point out, the IHS did little to recognize or work with Indigenous knowledges associated with health care or healing.[6] Yet McPherson suggests that, in the field and in practice, IHS nurses and health practitioners worked around the coercive colonizing structures of the IHS to provide Indigenous peoples chances to assert their own definitions of health and care.[7]

On the one hand, it is clear that local Indigenous medical practices continued to co-exist alongside formal Western medicine despite the countervailing forces of federal Indian policy, law, and the biomedical treatments offered to Indigenous peoples through the IHS. On the other hand, it is less clear *how* First Nations' medicines and healing practices fared and *how* they operated in a context where IHS administrators and health care providers officially dismissed their value. My interviews with First Nations community members in the central Vancouver Island region between 2005 and 2009 reveal that these remedies continued to be administered and shared in the same time and space as the formal Western medical treatments offered by the IHS from 1945 to the 1970s. As such, "Indian medicine" is part of the rich and culturally diverse Canadian medical history. This small case study of the use of local First Nations medicine within the IHS Nanaimo Indian Hospital in Nanaimo, BC, during the postwar period provides a glimpse into the nature of co-existing medical practices, using Indigenous perspectives.

A central theme conveyed in the oral histories is that "Indian medicines" moved fluidly in and out of the Indian hospital setting. These treatments were sometimes highly visible; at other times, they were practically invisible to everyone but their provider and recipient. Sometimes IHS doctors encouraged the use of "Indian medicines," while at other times they were unaware of their presence. As a result, there was more than one form of medicine in the Nanaimo Indian Hospital. The Indian hospital offered a space where medicine moved in and out, depending on the availability of practitioners and the needs of patients. As Kelm points out, "Aboriginal people did not relinquish their belief in their own medicine and its role in preserving their health."[8] Kelm's thesis is supported here but needs to be refined. In fact, based on oral history evidence, local First Nations' medicines made their way into—and operated within— the government facilities created to subvert them.

Indian Health Services and Hospitals

The Canadian government did not always tolerate Indigenous self-determination in health care, especially when it concerned infectious and communicable diseases such as TB. In fact, as early as 1914, sections of the Indian Act allowed the government to apprehend patients by force if they did not seek medical treatment.[9] Not only could a person be arrested for avoiding treatment, but any person subject to the Indian Act was also personally responsible for seeking treatment from a "properly qualified physician."[10] Such regulations did not recognize treatments given by family or community members. In this way, both federal and provincial law applied their weight to Indigenous communities, forcing the acceptance of Western medicine and its attendant institutions for the sake of public health.

After 1945, IHS became the new instrument through which the federal government would take care of Indian peoples and their health issues. Underlying the IHS was the attitude that Indian and Inuit peoples would not have autonomy in health care. The IHS would take care of Indian and Inuit health; it would provide "a complete health service for these [Status Indian and Inuit] peoples" based on a moral, not a legal, imperative. In the words of the IHS, "Canada's Indian Health Service . . . has arisen, not from legislative obligation, but rather as a moral undertaking to succor the less fortunate and to raise the standard of health generally."[11]

The IHS also sought to "improve assimilation" of Indian peoples into mainstream non-Native society. Healthy Indian people were deemed to be more economically independent, less dependent on government, and thus better able to join Canada as workers rather than wards.[12] Finally, within this new health care system there was no support or understanding for traditional Indigenous health practices. Until at least the 1960s, traditional medicines and practices were viewed as backward and as based on superstition and ignorance. The aim of the IHS was to "correct" the traditional medical and health practices of Indigenous peoples.

As part of the new health care system, the number of IHS hospitals operated directly by the Department of National Health and Welfare grew from 17 to 21 between 1945 and 1950.[13] Funding also grew: in 1937, Parliament approved $750,000 for the medical branch of Indian Affairs; by 1948, that amount had increased to $7.5 million.[14] Although some mission and public hospitals remained available to First Nations, the IHS institutions were specifically for registered Indian and Inuit patients. Of all Indian hospitals within the IHS, the largest were located in British Columbia and Alberta. Important questions remain, however: how did Indigenous people experience IHS policies and facilities, and what was the impact of IHS on Indigenous medical traditions?

Coast Salish Medicine

Hul'qumi'num-speaking peoples, from the central Vancouver Island region, possess a deep and complex philosophy pertaining to the human body and how to best maintain an individual person's health and wellness. As part of this philosophy, a myriad of individual and communal cultural practices serve to enhance a person's well-being, build his or her strength, and support his or her ongoing health. These activities might include bathing, performing specific training exercises, eating particular foods, and engaging in prayer, singing, and specific rituals. Herbal preparations and their application often form another element in treating illness and supporting healthiness in people.

Although many of the practices and preparations are commonly known and communally shared among members of the mid-island First Nations communities, some practices and treatments are kept within specific families, to be used only by those families or by special request. Some practices and preparations are deeply private and never shared, except in special circumstances. Taken together, these elements form the medicine upon which many First Nations peoples draw during challenging times and illnesses. Generalizations about the nature and implementation of this medicine are difficult to make, given the sometimes confidential and often private way in which it is shared and used. What is clear is that there exists a body of thought and of practice that support each other in offering humans a way to be a good person and to stay physically, mentally, and spiritually well.

Perhaps one of the more public aspects of this philosophy of maintaining good health is the body of wisdom known in the Hul'qumi'num language as *snuwuyulth*.[15] *Snuwuyulth* is the teachings, offered by Elders to those individuals who are willing and open to listening, that present guidelines or lessons that convey the life skills necessary to be well and a good person. *Snuwuyulth* is usually offered through storytelling, from which listeners can draw the information they need to help themselves. Shared both publicly and privately, the teachings are all-encompassing, addressing the mental, physical, and spiritual aspects of a person. If an individual is not feeling well, mentally or physically, these teachings assist in rebalancing him or her, including his or her energies, body, and mind. For example, some teachings deal with anger management or offer techniques on how to cope with negative emotions. Other teachings emphasize how people should relate to one another in order to maintain healthy communities, such as including children in daily chores and knowing who one's family is. Still others deal with food or with care of the body. If a person follows the teachings, he or she is sure to have a strong mind, heart, and body and will benefit by being "well." Sometimes, if a person is feeling unwell, family or community members offer him or her *snuwuyulth* as a balm or a healing. In this way, *snuwuyulth* forms a type of medicine and is understood and practised as such.

Coast Salish communities also have a long history of understanding the biomedical properties of plants. In various families, traditional knowledge about what plants can be harvested, combined, and prepared to offer remedies for a range of illnesses remains. Some of these remedies have been documented by ethnobotanists, including Nancy Turner, as part of ethnobotanical and traditional ecological knowledge studies. Thus, in the Coast Salish communities of central Vancouver Island, well-established sets of practices dealing with all types of illness and sickness continue to exist and flourish. In contemporary times, these practices can and are frequently used in conjunction with formal Western medical treatments.

Nanaimo Indian Hospital

The Nanaimo Indian Hospital (NIH) was opened in 1945 as part of the IHS hospital network. Located on an old military property in Nanaimo, BC, this particular hospital served First Nations patients from central and north Vancouver Island, as well as the central northwest coast of British Columbia. The NIH was one of the larger hospitals in the IHS system, consisting of over 200 beds in its first decade of operations. It offered surgeries and drug treatments for TB as well as other illnesses, although the vast majority of its patients were admitted for TB treatment and convalescence. As new antibiotic drug treatments emerged to address TB, the Indian hospitals adopted and administered them to their patients. Standard medicines offered to tubercular patients between 1945 and the 1970s included the drugs streptomycin, para-aminosalicylic acid (PAS), and isoniazid (INH). Another important component of the TB treatment regime was mandatory rest, and patients often found themselves on enforced bed rest for months—even years—at a time. In the early years of the NIH's operation, patients were rarely allowed to venture outdoors; however, by the 1950s, fresh air and light outdoor activity for patients became a regular part of the routine implemented by the staff.

Patients of the NIH during the 1950s and 1960s and their family members have rarely spoken publicly about their experiences within this federal facility. In 2005, I began to actively canvass for oral histories related to the institution from both former patients and former employees. The resulting interviews were far-ranging in subject and tone, yet a common theme that emerged was that First Nations peoples continued to practise their own remedies, both inside and outside the hospital, despite the availability of Western medicine through the hospital and its staff. Although Kelm's examination of the IHS in British Columbia discusses at some length

Tuberculosis patients on the hospital steps, Blackfoot (Siksika) reserve, Alberta, 1938; Back row: Howard McMaster and Emil Medicine Traveller. Front row: Herbert Eagle Ribs and Marie Many Bears (Chief's daughter). Photographed by Jane and Lucien Hanks. (Picture: PA-3385-147; Glenbow Archives.)

how First Nations' healing traditions persisted in spite of the presence of the IHS and its treatments, just *how* local medicines were employed remains vague. Based on the interviews collected, it appears that First Nations people brought their own treatments to the hospital in Nanaimo, whether or not they were invited to do so by physicians or nurses. In many instances, these medicines may have been entirely invisible to hospital staff, who may not have even realized that local medicines were being offered to patients by their visiting family members. Indeed, it is quite likely that staff members did not recognize the activities of family as constituting the administration of medicine. In this way, the bringing of food, the sharing of time and attention, and the administration of herbal remedies and special rituals went on in the NIH without much notice.

The first person to speak to me about Coast Salish medical practices was Ellen White, a beloved Elder, author, and teacher of the Snuneymuxw First Nation. As a young child, White was trained in the preparation and use of certain herbal medicines, as well as in midwifery, by her grandmother. Today, her community recognizes her as a powerful spiritual person and as someone who has specific knowledge of health and healing. White took the time to speak with me about her interaction with the NIH and the staff who worked there in the 1950s. A small excerpt of our conversation is as follows:

> My granny trained us in all the medical things by telling us story after story. Some
> stories are about childbirth. Or about behaving properly. Another story would be the

power of words and how to cause problems for yourself. She also talked to us about the dangers of using certain words when it's not right to do so, not proper. Words go with certain things and you are supposed to do it right.

The stories train us how to do things—we always say, "Remember that story?" when we are trying to do something. It's a lot like when you are being trained in the hospital to be a nurse. The stories taught us. We learned about kinds of medicines, how to stop bleeding with things like plantain, and a lot of other things.

I went up to the Nanaimo Indian Hospital now and then. I was called up there and did deliver a couple of babies. Some patients were sent out of the hospital. The hospital, I heard later, didn't want to have some of the women that were really badly affected with TB and refused them. It also didn't want some of those women to give birth. The Doctor, Dr Drysdale, would come in and later on, Doctor Schmidt. Dr Schmidt used me a lot. He was always encouraging me, and came down to the reserve. He encouraged some of us from the reserve to train as health aides. I remember that hospital. I recall how one time Doug carried a ladder up the hill, and how he used it to climb in one of the windows to visit a friend there. That's how he got inside! I was pregnant at the time and wanted to stay away. I didn't really like that place much and I got into trouble with one of the nurses so I had an excuse. I think she wanted me to stay away. She said, "It's filthy stuff you're putting on the patients."[16]

In a separate conversation, White mentioned how she was invited to the hospital at times to help with "cleansings," a local First Nations ritual of sweeping out negative forces or energies from places, thereby purifying a space or person. The hospital staff allowed her to come in and work through the ceremony for the benefit of the patients in the hospital. Undoubtedly, White also brought stories and teachings to those she treated in the hospital.

In these ways, White brought her traditions of healing into a Western medical facility that otherwise appeared separate from, and in many ways ran counter to, local First Nations' healing practices. As she mentions, one particular doctor—Dr Schmidt—supported her activities. However, some nurses were less than appreciative of what she brought to the hospital in the form of knowledge or herbal remedies, and it was these individuals who eventually encouraged White to stay away from the facility.

Much like Ellen White, Delores Louie (Chemainus First Nation) was a visitor to the NIH in the 1960s. Unlike White, she was not invited by the staff to offer any specific treatments but instead came to the hospital every weekend to visit her family: her father, her brother, her sister, and a niece were all patients within the institution. Along with her mother and sisters, Louie visited the hospital every weekend during the extremely limited visiting hours. In this way, she was able to spend valuable time with her family despite the considerable distance of the hospital from her home on the reserve in Cowichan (Duncan, BC). In her words:

Back in '59 or '60, when my Dad, Basil Alphonse, ended up in the TB hospital . . . what I can't remember is who was first, my brother Leo Alphonse or Dad . . . anyway,

Dad was in there for a number of years. I used to go see him. We were only allowed on the weekends. A certain day we had to be there. We had an old vehicle. I used to drive for Mom. Seems like we were there all afternoon, for visiting!

The importance of family, and sharing time together, is part of the Hul'qumi'num understanding of how to live well. Louie spent many hours visiting her relatives on weekends in the hospital and brought them materials so that they could work on crafts as they rested, crafts that they subsequently sold for pocket money. Through visiting and bringing them work to do, Louie offered her relations a chance to remain active and connected to the outside world. Indeed, she was helping her family in a manner that was consistent with her cultural values and teachings. Her family also assisted its sick members with herbal treatments, although those were not brought into the hospital:

> My brother Leo was only in there for eight months. He didn't have TB, so it's strange that he ended up in there. He mentions that one nurse, Mrs Langlois, just brought him in there to be checked and they kept him. He just had pleurisy. He walked out. He got tired of it and just left one day. Walked out. He said he'd never return. But he went on herb medicine [traditional medicine]. He got better in no time. His mom, our mom, made the medicine! And his wife. Those herbs are really interesting. It was pine tree bark, and gosh, a few other ingredients. Three ingredients in it. He mentions that when he had three gallons, he drank that completely. They checked him months after and there was nothing. He went back to logging! He was a logger . . .

Louie's family used herbal medicines when the hospital treatment failed to meet their needs, taking care of the health problems themselves. The hospital was not criticized overtly, but the perception in her family was that the hospital was a place where people were not treated in a manner that might always help them:

> That hospital, it seems like it just existed and that we just accepted it. We accepted what was happening to our people. It wasn't good or bad. My sister never ever complained about it. But when she did come out she just said she just never ever wanted to go back. Same with Dad. He never ever wanted to go back in there! Even my brother, today I tried questioning him, and he just never wanted to be there. I guess because they weren't allowed to walk and they couldn't visit who they wanted, or needed. It was most likely that stressful regime in there. They were kept busy in there, but it was not good.[17]

It is important to note that Louie emphasizes the significance of visiting and staying busy but that the hospital interfered with those important activities that, according to Coast Salish tradition, are considered good and healthy for a person.

A third way in which local First Nations' ways of maintaining and supporting health were brought into the hospital was by bringing patients gifts of food. Officially, the NIH provided meals for all its patients; however, many family members brought their ailing relatives local and preferred foods to help them get better. Violet Charlie, well-respected Elder of the Cowichan Tribes in Duncan, BC, spent four years at the NIH while she was treated for TB. In conversation with me in May 2008, she mentioned how families brought food to their relations in hospital, especially the much prized "superfood" commonly consumed in the north central coast First Nations communities of British Columbia: oolichan and oolichan oil, called "grease":

> LMD: Someone would bring it in, a family member would bring it in?
>
> VC: Uh-huh. A family member would bring it—this grease.
>
> LMD: And did they bring in fish and things like that, for people?
>
> VC: Ya, they got dried fish, abalone—I never tried that—and they called it candle-fish, tiny. I tried it and it's really rich. The nurses didn't object. Mind you, that was the four years I spent in there.[18]

Grease is rich in Vitamin A and is a traditional food that many coastal First Nations community members consider vital to their well-being.[19] In addition to being consumed as a food, the grease can be used to treat skin conditions such as psoriasis or inflammation and even stomach ailments.[20] In this case, the NIH allowed family members to bring food in, although this was done at the discretion of the nursing staff and doctors of the facility.[21]

Conclusion

In these three seemingly small ways, First Nations people, who were either patients or family associated with patients in the NIH, found ways to bring their cultural knowledge and understandings of health and well-being into an institution that otherwise did little to recognize Indigenous cultural practices. The perception by First Nations people that these activities had a positive impact on the health and well-being of First Nations patients is evident in the stories shared here.

From 1945 to the 1970s, Indian hospitals in Canada were authoritarian institutions where the health workers and hospitals possessed the legal power to admit and treat individuals suspected of illness, with or without patient consent. The medical system operating within the hospitals was hierarchical, with clear lines of command and obedience: doctors were at the top, followed by nurses, and then the various support staff. Patients stood outside this hierarchy yet were viewed as subject to the power and authority of the hospital staff. In addition, biophysical diagnoses and treatments held supremacy in this system, and the social or spiritual causes of illness were considered either unimportant or irrelevant, as were cultural perspectives on health and healing. In fact, "Indian medicine" was deemed to be virtually non-existent in the post–Second World War period. In 1974, a visiting anthropologist studying Coast Salish communities commented, "with the near extinction of other forms of native healing, the winter spirit ceremonial has become the only major non-Western therapy at the disposal of the Coast Salish Indians."[22] As discussed, First Nations brought some of their own healing techniques into this system, generally with the consent of the medical staff. From a contemporary perspective, it seems contradictory that medical staff who sought to isolate and treat Indigenous peoples within an institutional setting rather than their home communities (which were viewed as being unhygienic and unhealthy) allowed significant elements of that community to "leak" into the tightly controlled hospital setting. Perhaps hospital staff allowed family visits for compassionate reasons or simply lacked interest in, or insight into, what visitors actually brought into the facility. The fluidity of "Indian medicine," its rootedness in relationships, and in practices or foods not readily recognizable by doctors and nurses, made for its portability and facilitated its implementation in an otherwise generally hostile environment. "Indian medicine" quietly flowed from person to person, healing as it moved.

Another irony also emerges from the stories about the health care offered by the First Nations Elders interviewed on this subject. Although their collective experiences with the NIH were generally negative, they all shared their memories with a great deal of humour. The humorous retelling of experiences that very likely took place under trying circumstances reflects First Nations' sense of self-determination and resilience in recalling situations where their dignity and self-reliance were being tested. The success of local medicines in a person's life seems to add to that person's sense of power and self-esteem and to their ability to overcome difficult situations. Such retelling also underscores the significant power of the medicines themselves.

In the end, the treatments and activities related to health care operations within the Indian hospitals were far more diverse than the official record or even anecdotal accounts provided by doctors and nurses suggest. For this reason, it is important to investigate the perceptions and personal experiences of those people whose bodies were subject to the care of institutions. Canadian medical history is a rich field with many different perspectives and experiences, all of which deserve exploration and consideration. Historian Kathryn McPherson argues that it is important to research and theorize the diverse, and often oppositional, ways women relate to their health care systems;[84] by extension, it is important to research and theorize how cultural minorities relate to those same standard systems in society. In this case, Coast Salish perspectives on health care reveal that, contrary to the perceptions of "outsiders," Indigenous medical practices took on many different forms, were highly portable, and continued to be implemented even when members of that community were perceived by medical "experts" to be lacking in the ability to deal adequately with illness. As academics, we might presume that specific cultural practices related to health care survive and operate, but we rarely seek to describe or explain *how* they operate within our universal and formal Canadian health care system. Sometimes we have much to learn before we can see.

Notes

1. Although used throughout this article in reference to Indigenous health practices, *medicine* is a western biomedical term. The traditional meaning of the word does not capture the range of therapeutic practices and understandings used by Indigenous peoples.

2. Until 1945, the piecemeal but growing services to Indigenous peoples operated as a marriage of church and state. Indigenous populations in the southern provinces were served primarily by federal Indian hospitals. Northern locations, like the Northwest Territories, were served entirely by mission hospitals, which were partially, although inconsistently, funded through the federal department of Indian Affairs. In 1945, Indian Health Services (IHS) consolidated and reorganized health services for Canada's Indigenous communities. Creation of the IHS reflected attempts by the federal government to prioritize public health care services for *all* Canadians—including Indian people. Under this new bureaucratic regime, Indian Affairs

was no longer directly responsible for Indian health care. See James B. Waldram, D. Ann Herring, and T. Kue Young, *Aboriginal Health in Canada: Historical, Cultural and Epidemiological Perspectives* (Toronto: University of Toronto Press, 1995); T. Kue Young, *Health Care and Cultural Change: The Indian Experience in the Central Subarctic* (Toronto: University of Toronto Press, 1988); G. Graham-Cumming, "Health of the Original Canadians, 1867–1967," *Medical Services Journal of Canada*, 23, 2 (1967): 115–66.

3. Few researchers have taken on the challenge of investigating Indigenous epistemologies in relation to definitions of "health" and engagement with formal Western-style health care systems; however, in the field of medical anthropology Naomi Adelson's *"Being Alive Well": Health and the Politics of Cree Well-Being* (Toronto: University of Toronto Press, 2000) is an excellent example, as is Young's *Health Care and Cultural Change*. Other relevant histories include Dara Culhane Speck, *An Error in Judgment* (Vancouver: Talonbooks, 1987), and Lux, *Medicine That Walks*. Doctoral dissertations include Sally M. Weaver, "Medicine and Politics among the Grand River Iroquois," University of Toronto, 1967; and Kristin Burnett, "The Healing Work and Nursing Care of Aboriginal Women, Female Medical Missionaries, Nursing Sisters, Public Health Nurses and Female Attendants in Southern Alberta First Nations Communities, 1880–1930," York University, 2006.

4. Mary-Ellen Kelm, *Colonizing Bodies*, 127–9.

5. Kathryn McPherson, "Nursing and Colonization: The Work of Indian Health Service Nurses in Manitoba, 1945–1970," in Georgina Feldberg, Molly Ladd-Taylor, Alison Li, and Kathryn McPherson, eds, *Women, Health, and Nation: Canada and the United States Since 1945* (Montreal & Kingston: McGill-Queen's University Press, 2003), 223–46, 232–4.

6. Kelm, *Colonizing Bodies*, 153; McPherson, "Nursing and Colonization," 234.

7. McPherson, "Nursing and Colonization," 235.

8. Kelm, *Colonizing Bodies*, 164.

9. Ibid., 122.

10. Canada, Indian Health Services and Indian Affairs Branch, *Circular Letter to All Superintendents, Indian Agency, Regional Supervisors, and the Indian Commissioner for BC, and to all Medical Officers, Indian Health Services*. File L.3 (Ottawa: Claims and Historical Research Centre, 1953).

11. Canada, House of Commons, Sessional Papers, Department of National Health and Welfare, *Annual Report, Indian Health Services, 1949–50*, 80.

12. Canada, House of Commons, Sessional Papers, Department of National Health and Welfare, *Annual Report, Indian Health Services, 1947–8*, 41.

13. Graham-Cumming, "Health of the Original Canadians," 123. He points out how governmental services for Indian health grew "under pressure of growing need and public outcry."

14. Provincial Archives of Alberta, Accession No. 96.2/7, file 1, "Indian Health Services," speech, 1949, 4.

15. This discussion of *snuwuyulth* is based on information shared with me by Florence James (Penelekut First Nation), Ray Peter (Cowichan Tribes), Delores Louie (Chemainus First Nation) and Ellen White (Snuneymuxw First Nation) between 1999 and 2009 as part of my work in the First Nations Studies Department, Vancouver Island University. Interestingly, descriptions of such teachings are missing from the standard ethnographies dealing with Coast Salish cultures, including Homer G. Barnett, *The Coast Salish of British Columbia* (Eugene, OR: University of Oregon, 1955); Wayne Suttles, *Coast Salish Essays* (Vancouver: Talonbooks, 1987).

16. Interview with Ellen White, Nanaimo, BC, 25 Oct. 2007.

17. Interview with Delores Louie, Cedar, BC, 28 May 2008.

18. Interview with Violet Charlie, Duncan, BC, 14 May 2008.

19. Information derived from www.wellsphere.com/healthy-eating-article/oolichan-grease-and-my-big-fat-diet/548833, accessed 16 May 2009.

20. Information derived from www.cbc.ca/thelens/bigfatdiet/grease.html, accessed 16 May 2009, and www.livinglandscapes.bc.ca/northwest/oolichan_history/preserving.htm, accessed 16 May 2009.

21. Kelm also mentions the importation of grease into the Indian hospital setting in her work on Indian Health Services before 1950. See Kelm, *Colonizing Bodies*, 163–4.

22. Wolfgang G. Jilek, *Salish Indian Mental Health and Culture Change* (Toronto: Holt, Rinehart and Winston of Canada, 1974), 105.

23. McPherson, "Nursing and Colonization," 241.

Primary Document

Excerpt from an Interview with Violet Charlie

Interview by Laurie Meijer Drees (LMD), 14 May 2008, Duncan, BC. Others present at the interview were Delores Louie (DL) and Violet Charlie (VC)'s daughter, also named Violet Charlie.

LMD: Someone would bring it [oolichan oil] in [to the hospital], a family member would bring it in?

VC: Uh-huh. A family member would bring it—this grease.

LMD: And did they bring in fish and things like that, for people?

VC: Ya, they got dried fish, abalone—I never tried that—and they called it candle-fish, tiny. I tried it and it's really rich. The nurses didn't object. Mind you, that was the four years I spent in there.

LMD: What years were those?

VC: [laughing] I don't remember!

LMD: We can figure it out from the photos maybe.

DL: She was born in 1925, so . . .

LMD: So the photo must have been in the late 1940s. That makes sense.

VC: There were quite a few of us.

LMD: Were you in there with friends?

VC: Not all of them. We became friends . . .

LMD: You were on a ward then, with all young women?

VC: Yes. The ward was barracks, divided. There was a wall and glass . . . there were four or six beds to one cubicle, would you say?

DL: Yes.

VC: I had a corner. You would be so happy if you got the window side! So you could look outside! [laughing] It was very boring. Yes.

LMD: Did they do any activities with you?

VC: Well, not until you're getting better. Then you can do craftworks. I never beaded before I went in for TB. I did do knitting before I went in. When I was knitting the nurse brought me some wool.

LMD: After a while you were allowed up, to walk around?

VC: I don't know, after maybe two years I was allowed to get up. To go to the washroom. Otherwise I couldn't get up.

LMD: Did they allow you to go out on little day trips?

VC: When I was in Coqualeetza I was out for a couple of hours. Out with the bus. I was in Nanaimo first, and then for surgery I went to Coqualeetza, I had a lobectomy.

DL: They didn't take any ribs off, eh?

VC: I wouldn't let them! [laughing] They were going to take five, and I said, "No way!' Ya, you really get lopsided.

DL: I think Dad's was three ribs.

VC: Did they take them out too?

DL: Ya. His turned to cancer after.

LMD: Did they explain to you, what they were doing?

VC: Oh yes, they explained. I didn't want to come home after seeing the X-ray, and seeing the spots. I decided they should take it off. They explained that it might just come back.

LMD: So you stayed longer?

VC: I had two lobes taken off. And which made it difficult to have surgeries after.

LMD: Was your family able to come and visit you?

VC: Yes, they were. Those that were able to come.

LMD: I heard of some people trying to escape from the hospital.

VC: Ya, I wanted to. Because my mother was very very sick . . . and I couldn't even walk. I couldn't even walk to the end of my bed. I wanted to, but I couldn't.

DL: How did you find out you had TB?

VC: My mother kept giving me Indian medicine. She knew there was something wrong with me. She kept changing it. Try it for one month and then change it again. But I started throwing up blood . . . and the doctor was watching me . . . it was terrible . . . I was afraid I would spread it on the children. . . . I had to get away then.

DL: Was that Goodbrand?

VC: Ya, that's right.

LMD: Was he at the hospital? Or here?

VC: He was the Indian doctor here.

LMD: So who looked after your children?

VC: My husband took care of them, and my late niece took care of them, and my mother took care of my baby.

LMD: That was a big worry for you, I'm sure.

VC: I don't know how many days I cried. It is a lot of stress, all the way around. Having someone gone.

LMD: When you returned did you feel healthy again?

VC: It's kind of difficult, after being . . . I don't know what the English word is . . . being told what to do every day. And all of a sudden I had to decide for myself, and it's different again.

LMD: There must have been a lot of rules?

VC: No, not really. The rule was that we shouldn't exert ourselves if we wanted to get better.

VC: It was not much different than going to Residential Schools. Start listening to the staff.

LMD: The staff that were in the hospital, were they mostly white people?

VC: The patients or the staff?

LMD: The staff.

VC: The workers were Natives, the nurses were non-Native. I know one was German. I couldn't understand her. There were quite a few of them. Campbell was our head doctor. And Dr Gamble. . . . Dr Greer . . . and Dr Schmidt, he was there too! [laughing]

LMD: [talks about Auntie Ellen and how she was allowed to do some of her work in that hospital, on the invitation of Dr Schmidt, until she got into a fight with one of the nurses there.]

VC: [laughing] You had to get into a fight! They weren't very nice! Because we were lying flat, they could see anything they wish! You'll answer them one way or the other. It was something we had to put up with. It wasn't so bad. . . .

LMD: I tried to imagine what it was like.

VC: I don't know, it was . . . I was already doing bad because I had TB, which was likely my own fault because I didn't rest enough.

LMD: Was there anyone in there that didn't have TB?

VC: That's what it is, a TB hospital. My daughter didn't have TB—she had a bone problem—she did the Solarium first, and after I asked her to be brought into Nanaimo.

LMD: Where is the Solarium? What facility was that?

VC: It's somewhere near Sidney. It was a San or something.

DL: Ah, that's right!

LMD: A little hospital over there?

VC: Ya . . . it wasn't an Indian Affairs facility.

LMD: I don't know when Nanaimo closed, as a hospital.

VC: I don't know. I guess I just shut my mind away from it all. Tried to forget about it. I went to see it after, though.

DL: It was 1961, it was still there. Cause that's when Percy and I got married and Dad was still there. In 1962, he walked out. [laughing]

LMD: For your wedding?

DL: Ya.

VC: Quite a few of them walked out. Some came back again.

LMD: Were people sneaking in Indian medicine too? Or no?

VC: They could have been. Uh-huh.

VC: When people walked away from Coqualeetza, they locked the doors and they weren't allowed back in. Even if it's raining!

LMD: Was Coqualeetza bigger than Nanaimo?

VC: I would imagine that it would be about the same size, except that it was high. A different kind of building. Four or five stories. The Nanaimo was just one story.

VC: When you look back on all of this. Do you ever find out why it was that the Natives got TB?

LMD: What causes them to have it more? It's a good question. . . .

DL: [listing people who had TB and who may have passed it on to others, unknowingly]

VC: It depends on your immune system.

LMD: Do you remember what drugs they gave you?

VC: Streptomycin. After two years of that we switched to something else . . . then I went colour blind from that. Then it was pills. The streptomycin was with needles.

LMD: When you went home, after your four years, did you have to keep taking medication?

VC: No, no.

DL: You didn't go on herb, eh?

VC: No.

LMD: Was there a problem there with language? Maybe some of the patients didn't speak English? Was that a problem there?

VC: No, not really. There was one granny there that didn't speak English, but she understood. She used to sing in her own language sometimes [laughter]. I don't know where she was from. But she understood very good what to do.

DL: There was quite a few different wings, eh?

VC: There were quite a few wings.

DL: I remember because I'd go see Adeline, and then I'd take off and get lost and end up in another wing.

VC: There were three or four from the front. I think the front was "G"—Ward G. They were all attached by hallways. The kitchen was around the middle.

DL: Did they have men, what do you call them, orderlies?

VC: Yes, that would be. There was quite a few orderlies. Native. Not many, but a few of them.

DL: So all the nurses, they were pretty well friendly, eh?

VC: Very few were not. Most of them were very friendly. We argued with some of them. Then they would go to the doctor, and the doctor would come and talk to us!

LMD: Tell you to smarten up?

VC: Yeh, tell us to smarten up!

LMD: Do you remember specific nurses? Would you stay friends with some of those nurses? If you'd been there for so long?

VC: Well . . . we would tolerate them, I guess would be the word. They couldn't become friendly with us . . . not really. Some of the staff we could really be friends with. Very few. I couldn't anyways, because of myself, really.

LMD: But they didn't come and visit you at home, years later, or anything.

VC: No.

DL: I just remember that nurse that raised Leona, eh? She had a real strong English accent.

VC: Violet [daughter] had an English nurse. She was speakin' like an English person when she got home! [laughing]

DL: That's the way my little niece was too. A strong accent!

VC: They would bring her over to see me, but I wasn't allowed to touch her. She had to stand way back.

LMD: That would be hard. That would make me cry!

VC: Ya. [laughter]

Secondary Source

Government Policy, Food Insecurity, and Indigenous Peoples in Northern Canada

Kristin Burnett, Travis Hay, and Kelly Skinner

In 2012, the United Nations' Special Rapporteur on the Right to Food, Olivier De Schutter, issued a report on his visit to Canada. In the report, De Schutter noted that

60 per cent of on-reserve Indigenous households in northern Manitoba were food insecure, as were 70 per cent of Inuit adults in Nunavut. These rates of food insecurity are six times higher than the national average and "represent the highest documented food insecurity rate for any Indigenous population in a developed country."[1] Food Insecurity is defined as the "condition of not having regular access to enough nutritious food for a healthy life"[2] and it is an urgent and pervasive issue for many Indigenous communities, particularly in Canada's northern regions.

The cost of commercial foods is prohibitive in northern Indigenous communities: in September of 2011, the reported cost of the Revised Northern Food Basket intended to feed a family of four for one week was $546 (Canadian).[3] What is more, for many individuals, access to forest and freshwater foods is either non-existent or limited and unreliable due to life circumstances such as the need to provide childcare or the conditions of their employment; the prohibitive costs of equipment and environmental degradation due to resource development and industrial pollution provide another barrier. As a result, many northern households struggle to put food on the table and often have no idea what they will eat next and when. Chronic malnutrition is the leading cause of anemia, tooth decay, rickets, heart disease, high blood pressure, obesity, and type 2 diabetes; malnutrition at an early age leads to reduced physical, mental, and social development during childhood. Clearly the health consequences of chronic malnutrition are enormous and will continue to have long-lasting effects on the health and well-being of Indigenous communities.

The making of food insecurity in northern Indigenous communities is not a naturally occurring phenomenon: it is a problem whose origins are cultural, social, and, above all, political. In this way, the situation in the Canadian North conforms to what well-known Indian economist Amartya Sen notes about food crises: mainly, that they almost always have more to do with political and economic practices than environmental or natural factors.[4] Quite simply, the manufacturing of food insecurity among northern Indigenous peoples is a symptom of colonial power relations in general and the intersection of government policies and corporate monopolies in particular. Using food as a lens to track the institutional presence of the Canadian state in the North, this chapter seeks to illuminate the impact that over a century of governmentality[5] (how states think about, organize, and carry out the act of governing) and corporate monopolies has had, and continues to have, on the health and well-being of Indigenous peoples living in Northern Canada.

The connections between colonialism, food, and power have been touched upon in other national contexts. Australia has a rich body of literature that draws the links between food and colonial practices. Tim Rowse, in his illuminating *White Flour, White Power: From Rations to Citizenship in Central Australia*, sketches out how ration policies implemented against Indigenous peoples were and are "a site of rich meanings, a central generator of colonial ideology."[6] Significantly, Rowse looks at rationing as a method of controlling, surveilling, and disciplining Indigenous peoples that is easily "transferred across a diversity of institutions: the scientific party, the pastoral lease, the mission enclave, the police station, the welfare settlement."[7] In *A Workman Is Worthy of His Meat: Food and Colonialism in the Gabon Estuary*, Jeremy Rich takes Rowse's work further and uses it to examine the history of food supply in colonial contexts. Rich notes that unlike the consumption of other goods (like blankets, guns, steel), food is a "product that people must have, and if consumers lack the leverage or the resources to obtain sustenance, then they have to accept the choices of those who have control over food supply."[8] Combined with the destruction of Indigenous foodways, then, control over food systems and lines of supply make food a "technology of power," or a tool of governance that allows the state to simultaneously act out and reinforce its own control over a given population.

Food as a technology of power and its portability across institutional environments is particularly important in the Canadian context, and for this study in particular. In Canada, food was used by the North-West Mounted Police (NWMP), the Department of Indian Affairs (DIA), the residential school system, and Indian Health Services (later the Department of Health and Welfare and Health Canada) both to control Indigenous bodies and to produce scientific knowledge about them. The most recent and infamous example of this was recently publicized through Ian Mosby's article on the nutritional experiments that were carried out on Indigenous children in residential schools in the post–Second World War period.[9] Mosby echoed historians Maureen Lux and Hugh Shewell in showing that food served as a means to both control and resolve the so-called Indian problem. Shewell's work, in particular *Enough to Keep Them Alive: Indian Welfare in Canada, 1873–1965*, outlined how the issue of food and relief "had become a tool for subjugating Indians. The government was using it to force the treatied back onto the reserves and to make the taking of treaty seem a better choice than hunger."[10] Given this history of imposed starvation, it is clear that an accounting of food insecurity crises in the North is necessary in order to understand current problems and elucidate how colonial power functions in the region.

Framing Agency and Resistance in the Colonial Context

Indigenous communities have never been passive recipients of government policy. Some historians, in their attempts to address the violence of colonial policies in Canada, have often obscured this fact and constructed settler colonial history as a one-way street wherein the power, survivance, and resistance of Indigenous peoples remained largely invisible. According to Indigenous scholar Sonya Atalay, there "can be no stories of survivance without an understanding of extreme struggle and survival in the face of horrific circumstances."[11] Conversely, however, as settler historians we need to be cautious about becoming preoccupied over questions of Indigenous agency to the extent that we misrepresent the unequal power relations that characterize colonial histories in Canada.[12] Thus, before we begin our examination of settler colonial governmentalities and technologies of power, we will start with a brief review of the ways in which some Indigenous peoples are currently acting to regain control of their food economies, and respond to the failure of current government programs.

Community members are forced to respond to and resist hunger in their communities when state policy or system level responses fail to provide the basic necessities of life. These include a variety of initiatives such as food banks, food co-operatives, good food boxes, community kitchens, community gardens and greenhouses, community freezers, school food programs, hunter support programs, and food sharing.[13] The most effective programs in communities where size and geographical location makes the establishment of food banks or similar organizations almost impossible empower communal responses to widely experienced problems of food insecurity. For instance, First Nations and Inuit peoples continue to practise food sharing widely in many communities; in Fort Albany, community members describe food sharing as a "normal part of daily life" that is most common "during hunting seasons when game meat was made available by hunters."[14] Indigenous peoples in remote locations also use community freezers as part of the food sharing strategy. The community freezers enable individuals to have access to forest and freshwater foods that have been donated and stored in the freezers.[15] Some communities have also implemented hunter or harvesting support programs. These programs provide funds to help offset the high costs of provisioning hunters/harvesters, and a portion of the hunt is redistributed to those community members most in need.

In 2007, community food champions from Fort Albany First Nation, a Cree community in Northern Ontario along the west shores of James Bay, began to organize a nonprofit "farmers' market" every few months. The alternative market has received attention from a broader non-Indigenous audience, is now held biweekly, and is supported by external agencies.[16] Other communities in the region, such as Attawapiskat First Nation, want to establish their own alternative food markets, and are learning from the actions of food activists in Fort Albany about transportation routes and buying depots.[17]

Perhaps the best-known example of Indigenous grassroots activism around the issue of food insecurity in northern Canada is the Feeding My Family Facebook group. A freely associated group of community stakeholders launched Feeding My Family on 29 May 2012 to raise awareness about the excessively high costs of market food in northern communities; it has grown to include more than 23,000 members and has received national media coverage. The page has become a "community activism command centre" wherein engaged members use the group as a tool for organizing protests at local stores, building awareness of northern food security issues for people living in southern Canada, share tips about how to make food stretch further, and to build action, advocacy, and garner media attention.[18] However, despite the impact of community action, food security in the North remains a serious problem.

Treaties, Reserves, and Hunting in the Post–Second World War Period

Although treaties in Northern Ontario were negotiated in the early part of the twentieth century, permanent settlement on reserves in the northern regions of Canada did not take place for many communities until the late 1950s and later.[19] For instance, the northern portion of Treaty 5 was negotiated in 1908 but Poplar Hill First Nation (located on the Ontario–Manitoba border 120 kilometers north of Red Lake) did not receive full band and reserve status until 1978 when it separated from Pikangikum First Nation. When the federal government resettled Indigenous peoples on reserves, it did little to ensure that Indigenous peoples continue to have access to hunting territories; nor did authorities consider whether reserves were located in areas appropriate for permanent all-season settlement (the advice of people who had lived on these territories since time immemorial about the unsuitability of sites chosen by the government was ignored and many northern communities experience seasonal flooding).

Further, Canadian officials and leaders did not factor into their decision-making how limited Indigenous peoples' access would be to building materials, medicines, and clean water, with predictable results.

Compounding the difficulties produced through the creation of fixed reserves was government policy on hunting, fishing, and natural resource management. Provincial hunting laws, for example, criminalized the hunting of certain animals and prevented Indigenous peoples from hunting in specific seasons; moreover, the creation of bag limits inscribes European notions of conservationism and "hunting for sport" onto Indigenous peoples who lived in a harsh northern climate where it was necessary to gather and harvest meats in the warmer seasons.[20] Such restrictions on hunting were endorsed by organizations and individuals whose interests lay primarily in conservation or hunting for sport rather than as a household's main source of income or sustenance.[21]

The Hudson's Bay Company: Corporate Policy

The first corporation to shape the food economies of Indigenous peoples in the North was the Hudson's Bay Company (HBC). Indeed, the HBC has a long history in Indigenous communities, and although a great deal of it has been documented, the role that the HBC played in the introduction of non-Indigenous or market-based foods into remote-access northern communities after the Second World War is less well-known. Histories of the HBC have focused almost entirely on the fur trade and overlooked the introduction of market foods except to show that Indigenous people's participation in the fur trade inevitably led to the replacement of their foodways.[22] Representative of this kind of fur trade history is Arthur Ray's explanation that the trade "made the Indians dependent on the company not only for clothing, as has been the case for nearly 50 years by 1870, but also for food—and not just Pemmican, but so-called 'store food' as well, such as flour and biscuits."[23] Though groundbreaking for the early 1970s, this articulation of changing foodways constructs colonial food histories as monolithic and simplistic. We now know that this is a much more complicated story and that this process occurred in different ways and at different times depending upon geography, the Indigenous peoples involved, and the presence and/or relationship of the community to state authorities and/or the HBC.[24]

Until the Second World War, the HBC was often expected by the federal government to serve as its surrogate in the North while simultaneously operating as a corporate entity with shareholders and profit margins. In addition to running over 200 stores in the North out of its Fur Trade Department, the HBC often provided rations or basic medical services to Indigenous peoples during periods of crises. In 1959, the Fur Trade Department was renamed the Northern Stores Department because it had expanded into selling general merchandise and food.[25] This shift in focus also coincided with declining international fur trade prices. Retailing became the main focus of the Northern Department and was administered separately from the rest of the company, based on the belief that retail in the North was fundamentally different from the rest of Canada.

In 1987, the HBC sold its Northern Department to its employees and private investors. It was renamed the North West Company (NWC) (popularly known as the Northern Store or the Northern). This new company built supermarkets on the foundation of extant HBC stores. Since 1987, the NWC has expanded and is the main, and often the only, retailer in northern and remote access Indigenous communities. The Northern Store's mandate is to operate in areas and communities where the fur trade played a substantial role and where the population is between 500 and 5000.[26] The services provided by the Northern Store in many communities are broad and have increased dramatically over the last couple of decades. In addition to the sale of food and general merchandise, the Northern Store is often the only provider of the following: banking and postal services, bulk fuel, fast food, nutrition guidance, special orders, pharmacies, and auto parts or materials necessary for home renovations and upkeep.[27] The history of the HBC in North America, and especially as a service provider in the North, has uniquely positioned the current iteration of the NWC to operate as a virtual monopoly for most goods and services in northern Indigenous communities.

The NWC also operates as, or at least perceives itself to operate as, a cultural broker for northern communities that are distant from southern locales. The NWC applaud itself in its annual reports for offering communities important connections to the south through the purchase of commercial luxuries: "not every remote community has a restaurant" and therefore a trip to the frozen-food aisle brings the world to the isolated North through "14 varieties of frozen Chinese dinners."[28] The company also sees itself as acting as an intermediary for the community between the young and old (read modern versus traditional). For customers 5 to 18 years of age the NWC sets the fashion for "snack and fast foods, toys, clothing, sports equipment, music and entertainment"; for 18 to 25 year olds, the NWC means "being accessible to them through credit financing"; and for their older costumers the NWC is a "trusted, reliable source for more traditional lifestyle needs amidst the rapid influx of southern trends and technology."[29] The NWC describes itself as making life in the North possible, that is, by providing modern amenities as well as "traditional lifestyle needs." This is somewhat troubling given the disparity in community health and corporate wealth generated by these market operations. As a reference point, since 1987, NWC profits from food have increased dramatically from 40 per cent to more than 80 per cent.[30] Not surprisingly, given its dominant market share of northern food sales, the North West Company reported a record trading profit for 2012 of $134.3 million. Profits were up 12 per cent or 65 million from the previous year.[31]

Federal Programs and Food Purchasing in the North

The post–Second World War period witnessed the federal government undertaking a series of federal initiatives intended to transform the foodways[32] of Indigenous peoples—the Family Allowance Program and food subsidy programs. Ostensibly, these programs were designed to address public concerns about malnutrition and hunger in the North that had been produced as a result of the depression of the 1930s, the erosion of the international price of furs in the immediate post–Second World War period, and over-hunting and trapping in northern regions. This period also witnessed repeated efforts by the federal government to establish game preserves and western-style animal husbandry regimes in order to boost declining fur yields. These events combined significantly affected annual incomes and were used by the government to shape how families and communities fed themselves.

The Family Allowance Program, initiated in 1944, was heralded as the first significant universal social welfare measure to be passed by the federal government in Canada.
Under the family allowance program, Canadian mothers were entitled to monthly payments through cheques issued in the woman's name and based on the age of her children
(five dollars for children under the age of six and eight dollars for children from 13 to 16
years of age). Most Canadian women were able to spend their family allowance cheques
on whatever they needed; however, this was not the case for many Indigenous women
living in Northern Canada, who were not allowed the freedom to spend that money as
they saw fit. As Peter Kulchyski notes, regulations put in place by Percy Moore (the head
of Indian Affairs' Medical Services Branch) and others limited the kinds of goods that
could be purchased with family allowances in the North.[33]

Regulations were set on how family allowance monies could be cashed and on
what they could be used. Indigenous women could only cash the cheques at limited locations (usually the HBC) and purchase items from a select list of groceries and
goods such as clothing. Foods were restricted to items considered to be of "high nutritive value" such as "canned tomatoes (or grapefruit juice), rolled oats, pablum, pork
luncheon meat (such as Spork, Klik or Prem), dried prunes or apricots, and cheese
or canned butter."[34] These forced purchasing lists had a huge impact on the types of
foods purchased by Indigenous families. For instance, a survey of foods on the allow-
able items on the family allowance list from 1948 to 1955 showed that the purchase of
pablum and powdered milk by the Inuit had gone from 60 to over 1400 units in less
than eight years.[35]

Family Allowances were also used in other regulatory ways. For instance, in
order to be eligible for the program, families had to register the birth of their children, and once registered, these children became visible to the state. As a result,
family allowances were used to force children to attend school.[36] Parents could not
collect the allowance (necessary for their income) unless children were attending
school; often this meant the removal of children and their internment in residential
schools. Miriam McNab, in her study of First Nations and Métis women and their
children's adaptation to urban environments, found that a major reason for settlement and the creation of towns or villages in northern Manitoba was the introduction of family allowances and the compulsory attendance of children at schools.[37] In
spite of family allowances, the cost of food in the North remained prohibitively high
and northerners were increasingly unable to afford to participate in the southern
commercial economy.

Federal Government Food Subsidy Programs

Since the sixties, the federal government has instituted two subsidy programs designed
to reduce the cost of food in northern communities. The first program, officially called
the Northern Air Stage Program but popularly known as the Food Mail Program (FMP),
began in the late 1960s, and the second program, Nutrition North Canada, replaced
the FMP in 2011. The FMP was intended to address the enormous costs of shipping
southern commercial foods into northern communities.[38] The FMP operated as a transportation subsidy that was run through Canada Post. In 1991, the FMP came to be
administered by the Department of Indian Affairs (INAC).[39] The transfer of the program

to INAC represented an effort to reduce costs and to focus the program more effectively on nutritious food. However, the implementation of the program was unequal and access to the subsidy before 1991 varied greatly across the North, and there was no systematic process through which communities could become eligible for the subsidy. Although the service was made available to all regions in October of 1991 at a uniform rate ($0.80 per kilogram for perishable foods), it remained poorly used by communities.[40] A report released by INAC in 2009, offering food frequency questionnaires conducted in 1996–7 among women in Pond Inlet, revealed that the revised shipping rates under FMP had affected food consumption patterns, with the result that women reported eating more types of fruits and vegetables in 1997 than before 1992.[41] However, few communities applied for the subsidy through Canada Post, especially in the provincial Norths. The reason for this lack of community participation is unclear but several reasons can be suggested. First, the FMP was poorly advertised and little awareness of it existed in many northern regions or outside of the major retailers (few of whom participated in the program). Second, it was difficult for people who did not speak English or French or possess credit cards, and third, Indigenous people had a general belief that the FMP was something used only by "white people from the south."[42]

Initially, the foods subsidized were based on the Thrifty Food Basket (later called the Northern Food Basket and the Revised Northern Food Basket) developed by Agriculture Canada and Health and Welfare Canada and based on the spending patterns of low-income Canadians. A 1993 report noted that the "basket was not intended to be promoted as an ideal diet and should not be considered as such. Rather, it represents a price monitoring tool which meets the nutrient requirements of a family of four."[43] In 1998, INAC revised the nutritious food basket (RNFB) to reflect the results of "nutrition surveys conducted in a number of northern communities during the 1990s" to more accurately reflect what was available in communities and household purchasing patterns.[44] These surveys also clearly showed that the Nutritious Food Basket (NFB)[45] was not "affordable for families living on social assistance in some northern communities" and posed a particular concern for pregnant women and children.[46] Further modifications were made to the basket in 2004–05 and April 2007 to reflect recommendations made by the Dietary Reference Intakes Committee and the release of the Indigenous version of the new Canada's Food Guide, respectively.[47]

Continuing Food Insecurity: The Twentieth Century

In spite of the federal government's best efforts, or perhaps because of them, the cost of foods in the North remained prohibitively high and unaffordable for most northerners. In a review of the FMP in 2004 by the federal government, Judith Lawn and Dan Harvey found that food costs were 82 per cent higher in Fort Severn[48] than in Ottawa; that two-thirds of the households in the community were considered "food insecure"; and that at least one-quarter of the families had experienced hunger in the past 12 months because they were unable to afford food.[49] This was not a new state of affairs for the community of Fort Severn. Indeed, INAC had undertaken a nutrition survey 12 years earlier and found that food insecurity had been a "serious concern" for women and that "approximately 45 per cent of women in Fort Severn reported running out of money to buy food at least once a month in the past year, 39 per cent reported not having enough to eat in the house in the past month, and about 40 per cent of women were extremely concerned about not having enough money to buy food."[50] Nor was this situation unusual across the Canadian North. In the Yukon and northern Alberta, the cost of the Northern Food Basket was 80 to 200 per cent higher than in the South.[51] In 1997, 80 per cent of the Inuit women in Pond Inlet and Repulse Bay said that at least once a month they ran out of money to buy food.[52]

Concerns over the high costs of the FMP led to a series of program reviews from 2007–09 and on 21 May 2010, the federal government announced the end of Food Mail and the introduction of a "new" federal subsidy program, Nutrition North Canada (NNC). This new program was said to offer a "market-based solution"; however, the actual framework of NNC was to give the subsidy directly to retailers, who were then supposed to pass it on to consumers at the point of purchase. Unfortunately, these new subsidies applied only to those foods deemed eligible and only in those communities that qualified for NNC. Most disturbingly, the number of communities and items listed as eligible to receive subsidies was grossly reduced: most communities were deemed ineligible, and items such as bottled water, hunting ammunition, and dental hygiene products were no longer subsidized.[53] This means that the already precariously positioned food-insecure families in the North are now subject to even more governmental regulation of their foodways: food insecurity is getting worse, not better, in the Canadian North.

Conclusion

Clearly, there is a need to examine the manufacturing of food insecurity in Indigenous communities in northern Canada. The making of Indigenous food insecurity is and has been a colonialist process that not only includes a long history of government policies and corporate practices that traverse a number of institutional boundaries but also relies on characterizing Indigenous knowledge as simultaneously in need of government intervention and as unable to manage their own health and well-being. Dene theorist Glen Coulthard has suggested that the newest paradigm of Canadian colonialism functions to "discipline Indigenous life to the cold rationality of market principles." Nowhere is this more evident than in the "market-based solution" that the Canadian government has conjured up to address food insecurity in the North.[54] Although the history presented in this chapter is messy and involves a complex intersection of state and corporate entities, the way in which the federal government forces Indigenous communities to live without sufficient food or food that is rotten and prohibitively expensive is simple to understand. Moreover, the use of food and health as technologies of control and power persist today through federal legislation like the First Nations Financial Transparency Act (FNFTA). If First Nations do not comply with the FNFTA by posting their financial information on a public website, their funding for "food, water and health care" will be cut.[55] Such threats to withhold the necessities of life are criminal. Food is not something that people can choose to go without and thus they must always "accept the choices of those who have control over the food supply."[56]

Notes

1. UN Human Rights Council, "Report of the Special Rapporteur on the Right to Food, Olivier de Schutter: Addendum, Mission to Canada," 24 December 2012, A/HRC/22/50/Add.1, p.16. Available at www.refworld.org/docid/511cb0422 .html, accessed 3 January 3015.

2. United Nations, Food and Agriculture Organization, "Rome Declaration on World Food Security," 13–17 November 1996. www.fao.org/ wfs/index_en.htm, accessed 3 January 2015.

3. Fred Hill and Michael Fitzgerald, "What really happened to food costs under Nutrition North," *Nunatsiaqonline,* 4 March 2013. www .nunatsiaqonline.ca/stories/article/65674what_ really_happened_to_food_costs_under_ nutrition_north/

4. Amartya Sen, *Poverty and Famines: An Essay on Entitlement and Deprivation* (Oxford: Oxford University Press, 1983), 8.

5. Gordon defines governmentality as "a way or system of thinking about the nature of the practice of government (who can govern; what governing is; what or who is governed), capable of making some form of that activity thinkable and practicable both to its practitioners and to those upon whom it was practiced"; Graham Burchell and Colin Gordon, eds, *The Foucault Effect: Studies in Governmentality* (Chicago: University of Chicago Press, 1991), 3.

6. Tim Rowse, *White Flour, White Power: From Rations to Citizenship in Central Australia* (Cambridge: Cambridge University Press, 2002), 4.

7. Rowse, *White Flour, White Power,* 5.

8. *Jeremy Rich, A Workman Is Worthy of His Meat: Food and Colonialism in the Gabon Estuary* (Lincoln: University of Nebraska Press, 2007), 148–9.

9. For discussions of nutrition experiments, see Hugh Shewell, *Enough to Keep Them Alive: Indian Welfare in Canada, 1873–1965* (Toronto: University of Toronto Press, 2004), 208; also, see Shewell's "What Makes the Indian Tick?" The Influence of Social Sciences on Canada's Indian Policy, 1947–1964," Histoire sociale / Social History, 34, 67 (May 2001): 146.

10. Shewell, *Enough to Keep Them Alive,* 70.

11. Sonya Atalay, "No Sense of Struggle: Creating a Context for Survivance at the NMAI," *American Indian Quarterly,* 30, 3/4 (2006): 597–618. Atalay describes survivance as the following: "Native societies that survived the firestorm of Contact faced unique challenges. No two situations were the same, even for Native groups in the same area at the same time. But in nearly every case, Native people faced a contest for power and possessions that involved three forces—guns, churches, and governments. These forces shaped the lives of Indians who survived the massive rupture of the first century of Contact. By adopting the very tools that were used to change, control, and dispossess them, Native peoples reshaped their cultures and societies to keep them alive. This strategy has been called survivance."

12. For a broader discussion of this, see Robin Jarvis Brownlee and Mary-Ellen Kelm, "Desperately Seeking Absolution: Native Agency as Colonialist Alibi?" *Canadian Historical Review,* 75, 4 (December 1994): 543–56.

13. David Boult, *Hunger in the Arctic: Food (In) Security In Inuit Communities* (Ottawa: National Aboriginal Health Organization, 2004). Retrieved from www.ruor.uottawa.ca/handle/10393/30217; Dietitians of Canada, *Individual and household food insecurity in Canada: positions of Dietitians of Canada* (Dietitians of Canada, 2005). Retrieved from www.dietitians.ca/Downloadable-Content/ Public/householdfoodsec-position-paper.aspx.

14. Kelly Skinner, Rhona Hanning, Ellen Desjardins, and Leonard Tsuji, "Giving Voice to Food Insecurity in a Remote Indigenous Community in Subarctic Ontario, Canada: Traditional Ways, Ways to Cope, Ways Forward," *BMC Public Health,* 13, 427 (2013): 7.

15. Noreen Willows, "Determinants of Healthy Eating in Aboriginal Peoples in Canada," *Canadian Journal of Public Health, 96/Suppl 3,* (2005): S32–6.

16. Joseph LeBlanc and Gigi Veeraraghavan, "Food Program a Hit in Fort Albany," *The NAN Advocate.* (2012). Retrieved from www.nan.on.ca/

17. Food Secure Canada Conference. (2012). "PoweringUP—Food for the Future!" Retrieved from http://storify.com/milzofsmilz/pwrup2012-food-secure-canada-conference-poweringup.

18. Alexandra Townsend, "Iqaluit, Nunavut: A Northern Diet," www.facebookstories.com/ stories/1579/iqaluit-nunavut-a-northern-diet.

19. John Long, *Treaty No. 9: Making the Agreement to Share the Land in Northern Ontario in 1905* (Montreal & Kingston: McGill-Queens University Press, 2010).

20. According to a study undertaken in 1987, the annual cost of outfitting a full-time hunter in Arctic Bay was estimated at over $10,000. INAC, *Food for the North: Report of the Air Stage Subsidy Review,* (Ottawa: Minister of Supply and Services, 1990), 31. Also, see Anthony Gulig, 'We beg the government': Native People and

Game Regulation in Northern Saskatchewan, 1900–1940," *Prairie Forum,* 28, 1 (2003): 82 and Frank Tough, "Introduction to documents: Indian hunting rights, natural resources, transfer agreements, and legal opinions from the department of justice," *Native Studies Review*, 10, 2 (1995): 121–49. Finally, see M.A. Robioux, et al., "Traditional Foodways in Two Contemporary Northern First Nations Communities," *The Canadian Journal Native Studies,* 32, 1 (2012): 66.

21. Government websites underscore this understanding of multiple numbered treaties; for example, Treaty No. 9 is specifically discussed as reactive to a crisis of starvation and country food availability on INAC's website on the history of the treaty, available at www.aadnc-aandc .gc.ca/eng/1100100028859/1100100028861. Retrieved 23 February 2014.

22. Arthur Ray, *Indians in the Fur Trade: Their Roles as Trappers, Hunters, and Middlemen in the Lands Southwest of the Hudson Bay, 1660–1870* (Toronto: University of Toronto Press, 1974).

23. Ray, quoted in Shewell, *"Enough to Keep Them Alive,"* 35.

24. Peter Kulchyski and James Tester. *Tammarniit (Mistakes): Inuit Relocation in the Eastern Arctic, 1939–1963.* (Vancouver: UBC Press, 1994).

25. Geraldine Alton Harris, "An Archival Administrative History of the Northern Stores Department, Hudson's Bay Company, 1959–1987," *Archival Studies*, University of Manitoba, 1994.

26. NWC, *Annual Reports* 1987–2013.

27. North West Company (NWC), Annual report for the year ending 1990, 6.

28. NWC, Annual Report, 1993, 7.

29. NWC, Annual Report, 1998, 6.

30. NWC, Annual Report, 2013, 9.

31. "North west company reports record profit," *CBC News*, 25 April 2013.

32. Foodways are defined as a "series of moments (or complex web of processes) in which food is first produced in close interaction with the natural world (farming, fishing, hunting), processed to varying degrees, and then distributed to and procured by individuals, households, or organizations that then prepare, serve, and/or consume it." See Amy Guptill, Denise Copelton, and Betsy Lucal, *Food and Society: Principles and Paradoxes* (Cambridge: Polity Press, 2013), 5.

33. Kulchyski and Tester, *Tammarniit.*

34. Library and Archives Canada (LAC), Record Group (RG) 29, Vol. 973, File 388-6-1, "Indian affairs list of special food and clothing, family allowances Act," 27 October 1945.

See also Ian Mosby, "Administering Colonial Science: Nutrition Research and Human Biomedical Experimentation in Aboriginal Communities and Residential Schools, 1942–1952," *Histoire sociale/Social History* XLVI, no. 91 (May 2013): 156.

35. Archives of Manitoba, Hudson's Bay Company Archives (HBCA), Northern Stores Department (NSD), Native Welfare, RG 7 box 1, file 1764,

36. This is pursuant to *The Indian Act*, Sect. 116, which states that "every Indian child who has attained the age of seven years shall attend school."

37. Miriam McNab, "From the Bush to the Village to the City: Pinehouse Lake Aboriginal women Adapt to Change," in David De Brou and Aileen Moffatt, eds, *"Other" Voices: Historical Essays on Saskatchewan Women* (Regina: Canadian Plains Research Centre, 1993), 139.

38. Sonya Grier and Kashef Majid, "The Food Mail Program: 'When Figs Fly': Dispatching Access and Affordability to Healthy Food," *Social Marketing Quarterly,* 16, 3 (August 2010): 77–95.

39. Interview #3, August 2014.

40. Jody Glacken and Frederick Hill, *The Food Mail Pilot Projects: Achievements and Challenges* (Ottawa: INAC, 2009), 1.

41. Ibid., 3.

42. G. Dargo, *Food Mail Program Review: Findings and Recommendations by the Minister's Special Representative.* (Ottawa: Dargo and Associates, 2008), 17, Interview #3, August 2014.

43. Judith Lawn, *Air Stage Subsidy Monitoring Program Final Report*, Vol. 1 (Ottawa INAC, December 1993).

44. INAC, *The Revised Northern Food Basket* (Ottawa: 2007), 1.

45. The NFB was introduced to Canada in 1974, and is a tool that is used by government and community stakeholders to monitor the cost and affordability of healthy eating. For more information see http://hc-sc.gc.ca/fn-an/surveill/ basket-panier/index-eng.php.

46. Judith Lawn and Frederick Hill, *Alternative Northern Food Baskets* (Ottawa: Department of Indian and Northern Development, March 1998), 2.

47. INAC, *The Revised Northern Food Basket* (Ottawa: 2007), 1–2.

48. Fort Severn First Nation is a fly-in Cree community located in Northern Ontario.

49. Judith Lawn and Dan Harvey, *Nutrition and Food Security in Fort Severn, Ontario: Baseline Survey for the Food Mail Pilot Project* (Ottawa: Ministry

of Indian Affairs and Northern Development, 2004), ix.

50. Lawn and Harvey, *Nutrition and Food Security in Fort Severn*, 1.

51. INAC, *Nutrition and Food Security in Kugaaruk, Nunavut: Baseline Survey for The Food Mail Pilot Project*, (Ottawa: 2003), 2.

52. INAC, *Nutrition and Food Security in Kugaaruk, Nunavut*, 1.

53. Nutrition North Canada, "Eligible Communities and Subsidy Rates," available at www .nutritionnorthcanada.gc.ca/eng/1366896628975/ 1366896685293, retrieved 23 October 2013.

54. Glen S. Coulthard, *Red Skin, White Masks: Rejecting the Colonial Politics of Recognition in Canada* (Vancouver: UBC Press, 2014).

55. See Pam Palmater's weblog post of 26 November 2014 entitled "Stephen Harper and the Myth of the Crooked Indian"; This source is available online. See http://rabble.ca/blogs/bloggers/ pamela-palmater/2014/11/stephen-harper-and-myth-crooked-indian [accessed 23 January 2014].

56. Jeremy Rich, *A Workman Is Worthy of His Meat: Food and Colonialism in the Gabon Estuary* (Lincoln: University of Nebraska Press, 2007), 148–9.

Primary Document

LAC, RG29, file 2989, Part 1—Directions for Feeding Indian Babies

Memorandum from Mrs Ruth Curried "Health Rules for Indians," n.d.

Department of National Health and Welfare

Indian Health Services

Directions for Feeding Indian Babies

The Doctor says: "Family Allowances are given so that you can give good care to your children, helping them to grow up strong and healthy. Nature's free gifts of sunshine, fresh air and pure water are essential. Also, you should feed the Baby according to the following instructions.

During Second Month

Feed 1 teaspoonful COD LIVER OIL every day (the OIL can be obtained from Indian Health Services supplies).

Feed 1 teaspoonful of ORANGE JUICE or 2 teaspoonfuls TOMATO JUICE each day (dilute the juice with an equal amount of water which has been boiled and cooled). You should give water which has been boiled and cooled several times daily, but always about 1 hour away from feedings.

Feed the baby from the mother's breast or give canned evaporated MILK 5 times during the day. Always mix evaporated MILK with an equal amount of boiled water.

During Third, Fourth & Fifth Months

1 Teaspoonful COD LIVER OIL (always give 1 hour before or after feeding).

3 teaspoonful of ORANGE JUICE or 6 teaspoonfuls of TOMATO JUICE which was been diluted with a small amount of water which has been boiled and cooled.

½ tablespoonful PABLUM mixed with MILK twice each day. Give this off a spoon, just before the morning and evening feedings. Give several times each day 3 or 4 ounces of WATER which has been boiled and cooled.

Feed at mother's breast or give canned evaporated MILK or powdered MILK 5 times each day. (always mix with water which has been boiled).

During the SIXTH, SEVENTH, AND EIGHT MONTHS

1 teaspoonful COD LIVER OIL 2 times each day.

2 tablespoonfuls of ORANGE JUICE or 2 tablespoonfuls of TOMATO JUICE.

2 Tablespoonfuls of PABLUM 2 times each day.

2 tablespoonfuls of STRAINED VEGETABLE SOUP or the same of MASHED VEGETABLES.

Feed at the mother's breast 5 times each day or give proper amount of canned evaporated MILK or powdered MILK mixed with boiled water.

Give 2 or 3 times each day WATER which has been boiled and cooled.

During the NINTH, TENTH, ELEVENTH, AND TWELFTH Months

Give the same amount of COD LIVER OIL and ORANGE or TOMATO JUICE as given at 6 months.

Give 2 tablespoonfuls of PABLUM 2 times each day. The PABLUM should be made with MILK.

3 Tablespoonfuls of STRAINED VEGETABLE SOUP or MASHED VEGETABLES.

1 EGG which has been boiled but is soft or 1 EGG scrambled.

2 or 3 tablespoonsful STEWED FRUIT (APPLESAUCE, PRUNES, APRICOTS, PEACHES).

At this age the Baby should be weaned from the breast and fed from a cup of canned evaporated MILK or powdered MILK mixed with boiled water 4 times each day.

From the Age of ONE Year

Give the same amount of COD LIVER OIL and ORANGE or TOMATO JUICE as at 6 months.

Give 4 tablespoonfuls of PABLUM or OATMEAL mixed with milk twice each day.

2 or 3 ounces of MEAT SOUP or VEGETABLE SOUP.

2 tablespoonfuls of VEGETABLES (PEAS, CARROTS, SPINACH, WAX BEANS, BEETS).

1 EGG which has been soft-boiled or scrambled.

3 tablespoonfuls of MILK PUDDING.

2 or 3 teaspoonfuls of COOKED FISH or LIVER from rabbits or other animals, well-chopped or ground. The Baby should have 1 cup of MILK 3 times each day at the end of the meal.

Mother's Milk

MOTHER'S MILK should be given up to 9 months. At 9 months of age do not nurse from the mother's breast any longer but give either canned evaporated MILK or powdered MILK, mixed with water which has been boiled.

Canned Milk

The CANNED MILK must always be mixed with an equal amount of WATER which has been BOILED and COOLED.

Powdered Milk

The POWDERED MILK is prepared by mixing ½ cup of POWDERED MILK with 2 ½ cups of WATER which has been BOILED and COOLED. Children of 1 year of age or over should have 3 to 4 cups of MILK each day.

Additional Food

When a Baby has 4 teeth give crisp TOAST or PLAIN BISCUITS at the end of the meal if he is still hungry. From the Third month on the Baby should eat PABLUM, VEGETABLES, and FRUIT every day. BISCUITS made from Family Allowance Flour and Butter are especially good for children and the children should start to eat them at one year of age. COD LIVER OIL and FRUIT JUICES should be given to every child every day. This prevents sickness. After the child is 1 ½ years old he may be fed all kinds of MEAT but the meat must be well cooked. As the child gets more teeth, foods do not need to be chopped as much.

If you follow these directions your children will be much healthier and stronger and they will not have so much sickness.

THE DOCTOR

Questions for Consideration

1. What effects did the opening of the Dauphin River hatchery have on the Indigenous peoples of the area and the aquatic environment?
2. In Piper's analysis, what were the failings in the design of the Dauphin River hatchery? To what does Piper attribute these problems?
3. Why did the Canadian government extend health care services to Indigenous peoples?
4. How does Meijer-Drees's research on the Nanaimo Indian Hospital challenge the traditional view of such institutions and federal Indian Health Services? How were the patients able to practise their own medical treatments while at the NIH?

5. Does Meijer-Drees's interview with Violet Charlie and Delores Louie support her view about the co-existence of Western and Indigenous medical practices? Does Charlie appear to use humour because of a "sense of self-determination and resilience"? Give reasons to support your answers.
6. In what ways has the Canadian government sought to use the provision of food to northern communities as a tool in its assimilationist project?
7. How have Indigenous communities in the North resisted government food policies? What strategies have they tried and continue to try to gain access to plentiful, nutritious, and affordable foods?
8. How would you characterize the Department of National Health and Welfare Indian Health Services' "Directions for Feeding Indian Babies"? What can we learn from this document about the Canadian government's attitude towards and its goals for Indigenous peoples?
9. Collectively, how does the material in this chapter challenge traditional interpretations of Indigenous health and well-being?

Further Resources

Books and Articles

Burnett, Kristin. *Taking Medicine: Women's Healing Work and Colonial Contact in Southern Alberta, 1880–1930*. Vancouver: UBC Press, 2010.

Green, Adam J. "Telling 1922's Story of a National Crime: Canada's First Chief Medical Officer and the Aborted Fight for Aboriginal Health Care," *The Canadian Journal of Native Studies* 26, 2 (2006): 211–28.

Ilyniak, Natalia. "Mercury Poisoning in Grassy Narrows: Environmental Injustice, Colonialism, and Capitalist Expansion in Canada," *The McGill Sociological Review*, Vol. 4 (February 2014): 43–66.

Kelm, Mary-Ellen. *Colonizing Bodies: Aboriginal Health and Healing in British Columbia, 1900–50*. Vancouver: University of British Columbia Press, 1998.

Lux, Maureen. *Medicine that Walks: Disease, Medicine, and the Canadian Plains People, 1880–1940*. Toronto: University of Toronto Press, 2001.

Marchildon, Gregory and Renée Torgerson. *Nunavut: A Health System Profile*. Montreal and Kingston: McGill-Queen's University Press, 2013.

Martin-Hill, Dawn. *The Lubicon Lake Nation: Indigenous Knowledge and Power*. Toronto: University of Toronto Press, 2008.

Piper, Liza. *The Industrial Transformation of Subarctic Canada*. Vancouver: UBC Press, 2009.

Tough, Frank. *"As Their Natural Resources Fail": Native Peoples and the Economic History of Northern Manitoba 1870–1930*. Vancouver: UBC Press, 1996.

Waldram, James D., Ann Herring, and T. Kue Young. *Aboriginal Health in Canada: Historical, Cultural, and Epidemiological Perspectives*, 2nd edn. Toronto: University of Toronto Press, 2006.

Walters, Krista. "A National Priority": Nutrition Canada's Survey and the Disciplining of Aboriginal Bodies, 1964–1975," in Franca Iacovetta, Valerie Korinek, and Marlene Epp, eds. *Edible Histories Cultural Politics: Towards a Canadian Food History*, Toronto: University of Toronto Press, 2012, 433–52.

Willow, Anna. *Strong Hearts, Native Lands: Anti-Clearcutting Activism at Grassy Narrows First Nation*. Winnipeg: University of Manitoba Press, 2012.

Printed Documents and Reports

Health Canada. *First Nations and Inuit Health. Health Promotion—Reports and Publications*. www.hc-sc.gc.ca/fniah-spnia/pubs/promotion/index-eng.php
———— *Food and Nutrition Surveillance in Canada: An Environment Scan*. March, 2000.
Rich, E.E. ed. *Journal of Occurrences in the Athabasca Department by George Simpson, 1820 and 1821, and Report*. London: Hudson's Bay Record Society, 1938.
That is what happened. Timmins: Ojibway and Cree Cultural Centre, 1999.
UNICEF, Canada. Canadian *Supplement to the State of the World's Children, 2009—Aboriginal Children's Health: Leaving No Child Behind*. Canadian UNICEF Committee, 2009.
Williams, Glyndwr, ed *London Correspondence Inward from Sir George Simpson, 1841–42*. London: Hudson's Bay Record Society, 1973.

Films

Band-Aid. DVD. (Documentary). Directed by Daniel Prouty. NFB, 1999.
Battle for the Trees. DVD. Directed by John Edginton. NFB, 1993.
The Canary Effect. DVD. Directed by Yellow Thunder Woman and Robert Dave. Weapons of Mass Entertainment Productions. 2006
The Gift of Diabetes. DVD. Directed by John Paskievich and O. Brion Whitford. NFB, 2005.
The Invisible Nation: The Story of the Algonquin. DVD (documentary). Directed by Richard Desjardins and Robert Monderie. National Film Board of Canada. 2007.
March Point. DVD. Directed by Tracy Rector and Annie Silverstein. Longhouse Media, 2008.
My Big Fat Diet. DVD. Directed by Mary Blissel. Bare Bones Productions. 2008.
Paola Loriggio, "Grassy Narrows First Nation Says Mercury Poisoning Report Never Released," *The Canadian Press*, 28 July 2014; available online. See www.huffington-post.ca/2014/07/28/grassy-narrows-mercury-poisoning_n_5626920.html
Toxic Trespass. DVD. (Documentary). Directed by Barri Cohen, NFB, 2007.
Uranium. DVD. Directed by Magnus Isacsson. NFB, 1990.
Wasting Away. APTN Investigates. 2014. http://aptn.ca/news/2014/11/21/wasting-away/

Websites

Feeding My Family
www.feedingnunavut.com/feeding-my-family/

Health Canada Aboriginal health policy
www.hc-sc.gc.ca/ahc-asc/branch-dirgen/fnihb-dgspni/index-eng.php

Peoples' Experiences of Colonization: Indian Hospitals
http://web2.uvcs.uvic.ca/courses/csafety/mod1/notes4.htm

Canadian Association on Water Quality (CAWQ)
www.cawq.ca/en/index.html

Health Canada. First Nations and Inuit Health Branch. "Drinking Water Advisories in First Nations Communities."
www.hc-sc.gc.ca/fniah-spnia/promotion/public-publique/water-dwa-eau-aqep-eng.php

Mining Watch Canada
www.miningwatch.ca/

Treaties, Self-Governance, and Grassroots Activism

Introduction

The contemporary political activism of Indigenous peoples is long-standing and well-documented. Some of the most celebrated examples of the twentieth and twenty-first centuries include the 1970 Red Paper, the 1990 Oka Crisis, the 1995 Ipperwash Crisis, the 1995 Gustafsen Lake Standoff, the assertion of Mi'kmaq fishing and lobster-trapping rights following the **Marshall decision** of 1999, the Kitchenuhmaykoosib Inninuwug's more than decade-long battle to prevent drilling for platinum on its traditional lands, the ongoing Grand River land dispute, the anti-fracking campaigns, and Idle No More. These examples illustrate a clear pattern of Indigenous peoples' defence of their rights, lands, and traditions.

However, historians examining the political activism of Indigenous peoples in Canada have tended to draw links between the participation of Indigenous peoples in the Second World War and the development of a "new political consciousness."[1] As a result, groups such as the Assembly of First Nations, the League of Indians of Canada, and the Indian Association of Alberta, and the men who organized and ran these groups, have received a disproportionate amount of attention. This focus on recent history has overshadowed centuries of defiance by Indigenous peoples. Furthermore, these very public forms of resistance have eclipsed more private acts, such as hiding one's children when the Indian agent came to take them away to residential school or continuing to hunt and trap on ancestors' land despite the fact that it had become the Minai-nipi bombing range.[2] Unfortunately, much of this resistance went unreported and has, accordingly, remained unacknowledged, especially when listening to or searching for these stories threatens the interests of capital and the state.

Shiri Pasternak's piece looks at the ongoing struggle of the Algonquins of Barriere Lake (ABL), a First Nation located three hours north of Ottawa, to assert control over their territories. Since 1991, ABL has been struggling to get the federal and Quebec governments to acknowledge and implement the Trilateral Agreement. The ABL First Nation has resisted the efforts of both governments to undermine its sovereignty and appropriate its land through the Comprehensive Land Claims Policy (CLCP). The CLCP is a federal policy intended to settle all outstanding grievances concerning unceded First Nations lands. Pasternak argues that the CLCP does not benefit First Nations and instead of "recogniz[ing] the distinct relationship First Nations have to their home-lands and to the Crown, [Aboriginal rights and title] are transformed from a nation-to-nation relationship with the federal government into a set of circumscribed practices and regulations that fall under provincial and municipal jurisdictions."

Paul Rynard looks at the very process that Pasternak is critiquing in his exam-ination of the James Bay and Northern Quebec Agreement signed by Quebec, the federal government, and the Cree and Inuit of northern Quebec in 1975. Initially, most commentators heralded this agreement as a breakthrough for Indigenous peoples because it included significant provisions for self-government and participation in the development of the region. However, there was a significant difference between prac-tice and discourse. The failure of the agreement and the "reluctance" of either level of government to enforce the provisions of the treaty have resulted in the sorts of outcomes that ABL is fighting to prevent. Clearly, when it comes to choosing between upholding Indigenous treaty rights and advancing capitalist development, the state will favour the latter every time.

The final article, by Martha Stiegman and Sherry Pictou, picks up on the con-cerns raised by Pasternak and critiques the use of the legal system by Indigenous peoples in their attempts to reclaim self-government and federal government recog-nition of their land rights. The authors argue that such methods support the status quo, underpinning a system that facilitates the appropriation of Indigenous land. By using this system, First Nations are forced to adopt and internalize those under-standings and identities of Aboriginality that the state has defined for them. As a result, the legal system in Canada remains geared towards the extinguishment of Indigenous cultures and the assimilation of Indigenous peoples. Continuing to work within this framework will ensure that inequities will never be addressed. In the words of Bonny Ibhawoh, "Discussion about rights within [the] context of colonial law [is] merely part of the many discourses employed to legitimize the colonial state."[3] Ergo, Stiegman and Pictou believe that Indigenous activists should disdain the mechanisms for redress designed and provided by the state and thereby deny them legitimacy, because the system is the problem.

Chapter Objectives

At the end of this chapter, you should be able to

- identify how and why Indigenous peoples continue to struggle for self-governance; and
- appreciate the problems of seeking redress through official processes and channels such as the Comprehensive Land Claims Policy for Indigenous peoples.
- identify alternative methods employed by Indigenous peoples to advocate for change.

Notes

1. Robert Alexander Innes, "I'm On Home Ground Now. I'm Safe": Saskatchewan Aboriginal Veterans in the Immediate Postwar Years, 1945–1946," *American Indian Quarterly* 28, 3&4 (2004): 685–718.

2. In the late 1980s and early 1990s, Innu men, women, and children occupied the Minai-nipi bombing range and the runway at CFB Goose Bay to stop the bombing of the territory in which they had hunted and trapped for centuries.

3. Bonny Ibhawoh, "Stronger than the Maxim Gun: Law, Human Rights and British Colonial Hegemony in Nigeria," *Africa: Journal of the International African Institute* 72, 1 (Jan. 2002): 55.

Secondary Source

A Tale of Two Visions for Canada: The Trilateral Agreement versus the Land Claims Policy

Shiri Pasternak

In Canada, close to 100 First Nations groups are currently attempting to reach a final settlement regarding their lands and resources through the Comprehensive Land Claims Policy (CLCP).[1] The CLCP is a federal policy that was introduced to settle all outstanding grievances relating to unceded traditional First Nations lands. The Canadian government cites the sheer number of ongoing land claims negotiations as evidence of the policy's success. But although the CLCP is designed to resolve disputes, it will do so at the cost of Aboriginal rights and title to these lands. Under the CLCP, these special legal rights that recognize the distinct relationship First Nations have to their homelands and to the Crown, are transformed from a nation-to-nation relationship with the federal government into a set of circumscribed practices and regulations that fall under provincial and municipal jurisdictions. First Nations collectively held territories, which both embody and produce the social, political, and ecological relations of each nation to their lands, are also transformed through the policy into an individualized form of land ownership. Determined to avoid this fate, the Algonquins of Barriere Lake are among a number of communities who have refused to negotiate under the CLCP policy, and among an even smaller group who have put forth their own comprehensive plan for resolving land grievances with the state.

Insisting on a very different kind of process to resolve overlapping jurisdictional claims with federal and provincial state authorities over their lands and resources, the Algonquins of Barriere Lake developed a sophisticated and viable alternative to the land claims policy that could mark a new path of co-existence between settler Canadians and Indigenous peoples. Their vision involves a tripartite agreement for resource co-management between the federal, provincial, and Algonquin governments. This agreement proposes a solution that would guarantee the Algonquins the final decision over resource extraction on their territory, protect their traditional ways of life, and offer them a modest share of the revenues extracted from their lands, so they are able to develop and independently run cultural programs and generate socio-economic opportunities appropriate for their community.

In 1991, under the Trilateral Agreement, Canada and Quebec agreed to such an arrangement. However, due to growing concern that the Trilateral Agreement would call the CLCP into question, setting it as a dangerous precedent for other bands to consider, the settler governments failed to honour the agreement. As one high-profile government official put it, the development of alternative models like the Trilateral Agreement might lead other bands to ask "why bother negotiating a land claims agreement" when they can obtain jurisdictional control over their lands and resources without extinguishing their Aboriginal rights and title?[2]

The Trilateral Agreement can teach us a great deal about the serious problems with the CLCP, as well as provide a powerful reconstructive vision for co-existence in Canada between Indigenous peoples and settler society. This chapter sets out to examine some of the core forms of extinguishment of Aboriginal rights that are embedded in the CLCP and the ways in which the Algonquins of Barriere Lake developed the Trilateral Agreement as an alternative in response to this process. I examine both the unique features of the Agreement and the coercive force employed by the federal and provincial governments to terminate their obligations of resource co-management on Algonquin territory. The refusal of settler governments to implement the Trilateral Agreement and the coercion they have used to push the Algonquins into the CLCP process demonstrates the goal of state policy to extinguish Indigenous jurisdiction over lands and resources in Canada.

The Land Claims Policy

To fully understand the political implications of the tripartite vision for co-existence that Barriere Lake has proposed, we must first place it in the context of the process the ABL has refused to participate in and continues to reject. Here I focus on the principal and most controversial element of the CLCP—the *extinguishment* requirement of all final modern treaty agreements—as will be explained below.

In 1973, the modern treaty process was ushered in with some excitement. It emerged as a result of the considerable efforts of First Nations peoples to gain formal recognition of their jurisdiction over their traditional territories. The CLCP was the Government of Canada's response to a ruling handed down by the Supreme Court of Canada in a case brought by the Nisga'a tribal council (hereafter referred to as *Calder*) against the government of British Columbia (BC) in 1967.[3] The Nisga'a asserted that they had never surrendered their lands or their authority to govern them, despite the imposition of Crown sovereignty and the province's claims that its establishment in 1871 made it the de facto authority over land. But the lower courts were not able to grasp the concept of Indigenous land ownership. The Chief Justice in the case, H.W. Davey, stated that First Nations peoples were far too primitive to have any notion of private property——the sign of civilization—and therefore must be denied any right to claim underlying title.[4] However, the Supreme Court of Canada found otherwise. Although a split decision of 3:3:1 (three in favour of the plaintiffs, three against, one dismissal based on a technicality), it opened up the possibility of "Aboriginal title" in BC and on unceded lands nationwide. Emmett Hall, the most outspoken Supreme Court judge, recognized that the Nisga'a's title predated Confederation and argued that it was never extinguished and could still be asserted.[5] Hall urged the Court to adopt a progressive view of Indigenous peoples and not be bound by outdated notions of "Indians" from the past.

Specifically, to assertions of sovereignty by the Crown, Hall defined Aboriginal title as a pre-existing form of land-holding. He famously wrote that "the fact is that when settlers came, the Indians were there, organized in societies and occupying the land as their forefathers had done for centuries."[6] This conclusion shocked then Prime Minister Pierre Elliott Trudeau, who confessed, "Perhaps you [First Nations peoples] had more legal rights than we thought you had." Trudeau was forced to reverse his denial of special rights for First Nations peoples as articulated in the Department of Indian Affairs' 1969 White Paper.[7]

But, as Johnny Mack writes, while the *Calder* decision marked a step away from the harsh denial of First Nations rights represented by the White Paper, it was also a movement towards a "soft imperialism," "characterized by a rejection of a colonial apartheid/assimilation mode of operation in favour of one marked instead by integration and selective toleration of indigenous difference."[8] This soft imperialism was signalled by the introduction of a settlement process for outstanding land grievances. Within six months of the *Calder* decision, a new policy to deal with all Indigenous nations that had not signed treaties was introduced. In August of 1973, the federal government issued a "statement of policy," demonstrating a willingness to negotiate for land with Indigenous peoples and acknowledging its obligations under the Royal Proclamation.[9]

The Supreme Court first heard *Calder* the same year that Premier Robert Bourassa announced the James Bay hydroelectric project in Quebec. Gravely concerned over the potential effect of hydroelectric development on their territory, the James Bay Cree and Inuit of Quebec took the government to court, ordering a halt to the massive construction project which would damage their lands and ways of life. Although Quebec first denied that Indigenous peoples had any such rights of claim to the land, the *Calder* decision forced the province to reach a settlement as quickly as possible with the Cree and Inuit so that the hydroelectric project could proceed.[10] The James Bay and Northern Quebec Agreement (JBNQA) was signed in 1975, the first land claim settlement signed in Canada since 1930. The JBNQA was not signed under the CLCP, but it set a crucial framework in place that continues to set the precedent for all other land claim negotiations across Canada. Article 2.1 of the JBNQA reads as follows:

> In consideration of the rights and benefits herein set forth in favour of the James Bay Crees and the Inuit of Quebec, the James Bay Crees and Inuit of Quebec hereby *cede, release, surrender, and convey* all their Native claims, rights, title, and interest, whatever they may be, in and to land in the territory.[11]

From that day forth, all Indigenous parties negotiating "modern treaties" have been forced to extinguish "their Native claims, rights, title, and interest" over their lands.

This requirement was made even clearer under the CLCP policy statement released in 1981. The revision stated that the policy's objective was "to exchange undefined aboriginal rights for concrete rights and benefits," calling for the "*extinguishment of all aboriginal rights and title as part of a claim statement.*"[12] The requirement of Indigenous nations to extinguish their land rights upon settlement was met with protest from the start, but a pattern of policy revision without substantial reform to the extinguishment clause has persisted.[13]

The federal government has tinkered with the language of the policy, but has never changed the underlying extinguishment requirement. This feat is quite significant, given the constitutional, judicial, and international developments in Indigenous rights that have unfolded since the CLCP was first introduced. In 1982, under section 35(1), Aboriginal and treaty rights were "recognized and affirmed"[14] in Canada's patriated *Constitution*. Extinguishment, on the other hand, is the antithesis of the recognition and affirmation of Aboriginal rights under section 35(1). On the judicial front, the Supreme Court of Canada recognized Aboriginal title as an Aboriginal right protected under section 35(1)[15] when the Court in *Delgamuukw* ruled that "Aboriginal title is a right to the land itself."[16] The recent *Tsilhqot'in Nation v. British Columbia* (2014) decision ruled that timber on Aboriginal title lands can no longer be considered Crown timber; the implications here are that provinces across the country have lost—to a hitherto-unknown extent—exclusive legislative jurisdictional authority over vast amounts of natural resource development, thus empowering First Nations to assert their authority to govern in the face of extinguishment policies.[17] In the international arena, the United Nations (UN) and other human rights bodies have passed protocols that protect ancestral Indigenous lands from state expropriation.[18] UN human rights bodies have further advised Canada that they need to stop requiring Indigenous peoples to surrender or extinguish their land rights.[19] It is not an exaggeration to state that these substantial improvements in the scope of recognition for Indigenous rights have not affected the scope of the CLCP at all.

What did change in the policy was the language used to require extinguishment. A language of "modification" and "exhaustion" was adopted in the Nisga'a Final Agreement—the first treaty signed in BC under the CLCP (more specifically, under the regional form of the CLCP, the British Columbia Treaty Process [BCTC]), in May 2000.[20] The concept of this new language was that Aboriginal rights were being modified, but not extinguished. What is sometimes called "certainty language" by negotiators substitutes the languages of "modification" and "non-assertion" for "cede, surrender, and release," but like extinguishment, requires full cession of Aboriginal rights and title in exchange for narrowly and exhaustively defined "treaty rights."[21] Perhaps the most troubling aspect of current negotiations is that the government refuses to release an exact and accurate description of the policy. In the spring of 2015, the federal government announced that it would soon introduce the first policy revisions in almost 25 years. In the meantime, interim policy statements contain no mention of its core elements, such as the transformation of collective, *sui generis* Aboriginal title land into fee simple (private) property.[22] The formula for the government's final terms of offer must instead be discerned by combing through signed agreements to calculate average land and cash settlements, non-negotiable items, and other key parameters for negotiation.

Factoring in all the modern treaties, agreements in principle, and final agreements prepared to date, we can state conclusively that according to these agreements, Indigenous peoples must give up their constitutional protections, however undefined, in exchange for ceding approximately 95 per cent of their lands.[23] The band also becomes a new legal entity, as one analyst explained: "[t]he "corporation" will replace the First Nation as the land holding entity, and this will formally break the link between the First Nation and its Aboriginal title."[24] These privately held lands (by the corporation or by individual members) become part of the provincial land system and are subject to taxation. The cash component of agreements is tied relative to the amount of land: the more land, the less money, and vice versa. This money is referred to as "compensation" though it is not tied to past losses or to a substantive figure representing the current economic value of resources on the land. Rather, it is a fixed amount of approximately $45,000 per person.[25]

For a band the size of Barriere Lake, the one-time payout would be around $1 million in exchange for the permanent renunciation of their Aboriginal rights and title. Compare that sum to the $100 million of resources extracted from the territory on an annual basis, or to the $1.5 million in annual resource revenue sharing laid out in the Trilateral Agreement. In this light, the CLCP represents a substantial discount for governments on Indigenous land value.

The Trilateral Agreement anticipated these failures and shortcomings of the federal policy. It was carefully designed to avoid the pitfalls of state models of recognition for Indigenous lands. Although this strength may explain the government's opposition to it, the Trilateral Agreement offers a viable alternative to a widely criticized state solution of dealing with unceded Indigenous lands.

The Trilateral Agreement: An Economy of Inherent Jurisdiction

Clear-cut logging had been devastating much of Barriere Lake's traditional territory for decades before a campaign of logging road blockades finally brought the governments and forestry companies to the table. In the shadow of the Oka Crisis in 1990, with politicians anxious that the insurgency could spread, government negotiators finally agreed to allow the Barriere Lake Algonquins to have a say in resource management on their lands. In August 1991, the Trilateral Agreement was signed. The Royal Commission on Aboriginal People report called the Trilateral Agreement a model for co-existence, commending the fact that it overturned the common insufficient conventions of co-management.[26] Rather than simply institutionalize a joint management plan over a particular region and species, the Trilateral Agreement laid the groundwork for co-operation between parties to develop an integrated resource management plan for over 10,000 square kilometres of land, covering a major portion of Barriere Lake's traditional land base.[27]

The Trilateral Agreement is technically a study and recommendation process agreement, referred to in the agreement text as a "pilot project." Though the agreement clearly states that it is without prejudice to Aboriginal rights and brackets the issue of title outside of negotiation parameters, in a mediator report in 1993 Quebec Superior Justice Réjean Paul acknowledged that the Agreement would likely be recognized as having "treaty-like" status if challenged in the courts.[28]

This treaty agreement was designed to give the community a decisive voice in the management of 10,000 square kilometres of their traditional territory, protect Algonquin land uses, and grant them a share in the resource revenue from natural resource development on their land. But what made all the difference between the Trilateral Agreement and other resource co-management agreements (and especially the land claims policy) was the funding the Algonquins secured under the agreement to undertake traditional land use and occupancy research and mapping. The lack of financial, administrative, and technical capacity in Indigenous communities erodes their ability to negotiate for land on a level playing field with governments and industry. Likewise, without detailed maps of traditional land use, having a "say" at the table over resource management would mean undertaking lengthy consultations with Elders for each individual proposal to log or engage in resource extraction, which would be quickly dismissed as unworkable. With the financial resources to collect, correlate, and map the community's traditional knowledge of their land, the Barriere Lake Algonquins possessed a blueprint for how the territory could be collectively managed, based on a transparent, easily referenced, common base of ecological understanding and knowledge of the territory. In article 3 of the Agreement, Quebec and the Algonquins agreed to share the costs of the study and recommendation phases, and Canada further agreed to pay all of Barriere Lake's costs, including the costs incurred during negotiations.

According to the Agreement, the collection, inventory, study, and analysis of data on renewable resources and their uses constituted the first phase of the Trilateral Agreement. The preparation of a draft Integrated Resource Management Plan (IRMP) was the second phase. The IRMP was the outcome of thousands of hours of interviews with land users, in particular Elders, whose education was derived almost exclusively from the bush.

To give a sense of the sophistication of this arrangement, one component of phase one in the Agreement is worth singling out. The Indigenous Knowledge agenda of the Trilateral Agreement involved individual and joint interviews with harvesters, Elder field trips, and extensive date collation and analysis. For example, Elders identified each tree species found on the territory, then described to what ends they were best used, in the construction of which specific implements, the season to harvest their bark, and how best to undertake this harvest. This work overlapped with Sensitive Area Studies mapping for the (second) IRMP phase of the research, which also relied on extensive interviews and field trips. Scholar Sue Roark-Calnek produced three major reports—on family narratives, toponymy, and social custom—which formed the major ethnographic synthesis of the data. For example, Roark-Calnek's toponymy report presents a complex geomorphology of historical ecological knowledge, including information on family traplines, territorial boundaries, animal life, and medicines. The collation of this research data was equivalent to binding an encyclopedia of oral knowledge of the territory.[29]

The third phase of the Trilateral Agreement research would have involved formulating recommendations for carrying out the draft plan of Phase 2, including IRMPs and a plan for resource revenue sharing. Although the Trilateral set the schedule for completion of the plan by 1995, because of delays in the agreed-upon process, caused first by Quebec (1991–3) and then by Canada (1996–7), the 1995 goal was not reached. Although Barriere Lake believed that the signing of this Agreement, for which they had fought and sacrificed so much, was the end of their struggle to protect the forest, they soon discovered that it was just the beginning.

Breaking Treaty

The Trilateral Agreement specifies that the Agreement is between parties from "within their respective jurisdictions."[30] The fact that the Algonquins are implicitly recognized as being under their own jurisdiction is a respectable basis for negotiation. But the new relationship the Algonquins had hoped would restore ecological integrity and social harmony to their lands quickly disintegrated. Algonquin input on Quebec's Action Plan for Trilateral work was mostly ignored, logging plans went forward in sensitive and sacred forested areas without Algonquin consultation, and funding from the federal government was not forthcoming for the traditional land use studies, which were meant to have been completed in the first phase of the Trilateral process.[31] Quebec refused to acknowledge what they considered "outside interference" to their ministries by Barriere Lake's insistence on participating in forest management, and the province's Special Representative repeatedly made promises and assurances he did not keep.[32]

An exchange in 1992 between Chief Jean Maurice Matchewan and the Quebec Minister of Native Affairs is telling about what jurisdiction meant to the Algonquins compared to what it meant in provincial land management, where the exercise of provincial jurisdiction was resulting in widespread ecological destruction on Barriere Lake's lands. Customary Chief Jean Maurice Matchewan wrote,

> Our authority derives from the traditional knowledge of our elders which has been passed down from generation to generation and accumulated over hundreds of years of occupation of our lands. It derives from our sense of responsibility to the land and forests and wildlife and our desire to maintain the integrity of those things so that we may continue to benefit from them in our traditional pursuits.[33]

The letter urged a mutual respect of views on the matter of jurisdiction and authority, concluding that the parties had seemingly reached an impassable section of the road. Chief Matchewan proposed that Quebec and the Algonquins move forward through a mediation process overseen by a Quebec Superior Court judge.

After a protracted struggle with Quebec, Justice Réjean Paul of the Quebec Superior Court was finally brought in to mediate, forcing the province back to the table. Justice Paul was shocked by the conditions in which negotiations were unfolding. He wrote, "[t]he Algonquins of Barriere Lake have, from their own Band budget and to the detriment of their other programs, unilaterally funded certain anthropological studies and have produced maps of an excellent quality indicating, among other things, their sensitive zones and their sacred territories. . . . *It is David and not Goliath who is attempting to sustain the Agreement.*"[34]

In spite of the mediator's report, Quebec unilaterally withdrew support for the Agreement again in 1993, and the process nearly collapsed.[35] Quebec continued to allocate logging permits and sensitive and sacred areas continued to be logged without regard for the Algonquins. Against overwhelming odds, Barriere Lake continued their fight to force the province to implement the agreement. They invited human rights and religious organizations as well as Ovide Mercredi, the National Chief of the Assembly of First Nations, to tour the logging camps on their territory. Media were also invited to attend. Just when it seemed that the Trilateral Agreement was on the brink of collapse, the government relented. Public support was on the Algonquins' side, and as a result of ongoing logging blockades, the increasingly litigious industry pressure on government negotiators was mounting.[36] This temporary act of government reprieve reveals, as well, how constitutive *accommodation* can be of settler colonial structures of domination as modes of *coercion*.

Work began in earnest on the measures to harmonize forestry operations with Algonquin land use. For possibly the first time in Canadian history, Indigenous knowledge was being integrated into land use management plans and natural resource operations by non-Indigenous authorities. Although Trilateral protocols are still in use at times on the territory by logging companies and the province,[37] twenty years of disruption have marred the legacy of the Agreement. A Bilateral Agreement, signed in 1996, temporarily resolved Quebec's earlier interference, though to this day the Algonquins are still in talks with the province to see it fully implemented.[38] It was Canada, in fact, that became the major barrier to the implementation of the Trilateral Agreement, though Quebec certainly played its part.

In 2001, Canada signed a follow-up agreement in the form of a Memorandum of Understanding (MOU) in an effort to repair the financial, political, and emotional devastation of the federal government's role in dishonouring the Agreement. Specifically, the MOU followed federal interventions into Barriere Lake's customary leadership selection process in 1994. This political intervention led to a major derailment of Trilateral work and pointed to Canadian attempts to coerce Barriere Lake into land claims negotiations under the CLCP. It took years for evidence to surface that confirmed Barriere Lake's conviction that the 1994 coup d'état, and other leadership interventions that placed dissident factions who were against the Trilateral Agreement into power, were, in part, the product of Canada's change of heart regarding the Trilateral Agreement. In 1999, in relation to a labour dispute at Barriere Lake adjudicated by Madam Justice Tremblay, a matter of fact in her ruling stated that Indian Affairs was advising a group of dissidents on how to seize power.[39] Another indication of the government's prerogative followed a few years later. In 2002, Barriere Lake received a letter from Prime Minister Jean Chrétien's office in response to concerns raised by Barriere Lake's Special Representative at the time, Michel Gratton, questioning the federal government's commitment to the Trilateral process. Chrétien blatantly expressed his preference for the land claims process as a "solution" to the crisis. He wrote, "I am . . . confident that a positive long-term solution can be found, specifically through negotiations concerning global territorial claims."[40]

More definitive evidence of such federal concern surfaced in a "protected" document brief released accidentally through court disclosure in another matter. A high-profile government official acknowledged the threat the Trilateral Agreement could pose as an alternative to an unpopular land claims policy. Former diplomat Marc Perron counselled Chuck Strahl, the Minister of Indian Affairs at the time, to reject the terms Barriere Lake continued to set for negotiation:

> The former Chief clearly indicated that the ABL [Algonquins of Barriere Lake] had no interest in comprehensive claims. They hoped to maintain Federal responsibility (and their obligations) and to obtain rights and co-management on the territory (including royalties). . . . A question we could ask: why bother negotiating a land claims agreement when we can obtain benefits (at least partially) through a partial accord like a trilateral agreement? Other First Nations would be justified in questioning this matter. *And it's the current overall comprehensive lands claims and self-government negotiations which could be questioned.*[41]

This document exposes an alarming admission that a central threat posed by the Trilateral is its insinuation of an alternative to the CLCP.

Rather than implement this landmark agreement promoting co-existence between Indigenous and settler governments, Canada spent years trying to destroy the credibility of the community. Some of these tactics include defunding the process and engaging in leadership intervention, but it also pursued many others: sexual abuse allegations and fruitless investigations; the criminalization and incarceration of community spokespeople and leadership; and claims of financial misconduct, followed by the imposition of external accountants for debts accumulated due to Trilateral defunding. The list is endless.[42]

Conclusion

One vision of resolving the jurisdictional overlap between Indigenous and settler claims to land is represented here by Canada and Quebec. By all accounts it is a dishonourable vision, one that does not recognize Indigenous forms of authority, and actively works to dismantle them. Governments prefer that bands living on unceded lands settle their outstanding claims through the federal land claims policy. This policy treats Indigenous land rights precisely as "claims" against federal and provincial authority, disregarding domestic and international law that speaks, to the contrary, to the prior territorial ownership and proprietary interest of Indigenous nations.[43]

The governments' perspective further degrades inherent Indigenous authority to land, based on the terms described by Chief Matchewan as the accumulation of knowledge and responsibility born of centuries' occupation, sustenance, and, not incidentally, a deep love of the land. To force Indigenous peoples to cede responsibility to 95 per cent of their lands and extinguish Aboriginal rights and title to these lands is an act tantamount to genocide to many Indigenous peoples contesting the policy. This is what colonialism looks like in Canada, quips Russell Diabo, a Mohawk policy consultant, who worked with the community for over 25 years to see the Trilateral Agreement implemented.

The Algonquins of Barriere Lake and their Trilateral Agreement represent another vision for resolving conflicts over land. The Trilateral Agreement allows for sustainable development of their traditional territories as defined by extensive land use and occupancy studies—the encyclopedic knowledge of peoples inhabiting those lands since time immemorial. The diplomatic arrangement of co-management is the embodiment of a wampum agreement among the French, British, and Algonquins made in the eighteenth century that first inspired the Elders' vision of the Trilateral Agreement. It depicts three figures in white against a purple background—the Anishnabe in the middle, with French and British representatives on either side—a white Christian cross to the left of the figures. The belt depicts an understanding, under the sign of the cross, but through an Indigenous protocol of alliance, that no interference would be made into the local Anishnabe ways of life. Reinterpreted in 1991 as a partnership between Canada, Quebec, and the Algonquins, the community has been an honourable partner in their treaties and tenaciously awaits the settler governments to be the same.

Notes

1. For a full list of the "Aboriginal groups" participating (there is considerable variation in the number of Aboriginal communities participating in each "group"), see Aboriginal Affairs and Northern Canada here: www.aadnc-aandc.gc.ca/eng/1346782327802/1346782485058.

2. Marc Perron, "Report by Special Ministerial Representative to the Algonquins of Barriere Lake," submitted to the Honourable Chuck Strahl, Minister of Indian and Northern Affairs Canada, 20 December 2007, 5, *emphasis added*. See also Martin Lukacs, "Top Diplomat's Report to Minister Laid Out Strategy for Government Subversion of Algonquin Community," *Znet*, https://zcomm.org/znetarticle/top-diplomat-s-report-to-minister-laid-out-strategy-for-government-subversion-of-algonquin-community-by-martin-lukacs/, 3 July 2015.

3. *Calder v. British Columbia (Attorney General)* [1973] S.C.R. 313, [1973] 4 W.W.R [Hereafter, *Calder*].

4. Thomas R. Berger, *A Long and Terrible Shadow: White Values, Native Rights in the Americas, 1492–1992* (Vancouver; Toronto: Douglas & McIntyre, 1991), 140–56.

5. Berger, *A Long and Terrible Shadow*, 154.

6. *Calder* at para 328.

7. Canada, Indian and Northern Affairs. *Statement of the Government of Canada on Indian Policy.* Ottawa: Department of Indian and Northern Affairs, 1969. Accessed on 1 May 2013: http://epe.lac-bac.gc.ca/100/200/301/inac-ainc/indian_policy-e/cp1969_e.pdf. Trudeau's line is quoted in J.R. Miller, "Great White Father Knows Best: Oka and the Land Claims Process, *Native Studies Review* 7, 1 (1991), 38. The full quote ends with the phrase "When we did the White Paper." The "White Paper" of 1969, introduced by Trudeau's government, attempted to erode Indigenous peoples' distinct status in Canada, for example by scrapping the Indian Act and reserve system, under the auspices of liberal equality.

8. Johnny Mack, "Hoquotist: Reorienting through Storied Practice," *Storied Communities: Narratives of Contact and Arrival in Constituting Political Community*, Hester Lessard, Rebecca Johnson, and Jeremy Webber, eds (Vancouver: UBC Press, 2011).

9. Department of Indian Affairs and Northern Development, "Statement Made by the Honourable Jean Chrétien, Minister of Indian Affairs and Northern Development on Claims of Indian and Inuit People," *Communiqué*, 8 August 1973. The policy was reaffirmed in *In All Fairness: A Native Claims Policy—Comprehensive Claims*, Department of Indian Affairs and Northern Development, Ottawa, 1981.

10. Paul Rynard, "'Welcome In, but Check Your Rights at the Door': The James Bay and Nisga'a Agreements in Canada," *Canadian Journal of Political Science*, 33, 2 (June 2000): 211–43.

11. James Bay and Northern Quebec Agreement, Section 2: Principal Provisions, 2.1, *emphasis added*. Accessed online 1 May 2013: www.gcc.ca

12. Government of Canada, *In All Fairness: A Native Claims Policy—Comprehensive Claims*, Department of Indian Affairs and Northern Development, Ottawa, 1981, *emphasis added*.

13. Government-commissioned policy reviews include Hon. A.C. Hamilton, "Canada and Aboriginal Peoples: A New Partnership," Ottawa: Minister of Indian Affairs and Northern Development, 1995, and "Honouring the Spirit of Modern Treaties: Closing the Loopholes, Interim Report: Special Study on the implementation of comprehensive land claims agreements in Canada," Standing Senate Committee on Aboriginal Peoples, May 2008. Indigenous critiques of the policy were also largely ignored. Key reports include Assembly of First Nations, "Doublespeak of the 90's: A Comparison of Federal Government and First Nation Perception of Land Claims Process," 1990, and Russell Diabo, "Harper Launches Major First Nations Termination Plan: As Negotiating Tables Legitimize Canada's Colonialism," *First Nations Strategic Bulletin*, 10.7–10, (June–October 2012): 1–9.

14. *Constitution Act, 1982* (Schedule B to the *Canada Act, 1982*, (U.K.) 1982 c. 11), Part II: "Rights of the Aboriginal Peoples of Canada." Subsection 35(1) reads: (1) The existing aboriginal and treaty rights of the aboriginal peoples of Canada are hereby recognized and affirmed.

15. For a good summary, see AFN, *Executive Summary of Memorandum Regarding Canada's Comprehensive Claims Policy*, prepared by Mark L. Stevenson and Albert Peeling for the Delgamuukw Implementation Strategic Committee, 15 February 2002.

16. *Delgamuukw*, supra note 1 at para. 140.

17. *Tsilhqot'in Nation v. British Columbia*, 2014 SCC 44.

18. For the best example of these international developments, see the United Nations Declaration on the Rights of Indigenous Peoples (UNDRIP), Article 8.2: "States shall provide effective mechanisms for prevention of, and redress for:

(b) Any action which has the aim or effect of dispossessing them of their lands, territories or resources." Canada voted twice against the UNDRIP, once as a member of the United Nations Human Rights Council on 26 June 2006 and once at the United Nations General Assembly on 13 September 2007. However, Canada endorsed the declaration on 3 March 2010 in Prime Minister Stephen Harper's *Speech from the Throne*, then issued a Statement of Support endorsing the UNDRIP on 12 November 2010. Canada is also a signatory to the International Labor Organization's Convention 169, the UN Committee on the Elimination of Racial Discrimination, and the Convention on Biological Diversity.

19. Canada is a signatory to the International Covenant on Economic, Social and Cultural Rights (ICESCR), a treaty adopted by the UN General Assembly. The BC-based Indigenous Network on Economies and Trade submitted a shadow report on Canada's performance regarding their treatment of Indigenous peoples in 2007 and Canada responded that they no longer require Indigenous groups to extinguish their Aboriginal rights and title upon settlement. However, the Special Rapporteur of the Commission on Human Rights responded by saying that "the inclusion of clauses in land claims agreements requiring Aboriginal peoples to "release" certain rights has led to serious concerns that this may be merely another term for extinguishment" (UN Committee on Economic Social and Cultural Rights (CESCR) Concluding Observations on Canada," 2006, cited in INET to Olga Nakajo—CERD Secretariat, "Consideration of State Reports: Canada," 19 Feb. 2007).

20. Para 2.23 of Nisga'a Final Agreement reads: "This Agreement *exhaustively* sets out Nisga'a section 35 rights, *the geographic extent of those rights, and those limitations to those rights,* to which the parties have agreed, and those rights are: a. the aboriginal rights, including aboriginal rights, including aboriginal rights, *as modified by this Agreement*, in Canada of the Nisga'a Nation and its people in and to Nisga'a Lands and other lands and resources in Canada; b. the jurisdictions, authorities, and the rights of Nisga'a Government; and c. the other Nisga'a section 35 rights" (*emphasis added*).

21. As Aboriginal Affairs and Northern Development explain, certainty over ownership is a key goal of the CLCP. To accomplish this task, modification and non-assertion clauses are necessary: "Under the modified rights model, aboriginal rights are not extinguished, but are modified into the rights articulated and defined in the treaty. Under the non-assertion model, Aboriginal rights are not extinguished, and the Aboriginal group agrees to exercise only those rights articulated and defined in the treaty and to assert no other Aboriginal rights" (Canada, Resolving Aboriginal Claims, 2003).

22. The long lag in policy revisions is particularly problematic due to the widespread changes to the policy itself, such as the inclusion in 1995 of self-government provisions.

23. Rudolph C. Rÿser, *Indigenous Nations and Modern Nation States: The Political Emergence of Nations Challenging State Power* (New York; London: Routledge, 2012), 85.

24. Algonquin Nation Secretariat AFN Briefing, "Briefing Note: Comprehensive Claims Policy and Process," 18 April 2002, 4.

25. See supra note 22.

26. Claudia Notzke, "The Barriere Lake Trilateral Agreement," A Report Prepared for the Royal Commission on Aboriginal Peoples—Land, Resource and Environment Regimes Project (Barriere Lake Indian Government—October 1995) 21.

27. Notzke, "The Barriere Lake Trilateral Agreement," 21.

28. The Honourable Rejean F. Paul, "Mediation Report," Longeuil, 14 September 1992.

29. Core data sets included Scott Nickels, "Traditional Knowledge of the Algonquins of Barriere Lake, Volume 1 and 2," Report. Prepared for the Trilateral Secretariat, Algonquins of Barriere Lake, August 1995; and Terry Tobias's data on household and cabin cluster composition, trapping partnerships, and moose hunting task groups.

30. Canada, Quebec, Algonquins of Barriere Lake, "The Trilateral Agreement," 22 August 1991, 2.

31. Algonquins of Barriere Lake, "Declaration and Petition," 26 November 1992.

32. Clifford Lincoln (Special Representative, ABL) to Secrétaire general associé, Secretariat aux Affaires autochtones, Letter, 22 March 1992.

33. Christos Sirros (Quebec Minister Indian Affairs) to Jean Maurice Matchewan (Chief, ABL), 22 July 1992.

34. Justice Paul, "Mediation Report," 1992, 8, *emphasis added*.

35. Boyce Richardson, in collaboration with Russell Diabo, "Canadian Hunters Fights for the Forest: The Algonquins Striving for Territory and Good Management," in *Forests for the Future: Local*

Strategies for Forest Protection, Economic Welfare and Social Justice, ed. Paul Wolvekamp (Zed Books, 1999), 209.

36. Notzke, "The Barriere Lake Trilateral Agreement," 2.

37. On 5 June 2012, Barriere Lake community member Norman Matchewan went to court on indictable charges of mischief and trespass on his lands for informing loggers that there would be no cutting on the territory without Algonquin consent. The charges were dropped that day, but the remarkable aspect of the trial is revealed in the discrepancy between the court's interpretation of the Trilateral Agreement versus the government's spin on Barriere Lake's "utopic" fantasy that the Trilateral still exists. *All the interim measures of consultation were evaluated by the court based on the terms of the Trilateral Agreement.* Furthermore, as per the Trilateral Agreement, the forestry company had obtained a permit from Quebec, submitted a cutting plan, and obtained approval from MNR about where they could cut, all of which should have been based on "measures to harmonize" with Algonquin land use.

38. There are ongoing negotiations with the province. Author will update when publication date is set.

39. *Mitchikanibikok Inik v. Michel Thusky* [1999] Federal Court of Canada, T-1761-98, at paras 5 and 6.

40. Jean Chrétien (Prime Minister of Canada) to Michel Gratton (Special Representative for Barriere Lake), 29 August 2002.

41. Perron, "Report by Special Ministerial Representative to the Algonquins of Barriere Lake," 5, *emphasis added.*

42. For a full account of this history, see my dissertation: Shiri Pasternak, "Jurisdiction and Settler Colonialism: The Algonquins of Barriere Lake Against the Land Claims Policy," Dissertation, University of Toronto, 2013.

43. See, for example, in the recent *Tsilhqot'in Nation v. British Columbia*, 2014 SCC 44, para 69, where Justice McLachlin submits that *terra nullius* never existed in Canada.

Primary Document

Memorandum of Mutual Intent between the Algonquins of Barriere Lake and the Department of Indian and Northern Affairs Canada

Global Proposal for Rebuilding the Community

1. Background

Mitchikanibikok Inik, also known as the Algonquins of Barriere Lake, is a First Nation whose traditional territory is in Northwestern Quebec, in the area of La Verendrye Wildlife Reserve.

The First Nation has a 59-acre reserve at Rapid Lake, which was created in 1961. The reserve serves as a home base and administrative centre for approximately 450 community members who continue to use their traditional lands in the outlying area of the reserve for traditional pursuits.

The community subsists on a "mixed economy" based on traditional activities and government transfers. However, many opportunities exist in the resources and tourism sector, due to the particular position of the Algonquins and the resource richness of their location.

The Algonquins of Barriere Lake possess Aboriginal title which has never been surrendered pursuant to treaty. Rather than advance a land claim, the Algonquins signed the Trilateral Agreement in 1991, with the federal and Quebec governments which encompass their traditional territory. This should lead to a stronger role for the Algonquins in the management of their traditional territory and facilitate equitable access to resources which would enable them to realize economic opportunities.

2. Vision for the Future

The Algonquins of Barriere Lake see a bright future based on a vision which incorporates four fundamental orientations:

(1) Strength through the retention and enhancement of their culture, language and traditional way of life, augmented by improved training and education geared to needs;

(2) Self-government through adherence to their customary system of government and continued respect for their customs adapted to meet contemporary circumstances;

(3) Community development which includes positive social development, economic self-sufficiency and modern infrastructure; and

(4) A decisive voice in resource management decisions within their traditional territory, guided by the principles of sustainable development and equitable sharing of resources.

3. Needs, Priorities

In order to meet their vision, the Algonquins require a comprehensive support and development package from the federal government. What follows is a brief description of the elements of this package, together with estimates. It is important to underline that these are only estimates which require detailed costings by experts in the field.

(1) Housing and Infrastructure

A positive physical environment is required to encourage emotional and spiritual well-being within the community. The community is in need of housing, due to the inadequacy of the existing stock which causes serious overcrowding. Corresponding improvements must also be made to infrastructure.

Housing (10 new houses/year for 5 years at $650,000/year)	$ 3,250,000
Housing Renovations (60 houses over 2 years at $20,000/house)	1,200,000
Roads (access road and streets to be paved)	350,000
Water, Sewage and Fire Protection (over 2 years)	3,500,000

(2) Multi-functional Community Centre/Administration Building

The Algonquins need a community centre they can be proud of, where community activities such as general assemblies, social events and feasts, can take place. The centre could accommodate day care services and activities for Elders, women and youth. Barriere Lake has never had a community centre and one is desperately needed.

The First Nation also needs a modern administration building which is equipped to meet contemporary and increasing communications and business needs. The existing band office is structurally defective and inadequate in any event. Administrative offices are being set up on a temporary basis in a portable unit.

The Building would also serve as office space for policing, child welfare and social services.

Multi-functional Building   1,700,000

(3) Education Facilities

The children of Barriere Lake have gone without for too long. In order to foster education within the community, the children need to be provided with a positive, healthy, up-to-date learning environment. The existing elementary school at Rapid Lake is old and inadequate. It lacks basic modem amenities such as a gymnasium and a library.

The children of Barriere Lake are also entitled to be educated at home near their parents. At the current time, secondary students have to board in Maniwaki or even further away. This creates loneliness, alienation and does not encourage educational development.

Construction of a new Combined Elementary and Secondary School with Gymnasium, a library and Recreational Facilities   3,500,000
Construction of a remote learning centre located on their traditional territory away from Rapid Lake Reserve to serve as a centre for traditional teachings $ 237,000

(4) Community, Social and Educational Development

Studies indicate serious age–grade deficits amongst school-age children, which must be addressed through major remedial programs (for over 5 years)   1,355,000
Specialized curriculum development incorporating traditional knowledge using existing research materials developed under the Trilateral process   100,000
Education and literacy levels in adults reflect the shortcomings in the provision of education programs and services in the past. Adult education and training programs will be required (0 redress these problems ($166,000/year for 3 years)   498,000
A healing process will need to be undertaken, which has as its objective the taking back responsibility for child welfare and community justice. This will require an emphasis on training community members in relevant skills (over 2 years)   627,400

(5) Governance and Administrative Development

Traditional government structures continue to predominate within Barriere Lake governance and serve as a foundation for emerging structures which are adapted to contemporary circumstances. Seen positively, the events of the past 18 months initiated a process which required the Algonquins to codify their customs and to give thought to changes which were needed to update their system.

The work to codify and update the customs is complete, however resources will be required during a period to two years to establish an administrative system and to train personnel in management and administration.

Joint-Administrator/Trainer and management training (for 2 years)   220,000

(6) Restoration and Consultation Costs

The events of the past 18 months have created setbacks, both for individuals and for the community generally. A major disruption to the community economy occurred with the loss of federal transfers for this period. This was most acutely felt in the loss of wage income in the amount of approximately $1,500,000. Added to this are consultation costs which were incurred by the Algonquins in the amount of approximately $600,000, as well as claims for loss of wages by teachers in the amount of $260,000.

Restoration and Consultation Costs   2,360,000

(7) Trilateral Agreement

The Trilateral Agreement is fundamental to the future of the First Nation. What is contemplated are negotiations with Quebec respecting resources within their traditional territory in a framework which provides for.
(a) an expanded area of land for the exclusive use of the Algonquins for the community and administration;
(b) the development of an integrated resource management plan which provides for sharing and co-existence of traditional Algonquin uses with non-Algonquin uses;
(c) resource revenue sharing arrangements with the government of Quebec for resources within the traditional territory of the Algonquins; and
(d) partnerships with public and private sector interests with respect to forestry and tourism within the Trilateral Agreement territory.

However, these negotiations cannot take place until the objectives of the Trilateral Agreement are fulfilled, including the completion of Phases I, II and III. It is estimated that this will take two years at $800,000 per year.
Total Estimated Costs: 1,600,000

(8) Expanded Land Base and Electrification

The 59-acre Reserve at Rapid Lake is not adequate to meet the existing or future needs of Algonquin residential and community development. The Algonquins are not looking for an addition to Reserve, they foresee an expansion to their land base through negotiations under the Trilateral Agreement.

Further capital development at the Rapid Lake Reserve site is limited by constraints related to electrification. Options will have to be considered to expand electrical capacity, including development of a mini-hydro dam, connection to the hydro grid, as well as alternative sources of energy. However, maintenance of the diesel generation system will be required until a suitable replacement is decided upon and developed.
Total Estimated Costs: $20,497,400

4. Implementation and Schedule

What is contemplated for the implementation of this proposal is as follows:

(1) Acceptance-in-principle by the federal government;
(2) Identification of estimated resources to carry out the proposal;
(3) Evaluation of the existing site at Rapid Lake Reserve by a town/municipal planner;
(4) Development of detailed costs and plans for all elements by experts; and
(5) Construction and Development.

The Schedule Contemplated for the completion of this proposal is 5 years. However, the approval in principle and planning phase needs to be completed by this Fall.

Secondary Source

Ally or Colonizer?: The Federal State, the Cree Nation, and the James Bay Agreement

Paul Rynard

I. Introduction

This paper argues that current public policies on Aboriginal rights may be insufficient to help ensure that First Nations can thrive as distinct peoples. There are widespread fears that many distinct First Nations cultures will soon disappear, and the evidence suggests that the manner in which governments have interpreted and implemented the James Bay Agreement poses a very real threat to the viability and distinctiveness of the eastern Cree Nation. In turn, this situation is rooted in a deeply entrenched historical pattern of federal evasion of the constitutional and moral obligations owed to First Nations. Finally, it is argued that to best understand this situation public policy needs to be analyzed in light of the Canadian state's chronic subservience to the needs of powerful social interests and the exigencies of the market economy.

Two qualifications are in order: first, the Inuit of northern Quebec (Nunavik) are, of course, partners in the James Bay Agreement, but I do not comment on their unique experience with the treaty here;[1] and second, the focus is primarily on the record of the federal government, partly for reasons of manageability, partly because its actions are of general significance for First Nations and for all Canadians across the country, and also because I make extensive use of Alan Penn's important analysis,[2] which emphasizes the province–Cree relationship. Finally, Aboriginal lands and treaties are federal matters under the Constitution.

II. The Historical Setting for the James Bay Agreement

Background

The Cree to the east of James Bay have been trading furs with the Hudson's Bay Company since the early seventeenth century, and missionaries have been active in the region since the mid-nineteenth century. The charter granted by King Charles II of England to the Hudson's Bay Company in 1670 covered a vast territory, including the Cree portion of what is now northern Quebec or **Eeyou Istchee** (the Cree traditional lands). In 1871 the company sold its chartered territories to Canada, but an 1870 Imperial order-in-council stipulated that "the Indian title" still had to be obtained by the Government of Canada. In 1898, Canada transferred much of the present Cree territory to Quebec, and the rest of present-day northern Quebec in 1912.

The 1912 transfer—the Quebec Boundaries Extension Act—explicitly reiterated the requirement to negotiate treaties: ". . . the Province of Quebec will recognize the rights of the Indian inhabitants . . . and will obtain surrenders of such rights. . . ."[3] In a sense, then, Canada transferred lands that were not its own, since they had never been ceded by the Cree. The stipulation to negotiate treaties provided an eventual legal basis for clear and "unburdened" provincial ownership (west of James Bay, Treaty 9 had been "negotiated" in 1905 and 1929). The transfer also involved an attempt to avoid, perhaps unconstitutionally, the federal government's obligations, given that section 91(24) of the Constitution Act of 1867 declares "Indians, and Lands reserved for the Indians" to be federal jurisdiction.[4] In contrast, in the numbered treaties covering Northern Ontario and most of Manitoba, Saskatchewan, and Alberta, federally appointed treaty commissioners representing the Crown conducted the negotiations. So the transfer of the requirement to negotiate treaties in northern Quebec (which was absent Native consent) was an early federal off-loading of responsibilities, not unlike more recent betrayals of the Cree. This understanding of the transfer is also in keeping with a view of the Canadian state that sees both its policies and the evolving shape of its federalism as results of its chronic need to rank the priorities of capitalist accumulation ahead of other concerns and interests, such as the rights and well-being of First Nations. After 1912 in Quebec it was the province that was responsible for rights relating to Indian title.

It was not until the 1930s that either the province or the federal government established a limited presence in Eeyou Istchee. The provincial presence was confined to the regulation of some hunting and trapping in the extreme south of the territory. In the late 1930s the federal Department of Indian Affairs began to draw up band lists amongst the Cree and to create, or in most cases to recognize, band councils headed by chiefs.[5] There was no consultation or negotiation about the political implications of the government's new presence and the modified Cree institutions. Indian Affairs came to control the political affairs of the Cree under the Indian Act, and minimal social services such as pensions became available to many. Residential schools were also established as church and state co-operated in a misguided attempt to educate and socialize, sometimes with horrifying consequences.

After 1945, as part of the pan-Canadian use of northern resources to fuel the postwar economy, mining enterprises and some forestry spread into the southern extreme of Eeyou Istchee. Yet although these are provincially regulated industries, it was only in the 1960s that the provincial government began to be a significant presence in most of the Cree territories and in the communities. Prior to the hydro projects, then, the Quebec state lacked a physical presence, in terms of institutions and personnel, in most of Eeyou Istchee, thus underscoring the importance of the federal role and what could have been the basis for a more vigorous defence of Cree rights in the face of sudden massive hydro undertakings.

At the beginning of the 1970s, the Cree continued to live as a distinct people in their traditional homeland. The Cree were also increasing their contacts with the mainstream

Canadian economy through wage labour, especially in seasonal jobs with mining and forestry companies but also in guiding and with the Hudson's Bay Company. But the wage work of many Cree did not alter the fact that in 1971 the Cree "economy" consisted mostly of traditional trapping, hunting, and fishing. The Cree language, culture, and identity were being constantly renewed through traditional practices in ancient patterns—supplemented rather than replaced or threatened by wage work and some federal transfers. For most Crees, such income was used to outfit a family for hunting and not to provide an alternative source of subsistence.[6] The strength and relative autonomy of the traditional way of life were reflected in the stability of the Cree system of regulating hunting by dividing the land into traplines and hunting territories overseen by tallymen or stewards. Each tallyman controlled the use of and access to the wildlife in "his" territory, but under cultural and community pressure to be socially generous and ecologically responsible.[7]

Resistance and Negotiation

Quebec Premier Robert Bourassa announced the James Bay project in April of 1971 without bothering to consult the Cree and without considering their rights and title. A handful of young Cree leaders, fluent in English, enlisted community support and began to fight the project. With construction moving quickly ahead without Native consent, Cree and Inuit leaders went to court and won an injunction that stopped the entire project after a remarkable trial with 71 days of testimony from Cree and Inuit hunters. Justice Albert Malouf ruled that some sort of Aboriginal title and other rights were unextinguished and relevant, and that the hydro project posed a serious threat to the Indigenous peoples and their cultures. However, within only 10 days the project was back on track when the injunction was lifted.[8] The resulting legal uncertainty prompted the province to favour a negotiated solution. The James Bay and Northern Quebec Agreement (JBNQA) was signed in November 1975.

The Cree decision to negotiate has been analyzed by others in some detail, but it amounted to a recognition that they had very little choice.[9] Two important rulings made further court support for the Cree position seem extremely unlikely: in December 1973, the Supreme Court refused to overturn the suspension of the injunction against construction, and in November 1974 the Quebec Court of Appeal permanently overturned the suspended injunction (Malouf's sympathetic ruling). The Cree side saw their bargaining power undermined as the negotiations proceeded and as the project became unstoppable. There are other reasons, too, for concluding that the Cree were ultimately under duress during the negotiations. Before 1982, Parliament could unilaterally use legislation to extinguish Aboriginal rights, including title, and the Cree leaders were aware of this possibility.[10] Many basic provisions and the wording of the final agreement must be read in light of the lack of options and bargaining power on the Cree side.

III. Selected Provisions of the James Bay Agreement

The Land Regime

The JBNQA is more than 450 pages and now includes 10 supplementary agreements. Determining the amount of Cree land surrendered is especially complicated given that the agreement confirms varying degrees of Cree rights in the whole region.

Most of the region became category III lands—public lands available for use and development by all Quebecers (although regulated by other sections of the agreement). All the land and resources in category III belong to Quebec. But even on these lands the Cree retained exclusive rights to some species of fish and animals and significant rights to continue all of their wildlife harvesting activities under a regime set up by the agreement. Moreover, the provisions for environmental protection were designed to give the Cree a say in the development of these lands, and the Cree are also supposed to enjoy preferential treatment in the development of outfitting enterprises in category III lands.

Category II lands are defined by the exclusive rights of Native harvesters to hunt, trap, and fish—there is no legal non-Native competition here. However, beyond wildlife the Cree do not own any of the natural resources in these lands, which also became Quebec lands, nor do they control the development that takes place therein.

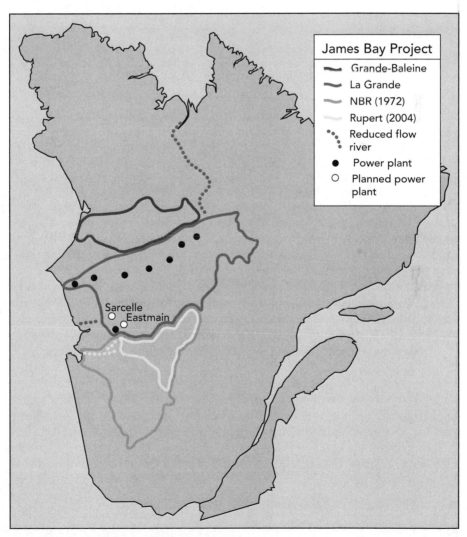

Map 14.1 Map of the James Bay Hydro Project.

Finally, category I lands are more under Native control, although even here Aboriginal title is not recognized, and Quebec has subsurface (mineral) rights and other specific development rights. But Cree band councils can pass a wide range of bylaws enforceable on these lands, and all the Cree communities are in category I lands. However, Cree category I lands total only 5600 square kilometres, or about 1.5 per cent of the land the Cree use (s.5.1). It must also be emphasized that the Cree faced substantial restrictions about which lands could be claimed as category I and II lands. Quebec and its Crown corporations effectively asserted priorities of hydroelectric and natural resource development as pre-existing plans were insisted upon.[11]

Extinguishing Aboriginal Rights

A central component of the treaty is its infamous extinguishment clause, which was presented by Canada and Quebec as absolutely non-negotiable. JBNQA section 2.1 reads:

> In consideration of the rights and benefits herein set forth in favour of the James Bay Cree and the Inuit of Quebec, the James Bay Cree and the Inuit of Quebec hereby cede, release, surrender and convey all their Native claims, rights, titles and interests, whatever they may be, in and to land in the territory.

The surrender is said to be in exchange for all the rights and benefits that are spelled out in the rest of the agreement, in the belief that the agreement then becomes a final and exhaustive list of rights—rights that *were* Aboriginal but have become treaty rights. This clause revived a nineteenth-century policy of using treaties to ensure that business interests and the state would never again have to deal with the issue of Aboriginal "rights, titles and interests . . . in and to land." The JBNQA's land regime is therefore effectively frozen even though it reflects, primarily, the interests of the Crown corporations and the province and even though it was negotiated under duress.

The JBNQA also contains a section devoted to "technical aspects" where the details of the La Grande complex and a variety of other remedial and possible future projects are spelled out. One clause is particularly disturbing in that it explicitly prevents the Native communities from referring to "sociological factors or impacts" in opposing any future developments (JBNQA 8.1.3). In other words, the clause suggests that the Crown corporations and governments involved are not interested in the human and cultural effects of their resource projects. The intent of this clause has become even more disturbing since we know that Hydro's development of the La Grande complex did in fact have unanticipated and extremely serious sociological impacts. Chisasibi is the Cree community most directly affected by the hydro projects because it is on the La Grande River. Due to an alteration in the river's natural flow because of flooding, the community was relocated. Then it was discovered that many of the residents of Chisasibi were suffering from mercury exposure. The mercury was accumulating in fish, a staple of the traditional Cree diet, as a direct but unanticipated consequence of the flooding required by the hydro developments. The sudden concentration of people in a new village, which had new road access to the south, was also a problem, as was the loss of a great deal of hunting territory.

What the Parties Achieved in the JBNQA

As noted, the mix of circumstances, threats, policies, and court rulings did not give the Cree side many real options, and the agreement that was finally ratified had some surprisingly promising provisions. The Cree Nation received some compensation and protection from a project they would not have been able to stop in any event, and they bargained for, amongst other things, a whole range of commitments for new services and programs and for increased Cree participation in administration. But, most important, the Cree also achieved provisions for wildlife harvesting, to help maintain and renew their traditional economy and way of life. Taken together, these sections of the agreement, in the eyes of the majority of Cree, overshadowed money and other considerations during the negotiations. For those Cree who would or could no longer make a living in the traditional manner, the agreement also contained promises to help them better integrate into the wider Canadian economy.

The agreement held considerable benefits for the provincial government, although it still met with significant resistance in Cabinet from those who seemed to deny the existence of any Aboriginal rights at all.[12] Quebec's negotiator and cabinet minister, John Ciaccia, sold the agreement largely by playing up its nation-building implications.

Quebec gained a legal and constitutional basis—however tainted by coercion—for its claims to the region, just as the hydro project itself and the array of services and programs promised in the agreement meant that the provincial presence in the region would be drastically expanded. All this was achieved at a cost that was a mere fraction of what would be invested in the construction of the project and eventually returned in electricity and other resource revenues.

Ottawa's role in the formation of the agreement is intriguing. Federal officials knew that the treaty-making conditions of the territory transfer agreements had not been met, yet when the hydro project was announced, the federal government did not oppose Quebec's unqualified assumption of jurisdiction and ownership. However, the Department of Indian Affairs had little choice but to fund some of the Cree's legal battles and the costs of negotiating, given the prevailing understandings of its constitutional obligations. In fact, in January 1974, Indian Affairs Minister Jean Chrétien threatened to cut off such funding in order to force the Cree to accept Bourassa's original offer of a settlement. According to Roy MacGregor, when it was made public editorial and public opinion forced Chrétien to back down on the threat.[13]

The wider context of federal–Indian relations was also relevant. The government had been forced to abandon—in public statements, at least—its 1969 policy paper, which had proposed an acceleration of the assimilation of Indians and denied the legitimacy of the concept of distinct and ongoing Aboriginal rights. In the summer of 1973, the federal government announced that it would consider negotiating Aboriginal title claims—a response to the Supreme Court's decision in the **Calder case**, in which three of the six judges who addressed the question argued that Nisga'a Nation's title to their homelands remained valid and unextinguished.

In sum, as the federal government apparently saw things, its role was to foster, not to undermine, economic development and capitalist investment, and this in turn required the elimination of the legal uncertainty created by Aboriginal land rights. In the case of James Bay, this broad goal did not conflict with that of trying to manage Quebec nationalism by co-operating with the Quebec Liberals.

IV. Implementation of the JBNQA

Delay, Negligence, and Review in the Initial Phase of Implementation

Neither level of government was ready to live up to the obligations agreed to in the treaty once it was signed. The main piece of federal enacting legislation was delayed for two years and only passed, just before the deadline, after the Crees pressed for action. Neither the financial nor the organizational resources necessary for implementation were made available in the years immediately following the signing, although work with Quebec on the harvesting regime in particular seems to have proceeded reasonably well.

It seems that the federal government was trying to proceed with a business-as-usual approach even though the JBNQA had codified and clarified many of its obligations to the Cree. Perhaps the most important event highlighting government negligence happened about five years after the treaty was signed. A gastroenteritis epidemic in several Cree communities killed several children and made others extremely ill. The deaths were the direct result of poorly planned and half-finished sewers built by the Department of Indian Affairs. Provision 28.11.1(b) of the agreement states that funding and technical assistance are to be provided for "essential sanitation services in each Cree community," subject to government funding capabilities. Yet initial Cree complaints about the situation were not acted upon until international pressure was applied. After such pressure, and after Cree and Inuit representatives testified before the House Standing Committee on Indian Affairs, the government ordered an internal review of its implementation of the treaty.[14]

The review, which looked at a variety of issues, unconvincingly argued that the government had not broken legal obligations—exaggerating the ambiguity of clauses like the sanitation clause while downplaying the government's fiduciary obligations on the advice of Department of Justice lawyers—but it still made clear that the government had violated the "spirit and intent" of the JBNQA. The report emphasizes what it sees as the ambiguity of most of the obligations in the agreement, and says the federal government was not prepared to implement the spirit and intent of the agreement whenever that required special or additional programs and structures.[15]

Warren Allmand, who was minister of Indian Affairs when the agreement was confirmed into law by legislation, told the Standing Committee on Indian Affairs that he had the same understanding of this issue as the Cree:

> [it] was crystal clear in the minds of the Crees at the time of the signing that all federal programs, services and benefits would continue, and would be in addition to, and without prejudice to, all the rights, benefits and privileges which the Crees would receive under the . . . Agreement.[16]

Inuit testimony has independently expressed precisely the same understandings of the text of the agreement and of its intent as stated by the negotiators.[17] Therefore, although many specific clauses are somewhat ambiguous and sometimes lack binding

language, the principle that the treaty committed both Canada and Quebec to recognize, fund, and provide both normal programs and additional treaty rights and
programs was firmly established—a reasonable enough principle if treaties are to be
aimed at reconciliation and renewal.

Allmand's testimony came to light in the wake of the gastroenteritis epidemics,
as did the implementation review. This public attention to the treaty resulted in the
establishment of an implementation office to oversee the JBNQA.

Self-Government for the Cree?

The JBNQA, in section 9, had set out guidelines for negotiations on Cree control
of local affairs and service delivery, although such powers were to be delegated
by legislation. Yet it was not until 1984, and after considerable lobbying efforts
by the Cree leaders, that the Cree–Naskapi Act was passed. This piece of federal
legislation replaced the Indian Act for the Cree and Naskapis, and recognized
significant powers of local governance, although they were limited to matters typically given to cities and municipalities. But another major limitation is that the
Cree–Naskapi Act only applies to the small parcels of category I lands, so that
the decisions made by the band councils are made in the context of their relative
isolation from the Quebec economy. This means that they lack of an adequate tax
base as well as a significant absence of Cree authority over 98.5 per cent of their
traditional territories.[18] The Cree–Naskapi Act also involved the creation of the
Cree Naskapi Commission. The commission is a panel with equal Cree and federal
representation and has usually been chaired by a judge from Quebec.

V. The Canadian State and Cree Nationhood

Explaining the Poor Record of JBNQA Implementation

One explanation for the poor record of federal implementation is fiscal priorities
and constraints.[19] The Department of Finance and Treasury Board have repeatedly
put pressure on federal officials to contain spending with respect to the JBNQA. But
it is not at all clear to what extent such policies and decisions reflect actual fiscal
capacities.

From the position of a middle-level bureaucrat with a fixed amount of money to
dispense, there may well be a logic and fairness about treating all recipients equally
and without reference to special rights, such as James Bay agreement entitlements.
For example, when the Cree–Naskapi Commission reviewed the capital-funding disagreements, the federal representatives told the commission that they felt obligated to
give the Crees only their fair share of normal Indian Affairs program funding so they
could avoid treating other Indians unequally. The commission correctly concludes,
"this implies that government funding is decided upon by policy and not in legal
accordance with an agreement."[20]

There is some ambiguity about the precise nature of the resistance to meeting
treaty obligations within Indian Affairs, but it is also true that this merely mirrors the
ambiguity about political will closer to the centres of power. Fiscal concerns, whatever

their origins, have consistently militated against a fair implementation of a legally binding treaty. The Ambassador of the Cree [notes] that there is such a poor record of treaty implementation simply "because it is cheaper to pay civil servants to fight Indians than it is to meet treaty obligations."[21]

Another explanation for poor implementation might be organizational. The government in general is not prepared to restructure operations to meet the new obligations taken on in the treaty,[22] and it has also failed to properly coordinate the various departments and agencies relevant to specific programs or treaty provisions.

Another distinct yet central factor in federal non-implementation is a concern to avoid conflicts with governments of Quebec, as much as possible, in order to check the separatist movement. Several commentators have shown how the Crees have seen the priority attached to their federal relationship subordinated to the general concerns of national unity.[23]

A number of factors are responsible for the history of poor treaty implementation. Taken together, they reveal an entrenched resistance to acting on the full range of obligations in the JBNQA, a resistance that has spanned nearly 25 years and run through numerous governments and Cabinets. The treaty-breaking can be seen as a contemporary version of the long-standing historical pattern of minimizing or denying Aboriginal rights.

Federalism, Capitalism, and Cree Land Rights

The JBNQA commits the federal government to confront certain powerful interests, most obviously the government of Quebec and Hydro-Québec, but also various corporate interests, like the forestry and mining companies, who directly benefit from the denial of Aboriginal rights by gaining easier and cheaper access to natural resources. The unwillingness to fundamentally restructure the relationship between the state and First Nations is very likely rooted in the limited capacity of, and the lack of incentive for, the federal state to compel all the interests who benefit from the status quo to behave differently.

The evaluation of public policies affecting the Cree is bound up with the complexities of Canadian federalism. The James Bay hydro developments and the other ongoing resource industries may be the most immediate and profound threats to the well-being of Cree communities, but they are provincial undertakings. It is in fact accurate to speak of a provincial colonization of the Eeyou Istchee, especially since there was such a notable absence of the provincial state from the region before expansion of the hydro projects.

Yet the federal jurisdiction over "Indians and lands reserved for Indians" means that provincial exploitation of the resources of James Bay could take place only with the co-operation of federal policies, even if the policies amounted to little more than an abrogation of responsibilities and the relatively passive negotiating stance of alert neutrality. The federal policy most obviously implicated here is the JBNQA's extinguishment clause, which immediately and decisively "cleared" the provincial ownership of lands and resources—excepting the limited and defined treaty rights of the JBNQA— from the "burden" of Aboriginal rights and title. Moreover, the Supreme Court has recently clarified that only the federal government can extinguish Aboriginal title,[24] thus reinforcing the dependence of provincial resource-based industries on federal policies that minimize Aboriginal land rights.

The specifics of Canadian federalism are only a partial explanation of the tendency for governments to minimize Aboriginal rights. At a deeper level the state–economy relationship of capitalism is structured so that governments face overwhelming pressure to allow for the continued plundering of lands and resources by capitalist interests. In Canada, these pressures can take on the form of provincial "rights." In Quebec, this compounds the unity crisis. The essential result of such intergovernmental conflict is a weakening of the capacity of the state to regulate resource economies in ways that oppose the interests of capital. This means that First Nations must sign treaties with state representatives, but in doing so they sign with only one component of the power structure with which they are dealing. Private capitalist interests—including Crown corporations like Hydro-Québec which may be arms of the state yet are designed and managed to act like corporations—pressure the state to ignore treaty and Aboriginal rights.

It is useful to consider some general estimates that can partly quantify and illustrate the situation in Eeyou Istchee. Cree reports estimate that electricity revenues from Eeyou Istchee are about $5 billion per year, and about $1 billion worth of lumber is cut annually from Cree traditional territories. In 1996–7, the federal government reports having spent $216 million on the Cree, Inuit, *and* Naskapis ($145 million from Indian Affairs and the rest from 12 other departments). These numbers exclude personal transfer payments—but it must be noted that the Cree band councils do not receive normal municipal transfers and are trying to cope with the legacy of colonial neglect, the social dislocation caused by the resource projects, and all the problems of youth unemployment and disaffection on the margins of the Quebec economy. The Cree portion of the annual federal expenditures is probably a little over half of the $216 million, whereas provincially owned corporations and the so-called private sector reap revenues of $6 billion from water and forestry resources on Cree lands. Of course, considerable tax revenues then flow back to the governments; about $250 million goes to the federal government from the GST collected on hydro sales alone.[25]

The government's inability and unwillingness to implement fully the James Bay Agreement sheds light on a central fact of the Canadian political economy: the much-discussed financial dependency of the First Nations on the Canadian state is the direct result of the often overlooked dependency of capital on the resources of First Nations' land. This is the contradictory context within which the state–First Nations relationship ought to be understood. However much the minister and the Department of Indian Affairs try to meet the needs of the dispossessed First Nations, they are part of a state that is structured to first serve the needs of those who benefit from the dispossession.

Implications of Rights Denied

It is important not to appropriate or misrepresent Cree experiences in confronting Canadian society, but we are obligated to listen, and Cree leaders have made public statements about Canada's inability to honour its treaties while being quite able to plunder the land's resources. Robbie Dick, former chief of Whapmagoostui, described what the Cree had encountered as "the bulldozer way of being."[26] Grand Chief Matthew Coon Come, referring to the plans to dam the Great Whale River, said that examining the reasons for the lack of a proper comprehensive and unbiased environmental review "questions the whole way that the dominant society does things."[27] Recent Cree testimony before the Senate Subcommittee on the Boreal Forests pointed out that "it is our opinion that the [forestry] companies are making decisions for Quebec."[28]

For the Cree east of James Bay, the agreement has meant that the development of the territory has proceeded in a manner not approved of by its residents. Nor has it given them a rightful share in economic benefits. Unemployment and poverty rates remain above the national average, as is the case in most other First Nations communities. The need for federal transfers is maintained and exaggerated by the JBNQA and public policies that deny Cree communities revenues and employment from the resources on their traditional lands. Hydro-Québec, for example, has fewer than 20 Cree on its payroll while continuously transferring hundreds of employees from southern Quebec and back.[29] Southern Cree communities like Waswanipi and Oujé-Bougoumou (a village relocated seven times in the twentieth century for the convenience of mining interests)[30] are surrounded by clear-cuts.

There are widespread fears about the strength and distinctiveness of Cree culture. For example, anthropologist Harvey Feit has emphasized the centrality of hunting to Cree culture and the seriousness of the threat to hunting posed by logging. He concludes that "rapid forestry development, as well as significant increases in non-Cree harvests of wildlife, directly threatens the Cree use of lands and the fabric of Cree society and economy."[31] The former deputy grand chief of the Cree, Kenny Blacksmith, put it this way:

> The arrogant assumption of all of the jurisdiction by the governments of Canada and Quebec, and their exclusion of the Cree people from both the determination of the regimes concerned and the implementation of the measures required, is a major threat to our society. I would say that, in tandem with megaprojects and forestry development, failure of the regulation of the management of wildlife resources is the major threat to our society, driving our culture towards extinction.[32]

The roots of these problems are deep and complex, but they cannot be explained sufficiently by referring to factors such as fiscal constraints, national unity concerns, or administrative organization. I think the evidence suggests that it is hardly a coincidence that the public policies threatening Cree culture are policies so well tailored to the needs of corporations.[33]

Notes

1. Evelyn J. Peters, "Native People and the Environmental Regime in the James Bay and Northern Quebec Agreement," *Arctic* 52, 4 (Dec. 1999): 395–410.

2. Alan Penn, "The James Bay and Northern Quebec Agreement: Natural Resources, Public Lands, and the Implementation of a Native Land Claim Settlement," Oct. 1995. Available in the "research reports" section of the RCAP (Royal Commision on Aboriginal People's) CD-ROM, "For Seven Generations," records 106607–106769.

3. Quoted in Billy Diamond, "Aboriginal Rights: The James Bay Experience," in Menno Boldt and J. Anthony Long, eds, *The Quest for Justice: Aboriginal Peoples and Aboriginal Rights*

(Toronto: University of Toronto Press, 1985), 273–4.

4. Renée Dupuis and Kent McNeil, *Canada's Fiduciary Obligation to Aboriginal Peoples in the Context of Accession to Sovereignty by Quebec*, vol. 2. Domestic Dimensions (Ottawa: Minister of Supply and Services Canada, 1995). (Also available on the RCAP CD-ROM, "For Seven Generations"), 29–33.

5. Harvey A. Feit, "Hunting and the Quest for Power: The James Bay Cree and Whitemen in the Twentieth Century," in R. Bruce Morrison and C. Roderick Wilson, eds, *Native Peoples: The Canadian Experience* (Toronto: McClelland & Stewart, 1995), 198.

6. R.F.A. Salisbury, *Homeland for the Cree: Regional Development in James Bay 1971–1981* (Kingston: McGill-Queen's University Press, 1986), 5–6; 20–3.

7. Harvey A. Feit, "Legitimation and Autonomy in James Bay Cree Responses To Hydro-electric Development," in Noel Dyck, ed., *Indigenous Peoples and the Nation State: Fourth World Politics in Canada, Australia and Norway* (St John's: Memorial University Institute for Social and Economic Research, 1985), 27–66.

8. Boyce Richardson, *Strangers Devour the Land* (Post Hills, VT: Chelsea Green Publishing Company, 1991), 301.

9. Harvey A. Feit, "Negotiating Recognition of Aboriginal Rights," *Canadian Review of Anthropology* 1, 2 (1980): 255–78; Diamond, "Aboriginal Rights," esp. 277.

10. See Grand Council of the Cree (GCC), *Never Without Consent: James Bay Crees' Stand Against Forcible Inclusion Into An Independent Quebec* (Toronto: ECW Press, 1998), 120–6; and Diamond, "Aboriginal Rights," 279.

11. See Penn, "The James Bay and Northern Quebec Agreement."

12. Roy MacGregor, *Chief, The Fearless Vision of Billy Diamond* (Markham, ON: Viking, 1989), 129.

13. Ibid., 115–16.

14. Wendy Moss, "The Implementation of the James Bay and Northern Quebec Agreement," in Brad W. Morse, ed., *Aboriginal Peoples and the Law: Indian, Metis and Inuit Rights in Canada* (Ottawa: Carleton University Press, 1989), 684–94; Evelyn J. Peters, "Federal and Provincial Responsibilities for the Cree, Naskapi and Inuit Under the James Bay and Northern Quebec, and Northeastern Quebec Agreements," in David C. Hawkes, ed., *Aboriginal Peoples and Government Responsibility: Exploring Federal and Provincial Roles* (Ottawa: Carleton University Press, 1989), 173–242.

15. *The Tait Review* (Department of Indian Affairs and Northern Development), The James Bay and Northern Quebec Agreement Implementation Review, "Report," 3 Aug. 1981, esp. 32–3; 68–9.

16. House of Commons, Minutes of Proceedings and Evidence of the Standing Committee on Indian Affairs and Northern Development (Respecting: Main Estimates 1980–81, Vote 1 under Indian Affairs and Northern Development, Issue No. 23:45, 1700–1735), Thursday, 26 Mar. 1981.

17. *The Tait Review*, 20–2.

18. J.P. Rostaing, as cited in Peters, "Federal and Provincial," 181.

19. Moss, "The Implementation of the James Bay and Northern Quebec Agreement," 688.

20. Cree–Naskapi Commission, "Report of the Cree–Naskapi Commission" (Ottawa, 1991), 50.

21. Ted Moses, "Address by Chief Ted Moses," Yellowknife, 13 June 1988, 6.

22. Peters, "Federal and Provincial."

23. Penn, "The James Bay and Northern Quebec Agreement."

24. *Delgamuukw v. British Columbia*, paragraph 173.

25. The resource revenue and GST estimates are from GCC, "1997–8 Annual Report." The federal spending figures are from Indian and Northern Affairs Canada, *The 1997 Annual Report: The James Bay and Northern Quebec Agreement*, 14.

26. As quoted in Michael Posluns, *Voices from the Odeyak* (Toronto: NC Press Ltd, 1993), 93.

27. GCC, Presentation to the RCAP, Montreal, 18 Nov. 1993, 978.

28. Jack Blacksmith in GCC, To the Subcommittee on the Boreal Forest. Proceedings of the Subcommittee on the Boreal Forest, Issue 17, Evidence. 2 Dec. 1998; and Issue 9, Evidence, Morning Sitting, Rouyn-Noranda, 28 Oct. 1998.

29. This figure comes from the Cree magazine, *The Nation* 4, 16 (4 July 1997): 11.

30. John Goddard, "In From the Cold: The Oujé-Bougoumou Crees Build a Model Community After 60 years of Mistreatment and Dislocation," *Canadian Geographic* (July/Aug. 1994): 38–47.

31. Feit, "Hunting," 218.

32. Kenny Blacksmith, to the House Standing Committee on the Environment and Sustainable Development, Evidence, 25 Apr. 1995.

33. At the time of the final revisions of this essay a major agreement-in-principle between the Grand Council of the Cree and the Government of Quebec was announced. It commits Quebec to funding a Cree Development Corporation and to revised forestry practices with Cree input into forestry management. In exchange, the Cree

have agreed to a new hydro undertaking and to drop several legal actions. The agreement is not yet ratified, but it appears to be a significant breakthrough in Cree–Quebec relations. However, it is also, in part, a response to the ongoing court proceedings over breaches of JBNQA and to the public campaign in the United States against provincial forestry practices. See Kevin Dougherty, "Crees get $3.5 billion," *Montreal Gazette*, 24 Oct. 2001.

Primary Document

Excerpt from *Cree Regional Authority et al. v. Attorney-General of Quebec*, 1991

Cree Regional Authority and Bill Namagoose (Applicant)
v.
Raymond Robinson (Respondent)

Indesec as Cree Regional Authority v. Canada (Federal Administrator)

Trial Division, Rouleau J.—Montreal, March 11 and 13, 1991

. . . In recent months, the government of Quebec along with the James Bay Corporation and Hydro-Québec have made public their intention to proceed with Phase II of the development called the Great Whale River Hydroelectric Project. It was recently disclosed that the corporation responsible for the development of the project called for the tenders for the clearing of an access road as well as its construction. The **Grand Council of the Cree** became aware of this initiative and were pressing federal authorities to initiate environmental review procedures in the area before the construction was to begin. Conscious of the imminent commencement of site preparation for the road, the Grand Council of the Cree instructed their lawyers to bring proceedings before this Court seeking *mandamus* or an injunction against the appointed federal administrator, Mr. Raymond Robinson. Ultimately the relief requests that he conduct environmental and social impact assessment and review procedures pursuant to sections 22 and 23 of the Agreement.

In a letter dated October 3rd, 1989 and directed to the Minister of the Environment of the Province of Quebec, the federal minister, Lucien Bouchard, indicated that since the federal authorities had become aware of the development of the Great Whale River Hydroelectric Project, it was its view that an environmental assessment should be undertaken since the project involved matters of federal jurisdiction. He contended that sections 22 and 23 of the Agreement applied and he suggested a cooperative approach between both levels of government. The letter went on to indicate that federal officials would look forward to hearing from Hydro-Québec and hoped to receive from them an outline of the proposed project. He further suggested that taking into account the considerable magnitude of the project, it was extremely important that an environmental assessment be conducted as objectively and independently as possible.

On November 28, 1989, the federal Minister of the Environment once again wrote to the newly appointed Minister of the Environment of the Province of Quebec bringing to his attention that urgency of the environmental review and enclosed a copy of the letter previously forwarded to his predecessor. By a letter dated the 23rd of November 1989, Mr. Raymond Robinson, the federal administrator, corresponded with the vice-president of the environment of Hydro-Québec and reiterated that this project was subject to a federal environmental review pursuant to sections 22 and 23 of the Agreement. He further requested a summary or outline of the project and confirmed that pursuant to his mandate, he had appointed a tribunal to initiate a study. He also confirmed that he considered that the federal government had an obligation to undertake these studies in light of recent decisions of the Federal Court of Canada, and more particularly, in light of the EARP Guidelines [*Environmental Assessment and Review Process Guidelines Order*, SOR/84-467] which came into effect in June of 1984. He also suggests a co-operative study.

An extensive period of silence then prevails. On the 19th of November 1990, Mr. Robinson wrote to Michel Chevalier of Environment Canada, president of the evaluation committee responsible for the James Bay and Northern Quebec Development. He outlines the federal responsibility with respect to the Great Whale Project and the impact it may have in areas of federal jurisdiction, such as fisheries, migratory birds and the ecology of Hudson's Bay. He advises that the federal appointees are prepared to work in collaboration with their provincial counterparts and he is anxious that a joint agreement be ratified. Should Quebec fail to act, the federal government would be obliged to act unilaterally, he wrote. On November 23, 1990, Mr. Robinson again advises the vice-president of the environment for Hydro-Québec that this project is subject to federal evaluation pursuant to sections 22 and 23 of the Agreement and he seeks a cooperative effort.

At a meeting in November of 1990, Mr. Robinson changes his position and informs the Cree that he has no mandate to apply federal impact assessment review procedure under the Agreement. As a result of this turn of events, this motion was launched against Mr. Robinson, the federal administrator responsible for environmental evaluation pursuant to section 22 and 23 of the Agreement. Shortly thereafter, having been made aware of the motion, Hydro-Québec, the federal Department of Justice, and the Attorney General of Quebec sought leave to be added as intervenors. This was granted by the Court without objection by the applicant. The respondent as well as the intervenors challenge the jurisdiction of this Court to grant the relief sought.

It is the applicant's position that the Agreement, which was ratified by the Parliament of Canada, is the law of Canada, that Mr. Robinson, appointed pursuant to the enabling Act of Parliament, has a statutory obligation to appoint Review Panels which he has failed to do; that, pursuant to subsection 3(5) of the ratifying Act, Mr. Robinson, appointed by Order in Council, was a "federal board, commission, or other tribunal" pursuant to paragraph 2(g) of the Federal Court Act . . . and that this Court has jurisdiction to entertain the motion and grant the relief claimed.

The respondent, as well as all intervenors, submit that the Parliament of Canada, has not incorporated the Agreement *per se* into its confirming legislation. They submit that as a result, the appointment of Mr. Robinson was not pursuant to federal legislation and that his powers are derived from a joint provincial and federal authority; and finally, that this Agreement was not an Act of Parliament and therefore this Court does not have jurisdiction.

As mentioned earlier, this rather extensive and complex Agreement involved not only the federal and provincial authorities, but included as signatories Hydro-Québec, the James Bay Development Corporation, and more importantly, the Grand Council of Cree and Inuit of Northern Quebec. In the document, the aboriginal peoples relinquished their traditional rights over some 3/5 of the territory of the province of Quebec in return for certain assurances and guarantees included in the Agreement. It specifically recognizes the Cree's rights to trapping, fishing, and hunting grounds; considers the social and economic impact that any future development may have, and enshrines, in sections 22 and 23, a procedure to be followed with respect to environmental impact studies which are to be conducted in the event of further projects.

Section 22 refers to the Environment and Future Development Below the 55th parallel, and section 23 refers to the Environment and Future Development North of the 55th parallel. There is no doubt that some of the initial infrastructure development may be undertaken south of the 55th parallel, but nevertheless the major hydroelectric development will occur north of the 55th parallel.

Pursuant to the terms of this Agreement, all parties are to derive certain benefits, and there is no doubt that the Cree and Inuit of the territory were given some guarantees for having surrendered certain rights. The ultimate aim was to provide future safeguards for the occupying aboriginal peoples.

According to sections 22 and 23 of the Agreement, a federal administrator is to be appointed for the purposes of supervising the environmental impact of any future development and to see to the protection of areas of federal jurisdiction which includes, of course, the Indian people of the region. The Agreement specifically indicates that the Administrator is to set up evaluating committees to determine if the development is to have any significant impact on the native people or the wildlife resources of the territory. He is under no obligation to proceed with an assessment in the event that the development contemplates no significant impact. I doubt that anyone can suggest that Phase II of the James Bay Hydroelectric Development Project will not affect both the social and economic future of the native peoples and will certainly interfere with wildlife and its habitat, resulting in drastic changes to the traditional way of life.

As a schedule to the Agreement, it was indicated that future amendments were to be approved by all parties and ratified by the Quebec National Assembly as well as the Parliament of Canada when changes concerned their respective jurisdictions. This would appear to me to indicate that all parties presumed legislative authority or ratification.

The initial submission put forth by the respondents, as well as the intervenors, was to the effect that the statute passed by the Parliament of Canada ratifying the Agreement did not of itself incorporate all terms of the Agreement; was not an enactment and therefore created no federal jurisdiction; it was not a statute, therefore the appointment of Mr. Robinson, by an Order in Council, was not by enactment, and could not clothe this Court with jurisdiction to grant the relief sought. . . .

The preamble [of the Agreement] goes on to state, that in consideration of the surrender of the native claims to this portion of the territory of Quebec, the government of Canada recognizes and affirms a special responsibility to protect the rights, privileges, and benefits given to the native peoples under the Agreement . . . The Agreement was tabled by the Minister of Indian Affairs and Northern Development and approved and declared valid by Parliament. . . .

In reaching this conclusion, I cannot help but be directed by the words of Dickson C.J. in *R. v. Sparrow*, [1990] 1 S.C.R. 1075, in which courts are directed that "the Sovereign's intention must be clear and plain if it is to extinguish an aboriginal right."

I feel a profound sense of duty to respond favourably. Any contrary determination would once again provoke, within native groups, a sense of victimization by white society and its institutions. This Agreement was signed in good faith for the protection of the Cree and Inuit peoples, not to deprive them of their rights and territories without due consideration. Should I decline jurisdiction, I see no other court of competent jurisdiction able to resolve this issue.

Secondary Source

Recognition by Assimilation: Mi'kmaq Treaty Rights, Fisheries Privatization, and Community Resistance in Nova Scotia

Martha Stiegman and Sherry Pictou

In *R. v. Marshall* (1999), the Supreme Court of Canada recognized the treaty rights of the Mi'kmaq and Maliseet to earn a "moderate livelihood" through commercial fishing. The case is part of generations of Maritime First Nations' struggle to gain recognition of the eighteenth-century Peace and Friendship treaties and the inherent rights they were negotiated to protect. Following the Marshall Decision, many initial Mi'kmaq forays onto the water were met with violent backlash from non-Native fishers, who were struggling after the collapse of the northern cod stocks and battle-worn from a decade of mobilization against neoliberal Fisheries and Oceans Canada (popularly known as DFO) policy. While the media focused on clashes in Burnt Church, NB, discussions in other places, such as L'sɨtkuk, also known as Bear River First Nation (BRFN) in Nova Scotia, focused on potential collaboration between small-scale fishers and First Nations. For those advocating community-based management, the Marshall Decision represented hope that such a political alliance might reverse the neoliberal privatization and rationalization of the fisheries. That window of opportunity quickly slammed shut, however, as DFO negotiated interim agreements on a band-by-band basis, integrating First Nation harvesters into the fishing industry under DFO jurisdiction rather than negotiating with provincial and First Nation governments to establish a treaty-based fishery. This process has undermined Aboriginal and treaty rights, consolidated neoliberal transformations, and left no room for BRFN's vision of sustainable practices and Mi'kmaq ecological knowledge. L'sɨtkuk's vision for a livelihood fishery under Mi'kmaq jurisdiction has yet to be established. In Nova Scotia, the parameters of such a treaty-based fishery are supposedly being negotiated within the Kwilmu'kw Maw-klusuaqn (KMK), or Mi'kmaq Rights Initiative (MRI) the forum for ongoing tripartite negotiations to implement the historic Peace and Friendship treaties.

The treaty rights affirmed through *R. v. Marshall* and debated within the KMK/MRI are by no means limited to the fisheries; separating fishing from other traditional practices based on an entire way of life is problematic for many Indigenous peoples. However, in this article we present BRFN's experiences of fisheries negotiations in the post-Marshall environment to highlight concerns about the larger KMK/MRI process and Crown–First Nation negotiations in general. Neoliberal ideology now permeates government policy, as demonstrated by the vicious paces of privatization, commodification, and deregulation in the Atlantic fisheries. In BRFN's traditional territory of Kespukwitk, industrial overexploitation and the resulting species collapse are advancing to such a degree that survival for subsistence harvesters and independent commercial fishers outside neoliberal market relations (such as capital-intensive high-volume harvesting and aquaculture) has become nearly impossible. The post-Marshall process has essentially been integrated into this agenda of fisheries rationalization. This enclosure movement, matched with a negotiation policy framework determined to feed into these neoliberal transformations, presents Aboriginal leaders with a very limited set of options at the negotiation table. It is a political and economic context that places unacceptable limits on the exercise of Indigenous sovereignty.

For Dene political philosopher Glen Coulthard, Canada's once unapologetically assimilationist policy framework has evolved into a deceptively innocuous "politics of recognition." Over the last 30 years, recognition—of Canada's treaty obligations and of Indigenous peoples' inherent rights to self-government—has become the main goal of the Aboriginal rights movement, with economic development initiatives, comprehensive land claims, and self-government negotiations resulting in land, money, and political power being delegated from Ottawa to First Nations. Like Taiaiake Alfred, Coulthard sees such legalist strategies as short-sighted. They ease the pain of colonialism but do nothing to challenge its generative roots, namely a liberal capitalist economy and colonial state, or the Eurocentric world view underpinning them. Instead, the current arrangement creates Aboriginal citizens who define their identities and rights in relation to the Canadian state, a process Alfred calls "Aboriginalism." This consequence does nothing to challenge the subjective, internalized oppression of Indigenous people—an equally significant dynamic in colonial power relations.[1]

Anthropologist Paul Nadasdy argues that the co-management regimes emerging from such negotiations reinforce state domination over the Aboriginal communities they seek to empower because colonial power dynamics are unacknowledged and therefore unaddressed. The task of improving science-based "resource management" by partnering with First Nations and including their "traditional ecological knowledge" is generally viewed as a technical exercise; its political dimensions are obscured. Nadasdy reminds us that all knowledge systems—including western science—derive from and depend on an epistemologically distinct social and political context for meaning. In other words, "resource management" regimes express a world view and belong to a political-economic system that is neither universal nor neutral; the name itself implies a commodification of and domination over nature that makes no sense from an Indigenous perspective. Indigenous people internalize this world view because they are "empowered" to participate in management.[2]

This cognitive dimension of colonialism is pivotal for Indigenous scholars such as Linda Tuhiwai Smith, Marie Battiste, and Taiaiake Alfred, who argue that the self-determination struggles of Indigenous Peoples must target the Enlightenment ideology driving European imperialism.[3] This ideology includes the "imperial imagination"[4] that conceives of the world as *terra nullius*, an empty wilderness waiting to be claimed by Europe; the ideal of progress that relegates authentic Indigenous people to history; the cult of science that alienates nature from culture and aspires to control the environment; and the fetishization of the individual as rational, free, and compelled to pursue his or her self-interest in a capitalist economy founded on the myth of private property. Alfred argues that, at the heart of Indigenous nations, there is "a set of values that challenge the homogenizing force of western liberalism and free-market capitalism; that honor the . . . deep interconnection between human beings and other elements of creation."[5]

There is debate within Indigenous communities across Canada about how to negotiate a balance between "traditional" ways of life and integration into the modern global economy, and about the degree of political compromise acceptable when negotiating with the Canadian state. Certainly the Marshall case, with the emphasis the tribal organizations supporting the case placed on commercial fishing, is part of that discussion; as are the ongoing treaty implementation negotiations the decision opened. From Bear River First Nation's perspective, both are poignant examples of the extent to which the politics of recognition has steered the current of Indigenous resurgence away from a path towards self-determination grounded in a recognition of Indigenous land rights, and self-governance anchored in Indigenous world views.[6] If we take the Aboriginal commercial fishery opened by *R. v. Marshall* as a litmus test, Mi'kmaq treaty rights are being equated with assimilation into the globalized economy and the Canadian state.

Of fundamental concern to BRFN is the world view that this model of development imposes and the respectful relationship with the land—known in Mi'kmaq as *Netukulimuk*—that it severs. In the 15 years since the Marshall Decision, BRFN's struggle to assert *Netukulimuk* has a new battlefront, a process that we term treaty right recognition by assimilation. This chapter tells the story of BRFN's more than a decade of struggle, of grassroots renewal and engagement with traditional values to ground the community's vision, and of the alliances built to defend that vision. It is a cautionary story that reveals the vulnerability of Indigenous self-determination struggles in the context of neoliberal transformations and questions the limited potential of negotiations that are driven by the current policy framework. It is also a story of hope that points to the potential of alliances between Indigenous self-determination struggles and broader resistance to neoliberalism.

We begin with an analysis of DFO's management regime and its success in extending and deepening state control and capitalist relations in non-Native fishing communities—developments that foreshadow the "Aboriginalism" agenda that Alfred sees as crafting Aboriginal-Canadian citizens of the globalized economy. We then ground our discussion of these dynamics as they are illustrated in the BRFN and the Mi'kmaq people's struggle for self-determination. Taking the Marshall Decision as a watershed moment in that movement, we explore the ways in which the federal government's response has undermined the rights that *R. v. Marshall* affirmed. Finally, we present BRFN's strategy of resistance to this recognition by assimilation and explore the potential of the alliances that this First Nation is building with non-Indigenous communities and social movements resisting neoliberal globalization.[7]

Fisheries Privatization and Resistance in Non-Mi'kmaq Communities

Fishing has long defined the culture, economy, and social fabric of coastal communities in Atlantic Canada. Viewed as a barrier to capitalist development, these attributes have been dismantled over the last 30 years by DFO policy aimed at integrating small-scale independent producers into an ever-expanding market and on developing a centralized, corporate-owned fleet capable of large-scale harvesting and processing for international trade.[8] The current policy thrust is consistent with a wider neoliberal agenda: privatize Crown-owned resources, downsize government services, and deregulate management. These objectives have been achieved primarily through the imposition of individual transferable quotas (ITQs), intended to create market competition for control of quota, resulting in the survival of only the most "efficient" and "competitive" fishers. As a result, Atlantic Canada has experienced a dramatic consolidation of corporate ownership in the fisheries and the near extinction of the family-owned businesses that characterized the industry for generations.[9]

The Atlantic fisheries have always been integrated into an international capitalist market: this association defined the opening phase of the colonial project in Eastern Canada. But Anthony Davis describes how the intensification of capitalist relations in the fisheries during the 1980s systematically dehumanized coastal communities, changing fishers' identities, their relationships to the water, and to each other. Fishing used to be anchored in a deep attachment to place, to provide a sense of collective destiny, and to be central to the subsistence economy. Fishing rules and access were things harvesters negotiated with their neighbours. With DFO's drive for professionalization, fishers became businesspeople and clients of the state, accountable to the government and their creditors. Competition was embedded in a management regime that both presupposes and creates the atomized, self-interested, rational individual at the heart of liberal capitalist theory. The system also fractures fishers along lines of geography, technology, and fish species, making large-scale collective action difficult.[10]

Davis depicts this shift as one from "livelihood harvesting," made up of small-scale fishers with control over their means of production, to capital-intensive "accumulation harvesting," where workers on the water engage in resource extraction for profit.[11] It is a tragic irony that the Marshall Decision affirmed the treaty right to a "livelihood" fishery, the same sector being actively dismantled by the very resource management regime that DFO would impose on First Nations.

David Harvey calls the process driving the expansion and deepening of capitalist relations "accumulation by dispossession," a movement that dispossesses people of the means of production as it coerces them into labour market relations.[12] Resistance in non-Indigenous communities to this enclosure of the ocean commons has been well documented.[13] It has also created painful divisions between fishers who have accepted the ITQ system and those who have fought to establish community-based fisheries management as a strategy of resistance to this privatization. The outrage and sense of betrayal among this former group is so raw that some non-Indigenous fishers feel they can identify with the displacement and loss of sovereignty experienced by their Mi'kmaq neighbours as a result of Canadian colonialism. But if the management regime enacting this accumulation by dispossession is offensive to non-Native fishers, it is even more threatening to the Mi'kmaq for whom assimilation into this development model amounts to an intensification of the colonial project that they have confronted for over 400 years.

L'sɨtkuk and Mi'kmaq Struggles for Self-Determination

L'sɨtkuk, or Bear River First Nation, is a tiny community of 150 people[14] located at the headwaters of Bear River, which flows into the Bay of Fundy. In the Mi'kmaq language, *L'sɨtkuk* means "water that cuts through" or "flowing along high rocks." The name describes the trajectory of the river well, which cuts a swathe through the steep hills. The area was a fishing camp where families gathered over the warm months after spending the winter dispersed, hunting across Kespukwitk. The community was largely cut off from its fishing grounds and confined to a reservation in 1801. The reserve is now a postage stamp of green in a sea of clear-cut logging, and most of the fish and animals that the community once relied on for subsistence are now either severely depleted or extinct.

L'sɨtkuk is also a stone's throw from Port Royal, where the French (the first colonial powers in Mi'kmaki) established a settlement in 1604. Colonialism is long-standing in this part of North America: the **Covenant Chain** of treaties that the Mi'kmaq and their Wabenaki allies negotiated with the British Crown stretches back to the 1600s, with the last of the Peace and Friendship treaties negotiated in 1761.[15] Unlike the post-Confederation treaties, these agreements contained no land surrender provisions. They enshrined a vision of sharing the land as "two states under one crown,"[16] with the Mi'kmaq adding an eighth point to the star symbolizing the seven traditional districts of the Mi'kmaq nation.[17] As long as the sun shines and rivers flow, the Mi'kmaq could maintain their way of life; in exchange, they accepted the newcomers to Mi'kmaki. These promises were forgotten by the British as soon as the ink had dried on the page. And so began the Mi'kmaq peoples' long-standing struggle to decipher the doublespeak of the British and Canadian governments, to maintain Mi'kmaq values while adapting to non-Mi'kmaq economies, and to negotiate a balance between resisting assimilation and integrating into non-Indigenous society in a self-determined way. Incredibly, the Mi'kmaq have survived over 400 years of relentless colonization despite several obstacles, including the outlawing of traditional government under the Indian Act, the criminalization of Mi'kmaq language and ceremonies until the early 1950s, the residential school at Shubencadie, and Nova Scotia's attempts in the 1940s to centralize the Mi'kmaq on two reserves at Indian Brook and Eskasoni.

Court cases and police case files provide a public record of Mi'kmaq resistance, from the trial of Grand Chief Syliboy, who was charged in 1928 with illegal hunting and who referred to the 1752 Treaty to defend the Mi'kmaq's right to hunt and trap, to the 1973 and 1981 armed raids by Quebec Provincial Police and DFO wardens on the people of Listiguj, who were defending their traditional fishery.[18] But historical records fail to capture the spirit driving these events: the intention of Mi'kmaq people to live—as Kerry Prosper, an Elder from Paq'tnkek Mi'kmaw Nation, would say—according to the laws that are rooted in the land and waters of Mi'kmaki.

The Marshall Case

This tradition of resistance is the context for the late Donald Marshall Jr's act of community-supported civil disobedience in 1993 when he fished for *K'at* (eel), a creature and food of tremendous medicinal and spiritual significance.[19] Marshall was arrested for fishing out of season, for not having a licence, and for selling his catch. Marshall held that he was asserting his inherent right to fish, a right protected by the treaties his ancestors had negotiated with the Crown. Responding to the DFO officer who stopped him, demanding to see his fishing licence, Marshall replied: "Licence?! I don't need a fishing licence. I have a treaty!"[20]

Under the 1982 Constitution Act, this right is protected by section 35(1), which recognizes and affirms Aboriginal and treaty rights—a constitutional addition that First Nations across Canada fought hard to have included. The purpose of this section is to reconcile pre-existing Aboriginal and treaty rights that derive from Indigenous peoples' presence on and responsibility for the land since time immemorial, with the underlying sovereignty and title claims of the Crown established through the doctrine of discovery based upon the legal fiction of *terra nullius*. Section 35(1) has provided a powerful, though controversial, legal tool for First Nations. Critics point out that Canada acts as defendant, judge, and jury within a framework of colonial state institutions that undermine Indigenous sovereignty and are grounded in a liberal ideology hostile to Indigenous cultures. Nevertheless, appealing to the courts has proven an important strategy for First Nations in dealing with a federal government reluctant to acknowledge, let alone negotiate, their claims.[21]

In the Maritimes, the focus of First Nations' legal activism has been on establishing access to natural resources, based on the contemporary relevance of the historic Peace and Friendship treaties. Until Donald Marshall Jr went fishing, the Mi'kmaq treaty rights recognized by the Crown included the right to hunt, established through *R. v. Simon* (1985), and the right to fish for food and ceremonial purposes, established by *R. v. Sparrow* (1990).[22] Though Mi'kmaq access to resources was increasing, the Union of Nova Scotia Indians and the Confederacy of Mainland Mi'kmaq were frustrated with the limited management authority granted by DFO and the department's unwillingness to discuss Mi'kmaq commercial fishing access. These organizations supported the Marshall case as a means of expanding access to the commercial fisheries.[23] Marshall's defence, referring to clauses in the 1760–61 treaties, asked the court to affirm the Mi'kmaq's constitutionally protected right to earn a living from the land and waters of Mi'kmaki.[24] The Supreme Court affirmed the currency of the Peace and Friendship treaties and the collective rights recognized therein for the Mi'kmaq and Maliseet to obtain a "moderate live-lihood" through participation in the commercial fisheries. The ruling recognized the Crown's prerogative to regulate such rights for the purposes of conservation, though the current regulations were considered an infringement of those rights because they failed to explicitly acknowledge them.[25]

The traditional leadership in Esgenoopotitj, or Burnt Church First Nation, rejected the subjection of inherent Mi'kmaq rights within Canadian domestic law, citing the spirit and intent of the treaties as nation-to-nation alliances of peace and friendship, not sur-renders of land or sovereignty. Given DFO's poor conservation record, community leaders judged the department incompetent and its move to place Mi'kmaq fishers under federal jurisdiction illegitimate.[26] It was a stand that resonated with Mi'kmaq across the region and grassroots Indigenous people across the country, as reflected by the hundreds of supporters who came to stand with Esgenoopititj during the fishing seasons of 2000 and 2001.[27] In 2000, the Esgenoopotitj Fisheries Act was drafted through community consul-tation and blended science, harvester knowledge, and Mi'kmaq traditional teachings.[28] It articulated a vision for broad community involvement and resource sharing, one that was radically different from the trickle-down model of economic development dictated by the DFO management regime. It won the support of conservation groups but was met with violent backlash. Shocking images of RCMP officers beating Esgenoopititj fishers and DFO boats ramming Mi'kmaq dories made headlines for two consecutive summers.

While the media focused on these clashes, fishers around BRFN were quietly negotiat-ing the entry of Mi'kmaq harvesters.[29] This relationship-building approach was motivated by the simple fact that, as one community member put it, "We have to live here year round. Our children go to school in the neighboring community, and if we can't share the resource there's no point in our even having access."[30] We have written elsewhere about the remarkable conflict mediation process in southwest Nova Scotia that defused the near-violent crisis triggered by the Marshall ruling.[31] After dialogue was initiated, BRFN discovered that neighbouring fishers shared a similar vision for ecologically sustainable, community-based fishery management grounded in local self-governance, and that they had developed a rich critique of the neoliberal fisheries management regime through years of resistance to the regulations dismantling their local fisheries. Their analysis would provide BRFN with crucial insight in navigating the post-Marshall environment.

Government Response

The government response to *R. v. Marshall* was twofold. Over the long term, the par ameters of a treaty-based commercial fishery are to be established as part of formal negotiations between First Nations and provincial and federal governments to imple-ment the historic Peace and Friendship Treaties in a present-day context. As previously mentioned, this process is being carried out in Nova Scotia through the KMK/MRI. This part of the response comes after three decades of activism on the part of the Nova Scotia Mi'kmaq to have governments address outstanding title and rights questions in Mi'kmaki.[32] A framework agreement was signed in 2007 to guide the negotiations; a final agreement that was initially anticipated in 2011 is still under negotiation.

In the short term, DFO negotiated interim fishery access agreements, both as an immediate means of responding to First Nations demands for fishing access, and to restore calm on the waters. These agreements, negotiated on a band-by-band basis, offered money for communal commercial licences, vessels, gear, and training. Signing bands agreed to "shelve" their right to manage their fisheries for the duration of the agreements and to fish by DFO regulations.[33] This paternalistic response triggered resentment within Mi'kmaq communities: the federal government was not so much recognizing treaty rights as pressuring bands to put them aside. There was also dissatisfaction with the funds and the quota put on the negotiating table, as well as with the rushed pace of negotiations and DFO's inflexibility, which gave the department effective control of the negotiation agenda.[34]

BRFN's negotiations with the department are a revealing case in point. For the people of L'sɨtkuk, the Marshall Decision represented a deep affirmation of Mi'kmaq identity. It also triggered a renewed exploration of *Netukulimuk* and a grassroots effort to envision a treaty-based livelihood fishery anchored in a renewal of this traditional concept. BRFN's fisheries management plan was drafted with support from neighbouring fishing groups through a community-organizing process that strengthened self-governance, built relationships with neighbouring communities, coordinated BRFN's fishing activities with those of surrounding fishers, and went much farther than DFO regulations in terms of conservation. However, it was completely rejected by DFO, which insisted on assimilating BRFN's fishing activities into the privatized fisheries management regime.

Negotiations around scallop harvesting are a poignant example. BRFN proposed to share the scallop license offered by DFO between several community harvesters, who would use traditional and ecological methods, such as diving, to harvest scallops. Instead, DFO insisted the licence be assigned to a single (and much larger) boat. This would have effectively forced Bear River to contract a corporate-owned dragger to fish their quota in the band's name—a move that would have disenfranchised Bear River harvesters while forcing the community to use ecologically destructive fishing technologies.

Given the sharp contrast between BRFN's vision for a livelihood fishery rooted in *Netukulimuk* under Mi'kmaq jurisdiction, and the social, political, and ecological relationships imposed through DFO's regulations, BRFN refused to sign an agreement. However, 32 of the 34 eligible bands in the Maritimes did sign interim agreements with DFO. Some have been able to develop innovative community-based fisheries, but, for the most part, First Nations in Nova Scotia have been given little more than local control over the implementation of DFO policy and a token advisory role at the local fisheries management level.[35]

It bears repeating that these interim agreements were supposedly without prejudice to the exercise of Mi'kmaq treaty rights while KMK/MRI negotiations are ongoing. However, BRFN's concern has been that the federal government will consider these agreements as consultation in retrospect, and the funds associated with these agreements as compensation for the infringement of treaty rights. Recent frustrations expressed by the 13 Nova Scotia chiefs at the federal government's reluctance to negotiate a treaty-based fishery within the KMK/MRI, signal that those fears are now confirmed.[36] In 2013, 14 years after the Marshall Decision and six years after a framework agreement was signed with the provincial and federal governments to enter into formal negotiations, the 13 Nova Scotia Mi'kmaq chiefs were forced to file court proceedings declaring the government's unwillingness to negotiate a treaty-based livelihood fishery, beyond the scope of the programs established through interim access agreements. Only the pressure of litigation was enough to force DFO to concede a mandate to negotiate a livelihood fishery.[37]

A comprehensive evaluation of the Aboriginal commercial fishery that the interim access agreements and the KMK/MRI process put in place has yet to be undertaken. However, it appears that if the process was successful in easing tensions and helping bands enter the commercial fisheries, it was equally successful at establishing DFO control over the orientation and management of this Aboriginal fishery, and at creating a set of commercial interests within communities that, once established, are very difficult to uproot. L'sɨtkuk's vision for a treaty-based livelihood fishery under Mi'kmaq jurisdiction has instead been implemented as a de facto program and service of the federal government. While the department uses conservation as justification for this infringement of Aboriginal rights, many suggest that its primary motivation is retaining control over management to further privatizing and rationalizing the fishing industry.[38] In the words of one leader in BRFN, "We don't see any evidence of DFO supporting conservation; we see them supporting big business."[39]

Resisting Privatization: Towards an Anti-Colonial Commons

Though Mi'kmaq and non-Mi'kmaq communities are affected very differently by this neoliberal enclosure movement, it is important to frame these experiences of dispossession as moments in the same story—the history of the expansion and intensification of capitalism driven forward by a system of colonial political control. This helps us better understand the forces that BRFN and allied non-Indigenous groups in Kespukwitk are resisting as they struggle to assert what could be viewed as an informal treaty relationship between their peoples. It also forms a deepening basis of unity between the various groups.

For BRFN, resistance to this neoliberal intensification of colonialism begins with what Coulthard would describe as "on-the-ground practices of freedom," trading the politics of recognition for a process of self-recognition and building a radical alternative to the current neo-colonial arrangement through a critical engagement with traditional culture. Coulthard notes that such a "transformational praxis" would not only address the internalized oppression of Indigenous people, but would contribute to the wider society as well. He writes, "[O]ur cultures have much to teach the Western world about the establishment of relationships within and between peoples and the natural world that are profoundly non-imperialist."[40]

A key element of BRFN's transformational praxis is working with neighbouring communities to learn how the colonial–capitalist project has pitted the interests of Mi'kmaq and non-Mi'kmaq communities against one another and to overcome the de facto segregation that characterizes much of rural Nova Scotia.[41] In Bear River's traditional territory, the conflict mediation sparked by the Marshall ruling opened a dialogue that has matured over the past decade into cross-cultural alliances resisting the successive waves of privatization affecting local communities. The most successful example of this joint action is the opposition that BRFN and non-Mi'kmaq groups mounted against the White Point Quarry project, which forced an environmental assessment process that has delayed, if not thwarted, the mining project.[42] Although that political victory is significant, the deepening relationships and political analysis that have resulted from these joint actions are of equal importance.

Battiste sees a liberating potential in dialogue between western and Indigenous traditions.[43] Together, we can more accurately diagnose colonialism as we imagine and invoke a new society. Creating spaces for such cross-cultural pedagogy is an integral part of BRFN's political action, be it through cultural production, learning circles, or other forums for reflection and cultural sharing. Broadening this discussion to include harvesters, activists, researchers from across the country, and internationally through BRFN's association with the World Forum of Fisher Peoples (WFFP) is helping this First Nation to recognize its position within broader struggles against the neo-colonial agenda of accumulation by dispossession. Together, we are imagining a response to neoliberal enclosures that resists retrenching the colonial relations embodied in Crown "public" resources.

Meanwhile, the privatization of the resource base that the treaty relationship is meant to protect continues. The most recent example is the de facto privatization of 14 beaches in Kespukwitk through 10-year leases signed between the provincial government and Innovative Fisheries Products Inc., a move that gives the latter monopoly control over the clamming sector as it expropriates ancestral clam beds used by BRFN.[44] Though there is a legal duty to consult First Nations on issues that might infringe upon their rights, these consultations happen in a top-down manner through the centralized KMK/MRI process, sidestepping and undermining the local alliances so crucial to BRFN's strategy to protect Kespukwitk.

Conclusion

The Marshall Decision was a moment of hope in the Mi'kmaq's struggle for self-determination that could have led to many things. It could have led—as early declarations from the Atlantic Policy Congress of First Nations Chiefs demanded[45]—to strengthened self-governance and cultural renewal, increased access to hunting and fishing for traditional harvesters, and a meaningful voice for the Mi'kmaq nation in shaping the regulations that govern the fisheries. It could have been, as BRFN hoped, the grounds for alliance, as well as a fundamental challenge to the privatization of marine resources and the intensification of capitalist relations in the fishing industry. Instead, the window of opportunity opened by the Marshall Decision slammed shut. In theory, the ongoing KMK/MRI negotiations have the power to pry that window open, but the prevailing neoliberal climate and limited negotiation policy framework leave little room for optimism.

So where do communities who are unwilling to choose between the limited set of options available through such compromised political negotiations find a voice? For BRFN, action at the international level, through participation in social movements such as the World Forum of Fisher People (WFFP, an international alliance of small-scale and Indigenous fishers) has proven crucial. Within Canada, there is a collective denial of the colonial origins of this settler-state. This "Canadian psychosis"[46] is buttressed by a constitution that supposedly enshrines Aboriginal and treaty rights, despite a modern treaty negotiation framework in which the Canadian state recognizes such title and rights only after First Nations agree to extinguish them. This situation creates a veneer of democracy that makes Canadian colonialism hard to diagnose, let alone confront. But WFFP colleagues in the global South have no problem identifying their resistance to neo-colonialism and globalization with BRFN's experience.

"We were happy—for five minutes." That is how a South African WFFP comrade describes the euphoria in his country at the fall of apartheid. John Pilger tells the story of the economic conditions that the once-socialist African National Congress (ANC) leadership was pressured to accept in negotiating the end of that system. In exchange for political control of the country, the ANC leadership quickly implemented savage neoliberal reforms that have seen income for blacks decrease by 19 per cent and for whites increase by 15 per cent in the 21 years since. "Economic apartheid replaced legal apartheid with the same consequences," notes Pilger, "yet is greeted as one of the greatest achievements in world history."[47] It is an ominous tale for those struggling for Indigenous self-determination in Canada.

Across the global South, overt colonial rule has been replaced by neo-colonial arrangements characterized by the now familiar neoliberal prescription of privatization, trade liberalization, and deregulation imposed through the International Monetary Fund's structural adjustment programs and World Trade Organization-enforced trade agreements. These are the tools of what Harvey calls "the 'new' imperialism," designed to extend the borders of global capital's reach.[48] While trade agreements drive this agenda of accumulation by dispossession forward in the South, the displacement and dispossession of Indigenous peoples in Canada represents a major frontier of capitalist expansion.

BRFN's challenges in asserting *Netukulimuk* demonstrate how Crown negotiations with First Nations continue Canada's long-standing project of assimilating Indigenous nations and extinguishing their rights and title in the interests of capitalist development. We do not mean to understate the tremendous victory that the Marshall Decision represents or to underemphasize how hard the Mi'kmaq have fought to force the Crown to acknowledge and then honour the Peace and Friendship treaties and to negotiate a modern interpretation of these nation-to-nation agreements. Our intention is to clarify how the dynamics of accumulation by dispossession, matched with a policy framework determined to feed into these neoliberal transformations, limit negotiations to such an extent that the notion of self-determination in the current context is highly problematic. This limitation presents a tremendous challenge for First Nations leaders working within established legal channels to find an acceptable compromise. It also points to a need for non-Indigenous social movements challenging neoliberal globalization to learn from and ally with Indigenous anti-colonial struggles.

Notes

1. Taiaiake Alfred, *Wasáse. Indigenous Pathways of Action and Freedom* (Peterborough: Broadview Press, 2005); Glen Coulthard, "Subjects of Empire: Indigenous Peoples and the 'Politics of Recognition' in Canada," *Contemporary Political Theory* 6 (2007): 437–60.

2. Paul Nadasdy, *Hunters and Bureaucrats: Power, Knowledge, and Aboriginal–State Relations in the Southwest Yukon* (Vancouver: UBC Press, 2003).

3. Taiaiake Alfred, *Peace Power Righteousness: An Indigenous Manifesto* (Toronto: Oxford University Press, 1999); Marie Battiste, "Introduction, Unfolding the Lessons of Colonization," in Battiste, ed., *Reclaiming Indigenous Voice and Vision* (Vancouver: UBC Press, 2007), xvi–xxx.

4. Linda Tuhiwai Smith, *Decolonizing Methodologies: Research and Indigenous Peoples* (New York: St Martin's Press, 1999), 22.

5. Alfred, *Peace Power*, 60.

6. Cliff Atleo, Jr, "From Indigenous Nationhood to Neoliberal Aboriginal Economic Development: Charting the Evolution of Indigenous-Settler Relations," *Canadian Social Economy Hub* (Oct. 2008). Available at www.socialeconomyhub .ca/?q=content/indigenous-nationhood-neoliberal-aboriginal-economic-development-charting-evolution-indigeno (accessed 23 Nov. 2009).

7. This article is a product and an embodiment of these alliances, written collaboratively by Martha Stiegman, a non-Indigenous doctoral student at Concordia University, and Sherry Pictou, a grassroots community leader and former chief of Bear River First Nation. The analysis presented here comes out of three decades of Pictou's community-based political work, as well as the last six years of Stiegman's participatory-action doctoral research. For a detailed presentation of the authors' collaborative, video-based research methodology, see Stiegman and Pictou, "How do you say Netuklimuk in English? Using Documentary Video to capture Bear River First Nation's Learning through Action," in Aziz Choudry and Dip Kappoor, eds, *Learning from the Ground Up: Global Perspectives on Social Movements and Knowledge Production* (New York: Palgrave Macmillan, 2010).

8. Henry Veltmeyer, "The Restructuring of Capital and the Regional Problem," in Bryant Douglas Fairley, Colin Leys, and R. James Sacouman, eds, *Restructuring and Resistance from Atlantic Canada* (Toronto: Garamond Press, 1990), 79–104.

9. Patrick Kerans and John Kearney, *Turning the World Right Side Up: Science, Community, and Democracy* (Halifax: Fernwood, 2006): 100–02; 180–5.

10. Anthony Davis, "Insidious Rationalities: The Institutionalisation of Small Boat Fishing and the Rise of the Rapacious Fisher" (1991). Available at http://people.stfx.ca/rsg/gbayesp/insidious_report.htm, accessed 6 Jul. 2015.

11. Anthony Davis, "Barbed Wire and Bandwagons: A Comment on ITQ Fisheries Management," *Reviews in Fish Biology and Fisheries* 6 (1996): 97–107.

12. David Harvey, *The New Imperialism* (New York: Oxford University Press, 2003), 137–82.

13. Kerans and Kearney, *Turning the World*; M. Stiegman, *In the Same Boat?* 39 min. Canada: V-Tape.

14. There are roughly 300 registered band members of Bear River First Nation, approximately half of whom live on-reserve.

15. Grand Council of Micmacs, Union of Nova Scotia Indians, and Native Council of Nova Scotia, *The Mi'kmaq Treaty Handbook* (Sydney & Truro: Native Communications Society of Nova Scotia, 1987).

16. Donald Marshall Sr, Alexander Denny, and Simon Marshall, "The Covenant Chain," in Boyce Richardson, ed., *Drumbeat: Anger and Renewal in Indian Country* (Toronto: Summerhill Press, 1989), 71–104.

17. Grand Council et al., *The Mi'kmaq Treaty Handbook*, i.

18. Alanis Obomsawin, *Incident at Restigouche*, 45 min 57 s. (Canada: National Film Board of Canada, 1984).

19. Kerry Prosper, Mary Jane Paulette, and Anthony Davis, "Traditional Wisdom can build a Sustainable Future," *Atlantic Fisherman* (Aug. 2004): 2.

20. McMillan, J., Prosper, K., Davis, A., Stiegman, M. (Producers), Stiegman, M., and Prosper, K. (Director). (2013) *Seeking Netukulimk*. [Documentary Video]. 22 min.

21. J. Marshall, "Kmitkinu aq Maqmikewminu— Our Birthright and our Land," *Mi'kmaq Maliseet Nations News* 13, 3 (2006): 3.

22. Thomas Isaac, *Aboriginal and Treaty Rights in the Maritimes: The Marshall Decision and Beyond* (Saskatoon: Purich Publishers, 2001), 54–60.

23. William C. Wicken, *Mi'kmaq Treaties on Trial: History, Land, and Donald Marshall Junior* (Toronto: University of Toronto Press, 2002), 3–6.

24. Ken Coates, *The Marshall Decision and Native Rights* (Montreal & Kingston: McGill-Queen's University Press, 2000), 3–7.

25. *R v. Marshall*, 1999.

26. Kwegsi, "Modern Day Treaty (Self-assimilation)" (2001). Available at www.turtleisland.org/news/kwegsi.doc; Kwegsi, "Injustice? Duress and the Burnt Church First Nation Fisheries Agreement with Canada" (2002). Available at www.turtleisland.org/news/news-onemans-kwegsi.htm (accessed 12 Jan. 2003).

27. Alanis Obomsawin, *Is the Crown at War with Us?* 96 min 31 s. (Canada: National Film Board of Canada, 2002).

28. James Ward and Lloyd Augustine, "Draft for the Esgenoopotitj First Nation (EFN) Fishery Act" (2000). Available at www.cifas.us/page/draft-esgenoopotitj-first-nation-efn-fishery-act-fisheries-policy-may-2000, accessed 6 Jul. 2015.

29. Pauline McIntosh and John Kearney, "Enhancing Natural Resources and Livelihoods Globally through Community-Based Resource Management," *Proceedings from the Learning and Innovations Institute* (6–9 Nov. 2002).

30. Interview with Martha Stiegman, 2005.

31. Stiegman and Pictou, "How do you say...."

32. Marshall, "Kmitkinu."

33. Chris Milley and Anthony Charles, "Mi'kmaq Fisheries in Atlantic Canada: Traditions, Legal Decisions and Community Management." Unpublished paper presented at "People and the Sea: Maritime Research in the Social Sciences: An Agenda for the 21st Century, Amsterdam" (2001).

34. Martha Stiegman, "Fisheries Privatization Versus Community-Based Management in Nova Scotia: Emerging Alliances between First Nations and Non-Native Fishers," in Laurie Adkin, ed.,

Environmental Conflict and Democracy in Canada (Vancouver: UBC Press, 2009), 69–83.

35. Atlantic Policy Congress of First Nations Chiefs, "The Management of Fisheries on Canada's Atlantic Coast: A Discussion Document on Policy Direction and Principles" (2001). Available at www.apcfnc.ca (accessed 14 Apr. 2006).

36. Maureen Googoo, "NS chiefs Want Feds to Implement Marshall Decision" (2009). http://radiogoogoo.ca/2009/09/17/ns-chiefs-want-feds-to-implement-marshall-decision/, accessed 5 Dec. 2009.

37. A. Bernard, 2013. *Moderate Livelihood Fishery: A Mi'kmaq Way of Life.* Retrieved from http://smallscales.ca/2013/04/05/mlf/. Mi'kmaq Rights Initiative (2013 a). *Nova Scotia Mi'kmaq Leaders Meet to Discuss Fisheries Mandate.* Press Release. 3 October 2013. Retrieved from: http://mikmaqrights.com/uploads/fisheriesreleaseoct3.pdf.

38. Anthony Davis and Svein Jentoft, "The Challenge and the Promise of Indigenous Peoples' Fishing Rights—From Dependency to Agency," *Marine Policy* 25, 3 (2001):

223–7; Melanie G. Wiber and Julia Kennedy, "Impossible Dreams: Reforming Fisheries Management in the Canadian Maritimes after the Marshall Decision," *Law & Anthropology* 11 (2001): 282–97.

39. Interview with Martha Stiegman, 2003.

40. Coulthard, "Subjects of Empire," 457.

41. Sherry Pictou and Arthur Bull, "Resource Extraction in the Maritimes: Historic Links with Racism," *New Socialist* 1 (2009): 38–9; Stiegman and Pictou, "How do you say...."

42. Sherry Pictou, "How Deep Are Our Treaties?" *Samudra* 54 (2009). Available at http://icsf.net.

43. Battiste, "Introduction."

44. Wiber and Bull, "Rescaling Governance."

45. Atlantic Policy Congress, "The Management of Fisheries."

46. Joyce A. Green, "Towards a Détente with History: Confronting Canada's Colonial Legacy," *International Journal of Canadian Studies* 12 (1995): 85–105.

47. John Pilger, *Freedom Next Time* (Ealing: Bantam Press, 2006), 287.

48. Harvey, *The New Imperialism.*

Primary Document

Guides, 1899. Left to right, top row: Louis Peters, John Peters, John McEwan, John Louis; left to right, bottom row: John Labrador, Malti Pictou, Eli Pictou. These men guided a group of sports fishermen into the interior of Digby County, presumably in early May, as the leaves are not yet showing on the trees and bushes, yet there is no snow on the ground. Late April and early May are the best times for going after trout in this area. This picture, one of a series documenting the expedition, was taken at the beginning of the trip, which most likely took place in 1899. (Ethnology Collection, Nova Scotia Museum.)

The Guides, 2009. Harvesters from Bear River First Nation, Bear River First Nation Descendants. (Martha Stiegman and Sherry Pictou.)

Questions for Consideration

1. What was the Trilateral Agreement and why was, and is, it significant?
2. Why have the federal and provincial governments failed to live up to their obligations in the Trilateral Agreement? Why has Barriere Lake First Nation tried to force the governments to honour the agreement?
3. What is being agreed to in the "Memorandum of Mutual Intent between the Algonquins of Barriere Lake and the Department of Indian and Northern Affairs"? What rights does the agreement attribute to Barriere Lake First Nation? What obligations does it impose on the Canadian and Quebec governments?
4. Why was the James Bay Agreement hailed as a landmark agreement for Aboriginal rights?
5. Has the James Bay Agreement served the interests of the Cree in northern Quebec? Does the Quebec government and Hydro-Québec behaviour seem consistent with the analysis of treaties, rights, and the politics of recognition offered by Stiegman and Pictou? Give reasons to support your answers.
6. Why did Judge Rouleau rule in favour of the applicants in the Cree Regional Authority case? What, if any, evidence of duplicity on the part of the federal and/or provincial governments exists in the trial record?
7. What criticisms do Stiegman and Pictou offer of the strategy of fighting for Canadian government recognition of Indigenous treaty rights?
8. What, in Stiegman and Pictou's view, motivates the Canadian government's attempts to dispossess Indigenous peoples of their rights, lands, and resources? Do you agree with their assessment? Why or why not?

9. Discuss whether treaty-making with the Canadian government has been a positive or negative experience for Indigenous peoples and whether treaty-making can be a strategy for advancing their rights and positions.

Further Resources

Books and Articles

Alfred, Taiaiake. *Peace Power Righteousness: An Indigenous Manifesto*. Toronto: Oxford University Press, 1999.

Alfred, Taiaiake and Corntassel, Jeff. "Being Indigenous," *Government and Opposition: An International Journal of Comparative Politics* 5, 2 (Spring 2006) 112–34.

Boldt, Menno, and J. Anthony Long, eds. *The Quest for Justice: Aboriginal Peoples and Aboriginal Rights*. Toronto: University of Toronto Press, 1985.

Ladner, K. and Leanne Simpson, eds. *This Is an Honour Song: Twenty Years Since the Blockades*. Winnipeg: Arbiter Ring Publishing, 2010.

Lambertus, Sandra. *Wartime Images, Peacetime Wounds: The Media and the Gustafsen Lake Stand-Off*. Toronto: University of Toronto Press, 2004.

Morse, Brad W., ed. *Aboriginal Peoples and the Law: Indian, Metis and Inuit Rights in Canada*. Ottawa: Carleton University Press, 1989.

Nadasdy, Paul. *Hunters and Bureaucrats: Power, Knowledge, and Aboriginal–State Relations in the Southwest Yukon*. Vancouver: UBC Press, 2003.

Peters, Evelyn J. "Native People and the Environmental Regime in the James Bay and Northern Quebec Agreement," *Arctic* 52, 4 (Dec. 1999): 395–410.

Simpson, Audra. *Mohawk Interruptus: Political Life Across the Borders of Settler States*. Durham: Duke University Press, 2014.

Simpson, Leanne. *Dancing on Our Turtle's Back: Stories of Nishnaabeg Re-Creation, Resurgence, and a New Emergence*. Winnipeg: Arbeiter Ring Publishing, 2011.

Printed Documents and Reports

Amnesty International. Canada: Indigenous Protest Movement Highlights Deep-Rooted Injustices. www.amnesty.org/en/articles/news/2013/01/canada-indigenous-protest-movement-highlights-deep-rooted-injustices/

Canada, Aboriginal Affairs and Northern Development. Renewing the Comprehensive Land Claims Policy: Towards a Framework for Addressing Section 35 Aboriginal Rights. Ottawa: September 2014.

Grand Council of Micmacs, Union of Nova Scotia Indians, and Native Council of Nova Scotia. *The Mi'kmaq Treaty Handbook*. Sydney & Truro: Native Communications Society of Nova Scotia, 1987.

Grand Council of the Cree. *Never Without Consent: James Bay Crees' Stand Against Forcible Inclusion Into An Independent Quebec*. Toronto: ECW Press, 1998.

Manuel, Arthur. "Federal Comprehensive Land Claims Policy: A Dead End for First Nations." Defenders of the Land. www.defendersoftheland.org/story/188

Films

Dancing around the Table. DVD. Directed by Maurice Bulbulian. NFB, 1987.

Encounter with Saul Ralinsky, Part II: Rama Indian Reserve. DVD. Directed by Peter Pearson. NFB, 1967.

Hi-Ho Mistahey. DVD. (Documentary). Directed by Alnis Obomsawin. NFB, 2013.

Incident at Restigouche. DVD. Directed by Alanis Obomsawin. NFB, 1984.

In the Same Boat? Film. Directed by Martha Stiegman and Sherry Pictou. Bear River First Nation, 2007.

Is the Crown at War with Us? DVD. Directed by Alanis Obomsawin. NFB, 2002.

Kanehsatake: 270 Years of Resistance. DVD. Directed by Alanis Obomsawin. NFB, 1993.

Rocks at WHISKEY Trench. DVD. Directed by Alanis Obomsawin. NFB, 2000.

Starblanket. DVD. Directed by Donald Brittain. NFB, 1973.

Websites

Idle No More
www.idlenomore.ca/

Barriere Lake Solidarity
www.barrierelakesolidarity.org/

Feeding My Family
www.facebook.com/groups/239422122837039/

Free Grassy Narrows: Support Grassy Narrows First Nation
http://freegrassy.net/

Indigenous Environmental Network: Working for the Rights of Indigenous Peoples and for Environmental and Economic Justice
www.ienearth.org/what-we-do/tar-sands/

Settlers in Support of Indigenous Sovereignty
http://sisis.nativeweb.org/

Walking With Our Sisters
http://walkingwithoursisters.ca/

Glossary

1885 Rebellion Also known as the 1885 Resistance, North-West Rebellion, or North-West Resistance, an armed resistance to Canadian expansion in the North-West territory (particularly present-day Saskatchewan) among some of the Indigenous peoples of the region. Beginning in March and ending in May and June 1885, the rebellion is often considered an extension of the earlier Red River Resistance.

Abenaki An Algonquian-speaking Indigenous people living in the present-day Maritimes and Northeastern United States who are also members of the Wabanaki Confederacy.

Aboriginal The original inhabitants of a particular territory and their descendants. In Canada, the word refers collectively to First Nations, Inuit, and Métis peoples. *Aboriginal* is the term used in the Charter of Rights and Freedoms and is thus the preferred term of official Canadian government documents and legislation. The editors of this collection use Indigenous; however, the individual authors frequently use *Aboriginal* depending on context or personal preference.

Acadians The Francophone settlers and inhabitants of present-day New Brunswick, Nova Scotia, and Prince Edward Island, many of whom were expelled by the British following the French defeat in the Seven Years' War.

Adopt Indian Métis (AIM) The agency created by the Saskatchewan government that oversaw the adoption of Indigenous children by non-Indigenous families. It was one of many government agencies that participated in the Sixties Scoop.

Algonquian (also **Algonkian**) One of the largest and most widespread Indigenous linguistic groups, located from the East Coast all the way to the western Plains.

American Fur Company Founded by John Jacob Astor in 1808, the company monopolized the fur trade in the United States and, by 1830, was one of the largest businesses in the country.

American Revolution (1775–83) Also known as the Revolutionary War or the War of American Independence, this was a rebellion against the authority of the British Empire among the 13 colonies of the present-day eastern United States. The British conceded American independence in the Treaty of Paris (1783). Notably, neither side's Indigenous allies were included in the peacemaking process and, accordingly, their concerns went unconsidered.

Anishnabe (also **Anishinaabe, Anishinabe,** or **Anishinaabeg**; *plural* **Anishinabek**) Meaning the "first" or "original" peoples, the name used by the Ojibwa, Odawa, and Algonquin peoples to refer to themselves.

Assembly of First Nations (AFN) A national organization, formerly known as the National Indian Brotherhood (NIB), representing First Nations in Canada.

Attawapiskat First Nation A Cree First Nation located on the western shores of James Bay.

Bagot Commission (1842–44) Established by Governor General Sir Charles Bagot after the union of the Canadas, the commission's mandate was to review the operations of the Indian Department in Canada and suggest reforms that would facilitate the assimilation of Indigenous peoples while simultaneously reducing expenditures. The commission's report led to the centralization of all Indian affairs, especially record-keeping, and laid the foundation for provisions in the Indian Act pertaining to Indian status, band membership, and enfranchisement.

band A collection of interrelated nuclear families combined to form a larger unit. According to the Government of Canada, a band is a body of "'Indians' for whose collective use and benefit lands have been set apart, money is held by the Crown, or declared to be a band for the purposes of the Indian Act." Each band has its own governing council and Chief.

band council The governing body of a band, which usually consists of a chief and councillors selected through either custom or (under the Indian Act) elections. Elected officials hold office for two to three years. Under the Indian Act, the band council is responsible for providing services such as education, water, sewer and fire services, community buildings, schools, roads, and other community businesses and services, without the same funding and infrastructure as non-Indigenous municipalities.

Barriere Lake The home of the Algonquins of Barriere Lake located in present-day western Quebec.

Battle of Seven Oaks Also known as *la Victoire de la Grenouillière*, or the Victory of Frog Plain, a battle that was part of a long-term dispute between the North West Company (NWC) and the Hudson's Bay Company (HBC). In January 1814, Miles Macdonell, governor of Selkirk Colony, issued the Pemmican Proclamation, prohibiting the export of food from the colony. The NWC refused to abide by Macdonell's proclamation and accused the HBC of unfair business practices. On 19 June 1816, a group of Métis led by Cuthbert Grant was transporting a shipment of pemmican from the upper Assinboine River to Lake Winnipeg in order to sell it to the NWC. They were met by Robert Semple (the new governor) and a group of HBC men and local settlers at Seven Oaks. When Semple tried to arrest the Métis, a fight broke out. The Métis defeated Semple, killing him and 20 of his men while sustaining only one casualty of their own. The battle is often referred to as a foundational moment in the development of Métis nationalism.

Bill C-31: An Act to Amend the Indian Act Passed by the Canadian Parliament in 1985, an Act that was intended to address the discriminatory membership provisions of the Indian Act that disproportionately affected women. Most significantly, status Indian women who married non-status men would no longer lose their Indian status; Indigenous women who married a member of another band would no longer automatically became a member of that band and lose membership to their natal band; and bands could establish their own membership rules.

Bois-Brûlés A term applied to those of mixed European and Indigenous heritage that predated the formation of Métis national consciousness on the Plains. Translates literally as "Burnt-Wood."

British Columbia Treaty Commission A commission established in 1993 to oversee land claims disputes in British Columbia.

Calder case (*Calder v. British Columbia* [1973]) A Supreme Court decision that acknowledged the existence of Aboriginal title to the land prior to the arrival of Europeans. In 1967, Frank Arthur Calder and the Nisga'a Nation Tribal Council brought an action against the BC government contending that that Aboriginal title to most of the land in the province had never been lawfully extinguished.

cama A plant commonly eaten by the Indigenous peoples of the West Coast.

castor gras d'hiver Greasy winter beaver fur, in high demand on the European market in the 1600s and therefore a key trade good in the early fur trade.

Charter of Rights and Freedoms Legislation that guarantees Canadian citizens certain rights and extends civil rights to everyone in Canada, regardless of their citizenship. The Charter was enshrined in the Canadian Constitution and signed into law in April 1982.

comprehensive land claims Agreements negotiated in regions of the country where Aboriginal rights and title have not been extinguished through treaties with Canada or the British Crown. These agreements are considered modern-day treaties between Indigenous groups, the federal government, and the relevant province or territory.

Comprehensive Land Claims Policy (CLCP) The federal government policy that is supposed to govern the resolution of Aboriginal land rights in those territories of present-day Canada where treaties were not negotiated.

Constitution Act (1982) Part of the process by which Canada "patriated" its Constitution, reforming and renaming the British North America Act (1867) as the Constitution Act. The Charter of Rights and Freedoms is usually seen as the most significant reform within the Act. Section 35 of the Act states that "'existing Aboriginal and treaty rights of the Aboriginal peoples of Canada are hereby recognized and affirmed' and that "'Aboriginal Peoples of Canada' includes the Indian, Inuit, and Métis peoples of Canada."

Covenant Chain An alliance between the Haudenosaunee (Iroquois Confederacy) and the British Colonies.

Cree (*Eeyouch*) One of the largest groups of Indigenous peoples in North America. The Cree live in territories that stretch from present-day Alberta to Quebec, a geographic distribution larger than that of any other Indigenous group in Canada.

Cree Regional Authority (CRA) The political body that represents the approximately 14,000 Cree of eastern James Bay and southern Hudson Bay in northern Quebec. The CRA was created by the Act respecting the Cree Regional Authority, which was passed by the Quebec National Assembly in 1978. The CRA and the Grand Council of the Crees are two distinct legal entities; however, they have identical membership, board of directors, and governing structures and are de facto managed and operated as one organization by the Cree Nation.

Dene (Dené) Indigenous peoples who live in the northern boreal and Arctic regions of present-day Canada.

Department of Indian Affairs (DIA) Formally created in 1880, one of the departments within the federal government that is responsible for meeting the Canadian government's obligations and commitments to First Nations, Inuit, and Métis. In 1966, the DIA became the Department of Indian Affairs and Northern Development. Since May 2011, the department has been known as Aboriginal Affairs and Northern Development Canada.

Eeyou Itschee (Cree for **"the People's Land"**) The territorial equivalent to a regional county municipality located in northern Quebec. It was created on 20 November 2007 and is governed by the Grand Council of the Crees.

enfranchisement A term that usually refers to giving someone the right to vote. It can also mean, more broadly, to include someone as a full member of the community with all the rights that entails. In relation to Indigenous peoples in Canada, the word often meant losing Indian status as defined under the Indian Act in exchange for the ability to vote and the other rights of Canadian citizenship.

factory A trading post. Factories served as markets, warehouses, defensive fortifications, centres of government (as understood by Europeans), and sometimes ports.

Feeding My Family A Facebook group established by activists living in Nunavut to try to use co-operative strategies to obtain healthy and affordable food for northern Indigenous peoples.

First Nations The original inhabitants of a particular territory and their descendants. The term came into common usage in the 1970s to replace the word *Indian*, which many people found both historically inaccurate and offensive. Some groups have adopted the term *First Nation* to replace the word *band*.

Frog Lake Massacre A Cree uprising that took place during the 1885 Resistance. It occurred at the village of Frog Lake in present-day Alberta on 2 April 1885.

Grand Council of the Crees The political body that represents the approximately 14,000 Cree of eastern James Bay and southern Hudson Bay in northern Quebec. The Grand Council has 20 members: a grand chief and deputy-grand chief elected at large by the Eeyouch; the chiefs elected by each of the nine Cree communities; and one other representative from each community. The Grand Council of the Crees and the Cree Regional Authority are two distinct legal entities; however, they have identical membership, board of directors, and governing structures and are de facto managed and operated as one organization by the Cree Nation.

half-breed A derogatory term used to refer to an individual who is of mixed-race descent. Historically, the term was used to describe individuals who were of Indigenous and European ancestry. *Métis* is the more common and acceptable term though, in turn, many such as Adam Gaudry argue that Métis should only be used to refer to those who are descendants of the historic Métis Nation of the plains.

Haudenosaunee The People of the Long House, also known as the Iroquois, the Iroquois Confederacy, and the Six Nations.

Hawthorn Report A report commissioned by the federal government to examine the socio-economic, political, and constitutional conditions of Status Indians in order to advise policy-makers on how to improve the lives of Indigenous peoples in Canada. Issued in 1966, the report recommended a "Citizens Plus" approach, which would give Indigenous peoples the same rights and benefits as other Canadians while simultaneously acknowledging that they have special rights and privileges as the original inhabitants of North America and as the signatories of treaties with the British and Canadian governments. Prime Minister Pierre Elliott Trudeau rejected the report.

Hispaniola The second-largest island in the Caribbean and the present-day site of the Dominican Republic and Haiti. Christopher Columbus founded a settlement in Hispaniola in 1492. Some historians argue that the island's Indigenous peoples were entirely wiped out by the end of the sixteenth century.

Hochelaga An Iroquoian village located at the site of present-day Montreal. Jacques Cartier visited Hochelaga in October 1535.

Hudson's Bay Company (HBC) The HBC was incorporated by royal charter in 1670 as "The Governor and Adventurers of England trading into Hudson's Bay." The HBC played a central role in the history of Turtle Island generally and in the fur trade particularly.

Idle No More A grassroots protest movement founded by four women (three Indigenous, and one non-Indigenous ally) in Saskatchewan in December 2012.

Inca (or **Inka**) A group of Indigenous peoples originally located in present-day Cuzco, Peru. In 1442, the Incas expanded their geographic territory under the leadership of Pachacutec, who also founded the Inca Empire, or Tahuantinsuyo. The Inca Empire was the largest empire in the Americas prior to a significant European presence.

Indian Act Canadian federal legislation that governs the lives of Registered/Status Indians "from cradle to grave" and regulates reserve land, money, and other resources. The Act was formally created in 1876, when all legislation pertaining to Indians was consolidated, and has since undergone over 20 major revisions. In particular, the Act defines who is an "Indian."

Indian agent The chief administrator of Indian affairs within a particular district, reserve, or treaty area. Indian agents wielded a great deal of power over all aspects of Indigenous people's lives. The term is no longer used.

Indian Homemakers' Clubs Established on reserves by the federal government in the late 1930s, the clubs were intended to teach Indigenous women European-Canadian domesticity; however, Indigenous women often shaped their local club's activities to fit their own needs.

Indian Residential Schools Settlement Agreement (IRSSA) The largest class-action settlement in Canadian history. Brought into effect on 19 September 2007, the IRSSA is the result of former residential school students, with the support of the Assembly of First Nations (AFN) and Inuit organizations, taking the federal government and the churches to court. The agreement includes the following individual and collective measures to address the legacy of the residential school system: a "common experience" payment to be paid to individuals who attended the schools; the establishment of a Truth and Reconciliation Commission; the creation of an Independent Assessment Process (IAP); the commemoration of the history of residential schools; and the establishment of an Aboriginal Healing Foundation.

Indigenous peoples The original inhabitants of a particular territory and their descendants.

Innu One of the Indigenous inhabitants of present-day northeastern Quebec and Labrador. Innu refer to their territory as Nitassinan.

Inuit One of the Indigenous inhabitants of the Arctic and subarctic regions of present-day Northwest Territories, Nunatsiavut (coastal region of Labrador), Nunavik (northern Quebec), Nunavut, Nunatukavut (coastal region of Labrador), Denmark (Greenland), Russia (Siberia), and Alaska.

Inuk The singular of *Inuit*.

Iroquois Confederacy An alliance formed in the sixteenth century by the Seneca, Cayuga, Oneida, Onondaga, and Mohawk, the Iroquois tribes that originally inhabited the northeastern part of present-day New York state. The confederacy was also known as the Five Nations until 1722, when the Tuscarora joined. Thereafter, it has been known as the Six Nations.

James Bay and Northern Quebec Agreement (1976) The first land claim agreement signed between an Indigenous nation or nations and either the federal or a provincial government since 1930. The agreement was struck by the government of Quebec and the Crees and Innu of northern Quebec and was crucial in allowing Quebec's James Bay hydroelectric project to proceed.

Jay Treaty Also known as the Treaty of London (1794), a treaty between the United States and the British Empire. The treaty is credited with preventing war between the two anglophone powers during the upheavals in revolutionary France. Notably, the British agreed to relinquish several forts in what became the American Midwest, including in the Ohio Valley and present-day Michigan. Article 3 guaranteed Indigenous peoples the right to cross the boundary between British North America and the United States.

Jesuit A member of the Society of Jesus, a Catholic order of priests and brothers founded by Ignatius Loyola in 1534. Following Loyola's initial vision, the Jesuits were organized along military lines and highly disciplined. Jesuits played a central role in missionary and educational activity in what became Canada, particularly during the period of French colonial rule.

Jesuit Relations A publication compiling Jesuit missionaries' reports from over 200 years, beginning in 1611. Jesuit missionaries reported regularly to their superiors about the progress of their missionary work, and these documents constitute an invaluable source of information for historians about missionary activity and Indigenous–Jesuit relations as seen from the Jesuits' perspective.

Lac Saint-Jean A large lake located on the Saguenay River; the location of the communities of Mashteuiatsh and Roberval.

League of Indians of Canada A national political organization created by Indigenous peoples. The league was formed in 1919 in Ontario by Fred Loft (Haudenosaunee), who wanted to create an organization that could collectively advocate for Indigenous peoples across Canada.

Lorette A Wendat community near Quebec City.

Louisbourg A French fortress on present-day Cape Breton Island, from which the French protected their trade routes in the Gulf of St Lawrence and access to the St Lawrence River. It was also the centre of Indigenous–European trade in the region. Louisbourg was captured by the British in 1758 and destroyed in 1760.

Magna Carta An English charter, first issued in 1215, that bound the monarch to respect certain liberties among the aristocracy. The Magna Carta is often hailed as the first document in which an English monarch pledged to respect, to some degree, the rule of law, which provided a check on his or her power.

Maliseet An Algonquian First Nation and member of the Wabanaki Confederacy inhabiting areas in present-day New Brunswick, Maine, and Quebec, but most heavily concentrated in the St John River Valley.

Manitoba Act (1870) Legislation that created the province of Manitoba. Given Royal Assent on 12 May 1870, the Act was adopted by Parliament in response to the Métis resistance and the provisional government led by Louis Riel. The Act was based, in part, on Riel's list of Métis rights.

Marshall decision (*R. v. Marshall* [1999]) A landmark Supreme Court decision that recognized the constitutionally protected treaty rights of the Mi'kmaq in Nova Scotia. The decision responded to Donald Marshall Jr's assertion of Aboriginal fishing rights after he had been arrested in 1993 for catching and selling eels out of season and without a licence.

Mashteuiatsh An Innu community on Lac Saint-Jean.

Mayan The Indigenous peoples of present-day southeastern Mexico and parts of Central America.

Mesoamerica A region and culture area in the Americas inhabited by a thriving group of Indigenous peoples prior to the arrival of the Spanish in the sixteenth and seventeenth centuries. The area extends from present-day central Mexico to Belize, Guatemala, El Salvador, Honduras, Nicaragua, and Costa Rica.

Métis Indigenous peoples who trace their descent to mixed First Nations and European parentage. The Métis on the plains developed a national consciousness in the nineteenth century and played a key role in the fur trade.

Métis National Council The council representing the national voice of the Métis comprising organizations from five provinces: British Columbia, Alberta, Saskatchewan, Manitoba, and Ontario.

Michif A combination of Cree and French that is the language of the Métis people of Canada and the United States.

Mi'kmaq (also **Mi'kmaw** or **Micmac**) Indigenous peoples who inhabit the present-day Maritimes, particularly Nova Scotia, and are members of the Wabanaki Confederacy.

Mississauga The name of an Anishnaabe First Nation settled on the northern shore of present-day Lake Ontario.

Mohawks (Kanien'gehaga) The most easterly tribe of the Haudenosaunee or Six Nations.

Montagnais The French term for the Innu settled in the St Lawrence Valley, the Gulf of St Lawrence, and in present-day Labrador and northern Quebec.

National Indian Brotherhood (NIB) An organization created in 1968 to represent treaty/status groups. In 1981, the NIB changed its name to the Assembly of First Nations.

***Natural Parents v. British Columbia (Superintendent of Child Welfare)* (1976)** A Supreme Court decision, which decided that it was legal for non-Indigenous people to adopt Indigenous children and that the children did not lose their Indian status as a result of such adoptions.

New France The area colonized by France on Turtle Island. The territory of New France extended from present-day Newfoundland to the Rocky Mountains and from Hudson Bay to the Gulf of Mexico. France ceded New France to Great Britain and Spain in the Treaty of Paris (without consulting Indigenous peoples) in 1763.

Non–status Indian A person who self-identifies as "Indian" or is a member of a First Nation but is not recognized as such under the Indian Act. Non-Status Indians do not enjoy the same rights and benefits as Status Indians.

North West Company (NWC) A fur-trading business headquartered in Montreal and in operation from 1779 to 1821, when it merged with the Hudson's Bay Company. Before the merger, the rivalry between the two companies resulted in several armed clashes between their respective agents, including the Battle of Seven Oaks.

North-West Mounted Police (NWMP) A paramilitary police force created by the Canadian government in 1873 to maintain order in the newly acquired North-West territories, including present-day Saskatchewan and Alberta. The force was renamed the Royal North-West Mounted Police in 1904 and merged with the Dominion Police in 1920 to create the Royal Canadian Mounted Police (RCMP).

Northwest Territories Territory created when the Hudson's Bay Company transferred Rupert's Land and the North-Western Territory to the Government of Canada in June 1870. The area comprised all non-Confederation Canada except for British Columbia, the coast of the Great Lakes, the Saint Lawrence River Valley, and the southern portions of Quebec, the Maritimes, Newfoundland, and the Labrador coast.

North West Company (aka "**The Northern Store**") A retailer of food and general merchandise in northern Canada, rural Alaska, the South Pacific Islands, and the Caribbean. The Company specializes predominantly in smaller, rural, and Indigenous communities.

Numbered Treaties The term given to eleven treaties signed between different First Nations and the Crown between 1871 and 1921, which are seen as a critical component of Canadian colonization of the West and the North in particular.

Oblate A member of a male Roman Catholic order who has dedicated his life to the service of God.

Ojibwa (also **Ojibwe** or **Ojibway**) One of the largest Indigenous groups north of Mexico. The group's territories include parts of present-day Manitoba, Ontario, Quebec, Ohio, Michigan, Illinois, Wisconsin, Minnesota, and North Dakota.

Passamaquoddy Indigenous peoples who live near the border of present-day Maine and New Brunswick. They are a member of the Wabanaki Confederacy.

Peace of Paris, 1763 The treaty concluding the Seven Years' War, which saw France cede most of its North American possessions to Britain.

peltry Pelts or furs usually in an unfinished state.

pemmican A concentrated mixture of meat (such as bison, moose, elk, or deer) and fruit (such as cranberries and Saskatoon berries) made by Indigenous peoples. Pemmican was widely adopted by fur traders as a light and easily transportable high-energy food.

Penner Report The report of a special committee struck by the House of Commons in 1982 to examine Indian self-government. The committee was chaired by Member of Parliament Keith Penner and recommended recognizing First Nations as self-governing.

Penobscot A First Nation residing principally in present-day Maine who are part of the Wabanaki Confederacy.

Poundmaker (**Pîhtokahanapiwiyin**) A Plains Cree Chief born in 1842, who is well known as a great leader and diplomat. He is best known for his unwilling role in the 1885 resistance against the Canadian government.

potlatch A gift-giving ceremony practised by the Indigenous peoples of the Pacific Northwest Coast. The ceremony was banned by the Canadian government in the 1890s.

Pueblo Revolt of 1680 (**Pope's Rebellion**) An uprising against the Spanish in New Mexico by the Pueblo.

Racine v. Woods (**1982**) A Supreme Court decision that gave precedence to the "psychological bonding" between Indigenous children and adoptive non-Indigenous parents over the cultural heritage of the children.

Récollet(s) A member of the French branch of the Franciscans, a Roman Catholic order of monks. The Franciscans developed in the fifteenth century out of a reform movement in the Catholic Church.

Red Paper (1970) The Indigenous response to the federal government's 1969 White Paper that, without Indigenous consultation, recommended the abolition of the Indian Act and any special status for Indigenous peoples in Canada. A few of the main points of the Red Paper, also known as *Citizens Plus*: that the legislative and constitutional basis of Indian status and rights remain as is until Indigenous peoples are ready to change them; that the only way to maintain Indian culture is to remain as Indians; and that Indigenous peoples should have self-government and control over their own land and resources.

Red River Resistance The resistance, popularly remembered as the Red River Rebellion, that occurred in the Red River Settlement in present-day southern Manitoba in 1869–70. Following its purchase of Rupert's Land, Canada sent an English-speaking governor to the settlement to survey the land. The French-speaking Métis of the region, led eventually by Louis Riel, refused to give the governor access to their settlement. Riel and his co-resistors then negotiated the terms of Red River's entry into the Canadian federation, laying the groundwork for the founding of the province of Manitoba. The resistance came to an end with the passage of the Manitoba Act in May 1870 and the arrival of a British military expedition to impose Canadian authority in August of the same year.

Red River Settlement Also known as the Selkirk Settlement or the Red River Colony, a colonization project undertaken by Thomas Douglas, the Fifth Earl of Selkirk, in 1811 along the northern branch of the Red River in present-day southern Manitoba. The settlement became the centre of the Red River Resistance in 1869–70.

reserve Defined by the Indian Act as "a tract of land, the legal title to which is vested in Her Majesty, that has been set apart by Her Majesty for the use and benefit of a band." There are over 600 reserves in Canada.

residential school apology The apology made on behalf of the government of Canada by Prime Minister Stephen Harper to the former students of Indian residential schools. Harper's statement of apology was delivered in the House of Commons on 11 June 2008.

residential school system A school system established in the nineteenth century by the federal government in partnership with churches of various Christian denominations and designed to assimilate Indigenous peoples into European-Canadian society. The schools forcibly separated Indigenous children from their families, communities, and cultures in order to "kill the Indian in the child."

Roberval A community on Lac Saint-Jean that was the centre of the regional fur trade in the late nineteenth and early twentieth century.

Royal Commission on Aboriginal Peoples (RCAP) A Canadian royal commission established in 1991 to examine issues related to Indigenous peoples that had come to light as a result of recent events such as the Oka Crisis. The final report was released in 1996 and set out a 20-year agenda for implementing changes. To date, the recommendations of the RCAP have not been implemented.

Royal Proclamation of 1763 A decree issued by King George III after Britain acquired the territories of New France. The proclamation was intended to organize Britain's empire in North America and stabilize relations with First Nations through the regulation of trade, settlement, and land purchases. The Royal Proclamation continues to be of legal significance to First Nations in Canada and the United States.

Rupert's Land A vast territory in British North America that consisted of all the land connected to the Hudson Bay drainage basin. Charles I of England granted the territory to the Hudson's Bay Company in a 1670 royal charter. The HBC sold Rupert's Land to Canada in the late 1860s, although Canada did not formally acquire the land until 1870. The Indigenous peoples who lived in the territory were not consulted and disputed Canadian sovereignty of the area.

scurvy A disease that results from a deficiency of vitamin C, which is required for the synthesis of collagen in humans. The disease was common among sailors and others who had little or no access to fruits or vegetables for long periods of time.

self-government A system considered to provide Indigenous people with the power to design, establish, and administer their own governments under the Canadian Constitution through a process of negotiation with Canada and, where applicable, the provincial governments.

Seven Fires A Confederacy of Indigenous peoples, including the Wendat of Lorette, living in the St Lawrence Valley at the time of the American Revolution. The Seven Fires remained loyal to the British Crown.

shaman A member of an Indigenous group who possesses a deep connection to both the material and sacred worlds. Some shamans have medicinal skills and/or healing powers. Some scholars consider the term to be outdated.

Six Nations An association of six Iroquois (Haudenosaunee) tribes. The original Iroquois League, known as the Five Nations, consisted of the Mohawk, Oneida, Onondaga, Cayuga, and Seneca. The name changed in 1722, when the Tuscarora joined.

Sixties Scoop A term referring to the mass removal of Indigenous children from their families and homes in Saskatchewan beginning in the 1960s; many were adopted into families of European heritage; many others suffered in foster care. Although the term was coined in reference to Saskatchewan, similar policies and practices were pursued across Canada.

Spence, Theresa (Chief of Attawapiskat First Nation) Chief Spence undertook a protest in late 2011 and early 2012 to draw attention to the housing crisis in her community. A state of emergency, the third one in three years, was called in Attawapiskat First Nation on 28 October 2011.

St Lawrence Iroquoians A group of Iroquoian peoples who lived along the shores of the St Lawrence near present-day Quebec City from the fourteenth to the late sixteenth centuries.

Stadacona A sixteenth-century St Lawrence Iroquoian village near present-day Quebec City.

Status Indian An individual who is registered as an Indian under the Indian Act.

terra nullius A Latin expression derived from Roman law, meaning "empty land" or "land belonging to nobody." Europeans used this concept to justify their claim to the Americas.

treaty An agreement recognized under international law and entered into by sovereign parties. In regard to Indigenous peoples, treaties refer to agreements between the Crown and First Nations. In Canada, treaties are constitutionally recognized.

Treaty of Paris (1783) Treaty that formally ended the American Revolution. Indigenous allies on both sides were not consulted during the peacemaking process, and the consequences for many Indigenous peoples were catastrophic.

treaty rights Refers to Indigenous rights as set out in a treaty. These rights are protected under section 35 of the Constitution Act, 1982.

Trilateral Agreement A treaty negotiated between the Algonquins of Barriere Lake, Quebec and the federal government, which superseded the Comprehensive Land Claims Policy.

Truth and Reconciliation Commission (TRC) A commission whose mandate was to learn the truth about what happened in the residential schools and to disseminate this information to all Canadians. The establishment of the TRC was one of the conditions of the Indian Residential Schools Settlement Agreement.

United Empire Loyalists Those living in the American colonies who remained loyal to the British Crown during the American Revolution, many of whom migrated northward to British-controlled territory in what became Canada.

voyageurs Persons engaged in the transportation of furs by canoe during the fur trade.

Wabanaki Confederacy A Confederacy joining together five Indigenous nations: the Abenaki, the Maliseet, the Mi'kmaq, the Passamaquoddy, and the Penobscot.

wampum belt Belts made of small cylindrical beads used by certain eastern tribes to commemorate treaties, record historical events, and act as currency in both social and material transactions.

Wendat (also **Wyandot, Huron**) Indigenous peoples once inhabiting parts of present-day south-central and central Ontario; originally a confederacy of four distinct but related nations. The Wendat, known as the Huron to the French and subsequently the British, were dispersed in the 1600s following conflict with the Haudenosaunee, and eventually resettled principally in four distinct areas, including near present-day Quebec City.

White Paper (1967) A policy paper put forth by the Minister of Indian Affairs Jean Chrétien, without consultation with Indigenous peoples, which proposed the abolition of the Indian Act and the rejection of all land claims. Ultimately, these measures attempted to assimilate Indigenous peoples into European-Canadian society. Indigenous peoples responded to the policy paper with the Red Paper.

Wustukwiuk (also **Wuastukwiuk**) Indigenous peoples settled in present-day Eastern Canada.

Credits

Chapter One

Joseph Boyden, *The Orenda* (Toronto: Penguin Books, 2013), 273.

Reuben Gold Thwaites, ed., *The Jesuit Relations and Allied Documents: Travels and Explorations of the Jesuit Missionaries in New France 1610–1791* vol. 34 (New York: Pageant Books, 1959), 9–35.

Deborah Doxtator, "Issues in Writing Native History," in *Indigenous Learning: Proceedings from the First Biennial Aboriginal Peoples Conference*, Sylvia O'Meara, et al., eds, (Thunder Bay, ON: Lakehead University Aboriginal Resource and Research Centre, 1996), 115.

Jace Weaver, *That the People Might Live: Native American Literature and Native Community* (New York: Oxford University Press, 1997), 32–3. By permission of Oxford University Press, USA.

William Douw Lighthall, *The Master of Life: A Romance of the Five Nations and of Prehistoric Montreal* (Toronto: The Musson Book Co. 1908), 143.

Patricia Vervoort, "Re-present-ing Rock Art," *American Review of Canadian Studies* 31, 1–2, (2001): 209.

Chapter Two

Daniel K. Richter, "Imagining a Distant New World," in *Facing East from Indian Country: A Native History of Early America* (Cambridge: Harvard University Press, 2001). Copyright © 2001 by the President and Fellows of Harvard College.

Dorothy Harley Eber, "Into the Arctic Archipelago: Edward Parry in Igloolik and the Shaman's Curse," in *Encounters on the Passage: Inuit Meet Explorers* (Toronto: University of Toronto Press, 2008), 12–36, 145–8 with some deletions from the original material. Reprinted with permission of the publisher.

Louis Tapardjuk, interviewer and trans. Leah Otak, ed. "Excerpt from an Interview with Rosie Iqallijuq," Igloolik Research Centre, Inullariit Elders' Society Archives, Tape Number: IE-204, 8 October 1991.

Chapter Three

Sweet Grass, "Message of Sweet Grass, Kihewin, Little Hunter, and Kiskion to Governor Adams Archibald," Red River, 13. April 1871, in Morris, Treaties, 170–1. The portion quoted here is the message of Sweet Grass, the most senior of these chiefs.

Alexander Morris, "The Treaties of Canada with the Indians of Manitoba and the North-West Territories, including the Negotiations on which they were based, and other information relating thereto" (Toronto: Belfrods, Clarke, 1880), 170–1.

Articles of Peace and Agreement: Annapolis Royal 1726. London, England, Public Record Office, Colonial Office Series 217/5: 3r–5r.

Chapter Four

Brett Rushforth, "Slavery, the Fox Wars, and the Limits of Alliance," *William and Mary Quarterly* 63, 1 (2006): 53–80.

"Baptism, Sept. 21, 1713," in Gaeten Morin, ed., *Repertoire des actes de baptême, mariage et sepulture du Québec ancien, 1621–1799*, CD-ROM, entry # 44145. Archives nationales du Québec, Centre régional de Montréal, Registres Notre-Dame de Montréal, film 111.

The present State & situation of the Indian Tribes in the Province of Quebec, May [20] 1779, Rauner Special Collections Library, Dartmouth College, 779301.

Chapter Five

John Work, Report from Colvile District, "Answers to Queries on Natural History," 1829. Hudson's Bay Company Archives [HBCA], B.45/e/2, fos. 1, 4, 5, 12 [extracts].

Dominion of Canada Annual Report of the Department of Indian Affairs for the Year Ended March 31 1910. Printed by Order of Parliament Ottawa. Printed by C.H. Parmelee, Printer to the King's Most Excellent Majesty 1910.

Chapter Six

Jacqueline Peterson, "Red River Redux: Métis Ethnogenesis and the Great Lakes Region," in *Contours of the People: Métis Family, Mobility, and History*, Nicole St-Onge, Carolyn Podruchny, and Brenda Macdougall, eds (Norman: University of Oklahoma Press, 2012), 39–40.

Louis Goulet, *Vanishing Spaces: Memoirs of a Prairie Métis* (Winnipeg: Editions Bois-Brules, 1976), 43.

Métis National Council, *Métis Registration Guide*, 2011, 2.

"The Insurrection in Manitoba," *Brisbane Courier*, Saturday, 16 May 1885, 1.

Chapter Seven

"Civilizing Influences," a proposed pamphlet by Thomas Deasy, Indian Agent. Library and Archives Canada. LAC, RG-10, Black Series, V. 4093, File 570970. 1920.

Christine Smith (McFarlane), "A Legacy of Canadian Child Care: Surviving the Sixties Scoop," *Briarpatch Magazine*, 1 September 2013. http://briarpatchmagazine.com/articles/view/a-legacy-of-canadian-child-care.

Chapter Eight

Indian Act, 1876, Sections 3(3)–3(6). Statutes of Canada, 39 Vict., c. 18, 1876.

Excerpt from an Interview with Life History Respondent 12, Interview by Jaime Mishibinijima, 28 July 2008.

Chapter Nine

'Program of Studies for Indian Schools, 1897,' from Canada, 'Annual Report of the Department of Indian Affairs for the year Ended June 1897', *Sessional Papers*, 1897, 398–9.

Excerpt from the Indian Residential Schools Settlement Agreement, May 2006. Available at http://www.residentialschoolsettlement.ca/SCHEDULE_N.pdf (accessed 5 Jan. 2011).

Chapter Ten

Cornelius H.W. Remie and Jarich Oosten, "The Birth of a Catholic Inuit Community," *Études/Inuit/Studies* 26, 1 (2002): 109–41.

Excerpt from *Codex Historicus* Mission Pelly Bay, Volume I: 25 December 1940 entry, Archives Deschâtelets, Oblats de Marie Immaculée.

Robert Robson, "Housing in the Northwest Territories: the Post-War Vision," *Urban History Review/Revue d'histoire urbaine*, 24, 1 (1995): 3–20.

Pia Kooneelusi, Royal Commission on Aboriginal Peoples – Transcriptions of Public Hearings and Round Table Discussions, 1992–1993, volume 1 Pangnirtung, Northwest Territories (Ottawa: Minister of Public Works and Government Services 2008), 136–142.

Chapter Eleven

Excerpts from the Diary of Arthur Wellington Clah (T'amks), 1860–1916. (London: Wellcome Institute, MS American 140).

Indian Girls Achieve Successful Careers—Pave Way for Others. *Indian News* (June 1958): 6–7.

Chapter Twelve

Sarah Carter, "Categories and Terrains of Exclusion: Constructing the Indian Woman in the Early Settlement Era in Western Canada," is reproduced from *Great Plains Quarterly* with permission from the University of Nebraska Press. Copyright 1993.

LAC, RG 10, vol. 11339 part 1, file 13/7-2-7, Mrs. Meawasige to Superintendent O'Neil, 9 May 1956.

Constitution and Regulations for Indian Homemakers' Clubs, Department of Citizenship and Immigration.

Excerpt from the Indian Act, 1951. Statutes of Canada, 1951, c. 149.

Chapter Thirteen

Letter from Chief Pierre Freezie to S.J. Bailey. Library and Archives Canada. LAC, RG 85, Series D-1-A, vol. 1254, file 431-178, part 2.

Excerpt from an Interview with Violet Charlie. Interview by Laurie Meijer Drees, 14 May 2008. Reprinted by permission of Laurie Meijer Drees.

Textual: RG29 volume 2989 file part 1–"Directions for Feeding Indian Babies." © Government of Canada. Reproduced with the permission of Library and Archives Canada (2015). Source: Library and Archives Canada/Department of Health fonds/File 851-6-2.

Chapter Fourteen

Memorandum of Mutual Intent between, the Algonquins of Barriere Lake and the Department of Indian and Northern Affairs Canada: Global Proposal to Rebuild the Community, 1997 Indian and Northern Affairs Canada.

Rynard, Paul. 'Ally or Colonizer: The Federal State, the Cree Nation and the James Bay Agreement', *Journal of Canadian Studies* 36, 2 (Summer 2001): 8–48.

Excerpt from *Cree Regional Authority et al. v. Attorney-General of Quebec* (1991) 42 Federal Trial Records, p. 168.